The GLOBAL PUZZLE

The GLOBAL PUZZLE

ISSUES AND ACTORS IN WORLD POLITICS

Third Edition

Richard W. Mansbach

Iowa State University

HOUGHTON MIFFLIN COMPANY   Boston   New York

Sponsoring Editor: Melissa Mashburn
Associate Editor: Katherine Meisenheimer
Senior Project Editor: Carol Newman
Senior Production/Design Coordinator: Jennifer Waddell
Senior Cover Design Coordinator: Deborah Azerrad Savona
Senior Marketing Manager: Sandra McGuire

Cover Design: Walter Kopec
Cover Image: Reza Estalchrian/Tony Stone Images

Printed in the U.S.A.

Library of Congress Catalog Card Number: 99-71948

ISBN: 0-395-96374-5

2 3 4 5 6 7 8 9-DSG-04 03 02 01 00

Contents

PART TWO: ACTORS AND ISSUES IN THE POSTINTERNATIONAL WORLD 133

6. The Janus Faces of Foreign Policy 164

PART THREE: COOPERATION AND CONFLICT: A CHANGING BALANCE   261

PART FOUR: THE SEARCH FOR SOLUTIONS 449

Maps

Figures and Tables

The five chapters in Part Three, "Cooperation and Conflict: A Changing Balance," move beyond the theoretical perspectives of the previous sections to examine the mix of conflict and cooperation in global politics. Chapter 9, "Going It Alone or Working Together in Global Politics?," focuses on the implications of anarchy in global politics, arguing that even in the absence of world government, informal rules, international law, and international regimes foster cooperation and provide the bases for global society. Chapters 10 and 11, "Force in World Politics: A Changing Role" and "The Special Case of Nuclear Weapons," discuss the changing role of military force in global politics. The final chapters in this section, "International Political Economy: Where Economics and Politics Meet" and "Economic Competitors or Partners: The United States, Japan, China, and Europe," focus on the growing role of economic factors in global politics. Chapter 12 examines the assumptions and concepts of international political economy and looks at the implications of globalization. Chapter 13 focuses on the relations among the world's leading economic powers, stressing the pressure the global economy exerts on actors to coordinate goals and policies.

The final section of the book, "The Search for Solutions," examines issues that are overwhelming sovereign states or in which states themselves are a big part of the problem. Chapter 14, "The State and the Species: Environmental Dilemmas," looks at a series of environmental issues—such as the population explosion, global warming, growing scarcities of food and water, and nuclear waste—that threaten everyone's survival. Chapter 15, "States Versus the Individual: Human Rights in the Global Arena," examines the relationship between the state and individual citizens in the context of human rights abuses, with special emphasis on the global status of women and on the trade-off between human rights and economic relations in the case of China. The final chapter, "From International to Postinternational Politics," revisits the book's key themes, especially the trends of globalization and localization, and interprets some of the book's key concepts in the context of these trends.

New to the Third Edition   Coverage has been updated throughout the book to take account of the global economic crisis, economic and political turmoil in Russia, and growing terrorism against American interests, for example in Africa. Data in all tables and figures have been updated, and the format and purpose of the "Actors Speak" boxes have been altered to highlight conflicting views on key issues. As noted earlier, two important themes have been highlighted and carried through in all chapters: the evolution from an *international* to a *postinternational* world and the simultaneous presence of fragmentation and integration in political communities. Attention is paid to the impact and implications of globalization throughout the text, and actors and issues are assessed in terms of their impact on globalization and localization. The theme of *old* and *new* worlds in the first two editions has been replaced with a comparison of *international* and *postinternational* politics.

A number of more specific changes have also been made to the third edition. Chapter 3 contains an updated section on neorealism that has been moved to this chapter from old Chapter 5. The discussion of Russia in Chapter 4 has been extended to take account of the economic and political turmoil that has engulfed the country in recent years and of the changing nature of Russo-American relations. Chapter 6 contains new figures to illustrate better the several perspectives introduced for assessing foreign policy.

Old Chapter 7, which dealt with both nonstate actors and international organizations, has been divided into two chapters. New Chapter 7 contains expanded materials about nonstate actors. A new subsection has been added that presents the case of terrorism in the Middle East. A new section on religious actors, emphasizing the role of religious fundamentalism, and a new section on individuals as actors, focusing on the Saudi terrorist Osama bin Laden, have also been added. New Chapter 8 deals with international organizations. Materials on the United Nations have been updated to take account of changes in peacekeeping and humanitarian operations and in institutional financing in recent years; greater attention is paid to the U.N.'s economic and social roles; and a new section has been added on commodity cartels, focusing on OPEC.

Chapter 9 features new material on the individual and international law. Chapter 10 has a longer section on "Postmodern War" to take account of events in Central Africa and Kosovo, and a subsection on the global arms trade, formerly in Chapter 11, has been moved to this chapter. Chapter 11 has a new subsection on the proliferation of chemical and biological weapons and the threats they pose. Chapter 12 features new sections on globalization and on the economic "contagion" in Asia and its spread first to Russia and then to South America. In Chapter 13, the section on Japan has been revised to reflect Japan's economic recession and banking problems, and the Japanese experience is contrasted to the economic boom in the United States. More importantly, a new section has been added on China, including China's recent history from Mao to Deng, its role in the global economic system, and its relations with the United States. Chapter 15 includes an expanded section on gender, and new subsections have been added dealing with the gender gap, women in traditional societies, rape, and the U.N.-sponsored Beijing Conference. Finally, the title of Chapter 16 has been changed to reflect its new focus on the transition from international to postinternational politics. New sections have been added on "The Globalized Side of Things" and "The Localized Side of Things."

Aids for Students and Instructors

To assist students in understanding the complexities of global politics, the text employs a variety of visual and pedagogical aids. The extensive use of maps, for example, not only locates peoples in a conventional sense, but also reflects the changing impact of phenomena like global population and conflict. Tables and figures throughout the text provide students with contemporary data that reinforce and illustrate substantive points, such as the extent of environmental damage suffered by the planet. Photographs and cartoons with instructive captions bring to life some of the people and issues described in the text. Substantive endnotes provide students with the background to key issues and with additional sources to consult if they wish to do so. Finally, lists of key terms at the end of chapters and a glossary at the end of the text assure that students understand the basic concepts in the text and will aid them in studying for exams.

A web site has been created for the Third Edition. It contains a variety of features, including links to additional sites that provide information relevant to the chapter's content and that will be valuable for researching papers. The site also provides chapter outlines and review questions that test students on their understanding of key points and that instructors can use in class to spur discussion or can assign to students as essay topics. ACE self-quizzes are also included so that students can test their knowledge of a chapter's content. Finally, the site enables instructors and students to contact me with questions or comments.

I have also written an accompanying Instructor's Resource Manual that will make it easier for instructors to use this text effectively. To facilitate preparation of lectures, it includes chapter summaries and detailed lecture outlines. It also includes a number of illustrative syllabi that suggest how the text can be used in both introductory and more advanced settings. These syllabi contain additional suggested readings as well as suggested activities that I have found useful. The manual also contains sample essay and multiple choice questions for exams; these are also available on disk.

Acknowledgments

My thanks go to many colleagues and students whose advice and assistance over the years have informed this book. Thanks go, too, to those at Houghton Mifflin who have been so generous with their time and effort, including Melissa Mashburn, Katherine Meisenheimer, Jean Woy, Carol Newman, and Sandra McGuire. Thanks also goes to those who, in reviewing this manuscript, have improved it by their suggestions and emendations: Patrick M. Boyle (Loyola University–Chicago), Nicholas Damask (Scottsdale Community College), Joseph Lepgold (Georgetown University), and Larry F. Martinez (California State University–Long Beach).

In the end, neither sentimental optimism nor paralytic despair will serve our needs. It takes courage to confront the daunting issues of global politics that threaten our survival, not merely as individuals but as a species. Let us show that courage so that our children and our children's children can say that we did what we could to make their lives better than ours. It is for this reason I dedicate this book to my daughter, Rachael Alexandra.

Richard W. Mansbach
July 1999

The GLOBAL PUZZLE

Part One

The Past as Prologue

Part One introduces the momentous changes that have reshaped global politics in recent years, the sources of those changes, and the need to readjust our theoretical perspective to make sense of those changes. This section also introduces the key concepts used in the study of global politics—political systems, power, actors, and issues. Chapter 1 describes the world before and after the Cold War and examines many of the key changes in global politics that explain why we speak of a postinternational world. Chapter 2 emphasizes the critical role of the past in understanding the present and the future by looking briefly at ancient Greece, imperial China, medieval Islam, and medieval Europe. Chapter 3 examines the emergence and evolution of the territorial state, as well as challenges to it. And Chapter 4 examines how alternative theoretical lenses explain the outbreak and resolution of the Cold War and summarize events in Russia since the Cold War's end.

Chapter 1

A World Turned Upside Down

Imagine having boarded a machine that can accelerate backward or forward in time. At first, you lurch back to 1945; next, you slowly move forward a few years and observe the changing world, and then surge ahead to the present. The worlds even in that short a time will look markedly different from each other.

For students of global politics, this journey would be even more startling. After World War II, the world was divided between two superpowers. Virtually all of global politics revolved around the interaction of these two states, and the tense and dangerous standoff between the communist East (the Soviet Union and its allies) and the capitalist West (the United States and its allies) dominated global politics. Each side expended vast resources on military establishments, funneled military and economic assistance to friends, and built competing alliances. This struggle would last over forty years. Today, "where the largest tank brigade in the United States Army was once stationed, there is . . . only a vast, empty parking lot . . . ."[1]

As recently as 1983, President Ronald Reagan called the Soviet Union an evil empire as Washington engaged in a massive arms buildup aimed at closing what the president called a window of vulnerability between the two countries. President Reagan blamed heightened tension on Soviet deployment of a new generation of large and accurate intercontinental ballistic missiles (ICBMs).[2] The United States deployed intermediate-range nuclear forces (INF) in Western Europe and assisted the Nicaraguan "contras," the Mujahedeen in Afghanistan, Jonas Savimbi's UNITA rebels in Angola, and other insurgents in Mozambique, Cambodia, and Ethiopia who were rebelling against Soviet-supported clients. The purpose was to bleed the Soviet Union much as Moscow had bled the United States by aiding "national liberation movements" in Vietnam and elsewhere. In this respect, the mid-1980s world looked little different from that of the 1950s. Who would have guessed that a few years later Americans would be lured as tourists to fly Soviet MIG fighters,[3] or that American spy satellites would be used to monitor climatic changes and ecological threats?[4]

From International to Postinternational Politics

The premise of this book is that the dramatic changes that have transformed global politics in recent years make the theoretical tradition that dominated thinking for

This Belorus stamp reflects the monumental shift in global politics in recent years. Instead of Karl Marx and Vladimir Lenin, the pioneers of Marxism-Leninism, the stamp pictures two famous Western entertainers, the comedian Groucho Marx and the Beatle John Lennon. (NYT Pictures)

over three centuries obsolete. *That tradition of international or interstate politics focused solely on a world of sovereign territorial states (or, more correctly, a few powerful states) that were seeking security defined largely in military terms. In this system, an increase in one state's security meant a decrease in another's.* The tradition developed alongside the growth of states in Europe following the Middle Ages, and its theories tried to explain the behavior of and relations among those states. In this world, kings sought to increase their power and wealth, usually at the expense of neighbors. Territory was the main source of wealth and military capability, and wars among states were frequent. This interstate violence was in vivid contrast to the world *within* the states, in which kings exercised sovereign authority over subjects and controlled the means of coercion.

The world of international politics—that is, a political universe monopolized by territorial states—is eroding and is being replaced by a world of *postinternational politics*.[5] *In this world, state authority and capacity have eroded, states must share authority with nonstate and nonterritorial actors, territory and physical distance have become less important, boundaries between states and peoples are increasingly irrelevant (especially because of revolutions in telecommunications and transportation that facilitate the rapid movement of persons, things, and ideas), and the distinction between the domestic and global arenas is disappearing.*

Although states exist in the postinternational world, their authority and capacity are diminished by integration into larger political communities on the one hand and fragmentation into tiny islands of self-identification on the other. Where individuals once defined themselves mainly as subjects, citizens, or nationals of a state, today they have multiple and sometimes conflicting loyalties to states, religions, professions, ethnicities, genders, age cohorts, and so forth. *Globalization, that is, the proliferation of worldwide economic, social, and cultural networks and people's dependence on these global networks for prosperity and security,* illustrates the loss of authority by states to more encompassing systems of authority. At the same time, the collapse of the Soviet Union and Yugoslavia and the worldwide upsurge in religious fundamentalism, ethnic self-consciousness, and civil strife, especially in Africa and the Balkans, reflect the fragmentation side of the equation. The parochialism of many ethnic, national, and religious groups and movements is partly a backlash to globalization and the undermining of traditional values and culture.[6]

One reason that state authority has eroded is that the meaning of security has changed and states are unable individually or even collectively to cope with contemporary threats to security. Although states are still responsible for protecting citizens from external military threats, such threats are no longer the most important security issues. In many of the less-developed countries, the threat of violence is internal, not foreign: crime, terrorism, and ethnic and religious conflicts. This threat is partly a consequence of state weakness. By contrast, military threats, both internal and external, are less important to much of Europe, North America, and Japan. Finally, the security of people in both rich and poor countries is threatened by new diseases, the flight of capital investment and currency speculation, deepening poverty, human rights abuses by police and armed forces acting in the name of governments, and environmental catastrophe. Such threats have revised the security agenda away from the traditional concerns of states, and many are beyond the competence and capacity of states to resolve.

Fortunately, the erosion of state capacity is accompanied by the emergence and growing authority of other institutions that assist and advise states or perform some of the tasks states once performed. A vast array of nongovernmental and intergovernmental actors now deal with environmental, human rights, economic, gender, and humanitarian issues that are beyond the competence of many governments, and together they are creating a global civic society. Thus we increasingly speak of *governance* rather than government. According to political scientist James Rosenau, "governance encompasses the activities of governments, but . . . also includes any actors who resort to command mechanisms to make demands, frame goals, issue directives, and pursue policies."[7]

The world has become more complex in recent decades, and in what follows, we describe how the pieces of this global puzzle fit together. Who will be the major actors in the world in the twenty-first century, and what will their relationship be like? What are the big issues in the postinternational world? How have power and security changed? How are economic and political issues related? What will the global political system and structure be like? For the moment, let us examine how world politics has been turned upside down in recent decades. We will discover that the worlds before and after the Cold War are vastly different and that our theories must change to reflect these differences. Let us now examine more closely the transition from the international to the postinternational world and some of the features that distinguish the two.

The Cold War: The Last Great "European" War

We are entering an era in global politics that differs as much from the old as frontier America differed from cosmopolitan Europe at the time of the American Revolution. We are leaving behind a long, intense, and hostile competition between the United States and the Soviet Union. For decades, crises, the use of proxies in local conflicts, the arms race, and competition in other realms substituted for direct military conflict between the two superpowers. Despite limited "hot" conflicts such as the Korean (1950–1953) and Vietnam (1960–1976)[8] wars, the two main players were able to avoid direct military confrontation that might have escalated into World War III.

Although the Cold War became worldwide, like World Wars I and II, it originated in Europe. The Cold War began as a dispute over control of Germany and Poland, its key actors were European states,[9] and the ideologies of its chief actors—Marxism and capitalism—were of European origin. In many ways, the Cold War was an outgrowth of the great wars Europe had fought earlier in the twentieth century.

The Cold War is often said to have begun when the Grand Alliance of World War II—the United States, Great Britain, and the Soviet Union—broke down, but the seeds of the conflict were sown earlier. The 1917 Bolshevik Revolution in Russia and Russia's withdrawal from World War I made the Western democracies suspicious of Lenin's communist regime. Mutual mistrust was intensified by Soviet efforts to foster revolutions in Europe and Western military intervention in Siberia and northern Russia. An ideological gulf separated those who followed Lenin and Stalin, who believed in *economic socialism* and denied *political democracy,* from Western elites, who advocated *free-market capitalism* and democracy.

Rising fascism in Germany, Italy, and Japan deepened Western-Soviet mistrust. The European democracies and the Union of Soviet Socialist Republics (hereafter, U.S.S.R.) believed that each was prepared to let the dictators Adolf Hitler and Benito Mussolini devour the other. Mutual suspicion was heightened by the 1939 German-Soviet Nonaggression Treaty by which Poland was to be divided between them. Two years later the Nazis attacked the U.S.S.R. These events, along with the Japanese attack on Pearl Harbor, threw the United States, Great Britain, and the Soviet Union together in an alliance of convenience and survival.[10] With their enemies crushed in 1945, the bond that had united them disappeared, and changed circumstances revived old grudges and aroused new ones.

The most profound change was the emergence of the United States and the Soviet Union at the top of the global hierarchy. Their resources, populations, industrial capacity, and military might elevated them above others like colossi. That each alone could harm the interests of the other produced perceptions of threat. Germany, Japan, and Italy had been devastated by war, and most of Western Europe had been occupied and was in economic shambles. An enfeebled Europe was losing its grip on its colonial empires in Asia and Africa. Much of China had been occupied. Even as the invaders withdrew, that country was engulfed by civil war.

The war was not yet over when misunderstandings arose. Soviet leader Josef Stalin, U.S. President Franklin Roosevelt, and British Prime Minister Winston Churchill, meeting at Yalta in February 1945, agreed to establish "democracies"[11] in the Eastern European countries that were occupied by the Red Army as it advanced toward Berlin. Moscow imposed communist dictatorships in those countries to ensure that they would be governed, as also agreed at Yalta, by "friendly regimes."[12] Romania (1945) and Bulgaria (1946) were the first to succumb, and Hungary (1947) and Czechoslovakia (1948) were the last. Although Yugoslavia remained beyond the Red Army's reach, a radical communist regime under Marshal Josif Broz (Tito) took power.[13]

Americans felt that imposing *communism—state ownership of the means of production directed by an authoritarian party that took orders from the Soviet Communist Party*—on Eastern Europe betrayed the wartime alliance and threatened Europe's security. Poland's fate was symbolically important because Hitler's invasion in September 1939 had precipitated World War II, an act in which Stalin was implicated by virtue of having signed a pact with Hitler that included a secret protocol dividing Poland into German and Soviet spheres of influence. United States voters of East European extraction, especially Polish-Americans in such cities as Chicago, Buffalo, and Pittsburgh, were incensed. The fall of Czechoslovakia also had great impact on Western consciences. The West had failed to help that country resist Hitler's demands for the Sudetenland at the Munich conference of 1938 and then in the following year when the Nazis occupied the rest of Czechoslovakia. The United States had provided the U.S.S.R. with billions of dollars in military and economic assistance through "lend-lease" in the war, and British and American women had spent long evenings "knitting socks for Uncle Joe" (Stalin). Soviet actions in Eastern Europe were not the gratitude Americans expected.

Defeated Germany was the crucible in which the Cold War was forged. Germany had been the most powerful state in Europe, and control of Germany was seen as the key to control of Europe as a whole. Until 1947, both sides paid lip service to reuniting Germany, but for incompatible reasons. Stalin wanted to make sure that Germans would never again threaten his country and would pay for the havoc they had wrought. By contrast, the West[14] felt it necessary to restore the German economy as quickly as possible so that Germany could lead Europe's economic recovery.

At the Potsdam Conference (July–August 1945), General-Secretary Stalin, President Harry Truman,[15] and British Prime Minister Clement Attlee[16] agreed to divide Germany into zones of occupation reflecting the location of the conquering armies but to administer the country as an economic unit. This agreement quickly broke down as the Soviets sought large reparations from the Germans and as the Americans and British tried to reinvigorate Germany's moribund economy.

This contest, along with a communist insurgency in Greece, was the first act in the Cold War drama and triggered, in early 1947, a new policy toward the Soviet

Union by which the United States was committed to assist "free peoples" everywhere who "must choose between [two] alternative ways of life," one "based upon the will of the majority" and the other "based upon the will of the minority forcibly imposed upon the majority." President Truman's announcement of this policy was more than any other single act an official declaration of the Cold War.[17]

With this declaration, Europe's division deepened, and the former allies established separate West and East German governments in the areas they occupied. With the division of Europe complete, Americans and Russians confronted each other warily. And, even as armies and armaments grew, the two came to understand that direct military engagement would be suicidal and that neither could dislodge the other from its sphere of interest.[18] Appreciating the risks of escalation—that a relatively minor incident might get out of hand—Russians and Americans continued to threaten one another across the line separating them but resisted the temptation to meddle in one another's sphere of influence.

By the end of 1991, the Cold War had been ended by agreements between the two sides, climaxing in the dissolution of the Soviet empire and the U.S.S.R. Bargains reduced many points of friction and promised major cuts in the superpowers' nuclear, chemical, and biological arsenals and their forces in Central Europe. A nonaggression pact between the two opposed alliances—the North Atlantic Treaty Organization (NATO) and the Warsaw Treaty Organization (WTO)—was signed late in 1990.

The most dramatic symbol of the end of the Cold War was the collapse of communist party rule in the Soviet satellite states in Eastern Europe—East Germany, Poland, Czechoslovakia, Romania, Bulgaria, and Hungary—beginning in 1989. The new governments in those countries dismantled the single-party system and the highly centralized political and economic controls that had dominated their societies and moved toward political democracy and market economies.

Even more remarkable, the Communist Party of the Soviet Union (CPSU)—the party of Lenin, Trotsky, Stalin, Khrushchev, and Brezhnev—voluntarily surrendered its constitutionally guaranteed monopoly over political power early in 1990. The CPSU had been discredited by a failed coup against Soviet President Mikhail Gorbachev in August 1991. An unforgettable image from those tense days is that of Russian leader Boris Yeltsin atop a tank promising to resist hard-line efforts to turn back the clock. Few observers realized that Yeltsin was taking advantage of events to outmaneuver Gorbachev and hasten the dissolution of the CPSU and the U.S.S.R. Immediately after the abortive coup, the three Baltic states—Estonia, Latvia, and Lithuania—were granted independence.[19] Other republics quickly sought to use political chaos in Moscow to reshape their relationship with the central Soviet government. The rigidly centralized Soviet structure soon dissolved into a loose union of republics, but even that reform proved insufficient for most of the constituent states. On Christmas day 1991, the Soviet Union was formally disbanded, and Gorbachev, who had initiated reforms beginning in 1985, had no country to rule.

Although Russia and three other former Soviet republics still had nuclear weapons, these developments reduced the prospect that global politics would return to the tense world of only a decade earlier. Seven decades of *Marxism-Leninism*[20] had left Soviet consumers with long queues, empty shelves, inadequate housing, shoddy goods, idle and surly employees, a degraded environment, and "hidden" inflation (higher costs caused by the need to repair or replace products). Year after year, despite highly publicized achievements in space and science, the Soviet society and economy fell further behind the United States, Western Europe, and Japan in critical areas of high technology.

Addressing pent-up consumer demands, yearnings for democracy, and revived ethnic rivalries would occupy the leaders of these new states more than involvement in foreign adventures. Almost a decade after the Soviet collapse, Russia's economy had not recovered; much of the economy's private sector was in the hands of organized crime; President Yeltsin was hobbled by political enemies, including former communists and strident nationalists; and regional governments in Siberia and elsewhere were paying little attention to Moscow. The precipitous decline in Russia's military capacity was revealed in the clumsy and brutal effort that began early in 1995 to crush the separatist regime in Chechnya.[21]

The most vivid symbol of the sea change in global politics was the Berlin Wall hacked to pieces by the Germans that it had kept apart. The Wall had been erected by the East German government in August 1961. Construction of the Wall and the killing of those seeking to flee the East symbolized the gulf between East and West. When the Wall opened on November 9, 1989, it foretold change in Germany, Eastern Europe, and the Soviet Union itself. Four months later, the communists were voted out of power in East Germany's first free election, and German reunification was under way. It was completed by October 1990, and in December reunified Germany had its first democratic election since 1933, when the Nazis had come to power.

International Politics During the Cold War

What were the outstanding features of international politics before 1991?[22] *First, the Cold War subsumed almost all other issues, and the game of global politics was played according to the rules set by East-West confrontation.* With stalemate in Europe, the Cold War spread to Asia, the Middle East, Africa, and the Caribbean and infected most global and regional issues. Washington and Moscow saw the world through the lens of this issue, asking how this or that event might alter the relative power of the two sides, and power-politics thinking admitted of only one type of issue that necessarily "relates to peace and war."[23] This claim's attraction lies in its simplicity, for it reduced everything in global politics to "the struggle for power and peace."[24] Regional and local strategies were largely designed to weaken the other superpower.

When one side backed a party to a local crisis, the other supported that party's adversary. If a local leader declared himself Marxist (whatever that might mean in the local context), Moscow would rush to his side; if he declared himself anti-Marxist, he could depend on U.S. aid. In Asia, Stalin backed Mao Zedong (Mao Tse-tung) and the communists, ensuring U.S. support of Jiang Jieshi (Chiang Kai-shek) and the Guomintang (Nationalists). Quarrels between allies could lead to shifts in alignments. Starting in the 1960s, the Sino-Soviet rift triggered a thaw in Sino-American relations. In the Middle East, Soviet leaders after 1955 wooed Egypt, first under Abdel Gamal Nasser and then Anwar Sadat, but in 1972 Sadat expelled the Russians, and the United States became Egypt's benefactor. Such behavior was frequent.

Second, Cold War thinking focused only on sovereign states, especially the superpowers. Not only did the Cold-War world emphasize just one script and plot line for the dramas of global politics, but it also seemed a world in which sovereign states, especially the few great powers, were the essential actors. "Nation states," wrote one observer, "are the essential actors ... because they are the actors that *engage in war and are essential in organizing the norms and institutions which provide more or less stability, security, order, and/or peace for the system.*"[25] In these respects, the Cold-War world was little different from the world in earlier centuries. In Hans Morgenthau's words:

> Today, no less than when it was first developed in the sixteenth century, sovereignty points to a political fact. The fact is the existence of a person or a group of persons who, within the limits of a given territory, are more powerful than any competing person or group of persons.... Thus the absolute monarch of the sixteenth and the following centuries was the supreme authority ... within his territory, not as a matter of theoretical speculation or legal interpretation, but as a political fact.[26]

Traditional thinkers reasoned that, because "the functions of states are similar," the only relevant differences among them are "their varied capabilities."[27] We describe this way of thinking as *state-centric* because states are seen as *unitary actors* that reach decisions rationally in response to their *national interest,* which is determined by relative power. According to such thinking, a state's national interest is more than the sum of citizens' interests, and domestic factors are irrelevant to state action. Statesmen, "as trustees of the national interest,"[28] are presumed able to discern the national interest through *rational analysis.* In a much-cited passage, Morgenthau argues: "We assume that statesmen think and act in terms of interest defined as power.... That assumption allows us to retrace and anticipate ... the steps a statesman—past, present, or future—has taken or will take on the political scene."[29]

Third, leaders on both sides believed the adversary was responsible for their problems. Each side believed the other was at the center of a conspiracy and, like a giant puppeteer, could pull strings all over the world and manipulate events. American leaders thought that those who opposed U.S. policies—at home or abroad—were part of a "communist conspiracy." Setbacks, such as the "fall of China" in 1949 or the U.S.S.R.'s exploding a nuclear weapon in the same year, had to be the result of "treason." Fanned by a previously little-known senator from Wisconsin, Joseph McCarthy, this belief led to witch hunts in the early 1950s against Americans in and out of government who might be engaged in "un-American" activities.

Belief in the enemy's responsibility (and omnipotence) led to decisions based on dubious assumptions. President Ronald Reagan, for example, spoke as though all terrorism directed at Americans and American interests by radical groups and governments around the world originated in Moscow.[30] Such beliefs made it difficult for leaders to respond creatively to challenges. Instability caused by nationalism, poverty, or ethnic rivalry was often misperceived as intentionally inspired by the adversary.

A fourth feature of the world during the Cold War was a perception that a gain for one side was equivalent to a loss for the other. The world was seen to be *bipolar* (divided into two blocs), and East and West were engaged in a *zero-sum game* (a loss by one equals the other's gain). American and Soviet leaders became involved in adventures in which their only interest was to hurt each other and from which it was difficult to extricate themselves because admitting defeat might give heart to the enemy. This concern largely explains U.S. involvement in South Vietnam after Congress passed the 1964 Gulf of Tonkin Resolution.[31] That act partly resulted from President Lyndon B. Johnson's belief that the communists must learn that "wars of national liberation" did not pay. A series of U.S. presidents, including Dwight D. Eisenhower, John F. Kennedy, and Johnson, failed to recognize that local nationalism was as much an enemy of the Soviet Union as of the United States.[32]

Just as U.S. leaders translated the fall of the "friendly" military government in Saigon (now Ho Chi-Minh City) as a Soviet gain, so Soviet leaders viewed the overthrow of an Afghan Marxist leader in the late 1970s as a triumph for Western capitalists. Viewing the world through Cold-War lenses, Soviet leaders believed that their only choice was to intervene. That action led to a protracted civil war in Afghanistan and a humiliating defeat for the U.S.S.R. The parallels with American action in Vietnam are striking; leaders on both sides were victims of a perception of reality that made a dangerous world still more dangerous.

A fifth characteristic of the Cold-War world was that security was largely defined in military terms. Immediately after World War II, the U.S. military establishment was reduced, but the Cold War reversed this trend. The major impetus militarizing the Cold War was the Korean War. The North Korean invasion of the South on June 25, 1950, was a shock to Americans. American leaders believed that the invasion was the first step in worldwide Soviet military expansion, and they argued that failure to resist would whet the appetite of a dictator as had the appeasement of Hitler in the 1930s. Unwittingly, the North Koreans provided legitimacy for a rapid American rearmament that had been recommended in April 1950 in a secret study by the Truman administration National Security Council-68 [NSC-68].

Thereafter, military expenditures remained high. To deter conventional war, conventional forces, it was believed, were necessary. On this belief U.S. troops were sent back to Europe and America's European allies rearmed, making NATO the most formidable peacetime military alliance in history. An arms race ensued. Each side, seeking a technological breakthrough, devoted more and more resources to stockpiling and improving weapons of mass destruction.[33] The race climaxed with President Reagan's idealistic fervor for the Strategic Defense Initiative (SDI) or Star Wars, which at vast cost would prevent Soviet missiles from reaching American cities. Efforts to slow the arms race were repeatedly stymied by mutual fear and suspicion.

The Cold War seemed to fit a theory of power politics imported to this country from Europe, which could neither predict nor explain the end of that conflict. With the emergence of a postinternational world, old theories need to be revised. Whether the world will be better or more peaceful is not clear. Certainly it will be unsettling to those accustomed to the old.

The Postinternational World

As the Cold War ended, different actors and different issues that did not fit the old mold came to the fore. Overwhelming dominance of global affairs by the two superpowers has ended. The Soviet Union has collapsed, and Germany and Japan have risen from the ashes of defeat and are pivotal in global economic and political life. However, not everything has changed. Although many observers believe that the United States no longer enjoys its former influence, the decisive role that country played in organizing a global response to economic crises in Asia and Latin America in 1997–1998 and 1999 reminds us that the United States remains a superpower. As President Bill Clinton declared about America's role in bringing an end to war in Bosnia-Hersegovina, "American leadership created the chance to build a peace and stop the suffering."[34]

Perusing our daily newspapers makes it clear that geographic maps dividing the world into neat territorial compartments called states do not exhaust political reality. The news repeatedly features terrorist groups like Al Qaeda ("the Base") led by Saudi millionaire Osama bin Laden, which bombed U.S. embassies in Africa in 1998. There are references to globe-girdling corporations like DaimlerChrysler, banks like CiticorpTravelers Group, and international organizations like the World Bank. We contribute time, energy, and money to dedicated and influential private groups like Greenpeace and a rich galaxy of other nonstate actors that affect our daily lives in myriad ways. Finally, our attention is drawn to dissatisfied and often violent ethnic and national groups like the Tamils in Sri Lanka and the Albanians in the Kosovo region of Serbia. Indeed, the disintegration of Yugoslavia becomes less surprising when we see the patchwork quilt of quarreling nationalities that live next to one another in that country (see Figure 1.1).

Of course, states, too, are in the headlines. When we see references to Indian nuclear tests or Iraqi-American hostility, we think of entities that occupy territorial spaces on geographic maps. Such headlines are deceptive, for it is not those territorial entities that are acting but rather some authoritative individual or group— the premier or the government—in the name of the state. As we shall see, groups may claim that they are acting on behalf of all the citizens of a state when, in reality, they are acting only for themselves or for a small segment of the population. In some cases we are observing the actions of government bureaucracies— Russia's Ministry of Agriculture, Nigeria's army—working against other bureaucracies in the same government. Some states even house competing governments, as in Cyprus, which is divided into Greek and Turkish enclaves, with rival authorities claiming to represent the Cypriot state.

We define a *state* as *an institutionalized and exclusive territorial entity that enjoys a monopoly of lawmaking and the means of coercion within frontiers that are recognized by other states.*[35] Rarely do real states meet all of the criteria in this definition. Those who claim to represent the state usually command only part of its resources and only a proportion of its citizens' loyalties. Unless some group controls the bulk of the resources and population within a state's boundaries and can do so on a sustained basis, it is deceptive to think in terms

FIGURE 1.1

Nationalities in the Former Yugoslavia Prior to the Eruption of Civil War (1990)

This map shows the degree to which the former Yugoslavia (Union of the South Slavs) is a patchwork of ethnic groups.

of unitary state-actors in global politics. When we think of China or France as actors, we are *anthropomorphizing* (ascribing human form or attributes to a thing not human). As long as we keep in mind that people, not states, act, we can avoid this trap.[36]

A state has only one legal government, though several may contend for this status. Some governments consist of fragile coalitions of bureaucracies, political parties, or ethnic groups in which individual ministers regard each other as political enemies.[37] Finally, a state may be coterminous with a single society or may consist of several societies and even nations (or parts thereof), and nationalism may take the form of efforts to make state and nation congruent.[38] The former, like Denmark and Iceland, are *homogeneous states*, and the latter, like Brazil and India, are *heterogeneous* (or plural). Most states are ethnically diverse, producing cleavages of which governments must take account. This is true even in stable countries. The population of Canada is divided into several language groups, and the country's politics reflects the efforts of each group, especially the French in Quebec, to guard jealously its cultural and linguistic prerogatives. Indeed, one observer writes "of more than two hundred ethnic and religious minorities throughout the world who are contesting the terms of their incorporation into 'the world order.'"[39]

Just as the cast of *actors* (individuals or groups whose behavior affects political outcomes) is changing, so is the range and nature of *issues* (contentions among actors over proposals for distributing valued objects and ends). The postinternational world features numerous issues, each forming a distinct arena. Imagine a world with many theaters (issue arenas), each featuring a drama (issue) with a unique plot and cast of actors. Every issue involves actors contending to achieve preferred outcomes. Some are violent, like the war in Kosovo, and others, like negotiations to slow global warming, are conducted peacefully. To the extent that some actors participate in several issues, those issues may be linked with actors bargaining among themselves to gain support on issues important to them.

Global politics is moving away from overriding preoccupation with military security, and that departure is likely to accelerate. New issues and old ones dormant in recent decades are moving to center stage. Economic and environmental questions in particular are demanding greater attention. Questions of trade and development are key issues, and the dangers posed by *hot money*— "a multitrillion dollar pool of capital that races around the world's stock, bond and currency markets in search of the highest returns each day"[40]—now receive the sort of attention formerly reserved for military issues. After the collapse of Mexico's financial markets in 1995, two observers wrote: "There's a growing worry among the Clinton administration, Federal Reserve officials and top Wall Street financiers that the international money markets could trigger a major financial crisis they might not be able to control."[41] The financial distress that struck Southeast Asia in 1997 almost proved to be that "major" crisis. Other important issues with economic consequences include enlargement of the European Union and creation of a single European currency, evolution of a market system in Russia, and integration of China into the global economy. Such issues will shape world politics in the future, much as military issues did in the past.

Theories of global politics in the postinternational world recognize the dangers to preserving planet earth. Environmental questions are challenging political-military rivalries for global attention. These issues were dramatically brought to the world's attention by the exploding nuclear reactor at Chernobyl in the Ukraine in April 1986 and by U.N.-sponsored meetings on the environment and economic development (the Rio meeting in 1992), world population (Cairo in 1994), and global warming (Berlin in 1995 and Tokyo in 1997).

The collapse of communism in Eastern Europe brought to light the environmental disaster that befell the region under communist rule. Communist regimes set out to industrialize their societies as quickly as possible, and the results were devastating. Across East Germany, Czechoslovakia, and Poland lie "barren plateaus . . . with the stumps and skeletons of pine trees. Under the snow lie thousands of acres of poisoned ground, where for centuries thick forests had grown."[42] Air and ground water grew toxic as acid rain was produced by industries without effective scrubbers. The air is laden with poisonous nitrogen oxide and heavy metals like lead, mercury, and zinc that are linked to cancer in humans, and in Hungary clinics have set up "inhalitoriums," small booths in which individuals with lung problems can breathe clean air. Environmental tampering produced a chain reaction. The forests are gone, the birds that used to eat mice have disappeared, and exploding mouse populations consume tree seedlings and prevent reforestation. Such conditions have created serious health problems. In the region around Volsk in southern Russia, efforts to destroy stockpiles of chemical weapons have led to dramatic increases in kidney disease among children, juvenile diabetes, bronchial asthma, cerebral palsy, hydrocephalus, and leukemia,[43] and north of the Arctic Circle, Russia's Kola Peninsula "has become one of the most poisoned spots on earth—relentlessly transformed by Russian industry into a laboratory of ecological destruction." The peninsula has spiraling rates of lung cancer, lead poisoning, emphysema, and spontaneous abortions.[44]

One feature of issues such as environmental degradation is that no single government can cope with them. "With prevailing winds blowing east, Czechs blame East Germans for half their pollution and Poles blame both neighbors for as much. Poland's fallout is also felt in the Ukraine and in Sweden."[45] When the Chernobyl nuclear power plant caught fire and released nuclear debris into the atmosphere, it poisoned land, animals, and crops as far away as Ireland. To reduce the threat to health, cattle and sheep were slaughtered, and milk was dumped throughout Europe. The nomadic Laplanders in Scandinavia, who depend on reindeer herds for survival, were among the most severely affected. The grass the reindeer forage was made toxic, so that their owners could not consume the animals or their milk. The global effects of the disaster, including higher cancer rates in Europe, will not be known for decades.

As leaders recognize that their citizens share the same fates as citizens elsewhere, they are also slowly redefining *security*. The traditional view emphasized safeguarding the state and its citizens from direct military threat. Governments channeled vast resources into building their own military establishments. Military threats, such as fear of a North Korean invasion of the South, still strongly influence government calculations, and enormous resources are poured into building military power; but leaders also are recognizing nonmilitary threats to security. Global warming, overpopulation, the spread of diseases like AIDS (acquired immune deficiency syndrome), proliferating illicit narcotics and transnational crime, and enmities caused by racial and economic inequalities are threats to security—even survival—from which military force can offer little protection. Referring to drug barons, a politician from the tiny Caribbean country of St. Vincent declared: "It's easy for them to take over one of these countries. They can undermine any government and implant another."[46] "During the cold war," declared a U.S. official,

> most security threats stemmed from state-to-state aggression, so most of the analysis was of factors that could produce state-to-state aggression. Now we're focusing more on internal factors that can destabilize governments and lead to civil wars and ethnic strife. Now we're paying much more attention to early warning factors, like famine and the environment.[47]

The growing economic dimension of security is captured by recognition that "a generation ago, the fear was over Vietnam and whether its fall to Communism would inevitably take Thailand or Malaysia or Indonesia with it. The Vietnam of the economic age is Mexico, and the insurgents are brandishing not AK-47's and ideology but 'hot money.'"[48] As a consequence of globalized markets, changing technology, and the enormous financial resources in private hands, in the space of a few weeks in 1995 private financial deals "swamped the dollar, sunk the Mexican peso, wrecked a 232-year-old British bank and pushed the Clinton Administration to propose lifting Depression-era American banking regulations."[49]

Another way of looking at the changed nature of security is to consider nuclear weapons. These weapons dramatically altered the world, providing a few governments with the means to incinerate each other almost instantaneously. But it is now apparent that the influence such weapons provide is less than was believed. Nuclear weapons can be used effectively for only one purpose—to deter an adversary from using similar weapons. Nuclear weapons are of little use in fighting conventional conflicts, as the United States discovered to its frustration in Korea and Vietnam. Finally, it appears that, if a nuclear war were ever fought, unintended results such as dust particles in the atmosphere might lead to environmental disaster.[50]

The postinternational world is the scene of *local and regional quarrels that had been ignored or suppressed during the Cold War.* The Cold War's end brought to light a host of bitter local contests and historical hatreds formerly hidden. Many of these grow out of ancient national and ethnic enmities, as in Eastern Europe and the former Soviet Union or in the arbitrary boundaries drawn by colonial authorities in Africa. As long as the U.S.S.R. controlled its satellites and its own ethnic minorities, quarrels that might siphon resources away from the Cold War confrontation were suppressed. As Soviet authority receded, bitter local enmities resurfaced. Says one observer:

> The 1990s will long be remembered as the "springtime of ethnicity" in Eastern Europe. After four decades of Marxist-Leninist uniformity, statist centralism, and enforced "socialist internationalism," a dramatic ethnic, cultural, and political reawakening accompanied the disintegration of Soviet domination and Communist rule.... After nearly half a century of dormant or disguised nationalism, virtually all the East European states have been profoundly racked by ethnic, regionalist, and autonomist movements....[51]

In the Balkans, hostility is again breaking loose among the mosaic of ethnic minorities that live cheek by jowl. The enmities are the same as those that enfeebled the Austro-Hungarian and Ottoman empires and helped start World War I in 1914 and that Hitler manipulated in the years leading up to World War II in 1939. Such enmities will continue to threaten world peace in the twenty-first century. A corollary of this threat is the changed nature of war. Formerly war was an interstate affair in which organized armies met in combat. Today, ferocious civil war is the norm. The military historian Martin van Creveld writes: "The characteristics of the new kind of warfare, of which Bosnia is an example, are that sophisticated modern weapons play little role.... But although sophisticated weapons are scarcely used, these *new wars tend to be very bloody because there is no distinction between armies and peoples, so everybody who gets in the way gets killed.*"[52]

The growing role of ethnic groups, some of which are domestic and others transnational, reminds us that another feature of the postinternational world is *the breaking down of the traditional wall separating the domestic and international*

The end of the Cold War was accompanied by the demise of authoritarian regimes in the East bloc and elsewhere and an explosion of democratic and nationalist demands around the world. *(Bill Day/Detroit Free Press)*

spheres of politics. In a later chapter we evoke the *Janus faces of politics*—the idea that foreign policy is produced by forces within and outside a country.[53] Domestic events like the demise of Soviet communism have an impact throughout the world, and global events like the end of the Cold War have far-reaching consequences for domestic politics in many countries.

Another feature is *the decline of some states and groups as global leaders and the rise of new ones.* The Soviet Union's collapse, despite its military power, and Russia's uncertain role in the new global hierarchy, exemplifies this transformation. The United States remains a military and economic superpower but exercises less global clout than it did in the years after World War II. More important, overall U.S. ability to control global events is declining. Economically, Japan, Germany, China, and a number of small countries known as the NICs (newly industrializing countries) or "tigers"—South Korea, Singapore, Malaysia, Hong Kong, and Taiwan—enjoy great economic influence (though less since Asia's 1997–1999 financial crisis). As the members of the European Union (EU) forge closer economic and political ties, they will rival in importance any other economic entity.

A corollary is that first the breakup of Europe's colonial empires and later the breakup of states such as the Soviet Union and Yugoslavia produced a *proliferation of states.* In recent years, U.N. membership has jumped to 185. Recent members include Armenia, Azerbaijan, Bosnia-Herzegovina, Croatia, Georgia, Kazakhstan, Kirgizstan, Moldova, San Marino, Slovenia, Tajikistan, Turkmenistan, Uzbekistan, and Palau. Some argue that this proliferation shows that people want to live in states and that the international era is far from over. However, the new states are small and weak, largely dependent for survival on other states or international institutions, and a far cry from Europe's earlier sovereign leviathans.

Many major actors in the postinternational world are not states. Giant transnational corporations and banks enjoy oligopolistic power over sectors of the global economy and control more assets than many countries, and their willingness to invest determines the prosperity of many societies. In some issues, international civil servants, private nonprofit organizations, and even secretive terrorist and criminal groups wield influence. For instance, the International Monetary Fund (IMF), an international organization affiliated with the United Nations, exerts considerable influence over the economic policies followed by countries that need its loans to overcome financial crisis. In recent years, the IMF has forced countries such as Russia, South Korea, and Indonesia to pursue economic policies that produced unemployment and anger among those countries' citizens.[54]

A final feature of the postinternational world is that *the nature of time and space is undergoing revolutionary change, and citizens are empowered as never before.* Geography no longer constrains the movement of persons, money, goods, information, missiles, or ideas. Distance is defined less by geography than by psychology, and information is available to anyone with a television or a computer. Microelectronics, satellite television, and facsimile machines epitomize this change, which portends a weakening of states' capacity to control their citizens.

By contrast, these technologies are a great resource to transnational corporations, investment firms, terrorists, and other groups that do not have "territory" in the traditional sense. Computer "mailboxes," declares a German author, "are a very good idea because you can communicate without the police being able to monitor."[55] Those on the Internet only occupy cyberspace, and national frontiers pose no barrier to instantaneous communication and the ability of individuals to organize globally.[56] The Internet allows political dissidents to communicate and organize even though they are scattered around the world; it "offers a solidarity in cyberspace that may be hard to achieve geographically. It is especially useful in developing a student movement, now that so many universities provide access to the Internet."[57] The Internet "is seamlessly global; whether a place on it is physically located in Atlanta or Amsterdam matters little to a cybernaut, who can 'visit' either with a click of the mouse."[58] Indeed, it was possible to use e-mail to stay abreast of the violence raging in Kosovo in 1999.

Governments can control neither what is transmitted on the Internet nor what citizens, using satellite dishes, can see on television.[59] This all adds up to "a skill revolution among individuals" that contributes to "authority crises in the relationships between citizens and their larger collectivities."[60] Thus, when Russian troops assaulted Chechnya in December 1994, Russia's citizens had their "first opportunity to watch a real war as it happens on officially uncensored Russian television." They saw "[w]ounded soldiers being interviewed in field hospitals. Bloody corpses being pulled from a shot-down helicopter. Russian officers refusing to advance. Baby-faced boys digging trenches in the snow. Women begging Russian soldiers not to kill their children or cursing the Russian President for trying to stamp out their independence."[61] These images contributed to public revulsion against the invasion.[62]

ACTORS SPEAK

Technology is revolutionizing the ability of people to communicate ideas across national boundaries and, in the process, is making state sovereignty obsolete. Access to information mobilizes people as never before and allows them to participate in global politics by sitting at their computers at home. It is no longer possible for rulers to act as gatekeepers for ideas and to control what citizens think and believe. Some argue that this technology is beneficial, whereas others fear its consequences.

The notion of using the Internet to transcend international boundaries that have been used to suppress information is a very visionary one. (Gara LaMarche, associate director of Human Rights Watch, as cited in Peter H. Lewis, "On the Internet, Dissidents' Shots Heard 'Round the World," *New York Times,* June 5, 1994, Section 4, p. 18)

It wasn't very long ago that Nazis and skinheads wouldn't get any mainstream press. . . . Along comes the Internet and not only do they have access to potentially 70 million people, but they can get it for next to nothing. (Kenneth McVay, director of the Nizkor Project, as cited in Tom Vogel, Matt Moffett, and Jed Sandberg, "Radical Groups Spread the Word On-Line," *Wall Street Journal,* January 6, 1997, p. A8)

Goals and Issues

Actors seek to satisfy basic goals—prosperity, happiness, freedom, justice, equality, peace, security, and knowledge—that reflect aspirations for a better life.[63] Each of the many dramas of global politics involves efforts to achieve greater satisfaction in one or more of these basic goals. Those who live in fear seek security, and those in poverty seek prosperity and dignity. Those who lack freedom wish it, and those who live in turmoil seek order and peace. Specific issues reflect the pursuit of such goals.

The Variety of Issues

Global politics has many kinds of issues. Some, such as U.S.-Russian arms negotiations or Syrian-Israeli peace negotiations, involve the quest for security. Others, such as negotiations on trade barriers, focus on economic matters. Still others, such as controversies about acid rain, are about threats to the environment. In other words, the enormous range of issues in global politics covers diverse topics. Increasingly, the global agenda is attracting nontraditional issues that either produce cooperation or necessitate collaboration if disaster is to be avoided.

Every issue is unique. Each has its own cast of actors and geographic domain. Some are global in scope, such as global warming. Others are regional, such as Europe's adoption of a single currency. Finally, some issues are local. The same actors may deal with one another in a number of issue arenas. Each actor, however, is likely to ascribe different weight to what is at stake in an issue. Thus U.S. relations with North Korea are dominated by Washington's preoccupation with Pyongyang's development of nuclear weapons. North Korean relations with the United States, though, derive from Pyongyang's economic needs and the country's desire for recognition by the West. Such differences mean that the way in which the same actors behave toward each other also vary by issue.

For example, the U.S. and French governments often cooperate in responding to crises in less-developed countries, and both sent troops to the Persian Gulf in 1990–1991, Somalia in 1992–1993, and Rwanda in 1994. At the same time, however, their relations are sometimes strained by trade differences, especially on subsidies provided to each country's farmers. Thus, at the very moment when French troops from Djibouti were coordinating their entry into Somalia with U.S. landings in Mogadishu, French farmers were burning American flags and attacking French McDonald's outlets in protest against U.S. pressure for reducing subsidies to French farmers.

This case illustrates how two actors can interact in dramatically different ways in different issue arenas. It illustrates, too, how actors can find themselves cooperating and competing at the same time. Finally, it illustrates how issues may remain relatively isolated from each other. Sometimes, however, they become entangled. One actor may change its position on an issue that is relatively unimportant to it but is important to a second actor in return for a similar concession on yet another issue that the first actor regards as vital. During the Cold War, for example, the United States consistently allowed its European partners to enjoy trade advantages in return for European support on political issues that pitted the United States against the Soviet Union or against the less-developed states. Issues may also become linked if relations between actors so deteriorate in one arena that the deterioration infects their relations in others. This is essentially what took place in U.S.-Soviet relations in the early years of the Cold War.

Even when issues remain unlinked, they may have an impact on one another, often because of the revolution in telecommunications. Thus individuals and groups may mimic what they see or learn about what others are doing. Terrorists often copy one another's methods, and politicians mimic one another's techniques. Chinese pro-democracy demonstrators in 1989 were inspired by what similar movements had done in the Soviet Union and Eastern Europe, and investors in South Korea and Hong Kong were sufficiently frightened by events in Southeast Asia in 1997 to withdraw their funds and convert local currencies into dollars, thereby triggering a financial panic in those countries as well.

In these ways, issues evolve and change their character. New actors become involved, and old ones leave the fray. Stakes may grow more or less important to some of the players, and issues may become entangled. Vietnam became a global issue after 1945 as a matter of decolonization, with President Franklin D. Roosevelt seeking to promote Vietnamese independence. After his death and the onset of the Cold War, the issue was transformed into a civil war against French colonialism; but, with growing U.S. assistance to the French in the 1950s, it became a Cold-War issue. After the French defeat in the decisive battle of Dienbienphu in 1954 and French withdrawal from Indochina, U.S. involvement deepened, in turn eliciting greater "fraternal" aid to North Vietnam from the U.S.S.R. and China.

The Postinternational World and Collective Goods

In many issues, including some of the most compelling threats to human survival, it is difficult for actors to prosper at the expense of one another, and, if they do so, they work against the interests of humanity as a whole. In earlier centuries, nomadic tribes could enrich themselves by stealing cattle and other goods from each other, and states could prosper by seizing each other's territory. Today's sources of prosperity and welfare cannot be acquired in such a predatory manner. Each society prospers only when other societies are able to buy its products, and the economic health of any actor depends on the health of the global economic system as a whole.

This was brought home forcefully after the dramatic increases in the price of petroleum in 1973 and 1979. Although higher prices initially increased wealth in oil-producing states, the increases had additional effects. Economic stagflation (simultaneous inflation and recession) reduced Western purchases of all goods (including petroleum), stimulated increased oil production and exploration around the world, encouraged energy conservation and the search for petroleum substitutes, and reduced the value of the U.S. dollar (the currency widely used to purchase petroleum). The global economic slowdown and fall in the dollar combined to create serious difficulties for oil producers, and matters grew worse when the world market was glutted with oil in the 1980s. The oil case also illustrates that *issues are increasingly placing actors in situations in which they win or lose jointly.*

These issues feature *public* or *collective goods,* so called because they *involve benefits that must be shared and made available to everyone if they are to be enjoyed by anyone.*[64] Clean air is a good that is difficult to deny to some citizens even if they refuse to pay for it. If air pollution is reduced, that benefit cannot be provided to a few while depriving the remainder.[65] In contrast, benefits such as trash collection or fire protection that can be given to some citizens and denied to others are *private goods.* They are available only to those who can afford them or who live in affluent areas.

Because collective goods benefit everybody, we all have a stake in them. The paradox is that because so many individuals benefit, no one has an incentive to pay for them voluntarily. Each, wishing the benefit, prefers that someone else pay and may conclude that, because the group is so large, one contribution will not be missed. The economist Mancur Olson, who is mainly responsible for the collective-goods idea, summarizes the paradox:

> It does *not* follow, because all of the individuals in a group would gain if they achieved their group objective, that they would act to achieve that objective, even if they were all rational and self-interested. Indeed, unless the number of individuals is quite small, or unless there is coercion or some other special device to make individuals act in their common interest, *rational self-interested individuals will not act to achieve their common or group interests.*[66]

Thus there is a tension between the general interests of a community and the particular interests of individuals in the community. This is why polls often indicate that citizens want more benefits *and* lower taxes. Everyone benefits from a common defense, yet many prefer not to pay taxes to support it or be drafted to fight for it.[67] Enforcing tax and draft-evasion laws is necessary to ensure national defense. Or some additional private benefit, known as a *side payment,* may be needed to get support from individuals for a collective goal. Defense contracts to local industries or military bases that employ local residents are examples of side payments.

In global politics, individual actors, though favoring the collective benefits that would flow from peace, a clean environment, and unfettered trade, may be averse to paying the price. This reluctance is especially strong if those who have to pay the highest cost do not expect to receive an equivalent share of the benefits. Since Americans will have to foot much of the economic bill to bring global warming under control but can expect no greater benefit than others, the United States has dragged its feet on this issue. On the one hand, with 4 percent of the world's population, the United States emits 20 percent of the world's greenhouse gases.[68] To stabilize emissions of greenhouse gases at 1990 levels by the year 2010 would cost the equivalent of an additional tax of 26 cents on a gallon of gas, 2 cents per kilowatt hour on electricity, $52.52 per ton of coal, and $1.49 per thousand cubic feet of natural gas[69]; by one estimate, reducing U.S. carbon-dioxide emissions by 20 percent from 1988 levels by the year 2020 would leave the U.S. economy 2.2 percent smaller than it would otherwise be.[70] Such trade-offs make it difficult to carry out reforms that, on the surface, everyone favors. Special interests face every issue, whether it is the lumber industry opposing efforts to save virgin forests or automobile manufacturers opposing stricter emissions standards.

Nationalism and patriotism seem out of place for collective-goods issues that may endanger human survival. In this context, the national interest is a cognitive trap for citizens, who are like residents of an earthquake zone—they cannot leave, even when dangerous tremors seem certain. National frontiers, border guards, tariffs, and nuclear weapons cannot keep disease and hunger from spreading, oceans and lakes from dying, soil from eroding, or salinization from transforming fertile regions into deserts. If loyalty to states is based on the belief that states can deliver the goods and protect citizens from danger, then governments everywhere are in trouble.

Plan for *The Global Puzzle*

The four parts in *The Global Puzzle* are designed to make sense of the changes that have swept world politics in recent years and to introduce students to the postinternational world. Part I reviews how the international world was and how it came to be as it is. Our focus must be on change in order to make sense of the present and prepare for the future, and understanding history, as the next chapter argues, is the only way to become sensitive to change. Two simultaneous processes—the fragmentation of some entities into smaller pieces and the integration of others into larger entities—dominate the present just as they did the past. The present makes little sense without understanding the historical conditions that gave rise to it. Chapter 3 shows how sovereign states were the products of historical change in a particular historical time and place during which small medieval principalities merged and large entities like the Holy Roman Empire decayed. It also shows how the power-politics tradition arose and why that tradition is less relevant to our needs than it was in the past. The chapter also reveals how different actors have assumed importance as conditions continue to change. Chapter 4, the last in this part, illustrates how observers ignored change during the Cold War, how the transition from the international to the postinternational world was accelerated by its end, and how, as a result, a variety of other issues—some new and some old—seized our attention.

Part II examines the units of analysis that explain global outcomes, starting from the most inclusive: the global system as a whole. Thus many theorists argue that much of global politics can be explained by such factors as the distribution of power among actors. In Chapter 5, we examine the global system and its most important attributes, including the absence of central authority and the elements of power, and explain how these attributes condition the behavior of actors. Chapter 6 examines states more closely, with an eye to explaining foreign policy by paying close attention to the interaction among factors *within* and *outside* their frontiers. Our examination suggests that the wall separating the two arenas has largely fallen and that neither arena alone explains policy fully. It illustrates how our understanding of events is altered when we focus on individuals, large government bureaucracies, or processes that cross state boundaries (transnational processes). Chapter 7 turns our attention from states to some of the many nonstate actors—corporations, terrorists, and ethnic and tribal groups—to which people are loyal and which have a substantial impact on global politics in the postinternational world, sometimes influencing the most powerful states in the world. Chapter 8 examines universal and regional international organizations, emphasizing how they represent the efforts of states to collaborate in the face of transnational problems and eroding sovereignty.

Part III focuses on how and why the balance between cooperation and conflict in global politics has shifted. One feature of the international world was fierce conflict over issues, especially those involving territorial disputes, in which some states were winners and others losers. As a result, theorists largely ignored the communitarian fabric that binds actors even without central authority. In Chapter 9 we examine how much of what goes on in global politics reflects cooperation. International law and international regimes are among the mechanisms that foster cooperation even in the face of anarchy. Nevertheless, war, so central to analyses of global politics until recently, remains a threat to cooperation. Chapter 10 reviews various explanations for war and describes how it, like other phenomena in global politics, has changed in recent centuries. Despite the many changes in global politics, nuclear weapons still pose a terrifying challenge to civilization. Chapter 11 reviews the impact of these weapons on global politics, the strategies designed to use them without triggering a global catastrophe, the efforts to reduce nuclear stockpiles, and the problems posed by the proliferation of weapons of mass destruction since the end of the Cold War. Nevertheless, recent years have witnessed declining preoccupation with the risks of war and increasing concern about economic well-being. The growing importance of international political economy is explored in Chapter 12, and, as Chapter 13 explains, the end of the Cold War has allowed contentious economic issues to drive a wedge between the United States, Japan, Western Europe, and China.

In Part IV, we turn to those issues that more than any other characterize the postinternational world because they necessitate global cooperation and make sovereign states the enemies of their own citizens and of humankind more generally. Chapter 14 describes environmental problems that threaten *Homo sapiens* as a species. Burgeoning populations, the demands they place on scarce resources, and the strain they put on the fragile global ecology pose one of history's greatest threats to our survival. Chapter 15 turns our attention from the threat we confront collectively to the injustices done to individuals by states. This chapter reviews the origins and development of human rights and the degree to which they are abused or honored in the postinternational world. Finally, Chapter 16 summarizes the relative impact of globalizing and localizing trends and considers whether these promise a brighter or more ominous future.

Key Terms

actors in global politics
anthropomorphizing
bipolar
collective goods
communism
economic socialism
free-market capitalism
globalization
governance

heterogeneous state
homogeneous state
hot money
international politics
issues
Janus faces of politics
Marxism-Leninism
national interest
political democracy

postinternational politics
private goods
rational analysis
security
side payment
state
state-centric
unitary actors
zero-sum game

End Notes

[1]Craig R. Whitney, "The Roar of Tanks Fades Out Where G.I.'s Guarded Europe," *New York Times,* November 11, 1993, p. A1.

[2]Although these missiles were permitted under arms-control agreements, the administration feared that America's arsenal of land-based missiles had become vulnerable to a Soviet attack.

[3]Peter Marks, "Tourists Invited to Fly in Soviet MIG Fighters," *New York Times,* May 10, 1995, p. A13.

[4]William J. Broad, "U.S. Will Deploy Its Spy Satellites On Nature Mission," *New York Times,* November 27, 1995, pp. A1, A14.

[5]The idea of a "postinternational" world is closely associated with James N. Rosenau. See Rosenau, "Global Challenges and Theoretical Challenges: Toward a Postinternational Politics for the 1990s," in Ernst-Otto Czempiel and Rosenau, eds., *Global Changes and Theoretical Challenges: Approaches to World Politics for the 1990s* (Lexington, MA: Lexington Books, 1989), pp. 2–3. The idea

is fleshed out in three subsequent books: Rosenau, *Turbulence in World Politics* (Princeton: Princeton University Press, 1990); Rosenau and Mary Durfee, *Thinking Theory Thoroughly: Coherent Approaches to an Incoherent World* (Boulder, CO: Westview Press, 1995); and Rosenau, *Along the Domestic-Foreign Frontier: Exploring Governance in a Turbulent World* (Cambridge, UK: Cambridge University Press, 1997).

[6]For an analysis of these two processes as historical engines of change, see Yale H. Ferguson and Richard W. Mansbach, *Polities: Authority, Identities, and Change* (Columbia, SC: University of South Carolina Press, 1996).

[7]Rosenau, *Along the Domestic-Foreign Frontier,* p. 145.

[8]Two Vietnam wars were fought. The first, against French colonial rule, lasted from 1945 until 1954. The second, climaxing in the 1976 unification of North and South Vietnam, began in

1960. Between 1965 and 1973, the United States heavily intervened in the war. Full relations between Hanoi and Washington were not restored until 1995.

[9]As a country dominated by the descendents of European immigrants, the United States was "European" in outlook, culture, ideology, religion, and ethnicity. Demographic shifts, including growing numbers of African-Americans, Hispanics, and Asian-Americans over the past fifty years have begun to alter this.

[10]During World War II, Stalin accused Roosevelt and Churchill of delaying a "second front" in the hope that Germany and Russia would bleed each other to death, and the Anglo-Americans and Soviets suspected that the other side was negotiating a separate peace.

[11]Marxists believed economic equality was a precondition for "democracy"; they saw free elections without economic reform as a sham. Roosevelt's political enemies, especially in the Republican Party, repeatedly accused him of having been duped by Stalin at Yalta and having sold out Eastern Europe. In fact, Roosevelt understood that because the Red Army was there, Stalin had no incentive to make concessions.

[12]In October 1944, Churchill and Stalin agreed to spheres of influence in Eastern Europe, but Roosevelt rejected the deal.

[13]When Stalin tried to exert control over the Yugoslavs, Tito broke with Moscow in 1948, and Yugoslavia became the first "national" communist society.

[14]Some Americans, including Treasury Secretary Henry Morgenthau, looked upon Germany in much the same way as Stalin. The French and others in Western Europe who had suffered much at the hands of the Nazis were anxious about Germany, and the Americans and British supported the formation of the Brussels Pact in 1948 to meet these anxieties. This pact was the precursor of NATO.

[15]Roosevelt had died suddenly from a stroke on April 13. Truman saw much less need than Roosevelt to maintain unity among the wartime allies and was determined to stand up to the Russians.

[16]Winston S. Churchill and his Conservative Party were voted out of office while the conference was under way, and Churchill was replaced by his Labour foe, Clement Attlee.

[17]For the East, the equivalent took place in September 1947 with establishment of the Cominform by representatives of the Soviet, East European, French, and Italian communist parties to act on behalf of international communism in the struggle against "imperialism."

[18]The major anomaly was Berlin, east of the main East-West line of demarcation. Repeated crises over Berlin (1948, 1959, 1960, 1961) pitted the Soviet Union and the United States against each other as the U.S.S.R. sought to use the city's vulnerability to bring pressure on the West and as the latter tried to ensure the integrity of West Berlin as an "outpost of freedom."

[19]Stalin seized the three countries in 1940 as security from Nazi Germany, but they were quickly overrun when the Germans invaded the U.S.S.R. in June 1941. The United States continued to recognize the independence of the three Baltic states.

[20]Marxism is the revolutionary doctrine of Karl Marx and Friedrich Engels based on a belief that history evolves by class struggle. Marxism-Leninism involves the addition to the doctrine of Lenin's teachings on how to bring about revolution.

[21]This episode moved one observer to argue that the United States provide assistance to Russia's armed forces to ensure stability in that country. Benjamin S. Lambeth, "An Ailing Army Needs Our Help," *New York Times,* February 28, 1995, p. A13.

[22]A number of these features characterize *only* the world of international politics during the Cold War and not earlier eras.

[23]K.J. Holsti, *The Dividing Discipline: Hegemony and Diversity in International Theory* (Boston: Allen and Unwin, 1985), p. 9.

[24]John A. Vasquez, *The Power of Power Politics: A Critique* (New Brunswick, NJ: Rutgers University Press, 1983), p. 18.

[25]Holsti, *Dividing Discipline,* p. 9. Emphasis in original.

[26]Hans J. Morgenthau, *Politics Among Nations: The Struggle for Power and Peace,* 6th ed. rev. by Kenneth W. Thompson (New York: Alfred A. Knopf, 1985), p. 335.

[27]Kenneth N. Waltz, *Theory of International Politics* (Reading, MA: Addison-Wesley, 1979), p. 97.

[28]Holsti, *Dividing Discipline,* p. 9.

[29]Morgenthau, *Politics Among Nations,* p. 5.

[30]The mix of assumption and fact that led to such conclusions can be found in Claire Sterling, *The Terror Network: The Secret War of International Terrorism* (New York: Holt, Rinehart and Winston, 1981).

[31]Alleged attacks by small North Vietnamese vessels on American aircraft carriers provided the excuse for a major buildup of U.S. military power in Southeast Asia.

[32]Almost three decades after the end of the Vietnam War, former U.S. Secretary of Defense Robert McNamara admitted that the Kennedy and Johnson administrations failed to understand the power of nationalism. McNamara with Brian VanDeMark, *In Retrospect: The Tragedy and Lessons of Vietnam* (New York: Time Books, 1995).

[33]The exploration of space, ostensibly a peaceful pursuit by the superpowers, was driven by military exigencies.

[34]"Clinton's Words on Mission to Bosnia: 'The Right Thing to Do,'" *New York Times,* November 28, 1995, p. A6.

[35]The state has many definitions, but the one provided here captures the key traits associated with states in global politics. See Yale H. Ferguson and Richard W. Mansbach, *The State, Conceptual Chaos, and the Future of International Relations Theory* (Boulder, CO: Lynne Reiner, 1989).

[36]In asking these questions, we should avoid the confusion among *state, government,* and *society.* A *society* is a group of individuals who perceive themselves as united by a culture that distinguishes them from others. If members of a society share a common language, ethnicity, history, and, most important,

a sense of destiny, they may regard themselves as a *nation*. Shared creation myths help produce national self-perception. The ancient Roman Republic fostered the myth that Rome had been founded by the twins Romulus and Remus. Emperor Augustus, wishing a more vigorous myth, commissioned the poet Virgil to write the *Aeneid* about how Rome had been founded by the hero Aeneas on his flight from the city of Troy after its destruction by the Greeks.

[37]It is important to distinguish between politicians who are elected and permanent professional bureaucrats who staff ministries and are expected to serve in a nonpartisan manner. In Japan, for example, bureaucrats have more policy influence than elected officials.

[38]E. J. Hobsbawm, *Nations and Nationalism Since 1780: Programme, Myth, Reality,* 2nd ed.(Cambridge, UK: Cambridge University Press, 1992), p. 9.

[39]Ted Robert Gurr, *Minorities at Risk: A Global View of Ethnopolitical Conflicts* (Washington, DC: United States Institute of Peace Press, 1993), p. ix.

[40]John M. Berry and Clay Chandler, "Trying to Cool the 'Hot Money' Game," *Washington Post National Weekly Edition,* April 24-30, 1995, p. 20.

[41]Ibid.

[42]Marlise Simons, "Pollution's Toll in Eastern Europe: Stumps Where Great Trees Once Grew," *New York Times,* March 19, 1990, p.A9.

[43]Judith Ingram, "Cribs Provide a Deadly Litmus Paper," *New York Times,* May 20, 1994, p.A5.

[44]Michael Specter, "Far North in Russia, the Mines' Fatal Blight," *New York Times,* March 28, 1994, p.A4.

[45]Simons, "Pollution's Toll," p.A9.

[46]Cited in "All This and Drugs," *The Economist,* June 13-19, 1998, p. 37.

[47]Cited in Steven Greenhouse, "The Greening of American Diplomacy," *New York Times,* October 9, 1995, p.A4.

[48]David E. Sanger, "Do Fickle Markets Now Make Policy?" *New York Times,* March 19, 1995, sec. 4, p. 3.

[49]Keith Bradsher, "Back to the Thrilling Trades of Yesteryear," *New York Times,* March 12, 1994, sec. 4, p. 5.

[50]See Carl Sagan, "Nuclear Winter and Climatic Catastrophe: Some Policy Implications," *Foreign Affairs* 62:2 (Winter 1983/84), pp. 257-292.

[51]Janusz Bugajski, *Ethnic Politics in Eastern Europe: A Guide to Nationality Policies, Organizations, and Parties* (Armonk, NY: M.E. Sharpe, 1994), p. xi.

[52]Cited in Roger Cohen, "In Sarajevo, Victims of a 'Postmodern' War," *New York Times,* May 21, 1995, sec. 1, p. 8. Emphasis added.

[53]Janus was the Roman god of beginnings and of the rising and setting of the sun and was depicted with two faces looking in opposite directions.

[54]Graham Bird, "The International Monetary Fund and Developing Countries: A Review of the Evidence and Policy Options," *International Organization* 50:3 (Summer 1996), pp. 477-511.

[55]Cited in Alan Cowell, "Neo-Nazis Now Network Online and Underground," *New York Times,* October 22, 1995, Sec. 1, p. 3.

[56]See David M. Herszenhorn, "Students Turn to Internet for Nationwide Protest Planning," *New York Times,* March 29, 1995, p. B8.

[57]"Arachnophilia," *The Economist,* August 10-16, 1996, p. 28. See also Chris Hedges, "Serbs' Answer to Tyranny? Get on the Web," *New York Times,* December 8, 1996, sec. 1, p. 1.

[58]"Censorship in Cyberspace," *The Economist,* April 8-14, 1995, p. 17.

[59]The U.S. government unsuccessfully sought to allow Internet eavesdropping by law enforcement agencies. John Markoff, "U.S. Fails to Win Global Accord on Police Internet Eavesdropping," *New York Times,* March 27, 1991, pp.A1, C3. And China is trying to limit "barbaric information" on the Internet by building a version that can be censored.

[60]James N. Rosenau, "New Dimensions of Security: The Interaction of Globalizing and Localizing Dynamics," *Security Dialogue,* 25:3 (September 1994), p. 257.

[61]Steven Erlanger, "Russians Watch War on Uncensored TV," *New York Times,* December 20, 1994, p.A7.

[62]Over two decades earlier, similar images on American television galvanized public opposition to the war in Vietnam.

[63]Richard W. Mansbach and John A. Vasquez, *In Search of Theory* (New York: Columbia University Press, 1981), pp. 57-58.

[64]See Mancur Olson, Jr., *The Logic of Collective Action* (New York: Schocken Books, 1965).

[65]In reality, no benefit is entirely collective. With sufficient ingenuity, it is even possible to deprive individuals of clean air and water.

[66]Olson, *Logic of Collective Action,* p. 2. Emphasis in original.

[67]Costs are not equally distributed. Those in higher tax brackets or with fewer exemptions have to pay higher taxes, and only the young are subject to conscription.

[68]James Bennet, "Clinton Defers Curbs on Gases Heating Globe," *New York Times,* June 27, 1997, p.A7.

[69]John H. Cushman, Jr., "Push Begins for New Global Warming Pact," *New York Times,* July 16, 1997, p.A10.

[70]Rose Gutfeld, "Agreement Is Near on Greenhouse Gases," *Wall Street Journal,* May 8, 1992, p.A2.

Chapter 2

The Richness of Historical Experience

I n a moment of contemplating history, the naturalist Henry David Thoreau observed, "To the philosopher, all news is gossip." Deluged by a flood of news about world events, we may forget that those have their origin in the past, a past sometimes only dimly recalled. The present is a bridge between past and future, and it is inexplicable without knowing how it came to be. Theory incorporates our perception of the world; it tells us what is important and what we can ignore. Only in this way can we simplify reality to make sense of why things happen. Yet our propensity is to assume that the world as we see it at any moment has always existed and always will; if that is wrong, theory will also be wrong.

Why Study History?

History informs us that change is continuous, altering the features of the global landscape.[1] Generations of students are accustomed to thinking of the sovereign state system as a permanent feature of global politics, yet this belief is wrong. The sovereign territorial state is an artifact of European politics. Just as that sovereign state was the product of the integration and fragmentation of prior political associations—what political scientist James Rosenau calls "fragmegration"[2]—so both processes are at work today, eroding the state. History focuses on change, forcing us constantly to reevaluate our theories.

Another assumption of many was that U.S.-Soviet hostility was a paramount feature of world politics. With that as context, it is clear why they also felt that military power wielded by a few governments is the overriding factor in global politics. The story of global politics has rarely had so simple a plot; mostly it has not been limited to a few powerful states engaged in life-and-death struggle, and the world after the Cold War is no exception.

It took a series of momentous events at the end of the twentieth century to remind us that the global arena is always in flux: Marxism-Leninism swept from Eastern Europe and the Soviet Union, Germany reunited, the end of apartheid in South Africa, and democracy a powerful symbol for peoples all over the world. However, global politics reflects continuity as well as change. Many of these events have earlier parallels, recognition of which helps us interpret and respond to them. Many of these historical roots grew in very different cultural soil, making it imperative that we study these cultures if we hope to respond wisely to the events they have produced. If we only use Western experience to make sense of the non-Western world, we are doomed to misunderstand events.

We need to learn about Chinese culture and politics, for example, to understand and explain that country's defensive reaction to the critical global response to imprisonment of political dissidents. The savage conflicts between Serbs and Muslim Albanians in Kosovo make sense only when we are aware of ancient rivalries between Turkey's Ottoman Empire and Christian Europe (see Figure 2.1). Whether we are preoccupied by conflict in Northern Ireland—its roots dating back as far as Henry VIII's efforts to pacify Ireland in the sixteenth century—or Muslim-Hindu violence in India—its roots in the sixteenth-century Mogul conquest of that country—today's problems make little sense outside their historical context.

Let us briefly look at several historically unique systems that reveal something of the variety of actors and issues in global politics. The cases have been selected because each has a different "architecture"—different actors, issues, and types of governance—and each represents a distinctive "civilization" in a world in which, according to one observer, "the great divisions among humankind and the dominating source of conflict will be cultural."[3] We start with the competition and interaction among the small Greek city-states in the fifth century B.C. to which subsequent Western civilization owes so much. Then we turn to a very different system: the centralized Chinese Empire from which stem contemporary Chinese views of their place in the world. We focus next on the expansion of medieval Muslim society and examine how the clash between integration and fragmentation in that context continues to echo in the Muslim world today.

In the second half of the chapter, we consider how global politics evolved in Europe, from the collapse of ancient Rome, through the Middle Ages, to the emergence of territorial states in western Europe. Examining Europe's transformation from a centralized political system during the Roman era to a decentralized one in the Middle Ages, climaxing in competitive territorial states, illuminates the impact of the past on our thinking today and provides clues about the future. Indeed, the fragmentation of states today and the spread of "subgroupism" "resemble the decentralized arrangements of the medieval era and its highly decentralized, conflictual, and disparate structures."[4]

Although the European system of states was only one form of international organization, it became significant because of Europe's outward expansion beginning late in the fifteenth century. "The global international society of today," declare Hedley Bull and Adam Watson, "is in large part the consequence of Europe's impact on the rest of the world over the last five centuries."[5]

Assumptions Critical to Understanding Global Politics

Before surveying these historical epochs, there are five assumptions we must share to understand today's global politics.

1815 to 1839: After the Congress of Vienna

The Ottoman Empire, having emerged from the Middle Ages predominant in the Balkans, controlled Serbia and Bosnia and Herzegovina at its northern fringes well into the 19th century.

1914: Eve of the First World War

The Turks were driven from most of the Balkans in the 19th century and were replaced by rival European powers. With Russian patronage, an independent Serbia was born alongside an Austrian-controlled Bosnia, where a Serbian nationalist ignited World War I by assassinating the Austrian crown prince.

Between the Two World Wars

The Versailles conference created a unified kingdom of the south Slavs—Yugoslavia. It encompassed Serbs, Croatians and Slovenians, with the capital in Belgrade and the lion's share of influence held by the Serbs. Bosnia's Muslims were not recognized as a distinct group.

November 1942: Height of Axis Occupation

The Axis powers occupied Yugoslavia, creating a puppet state in Croatia ruled by local fascists who fought and butchered Serbs, Jews, and Gypsies. Yugoslav Communist partisans led by Tito, as well as Serbian royalists known as Chetniks, fought the Nazis, and Tito emerged in control.

1945 to 1990: Cold War Stability

Under Tito, Yugoslavia held together as a federation of six autonomous republics, although Serbs retained great influence, notably in the military. As Communism collapsed, Serbia's President, Slobodan Milosevic, hastened Yugoslavia's disintegration with a blatantly nationalistic appeal to Serbs.

1991–1994: Open Warfare

Fighting broke out in 1991 when Slovenia and Croatia seceded, then spread to Bosnia in 1992. The key element was the determination of Serbs in Croatia and Bosnia, encouraged by Serbia, to expel non-Serbs from land they control in hopes of eventual union with Serbia.

1. *During much of history, communities have been largely isolated from one another, thereby limiting the exchange of ideas, persons, and things and minimizing the possibility of hostile interaction.* Through much of history, isolated pockets of people interacted only with those living close by, in ignorance of others elsewhere.[6] These pockets evolved unique cultures, religions, and political and moral beliefs, and often felt superior to outsiders. The ancient Greeks, for example, coined the word *barbarian* for those who did not speak Greek, because they considered them uncivilized.[7] The ancient Chinese had a similar attitude toward those who spoke other tongues and regarded China's empire as the center of the universe.

Contact with foreigners was impeded by geography, primitive transportation, and vulnerability to unaccustomed diseases.[8] Most cultures were agrarian, tying inhabitants to the land. Few people knew anything about the world beyond their immediate vicinity, and fewer cared. People in such *traditional societies* more willingly accepted such natural catastrophes as drought, flood, and famine than we do today. They assumed that the world was unchanging, in marked contrast to our belief that change is omnipresent. Ideas of progress had little influence on them, and only a few lived above the subsistence level.

Although economic exchange existed in prestate societies based on gift giving and barter, genuine markets "wherein goods and services are exchanged to maximize the returns to individual buyers and sellers"[9] only arose with the territorial state. Thus, until the end of the thirteenth century, the six annual Fairs of Champagne served as Europe's "central clearinghouse" for trade.[10] Originally such fairs were gatherings of merchants who met in the same place each year to exchange goods. In time, fairs such as those at Champagne were held year-round.

When previously isolated cultures came in contact, the mixture frequently was explosive, as during the medieval crusades between Christians and the Muslim Saracens and the Spanish collision with the indigenous peoples of the New World. Much of the global interconnectedness that we take for granted was produced by European imperialism, reinforced in recent decades by revolutions in transportation and communication. We cannot begin to understand the misperceptions and suspicions of disparate peoples today without recognizing that they retain beliefs and customs inherited from earlier centuries and that they persist in believing that their ways are superior to all others.

Tensions between Shi'ite and Sunni Muslims, Jews and Arabs in the Middle East, Chinese and Malays in Southeast Asia, Arabs and black Africans in the Sudan, Tamils and Sinhalese in Sri Lanka, and between many others date back to collisions in earlier centuries. So, too, do Japanese and Korean reluctance to buy foreign goods or accept immigrants and the Chinese sense of cultural superiority, characteristics that annoy, even infuriate, Westerners. Despite improved communications and transportation, many people remain isolated and rarely come in contact with foreigners, or do so only fleetingly when foreigners arrive as tourists.

2. *Western experience is not the only valid guide to global politics.* Bull and Watson write, "Europeans have never had any monopoly of knowledge or experience of international relations."[11] The model of global politics in which sovereign states are the principal actors, interacting only with each other, and military issues dominate derives from Europe's historical experience. Elements of that model,

FIGURE 2.1
History and the South Slavs

For Serbs, struggle and history are one. The map of the Balkans has changed time and again in the nineteenth and twentieth centuries. Empires rise and fall. Occupiers come and go. At the center, Serbia appears, in one guise or another, and sometimes dominates its neighbors, only to disappear and perhaps rise again. It is not a history that encourages feelings of security. SOURCE: *The New York Times*, April 10, 1994, sec. 4, p. 5. Copyright © 1994 by *The New York Times*. Reprinted by permission.

especially those dealing with power, are also found in writings by non-Western theorists,[12] but the state-centric bias of our thinking comes mainly from European history and philosophy. However well this tradition served in the past, it is no longer sufficient to understand global politics after the Cold War.

Scholars and practitioners also usually draw examples and recite "lessons" of global politics from Western experience. Even our understanding of ethics in politics is adduced from the Judeo-Christian tradition in the West. Our ignorance of other cultures, languages, and traditions makes this bias inevitable, but it also heightens the likelihood of misunderstanding when Westerners come in contact with non-Westerners. Until recently, the insights of non-Western history were often ignored. Only in recent decades have American schools and colleges routinely introduced us to non-Western ideas, history, and literature. Our leaders have often seen the world through *Eurocentric* eyes.

Western colonialism and dominance of global economics and politics during the nineteenth and twentieth centuries led many to assume that Western mores and ideas are inherently better than those of non-Western societies. Ideas like economic and political development have too often meant becoming more like "us in the West." Yet blindly emulating economic, political, and social policies that worked in the West perhaps a hundred years ago may be inappropriate for societies elsewhere that are confronting challenges that earlier generations of Europeans and Americans could hardly have imagined. Indeed, the modern state, featuring a government's centralized and exclusive control over a defined population in a clearly defined territory,[13] is a European invention, and efforts to impose this political organization outside of Europe, with competing tribal and ethnic traditions, have sometimes been disastrous. When the colonial powers imposed state structures in Africa on peoples with different tribal loyalties, they often unwittingly contributed to later authoritarian rule and civil strife. The consequence of forcing diverse *tribes*—groups whose members claim a common ancestry—and ethnic groups into Western-style "civilized cages"[14] is reflected in today's violence in the Balkans and in central Africa.

3. *People have organized themselves into a rich variety of groups other than territorial states.* The territorial state with its elaborate and impersonal bureaucracy is only one of many possible political forms. For a number of reasons, especially its capacity to mobilize large numbers of people with significant resources and to provide them with collective goods,[15] the state has proved a durable participant in global affairs. Where it collided with other forms in recent centuries, such as tribal groups in Africa and in North America, it triumphed.

The state is not, however, inherently superior to other forms of political organization. Other types of actors have also been effective and successful. Nomadic tribes—Arabs under the banner of Islam in the seventh century and Mongols in the twelfth century—swept across their worlds. The Arabs "conquered the civilized world from Spain to India, destroying one empire in the process and severely mutilating another, in some 50 years, while the Mongols destroyed states of every kind from eastern Europe to Burma, narrowly missing the conquest of Egypt in the west and Japan in the east, in less than a century."[16] "Arab scholars," declares one historian, "were studying Aristotle when Charlemagne and his lords were reportedly learning to write their names. Scientists in Cordova, with their seventeen great libraries, . . . enjoyed luxurious baths at a time when washing the body was considered a dangerous custom at the University of Oxford."[17]

Although the territorial state remains the dominant political actor in global politics, it is not the exclusive or even primary object of loyalty in all parts of the world. If history is a guide, we must assume that the state as we know it—a clearly defined territory with a locus of central authority—will be altered in the future. Other global actors such as transnational corporations (Exxon), interstate organizations (NATO), and even supranational organizations (the High Commission of the European Union) will grow in prominence.

4. *Political organization, ideological fervor, economic vitality, and technological capability help explain the waxing and waning of global influence.* History reveals that several factors account for the epochal shifts that occur from time to time in global power centers.[18] Such shifts include the decline of the Greek city-states and their absorption first by Macedonia and then by Rome, expansion and subsequent fragmentation of Islam, expansion of the Chinese Empire south of the Han River, the erosion of the Holy Roman Empire and medieval papacy and the triumph of states in Europe, and emergence of U.S.-Soviet bipolarity after World War II.

Political organization—the manner in which individuals and groups join one another and cooperate for political ends—is one factor that helps explain these great shifts. European organization into territorial states with efficient bureaucracies that could extract taxes from citizens and invest in economic and technological growth was a key element in successful expansion into tribal America and Africa. Successful and durable *ideologies*—deeply anchored and closed sets of beliefs that guide behavior—like religion, nationalism, or, more recently, capitalism and Marxism, are another factor in these shifts.

Finally, economic vitality and technology are critical in explaining shifts in power centers. One historian argues that the decline of "great powers" can be traced to their being overtaken and surpassed by others in economic and industrial performance and that their decline is accompanied by overexpenditure on nonproductive military ventures and underinvestment at home.[19] Competitive market economies took root in Western Europe early on, a major reason why Europeans were able to take advantage of and improve military technologies, including gunpowder and cannon, which were invented elsewhere. Lacking comparable weapons, such non-Europeans as the Aztecs of Mexico and the Ashanti of Ghana were unable to resist European imperialism. The collapse of communist regimes in Eastern Europe and the U.S.S.R. under faltering economies and technological obsolescence bears witness to the power of economic and technological factors.

5. *Theories of global politics are rooted in historical conditions.* The way we think about the world around us is determined by the real conditions we confront. In other words, political theories and philosophies—however abstract they seem—are *not* produced by dispassionate analysis of thinkers laboring in ivory towers. Instead, they represent efforts by people actively working to change those conditions in a manner consonant with their preferences.

We must distinguish between two branches of theory—*empirical* and *normative.* The first entails the search for knowledge by experiment and experience, and the second a search for that which is moral and right. A theory that stipulates the causes of war is empirical, and one addressing the injustice of war is normative. Scientific knowledge is empirical, and scientists argue for maintaining the boundary between the two branches of theory. The study of politics is not the same as the study of physics, however, even though some political scientists wish to emulate the physicist's certainty and precision.[20] Although it may be desirable to keep the empirical and normative aspects of problems as clearly separated as possible, political practitioners are so involved in the real world and are so interested in changing it that the boundary is difficult to maintain.[21]

Consider the Florentine Renaissance writer Niccolò Machiavelli. Machiavelli is famous for his treatise *The Prince.* Writing it as practical advice for a statesman, he argues that, because conditions make it impossible for leaders to trust each other, they must act in ways that most of us would consider immoral. His analysis is regarded as a key contribution to the power-politics approach because of its insistence that preserving and promoting the state ought to be the overriding objectives of leaders.

Far from being a disinterested scientist and observer of human nature, Machiavelli was a deeply committed statesman and Italian patriot. *The Prince* faithfully depicts how politicians in the small Italian city-states in the fifteenth and sixteenth centuries behaved and was a primer for a leader who Machiavelli hoped would unite the country to cast out the French and Spaniards who had invaded it. "So now," he concludes, "left lifeless, Italy is waiting to see who can be the one to heal her wounds . . . and cleanse those sores which have been festering for so long."[22]

Few modern scholars are so publicly passionate about their beliefs, but most are as deeply committed as Machiavelli. Their beliefs vary, but we cannot understand their work unless we recognize those beliefs and ideals. Thus those who study the causes of war are often at the same time scientists seeking truth and idealists trying to end the scourge they are studying. Inevitably, empirical theory is infused with normative values.

Classical Greece, Imperial China, and Theocratic Islam

Today's global politics owes much to systems that flourished in antiquity and in regions other than Europe. Those systems had their own cast of actors and their own issues, some of which have reappeared as the European epoch in global politics comes to an end.

Politics in Classical Greece   The Greek city-states (see Figure 2.2), which gave birth to many of the West's political ideas, lay in and around the Aegean Archipelago, with additional settlements along the Mediterranean shore to the east in Asia Minor and to the west in Italy, Sicily, southern France, and northern Africa. The Greeks are important because they "organized their external relations in very innovative and significant ways" and because they "exercised great influence on the European system, out of which the present system has developed; and for several centuries aspects of Greek practice

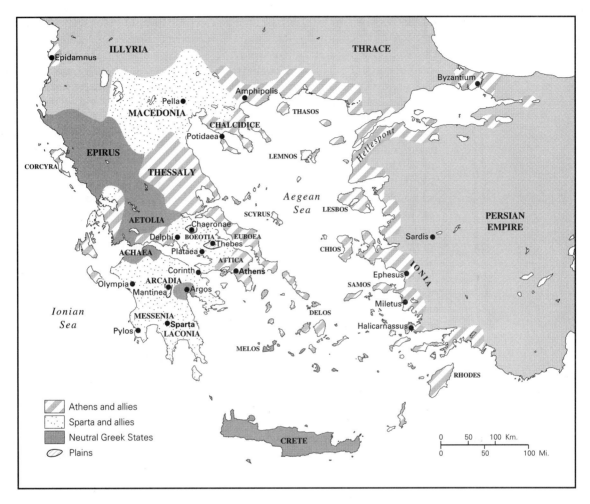

FIGURE 2.2
The Politics of Classical Greece

This map, which shows the alignment of states during the Peloponnesian War, vividly illustrates the large scale of the war and its divisive impact.

served as models for the European society of states."[23] Indeed, as we shall see in the next chapter, Greece was the home of one of the key founders of the West's tradition of power politics, the historian Thucydides.

Individual *city-states* were smaller than modern states and frequently were in conflict. Resources were widely distributed, although Athens and Sparta came to dominate the others. Greeks nevertheless felt a sense of community with each other that was reinforced by their tongue, their gods, their extensive trade, and their culture. Such rudimentary international institutions as the shrine to Apollo at Delphi and the Olympic Games reinforced the sense of Greekness. Their perception of a common identity proved potent when the Persian empire sought to conquer the

Greeks between 490 and 478 B.C. For a brief time the city-states were able to unite and defeat the common enemy, and the war was perceived as a conflict between Greeks from Europe and aliens from Asia. Successive efforts by the Persians to subdue Greece, culminating in an invasion led by Xerxes, were thrown back by an alliance of Greek city-states in the battles of Marathon (490 B.C.),[24] Salamis (480 B.C.), and Plataea (479 B.C.).

Once the Persians were repelled, the Greeks returned to their quarrelsome ways. Without the bond provided by a common enemy, little remained to keep them together. If Greeks viewed themselves as united by blood and culture, they were divided by type of political system and territorial jealousies. After the Persian defeat, Athenian influence grew, and an Athenian empire arose on the oars of a powerful navy. A countervailing alliance led by Sparta, which had the leading army in Greece, was formed to limit Athenian influence. The ensuing Peloponnesian War (431–404 B.C.) between the two alliances dragged on for almost three decades, nearly eliminating Athens and so enfeebling the Greek universe that the Persians reasserted their hegemony over the Greek communities in Asia Minor (see Figure 2.2).

The activities of the small Greek city-states offer insights into the causes of war between states. In the years leading up to the Peloponnesian War, resources and attitudes were divided into competing and exclusive alliances. Their competition resembled global politics after 1945, when much of the world divided into two rival camps. Observers feared that, just as war engulfed the Greek world in 431 B.C., the Cold War would end in a tragedy of nuclear proportions. The idea that war can be prevented if power is divided among several participants and no state is allowed to amass too much power is still propounded by some theorists.[25]

Another important parallel with today was the absence of a clear boundary between the domestic and foreign arenas. Like today, a good deal of *transnational* behavior—society to society rather than government to government—also appeared in the Greek world as leaders and soldiers frequently betrayed their city-state and changed sides.

China's Imperial System

China is home to the oldest continuous historical tradition and one of the richest civilizations (see Figure 2.3). Chinese ideas about global politics took their own shape, differing from Western ideas as those evolved from classical Greece. This divergence continues to contribute to misunderstanding between the Chinese and other peoples even today.

"The monumental Chinese achievement in the field of statecraft," declares Adam Watson, "is usually held to be the more or less effective imperial unity that has assured domestic peace and order for most of Chinese history."[26] The distinctive Chinese outlook on foreign affairs was forming long before Thucydides recorded the Athens-Sparta conflict in the fifth century B.C. "The ethical system that has largely determined the Chinese view of life, and therefore also the Chinese approach to foreign affairs, was already well established in its broad outlines in the first centuries of the Chou period (1027–221 B.C.)."[27] We associate this outlook mainly with the philosopher-sage Confucius, writing at a time of political turmoil in China.

The Chinese outlook was built on the conviction—reinforced by the age, continuity, and geographic isolation of the Chinese Empire and the sophistication of Chinese civilization—that the Middle Kingdom (as China styled itself) was the

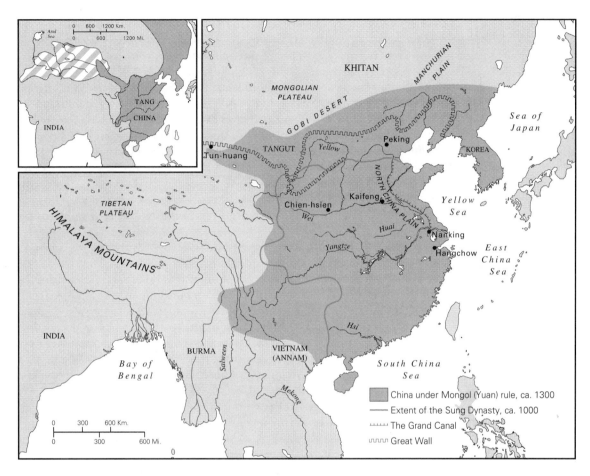

FIGURE 2.3
The Chinese Imperial System

This map and inset illustrate how the Táng Dynasty and its successors were able to sustain the expanded frontiers of the Han dynasty, although their hold in the west was always somewhat tenuous.

center of the world and that the Son of Heaven (as the emperor was called) was ruler of the universe. The Chinese Empire "remained the center of the world known to it, only vaguely aware of the other ancient centers to the west" and "never lost its sense of all-embracing unity and cultural entity."[28] The arrogance of this self-perception is apparent in a letter sent from the emperor to British King George III in the eighteenth century:

> Swaying the wide world, I have but one aim in view, namely, to maintain a perfect governance.... It behooves you, Oh King, to respect my sentiments and to display even greater devotion and loyalty in the future, so that by perpetual submission to our throne, you may secure peace and security for your country hereafter.... I do

not forget the lonely remoteness of your island, cut off from the world by intervening wastes of sea, nor do I overlook your excusable ignorance of the usages of our
Celestial Empire. . . . Tremblingly obey and show no negligence.[29]

The practical consequence of this egoistic view of the world was a belief that
the political universe was centrally and hierarchically organized and that all peoples were subjects of the Son of Heaven. This perspective contrasted vividly with
the dominant model of global politics that evolved in the West, which viewed the
political universe as consisting of numerous independent and competing states
with no superior to govern them. The Chinese view provided a basis for organizing China's relationship with small neighbors like the Koreans who were treated
as subject peoples. Such peoples had to provide symbolic tribute to the emperor,
and their representatives had to perform the kowtow (ritual bow) when coming
before the Son of Heaven.

With its imperial experience, the Chinese view of world affairs, unlike that in
the West, was unable to distinguish, at least in theory, between foreign and domestic politics. The Chinese had no conception of a world of sovereign actors. Instead,
all peoples were under the rule of Heaven, and the emperor was charged with governing them all, whether Chinese or not. The emperor's subjects, whether Chinese
or barbarian (non-Chinese), should be treated in the same way in accord with
Confucian norms, and all subjects should obey and respect the emperor.
The Chinese knew that theory and practice differed and that the emperor could
not govern foreigners as effectively as those who lived in China. Nevertheless, they
tried to force non-Chinese who wished to trade or negotiate with them to follow
the rituals of submission to the emperor. Occasionally, these efforts created tension with foreigners, especially when the latter were actually more powerful than
the Chinese.

The quality of rulership, taught Confucius, depended on adherence to traditional moral principles. In consequence, Chinese theories of world politics were
infused with a strong normative element; classical Chinese views of the world
were as preoccupied with what ought to be as with what was. John Fairbank
writes, "Adherence to the correct teachings would be manifested in virtuous conduct and would enhance one's authority and influence. . . . Right principles exhib-
ited through proper conduct . . . gave one prestige among others and power over
them."[30] In other words, moral behavior had the practical result of increasing imperial power. Right, one might say, makes might. By contrast, policy failures could be
traced to a ruler's lack of virtue and his loss of the Mandate of Heaven.

Since China's emperor, though in theory ruler of the world, had to govern in
accord with Confucian moral principles, he was obliged to educate barbarians in
the ethical precepts of Confucianism and extend to them the benefits of Chinese
culture and learning.[31] The Son of Heaven was expected to behave toward foreigners as he did toward his own people, in accord with the benign universal morality of Heaven. If he did so, the natural harmony of Heaven would prevail. Thus the
traditional Chinese perspective, unlike that of the West, saw harmony, not conflict,
as the natural condition of the political universe.[32]

Although harmony was believed to be a natural condition, the Chinese did *not*
assume that it would be automatic. "In the very nature of human relations," wrote

one observer, "superiors cannot expect automatic obedience from their inferiors. But since neither father nor husband, older brother nor emperor, was supposed to enforce subservience by reliance on the power that he inherited in his superior status, the exercise of control was traditionally viewed as an art requiring consummate knowledge and skill."[33] Moral suasion and patience, not coercion, were, Confucians believed, the way to maintain order.

China's sense of virtue and superiority and its rulers' effort to isolate the country from outsiders became sources of conflict with the Europeans and Japanese, especially in the nineteenth century, when the latter had the economic and military clout not only to disobey the emperor but to impose imperial rule over large areas of the country. The British,[34] Germans, Japanese, Russians, and others established trading zones in China's cities over which they exercised exclusive control. Chinese efforts to oust the "foreign devils," including the Boxer Rebellion (1900), were unsuccessful until after World War II.

China's military defeat at the hands of Japan in the Sino-Japanese War (1895) signaled the beginning of the end for China's last imperial dynasty, the Qing (also called the Manchus) and marked a giant step in Japan's effort to create an Asian empire for itself. After the overthrow of the Qing (1911–1912), Sun Yatsen, founder of the Guomintang (National Party), became provisional president of the Republic of China, but soon ceded power to the dictatorial General Yuan Shikai. Following Yuan's death in 1916, China descended into a warlord era that lasted until 1927, when the country was reunited under Jiang Jieshi and the Guomintang. As we shall see in Chapter 13, these humiliations weighed heavily on China in the twentieth century.

Chinese self-perception is still reflected in foreign-policy attitudes. Japanese economic power and Western military prowess are regarded as less important than Chinese cultural superiority. China's leaders still believe they have special rights and responsibilities toward neighboring states in Asia that were once their tributaries. Chinese refusal to embrace democratic reform or abandon communism and the Chinese leaders' rejection of foreign interference in their affairs after the 1989 massacre in Beijing's Tiananmen Square reflect their belief that China has little to learn from the West. China's suspicions of the West and of Russia are also intensified by the century of imperial interference in their internal affairs.

Rise and Decline of an Islamic Empire

Another historical system that still influences events was based on the religion of Islam (see Figure 2.4). Islam's adherents sought to make their religion universal. After the death of the Prophet Muhammad in A.D. 632, the Islamic Empire rapidly expanded, at its height stretching from western Asia and the Middle East, through northern Africa, and into Spain. In later centuries, Afghanistan, parts of central Asia, and much of the Indian subcontinent were added to the Islamic world. The consequences of Islam's expansion and of cleavages in the movement are still evident today. Almost a billion Muslims live in the Middle East, Turkey, Iran, Afghanistan, North Africa, India, Pakistan, Indonesia, Malaysia, central Asia, and even parts of the Philippines and sub-Saharan Africa. And many devoted Muslims still believe that the world is divided "into the *dar al Islam,* the area of acceptance (of the will of God) or the area of peace, and the *dar al harb,* the area of war, where conflict with non-Muslim powers was to be expected and where war to expand the *dar al Islam* . . . was not only legitimate but positively virtuous."[35]

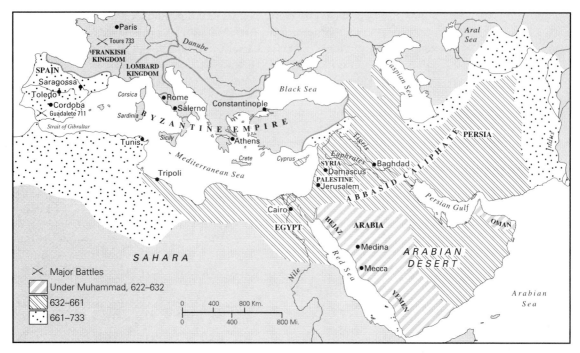

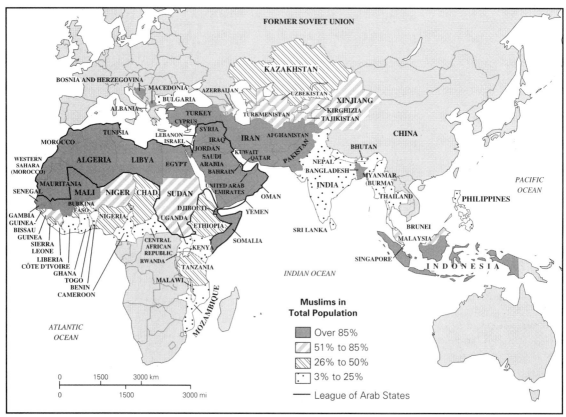

FIGURE 2.4
Medieval and Modern Islam

Political weaknesses in the territories they conquered, as well as superior fighting skills, help explain the speed with which the Muslims expanded. Initially spreading outward from Arabia into Persia and Egypt, Arab armies thereafter spread across North Africa and into Asia Minor, gaining a foothold and conquering the Byzantine and Sassanid (Persian) empires in the process. Although the Islamic heartland remains the Middle East and North Africa, Islam is growing steadily in black Africa and is the faith of heavily populated Indonesia.

Islam is based on the claim of the Prophet Muhammad that a message from Allah (God) had been revealed to him. Muhammad shared Allah's message with the Arabs of Mecca, and that message was recorded in the Koran. To understand the politics of Islamic societies, we must realize that "Muslims have always believed in the completeness of the Quran [Koran]; it is not to be supplemented by recurrent messages. . . . Among the Quran's truths is a prescription for regulating the political and social affairs of man. Islam makes no distinction between the state and the realm of believers. . . ."[36] Thus Islamic authority tended toward *theocracy* (government by religious leaders according to religious precepts).[37] Muslim behavior is guided by religion, and all Muslims are united by their faith regardless of national or class differences.

By the middle of the eighth century A.D., Muhammad's successors, the Umayyad caliphs, with their capital in Damascus, had transformed Islam's religious fervor into a workable Muslim empire. These caliphs often could not follow the principles of government and law as required by the theologians in the holy city of Medina, yet they were able to establish the needed political institutions for an expanding empire. With the conquest of Spain and Sicily, Islam collided with Europe's Christian Frankish emperors Charles Martel and Charlemagne. This was the high-water mark of Islam's spread as a united religion. Under the Abbasid caliphs (A.D. 750–1250), Islamic society reached its height. Greek, Roman, Persian, and Hindu works were translated into Arabic and became part of Muslim culture. The works of ancient jurisprudence, philosophy, science, and the humanities were preserved in Muslim culture and the Arabic language. Baghdad became a center of intellectual and cultural life.

This brief moment of glory soon faded, for the Islamic Empire fragmented into competing dynasties by the end of the tenth century. Rivalries grew among competing caliphs. The Seljuk Turks, hired as mercenaries, gained independent influence. Christian crusaders invaded the empire to recapture the Holy Land and controlled parts of the region for more than two hundred years (1094–1294). More important, Mongols from the east and the Mamelukes[38] from Egypt made inroads as well. Eventually, what remained of the Muslim empire was conquered by the Ottoman Turks.[39] Adda Bozeman writes:

> The remarkable success of [Islam] as an international association of coreligionists was offset by its equally remarkable failure as a political commonwealth. . . . The only pattern of political coalescence on the international level that Islamic history suggested was that of the unconsolidated empire-in-motion. It is not surprising to find, therefore, that expansion became the principal international policy of each separate Islamic sovereignty after the unified Empire had ceased to be a reality.[40]

In 1453, the Ottomans, a Turkish Muslim dynasty, conquered Constantinople, destroying the last vestiges of Christian Byzantium and creating panic in Europe. The Christian-Muslim conflict that had flared earlier began in earnest, and some of its consequences remain with us as tensions in the Middle East and the Balkans. Christians retook all of Spain by 1492 and expelled the country's Muslims and Jews. During the next two hundred years, the *Ottoman Empire* conquered much of the Middle East and North Africa and, until repelled, extended its rule into

Greece and the Balkans to the borders of Austria and Hungary (see Figure 2.5). The Ottoman Empire, writes Albert Hourani,

> was a bureaucratic state, holding different regions within a single administrative and fiscal system. It was also, however, the last great expression of the universality of the world of Islam. It preserved the religious law, protected and extended the frontiers of the Muslim world, guarded the holy cities of Arabia[41] and organized the pilgrimage to them.[42]

This great multinational empire expanded to the gates of Vienna in 1698 but then was gradually enfeebled until, late in the nineteenth century, it had earned the title "sick man of Europe." Until the middle of the eighteenth century, the relationship between the Ottomans and Europeans was still one of equality. Within a century, the societies composing the empire were being penetrated by Europeans and were becoming economically dependent on them. Ottoman mistreatment of Christians gave Europeans a handy excuse for intervening when they wished to.

During the nineteenth century, European conflicts with the declining Ottomans and with one another for the spoils of that empire were endemic.[43] In 1798 Napoleon seized Egypt, but the British drove out his forces three years later. The French conquest of Algeria (1830–1847) was the first important penetration of an Arabic society by Europeans, and the European powers also became deeply involved in the Ottomans' Balkan provinces. With their aid, Serbia gained independence in 1830 and Greece three years later. Thereafter, Tunisia (1881) and Egypt (1882), Morocco (1906), and Libya (1911)[44] were added to the European empires. World War I was set off by the last in a series of crises in the Balkans involving the struggle for control over areas being abandoned by the ebbing Muslim empire.[45] A flaming crisis in 1908 between Austria-Hungary and Russia over the former Ottoman province of Bosnia-Herzegovina brought the two powers to the verge of a war that finally erupted in 1914.[46]

Alliance with Austria-Hungary and Germany in World War I was catastrophic for the Ottomans, and the war set off an eruption of Arab nationalism. The British waged war against the Ottomans in Palestine, Syria, and Iraq, triumphing everywhere. Among their local allies was Hussein, the governor *(sherif)* of Mecca and leader of the Hashemite clan of Arab Bedouins,[47] who, encouraged by British promises of national independence,[48] launched an Arab revolt against the Ottomans in 1916. The revolt was aided by an adventurer of mythic proportion, T. E. Lawrence, known as Lawrence of Arabia. The Ottoman Empire collapsed in 1923 when the sultanate was overthrown by army officers led by Mustapha Kemal (Kemal Ataturk), who then established the secular Republic of Turkey.

Today, we are witnessing a revival of Islamic fundamentalism, which demands that people be ruled solely in accord with religious doctrine.[49] Under the Ayatollah Ruhollah Khomeini, Iran became a model for other efforts to Islamize societies. Today, Afghanistan is governed by the Taliban, a militantly Islamic movement founded by Islamic students from rural areas of the country. Algeria is in the grip of civil war between Islamic militants and a military government, and in Egypt, Sudan, Lebanon, Pakistan, and even Turkey, Islamists are trying to level secular institutions and govern according to Muslim principles. Islamists in Iran and the Sudan train, arm, and finance militant fundamentalists throughout the Middle East.[50] The idea of a stateless Islamic world is very much alive.

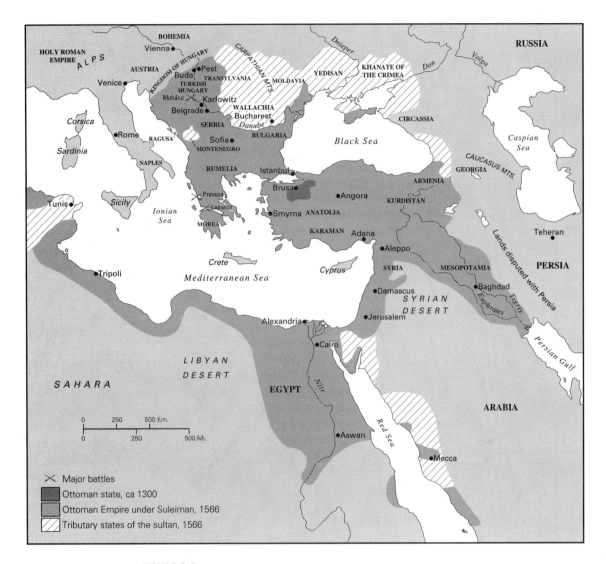

FIGURE 2.5
The Ottoman Empire at Its Height, 1566

The Ottomans, like their great rivals the Hapsburgs, rose to rule a vast dynastic empire encompassing many different peoples and ethnic groups. The army and the bureaucracy united the disparate territories into a single state.

Medieval Europe to Westphalia: Birth of the State System

The system of states that dominated global politics in the nineteenth and twentieth centuries evolved mainly in a western European context. That evolution was

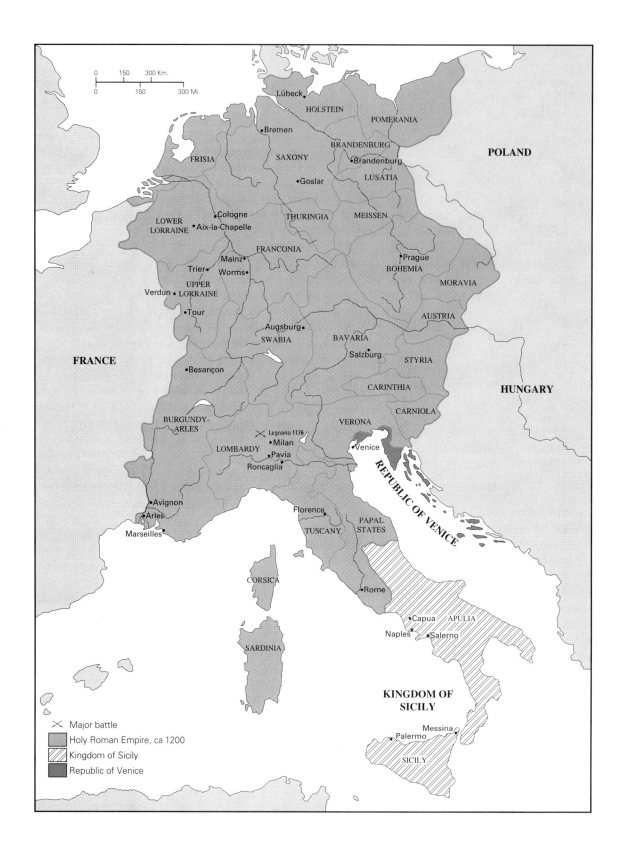

POLAND

HUNGARY

FRANCE

Lübeck
HOLSTEIN
POMERANIA
Bremen
BRANDENBURG
FRISIA
SAXONY
Brandenburg
LUSATIA
Goslar
MEISSEN
Cologne
THURINGIA
Aix-la-Chapelle
LOWER
LORRAINE
Prague
FRANCONIA
BOHEMIA
Mainz
Trier
Worms
MORAVIA
UPPER
Verdun LORRAINE
Tour
AUSTRIA
Augsburg
SWABIA
BAVARIA
Salzburg
STYRIA
Besançon
CARINTHIA
HUNGARY
CARNIOLA
BURGUNDY-
ARLES
VERONA
Venice
Legnano 1176
Milan
LOMBARDY
Pavia
Roncaglia

REPUBLIC OF VENICE

Avignon
Arles
Marseilles
Florence
PAPAL
STATES
TUSCANY

CORSICA

Rome

Capua
APULIA
Naples
Salerno

SARDINIA

KINGDOM OF
SICILY

Messina
Palermo
SICILY

Scale:
0 — 150 — 300 Km.
0 — 150 — 300 Mi.

✕ Major battle
Holy Roman Empire, ca 1200
Kingdom of Sicily
Republic of Venice

gradual and far from predictable, culminating in the great powers of Europe and their conquest of much of the rest of the world.

Statelessness in Medieval Europe

If classical Greece was an age of small city-states and ancient China the model of a centralized empire, then medieval Europe had characteristics of both. Over the centuries, it featured several empires, a universalistic religion, independent city-states and city-state leagues, successful trading companies, competing monarchies, and other independent or semi-independent entities that defy easy classification. In many ways, Europe during the Middle Ages (roughly the fifth to the fourteenth centuries) may seem more puzzling and remote to those who study world politics today than Greece, medieval Islam, or ancient China. Nevertheless, medieval Europe is the portal through which the European territorial state appeared, and it has features that are again appearing in world politics.[51]

If we think of global politics today as unfolding in an arena without a superordinate authority, in which overlapping groups compete with each other for people's loyalties, and in which the potential for violence is present, then the politics of medieval Europe may not seem so alien. If, on the other hand, we look only at interactions of states demarcated by territorial frontiers, then the medieval period will be almost unrecognizable.

In contrast to a division of the world into exclusive territorial states, medieval Europe was organized around social groups: nobles, burghers, and peasants. This sociopolitical organization, known as *feudalism,* appeared in Europe after the collapse of Rome and was built on an agrarian economic system based on landed wealth. The feudal system featured "a fragmentation of political authority, public power in private hands, and a military system in which an essential part of the armed forces is secured through private contracts."[52] Peasants owed obedience to powerful nobles who, in principle, held their estates in return for obedience to the Roman Church and the Holy Roman Empire (see Figure 2.6).

These two institutions were the principal successors to rule by Rome.[53] For the church, Christianity's triumph was proof that the pope was God's earthly agent. Secular authority, the church argued, could exist only with God's approval (provided by the pope). The German-based *Holy Roman Empire* was heir to Charlemagne's Frankish empire and dates from A.D. 962, when a Saxon king, having invaded Italy and aided the papacy, was designated Roman Emperor by the pope. The Italian poet Dante Alighieri defended the Holy Roman Empire by arguing that God had created all things in His image and that, because God was universal and unitary, humanity would most closely resemble Him "when it is united wholly in one body, and it is evident that this cannot be except when it is subject to one prince."[54]

In reality, powerful nobles, who were the society's military caste and often high church officials as well, were largely independent of both pope and emperor. Although the church was indisputable spiritual leader, like Islam's religious leaders, it discovered that transforming spiritual authority into secular power was difficult. The emperor's secular authority was circumscribed by his vassals as well as by the pope. Compared with imperial Rome, with an emperor who could command obedience by sending his legions to the farthest corners of his realm, medieval Europe was politically decentralized and the emperor's authority was limited.[55]

FIGURE 2.6
The Holy Roman Empire of Medieval Europe with Major Vassals, ca. 1200

With overlapping authorities, conflict was frequent in medieval Europe. Life for peasants and nobles alike might well be described, as the political philosopher Thomas Hobbes described the state of nature, as "nasty, brutish, and short." Subjects of imperial Rome expected their lives to be peaceful and orderly, but inhabitants of medieval Europe had no such assurance. "Insecurity became general; no region was able to claim immunity from war."[56] The absence of clear centers of authority also erased the distinction between the domestic and foreign realms: "Each individual, every social or family group, had to look to their own security. . . . The differences were obliterated between public warfare and private violence, between the feud or vendetta and a conflict waged by the king in the name of his people."[57] Because this description also fits a variety of "failed states"—Sierra Leone, Liberia, and Somalia—and rapidly growing "megacities"—Rio de Janeiro, Karachi, and Lagos, among others—some scholars draw analogies to medieval Europe to describe conditions.

From the tenth through the twelfth centuries, confronting an absence of law and order, the church tried to limit violence. These efforts—the Peace of God and the Truce of God—were clerics' attempts to pacify their unruly flock by restricting the times (the Sabbath day and religious holidays) and places (churches) for combat and by protecting classes of persons (unarmed clerics, merchants, and pilgrims). One cleric wrote: "Because we know that without peace nobody will see the Lord, we warn men in the name of the Lord that they should be sons of peace."[58] The code of chivalry with its obligations on knights to help the innocent was another effort to limit the depredations of war.

Another feature of this epoch was conflicts between the empire and the papacy. The church itself was divided among those who wished to purge it of venality and corruption, others who wished to assert papal primacy over earthly as well as heavenly affairs, and still others who wished to grow rich by cooperating with the empire. The empire, on the other hand, was torn by ducal families competing for the throne and by local nobles striving to exercise authority. In the end, neither pope nor emperor triumphed. Instead, both gave way to the territorial monarchs of France and England and the commercial city-states of Italy that took advantage of economic and military developments—money and firearms—and of the papal-imperial contest to assert their independence.[59] In this way the states in Europe emerged in a form that is familiar to us.

Territorial States in Europe

Europe's territorial state did not emerge full-blown overnight. It was the product of a process that began with the fall of Rome and continued in later centuries. The process continues even today with German reunification and with states like Bosnia, Slovenia, Croatia, and Macedonia appearing after Yugoslavia broke apart. Many contemporary states such as the Congo (formerly Zaire) are pale shadows of older centrally governed kingdoms. The European territorial state was unique in its ability to mobilize people and resources, and, as a consequence of Europe's colonial expansion, that state came to be thought a model for others.

With the waning of the Middle Ages and the enfeeblement of church and empire, two types of states appeared. One was the commercial city-state that grew up in Italy, such as Venice and Genoa, and the other was the territorial monarchic state that thrived in France, Spain, and England. Italy's city-states were already prosperous and independent by the eleventh century. The feudal system had never taken root in Italy, and Holy Roman emperors were unable to exert lasting authority south of the

Apennine Mountains.[60] The city-states, which controlled the countryside around them, and the cities of northern Europe were home to a new middle class whose wealth, accumulated through trade, was a challenge to feudal lords, whose prosperity was based on land. Gradually, this commercial class overthrew the local nobility, seized control of the countryside, and began to employ mercenaries to protect themselves. Crossbows and newly available gunpowder and artillery undermined the knights' military power; their stone castles, war horses, and armor were less and less decisive.

These developments dramatically changed political life. "The relative protection which the sway of certain moral standards and the absence of destructive weapons had afforded groups and individuals in the earlier Middle Ages gave way to total insecurity under the dual impact of the breakdown of common standards and the inven-tion of gunpowder."[61] Italy's urban centers, rediscovering ancient Greek and Roman learning, enjoyed a cultural flowering (the Renaissance) that complemented their financial power. As they grew more independent, the city-states, especially Florence, Venice, Milan, Naples, and the Papal States, began to compete among themselves for power and wealth and engage in elaborate *balance-of-power politics.* For almost two hundred years (1300–1494), they used diplomacy, alliances, and limited wars to augment their spheres of interest and to prevent anyone or any group from achieving preponderance over the others. They all "eagerly observed the slightest move on the political chess board and made a great fuss whenever the smallest castle changed its ruler."[62] Venice, on the Adriatic Sea, grew rich from commerce and invented modern diplomatic practices, including the use of permanent diplomatic missions.[63]

Italy's city-states were small, and it is probably a mistake to generalize from them to the larger states that emerged to the north. "Domestic" and "interstate" politics were not really separate in the city-states. Adversaries constantly meddled in each other's local affairs, cultivating local supporters, encouraging conspiracies, and aiding local factions. Few rules limited these struggles, and rulers routinely tried to assassinate each other.[64]

At the same time as Italy's city-states were flowering, a second type of state was forming in Europe. Local monarchs were asserting independence of empire and papacy and developing bureaucracies to unite and control large territories. These new monarchies traced their boundaries to those of the provinces of the Roman Empire, and ruling princes were the heirs of noble families that had increased their feudal holdings at the expense of neighbors. During the Middle Ages, they took advantage of papal-imperial hostility to assert their independence and, especially in England, France, and Spain, had evolved effective ways of collecting taxes from subjects and mobilizing them into large bodies of infantry that could hold their own against mounted knights. They forged alliances with the growing bourgeoisie that wanted trade regularized and protected and that was willing to lend money and pay taxes in return.[65]

The new monarchs had to overcome external and internal impediments to their independence. The sixteenth-century struggle of England's Henry VIII with the papacy illustrates how Europe's kings sought to assert prerogatives *simultaneously* against external and internal foes. One of the Catholic Church's most loyal servants, Henry had been named Defender of the Faith in 1521. To strengthen England's Tudor dynasty, he sought to divorce his wife, Catherine of Aragon, who had borne him no male heirs. The pope refused to grant Henry an annulment and then excommunicated the English king when he remarried. In retaliation, Henry forced the English Parliament to pass the Act of Supremacy (1534), naming him Protector and Only Supreme Head of the Church and Clergy of England. Having declared independence from the papacy's external control, the king went on to confiscate the English monasteries, took control of their income, and made the clergy dependent on him. By identifying the Catholic Church with such enemies of England as Spain, Henry fostered English nationalism.[66] He thus increased his own resources and acquired authority over the English clergy.

The movement toward independent states in Europe was accelerated by the political and religious sentiment known as the Protestant Reformation. The Reformation began with Martin Luther's rejection of the Catholic Church's authority in religious matters (1517). Once the church had been stripped of the awe in which it had been held in matters of faith, rejecting its authority in politics was easier. Local princes, especially in Germany, took advantage of the ensuing century and a half of religious war to foster a national consciousness among subjects and to assert practical independence of both pope and emperor.

The idea of *sovereignty* was a prerequisite to legitimizing independence for the young states. Monarchs like Henry VIII were known as sovereigns, and in time their states—originally territories that the king owned by personal conquest, dynastic inheritance, and marriage—were granted the unique legal status of sovereignty. Like the state itself, the idea of sovereignty evolved slowly. This development was a final step in carrying the monarchic state to the center of political life. Amidst political and religious turmoil in France, the lawyer Jean Bodin provided a modern definition of sovereignty. Bodin was one of a group of political moderates seeking to revive the French monarchy, enfeebled by fractious extremists, both Protestant and Catholic. In 1576, in *Six Books on the State,* Bodin defined sovereignty as "the absolute and perpetual power of the state, that is, the greatest power to command." The state, in the person of the monarch, was, Bodin argued, supreme within its territory, independent of any higher authority, and the legal equal of other states. Sovereignty was an attribute of the state itself rather than of an individual or a government. That the French state at the time did not possess "the greatest power to command" mattered little to Bodin; it *should* have such power to bring an end to chaos.

Religious conflict continued in Europe, and the period from 1618 to 1648—the *Thirty Years' War*—laid waste much of northern Europe and ended feudalism. The European state system is commonly dated from the Peace of Westphalia, which ended the war, but, as we have seen, that system had already been evolving for many years.[67] The Peace confirmed the *idea of a system of independent and legally equal territorial states* and abandoned the idea of a universal Christian commonwealth governed by pope or emperor. The Peace also regularized the system of permanent diplomatic missions, encouraged the growth of *international law among* legally equal states rather than divine law *above* them, and promoted a balance of power and system of rules governing diplomatic etiquette. Finally, Westphalia legislated *tolerance of diversity* in Europe, as it brought an end to the wars between Protestants and Catholics.

The Halcyon Era of the Sovereign State and the Balance of Power

In the decades after 1648, there emerged the crowded system of competitive European states that dominated world politics in ensuing centuries. These states sought to guard their internal affairs from external interference and vigorously competed among themselves for advantage in foreign affairs. During that same epoch, the Europeans conquered much of the rest of the world, and their ideas of global politics accompanied them.

The competition among European states encouraged observers to emphasize power distribution in the system. The heirs to this tradition remain transfixed by a belief that global politics is a struggle for power among sovereign states. Although the tradition of power politics seems dated in some ways, it does correspond to a historical reality in Europe. The perceptions and maxims of many contemporary theorists and practitioners reflect this bygone era. Some are also drawn to the period because it "was a period of order and progress." "An international society of states, or princes, functioned well, with rules and institutions and underlying assumptions which its members accepted."[68]

Although the idea of organizing people within defined and stable boundaries governed from the center by complex, autonomous, and anonymous bureaucracies had historical precedents, it reached its zenith and was idealized in Europe when territorial kingdoms formed. The European system as it evolved from medieval feudalism was unusual in that numerous independent states coexisted next to each other with none able to dominate the others. It was, to use the language of power theorists, a multipolar system. By contrast, important regions elsewhere were dominated by a single authority, as mainland Asia was by China and Mexico by the Aztecs before the Spanish conquest. As a result, rivalries were less intense and continuous than in Europe.

Intense rivalry and frequent wars in Europe fostered custom and law to keep participants from each other's throats. The eighteenth-century political philosopher Jean-Jacques Rousseau captured the spirit of states living cheek by jowl when he wrote that "they touch each other at so many points that not one of them can move without giving a jar to all the rest; their variances are all the more deadly, as their ties are more closely woven; their frequent quarrels are almost as savage as civil wars."[69] The almost continuous conflict compelled Europeans to compete in developing the economic and military innovations that later enabled them to conquer non-European peoples.

By the eighteenth century, the European monarchs had achieved nearly absolute power within their realms and had built a protective barrier around them. John Herz captures the essence of the sovereign state during this "halcyon era":

> What is it that ultimately accounted for the peculiar unity, compactness, coherence of the modern nation-state . . . ? It would seem that this underlying factor is to be found neither in the sphere of law nor in that of politics, but rather in that substratum of statehood where the state unit confronts us, as it were, in its physical, corporeal

ACTORS SPEAK

The idea of balance of power has been inherited from Western political thought in the eighteenth and nineteenth centuries and reflects the enormous debt that many of today's international-relations theorists owe to the European tradition. However, even in the era when balance-of-power theory dominated international-relations thought, it was a topic of fierce dispute that was attacked and defended with passion.

The balance of power—which has, for a hundred years been the burden of King's speeches, the theme of statesmen, the ground of solemn treaties, and the cause of wars—which has served, down to the very year in which we write, and which will, no doubt continue to serve, for years to come, as a pretense for maintaining enormous standing armaments, by land and sea, at a cost of many hundreds of millions of treasure—the balance of power is a chimera! (Richard Cobden, leading nineteenth-century English liberal, in M.G. Forsyth, H.M.A. Keens-Soper, and P. Savigear, eds., *The Theory of International Relations* [New York: Atherton Press, 1970], p. 309)

The European powers have formed a species of general law, which supersedes, in most instances, an appeal to the sword, by rendering such an appeal fatal to any power that may infringe upon the code; by uniting the forces of the rest inevitably against each delinquent; by agreeing, that any project of violating a neighbour's integrity shall be prevented or avenged, not according to the resources of this neighbour, but according to the full resources of all the other members of the European community; and by constantly watching over the state of public affairs even in profound peace. (Henry, Lord Brougham, nineteenth-century English radical thinker, in Forsyth, Keens-Soper, and Savigear, eds., *The Theory of International Relations,* pp. 272–273).

capacity: *as an expanse of territory encircled for its identification and its defense by a "hard shell" of fortifications.* In this lies . . . the "impermeability," or "impenetrability," or simply the "territoriality," of the modern state.[70]

The model state of the age was France under Louis XIV (the Sun King) (1643–1715). Aided by the great cleric-statesmen, Cardinals Richelieu and Mazarin, the king ensured the external security of his realm with a large professional army, the administrative and technical skills of a prosperous middle class, an economic system mobilized to amass military power, and a series of fortifications along France's frontiers.[71] France was a *great power* in an age when the label meant a state that could not be conquered even by a combination of the other states.[72] It was not the army alone that built a *hard shell of impermeability* around the great powers of the day. All pursued an economic policy known as *mercantilism*—the opposite of free trade—the aim of which was to become self-sufficient in the manufactures and agricultural products needed to wage war. No ruler wished to depend on imports from another, and all aided domestic industries by imposing import duties, providing subsidies to key industries, and forming state-owned monopolies. States sought self-sufficiency by encouraging exports and discouraging imports. Mercantilist states hoarded precious metals to pay for armies and weapons and sought empires in which they would enjoy exclusive trading rights. Though inefficient in an economic sense, mercantilism expanded the power of individual states.[73]

Louis XIV reinforced the internal side of French sovereignty by centralizing authority at his court in Versailles and by forcing French nobles to reside there. In this and other ways, the king made the formerly rebellious nobility dependent on him and his corps of central administrators.[74] The king kept his realm together by recruiting to government service members of France's middle class, who depended on and were loyal to the monarchy. This web of administrators successfully tamed independent nobles, economic guilds, and recalcitrant cities throughout France.

Europe's Classical Balance of Power

By the eighteenth century, Europe had evolved an institution among the great powers known as the *balance of power.*[75] The balance-of-power idea did not originate in Europe. Thucydides implied a balance among Greek city-states, and balance-of-power politics characterized Italy's city-states, as well as the princely states in ancient India and the warring states in ancient China.[76] Nowhere, however, did the balance-of-power metaphor and model become so embedded in the thinking of statesmen as in Europe. The balance-of-power idea was deeply rooted in the eighteenth-century mind and reflected the principles of the science of mechanics that were in vogue. Leaders viewed their states as having a defined role in the "game," which was often likened to chess. British statesmen thought of their country as a balancer that would intervene to tip the scales of the balance in the direction of the weaker alliance.

During the eighteenth century, Europe was dominated by a few major powers that competed for limited advantage. None was powerful enough to dominate the rest, and each respected others' right to survive. This mutual respect among the great powers did not extend to small countries. Their fate was a source of rivalry, and settlements among the great powers often meant fair division of the spoils—that is, of countries like Poland, which was partitioned on three occasions (1772, 1793, 1795). Each actor felt obliged to do what was necessary—including joining and switching alliances, increasing armaments, and going to war—to prevent any one state from dominating the others. This aim is reflected in a treaty between England and Spain that permitted the French king's grandson to become king of Spain but forbade the union of the two kingdoms. Unifying France and Spain was seen as a "great danger which threatened the liberty and safety of all Europe," a danger which could be avoided "by an equal balance of power (which is the best and most solid foundation of a mutual friendship)."[77]

Wars were frequent and often bloody, but they were short and had limited objectives. Defeated states were welcomed back into the fold by winners and treated as potential future allies. Peace was not the objective of balance-of-power politics, and, as one observer writes, "was no more essential to equilibrist theory than the barnacle to the boat."[78] Indeed, maintaining the balance depended on the threat of war. The powers used that threat—supplemented by flexible alliances,[79] compensations,[80] and arms races—to prevent any of them from upsetting the balance.

Recalling the indiscriminate slaughter that accompanied religious wars in the previous century, the conservative rulers of eighteenth-century Europe wished to avoid a major war that would destroy the system that was so beneficial to them and their class or that would disrupt the national economies on which prosperity was based. In a word, the policy of balance of power aimed to maintain the status quo among the great powers and therefore the stability of the system as a whole. In the eighteenth century, France under Louis XIV was the greatest threat to the balance, but, after his "bid for hegemony was broken by a coalition of states," no other state tried "to challenge the prevailing assumptions against hegemony and in favour of balance."[81] Rulers recognized that uncontrolled changes in the system might endanger their hold on power as well as the independence of their realms.

Theorists of the time regarded the balance of power with reverence. The Swiss legal scholar Emmerich de Vattel described it as a product of the "common interest" of the European monarchies united "for the maintenance of order and the preservation of liberty."[82] Rousseau declared that the balance flowed from a Europe "united by identity of religion, of moral standard, of international law,"[83] and the English radical Henry Lord Brougham likened it to a scientific breakthrough "as much unknown to Athens and Rome, as the Keplerian or Newtonian laws were concealed from Plato and Cicero."[84] The balance was also loudly praised by thinkers as diverse as David Hume, Immanuel Kant, Edmund Burke, and Friedrich von Gentz (adviser to Austria's Prince Klemens von Metternich).

Prerequisites for the Balance of Power

Although balance-of-power politics worked for Europe at a particular moment in its history, the conditions that allowed it to flourish had begun to disappear by the end of the eighteenth century with the French Revolution and Napoleon's wars. As Gulick says, the "theory was adjusted to work best through absolutism and under the warm sun of cosmopolitanism, since it demanded both flexibility and moderation."[85] What were these conditions, why were they necessary for the balance to function effectively, and what brought them to an end?

The first condition for a balance is a system of competitive states whose leaders are aware of their linked fates. Europe's states in the seventeenth and eighteenth centuries were tightly linked, and leaders were conscious of those links. Lord Brougham saw the connection between a successful balance-of-power system and "the perpetual attention to foreign affairs which it inculcates; the constant watchfulness which it prescribes over every movement in all parts of the system . . . ; the unceasing care which it dictates of nations mostly remotely situated, and apparently unconnected with ourselves; the general union . . . of all the European powers in one connecting system."[86] Eighteenth-century Europe was highly interdependent, and leaders' recognition of this interdependence made the balance effective.

The system requires a limited number of leading actors that are relatively equal in power. Eighteenth-century Europe included five great powers—Britain,

France, Austria, Russia, and Prussia—second-ranking states like Ottoman Turkey, Sweden, Spain, and the Netherlands, and smaller pawns such as Poland, Bavaria, Saxony, and Denmark. Although the military and economic capabilities of the great powers differed, they were sufficiently equal that, by adroitly shifting among alliances, each could make a significant difference. In a system with too many actors, their number alone would dilute the balance because none would have a sufficient impact. In a system with only two great powers (such as the bipolar system after 1945), a balance cannot function because no one can restrain a superpower except the other superpower.

Leaders must share an interest in preserving the system itself, and ideology must not reduce flexibility. Leaders must seek to preserve the status quo; neither ideology nor intense antipathy should be allowed to impede communication and negotiation. Effective balancing depends on adroit shifts in alliances and a willingness not to destroy enemies but to treat them to potential future allies after a war. If ideological differences or national passions bar cooperation, behavior will not be moderate, and flexibility will vanish.

When *nationalism*—consciousness on the part of people that they have in common some combination of cultural, linguistic, historical, or other traits that distinguish them from others—intruded, the system became rigid, and shifts in alliances were rare. After the Franco-Prussian War of 1870, intense French nationalism aroused by defeat and loss of the frontier provinces Alsace and Lorraine prevented Franco-German reconciliation and produced the conditions out of which a rigid alliance system evolved. This system contributed to starting World War I. In the years following the war, French and British nationalism isolated Weimar Germany and contributed to the German climate of opinion that brought Hitler to power in 1933. Ideological antipathy between Bolshevik Russia and the capitalist West also prevented an alliance among Britain, France, and Russia to balance Hitler before Germany's invasion of the Soviet Union.[87]

Eighteenth-century Europe was dominated by like-minded aristocratic elites that were linked by class interest in maintaining the system and the dynasties they represented. They were also bound by ties of marriage, language, education, and friendship. All "civilized" Europeans of the age spoke French, just as all civilized Europeans of the Middle Ages spoke Latin.[88] Europe's rulers understood that dominance by any one of them or unrestrained warfare could threaten the survival of dynastic interests. Thus their objectives and their wars remained moderate and limited.

The French Revolution unleashed forces of nationalism that made the balance of power obsolete. These forces erected new psychological barriers dividing states. French revolutionary leaders were pioneers in manipulating political symbols to intensify nationalist fervor. The word for "state" in French (*l'état*) was replaced by "fatherland" (*la patrie*), implying that citizens were part owners of their country. A new flag with the nation's colors—red, white, and blue—replaced the old one with the Bourbon monarchy's fleur-de-lis. A new national anthem—*La Marseilleise*—stirred the nationalist spirit of the masses.[89] The common form of address "sir" (*monsieur*) was replaced by "citizen" (*citoyen*).[90]

Foreign policy must remain in the hands of professional diplomats insulated from popular pressures. Another side to these symbols of popular nationalism was growing rigidity in diplomacy. Increasingly diplomacy was conducted with an eye on domestic politics, and the role of dispassionate professionals, so important to the system's smooth functioning, was diminished. When the balance of power functioned well, diplomacy was in the hands of a few professionals who understood how the balance worked, were alert to threats to it, and were willing to bargain with one another. Such diplomats were free of domestic pressures (except, of course, the whims of their royal masters) and were responsive *only* to external realities.[91]

Indeed, eighteenth-century diplomats could be persuaded to see virtue in each other's positions when provided with a nice fat bribe. The durable French statesman, Charles Maurice de Talleyrand, reflects the ideal of his age. He was flexible, serving Louis XVI as minister of foreign affairs, the revolutionaries who beheaded Louis, Napoleon Bonaparte who overthrew the revolutionaries, and the new king who was enthroned after Napoleon's defeat. Talleyrand died the wealthiest man in Europe from the bribes he received but thought himself an honest man because he never accepted a sou unless he could keep his end of a bargain.

Following Napoleon's defeat, a remarkable group of diplomats gathered at Vienna (September 1814–June 1815) to rebuild the shattered eighteenth-century balance by erecting a *Concert of Europe.* These diplomats—Talleyrand, Prince Metternich of Austria, Viscount Castlereagh of Great Britain, and Tsar Alexander I of Russia—appreciated "that something new and different must be devised to mitigate the increasingly chaotic and warlike balance-of-power system of the previous century."[92] Consonant with balance-of-power principles, the assembly readmitted France to their community and meted out a number of European territories to equalize the power of the leading states. More important, the victors (plus France) agreed that they should regulate Europe's affairs through periodic summit conferences and should prevent new revolutionary excesses that might, as had the French Revolution, imperil the status quo.[93]

The professional diplomats who made Europe's balance work and who created the Concert of Europe were agents of the *state,* not the *nation.* They could not function effectively and the Concert could not survive surges of public passion that inhibited policy or drove it in directions that were incompatible with principles of the balance. "State" and "nation" are different. Often states consist of peoples who identify with different nations, such as Austria-Hungary, which consisted of German-speaking Austrians, Magyar-speaking Hungarians, Serbian-speaking Slavs, and even Italians. Sometimes, nations do not possess a homeland (as was the case with the Jews before 1948 and the Palestinians today) and struggle to make one and create a state.

Nationalism forces leaders to earn popular approval for their actions. The merging of nation and state undermined the principle that wars should have only limited ends or should be waged to preserve the balance itself. Nationalism enables leaders to whip up fervor at home to draw attention away from a country's problems, and, if wars erupt, diplomats have a tough time limiting them because of the national passions wars trigger. As U.S. leaders discovered in the Korean and Vietnam conflicts and in the Somali intervention, it is hard for a democracy to wage limited wars for limited ends or reverse popular passions and make friends with former foes.

Modern technology has further reduced the freedom of diplomats. In the eighteenth century, ambassadors were pretty much on their own. They got sporadic instructions from their masters and had to base decisions on local conditions.

Revolutions in communication and transportation have undermined diplomats' freedom because they are now in constant contact with superiors back home. Those superiors are often more responsive to domestic polls, electoral considerations, or bureaucratic pulling and hauling than to conditions overseas. As a result, many ambassadors have become little more than cocktail-party hosts.

Some observers argue that the decline in diplomatic competence and independence has been most precipitous in countries like the United States and France, where democracy and nationalism have been united. For the balance of power to function well, they contend, diplomats must not only be independent but must be able to negotiate secretly and make deals without caring about moral conventions. Diplomacy cannot flourish where policies are made in public because impatient publics may be unwilling to sacrifice virtue to expediency. This is the problem President Clinton faced when, after taking office, he cited national interest to justify a retreat from his earlier pledge to aid Bosnia's beleaguered Muslims. Electoral politics, especially the demands of the Republican majority in Congress, also figured heavily in his 1995 decision to cut off U.S. trade with Iran. The nineteenth-century French observer Alexis de Tocqueville summed up the problem for democratic societies:

> Foreign politics demand scarcely any of those qualities which are peculiar to a democracy.... [A] democracy can only with great difficulty regulate the details of an important undertaking, persevere in a fixed design, and work out its execution in spite of serious obstacles. It cannot combine its measures with secrecy or await their consequences with patience.[94]

It must be possible to estimate power accurately. The eighteenth-century balance functioned well partly because leaders kept a close eye on changes in power distribution and reacted quickly to those changes. They carefully tracked the distribution of military capabilities—numbers of men, horses, and cannon, amount of territory, and size of harvest. Differences in power were *quantitative,* making it relatively easy to determine who should join with whom to maintain a balance.

By the nineteenth century, estimating power distribution had become more complex. *Qualitative* differences in capabilities became critical, and the pace of technological change accelerated. Improvements in weapons systems and proliferation of specialized and "smart" weapons made quantitative comparisons unreliable and complicated comparisons of military power. As a result, the calculations necessary for balance-of-power politics are close to impossible. As technological change quickens and qualitative differences among armies widen, it will become even more difficult to assess military balances.

War and the threat of war must be usable instruments of diplomacy. As Gulick reminds us, "the ablest theorists universally accepted the connection and thought of war as one more corollary of the balance of power."[95] The successful operation of the historical balance depended on war being "imaginable, controllable, usable."[96] Otherwise, how could one dissuade ambitious actors from disrupting the system? Great powers in the eighteenth century pursued limited ends partly because they recognized that pursuing grandiose goals would lead to war in which a preponderant coalition would form to prevent their attainment. Today, it is difficult to imagine anyone resorting to nuclear weapons to "restore a balance of power"; war is less and less "imaginable, controllable, usable."

Conclusion

"The Peace of Westphalia," declares one scholar, "marks the end of an epoch and the opening of another . . . the majestic portal which leads from the old into the new world."[97] The new world was that of the sovereign state and, like much of human history, it required abandoning old concepts in favor of new ones.

The era of the sovereign state engaged the attention of seventeenth- and eighteenth-century theorists of international law. Albericus Gentili (1552–1602), Hugo Grotius (1583–1645), and Emmerich de Vattel (1714–1767) sought to justify this new world and to explain to what, if any, limitations these new "leviathans" were subject. Sovereign states, limited only by expedience, became the basis of much of global politics in succeeding centuries. Balance-of-power theory seemed the key for preventing individual unlimited conflict that would destabilize the system, and it prevented states from gaining power over the rest. The balance-of-power system, for all its flaws, worked tolerably well in the eighteenth century. However, the conditions that allowed it to do so have disappeared.

The European experience of territorial states is only part of the story. Other places and epochs have much to teach us, especially as new actors proliferate, many with non-European roots. Even more important is that issues and passions that were born in these settings are resurfacing today.

Key Terms

balance of power
balance-of-power politics
barbarian
city-states
Concert of Europe
empirical theory
Eurocentric
feudalism
great power

hard shell of impermeability
Holy Roman Empire
ideologies
international law
mercantilism
nation
nationalism
normative theory

Ottoman Empire
political organization
sovereignty
theocracy
Thirty Years' War
traditional societies
transnational
tribe

End Notes

[1]Of course, historians offer competing interpretations of the past and recognize that no single theory can encompass history as a whole.

[2]James N. Rosenau, "New Dimensions of Security: The Interaction of Globalizing and Localizing Dynamics," *Security Dialogue* 25 (September 1994), p. 256.

[3]Samuel P. Huntington, "The Clash of Civilizations?" *Foreign Affairs* 72:3 (Summer 1993), p. 22. Huntington believes that wars between states were characteristic of an epoch in world history dominated by Europe. With the end of that epoch, interstate wars, he believes, will become rare.

[4]James N. Rosenau, *Along the Domestic-Foreign Frontier: Exploring Governance in a Turbulent World* (Cambridge, UK: Cambridge University Press, 1997), pp. 75-76.

[5]Hedley Bull and Adam Watson, "Introduction," in Bull and Watson, eds., *The Expansion of International Society* (New York: Oxford University Press, 1984), p. 1.

[6]Some historians argue that we have underestimated the extent and regularity of the contacts among different peoples in the pre-state epoch. See, for example, Robert S. Lopez, *The Commercial Revolution of the Middle Ages, 950-1350* (Cambridge, UK: Cambridge University Press, 1976).

[7]To Greek ears, non-Greek speakers sounded as though they were saying "bar-bar-bar," hence barbarian.

[8]William H. McNeill, *Plagues and People* (New York: Anchor Books, 1976).

[9]Robert Gilpin, "Economic Exchange and National Security in Historical Perspective," in Klaus Knorr and Frank N. Trager, eds., *Economic Issues and National Security* (Lawrence, KS: Regents' Press of Kansas, 1977), pp. 20-21. See Karl Polanyi, "The Economy as an Instituted Process," in Karl Polanyi, Conrad M. Arensberg, and Harry W. Pearson, eds., *Trade and Market in the Early Empires: Economic History and Theory* (New York: Free Press, 1957), pp. 256-270.

[10]R. H. C. Davis, *A History of Medieval Europe: From Constantine to Saint Louis,* 2nd ed. (New York: Longman, 1988), pp. 377-379.

[11]Bull and Watson, "Introduction," p. 1.

[12]See especially Chanakya Kautilya, a fourth-century B.C. Indian Brahman who wrote the *Arthashastra,* which outlines strategies for leaders that closely resemble balance-of-power politics and the Chinese legalist philosophers of the same period. The importance of force in early China is described by Sun-tzu, whose ideas had a great impact on Mao Zedong. *The Art of Warfare,* trans. Roger Ames (New York: Ballantine Books, 1993).

[13]Some social scientists would argue that to be sovereign states must also enjoy a monopoly of the means of internal and external coercion, but, as Janice E. Thomson points out, "The state's monopoly on external violence came very late ...." Thomson, *Mercenaries, Pirates, and Sovereigns: State-Building and Extraterritorial Violence in Early Modern Europe* (Princeton: Princeton University Press, 1994), p. 143.

[14]Michael Mann, *The Sources of Social Power,* vol. 1, *A History of Power from the Beginning to A.D. 1760* (New York: Cambridge University Press, 1986), p. 39.

[15]Hendrik Spruyt, *The Sovereign State and Its Competitors* (Princeton: Princeton University Press, 1994), esp. pp. 22-33.

[16]Patricia Crone, "The Tribe and the State," in John A. Hall, ed., *States in History* (New York: Basil Blackwell, 1987), p. 71.

[17]Philip Hitti, *The Arabs: A Short History* (Chicago: Regnery Company, 1956), p. 5.

[18]Such centers of power may be called *hegemons,* and their weakening is termed hegemonic decline.

[19]Paul Kennedy, *The Rise and Fall of the Great Powers* (New York: Random House, 1987).

[20]See Klaus Knorr and James N. Rosenau, eds., *Contending Approaches to International Politics* (Princeton: Princeton University Press, 1969). For a reconsideration of these issues two decades later, see Ernst-Otto Czempiel and James N. Rosenau, eds., *Global Changes and Theoretical Challenges: Approaches to World Politics for the 1990s* (Lexington, MA: Lexington Books, 1989).

[21]See Yale H. Ferguson and Richard W. Mansbach, *The Elusive Quest: Theory and International Politics* (Columbia, SC: University of South Carolina Press, 1988), pp. 32-48.

[22]Niccolò Machiavelli, *The Prince,* trans. George Bull (Baltimore: Penguin Books, 1961), p. 134.

[23]Adam Watson, *The Evolution of International Society* (New York: Routledge, 1992), p. 47.

[24]The marathon, a foot race of just over 26 miles, originated with the run Pheidippides made to carry the news of the Greek victory to Athens.

[25]See, for example, Morton Kaplan, *System and Process in International Politics* (New York: Wiley, 1957), pp. 22-36; and Kenneth N. Waltz, "The Stability of a Bipolar World," *Daedalus* 93:3 (Summer 1964), pp. 881-909.

[26]Watson, *Evolution of International Society,* p. 85. Watson points out that this unity was achieved only after 500 years of war among rival polities. Nevertheless, as in Greece, disunity did not prevent the growth of an inclusive cultural sense of being "Chinese."

[27]Adda B. Bozeman, *Politics and Culture in International History* (Princeton: Princeton University Press, 1960), p. 134. See also pp. 133-146.

[28]John K. Fairbank, "A Preliminary Framework," in Fairbank, ed., *The Chinese World Order* (Cambridge, MA: Harvard University Press, 1968), p.5. Because of a shared culture, this sense of unity persisted even during eras in which the empire was divided among warring competitors.

[29]Cited in Bozeman, *Politics and Culture*, pp. 145-146.

[30]Fairbank, "Preliminary Framework," p.6.

[31]After Genghis Khan and his Mongol warriors conquered China and established their own imperial dynasty (Yuan) in the thirteenth century, they were seduced by Chinese mores and in time were themselves "conquered" and absorbed by Chinese culture.

[32]A major exception was the fourth-century B.C. legalist school of thought, which viewed domination and conquest as the objectives of foreign policy. The most famous advocates of legalism were Lord Shang and Li Ssu, advisers to the rulers of the Ch'in state during the "warring states" era. Using harsh policies that they advocated, Ch'in conquered its competitors a century later.

[33]Bozeman, *Politics and Culture*, p.136.

[34]The British prevented Chinese authorities from disrupting the lucrative opium trade that helped finance British rule in India, the source of much of the opium.

[35]Watson, *Evolution of International Society*, p. 113.

[36]James A. Bill and Carl Leiden, *Politics in the Middle East*, 2nd ed. (Boston: Little Brown, 1984), p.40.

[37]Sixteenth-century Geneva ruled by the Protestant leader John Calvin was also a theocracy.

[38]Members of a military class that ruled Egypt between 1250 and 1517.

[39]Named after its first ruler, Othman.

[40]Bozeman, *Politics and Culture*, p. 385.

[41]Mecca and Medina.

[42]Albert Hourani, *A History of the Arab Peoples* (Cambridge, MA: Harvard University Press, 1991), p. 207.

[43]See Thomas Naff, "The Ottoman Empire and the European States System," in Bull and Watson, eds., *Expansion of International Society*, pp. 144-169.

[44]These events were part of the scramble for empire before World War I.

[45]The end might have come sooner except for Europe's balance of power. Only British and French intervention in the Crimean War (1853-1856) saved the Ottomans from disastrous defeat by Russia.

[46]Muslims living in Bosnia, Kosovo, and Albania are the remains of a community that once flourished under the Ottomans.

[47]Jordan's King Hussein was a Hashemite. His grandfather, Abdullah, was installed as ruler of Transjordan (1921-1951). Another Hashemite, Faisal, was king of Iraq (1921-1933).

[48]At the same time as the British were promising the Arabs postwar independence, the British foreign secretary Arthur Balfour was also promising to create an independent Jewish state. These contradictory commitments were important elements in producing friction between Jews and Arabs in Palestine.

[49]Islamic law is contained in the *shari'ah* (the sacred law). See James Piscatori, "Islam in the International Order," in Bull and Watson, eds., *Expansion of International Society*, pp. 309-321.

[50]Youssef M. Ibrahim, "Arabs Anxiously Accuse Iran of Fomenting Revolt," *New York Times*, December 21, 1992, pp. A1, A9.

[51]See Watson, *Evolution of International Society*, pp. 142-144.

[52]Joseph Strayer as cited in Spruyt, *The Sovereign State*, p. 36. Medieval Japan featured similar feudal relationships.

[53]The Roman or Catholic Church continues to influence millions of the faithful. It is no longer a territorial power, however, as it was in the Middle Ages. The Holy Roman Empire lingered on until Napoleon Bonaparte "officially" declared it at an end in 1806. Long before that, however, it had ceased to exercise political influence, and the French philosopher Voltaire satirically exclaimed: "This agglomeration which was called and still calls itself the Holy Roman Empire was neither holy, nor Roman, nor an Empire."

[54]Dante Alighieri, "De Monarchia," in William Ebenstein, ed., *Great Political Thinkers*, 4th ed. (New York: Holt, Rinehart and Winston, 1969), p. 252. The poet shows his contempt for the popes of his lifetime by putting them in the eighth circle of hell in *The Divine Comedy*.

[55]Marc Bloch, *Feudal Society*, trans. L.A. Manyon (Chicago: University of Chicago Press, 1961), p. 443.

[56]Philippe Contamine, *War in the Middle Ages*, trans. Michael Jones (Oxford, UK: Basil Blackwell Ltd., 1984), p.15.

[57]Ibid., p.15.

[58]Cited in ibid., p. 271.

[59]Some observers emphasize the ability of the state to extract resources from subjects to wage war as the decisive factor in the state's triumph over other political forms. Declares Charles Tilly: "Rulers squeezed the means of war from their own populations and others they conquered, building massive structures of extraction in the process." Tilly, *Coercion, Capital, and European States, AD 990-1990* (New York: Cambridge University Press, 1990), and Tilly, "War Making and State Making as Organized Crime," in Peter Evans, Dietrich Rueschemeyer, and Theda Skocpol, eds., *Bringing the State Back In* (Cambridge, UK: Cambridge University Press, 1985). Others emphasize "the economic transformation of medieval Europe" which permitted military advances as the key factor (Spruyt, *The Sovereign State*, p. 30).

[60]The German emperors did control Sicily and southern Italy for a time.

[61]John H. Herz, *International Politics in the Atomic Age* (New York: Columbia University Press, 1959), p. 45.

[62]Felix Gilbert, "Machiavelli: The Renaissance of the Art of War," in Edward Mead Earle, ed., *Makers of Modern Strategy* (New York: Atheneum, 1967), p. 8.

[63]Bozeman, *Politics and Culture,* pp. 457–477.

[64]Machiavelli provides a window through which to view the behavior of Renaissance princes, and the names Cesare and Lucrezia Borgia have become synonymous with political immorality.

[65]Holland's rise in the sixteenth and seventeenth centuries reflected the importance of the new middle class and of capitalist enterprise as factors in global power.

[66]F. H. Hinsley, *Sovereignty,* 2nd ed. (New York: Cambridge University Press, 1986), p.118.

[67]Stephen D. Krasner argues that "the Peace of Westphalia was not a decisive break with the past. It codified existing practices more than it created new ones. . . . Only in retrospect did Westphalia become an icon that could be used to justify further consolidation of the sovereign state against rival forms of political organization." "Westphalia and All That," in Judith Goldstein and Robert O. Keohane, eds., *Ideas and Foreign Policy* (Ithaca, NY: Cornell University Press, 1993), p. 246.

[68]Watson, *Evolution of International Society,* p. 198.

[69]Jean-Jacques Rousseau, "Abstract of the Abbé de Saint-Pierre's Project for Perpetual Peace," in M.G. Forsyth, H.M.A. Keens-Soper, P. Savigear, eds., *The Theory of International Relations* (New York: Atherton Press, 1970), p.136.

[70]John H. Herz, "Rise and Demise of the Territorial State," in Herz, ed., *The Nation-State and the Crisis of World Politics* (New York: McKay, 1976), pp. 100–101. Emphasis added. States were never fully impermeable. Peter Gourevitch writes: "The same hopelessly inter-penetrated quality of foreign and domestic issues was also present in . . . all the wars of the sixteenth and seventeenth centuries." "The Second Image Reversed: The International Sources of Domestic Power," *International Organization* 32:4 (Autumn 1978), p. 908.

[71]See Henry Guerlac, "Vauban: The Impact of Science on War," in Peter Paret, ed., *Makers of Modern Strategy* (Princeton: Princeton University Press, 1986), pp. 64–90.

[72]France and Britain were the leading great powers of the age, and Prussia under Frederick the Great was the smallest. Yet Prussia proved its credentials in the Seven Years' War (1756–1763), surviving the united effort of France, Austria's Habsburg Empire, and Russia, each of which had a population more than four times that of Prussia.

[73]See Edward Mead Earle, "Adam Smith, Alexander Hamilton, Friedrich List: The Economic Foundations of Military Power," in Paret, ed., *Makers of Modern Strategy,* pp. 217–261. Free trade was encouraged by entrepreneurs, and its growing popularity in the nineteenth century was a result of the dominance by one state—Great Britain—that could profit from it.

[74]This practice has been called the "Courtization of Warriors." Norbert Elias, *State Formation and Civilization,* trans. by Edmund Jephcott (Oxford, UK: Basil Blackwell, 1982), pp. 258–270.

[75]See Edward Vose Gulick, *Europe's Classical Balance of Power* (New York, W.W. Norton, 1955).

[76]The Italian balance of power deteriorated into a "theater in which the conflicts of the European powers were acted out." Winfried Franke, "The Italian City-State System as an International System," in Morton A. Kaplan, ed., *New Approaches to International Relations* (New York: St. Martin's, 1968), p. 448. The Hindu system lacked "stable patterns of collaboration" and was characterized by "rudimentary and unregulated" diplomacy. George Modelski, "Kautilya: Foreign Policy in the Ancient Hindu World," *American Political Science Review* 58:3 (September 1964), p. 556.

[77]Cited in Watson, *Evolution of International Society,* p. 199.

[78]Gulick, *Europe's Classical Balance of Power,* p. 35.

[79]Hans J. Morgenthau, *Politics Among Nations,* 6th ed. rev. Kenneth W. Thompson (New York: Knopf, 1985), pp. 209–213.

[80]If one actor increased its power, the balance (and peace as well) might be maintained by compensating other great powers. In some cases, compensation was used as the basis for policies of appeasement, using rewards to conciliate a potential adversary. German Chancellor Otto von Bismarck's effort to propitiate France in 1881 by dangling Tunisia as "a ripe plum ready to be plucked" illustrates how appeasement was used.

[81]Watson, *Evolution of International Society,* p. 199.

[82]Emmerich de Vattel, "The Law of Nations," in Forsyth et al., *The Theory of International Relations,* p.118.

[83]Jean-Jacques Rousseau, "Abstract of the Abbé de Saint-Pierre's Project for Perpetual Peace," in Forsyth et al., *Theory of International Relations,* p.133.

[84]Henry Brougham, "Balance of Power," in Forsyth et al., *Theory of International Relations,* p. 269.

[85]Gulick, *Europe's Classical Balance of Power,* p. 298.

[86]Brougham, "Balance of Power," p. 269.

[87]British and French leaders were so blinded by ideology that in the moment of their greatest peril, just before the invasion of France, they were trying to help Finland resist "Bolshevik" aggression.

[88]Some of Europe's rulers, including the Russian tsars and Hanovarian kings of England, spoke their country's language indifferently. Modern Russian still reflects that influence of French in words such as "royal" (meaning piano) that was the brand of the French piano played by the tsar.

[89]Fans of old films may recall the scene in *Casablanca* when the anthem is played, and all the French in "Rick's" stand to attention and sing, angering the Nazi onlookers.

[90]Similar symbolism characterized Russia after the 1917 revolution when "comrade" *(tovarich)* replaced "mister" *(gospadin).*

[91]See Inis L. Claude, Jr., *Power and International Relations* (New York: Random House, 1962), pp. 90–91.

[92]Richard B. Elrod, "The Concert of Europe: A Fresh Look At an International System," *World Politics* 28:2 (January 1976), p.161.

[93]René Albrecht-Carrié, *The Concert of Europe* (New York: Harper and Row, 1968), p. 48.

[94]Alexis de Tocqueville, *Democracy in America,* vol.1 (New York: Vintage Books, 1959), p. 243. Also Walter Lippmann, *The Public Philosophy* (New York: Mentor, 1955) and Hans J. Morgenthau, *Politics in the Twentieth Century,* abridged ed. (Chicago: University of Chicago Press, 1971), pp. 390–400.

[95]Gulick, *Europe's Classical Balance of Power,* p. 89.

[96]Claude, *Power and International Relations,* p. 91.

[97]Leo Gross, "The Peace of Westphalia, 1648–1948," in Robert S. Wood, ed., *The Process of International Organization* (New York: Random House, 1971), p. 42.

Chapter 3

The State and the Tradition of Power Politics

This chapter examines the sovereign state that has dominated global politics for over three centuries and the European intellectual tradition that accompanied it. One of the key differences between that tradition of international politics and the more recent approach of postinternational politics is that the former focuses on and generalizes from the European experience with territorial states and their repeated wars. However useful this approach was during the centuries of Europe's domination of global politics, it is less so today.

As we saw in the last chapter, the sovereign state "arose because of a particular conjunction of social and political interests in Europe,"[1] especially between the monarch and a growing commercial class that wanted protection. The sovereign state evolved gradually, and with it evolved a systematic theory of interstate politics sometimes called *realpolitik*[2] or simply *power politics.* Since state evolution was gradual, states managed to monopolize the means of coercion only "after some three hundred years of state-building."[3] Today, some states have surrendered that monopoly.[4] This does not suggest that states will become irrelevant or disappear. Rather they must share pride of place with other actors and must cooperate with one another if citizens hope to cope with today's challenges.

The Power-Politics Tradition

Although theories of power politics flowered in many societies, the European tradition owes much to classical Greece and the Italian Renaissance. Many of the ideas appear in the monumental *History of the Peloponnesian War,* written by a discredited Athenian general, Thucydides, and in *The Prince,* by the Florentine politician Niccolò Machiavelli. "The essence of realism as portrayed by Thucydides and Machiavelli," declares one theorist, "is the *replacement* of moral principle by compulsions or necessities, by 'laws' of behavior."[5]

Thucydides   Thucydides depicts Atens as declining from wealth, power, and glory to indigence and dependence. Analyzing the collision between Athens and Sparta that engulfed

Grecce in 431 B.C., Thucydides sought to understand the general causes of war. "It will be enough for me . . . if these words . . . are judged useful by those who want to understand clearly the events which happened in the past and which . . . will . . . be repeated in the future. My work is not a piece of writing designed to meet the taste of an immediate public, but was done to last for ever."[6]

Like a diagnostic physician, Thucydides describes the causes and symptoms of war. "What made war inevitable was the growth of Athenian power and the fear which this caused in Sparta"[7]—in other words, a change in the relative power of Sparta and Athens stirred Spartan suspicion and hostility and therefore destabilized the system. He reports that many city-states in Greece came to fear Athens because, after the Greeks defeated the Persians, the Athenians transformed their alliance into an empire. Changing the system's distribution of power left uncertainty about the future and made old expectations and identities obsolete. Sparta sought to balance Athenian power, and its effort made Athens suspicious of Spartan motives. Amid mutual fear and recrimination, it took only a spark to start a conflagration.

Thucydides is regarded as a father of power politics. First, he believes that distribution of power explains events. Second, his account of the *Melian Dialogue* seems to discount morality in global affairs. In a famous passage, the Athenians reject the Melians' appeal to justice and fair play. "We recommend," declare the Athenians, "that you should try to get what is possible for you to get . . .; since you know as well as we do that . . . the standard of justice depends on the equality of power to compel and that in fact the strong do what they have the power to do and the weak accept what they have to accept."[8] Some see this passage as praise of power pure and simple ("might makes right"), but they disregard Thucydides' most eloquent contributions, notably his account of the tragedy of Athens, and its fatal arrogance of power. This arrogance led Athens to overextend its empire until a disastrous expedition to Sicily culminated in Athens' defeat and a decline of classical Greek civilization.

Describing that decline, Thucydides suggests that democracies are poorly equipped to make foreign policy because in difficult times people turn to zealous demagogues for leadership. In his description of overextended Athens and the decline in civic virtue, some readers see a parallel to the United States in Vietnam. Echoing Thucydides' analysis of the decline of Athenian democracy, critics of U.S. intervention saw a close relationship between overextended capabilities abroad and turmoil at home.[9] America's leaders were victims of overweening pride, and, like Athenian leaders, they were undermining democracy at home to repress criticism of an overseas adventure.

Machiavelli   Like Thucydides' *History*, Machiavelli's *Prince* is recognized as an enduring contribution to the power-politics tradition. Machiavelli distinguishes between a prince's *private* obligations and his *public* duty as surrogate for a state's citizens, declaring that a prince "must not flinch from being blamed for vices which are necessary for safeguarding the state" and will find "that some of the things that appear to be virtues will, if he practices them, ruin him, and some of the things that appear to be wicked will bring him security and prosperity."[10]

This idea—called *reason of state* (*raison d'état* or *ragioni di stato*) because it was the direction an actor would take if its leaders behaved rationally—implied that the

ACTORS SPEAK

One of the most contentious issues in global politics is the role of the sovereign state. Some scholars argue that states remain the principal actors in global politics and continue to exercise control over other groups and institutions. Other scholars, however, contend that today's states are pale reflections of the leviathans that emerged in Europe in the seventeenth and eighteenth centuries. Today's states, they believe, no longer exercise a monopoly of the means of coercion in their territory and can no longer control what crosses their frontiers.

States are the units whose interactions form the structure of international-political systems. They will long remain so. The death rate among states is remarkably low. (Kenneth N. Waltz, *Theory of International Politics* [Reading, MA: Addison-Wesley, 1979], p. 95)

The territorial state is in a weak bargaining position because non-state actors with greater mobility can exploit resources, markets, and coalition-building opportunities available on a global scale....The boundaries of the state—the competencies it has, the resources it can command, the range of social conduct subsumable under its interests, and the limits on its authority—are thus seen to be dependent upon interactions with and among nonstate actors. (Richard K. Ashley, "Untying the Sovereign State: A Double Reading of the Anarchy Problematique," *Millennium* 17 [Summer 1988], p. 246)

citizens of a state *collectively* have interests that are greater than and different from the mere sum of their individual interests. Each state had a national interest, as it would be called later, which reflected its relative power, geography, and other factors unique to it that determined its survival and prosperity.[11] Both Thucydides and Machiavelli regarded power as the key determinant of *national interest,* the source of an actor's goals and actions.

Machiavelli, like other power-politics thinkers, starts from the belief that the world is a dangerous place. The source of danger, some feel, inheres in the defective nature of human beings, who are naturally aggressive and acquisitive.[12] Others emphasize human nature less and point to the absence of central authority in global politics—*anarchy*—that makes trust impossible and forces actors to rely on their own devices—the practice of self-help. Whatever the source of danger, all stress the central role of power in ensuring states' survival.

If conflict is an inevitable result of human nature or anarchy, two questions arise: Why are we not constantly at war, and how can war be prevented or its consequences mitigated? For many in this tradition, the answer is to be found in using power to thwart others who seek power. This is the core idea of balance of power.

Twentieth-Century Realism

Even though the historical balance of power ceased to function by the end of the eighteenth century, the revival of the power-politics tradition in the United States after World War II reawakened interest in the balance as a mechanism for maintaining order in a disorderly world. The publication of Han Morgenthau's *Politics Among Nations* in 1948 was a big step in reviving power-politics ideas in the United States. In his view, "the balance of power and policies aiming at its preservation are not only inevitable but are an essential stabilizing factor in a society of sovereign nations."[13]

George Kennan and Henry Kissinger are two other American scholar-statesmen who were influenced by Europe's tradition of power politics. Kennan, a prolific scholar of European and Russian history and politics and architect of America's postwar policy of "containing" the Soviet Union, was a career diplomat who served as ambassador to the U.S.S.R. and Yugoslavia and director of the State Department Policy Planning Staff. For much of his career, Kennan decried what he saw to be America's refusal to confront the realities of power. "I see the most serious fault of our past policy formulation to lie in something that I might call the legalistic-moralistic approach to international problems."[14] Americans, he argued, "tend to underestimate the violence of national maladjustments and discontents elsewhere in the world"[15] and try to make over the rest of the world in the image of U.S. democracy.

Henry Kissinger, a Harvard University political scientist, served as national security adviser between 1969 and 1975 and as secretary of state between 1973 and 1976. Kissinger is a European, steeped in the tradition of power politics, and his doctoral research dealt with early nineteenth-century European diplomacy.[16] Like Kennan, Kissinger criticized America's moralist tradition and deprecation of power and order. "It is part of American folklore," he observed sarcastically, "that, while other nations have interests, we have responsibilities; while other nations are concerned with equilibrium, we are concerned with the legal responsibilities of peace. We have a tendency to offer our altruism as a guarantee of our reliability."[17] Like Kennan, he sought to prevent America from trying to export its domestic values, and as a practitioner he forged policies similar to those of the European diplomats he admired, in which force and diplomacy were wedded to achieve objectives.

The efforts of power-politics advocates—*realists* as they called themselves—to popularize balance-of-power policies in this country were hampered because conditions for it to function well were absent. Also the concept has so many (often contradictory) meanings.[18]

Perhaps the most common modern usage of balance of power is to describe *any existing distribution of power.* When leaders argue that Israel's annexation of land near Jerusalem or the Iraqi invasion of Kuwait will overturn the Middle East balance of power, they mean merely that Israel or Iraq will become stronger. Neither usage corresponds to the eighteenth-century sense. Another common use of the phrase is to describe the *purposive policy* of actors, which is closer to its original meaning. In this usage, actors follow a policy of forming flexible alliances to prevent dominance by one of them. One expression of such a policy was British Foreign Secretary George Canning's explanation in 1826 of how, after the French occupation of Spain, he had restored Europe's balance of power without having to go to war. He had done so, he declared, by recognizing the independence of the Latin American states that were formerly part of the Spanish Empire and by having persuaded the Americans to issue the Monroe Doctrine. "If France occupied Spain, was it necessary, in order to avoid the consequences of that occupation that we should blockade Cadiz? No. I looked another way—I saw materials for compensation in another hemisphere.... I resolved that if France had Spain, it should not be Spain 'with the Indies.' I called the New World into existence, to redress the balance of the Old."[19]

A third use of balance of power is to denote a *relatively equal power distribution* among actors that ensures system stability. In this usage, the actors' intent or policy is unimportant. What counts is how power is distributed systemwide. The structural condition of the system as a whole, not the policy of its members, automatically brings about the desired balance. Structure, in this version, determines behavior.[20] Ultimately, however, power theorists must confront the knotty problem of explaining what power is so that we will know it when we see it.

Neorealism Starting from the premise that anarchy makes conflict likely, *neorealism* has tried to provide a more sophisticated version of power politics than realism. Differences exist among neorealists as well as among realists.

Some, like Kenneth Waltz, are called *structural realists* because they emphasize global structure as determining actors' behavior.[21] Waltz considers the following to be important: the distribution of capabilities, the hierarchic or nonhierarchic arrangement of the actors, and the functional similarity or diversity of the actors.[22] In contrast, Robert Gilpin emphasizes the rationality of states in designing policies to pursue their interests. "Actors enter social relations and create social structures in order to advance particular sets of political, economic, or other types of interests." Conflict ensues, and power determines which interests are satisfied: "Because the interests of some of the actors may conflict with those of other actors, the particular interests that are most favored by these social arrangements tend to reflect the relative power of the actors involved."[23] As a group, neorealists acknowledge their debt to the tradition from which they are descended, and they believe global politics is still a struggle for power. Gilpin writes, "international politics still can be characterized as it was by Thucydides."[24]

Although neorealists maintain much of the balance-of-power language, its meaning has changed. Power distribution remains prominent, but balance involving a number of states has just about disappeared. Both Waltz and Gilpin argue—though for different reasons—that *bipolarity,* the division of power into two camps as after World War II, provides stability and lessens the probability of war.[25]

As a concept, bipolarity (and polarity generally) suffers from some of the same confusion as balance of power. For some, it means dividing the world into two ideological blocs, thereby equating the division with an attitude cleavage between communism and capitalism. For others, it means that two countries (or alliances) have significantly more capabilities than others. Complicating matters is disagreement over which capabilities matter. Waltz emphasizes raw military power, especially nuclear weapons. But this interpretation has at least three problems. The first is that military capabilities, especially nuclear weapons, provide influence in few contexts, for example, in the case of economic or environmental issues. A second is that distribution of military power between two poles may be relatively equal or unequal.[26] The third is that if we count other capabilities—economic resources, for example—countries like Japan and Germany are major powers and Russia, despite nuclear weapons, is a declining one. As a result, it is difficult to agree on whether the world is bipolar, multipolar, or something else.

Waltz believes that *multipolarity*—the existence of three or more power centers—is a dangerous condition for two reasons:

> There are too many to enable anyone to see for certain what is happening, and too few to make what is happening a matter of indifference. . . . Second, in . . . a multipolar world, who is a danger to whom, and who can be expected to deal with threats and problems, are matters of uncertainty. Dangers are diffused, responsibilities blurred, and definitions of vital interest easily obscured.[27]

Although not all neorealists agree with Waltz on bipolarity, most share his belief that conditions of uncertainty generated by changes in status and power increase the likelihood of major *hegemonic war*—war between great powers for control of the system—in which "the declining power destroys or weakens the rising challenger while the military advantage is still with the declining power."[28]

By any standard, bipolarity is a thing of the past. The Soviet Union has broken into pieces. Those who believed that this change would make the world unipolar, with an "unchallenged superpower, the United States, attended by its Western allies,"[29] are coming to doubt this prediction, for the United States confronts intractable problems eveywhere, and its inability to achieve objectives such as isolating or altering the regimes in Cuba, Iraq, Serbia, and Iran reflects the limits of its power. Global power is becoming more dispersed. All in all, the end of the Cold War, a source of optimism for many observers, is viewed by neorealists as potentially dangerous. Some believe that the retreat of superpowers from global leadership is producing power vacuums that other actors will be tempted to fill. For neorealists, the paradox is that the breakup of Cold War alliances and loss of global control by the superpowers is frightening rather than comforting.[30]

Many scholars and policy-makers use neorealist theory for guidance for two reasons: (1) it is parsimonious; that is, it claims to explain the most important aspects of global behavior using only a very few power-related variables; (2) it requires relatively little accessible information, in contrast to theories that require knowledge about individual leaders or decision making within the inner sanctums of governments or other groups. However, the popularity of neorealism hides the fact that the world is more complex than neorealists believe and that the theory cannot account for the changing nature of global politics.

Let us summarize the European power-politics tradition. That tradition encourages observers to focus on issues that feature the following:

1. A dominant and authoritative role for the governments of states
2. Clear differentiation between domestic and international political activity
3. A direct or indirect military aspect with implications for national power and balancing of power among states
4. Deep conflict in which the gains (national interest) of one actor or set of actors are roughly equal to the losses of another
5. A propensity for actors to evaluate their gains and losses *relative* to the gains and losses of others[31]

An alternative perspective would focus on issues with these features:

1. A variety of state and nonstate actors that exercise direct and indirect influence in determining outcomes
2. Muddling and merging of distinctions between the international and domestic arenas so that it becomes unclear whether issues fall into one or the other
3. The declining value of military force for achieving goals
4. Reduced utility of national interest for understanding policy
5. Growing recognition of the presence of "public goods" so that no one actor or group of actors can profit (or lose) unless all do and recognition that profit depends on cooperation
6. A propensity for actors to evaluate gains or losses in *absolute* terms

---

The Puzzle of Power

It is hardly surprising that, in the power-politics tradition, relative power is the key determinant of behavior. Information about distribution of capabilities among states and their intentions toward each other is, in this tradition, pretty much all we need to know. The trouble is that we quickly discover that power is a slippery concept.

The stronger do not always win. During the Vietnam War, half a million American and more than a million South Vietnamese troops, supported by a naval armada with carriers and battleships and an air force flying B-52 bombers, spent nearly a decade (1965–1973) in a frustrating effort to prevent a communist victory in South Vietnam. America's nuclear arsenal and its high-technology weaponry were less useful than the Vietcong's and North Vietnam's low-tech bicycles and small arms, with which they fought as guerrillas. Despite U.S. military might, the last Americans fled Saigon helter-skelter in helicopters on April 30, 1975, the day the city fell to the communists.

Sometimes, the strong do not know their own strength. Following Iraq's invasion of Kuwait, the United States assembled a coalition of twenty-eight countries and more than half a million troops equipped with the most modern weapons in

America's arsenal.[32] The allies took no chances with the battle-hardened Iraqi army, armed with up-to-date weapons and concealed in fortifications along Saudi Arabia's border. Allied forces commanded by U.S. General Norman Schwarzkopf carried out a month of intense air bombardment before launching a ground invasion (Operation Desert Storm). Within 100 hours, President George Bush announced Kuwait's liberation. Iraq suffered as many as 400,000 casualties, including 100,000 dead and 4,000 lost tanks. Despite the "elephantine estimate" of Iraqi capabilities, "the Iraqi army put up almost no defense at all. . . . The sides were so mismatched that it was hardly a war at all."[33]

The Vietnam and Persian Gulf wars have in common a failure to assess an enemy's power well enough to guide policy. Despite an enormous intelligence community, the United States woefully *underestimated* the power of North Vietnam—a "third-rate" country—to endure hardship, absorb military blows, and defeat a superpower in a contest for Vietnamese political loyalties. Having learned the "lesson" of Vietnam—perhaps too well—the United States *overestimated* Iraq's power.

These miscalculations only begin to tell the story of the puzzle of power. Consider efforts to exert economic power. By the early 1970s, the Organization of Arab Petroleum Exporting Countries (OAPEC) controlled much of the world's oil—an all-but-irreplaceable raw material—and seemed to enjoy a stranglehold on the West's energy supplies. Following the 1973 Arab-Israeli war, OAPEC tried to use its oil power to force the West to change its Middle East policies. Yet the resulting embargo on OAPEC oil to the United States and the Netherlands and the threat of an embargo against others did not have the desired result.[34] Again, estimates of power and efforts to apply it to achieve objectives were off the mark.

Power is difficult to define and even harder to measure. Nevertheless, the concept is at the heart of a power-politics or realist tradition—wedding the idea of power to that of the territorial state in Europe. Complicating efforts to define and measure power is that the phenomenon changes before our eyes. A source of power in one historical period may vanish in another.

Defining Power

Although many would agree with Machiavelli that a prince "before engaging in any enterprise should well measure his strength, and govern himself accordingly,"[35] carrying out his advice is not easy. How tempting it is to conceptualize power as a thing, a tangible object the possession of which permits an actor to do as it wishes. Some claim that countries with nuclear weapons are powerful, but making nuclear weapons equivalent to power confuses the capabilities that might contribute to power with power itself. Those who make this error may then be surprised when a superpower like the United States fails to achieve its aims in a country like Vietnam.

Such observers are caught by surprise because, first, power is not a tangible thing, nor does it inhere in one actor. *Power is a psychological relationship in which one actor influences another to behave differently than it would have if left alone.* When we speak of an actor as powerful, we really mean it can exercise influence over someone or something.[36] A powerful actor presumably can *cause* another actor to do what it wishes.[37] The first actor's power over the second may not extend to other actors. In fact, the first actor may take power from conditions that apply to that relationship and to no other: a common frontier or a personal relationship among leaders.

A corollary is that the influence relationship is not general but *exists only in particular contexts*. An actor's capabilities may be useful for creating power in one context but not another. In other words, any influence relationship is limited and has a specific *domain* (the persons whose probable behavior is subject to it) and *scope* (those aspects of behavior that are subject to it).[38] Thus *power is the ability to get others to do what you want that is specific to particular contexts, issues, and actors*. It is not an attribute of one actor.

The Japanese government holds greatest influence over actors that depend on Tokyo for trade—the domain of its power. Japanese influence is greatest in countries that are single-mindedly preoccupied by economic development; it is less in countries like Russia in which nationalist sentiment is high. Strong Russian nationalism prevents Moscow from giving back to Japan the tiny northern islands of Kunashiri, Etorofu, Habomai, and Shikotan in the Kurile chain. Annexed after World War II, they could be swapped for the economic and technological assistance that Russia desperately needs. Japanese influence is much less where military force is necessary because its constitution forbids a large army, and memories of Japanese aggression in World War II make other countries nervous about Japanese troops overseas.

The fact that power is a contextual relationship makes it easier to explain why measuring it is so elusive. After all, how do we capture a psychological relationship? Instead, we must infer the relationship by analyzing its consequences (output) or looking at what is invested in it (input).

Inferring Power from Results. Inferring power by looking at "output" means observing the degree to which one actor is able to change the behavior of a target as a result of the actor's effort. A powerful actor is able to alter the behavior of those it seeks to influence, whereas a weak one is unable to do so. Analysis that is simple in theory, however, is complex in practice. First, even when one observes change in a target's behavior, it is difficult to identify the cause and confirm the presence of influence. A German chancellor may try to persuade other European leaders to accept a German proposal for enlarging the European Union. Even if those leaders accept the proposal, we cannot be certain that the chancellor *caused* the change. Perhaps other leaders were influenced by their advisers or some third party like a U.S. president, or some factor about which we remain in the dark. Whatever the reason, it is difficult to confirm the cause of a change in behavior *in any one case*. Only if a *pattern* is observed such that every time one actor seeks to alter another's behavior the latter does so can we conclude that a power relationship is present. Even when a pattern is present, we must be cautious. For instance, when a target of influence already intends to act as the influencer wishes, it would be wrong to conclude that power is present. This is the *chameleon effect*, so called after the small lizard that changes color to blend with its surroundings. The *satellite effect* is similar. Two actors may behave in tandem, and an observer may mistake which of the two is influencing the other.

A second problem in measuring results arises because a power relationship may exist without an observable change in behavior. We cannot infer that the German chancellor is powerless because his efforts to influence others bear no fruit. Prior to the chancellor's efforts, other European leaders may have been adamantly opposed to accommodating the chancellor's wishes. His exertions may have increased the probability of a change in their behavior, yet in the end they continued in the same old way.

In other words, power may be conceptualized as one actor's ability to alter the *probability* that another actor will behave in a certain way.[39] An actor requires greater power to change a target's behavior if the autonomous probability of such change starts out low, and the absence of change does not signify the absence of power. By contrast, if the probability of a certain outcome is high at the outset, its taking place does not mean that the actor is powerful.

Inferring Power from Capabilities.   Because inferring power from outcomes is difficult, scholars and practitioners lean heavily on the input side of the power equation—*capabilities*—in trying to estimate power; "power," argues one scholar, "has to be defined in terms of the distribution of capabilities."[40] Capabilities are resources available to an actor that can be used to influence others.

In turning from results to capabilities, we are trying to predict outcomes by measuring *potential power* because it is not clear that capabilities will be used to produce influence and, if so, whether the capabilities at hand are suitable. The U.S.S.R. continued to have enormous military capabilities throughout the 1980s but discovered that they did not produce prosperity at home or satisfy citizens' yearnings for democracy. By contrast, both the Europeans and Japanese, though they had enormous economic assets, discovered that they still had to depend on the United States to provide the military clout necessary to protect oil after Iraq invaded Kuwait. For its part, the United States discovered it needed financial support to carry out its military role in the Persian Gulf.

These cases show how capabilities are situationally specific. All capabilities are useful in providing an actor with influence in *some* contexts but are of little value in others. This variability explains why general comparisons of power may be misleading. Repeatedly actors err by concluding that amassing more capabilities will provide more influence overall. In fact, the opposite may occur. One actor, such as Athens in ancient Greece, acquiring greater capabilities, may frighten others into getting more themselves. In this way, the acquisition of greater capability may *reduce* an actor's ability to achieve its goals. This is the *paradox of power.*

German behavior following the country's first unification illustrates this paradox. Between 1870 and 1914, imperial Germany sought greater influence in world affairs ("a place in the sun"), commensurate with its growing military and industrial power. As part of this effort, Germany increased military capabilities, especially its navy. A strong navy, leaders reasoned, would enhance growth of an overseas empire and provide protection for German commerce. The naval effort confirmed, as one historian puts it, "important elements of British opinion in dark suspicions. . . . [W]hat was basically a German gesture of self-assertion was construed, and indeed could only be construed, as a threat to Britain."[41] The British responded to the German challenge by intensifying their own armament effort and joining an alliance that encircled Germany. As 1914 approached, Germany possessed greater capabilities than ever before yet suffered greater insecurity.

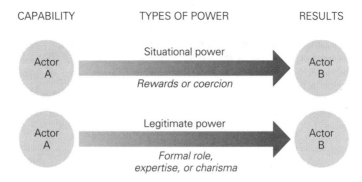

CAPABILITY   TYPES OF POWER   RESULTS

Actor A → Situational power / *Rewards or coercion* → Actor B

Actor A → Legitimate power / *Formal role, expertise, or charisma* → Actor B

FIGURE 3.1
The Power Relationship

Power is illustrated here as a relationship between specific actors in particular contexts. The two diagrams show the two major types of power—situational and legitimate—and the sources of each.

Types of Power In discussing power, several distinctions should be kept in mind. The first is between power that arises from the ability to manipulate the situation (*situational power*) of a target and the ability to alter a target's attitude (*legitimate power*). Situational power has two sources—*rewards* (positive incentives) and *coercion* (negative incentives). Legitimate power, as we see in Figure 3.1, has three sources—formal role, expertise, and charisma.

Situational Power. In order to achieve objectives, actors promise to reward or threaten to coerce each other. If a target submits, it does so not because it is convinced that the actor is justified but because it feels compelled to do so. Rewards and coercion generate power by altering the *situation* of a target. Rewards improve a target's situation contingent on obedience, and coercion involves a deterioration of that situation contingent on disobedience. If a target capitulates to the threat of force, it does so reluctantly because failure to obey would worsen its present situation.

Although we associate military force with coercion and economic assistance with reward, the distinction depends less on the capability being used than on *how* it is used. In practice, the distinction between threats and promises is murky. Suppose an actor promises to provide another with economic assistance if the latter votes in favor of its proposal in the United Nations. Such apparent generosity sounds like the promise of a reward, but are we sure? The answer is unclear until we learn more about the original situation. We may discover that the first actor has routinely provided the second with such aid for years without making it contingent on such support. What sounds like a reward is actually a threat.

Legitimate Power. Sometimes power is generated by persuading others of a policy's correctness; that is, getting the target to change its opinion rather than making it do so involuntarily. Many governments have accepted the compelling need to act quickly to avoid potential environmental disasters, such as depletion

TABLE 3.1
The World's
Priorities? (annual
expenditures)

Basic education for all	$6 billion
Water and sanitation for all	$9 billion
Reproductive health for all women	$12 billion
Basic health and nutrition	$13 billion
Military spending	$780 billion

SOURCE: *Human Development Report 1998,* (New York: Oxford University Press, 1998), Table 1.12, p. 37. Copyright © 1998 by the International Bank for Reconstruction and Development/The World Bank. Used by permission of the Oxford University Press.

of the ozone layer, less because of rewards or coercion than because of a genuine shift in opinion following persuasive scientific analysis.

One source of legitimate power is *formal role,* a belief that the actor has the right to demand a change in behavior. One might obey a parent or an elected official because the role confers authority. *Expertise* is a second source of legitimate power. Just as a doctor commands obedience in medical matters because of knowledge of medicine, so a scholar of international relations might influence the beliefs of students who study the subject. Finally, attitudes may be changed because of some *charismatic quality* that makes others wish to emulate an individual. The "star power" of famous actors in advertising and political campaigning illustrates charismatic influence, as did the profound influence of such religious leaders as Jesus, Moses, and Muhammad.

Costs of Power

The exercise of power entails *costs,* including the opposition that exercising influence arouses. High costs are also associated with producing and maintaining capabilities such as modern military forces. And resources expended for one purpose (such as military force) are not available for others (such as domestic welfare). Defense budgets give an idea of what it takes to be a modern military power. In 1989, the Soviet defense budget was about $311 billion and the U.S budget $304 billion, or an average $1,222 for each American and $1,077 for each Soviet citizen. The *relative burden* on the smaller Soviet economy was greater than on the American economy. In 1989, the Soviet Union spent almost 12 percent of its GNP on defense, compared with the United States, which spent less than 6 percent of its GNP for military purposes.[42] Using percent of GNP as a measure of cost, North Koreans bear the heaviest burden today, spending almost 29 percent in 1995 on the military (compared with 3.8 percent for the United States). The end of the Cold War eased military burdens, but the overall reduction is disappointing.[43] The impact of military expenditures is reflected in Table 3.1, which compares the additional annual funding to meet pressing global social needs with the amount spent for military purposes.

There are also invisible costs, such as time spent by decision-makers. Time spent on one issue is not available to spend on others. During the final months of his presidency in 1974, for example, Richard M. Nixon was so preoccupied with the Watergate scandal that he had little time to attend to the nation's business. In foreign affairs, Nixon, like his predecessor Lyndon B. Johnson, spent much of his time agonizing over Vietnam. In consequence, he paid little attention to the Middle East, where a war erupted between Egypt and Israel in 1973 that threatened a super-power confrontation.

Perhaps the most important cost associated with exerting power is the shadow of the future. If efforts to exert influence in the present offend or alienate others, it will prove difficult to cooperate with them in the future. If current behavior seems just and reasonable, future costs will be low. Thus U.S. efforts to exert pressure on countries like Iran and Pakistan because they are developing nuclear weapons may entail heavy opportunity costs for U.S. corporations that might have invested in these countries.

The Decline of Sovereignty[44]

As the concept of *state sovereignty* evolved, it came to mean that states, each with a defined and exclusive territorial area, were legal "persons" equal to one another under international law. States enjoy legal supremacy within their territory.[45] Each is supreme internally and subject to no higher external authority. As a result, a barrier stands between the intrastate and interstate political arenas. Because states are regarded as supreme in their own realm, they are forbidden to intervene in each other's domestic affairs. Article 2 of the U.N. Charter enshrines sovereignty by stating that organization is based "on the principle of *sovereign equality,*" prohibiting "the threat or use of force against the territorial integrity or political independence of any state," and forbidding U.N. intervention "in matters which are essentially within the domestic jurisdiction of any state."

Power-politics theorists argue that sovereignty continues to define the actors in global politics even though it was invented hundreds of years ago for a particular political purpose. International law transformed the reality of the monarch's personal property into the legal fiction of the sovereign state. Morgenthau captures the original idea, observing that the "doctrine of sovereignty" elevated the political realities of the age "into a legal theory and thus gave them both moral approbation and the appearance of legal necessity. The monarch was now supreme within his territory not only as a matter of political fact but also as a matter of law."[46] But is the concept of sovereignty still useful?

One difficulty resides in the vast differences in actors' autonomy and power today. How do we know when entities are sovereign and when they are not? The answer is that sovereignty is not a quality that inheres in an actor but is bestowed upon it by other states, especially large ones, which "recognize" it as sovereign.[47] *Recognition,* however, is a political act. Some actors may be deemed sovereign because they find favor with more powerful ones, but others may never become sovereign, even though they seem to have the same attributes. In recent years, tiny states like Nauru and Bosnia have been recognized as sovereign, but others such as Tibet were denied recognition to avoid offending China, which occupied the country in 1950.

Granting sovereign status to some less-developed countries (LDCs) reflects the expedient recognition of actors that were poorly prepared to become or remain independent. During the era of decolonizataion in the 1950s and 1960s, many

European colonies in Africa and Asia declared independence from their mother countries—Britain, France, Portugal, and Holland. At the strong urging of the U.S. and Soviet governments that were competing for influence in these regions, the "sovereign independence" of these new states was recognized by the global community.

Israel obtained international recognition only after much effort, and some of Israel's Arab neighbors for years refused to recognize the sovereign independence of what they called the "Zionist Entity." When the British Mandate in Palestine[48] ended on May 15, 1948, and the Jewish Agency in Palestine declared Israel's sovereign independence, it was not clear whether the global community would recognize the new state. A critical moment came when President Truman declared American recognition of Israel. At this time, there was little consensus about Israel's territorial boundaries, and the new government still did not enjoy control over its own frontiers. Israel did not look very sovereign.

The failure of a secessionist movement to attract external recognition of its statehood may contribute to its ultimate defeat. This was the fate of the Confederacy during the American Civil War (1860–1865) and of Biafra, the name taken by the eastern region of Nigeria during the bloody civil war that was waged in that country between 1967 and 1970. Biafra, consisting mostly of Christian members of the Ibo Tribe that was resisting dominance by the Yoruba and Hausa tribes, was recognized by four small African states—Gabon, the Ivory Coast, Tanzania, and Zambia. Although the Biafrans fought with courage and received aid from France and South Africa, the limited recognition accorded by the global community was a major factor in defeating the rebellion.

Strong, Weak, and Failed States

Strong states enjoy *autonomy* and *capacity.* An autonomous state can formulate and pursue goals that "are simply reflective of the demands or interests of social groups, classes, or society."[49] Capacity is a state's ability to tap and make use of citizens' resources as it wishes.[50] In a *strong state,* powerful bureaucracies ensure citizens' security and well-being and command their loyalties. In a *weak state,* government bureaucracies, if they exist, are mainly controlled by or are responsive to only a segment of society. Its *administrative capacity* is poorly developed, and the government can be manipulated by outsiders. A prototype weak state is the "united" Bosnia promised by the peace agreement concluded among Serbian, Croatian, and Bosnian Muslim leaders in November 1995. "The central government will have a parliament, a court and a central bank. It will also include. . . features such as a rotating presidency and the assignment of posts by nationality. This strange government will run foreign, trade and monetary policy. . . .The plan does not mention defence: presumably each of the three communities will keep its army."[51]

Overall, no region has as great a proportion of weak states as sub-Saharan Africa.[52] Unlike other regions, where states are able to make some progress in raising standards of living, sub-Saharan Africa is losing ground. Between 1980 and 1993, per capita gross national product fell annually in many African states, including

Mozambique, Sierra Leone, Malawi, Rwanda, Madagascar, Mali, Niger, Nigeria, Togo, the Gambia, Zambia, the Central African Republic, Benin, Mauritania, Zimbabwe, Ivory Coast, Lesotho, Cameroon, and the Congo (formerly Zaire).[53] Between 1988 and 1995, the Congo's economy fell by 40 percent, and per capita income has dropped 65 percent since 1958 (two years before independence from Belgium).[54] In the words of a European diplomat, "Zaire doesn't really exist anymore as a state entity."[55] States whose institutions of statehood, including the central government, have melted away and whose inhabitants rely on outsiders for the essentials of survival are call *failed states*. At one time or another Cambodia, Rwanda, Liberia, Sierra Leone, Angola, and the Congo fit this definition.[56]

Somalia as a Failed State

Consider Somalia, on the Horn of East Africa and bordering on the Red Sea and the Indian Ocean, which became a focus of world attention in 1992 as it vanished and civil war and famine engulfed the country. Declared one observer: "If there were a prize for the nation that had rolled back furthest the frontiers of the state, there could be only one winner: the Somalis."[57] So desperate was Somalia's condition that in November 1992 the United Nations authorized force to restore order and provide humanitarian relief. In December, an international force led by U.S. Marines landed in Somalia to carry out that mission, some of whom remained as part of a multinational U.N. force established in April 1993. The last U.S. units left in March 1994, and the U.N. operation ceased a year later, leaving behind a country divided into about 100 clans with no central government.

The Somali state, formed in 1960 by merging the British Somaliland Protectorate and the Italian Trusteeship Territory of Somalia, was weak even before its 1991 civil war, for its government was little more than an agent for the country's dominant clans. Two other factors help account for the deteriorating Somali state, and, more generally, for the difficulties faced by less-developed countries. First, Somalia was the setting for superpower rivalry. The country was wooed in the 1960s and 1970s by the U.S.S.R., which coveted a deep-sea naval base on the Red Sea. When, in the mid-1970s, a Marxist regime took power in Ethiopia, Somalia's neighbor and long its rival, the U.S.S.R. transferred its support to that regime and the United States began to aid Somalia. Both the Soviet Union and the United States poured weapons into Somalia, but when the Cold War ended, the Somali government was left to its own devices.

Second, the Somali government's corrupt policies did little to overcome the weakening of the state. That government, long led by the dictator Siad Barre, became increasingly unpopular. Finally, in 1991, Barre was ousted and fled the country, and the political void was filled by the militias of rival clans. Instead of order, their fighting produced anarchy. Despite efforts by foreign governments and other groups to end the suffering in Somalia, the looting of relief supplies by rival clans could not be prevented, and 350,000 Somalis died from starvation in 1992.

All States Are Sovereign, but Some More So Than Others

As Somalia shows, states, despite legal equality, are in practice very unequal, varying dramatically in their capacity to protect and command citizens. Unlike the great powers in eighteenth-century Europe, some states are more "sovereign" than others. At one extreme Russia occupies more than 17 million square kilometers stretching from the Baltic Sea in Europe to the Pacific Ocean, while the prosperous city-state

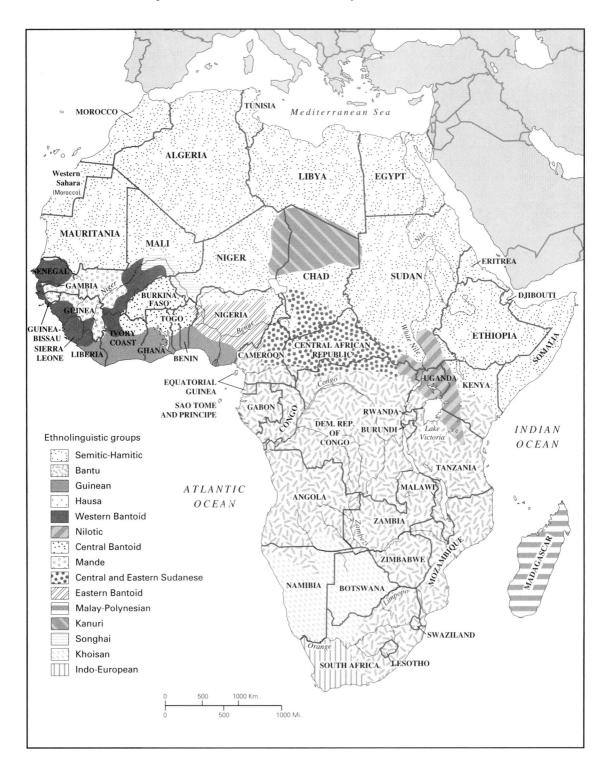

of Singapore consists of small islands totaling about 625 square kilometers off the south coast of the Malay Peninsula. China has a population of more than one billion, while tiny countries like Mauritius have populations that are scarcely above one million. As two observers suggest, some recently independent states "are not states in the strict sense, but only by courtesy."[58] They are "quasi-states," declares Robert Jackson, "a parody of statehood indicated by pervasive incompetence, deflated credibility, and systematized corruption."[59] Such states "disclose limited empirical statehood. . . . Their governments are often deficient in the political will, institutional authority, and organized power to protect human rights or provide socioeconomic welfare."[60]

These paragraphs only begin to tell the story of differences among today's states. Older states, especially in the West, remain a primary object of most citizens' loyalties. When asked to identify their primary affiliations, citizens list their state almost immediately, calling themselves French, Japanese, or Brazilian. Such citizens are more likely to obey and trust their government, pay taxes voluntarily, serve in the armed forces, and rally around their leaders during crises.

The situation in many postcolonial states is quite different. Unlike the gradual and natural evolution of states in Europe, these states were built on sand and, at independence, had few resources and skills to carry out the job. As a result, their citizens may identify principally with groups other than the state, for example, tribe, locality, ethnic group, race, or religion. And these affiliations may, for some issues, place them in opposition to their own governments. The state's frontiers are often only arbitrary lines on a map drawn by colonial governors with little meaning for inhabitants, especially if others with whom they identify live on the other side of the frontiers or if they interrupt traditional economic and social patterns. The map in Figure 3.2 shows the discontinuity between state frontiers and ethnic and tribal identities in Africa.

Sometimes an ethnic group is spread among several states and seeks to carve its own state in their midst. One example is the Kurds, who live in Iran, Iraq, and Turkey and whose efforts to establish an independent Kurdistan have been brutally repressed by authorities in all three countries. During the Iraq-Iran war (1980–1988), both sides tried to use the Kurds against one another, and once the war ended, Iraq turned with ferocity on Iraqi Kurds, forcing thousands to flee the poison gas that was used against their villages. Today Iraq's Kurds enjoy a precarious existence, protected from Saddam Hussein only by the threat of Western intervention. To preserve their status, they have cooperated with Turkish authorities against their Turkish brethren. In spring 1995, Turkey sent 35,000 troops into northern Iraq to crush Kurdish rebels who had taken refuge there.

Frequently, dissatisfied ethnic, tribal, and religious groups seek independence or greater autonomy, and such efforts—culminating in civil strife—have been among the bloodiest events in recent global politics. Since 1945 many more lives have been lost in civil strife than in interstate wars. And, as shown in Table 3.2, the most violent civil wars since 1945 have been fought in the less-developed countries.[61] The Nigerian conflict, the genocidic confrontations between the Tutsi and the Hutu in Rwanda and Burundi, and intertribal slaughter in African countries such as Liberia, Sierra Leone, Mozambique, and Angola reflect the ferocity of such warfare.

FIGURE 3.2
Africa: State Frontiers vs. Tribal Identities

This map illustrates the degree to which the frontiers of African states—largely imposed by European colonial authorities—are incompatible with the realities of tribal affiliations.

TABLE 3.2
*Bloodiest Civil Wars
Since 1945*

Civil War	Deaths
1. China, "Great Leap Forward" (1957–1962)	2.5–5,000,000
2. Nigeria (1967–1970)	2,000,000
3. Afghanistan (1979–1989)	1,300,000
4. Cambodian "Killing Fields" (1975–1978)	1–1,500,000
5. Sudan (1955–1972, 1983–)	1,006,000
6. China civil war (1946–1949)	1,000,000
6. China (government versus landlords) (1950–1951)	1,000,000
7. Ethiopa (1978–1990)	600,000–1,000,000
8. Mozambique (1978–1993)	400,000–900,000
9. Uganda (1971–1978, 1981–1986)	500,000–700,000
10. Chinese "Cultural Revolution" (1966–1968)	500,000
10. Indonesia (1965–1966)	500,000
10. Vietnam (1959–1965, 1973–1975)	500,000
10. Rwanda (1994)	500,000

SOURCES: *New York Times,* May 10, 1995, p. A3; Michael J. Sullivan III, *Measuring Global Values,* p. 34, Greenwood Press, an imprint of Greenwood Pub. Group, Inc., Westport, CT. Reprinted with permission.

Ethnic conflict is endemic in global politics today, especially in the developing world. The Kurds, the Basques in Spain, the Tamils in Sri Lanka, black Africans in the Sudan, and the Abkhazians in Georgia are only a few of the many dissatisfied ethnic minorities that have resorted to violence in recent years. The cruelties of apartheid in South Africa until 1993 and the urban explosions that rocked American cities like Los Angeles reveal the depth of racial mistrust that undermines national unity. Figure 3.3 illustrates how widespread civil strife has been in global politics since 1945. As of 1995, of 30 major armed conflicts in the world, all were intrastate.[62] Table 3.3 summarizes the most dangerous ethnic, religious, and national flash points in global politics today.

The centrifugal forces plaguing India epitomize the problems facing many less-developed countries. The British Indian empire included today's India, Pakistan, and Bangladesh. When independence was granted in 1947, fierce clashes between Muslims and Hindus forced the country to split into India and Pakistan. India was established as a secular state with a Hindu majority and Muslim minority[63] and Pakistan as a Muslim state. The partition did not end religious tension in India; it resurfaces with deadly regularity, as in the bloody riots that swept the country after Hindu extremists razed a sixteenth-century mosque at Ayodhya in Uttar Pradesh in December 1992 or after they burned a fifteenth-century Muslim shrine in Kashmir in May 1995.[64] The Hindu-Muslim cleavage is only one of many that jeopardize India's unity. Demands by Sikhs of the Punjab to have a separate state called Khalistan have led to repeated cycles of terrorism and civil violence, as has separatist agitation in northern tribal areas—Arunachal Pradesh, Mizoram, Assam, Nagaland, Tripura, and, most important, Kashmir and Jammu.[65] With people speaking

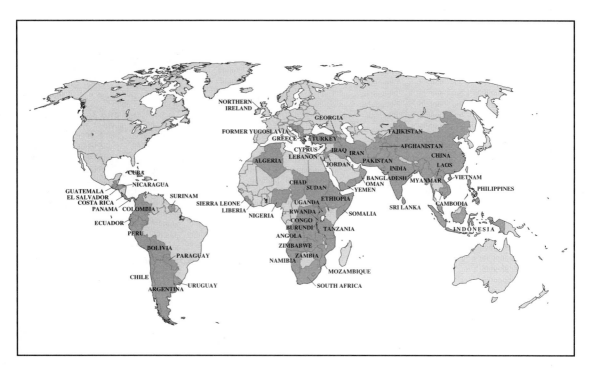

FIGURE 3.3
Victims of Major Civil Strife Since 1945

This map illustrates where widespread civil strife has been in the world since 1945. Virtually no region except North America and Oceania has been left unscathed.
SOURCES: Sullivan, *Measuring Global Values*, Table V1.1a, pp. 35–38; *SIPRI Yearbook 1994*, pp. 81–83; and *SIPRI Yearbook 1996*, pp. 16–21.

1,600 languages, vast economic gaps, and continued caste discrimination against "untouchables,"[66] the forces pulling India apart are strong indeed.

Loyalties to *ethnic* or *tribal groups* may undermine a state's capacity to govern itself, reducing the autonomy of the sovereign state. We must, therefore, exercise care not to confuse sovereignty's sweeping *legal* connotations with its limited *practical* consequences. It entitles states to legal privileges in international organizations and tribunals and in national courts of law. It also provides those who are legal surrogates for states with authority that others may lack. Thus we tend to regard representatives of sovereign states (even if they originally attained their positions by fraud and bloodshed) with awe, and they try to enhance this image by surrounding themselves with symbols of authority and power. These include music ("Hail to the Chief" is played whenever a U.S. president appears in public), uniforms (dictators often dress in gaudy military uniforms), and other accouterments of pomp and circumstance.

TABLE 3.3
Selected Ethnic, National, and Religious Tensions

Country	Current or potential adversaries
Afghanistan	Pathan, Tajik, Hazara, and Uzbek
Angola	Ovimbundu, Kimbundu, and Bakongo
Belgium	Walloon and Fleming
Bosnia	Serb, Croat, and Bosnian Muslim
Bulgaria	Bulgarian, Turk, Gypsy, and Macedonian
Burma	Burman, Shan, and Karen
Canada	British, French, and other European
Chad	Muslims (Arab, Toubou, Hadjerai, Fulbe, Kotoko) and non-Muslim (Sara, Ngambaye, Mbaye, Goulaye, Moundang)
Croatia	Croat, Serb, Muslim, Slovene, Hungarian, and Italian
Cyprus	Greek and Turk
Estonia	Estonian and Russian
Ethiopia	Oromo, Amhara, and Tigrean
Georgia	Georgian, Armenian, Russian, Azeri, Ossetian, and Abkhaz
Hungary	Hungarian (Magyar), Gypsy, German, and Slovak
India	Hindu, Muslim, and Sikh
Iran	Persian, Azeri, Gilaki, and Kurd
Iraq	Sunni Muslim, Shi'ite Muslim, and Kurd
Kenya	Kikuyu, Luhya, Luo, Kalenjin, and Kamba
Lebanon	Sunni Muslim, Shi'ite Muslim, Maronite Christian, and Palestinian
Liberia	Kpelle, Bassa, Gio, Kru, Grebo, Mano, Krahn, Gola, Gbandi, Loma, Kissi, Vai, Bella, and Americo-Liberians
Macedonia	Macedonian, Albanian, Turk, Gypsy, and Serb
Malaysia	Malay, Chinese, and East Indian
Nigeria	Hausa and Fulani (north), Yoruba (southwest), and Ibo (southeast)
Pakistan	Punjabi, Sindhi, Pathan, Baloch, and Muhajir
Peru	Indian, Mestizo, and European
Rwanda	Hutu and Tutsi
Serbia	Serb, Albanian, Montenegrin, Hungarian, Muslim, Gypsy, Croat, and Slovak
Sierra Leone	Mende and Temne
South Africa	Afrikaner, British, Xhosa, Zulu, Sotho, and East Indian
Spain	Spaniard, Basque, and Catalonian
Sri Lanka	Sinhalese and Tamil
Sudan	Muslim Arab and Christian or animist Black
United States	White, Black, and Hispanic

SOURCES: Central Intelligence Agency, *The World Factbook 1994-95* (Washington DC: Brassey's, 1994); and Brian Hunter, ed., *The Statesman's Yearbook 1994-95* (New York: St. Martin's Press, 1994).

BOSNIAN PARTITION PLAN

ETHNIC CLEANSERS

BARBARIAN RAPISTS

SONS OF ATTILA THE HUN

✳ GENOCIDAL MANIACS

WAR CRIMINALS

✳ THOSE WHO WISH TO LIVE IN PEACE

This cartoon parodies the effort to create a single multi-ethnic state in Bosnia, suggesting that years of civil strife and atrocities will make it almost impossible for Bosnian Serbs, Bosnian Croats, and Bosnian Muslims to live together. *(Signe/Cartoonists and Writers Syndicate)*

Sovereignty in some ways is a historical curiosity with declining importance for global politics. Although it continues to confer benefits, these have become less valuable. French recognition of the sovereign independence of the United States during its revolution against Britain in the late eighteenth century was a vital asset for the new republic. More recently it has been argued that the continued independence and territorial integrity of weak states in Africa owe much to *juridical statehood.*[67] Events such as the overthrow of Uganda's President Idi Amin in 1971 by the Tanzanian Army, the 1990 intervention in Liberia by peacekeeping forces of the Economic Community of West African States (ECOWAS), the entry of U.S. forces in Somalia in 1992, the U.N. 1994 operation in Rwanda, and the participation of Rwandan forces in overthrowing the Congo's President Mobutu in 1997 weaken even this argument. Indeed, the United Nations often does not follow Article 2 of its charter, and, from Cambodia to Bosnia, it intervenes in "domestic" affairs that it believes are threats to peace.

None of this means that sovereignty is disappearing. Actors continue to invoke it to prevent outsiders from dealing with such issues as the environment, human rights, drugs, and public health. The United States is still hampered by what two critics describe as the "talisman of 'sovereignty'."

That ill-defined and amorphous notion of international law has been used to denote everything from a state's political independence . . . to the more extreme view that all the internal affairs of a state are beyond the scrutiny of the international community.[68]

The National Interest

National leaders routinely justify their actions and elicit popular support for them by appealing to the *national interest.* Hitler declared that the decision to invade Poland in 1939, starting World War II, was taken to further German national interests, yet six years later German cities were in flames and Hitler had committed suicide. More recently, with the end of the Cold War, a debate has raged in the United States about whether the American national interest is better served by maintaining an active presence overseas or by concentrating on the country's domestic problems.

Is there a collective interest that binds citizens, differentiates them from citizens of other states, and can guide state behavior? And, if so, is there a rational and objective way of determining what that interest is? As we have seen, adherents of power politics argue that each state has a unique national interest that rational leaders should follow. Such interests are thought to arise out of the relative power of states. Powerful and weak states have different opportunities and are confronted by different constraints and perils and should, as a result, use different strategies adapted to their position in the world. The problem is that, at this level of abstraction, the national interest means little more than survival, independence, and security.

At that level of abstraction, it is difficult to use the concept of national interest to determine policies that should be followed to enhance it. Although many citizens of large or rich states are apt to perceive the world differently than those of small and poor ones, the real question is whether those perceptions of common interest are strong or detailed enough to overcome the interests they associate with being black or white, rich or poor, urban or rural, and male or female. In other words, are the interests of "their group" sufficiently compatible with the interests of other groups to produce a consensus about the state as a whole? On this logic, the national interest might be attacked as a rhetorical device that legitimizes whatever its leaders wish to do. It might also be attacked, as Marxists did, as identical with the interests of the group(s) of which leaders are members—class, gender, race, income bracket, and so on. Far from determining national interest in the deductive and rational manner described by power-politics theorists, it appears that the national interest is determined by the rough and tumble of groups and individuals striving to be heard and have their interests served.

Is it in the U.S. interest to raise tariffs and limit foreign imports or to lower tariffs and remove limits? If there were an objective standard for determining national interest, we could probably give a straightforward answer to this question, but instead we can only say that it depends. Owners and workers in industries that are suffering at the hands of foreign competition believe that limiting free trade is in the national interest. But stockholders and employees in export industries and consumers who want to buy products at the lowest price believe that limitations on free trade run counter to the national interest. Even if we had a standard that could determine the condition that the English utilitarian Jeremy Bentham called the greatest good for the greatest number, there would be winners and losers. The losers—whether a majority or a minority of the population—are unlikely to agree that a policy reflects the national interest. Cogent arguments can "prove" that any policy is in the national interest, but saying it does not make it so. People can reach opposite conclusions about the national interest, and as demonstrations and counterdemonstrations in the United States during the Vietnam War showed, such disagreements can elicit great passion.

The government itself rarely agrees completely about what the national interest is or how it can best be served. Bureaucrats may identify the national interest with what they believe to be in their agency's interest. Those responsible for defense believe that cuts in defense spending threaten the national interest, just as those responsible for agriculture, diplomacy, or the urban poor argue that budget cuts in their sector will hurt the country as a whole. The propensity for officials, both public and private, to merge parochial with general interests is probably universal and is expressed by the adage: Where one stands depends upon where one sits.

The national interest seems to change quickly even though it is thought to be determined by a systemwide distribution of power that changes slowly. In fact, changing definitions reflect changing popular moods, swings in public opinion, and shifting political conditions and coalitions. During the late 1940s and early 1950s when the American public was aroused against the "Red menace," the young Richard Nixon was a virulent anticommunist who argued that a hostile policy toward the Soviet Union and "Red" China was in America's national interest. As president, though, Nixon was responsible for détente with the U.S.S.R. and renewed American ties with China.

In the end, national interest, like sovereignty, is a fiction with an important function. Leaders use it as a symbol to gain citizens' acquiescence and support and to produce unity. The symbol is especially effective during crises but can also be used by unscrupulous authorities to justify almost anything. National interest, and its close relative, *national security,* were used to justify the illegal activities of Colonel Oliver North and his associates in their dealings with Iran and the Nicaraguan contras in the 1980s. The same symbols were brandished by Senator Joseph McCarthy during his anticommunist witch hunts in the 1950s to smear foreign-service officers and by cronies of President Nixon during the Watergate affair in 1972 to justify such bizarre activities as burglarizing the office of Daniel Ellsberg's psychiatrist.[69] In the words of two commentators: "Watergate . . . widened the fissures which the Vietnam War opened. . . . It . . . raised in bold type the biggest foreign policy issue of them all—what is 'national security'?"[70]

National-interest arguments have also been used by U.S. leaders to justify supporting brutal and corrupt leaders who turn around and justify their own actions as necessary because of alleged dangers to the state. The anticommunist credentials of dictators like Francisco Franco in Spain (1936-1975), Antonio Salazar in Portugal (1932-1968), Syngman Rhee in South Korea (1948-1960), Ngo Dinh Diem in South Vietnam (1955-1963), General Anastasio Somoza Debayle in Nicaragua (1967-1972, 1974-1979), and Ferdinand E. Marcos in the Philippines (1965-1986) were sufficient justification for many Americans to turn a blind eye to their repressive policies.

The Transnational Challenge to the State

The independence of states is circumscribed by proliferating links among people around the world that cross national frontiers and that can be severed only at great cost. The dependence of states on each other contrasts with the relative self-sufficiency of eighteenth-century European states. "Self-contained, centralized, internally pacified, they could rely on themselves for a high degree of external security."[71]

State autonomy is further limited by problems that do not respect state boundaries, for example, ecological disasters and drug trafficking. Not only are these problems that defy solution by individual governments, but they will be exacerbated if actors merely seek to increase their relative power. Such problems undermine the belief that one actor can enhance its interests without taking account of others' interests.

Technology and Diminishing Independence

The revolution in technology contributes to the decline in state autonomy. Military security is threatened by technology that enables "belligerents to overleap or bypass the traditional hard-shell defense of states."[72] The frontiers of *all* states—from the most insignificant like Vanuatu to the largest like Russia—are more penetrable in today's world than ever before. High-speed jet aircraft, space shuttles, spy satellites, and intercontinental ballistic missiles are only a few of the developments that make the frontiers of states more permeable than ever. The Internet, the facsimile machine, cellular phones, television, and radio have little respect for legal boundaries. Speculators move huge sums of money almost instantaneously from continent to continent. And during the Chinese government's brutal repression of pro-democracy demonstrators in 1989, students used fax machines to stay in touch with sympathizers overseas. Since governments cannot prevent radio broadcasts and television images from being beamed down from satellites, their efforts to restrict the spread of ideas are fruitless.

Television is especially powerful in breaking down national frontiers. Governments in China, Iran, and Saudi Arabia have banned satellite dishes in a largely fruitless effort to prevent citizens from being contaminated by foreign influences—"cheap alien culture" and the source of "family-devastating diseases of the West," thundered the Grand Ayatollah Mohammed Ali Araki.[73] In the two decades after 1965, the number of television transmitters globally exploded from 8,550 to 60,570 and the number of receivers from 55 to 137 per thousand inhabitants.[74] Stations like Cable News Network (CNN) give access to remote corners of the world, and the pictures they send have roused publics against starvation in Somalia and brutality in Bosnia. Iraqi dictator Saddam Hussein kept abreast of the effort to oust his forces from Kuwait by watching CNN, and CNN allowed us to watch Boris Yeltsin attack his parliamentary enemies in Moscow's "White House" in October 1993. People all over the world can witness dramatic events anywhere else, and they may mimic what they see (*demonstration effect*). Thus students demonstrating for democracy in China in 1989 were influenced by events in the U.S.S.R. surrounding Mikhail Gorbachev's steps to introduce democracy in his country.[75] Public opinion in one part of the world can influence public opinion elsewhere, sometimes almost instantly. As a result of technology, states have less and less ability to control the movement of things, ideas, and people entering and leaving their territory.

Mobilization of the Masses and Growing Global Society

The immense technological changes described above are not the only reasons for states' declining capacity and autonomy. The growing desire of private citizens to become directly involved in global politics, their unwillingness to leave foreign-policy decisions to government elites, and their abilities "to connect to world politics and cope with its complexity"[76] have produced a *participation explosion.* Earlier, mass publics were ignorant of or uninterested in politics, and their inertia was captured by Karl Marx's sarcastic description of the French peasantry as "homologous multitudes, much as potatoes in a sack form a sack of potatoes."[77]

Before the revolutions late in the eighteenth century in Europe and America, most inhabitants were so preoccupied with personal survival that they had neither the time nor information to participate in politics. The absence of mass participation in politics in much of Asia, Africa, Latin America, and the Middle East facilitated their conquest and pacification by relatively few European soldiers. Imperialists needed only to co-opt a small local elite or defeat relatively primitive local armies to win the day. Thus it took only a few thousand British soldiers and administrators to control hundreds of millions of Indians at the height of the British Raj.

Higher standards of living, wider education, and improved communication combined in this century to make many citizens throughout the world politically conscious. Once awakened, their energies were mobilized, first to oust colonial authorities and later to resist external control of their affairs. Thus the French in Indochina (1946–1954) and in Algeria (1954–1962) and the Americans in South Vietnam (1965–1973) were unable to pacify national movements despite a far larger military presence than their colonial predecessors. Formerly passive populations were transformed into intensely participant publics, willing to die if necessary to resist aggression. Thus conquest and occupation of one state by another has become difficult and expensive even though frontiers are porous. In sum, mobilizing the masses intensified nationalism and, by combining nation and state, propelled the nation-state to the forefront of human loyalties.[78]

But this is only part of the story of the participation explosion. More important is that, even while providing the raw material for nationalism, mass political consciousness has reduced governments' ability to shield foreign affairs from domestic passions, isolate the domestic arena from global politics, or manage foreign affairs without interference from below. Consider how each of us participates in global politics. Every day we make conscious and unconscious choices with implications for the world around us. For example, we decide whether to purchase products made overseas, decisions that affect the domestic and international economies and, indirectly, the political stability of the societies involved. Shall we buy a Toyota or Chevrolet? Shall we use Italian olive oil or American vegetable oil? Indeed, it is staggering to realize how much of what we eat, wear, and use is either partly or wholly foreign in origin.

We are also constantly exposed to cultural influences from abroad, whether rock stars, BBC television programs, French and Italian clothing designs, or, a more sinister example, neo-Nazi skinheads linked by rock bands, magazines, and electronic communication.[79] Similarly, U.S. cultural influences constantly bombard other societies, exasperating local leaders because such influences erode traditional mores and patterns of obedience, especially among the young. Jeans and rap music are now part of the youth culture from New York to Bombay, and from Lagos to Teheran. Thus McDonald's became part of the local scene in Moscow by opening the largest eating establishment in that city,[80] and a Euro-Disney theme park near Paris produced local controversy. Indeed, we may speak of a cultural globalization that accompanies economic globalization. Fear that such influences dilute national culture or undermine local values fuels authoritarianism in China, xenophobia in Burma, and Islamic fundamentalism in Iran, whose spiritual leader banned the consumption of Coca-Cola and Pepsi-Cola,[81] and where gangs of religious vigilantes roam the streets of cities searching for signs of Western culture.

Cultural exchange is also produced by growing numbers of people traveling and studying abroad. Expanding tourism, student and sports exchanges, foreign films, business and professional travel—facilitated by increased speed and capacity in communications and transportation—lead to homogenized lifestyles, especially among urban youths, business and professional classes, and political elites. Such exchanges may have profound political consequences, such as increasing consciousness of vital issues and greater sensitivity for other peoples' customs, and they have done much in mobilizing transnational environmental and feminist movements and creating a global economic market.

Occasionally, a news story from abroad is potent enough to persuade us to try to change foreign policy. We might write our member of Congress, contribute to a relief organization, or boycott foreign goods. Thus some Americans contribute to a group called Noraid to assist those seeking to oust the British from Northern Ireland, and others boycott Japanese goods because they believe imports take American jobs. We might even demonstrate for a cause, as many did, to urge U.S. and European firms to divest their holdings in South Africa to protest racial apartheid or against advertising baby formula in the less-developed countries.[82] Such passions produce political pressure on foreign-policy elites that would have been unthinkable in earlier centuries. On a few issues, individuals travel overseas to advance causes about which they feel strongly. In the 1930s, numbers of idealistic young Americans and Europeans fought for the Spanish Loyalists against General Franco's Fascists, and others joined Britain's Royal Air Force (RAF) to fight the Nazis before America's entry in the war. In recent years, Muslims from around the world have gone to fight alongside coreligionists in Afghanistan and Bosnia.

Transnational Relations   Until recently, theorists believed that to understand global politics it was sufficient to look only at relations between and among governments of sovereign states and between states and international organizations, as depicted in Figure 3.4. Nonsovereign entities or individuals were believed to affect global politics only indirectly, as by voting, lobbying, demonstrating, writing letters, or in other ways trying to persuade governments. Today, however, it is apparent that many issues are *transnational,* meaning they feature relations between nonsovereign social groups.[83] Figure 3.5 shows how the traditional model of global politics changes when we take account of *direct* involvement by nonstate actors—corporations, drug cartels, terrorists, and so forth—that are players in global politics, sometimes despite

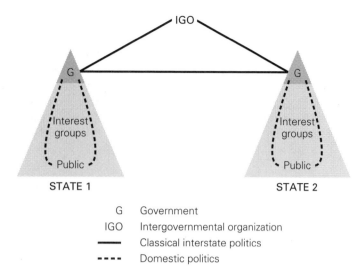

G	Government
IGO	Intergovernmental organization
——	Classical interstate politics
----	Domestic politics

FIGURE 3.4
Restricted Model of State-Centered Politics

The traditional model of global politics only allows domestic groups to influence the outside world *indirectly* by pressuring their government. The sum of global politics in this model is interaction among governments or between governments and IGOs like the United Nations. SOURCE: Copyright © 1971. Reprinted with permission of MIT Press.

government opposition. As one observer declares: "American law enforcement is being exported in response to the surge of international terrorism, narcotics trafficking, links between terrorists and drug dealers, illegal immigrant smuggling, money laundering and the potential theft and sale of nuclear material and chemically or biologically hazardous substances.[84]

Instead of a global hierarchy with sovereign states at the top, we can speak of a "web of world politics"[85] in which flows of goods, people, and ideas across national frontiers produce interdependence. This is the model of global politics that the president of the IBM World Trade Corporation had in mind when he declared:

> For business purposes, the boundaries that separate one nation from another are
> no more real than the equator. They are merely convenient demarcations of ethnic,
> linguistic, and cultural entities. . . . The world outside the home country is no longer
> viewed as a series of disconnected customers and prospects for its products, but as
> an extension of a single market.[86]

Transnational activity reduces governments' ability to carry out their own policies. In December 1994, foreign investors withdrew huge sums from Mexico to invest in Europe and the United States, where interest rates were rising.[87] Mexico was forced to devalue the peso, the value of which continued to fall. To stem the hemorrhage of investment, Mexico adopted a harsh austerity program that reduced citizens' standard

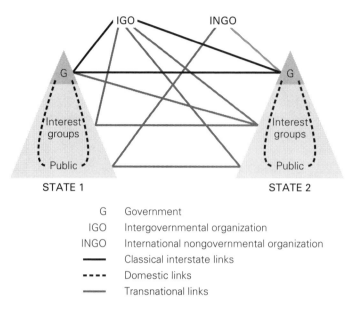

G   Government
IGO   Intergovernmental organization
INGO   International nongovernmental organization
─────   Classical interstate links
- - - - Domestic links
─────   Transnational links

FIGURE 3.5
Expanded Model of International and Domestic Policy Links

The expanded model of global politics allows for direct transnational interactions between societies, between societal groups and governments, and between societal groups and IGOs and INGOs. This model permits nongovernmental organizations like the PLO to behave as autonomous actors. SOURCE: Copyright © 1971. Reprinted with permission of MIT Press.

of living, and the United States, the International Monetary Fund, and other countries put together an aid package of $50 billion in loan guarantees to keep Mexico from defaulting on its bonds.[88] The impact of private speculators and investors in this case reflects the role of transnational activities. Governments thought they could maintain the value of their currencies as they had done in the past by ordering their central banks to buy and sell currencies. In fact, central banks had little idea how much cash was in private hands or how quickly it could be moved, and their resources were inadequate to cope with the enormous flows of private funds.

Some issues are really transnational rather than interstate. One is the global drug trade, worth some $400 billion a year (almost as much as global tourism), and the role played by organized crime. "In many Latin American countries," writes one observer, "drug-trafficking organizations, rather than the government, now represent the ultimate power in portions of a country if not the country as a whole."[89] To some extent, this description applies to Burma, Colombia, Afghanistan,[90] Kyrgyzstan, Morocco, and even Albania.[91] According to one report, the ancient Silk Road "now carries an ever-growing caravan of drugs through the damaged, lawless and often ungovernable countries of Central Asia."[92] Mexico has become both a major source

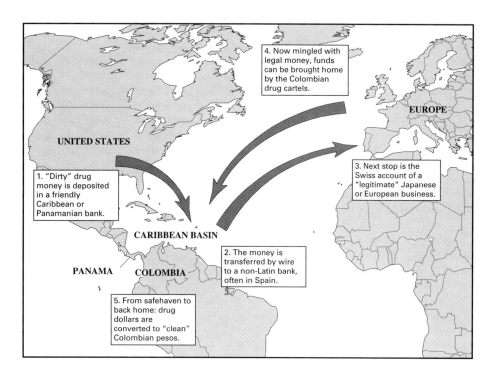

FIGURE 3.6
Colombian Hopscotch: How to Launder "Dirty" Billions

This map shows the transnational "laundering" of drug money earned by Colombia's drug cartels. SOURCE: David A. Andelman, "The Drug Money Maze," *Foreign Affairs* 73:4 (July–August 1994), p. 104. Map by Ib Ohlsson for *Foreign Affairs*. Reprinted with permission.

of and transit point for drugs in the United States, and drug corruption is rife within Mexico's police and armed forces.[93] Peruvian cocaine and heroin traffickers, with links to the Russian mafia, are coming to rival the Colombian cartels, and Colombian drug lords use American companies to launder illicit funds. What one author calls "the drug money maze," $100 billion worth, involves a complex and secretive transnational system (see Figure 3.6):

> The first step is the initial deposit, which must be made to a bank in a country where the launderer knows he and his associates will not be arrested within 24 hours and the money cannot be frozen quickly. This deposit is the single most important step, where the money is the dirtiest. . . . In the second stage the money is transferred to a bank controlled by a non-Latin. . . . Next, it is transferred to an account in the name of a Japanese or West European company. . . . In Colombia, the final stage is conversion into Colombian pesos. This series of transactions serves three purposes: it creates a complex paper trail, makes the origin and ownership of money dubious and commingles drug money with legitimate financial transactions.[94]

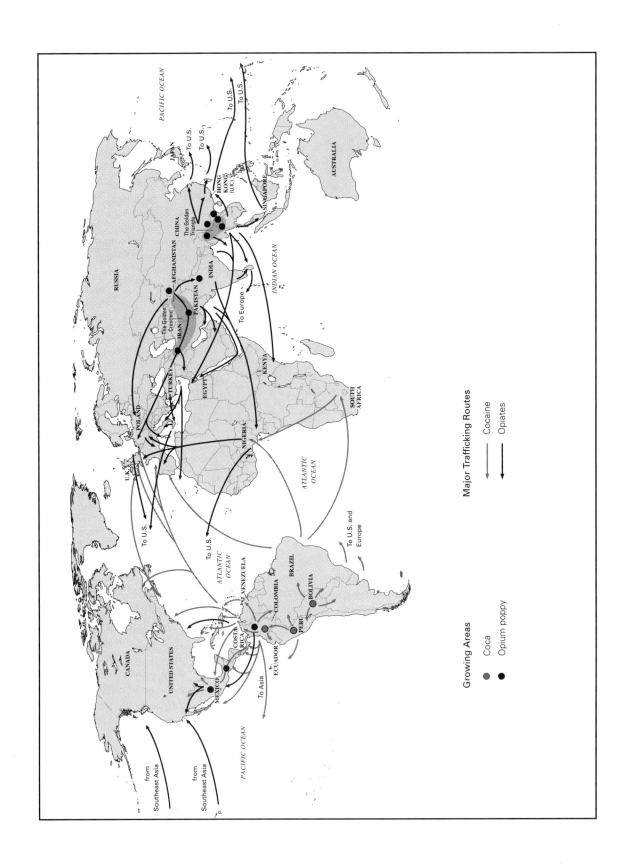

Growing Areas

Coca

Opium poppy

Major Trafficking Routes

Cocaine

Opiates

PACIFIC OCEAN

PACIFIC OCEAN

RUSSIA

CANADA

UNITED STATES

MEXICO

ECUADOR

COSTA
RICA

VENEZUELA

COLOMBIA

PERU

BOLIVIA

BRAZIL

ATLANTIC
OCEAN

ATLANTIC
OCEAN

U.K.

POLAND

TURKEY

IRAN

The Golden
Crescent

AFGHANISTAN

PAKISTAN

INDIA

CHINA

The Golden
Triangle

HONG
KONG
(U.K.)

SINGAPORE

JAPAN

AUSTRALIA

INDIAN OCEAN

EGYPT

NIGERIA

KENYA

SOUTH
AFRICA

To U.S.

To U.S.

To U.S.

To U.S.

To U.S.

To Europe

To U.S.

To U.S.

To U.S. and
Europe

To Asia

from
Southeast Asia

from
Southeast Asia

For its part, the U.S. government—notwithstanding the appointment of "drug czars," use of the military, and investment of large sums of money—seems helpless to control its own frontiers against the flow of drugs. Efforts to eradicate the sources of drugs are either unsuccessful or simply lead to their being moved to another region or country, and efforts to interdict the flow of drugs are largely useless. Some of these efforts have been imaginative: Americans have tested a fungus that destroys coca and "have also considered a coca-munching caterpillar."[95] Figure 3.7 shows the transnational nature of the drug problem by indicating the routes from cultivation areas in South America, the Middle East ("the Golden Crescent"), and Southeast Asia ("the Golden Triangle") to lucrative markets in North America and Europe. So serious has the threat of transnational crime become that the leaders of the major industrial states at their 1995 summit meeting in Halifax formed a task force to enhance cooperation in dealing with this "growing threat to the security of our nations."[96]

The Meaning of Interdependence

All this suggests how difficult it is for any state to close its frontiers to the movement of persons, ideas, and things or to shield citizens from the consequences of events far from home. From time to time states try to keep out foreign influences, but the costs are high because they cut themselves off from economic, technological, and informational benefits that accompany world trade, foreign investment, tourism, overseas education, global media, and other transnational activities.

Whether we like it or not, we live in an interdependent world. An actor is dependent if it is significantly affected by external forces. *Interdependence* is a situation of linked fates. In earlier centuries, interdependence was low. People were mainly self-sufficient and interacted infrequently with those outside their immediate locality. Today, all human beings depend, to some extent, on others outside their community. Thus the price Americans and Europeans pay for coffee and other primary products depends on events in Latin America and Africa, and prosperity in those regions depends on demand for their commodities in the developed world and the availability of substitutes from elsewhere that may depress prices for their products.

There are two sides to interdependence—sensitivity and vulnerability.[97] *Sensitivity* is the speed with which changes in one part of the world affect other parts and the magnitude of those effects. When the Clinton administration tried to help Mexico in early 1995 after the collapse of the peso, it had no time to consult allies because of what one official calls the "disjunction between the speed of the markets and the speed that deliberative bodies decide."[98] *Vulnerability* refers to the alternatives actors have in seeking to limit the effects of change. Many countries are vulnerable to changes in oil prices or supplies, so that labor unrest in Nigeria's oil fields in August 1994 produced a surge in global oil prices.[99]

There are quantitative indicators that can help us measure interdependence. The ratio of international to national trade is one measure of how embedded a people are in the global system. This ratio has increased for many actors, especially the United States, which until recently was relatively self-sufficient economically. Figure 3.8 illustrates the dramatic increase in U.S. foreign trade as a percentage of GNP, especially between the early 1970s and late 1990s, and shows how thoroughly the U.S. economy has been integrated into the global market. A similar conclusion becomes apparent from Table 3.4, which shows the increase of direct investment

FIGURE 3.7
Narcopolitics: A Transnational Issue

This map illustrates the transnational and global nature of narcopolitics. It shows the principal sources and markets of narcotics and the major trafficking routes from one to the other. As the drug trade has grown, the area of production has greatly expanded from the traditional Asian centers—the Golden Crescent and the Golden Triangle—to include many less-developed countries. Poverty provides the drug lords with an army of drug runners.

FIGURE 3.8

U.S. Foreign Trade as a Percentage of GNP

This figure reflects the growing importance of foreign trade to the U.S. economy and the growing participation of the United States in the interdependent global economy. By the mid-1970s, foreign trade accounted for 25 percent of the U.S. GNP.

from and to the United States between 1960 and 1997. Such indicators reveal "rapid acceleration in the development of ties linking nations, their institutional components, and the individuals who populate them" and "a general tendency for many forms of human interconnectedness across national boundaries to be doubling every ten years."[100]

The indicators of interdependence should not be confused with interdependence itself. Changes in factors like technology and trade create links across national boundaries and make it more expensive to go it alone. If people are prepared to pay a price, however, they may escape dependence.[101] Societies can sever economic and political ties if people are prepared to accept a lower standard of living, higher unemployment, and isolation more generally. Indeed, if a society is cohesive, citizens may be willing to bear high costs to escape dependence on others.

During World War I, Germans were cut off from the oil imports necessary to maintain their economy. Although Germany produced no oil at home and could not break Britain's naval blockade, the country did not capitulate. Instead, Germans found imaginative substitutes for oil, including vegetable-derived alcohol—beets and turnips—and animal energy, which they used even though the substitutes were inefficient and expensive. Fidel Castro's regime in Cuba—one of the few hard-line communist regimes in the world—refused to accept the consequences of its Soviet protector's collapse. Deprived of inexpensive Soviet oil and hard currency from

TABLE 3.4

U.S. Direct Investment Abroad, Foreign Direct Investment in the U.S. as a percentage of U.S. GNP

	U.S. direct investment abroad	Foreign direct investment in U.S.
1960	6.5%	1.4%
1965	7.2%	1.3%
1970	7.4%	1.3%
1975	8.0%	1.8%
1980	7.9%	2.5%
1981	7.7%	2.8%
1982	7.2%	4.1%
1983	6.9%	4.1%
1984	6.4%	4.5%
1985	5.7%	4.6%
1986	6.1%	5.2%
1987	6.8%	5.8%
1988	6.7%	6.4%
1989	7.2%	7.0%
1990	7.7%	7.1%
1991	8.1%	7.4%
1992	8.0%	6.9%
1997	10.6%	8.4%

SOURCES: U.S. Bureau of the Census, *Statistical Abstract of the United States* (Washington, DC: Government Printing Office, 1983–1994); *World Almanac 1999* (Mahwah, NJ: Primedia Reference, Inc., 1998), p. 125.

subsidized Soviet purchases of Cuban sugar, Cubans abandoned cars for bicycles and sought substitutes for other imports. Ultimately, then, dependence and interdependence are subjective phenomena. Independence today is costly, and the question is: *How high a cost are people prepared to bear to assert their independence?* Those who are prepared to bear higher costs are less dependent than those who are not.

Conclusion

Today's power-politics tradition has deep roots in European history. Sovereign states in Europe had to compete for scarce resources in limited geographic space. Under these conditions, war was common, and theorists and practitioners focused on questions of power. Power, however, is one of the most elusive concepts in studying global politics. There is some consensus that it entails relationships among particular actors in specific contexts and is not a general attribute. We cannot see power any more than we can see electricity. Like electricity, however, we can infer it from its results. We can also infer it from the resources that are invested in creating it. Having done so, and realizing that power cannot be applied indiscriminately, we must be alert to differences between using rewards and coercion to achieve goals and applying persuasion to that task. We must also recall that using power can have high costs.

The power-politics tradition helps make sense of issues that involve military security, in which actors' interdependence is low or negative, and in which the main players remain states. Increasingly, however, issues do not involve military security and involve actors other than governments that are highly interdependent. There have always been such issues, but they remained in shadow, receiving insufficient attention. They are poorly understood when viewed through the power-politics lens.

The power-politics perspective was dominant during the Cold War, and its end has made it easier to glimpse the features of an alternative perspective. The following chapter traces this transition from the international to the postinternational world. It summarizes the great confrontation between East and West, examines how and why it ended, and what this has meant for U.S.-Russian relations in ensuing years.

Key Terms

anarchy
bipolarity
capabilities
chameleon effect
coercion
costs of power
demonstration effect
domain of power
ethnic group
expertise
failed states
formal role
hegemonic war
interdependence
juridical statehood

legitimate power
Melian Dialogue
multipolarity
national interest
national security
neorealism
paradox of power
participation explosion
potential power
power
power politics
realism
realpolitik
reason of state
recognition

relative military-spending burden
rewards
satellite effect
scope of power
sensitivity interdependence
situational power
sovereign equality
state autonomy
state capacity
state sovereignty
strong state
structural realists
transnational relations
vulnerability interdependence
weak state

End Notes

[1]Hendrik Spruyt, *The Sovereign State and Its Competitors* (Princeton: Princeton University Press, 1994), pp. 18–19.

[2]The term is still used. See, for example, Frank W. Wayman and Paul F. Diehl, eds., *Reconstructing Realpolitik* (Ann Arbor: The University of Michigan Press, 1994).

[3]Janice E. Thomson, *Mercenaries, Pirates, and Sovereigns*

(Princeton: Princeton University Press, 1994), p. 11.

[4]See David Shearer, "Outsourcing War," *Foreign Policy* 112 (Fall 1998), pp. 68–81.

[5]Steven Forde, "International Realism and the Science of Politics: Thucydides, Machiavelli, and Neorealism," *International Studies Quarterly* 39:2 (June 1995), p. 158. Emphasis in original.

[6]Thucydides, *The Peloponnesian War,* trans. Rex Warner (Baltimore: Penguin Books, 1954), pp. 24-25.

[7]Ibid., p. 25.

[8]Ibid., p. 160. Thucydides would have been acquainted with the great tragedians of his time—Aeschylus, Sophocles, and Euripides.

[9]Economic inflation in the 1970s, upsurge in drug use, and the decay of the inner cities are in part viewed as the inheritance of the Vietnam War.

[10]Niccolò Machiavelli, *The Prince,* trans. George Bull (Baltimore: Penguin Books, 1961), p. 92.

[11]See Friedrich Meinecke, *Machiavellism* (New Haven: Yale University Press, 1957).

[12]There are variations in such claims. Christian theologians speak of man's fallen nature and original sin. Psychologists in the tradition of Sigmund Freud speak of a death instinct. Some anthropologists think human aggression has become dangerous because of incomplete evolution combined with mastery of weapons.

[13]Hans J. Morgenthau, *Politics Among Nations: The Struggle for Power and Peace,* 6th ed., rev. Kenneth W. Thompson (New York: Knopf, 1985), p. 187.

[14]George F. Kennan, *American Diplomacy 1900-1950* (New York: Mentor Books, 1952), p. 82.

[15]Ibid., p. 84.

[16]Kissinger's doctoral dissertation was published under the title *A World Restored: Metternich, Castlereagh and the Problems of Peace* (Boston: Houghton Mifflin, 1957).

[17]Henry A. Kissinger, *American Foreign Policy,* expanded ed. (New York: Norton, 1974), pp. 91-92.

[18]Inis L. Claude, Jr., *Power and International Relations* (New York: Random House, 1962), p. 13. Claude argues that the concept is used to refer to a "situation," a "policy," and a "system" (pp. 13-25). Also Ernst B. Haas, "The Balance of Power: Prescription, Concept, or Propaganda?" *World Politics* 5:4 (July 1953), pp. 442-477.

[19]Cited in Morgenthau, *Politics Among Nations,* p. 211.

[20]See Morton A. Kaplan, *System and Process in International Politics* (New York: Wiley, 1957), pp. 22-36.

[21]See Robert O. Keohane, ed., *Neorealism and Its Critics* (New York: Columbia University Press, 1986); and David A. Baldwin, ed., *Neorealism and Neoliberalism* (New York: Columbia University Press, 1993).

[22]He calls these three factors a system's *organizing principles.* Kenneth N. Waltz, *Theory of International Politics* (Reading, MA: Addison-Wesley, 1979), p. 88.

[23]Robert Gilpin, *War and Change in World Politics* (New York: Cambridge University Press, 1981), p. 9.

[24]Ibid., p. 228.

[25]Kenneth N. Waltz, "The Stability of a Bipolar World," in David Edwards, ed., *International Political Analysis* (New York:

Holt, Rinehart and Winston, 1970), and Waltz, *Theory of International Politics,* pp. 163-173. Gilpin declares that "Waltz's argument that bipolar systems are more stable and less subject to abrupt transformations than multi-polar structures has an impressive logic to it" (*War and Change in World Politics,* p. 89), but he suggests that Waltz overemphasizes "the static distribution of power in the system" at the expense of "the dynamic of power relationships over time" (ibid., p. 93).

[26]For most of the Cold War, the United States enjoyed military superiority over the U.S.S.R.

[27]Kenneth N. Waltz, "Will the Future Be like the Past?" in Nissan Oren, ed., *When Patterns Change: Turning Points in International Politics* (New York: St. Martin's Press, 1984), p. 17. An alternative argument is that multipolarity is more stable than bipolarity because the presence of more actors permits more complex interactions that produce crosscutting pressures, moderating conflict. Karl W. Deutsch and J. David Singer, "Multipolar Power Systems and International Stability," in James N. Rosenau, ed., *International Politics and Foreign Policy,* rev. ed. (New York: Free Press, 1969), pp. 315-324.

[28]Gilpin, *War and Change in World Politics,* p. 191. Some realists reverse this, arguing that the rising challenger starts the conflict.

[29]Charles Krauthammer, "The Unipolar Moment," *Foreign Affairs* 70:1 (1990/91), p. 23.

[30]See John J. Mearsheimer, "Back to the Future: Instability in Europe After the Cold War," *International Security* 15:1 (Summer 1990), pp. 5-56.

[31]Joseph M. Grieco, "Anarchy and the Limits of Cooperation: A Realist Critique of the Newest Liberal Institutionalism," *International Organization* 42:3 (Summer 1988), pp. 488-507.

[32]Among the weapons used for the first time in combat were sea-launched cruise missiles, Patriot antimissile missiles, and the Abrams tank (M-1). The array of modern U.S. aircraft included Stealth fighters and B-52s equipped with precision-guided "smart" bombs.

[33]Theodore Draper, "The True History of the Gulf War," *New York Review of Books,* January 30, 1992, pp. 41, 42.

[34]Roy Licklider, *Political Power and the Arab Oil Weapon* (Berkeley, CA: University of California Press, 1988), p. 279.

[35]Niccolò Machiavelli, *The Prince and The Discourses* (New York: Random House, Modern Library College Edition, 1950), p. 308.

[36]We use *power* and *influence* interchangeably. *Power* is more popular, but *influence*—unlike power—can be used as a verb and so connotes more fully that the phenomenon is relational.

[37]Defining power as a causal relationship is complicated because the influencer can have power without taking any action. An actor may refrain from doing something or take some action because it *anticipates* that this is the behavior a more powerful actor would wish. The cause of the actor's behavior is invisible, but a power relationship exists.

[38]Karl W. Deutsch, *The Analysis of International Relations,* 2nd ed. (Englewood Cliffs, NJ: Prentice Hall, 1978) pp. 32, 40.

[39]Objective probability exists only in reference to a series of events. The use of probability when referring to one event is metaphorical.

[40]Waltz, *Theory of International Politics,* p. 192.

[41]Laurence Lafore, *The Long Fuse,* 2nd ed. (New York: Lippincott, 1971), pp. 131-132.

[42]U.S. Arms Control and Disarmament Agency, *World Military Expenditures and Arms Transfers 1990* (Washington, DC: Government Printing Office, 1991), p. 36.

[43]Between 1983 and 1993, world military expenditures fell from 19% to 11.5% of GNP. U.S. Arms Control and Disarmament Agency, *World Military Expenditures and Arms Transfers 1993-1994* (Washington, DC: Government Printing Office, 1995), pp. 43, 68, 87.

[44]For an effort to establish empirical criteria for measuring sovereignty's decline, see Janice E. Thomson, "State Sovereignty in International Relations: Bridging the Gap Between Theory and Empirical Research," *International Studies Quarterly* 39:2 (June 1995), pp. 213-233. Since sovereignty is a legal concept, the claim that it is "declining" is metaphoric. It is actually state autonomy that is declining.

[45]Disagreement remains over which entities should be counted as sovereign. Should *microsovereignties* like Monaco and Andorra be counted as sovereign states? What about groups, like the Palestinian Liberation Organization, that aspire to become the governments of states and are recognized by some as having this status but that do not control the territory or people they claim as theirs?

[46]Morgenthau, *Politics Among Nations,* p. 329.

[47]Spruyt (*The Sovereign State and Its Competitors,* p. 28) argues that "sovereign states selected out and delegitimized actors who did not fit a system of territorially demarcated and internally hierarchical authorities."

[48]Mandates were territories formerly owned by the losers in World War I (1914-1918). They had been taken over by the League of Nations, which, in turn, had entrusted their administration to designated states.

[49]Theda Skocpol, "Bringing the State Back In: Strategies of Analysis in Current Research," in Peter B. Evans, Dietrich Rueschemeyer, and Theda Skocpol, eds., *Bringing the State Back In* (Cambridge: Cambridge University Press, 1985), p. 9.

[50]Ibid., p. 17.

[51]"Peace at Last, at Least for Now," *The Economist,* November 25-December 1, 1995, p. 23. See also Chris Hedges, "Bosnia's Checkerboard Partition: Instability More Likely," *New York Times,* March 20, 1996, p. A8; Chris Hedges, "Bosnia's Ethnic Fault Lines, It's Still Tense, but World Is Silent," *New York Times,* February 28, 1996, pp. A1, A6; and Chris Hedges, "Croatia Resettling Its People In Houses, Seized From Serbs," *New York Times,* March 14, 1997, pp. A1, A8.

[52]See, for example, Howard W. French, "Yes, Things Can Get Worse in Africa," *New York Times,* November 3, 1996, sec. 4, p. 3; "Polls to Nowhere," *The Economist,* November 23-29, 1996, pp. 20, 22; Howard W. French, "Zairian Crisis Part of Broad Web of African Subversion and Revolt," *New York Times,* November 23, 1996, sec. 4, p. 3.

[53]*World Development Report 1995* (New York: Oxford University Press, 1995), Table 1, pp. 162-163.

[54]Howard W. French, "Mobutu, Zaire's 'Guide,' Leads Nation into Chaos," *New York Times,* June 10, 1995, p. 6.

[55]Cited in ibid., p. 1.

[56]See Philip Shenon, "Cambodia Can't Shake the Legacy of Madness," *New York Times,* March 12, 1994, sec. 4, p. 3; "Paralysed," *The Economist,* May 31-June 6, 1997, p. 39; Howard W. French, "As War Factions Shatter, Liberia Falls into Chaos," *New York Times,* October 22, 1994, p. 6; Raymond Bonner, "Rwandan Needs Go Begging in Sea of Aid," *New York Times,* November 2, 1994, p. A6; "Rebel Without a Cause," *The Economist,* June 27-July 3, 1998, p. 48.

[57]"A Society Without the State," *The Economist,* September 16-22, 1995, p. 50. In the absence of functioning state institutions, Islamic leaders have come to play a major role in governing the country. James C. McKinley, Jr., "Islamic Movement's Niche: Bringing Order to Somalia's Clans," *New York Times,* August 23, 1996, pp. A1, A6.

[58]Hedley Bull and Adam Watson, "Conclusion," in Bull and Watson, eds., *The Expansion of International Society* (New York: Oxford University Press, 1984), p. 430.

[59]Robert H. Jackson, "Quasi-States, Dual Regimes, and Neoclassical Theory: International Jurisprudence and the Third World," *International Organization* 41:4 (Autumn 1987), pp. 526, 527.

[60]Robert H. Jackson, *Quasi-States: Sovereignty, International Relations and the Third World* (New York: Cambridge University Press, 1990), p. 21.

[61]The civil war in the former Yugoslavia was the first in Europe since World War II. Serbia itself is in danger of fragmenting as Albanians living in Kosovo seek independence. There is also a separatist movement in northern Italy that calls for an independent "Padania," Thomas Kamm and Maria Stupani. "Will Northern Italians Give Rome the Boot?" *Wall Street Journal,* September 13, 1996, p. A8.

[62]Margareta Sollenberg and Peter Wallensteen, "Major armed conflicts," *SIPRI Yearbook 1996* (New York: Oxford University Press, 1996), p. 15.

[63]Even after secession by Pakistan, Muslims still accounted for 11 percent of India's population, making it the third largest Muslim community in the world after Indonesia and Bangladesh. Bangladesh was created by the secession of East Bengal from Pakistan in the early 1970s.

[64]John F. Burns, "In a Kashmir Conflagration, India Faces a Turning Point," *New York Times,* May 14, 1995, sec. 1, pp. 1, 6. See also John F. Burns, "Bombay's Bleak Nationalism: 'Hindustan' for Hindus Only," *New York Times,* November 3, 1995, pp. A1, A6.

[65]See, for example, "Beyond the Brahmaputra," *The Economist,* January 4-10, 1997, p. 38.

[66]Caste remains a highly divisive factor in India. See Barbara Crossette, "Caste May Be India's Moral Achilles' Tendon," *New York Times,* sec. 4, p. 3; and "Casteing Stones," *The Economist,* July 19-25, 1997, p. 38.

[67]Robert H. Jackson and Carl G. Rosberg, "Why Africa's Weak States Persist: The Empirical and the Juridical in Statehood," *World Politics* 35:1 (October 1982), pp. 12-16.

[68]Gerald B. Helman and Steven R. Ratner, "Saving Failed States," *Foreign Policy* 89 (Winter 1992-93), p. 9.

[69]Ellsberg was a Pentagon analyst who made public the Pentagon Papers, which included official documents concerning U.S. decisions to intervene in Vietnam.

[70]Leslie H. Gelb and Anthony Lake, "Watergate and Foreign Policy," *Foreign Policy* 12 (Fall 1973), p. 177.

[71]John H. Herz, *International Politics in the Atomic Age* (New York: Columbia University Press, 1959), p. 96.

[72]Ibid., p. 97.

[73]Cited in Peter Waldman, "Iran Fights New Foe: Western Television," *Wall Street Journal,* August 8, 1994, p. A6. See also Patrick E. Tyler, "CNN and MTV Hanging by a 'Heavenly Thread,'" *New York Times,* November 22, 1993, p. A4; Philip Shenon, "A Repressed World Says, 'Beam Me Up,'" *New York Times,* September 11, 1994, sec. 4, p. 4.

[74]James N. Rosenau, *Turbulence in World Politics* (Princeton: Princeton University Press, 1990), pp. 339, 340.

[75]Two especially powerful images from the turbulent events in China were a photograph of a student wearing a T-shirt with the words "We Shall Overcome" in English (the title of the unofficial anthem of the U.S. civil-rights movement) and a picture of a replica of the Statue of Liberty in Tiananmen Square in Beijing.

[76]Rosenau, *Turbulence in World Politics,* p. 335. See also James N. Rosenau, *Along the Domestic-Foreign Frontier: Exploring Governance in a Turbulent World* (Cambridge, UK: Cambridge University Press, 1997), pp. 58-61.

[77]Karl Marx, "Excerpts from The Eighteenth Brumaire of Louis Bonaparte," in Lewis S. Feuer, ed., *Marx and Engels: Basic Writings on Politics and Philosophy* (Garden City, NY: Doubleday, 1959), p. 338.

[78]Rosenau argues that the growing sense of individual efficacy has reduced "loyalties focused on nation-states" (*Turbulence in World Politics,* p. 335). The contradiction is more apparent than real because, even as loyalties to nonstate entities proliferate, resentment of foreign control and capacity to organize resistance to it have grown. The answer in each instance depends on who is perceived as *we* and who as *they.*

[79]Marc D. Charney, "Some Music, It Turns Out, Inflames the Savage Breast," *New York Times,* July 2, 1995, sec. 4, p. 7.

[80]Between 900 and 1,200 new McDonald's restaurants open each year worldwide. "McDonald's Expects to Add Up to 1,200 Sites a Year," *New York Times,* November 23, 1993, p. C4.

[81]"Iran Attacks Coke and Pepsi," *New York Times,* January 11, 1995, p. C3.

[82]It is argued that advertising such formula contributes to malnutrition because mothers do not rely on their own milk and, when it is too late, discover they cannot afford expensive formula. Also, in less-developed societies, the water that is mixed with powdered formula is often impure.

[83]Joseph S. Nye, Jr., and Robert O. Keohane, "Transnational Relations and World Politics: An Introduction," in Keohane and Nye, eds., *Transnational Relations and World Politics* (Cambridge: Harvard University Press, 1971), p. xii.

[84]David Johnston, "Strength Is Seen in a U.S. Export: Law Enforcement," *New York Times,* April 17, 1995, p. A1.

[85]See Richard W. Mansbach, Yale H. Ferguson, and Donald E. Lampert, *The Web of World Politics: Nonstate Actors in the Global System* (Englewood Cliffs, NJ: Prentice Hall, 1975).

[86]Cited in Richard J. Barnet and Ronald E. Muller, *Global Reach: The Power of the Multinational Corporations* (New York: Simon & Schuster, 1974). See Christopher Bartlett and Sumantra Ghoshal, *Managing Across Borders* (Cambridge: Harvard University Press, 1989).

[87]Michael R. Sesit, "Global Capital Crunch Is Beginning to Punish Some Weak Economies," *Wall Street Journal,* January 12, 1995, pp. A1, A8.

[88]David E. Sanger, "Clinton Offers $20 Billion to Mexico for Peso Rescue: Action Sidesteps Congress," *New York Times,* February 1, 1995, p. A1. The IMF commitment ($17.5 billion) was the largest in that organization's history up to that time. See Chapter 12 for a discussion of Asia's economic crisis, which was in some way similar to Mexico's.

[89]Ethan A. Nadelmann, "U.S. Drug Policy: A Bad Export," *Foreign Policy* 70 (Fall 1988), p. 87. See also "Tremble, Medellin, Tremble," *The Economist,* June 13-19, 1998, pp. 45-46.

[90]Pakistan became a leading heroin source as a result of the Afghan war, which "created a nexus between the drug barons and a new generation of heavily armed gangs" in Karachi. John F. Burns, "Heroin Becomes Scourge for 1.5 Million in Pakistan," *New York Times,* April 5, 1995, p. A4. Afghanistan itself is a major source of opium. Barbara Crossette, "Opium Surge Threatens U.N. Aid to Afghans, Official Warns," *New York Times,* July 17, 1998, p. A3.

[91]Barry Newman, "Holland and Morocco Have Hash in Common, As World's View Differs," *Wall Street Journal,* April 23, 1996, pp. A1, A13; "The Albanian Connection," *The Economist,* October 29-November 4, 1994, p. 61.

[92]Michael Specter, "Opium Finds Its Silk Road in Chaos of Central Asia," *New York Times,* May 2, 1995, p. A1.

[93]Sam Dillon and Craig Pyer, "Warm Climate for Mexican Traffickers," *New York Times,* February 23, 1997, sec. 1, pp. 1, 4; Tim Golden, "A Joint U.S.-Mexican Drug Plan, Born in Hope, Is Hobbled by Disputes," *New York Times,* April 24, 1997, p. A9;

John Ward Anderson and Molly Moore, "Cornering the Market on 'Speed'," *Washington Post National Weekly Edition,* August 19-25, 1996, p. 14; Tim Golden, "In Breakthrough, Mexican Official Testifies in Texas," *New York Times,* July 15, 1998, pp. A1, A6. Honduras has become a key transit point as well. "Staging Post," *The Economist,* March 29-April 4, 1997, p. 50.

[94]David A. Andelman, "The Drug Money Maze," *Foreign Affairs* 73:4 (July-August 1994), pp. 99-100.

[95]"Downstream Drugs," *The Economist,* May 13-19, 1995, p. 44.

[96]Cited in David E. Sanger, "Seeking an Embrace, Yeltsin Is Rebuffed at Talks," *New York Times,* June 18, 1995, sec. 1, p. 5. The United States has concluded treaties with a number of Caribbean countries to shadow ships suspected of carrying drugs into their territorial waters. Larry Rohter, "9 Caribbean Nations Open Waters to U.S. Drug Pursuit," *New York Times,* July 20, 1996, p. 2. See also "Cleaning up Latin America," *The Economist,* April 6-12, 1996, p. 41. U.S. efforts to force Latin American countries to cooperate in Washington's war on drugs by an annual certification process of these countries has created considerable ill will. Douglas Farah, "Losing the Anti-Drug Seal of Approval," *Washington Post National Weekly Edition,* January 15-21, 1996, pp. 17-18; "Neighbours," *The Economist,* March 29-April 4, 1997, pp. 25-26. The U.S. is negotiating to retain bases in Panama for a "multilateral counter-narcotics centre." "A new base for a lost war?" *The Economist,* June 27-July 3, 1998, p. 36.

[97]Robert O. Keohane and Joseph S. Nye, *Power and Interdependence,* 2nd ed. (Glenview, IL: Scott, Foresman, 1989), pp. 11-19.

[98]Cited in Nathaniel C. Nash, "European Nations Abstain on Vote for Mexican Plan," *New York Times,* February 3, 1995, p. A4.

[99]Allanna Sullivan, "Crude-Oil Prices Surge on Turmoil in Nigeria," *Wall Street Journal,* August 2, 1994, p. C1.

[100]Alex Inkeles, "The Emerging Social Structure of the World," *World Politics* 27:4 (July 1975), p. 479.

[101]Some argue that the idea of a "national" economy is obsolete. See Robert Reich, *The Work of Nations* (New York: Knopf, 1991).

Chapter 4

Toward a New World: Onset and Exit of the Cold War

Just as the end of the Thirty Years' War (1648), the Napoleonic Wars (1815), World War I (1918), and World War II (1945) marked the end of epochs, so the end of the Cold War was a transition from one era in global politics to another. With the unification of Germany, the collapse of communism in Eastern Europe, and the dissolution of the multinational Soviet Union between late 1989 and the end of 1991, the *Cold War* was over.[1] The security problems that marked the preceding decades—communism and capitalism in conflict, the debate over the fate of Germany and Eastern Europe—had been addressed. The Cold War had injected rigidity and tension into global politics, but for many actors it had also produced stability and predictability. Suddenly, by 1990, the old rules and standards no longer worked. What could political actors use as the benchmark against which to judge their actions? Had we reached the *"end of history,"* from which democratic liberalism would emerge triumphant around the world?[2]

New issues would arise to shape foreign policy, but what those issues would be was far from clear. Would a dominant issue like the Cold War again emerge, or would many discrete issues pull global politics in different directions? Would new actors arise as well? We offer some tentative answers to these questions in subsequent chapters, but first we examine the rise and end of the Cold War, with special attention to the links between global and domestic politics in the superpowers.

The Issue Cycle[3]

One way to make sense of issues like the Cold War is to examine the steps through which issues typically pass—the *issue cycle*. That cycle has four stages: (1) *genesis,* an issue's passage onto the global agenda; (2) *crisis,* moment(s) of danger in which adversaries test each other's will; (3) *ritualization,* evolution of routinized patterns of behavior and rules to manage an issue; and (4) *resolution,* achievement of agreement and/or disappearance of an issue. Thinking of issues in terms of the issue cycle helps us understand why conflict erupts when it does and why apparently similar issues elicit very different types of behavior even though they seem superficially

97

similar. Thus, as we shall see, when an issue is in the crisis stage the likelihood of conflict is far higher than when the same or a similar issue is in ritualization.

Genesis   An issue's *genesis* places it on the global agenda by bringing it to the attention of leaders. The *global agenda* consists of matters that attract attention and to which participants are prepared to devote resources. Reading "prestige" newspapers—the *New York Times* or *Le Monde* (Paris)—can provide a reasonably accurate picture of which issues are on the global agenda at a particular time. Some issues remain in the headlines for long periods and reappear on the front pages or television news repeatedly. Others are seven-day wonders that enter our consciousness with dramatic quickness and disappear almost as suddenly.

Because attention and resources are limited, issues compete for a place on the agenda. President George Bush tended to pay attention to a few crucial issues, such as the collapse of the Soviet Union and Iraq's invasion of Kuwait, generally ignoring the domestic economy. By contrast, during his first three years in office, President Clinton spent most of his time on domestic issues. World leaders ignored the 1991 civil war and famine in Somalia and the 1994 genocide in Rwanda until televised pictures of victims forced the world community to take notice.

The appearance of major issues is part of a process in which some people try to bring a problem to the attention of others.[4] Thus U.S. Secretary of Health and Human Services Donna E. Shalala declared that a U.N. meeting in late 1994 had placed the AIDS crisis "higher on the world agenda."[5] Momentous events may also thrust an issue to world attention. Reports of a growing hole in the ozone layer above the North Pole in February 1992 pushed ecological problems higher on the agenda, and scenes of Chinese tanks crushing pro-democracy demonstrators in Tiananmen Square in June 1989 restored human-rights questions to the attention of the world.

Once an issue gains attention, it is still not assured of a place sufficiently high on the agenda to merit action by powerful world leaders. Individuals are drawn to issues because they are directly affected, perhaps because of nationality, profession, or gender. They seek to bring "their" issues to leaders' attention by writing letters, participating in demonstrations, or even performing acts of civil disobedience to get attention for a "cause." An example of this was provided by Jennifer Harbury, whose demonstrations in Guatemala and Washington finally led to the admission in March 1995 that her husband, a Guatemalan rebel, had been murdered at the behest of a Guatemalan army colonel with ties to the CIA.[6]

Nonstate actors play a particularly important role in gaining attention for important issues. The environmental group Greenpeace is effective in attracting attention to its causes. On one occasion, its members sailed into an area of the South Pacific in which France was to test nuclear weapons in order to disrupt these tests. Greenpeace vessels have interfered with Japanese and Norwegian whaling ships to publicize opposition to whale hunting. Greenpeace has even cut the nets of fishermen whose methods for catching tuna result in death for dolphins. Whatever one may think of its methods, the group succeeds in making "its" issues visible to political leaders.

Getting issues to the top of the global agenda requires the interest of high-status actors because what they say or do catches the attention of everyone else.

Minor actors try to interest major ones in their issues because, once the mighty have become interested, an issue will be dealt with. As a high-status actor, the U.S. government is constantly lobbied by others. Poor countries press U.S. leaders to attend to their poverty; environmental, corporate, and human-rights actors have issues that they want Washington to promote; and so on. Because even small countries have access to the United Nations and other international organizations, efforts are often directed toward getting these organizations to take up an issue.

Crisis   During the *crisis* phase, an issue assumes urgency—the belief grows that, unless something is done quickly, matters will deteriorate. The issue is seen to entail a high threat to actors. It surprises them with its implications for the future, and it demands rapid decisions to address it.[7] During a crisis phase, interactions among leading players increase, and new alignments form. Most important, this stage involves a frantic search for stable expectations and workable policies to ensure security.

The crisis stage is dangerous because actors do not know what to expect of each other and cannot predict the consequences of their own actions. One actor may make a decision that it views as justified or harmless, perhaps provoking another to retaliate. If care is not taken, a spiral of hostility may get out of hand with harm to all. Trade wars begin this way. One actor, perhaps under pressure from vocal domestic industries such as U.S. auto manufacturers or Japanese rice farmers, raises barriers to imports from other countries, and those countries then do the same.

Ritualization   If adversaries survive the dangerous recurrent crises that pit them against each other, an issue may enter the stage of *ritualization*.[8] Having groped in the dark to find mutually acceptable and stable norms of behavior, actors may acquire patterned and stable mutual expectations about how they should interact in the future. They have learned what they can safely do to each other without triggering hostile spirals. Their policies may be downright unfriendly; but those policies are expected by adversaries, regarded as posturing, and considered tolerable. In following the rituals of conflict, actors can satisfy constituents' demands without letting things get out of hand.

For many years before their conclusion of a peace treaty in 1995, Israeli-Jordanian relations over the Israeli-occupied West Bank were highly ritualized. Jordanian leaders could not afford to be seen as soft on Israel by the many Palestinians living in Jordan. Israel sought to prevent Jordan's moderate King Hussein from being overthrown and replaced by a more militant leader. Each side routinely denounced the other while carefully keeping the level of conflict stable. Israel kept the border between the West and East Banks of the Jordan River open as much as it safely could, and Jordan discouraged terrorist raids across the frontier by militant Palestinians. If an actor exceeds another's expectations, as did Hizbollah in April 1996 when it launched rockets from Lebanon against Israeli towns, it may trigger a conflict spiral. Israel retaliated with massive air and naval bombardments against Lebanese targets.

Resolution   A possible final stage in the cycle is *resolution* or removal of an issue from the agenda. Resolution can take several forms. An issue may be resolved by formal or informal agreements among competitors. For a complex issue, such as the Cold War, formal resolution may be required so that actors can revise deep beliefs and alter long-time policies. Alternately, an issue may defy formal agreement, but because leaders lose interest, it may fall dormant. Thereafter, the issue receives little attention and generates little heat.

The 1919 *Versailles Conference* was an international assembly that brought an end to World War I. In contrast, the 1962 Cuban missile crisis was informally resolved by a trade—withdrawing Soviet missiles in return for a U.S. promise not to invade Cuba and withdrawing U.S. missiles from Turkey at a later date. The war in Afghanistan illustrates how an issue may quietly fade from public view. Between December 1979, when Soviet troops marched into the country, and February 1989, when the last of those troops were withdrawn, Afghanistan was near the top of the global agenda. Although civil war continued after the Soviet withdrawal, most world leaders lost interest in it.

The Issue Cycle and the Cold War

The issue cycle is a useful framework for describing how the Cold War evolved. The conflict began in Europe as an ideological and strategic struggle between the United States and the Soviet Union shortly after the end of World War II, became routine after serious crises in the 1950s and 1960s during which both sides learned the rules of the game, and was finally resolved between 1985 and 1991. In the following pages, we focus on the Cold War issue cycle, emphasizing its genesis and resolution.

Stage 1: Genesis of the Cold War

For more than four decades the Cold War overshadowed profound changes in global politics. The number of states more than doubled, and the number of intergovernmental and nongovernmental actors more than tripled. Military destructiveness increased geometrically, and in economic capability all states grew impressively, but especially the United States, Japan, and Western Europe. All the while, environmental and demographic problems quietly grew, receiving little public attention.

The Soviet Union, the United States, and Postwar Europe.   The origin of the Cold War dates back to the 1917 Bolshevik[9] seizure of power in Russia. The young Soviet state was wary of Western intentions, especially after Western intervention in North Russia and Siberia in summer 1918. United States president Woodrow Wilson sought to justify intervention as part of an effort to keep the Russians fighting the Germans and Austrians in World War I, but Western actions owed much to a profound dislike for communism. Historian John Lewis Gaddis writes: "The fact is that a fundamental loathing for Bolshevism influenced all of Wilson's actions with regard to Russia and the actions of his Allied counterparts." This antipathy was mutual, for "the Bolsheviks made no secret of their fundamental loathing for the West."[10]

The enforced alliance between the U.S.S.R. and the West against Germany in World War II proved temporary, and the Cold War burgeoned as that war ended. In

RUSSIA'S COMMODITY EXCHANGE!

In the chaos of post-communist Russia, lax security at military installations and nuclear-power facilities have combined with economic distress to produce concern that plutonium, which can be used to build nuclear weapons, may be stolen and sold to pariah states such as Libya and Iran or even to international terrorist groups. *(King Features Syndicate)*

1945, the United States and the Soviet Union were the only powers still in a position to influence global politics. European states, traditional powers on the continent, had suffered indescribable economic and psychological damage. Great Britain had lost roughly a third of its wealth, and lacked food and coal to feed and heat itself, its troops in Europe, or the Germans for whom British occupation forces were responsible. France suffered even greater damage. Defeated Germany, Italy, and Japan were in ruins, and Germany was divided and occupied by the victors. All were heavily in debt, and all, to varying degrees, needed assistance from the United States to meet basic needs.

Politically, too, Europe was in shambles. The British Empire was unraveling as "the jewels in the crown," such as India, clamored for independence, and the British Mandate in Palestine was engulfed in civil war.[11] France faced political instability: Coalition governments were short-lived, and the powerful French Communist Party attracted many voters. France also had to deal with colonial rebellions abroad, first in Indochina and later in North Africa. The Netherlands too confronted an independence movement in Indonesia that would ultimately succeed in 1949.[12]

By contrast, the United States after World War II was economically vigorous and politically stable. United States industry, a chief source of allied victory, was booming, accounting for 45 percent of world manufactures, and the United States enjoyed large trade surpluses and huge gold reserves.[13] American military might was unsurpassed. Its troops occupied Western Europe and Japan, its navy was the world's largest, and it had a monopoly on a new and highly destructive weapon, the atom bomb. The Soviet Union had borne the brunt of the war against Germany, suffering more than twenty million dead and the devastation of over two decades of socialist construction. Nevertheless, 175 Soviet divisions remained in the heart of Europe, a fact that grew in importance as U.S. forces in Europe were demobilized. Politically, Stalin's ruthless regime had survived the Nazi onslaught, and no one dared oppose the aging tyrant. The Soviet Union, as one of the victors and with an army occupying Central Europe, expected to share in the spoils of war.

Continued United States–Soviet Postwar Cooperation?   The U.S.-Soviet-British alliance had won the war, and it seemed reasonable to believe their cooperation would continue. After all, "the Red Army . . . did more to destroy the evil of Nazism than any other single force. It lost millions of brave men—far more than all the other allies put together."[14] President Franklin D. Roosevelt had envisioned such agreement in his postwar plans. He expected the United States to remain an active participant in world affairs and hoped that the wartime allies would remain peacetime collaborators, especially in the new U.N. Security Council. Roosevelt also believed that power politics (a phrase he would not have used) would be a guiding principle in the postwar world, and his grand design looked and sounded much like a global balance-of-power system. Under his "Four Policemen" proposal, Britain, China, the United States, and the Soviet Union would be responsible for maintaining peace in their areas of the world. Although *spheres of influence* (areas of dominant influence for specific countries) and power politics were nowhere made explicit, they were implicit in the proposal.[15]

Several wartime summit conferences were held to iron out differences among the major powers. Meetings at Teheran (1943), Cairo (1943), Yalta (1945), and Potsdam (1945) addressed not only ways of prosecuting the war but also postwar arrangements in Europe and elsewhere. The most important of these, shaping postwar European politics and feeding the misunderstandings that accompanied the beginning Cold War, was the *Yalta Conference,* held in that Crimean city in February 1945. Several significant bargains were struck at Yalta to shape the postwar world. Although the commitments made there bore the imprint of balance-of-power politics, they also foreshadowed continued cooperation. The spirit of the time was reflected in a letter from George F. Kennan to Charles Bohlen just prior to Yalta in which Kennan asked: "Why could we not make a decent and definite compromise with it [the Soviet Union]—divide Europe frankly into spheres of influence—keep ourselves out of the Russian sphere and keep the Russians out of ours?"[16]

One set of Yalta agreements covered representation and voting arrangements for the proposed U.N. organization.[17] The Soviet Union wanted all of its republics seated in the U.N. General Assembly, but Washington objected. A bargain was struck whereby the U.S.S.R. was granted three seats in the General Assembly and the United States could have the same number if it wished. A second agreement provided for veto power in the Security Council, the principal peacemaking organ in the new organization. Under the veto arrangement, any of the five permanent members of the Council (the United States, U.S.S.R., Britain, France, or China) could halt any substantive action. That arrangement ensured that the permanent members would have to work together if the Council were to function.

Another agreement determined the four-power (British, French, U.S., and Soviet) zones of occupation in Germany. This arrangement was a compromise (France was given a zone only after much wrangling), but it ensured future U.S. participation in European affairs and made it less likely that America would return to prewar isolationism. The arrangement ratified the division of Germany among the victorious powers and was a first step in establishing spheres of interest between East and West in Central Europe.

Agreements were also reached on German war reparations and on establishing a coalition government including communists and noncommunists in Poland. The most controversial decision at Yalta, however, was the "Declaration on Liberated Europe," which pledged the Yalta participants to foster free elections and guarantee basic freedoms in all liberated countries. When the promise of Yalta was not honored by Stalin in Eastern Europe, it became a powerful rationale for U.S. suspicions about Soviet intentions.[18] One impetus for the United States to strike these deals at Yalta was to get a Soviet commitment to enter the war against Japan three months after the war in Europe came to an end.[19]

At the *Potsdam Conference,* held in a Berlin suburb in July 1945, further discussions were held on the future of Central Europe. Even though the question of Poland and its borders was to be a principal topic at Potsdam, the U.S.S.R. announced it had reached agreement with the Polish government on that country's new boundaries. This fait accompli reduced the prospects of fruitful bargaining among the parties, and disagreement was papered over in a statement indicating that the boundary question "shall await the peace settlement."[20]

Expectations still remained high that the Soviet Union would be willing to bargain over the future of Central Europe. The hope was that the *Yalta Axioms* would continue to guide U.S.-Soviet relations.[21] One of these was that the Soviet Union was much like any other state and thus driven fundamentally by power considerations. This axiom implied that the Soviet Union would seek to advance its interests but would also recognize that its power had limits. Rationally calculating its capabilities would thus restrain Soviet behavior. The United States hoped to use prospective economic aid and international control of atomic energy as inducements to obtain Soviet compliance with the Yalta Declaration on Liberated Europe and the agreement on unifying Germany.[22]

Ministerial meetings late in 1945 and early in 1946 proved disappointing, and Soviet actions in Eastern Europe raised doubts about its intentions. Free and democratic elections were not held, as promised at Yalta. Instead, first coalition, and, eventually, communist-dominated governments, came to power in Poland, Hungary, Bulgaria, Romania, and Czechoslovakia. These events profoundly affected U.S. public opinion. The Czech coup in 1948 and the murder of the country's foreign minister, Jan Masaryk, son of the country's founder, were the final steps in communizing Eastern Europe. All of Eastern Europe had fallen under the shadow of Soviet power. The Sovietization of Eastern Europe combined with Soviet rejection of proposals to reunify Germany,[23] along with actions limiting Western powers' access to Berlin in 1948–1949 (the first Berlin crisis), seemed to confirm Western suspicion that the Soviets intended to dominate Europe.

Growing Mistrust and Suspicion.   Soviet actions eroded Western belief in the Yalta Axioms and triggered wider acceptance of what Daniel Yergin calls the *Riga Axioms*.[24] Unlike the Yalta Axioms, the Riga Axioms assumed that the Soviet Union was driven by ideology (Marxism-Leninism) rather than power. According to these axioms, the Soviet Union's totalitarian structure was the ultimate source of its actions at home and abroad. One analyst said "doctrine and ideology and a spirit of innate aggressiveness shaped Soviet policy. . . . The U.S.S.R. was committed to world revolution and unlimited expansion."[25]

Emerging U.S.-Soviet perceptions of each other at the time are revealed in several documents. Nothing conveys more clearly the perception of the U.S.S.R. that was evolving in official Washington early in 1946 than the so-called *Long Telegram* sent by Kennan, then a counselor in the U.S. Embassy in Moscow. Kennan's image of the Soviet Union was almost entirely negative: Mistrust and basic incompatibility between the two superpowers were dominant themes. The Long Telegram portrays the deep suspicion with which this influential policy adviser viewed the Soviet Union.

First, Kennan assessed Soviet intentions toward the United States:

> We have here a political force committed fanatically to the belief that with the U.S.
> there can be no permanent modus vivendi, that it is desirable and necessary that
> the internal harmony of our society be disrupted, our traditional way of life be
> destroyed, the international authority of our state be broken, if Soviet power is to
> be secure.[26]

Thereafter he explained the role of ideology in Soviet behavior and how it warped the Soviet view of reality:

> It [the Soviet Union] is seemingly inaccessible to considerations of reality in its
> basic reactions. For it, the vast fund of objective fact about human society is not, as
> with us, the measure against which outlook is constantly being tested and
> reformed, but a grab bag from which individual items are selected arbitrarily and
> tendentiously to bolster an outlook already preconceived.[27]

Finally, he turned to the Soviet Union's challenge to the United States and the West generally:

> Efforts will be made . . . to disrupt national self-confidence, to hamstring measures
> of national defense, to increase social and industrial unrest, to stimulate all forms of
> disunity. . . . Where individual governments stand in [the] path of Soviet purposes
> pressure will be brought for their removal from office. . . . In foreign countries
> Communists will . . . work toward destruction of all forms of personal indepen-
> dence, economic, political, or moral.[28]

Although Kennan offered several general suggestions about what could be done to combat the Soviet threat in the Long Telegram, he had no specific prescription for U.S. foreign policy. That was to await publication of his "Mr. X" essay in *Foreign Affairs* a year later.

From documents released later, we learn that the Soviet Union at the time held a similar view of U.S. intentions. The Soviet ambassador to the United States, Nikolai Novikov, sent a secret report to Soviet foreign minister Vyacheslav Molotov in September 1946 outlining dangers from the United States.[29] The opening line in the *Novikov Telegram* set the tone: "The foreign policy of the United States, which reflects the imperialist tendencies of American monopolistic capital, is characterized in the postwar period by a striving for world supremacy." United States policy, Novikov argued, was particularly dangerous because its leadership had changed, and the United States had embarked on a course of action to achieve "global dominance." "The ascendance of President Truman, a politically unstable person but with certain conservative tendencies, and the subsequent appointment of [James] Byrnes as Secretary of State" gave power to "the most reactionary circles of the Democratic party." America had instituted a military draft, increased its defense expenditures, and placed military forces around the world, actions that Novikov believed had one purpose: "All of these facts show clearly that a decisive role . . . for world domination by the United States is played by its armed forces."[30]

The Novikov Telegram declared also that, though U.S. policy extended to all corners of the world, its principal "objective has been to impose the will of other countries on the Soviet Union." According to Novikov, U.S. policy was "directed at limiting or dislodging the influence of the Soviet Union from neighboring countries" and sought to "secure positions for the penetration of American capital into their economies." Even more ominous, the United States was undertaking preparations for a possible "war against the Soviet Union."[31]

The Novikov message is a *mirror image* of the Long Telegram. Soviet leaders saw the United States as driven by capitalist imperatives and bent on world domination. American leaders saw the Soviet Union as driven by Marxist-Leninist imperatives and bent on world revolution. Each side demonized the other as expansionist while failing to recognize that the other saw it in the same way.[32] The private images of the policy advisers were reflected in public pronouncements by their respective leaders. On February 9, 1946, in an address before elections to the Supreme Soviet that attracted Western attention, Stalin resurrected the Leninist view of the Western capitalist powers and the danger they posed:

> Marxists have repeatedly declared that the capitalist world economic system conceals in itself the elements of general crisis and military clashes as a result of which the development of world capitalism in our time proceeds not by smooth and even progress but by crises and military catastrophes.[33]

Stalin argued that war was inevitable among capitalist states and that an unbridgeable chasm separated the capitalist and Marxist systems.[34]

The mirror image appeared in a speech by Winston Churchill to a U.S. college audience in March 1946. Churchill responded to Stalin's suspicion of the West by assailing Soviet expansionism. The speech is best recalled for introducing the world to the phrase peculiar to the Cold War:

> From Stettin in the Baltic to Trieste in the Adriatic, an *iron curtain* has descended across the Continent. Behind that line lie all the capitals of the ancient states of Central and Eastern Europe. Warsaw, Berlin, Prague, Vienna, Budapest, Belgrade, Bucharest and Sofia, all these famous cities and the populations around them lie in what I must call the Soviet sphere, and all are subject in one form or another, not

only to Soviet influence but to a very high and, in many cases, increasing measure of control from Moscow.[35]

Churchill did more than introduce a powerful image; he also offered a new policy prescription for the West, built on confronting rather than appeasing the Soviet Union. Free peoples should cooperate against the Bolshevik menace by forming a "fraternal association of the English-speaking peoples" and building a "special relationship between the British Commonwealth and Empire and the United States." These actors, working under the "general authority" of the United Nations, should stand up to the Soviet challenge. If they did so, "there will be no quivering precarious balance of power to offer its temptation to ambition or adventure. On the contrary, there will be an overwhelming assurance of security."[36]

The unfolding of the Cold War has been interpreted in a variety of ways. As we noted earlier, theory conditions what we see and think, and necessarily omits much. This can be illustrated by looking at the steps in the Cold War's evolution through three different theoretical lenses.

Interpreting the Genesis of the Cold War

The Power-Politics Lens. From a power-politics perspective, the Cold War appears as the outcome of a sequence of moves and countermoves of two powerful states pursuing their national interest. Those interests were shaped and made incompatible by the postwar *power vacuum* created in Central Europe and East Asia by the defeat of Germany and Japan and the weakness of other European and Asian powers. Each superpower recognized that the only state powerful enough to do it real harm was the other. Neither wanted the other to enjoy a preponderance of power, and each sought to prevent this by arming and forging alliances with friendly states.[37] Efforts by each side to secure German occupation on its terms and create a buffer zone of friendly states in Europe[38] can be interpreted in a balance-of-power framework. A variant of this geopolitical argument is the view that the Cold War was a consequence of traditional Russian expansionism in search of warm water ports and defensible boundaries.

The Perceptual Lens. If we use only a power-politics lens, much cannot be explained, such as the ferocity with which the Cold War began, the deep ideological differences, and the role of many actors other than the two superpowers. As we have seen, the image that each set of decision-makers had of the other, and the yawning perceptual abyss that resulted, may have been pivotal in starting the Cold War. In wartime, Soviet-U.S. ideological hostility had been subordinated to the imperative of defeating a common foe, but once that task was accomplished, latent suspicion and mistrust dating from the 1917 Bolshevik Revolution quickly resurfaced. Wedding misperception and ideological hostility to changing power relationships in Central Europe provides a potent explanation of conflict.

The Transnational Lens. This framework moves beyond the perceptions of each country's leaders and elites and focuses on the competing worldviews that each society represented on behalf of communists and capitalists around the world. Seen thus, Americans and their allies and Soviets and their allies held incompatible beliefs about how societies ought to be organized politically and economically. The West looked on *capitalism* as the basic principle for organizing society, and the East favored *socialism.* The one defined democracy as individual political freedom and entrepreneurial activity, and the other as economic equality, collective responsibility, and centralized economic planning. Each regarded the other's version of democracy as a sham that gave power to the few at the expense of the many, and each feared that the other intended to impose its version of truth on the world.

The universality of both worldviews set the stage for the Cold War. Communists believed actions by the United States and its allies were a transnational "capitalist" effort to strangle socialism in general and the Soviet state in particular. "Capitalist encirclement" and "Western imperialism" summarized the belief that economic and class imperatives shaped Western policies after World War II. From this perspective, giant transnational corporations and banks, protected by Western governments that they controlled, were the engines driving capitalist expansion. One analyst writes: "Because of the irresistible pressures of American capitalism and the power of economic elites in the shaping of foreign policy, the United States pursued a policy of imperial anticolonialism rationalized in the language of humanitarianism and national self-determination but motivated by the quest for free markets essential to America's prosperity and well-being."[39]

Communists believed that capitalism's economic imperatives left little room for accommodation with socialism. Satisfying Soviet security interests in Eastern Europe necessarily challenged the free market and the economic open-door policies essential to capitalist interests.[40] In this perspective, the Cold War was caused by capitalism's transnational interests and its desire to maintain access to worldwide markets and resources. Because the U.S.S.R. and its socialist allies challenged those interests, conflict was inevitable.

A reciprocal interpretation of the Cold War in the West saw Marxism-Leninism, guided by the Soviet Union, which controlled a worldwide network of communist parties, as on the march, not only in Europe, but globally as well. One piece of evidence was Stalin's creation in 1947 of the Cominform (Communist Information Bureau) in Belgrade, consisting of the communist parties of the Soviet Union, Hungary, Romania, Czechoslovakia, Bulgaria, France, and Italy. The Western intellectual climate of the time is described by one observer:

> Never had the threat or promise of Communism loomed larger than it did three years after the conclusion of World War II. A century earlier two young German radicals introduced their fiery challenge to the old order on an exuberant note: "A specter is haunting Europe—the specter of Communism." . . . But what in 1848 had been an expression of youthful bravado became one century later only too true. . . . [T]he representative and carrier of the Communist idea, the Soviet Union, was the *dominant* power on the Continent. Eastern Europe lay under Moscow's domination, its vassal regimes rapidly transforming their societies in the Soviet model. No West European state, or all of them together, could match the strength of the Red Army. . . . Nor was the threat to Western Europe purely military. The French and Italian Communist parties . . . enjoyed a wide following in their countries.[41]

A National Security Council report, *NSC–68,* written in 1950, summarized the official Western perspective on the danger from the Soviet Union and international communism:

> The fundamental design of those who control the Soviet Union and the international communist movement is to retain and solidify their absolute power. . . . In the minds of the Soviet leaders . . . achievement of this design requires the dynamic extension of their authority and the ultimate elimination of any effective opposition to their authority.[42]

By this view, transnational communism sought absolute control worldwide and threatened human freedom and individual liberty everywhere. Under these circumstances, Western responses to communist actions were necessary and justifiable.

From this perspective, the Cold War owed less to competing Soviet-U.S. national interests or misperceptions than to the transnational movements and ideologies that the two societies represented. All three lenses have something to offer the analyst, and only by combining them can one understand why the Cold War began.

Stage 2: The Cold War as Crisis

The Cold War entered the crisis stage early in 1947. By enunciating the *Truman Doctrine,* the United States threw down the gauntlet and adopted a confrontational attitude toward the Soviet Union. The Truman Doctrine was the name given to a speech President Truman delivered to a joint session of Congress on March 12, 1947, in which he proclaimed a new policy and role for the United States in global affairs. Specifically, the president sought $400 million in economic and military assistance for Greece and Turkey, two strategic Mediterranean countries threatened by subversive forces supported by the Soviet Union, after the British said a month earlier that they could no longer provide the needed support.

The Truman Doctrine and Marshall Plan.   To justify aid for Greece and Turkey to a skeptical Congress, Truman placed the situation in the context of broader changes that he saw taking place in global politics. "The peoples of a number of countries," he declared, "have recently had totalitarian regimes forced upon them against their will." Although the United States had "made frequent protests against coercion and intimidation, in violation of the Yalta agreement, in Poland, Romania, and Bulgaria," those protests had proved insufficient. The United States must now be willing, Truman declared, "to help free peoples to maintain their free institutions and their national integrity against aggressive movements that seek to impose upon them totalitarian regimes."[43] The sweeping language of the speech and the worldwide commitment to assist any state threatened by totalitarianism gained it the status of a "doctrine" and a lasting policy for the United States. Yet the speech was more than that: It was a declaration of Cold War. The issue was beginning to overshadow everything else on the global agenda.

Following Truman's declaration, George F. Kennan, author of the Long Telegram, published an influential article under the pseudonym "Mr. X" in the journal *Foreign Affairs* in which he outlined a policy of *containment* against the Soviet Union. The strategy was designed to put enough pressure on the Soviet Union ("the application of counter-force at a series of constantly shifting geographical and political points") to produce a change in both its internal structure and its international conduct ("the break-up or the gradual mellowing of Soviet power").[44] Thereafter, the United States embarked on a global strategy to confront the Soviet Union. Notwithstanding changes in nuance and tactics, containment remained the basis for U.S. policy for four decades.

In ensuing years, the United States made global alliance commitments. The Inter-American Treaty of Reciprocal Assistance (Rio Treaty) was signed by Washington with twenty-one Western Hemisphere nations in 1947, the North Atlantic Treaty with twelve (later fifteen) European states in 1949, the ANZUS Treaty with Australia and New Zealand in 1951, and the Southeast Asia Treaty Organization with countries within and outside of the region in 1954. Bilateral pacts were completed with the Philippines, Japan, Korea, and Taiwan early in the 1950s. The United States also undertook economic and military assistance programs worldwide. Providing such aid linked U.S. security to that of recipients. A vigorous campaign began at home and abroad to warn against dangers from the Soviet Union.[45]

The *Marshall Plan,* named after a proposal put forward by Secretary of State George C. Marshall in a June 1947 Harvard commencement address, was enacted to provide economic assistance to help rebuild and unite Western Europe. Although the United States invited the Soviet Union and the Eastern European states to join, the chill in East-West relations prevented this from happening.[46] Instead, in 1949, the members of the East bloc created the Council for Mutual Economic Assistance (Comecon) to serve three purposes: (1) facilitate Soviet control over allies' economies, (2) create a socialist trade bloc, and (3) divide labor among socialist states so that each specialized in producing items desired by others. The West sought to deny the U.S.S.R. access to technology that might contribute to Soviet power, establishing in 1949 a Coordinating Committee, known as Cocom, to coordinate allied policy on embargoing strategic goods to the East.[47] Thus the economies of Eastern Europe were isolated from the West, subordinated to political interests, and made to depend on the U.S.S.R.

Two events now moved the Cold War into a crisis stage—the *Berlin blockade* (1948-1949) and the *Korean War* (1950-1953)—and a third, the *Cuban missile crisis,* marked a turning point in the Cold War.

Berlin, Korea, and Cuba.   In May 1948, anticipating the West's establishment of a new state from their zones of Germany, the Soviet Union began a rail, water, and road blockade around the former German capital, Berlin. The city, located deep inside the Soviet zone, was divided into occupation zones with Western access guaranteed. Soviet anger had been sparked by a unilateral Western currency reform in its zones that had been instituted because of Soviet refusal to treat Germany as a single economic unit. The West responded vigorously to this violation of the Quadripartite agreements.[48] Late in July, the Western powers began a massive airlift to the beleaguered city. By one estimate, U.S. and British aircraft transported "over 1.5 million tons of food, fuel and other goods into Berlin (the highest load in one day exceeded 12,000 tons)" during the ten months from July 1948 to the end of the blockade in May 1949.[49] The Berlin blockade was an important lesson in how West and East could confront each other without direct resort to arms.

The other event was the Korean War, which spread the Cold War to Asia. Like Berlin, divided Korea was an anomaly—it was in neither the Western nor the Eastern camp. In a January 1950 speech, U.S. Secretary of State Dean Acheson declared that South Korea was outside the U.S. defense perimeter in East Asia. Six months later, on June 25, 1950, North Korean troops suddenly invaded the south. United States leaders believed that the attack had been ordered by Moscow to test Western resolve. Following its containment strategy, the Truman administration thought it had few options except to help Syngman Rhee's regime in South Korea. The United States and its allies intervened under U.N. auspices[50] and were embroiled in a conflict that lasted three years and led to intervention by the Chinese communists. In the end, an armistice between North and South Korea around the 38th parallel was arranged and remains to this day. Although the Korean War's military outcome was inconclusive, its political impact was profound. The war, thousands of miles from Europe, confirmed that the Cold War was global. For Americans, the Korean War ended "the incoherence which characterized U.S. foreign and defense efforts in the period 1946-1950"[51] and propelled the United States in the direction of fully implementing the containment doctrine.

The Cuban missile crisis illustrated the potential danger of misunderstandings and the importance of crises for superpower learning. In 1962, the Soviet Union placed offensive missiles in Cuba—to protect Fidel Castro's communist regime and to intimidate the United States. This action violated U.S. expectations that neither superpower would meddle in the other's neighborhood. The ensuing showdown lasted a few tense days until Moscow capitulated. By any assessment, this episode was the most dangerous confrontation in the Cold War, yet its peaceful termination demonstrated that both sides still had learning capacity. This crisis, more than any other event, persuaded leaders that rules had to be created to lessen the chances of a war that neither wished.

Stage 3: Ritualization of the Cold War

Following the missile crisis, the superpowers tacitly concluded that their relations had to be governed by rules and procedures that would reduce the likelihood of mutual annihilation and allow them to coexist. Ritualization had set in. Ritualization does not mean peace, however, and superpower relations were still dominated by the threat of force, bargaining from strength, and a hostile climate.

Ritualization was evident in the spiraling defense burdens that both sides accepted, the interventionist policies that both pursued, and the fluctuations in tension between them. Despite such factors, which observers feared would bring on World War III, U.S. and Soviet leaders learned how to manage their mutual relations.

Military Spending, Intervention, and Ritualization. By 1953, U.S. defense expenditures had soared to more than 13 percent of GNP and remained above 8 percent during much of the 1960s.[52] These expenditures began to decrease in the 1970s, only to rise again in the 1980s as the Reagan defense buildup began. For the Soviet Union, estimates range from 10 to 20 percent of GNP (and even higher) throughout the Cold War. These expenditures fueled both a conventional and a nuclear arms race, but despite expectations that such races must end in war, they did not. Why? Because the U.S.-Soviet arms race was an expected and permissible ritual.

Direct military confrontation was too dangerous. Less dangerous and therefore permissible under the rules of the game were conflicts involving superpower proxies (such as Somalia versus Ethiopia) or conflicts between one superpower and a surrogate of the other (such as the United States versus North Vietnam). Such rules allowed intervention by the superpowers or their surrogates as long as it was limited and avoided direct superpower confrontation. Because communication in global politics is imperfect, these rules were endangered from time to time. United States bombing of the North Vietnamese port of Haiphong in May 1972 damaged Soviet vessels in the harbor and threatened U.S.-Soviet *détente* (lessening of tensions), and risk-taking by both sides during the 1973 Arab-Israeli war threatened to escalate out of hand. The rules also allowed other forms of Soviet-U.S. conflict: propaganda, espionage, and subversion; overt and covert economic, political, and military assistance; and other techniques for "informal penetration."[53]

The threat of communist expansion was the reason given for U.S. military action in Korea (1950), Iran (1953), Guatemala (1954), Vietnam (1961, 1965), Cuba (1961), the Dominican Republic (1965), and Grenada (1983). In all these, the Soviet response was restrained and did not directly challenge the U.S. position.[54] Fear that socialist control would be undermined motivated Soviet intervention in East Berlin (1953), Hungary (1956), Czechoslovakia (1968), and Afghanistan (1979). The United States, despite rhetoric about "rolling back" communism in Eastern Europe, did little more than offer moral support to Hungarian freedom fighters as Soviet tanks smashed into Budapest in November 1956. The United States again did nothing after the Warsaw Pact intervened in Czechoslovakia in August 1968 to crush the "Prague Spring." After Soviet intervention in Afghanistan in December 1979, Washington took limited political and economic steps against the U.S.S.R. but did not confront Moscow directly.[55] Churchill's iron curtain became a line of demarcation between the two sides, and even responses to interventions were ritualized.

Ritualizing by Confrontation and Accommodation. Superpower confrontations were another manifestation of the ritualization of the Cold War. Kenneth Waltz argued in 1964 that the "nearly constant presence of pressure and the recurrence of crises" were a source of superpower learning and actually stabilized their relations by serving as a substitute for war.[56] Dangerous crises flared in areas that were not in either superpower's sphere of interest, such as Berlin, Korea, Vietnam, Cuba, and Afghanistan. In time, recognizing the enormous costs that they would have to pay for a misstep, both sides sought to work out rules for these gray areas as well.

A variety of confrontations contributed to ritualization. In 1958 and 1961, the Soviet Union and the United States faced off again over Western access to Berlin. In August 1961, East Germany built the *Berlin Wall* to halt the flight of East Germans to West Berlin. The wall became a symbol of the abyss separating East and West and visibly staked out spheres of interest over which the adversaries enjoyed exclusive authority. Ultimately, the two sides recognized it was safer to leave things alone in Berlin. Gradually, "the main lines of expectations ... converged around the rough status quo"[57] as Moscow and Washington ritualized their disagreement over Berlin and set the issue aside.

Although hostility colored the ritualization period, those years also had East-West thaws and even a brief détente in the 1970s. These episodes, too, helped each side to accommodate the other. After Stalin died in 1953, superpower relations were warmed by the "spirit of Geneva" (named after a 1955 summit there). In the late 1950s, "peaceful coexistence" entered the global-politics vocabulary, and, after the Cuban missile crisis, efforts were stepped up to reach arms-control agreements.

While they worked at stabilizing the arms race, the superpowers also began to cooperate in other ways to reduce global tension. As a result, a period of Soviet-American détente began. Détente was short-lived. Relations were poisoned by a new Soviet arms buildup and by growing Soviet involvement in the Horn of Africa and southern Africa in the mid-1970s. The Soviets were surprised and angered by Jimmy Carter's human-rights policy and intrusive U.S. efforts to influence the Soviet Union to ease barriers to Jewish emigration from the U.S.S.R. The Soviet invasion of Afghanistan in December 1979 sounded the death knell for détente. In response, President Jimmy Carter embargoed grain exports to the U.S.S.R. even though U.S. farmers stood to lose a lucrative export market. A U.S. arms buildup began in the last year of the Carter administration and was accelerated by President Reagan, further burying détente.

Domestic Politics and Ritualizing the Cold War.   As Soviet and American societies developed a mirror image of each other, leaders sought to mobilize support for the struggle at home. As new leaders in both societies gained power, the Cold War pattern remained, but it became more and more routine.

The most dramatic case of virulent anticommunism in the United States was the witch hunt conducted by Senator Joseph McCarthy (R-Wisconsin) early in the 1950s "to root out communists" inside and outside of government and expose subversive activities at home. Although in the end McCarthy was censured by the Senate for attacks on colleagues, his actions chilled the foreign-policy debate in the country as a whole. A similar witch hunt was conducted by the House Un-American Activities Committee in the 1950s and into the 1960s. These hearings contributed to a charged and intimidating political atmosphere at home, and their effect was to enforce a foreign-policy consensus that helped shape the Cold War.

The *Cold War consensus* encouraged and legitimized vigorous U.S. actions, ranging from economic and military aid to regimes that appeared to be threatened by communist takeover—whether or not they were authoritarian—to the use of force.[58] It was also reflected in sustained support for high defense expenditures. In time, this consensus was modified by various American administrations and changing global events. Events such as the Sino-Soviet split late in the 1950s and progress in arms control in the 1970s modified public perceptions. Perhaps the event with the most profound effect on the Cold War consensus in the United States was the *Vietnam War.*

United States involvement in Vietnam began even before the expulsion of the French colonial authorities in 1954. American efforts to prop up a pro-Western government in South Vietnam took many forms and, after 1965, involved massive military intervention. The seemingly endless war challenged key assumptions behind the Cold War consensus, including those about "monolithic" communism, America's world role, the use of military power, the power of the American presidency, and bipartisanship (cooperation between Republicans and Democrats) in foreign policy. At the same time, the American public became more receptive to accommodation with the Soviet Union, even as it remained wary of Soviet power. American attitudes, too, became ritualized.

A parallel development occurred in the U.S.S.R. Using propaganda and coercion, Stalin instilled among the Soviet people great fear of the West. He sought to isolate Soviet citizens from Western influences and reinforce his personal power, and he intensified Soviet nationalism by painting a threatening "capitalist encirclement." A few years after Stalin's death, his successor, Nikita S. Khrushchev, shocked the Twentieth Congress of the Communist Party of the Soviet Union (CPSU) in 1956 by a secret speech in which he denounced Stalin's crimes, declared that war between the United States and U.S.S.R. was no longer inevitable, and initiated a policy of *peaceful coexistence* (a term originally coined by Lenin) with the West. In succeeding party congresses, other doctrinal changes were made to permit greater accommodation with the West.[59]

Other Soviet actions, however, seemed to contradict the thaw that followed Stalin's death. On one occasion, Khrushchev boasted to Americans that "we shall bury you," meaning that the Soviet economic system would outperform America's capitalist system, but his harsh rhetoric and melodramatic behavior—pounding his shoe on a desk during a United Nations debate, supporting wars of national liberation in the less-developed countries, and belittling President Kennedy after a 1961 summit meeting in Vienna—fed East-West hostility.

After Khruschev's ouster for "harebrained schemes" (one of which was placing the missiles in Cuba), his successor, Leonid Brezhnev, continued to boast of the U.S.S.R's growing military and political might. As the Soviet economy faltered in the 1970s, however, Brezhnev sought to reaffirm that the Soviet way of life was superior, and the Soviet leadership again embraced Leninist orthodoxy.[60] Ultimately, the centrally planned economy failed to modernize Soviet society, a failure that proved too much for the Soviet state.

Stage 4: Resolving the Cold War

Between 1989 and 1991, the Cold War issue that had dominated the global agenda for decades began to ebb, and by 1992, the U.S. Congress, no longer preoccupied by a "Red menace," was debating how much foreign assistance it should authorize for the Russian economy in its transition to a free market. Before this sea change, and perhaps as a prelude to it, however, the Cold War produced one last flurry of confrontation between the superpowers. Indeed, little happened early in the 1980s to make an observer predict anything but further chilly days.

The Reagan Years and the Cold War Revived.   The Reagan administration's initial strategy was to refocus U.S. policy on the Soviet threat. It set out to "win" the arms race by taking advantage of America's economic and technological superiority and challenging the U.S.S.R. in regional conflicts by supporting anti-Soviet proxies. Secretary of State Alexander Haig acknowledged a tougher line in 1981 when he described Soviet power as the "central strategic phenomenon of the post–World War II era" and added that the "threat of Soviet military intervention colors attempts to achieve international civility."[61] President Reagan's antipathy toward the U.S.S.R. was evident in a 1982 speech to the British House of Commons in which he echoed Churchill's earlier iron curtain speech:

> From Stettin on the Baltic to Varna on the Black Sea, the regimes planted by totalitarianism have had more than 30 years to establish their legitimacy. But none—not one regime—has yet been able to risk free elections. Regimes planted by bayonets do not take root.[62]

A year later, Reagan described the contest between the United States and the Soviet Union as a "struggle between right and wrong, good and evil."[63]

The heart of the tough U.S. policy was a massive arms buildup. A $180 billion nuclear modernization program was begun in which new land-based and sea-based missiles and long-range bombers were added to America's arsenal. New intermediate-range nuclear missiles (INF) were subsequently deployed in Western Europe to counter similar Soviet weapons and provide greater credibility to America's commitment to its allies. A new nuclear defensive system, the Strategic Defense Initiative (SDI), was proposed to protect the U.S. homeland from nuclear attack.

At first, the Soviet Union responded in kind, continuing to deploy mobile intermediate-range missiles, building new long-range missiles, and modernizing its nuclear submarine fleet. It also continued to assist Marxist forces in Afghanistan, Angola, Kampuchea (Cambodia), and Ethiopia. Finally, it abruptly broke off arms-reductions talks after U.S. INF deployments began in Western Europe in November 1983.

Nevertheless, even as Moscow continued to command a military establishment equal to that of the United States and to underwrite numerous foreign-policy ventures, it was becoming clear that cracks in the country's social and economic fabric required dramatic remedy. Economically, the Soviet Union was becoming a second-rate power. The system that was established in the 1920s and 1930s remained largely intact. It is aptly summarized by one observer:

> From the early 1930s onwards, the Soviet Union had a three-sector economy: heavy industry and defense as the priority sector, light industry a poor second, and then agriculture. . . . The economy was administered through a series of . . . nationalized industries, run from Moscow by ministries, each responsible for a different branch of industry, and issuing plans and instructions to the enterprises below. . . . This was subsequently, post-1985, rightly referred to as the Administrative-Command System. . . .[64]

Soviet GNP continued to rise through the 1970s, but overall economic performance was uneven. By the mid-1970s, "the momentum seemed to go; it was as though the system had run out of steam."[65] Mikhail Gorbachev's immediate predecessors, Leonid Brezhnev (1964–1982), Yuri Andropov (1982–1984), and Konstantin Chernenko (1984–1985)—all elderly and in poor health—were incapable of ending the economic stagnation. Corruption, alcoholism, poor service, and cynicism were widespread. Agriculture remained a great problem, and, by the 1980s, the U.S.S.R. had become dependent on Western grain imports to make up shortfalls at home. Finally, as the Soviet economy became more complex, "muscle power"—the key to rapid growth of the economy in the 1930s and 1940s—grew less important, and access to high technology became more critical.

One Soviet economist admitted that, in 1980, more than 25 percent of the Soviet population (68.7 million people) lived below the official poverty line, and that figure grew to about 28 percent by 1988.[66] The Soviet economy was afflicted by technological obsolescence, low productivity, and scarcity of consumer goods.[67] And the decline was continuing with no end in sight. Between 1971 and 1975, Soviet GNP grew at more than 3 percent per year; between 1981 and 1985, that rate declined to less than 1 percent. In short, the Soviet economy was no longer able to support adventures around the world.

Gorbachev and the Cold War's End.   Mikhail Gorbachev, who became general secretary of the Soviet Communist Party in March 1985, recast domestic and foreign-policy priorities. He inaugurated a period of *"new thinking"* about domestic and foreign policy. For domestic policy, he proposed three important concepts—*perestroika, glasnost,* and democracy. *Perestroika* meant "restructuring" Soviet society to address economic and social problems. It included changes in the country's economic and political bureaucracies. *Glasnost* called for opening up society to achieve internal democracy. More information about Soviet society would be made available, and greater criticism of policies would be allowed. Increased political democracy, Gorbachev believed, would enhance the legitimacy of Soviet institutions and reform the Communist Party.[68]

Domestic pressures were the incentive for Gorbachev to seek an end to the Cold War. Overseas adventures and unproductive investments in defense could not continue if domestic reform were to succeed. Gorbachev therefore set out to move Soviet thinking away from belief in the need for nuclear "superiority" toward acceptance of "sufficiency." He would reduce Soviet forces, adopt a new nonprovocative conventional-force posture, and scale back Soviet global commitments. All these actions provided greater flexibility to address the crisis at home. The barriers between domestic and foreign policy proved impossible to sustain.

By the second term of the Reagan administration (1984–1988), the stage was set for reordering superpower relations. A new U.S. attitude developed for several reasons. The U.S. arms buildup was under way and was creating alarming budget deficits at home. Continued increases in military spending no longer received wide support from the Congress or the American public, and the mood favored more cooperation with the Soviet Union, especially in arms control. Finally, the new leaders in Moscow had begun to talk about change. Accommodative moves by both sides quickly followed. New negotiations on intermediate, strategic, and defensive nuclear weapons began early in 1985, and the first summit meeting since 1979 between Soviet and American leaders was held in November. Additional summits followed, providing the impetus for Soviet-American rapprochement on a number of global and regional issues.

Major agreements were reached on arms control that raised the nuclear threshold. Genuine efforts were also made to address old regional differences. Agreement was achieved on ending the war in Afghanistan and hastening the departure of Soviet troops. The superpowers cooperated in obtaining a cease-fire in the Iran-Iraq War and ending the civil war in Angola so that Cuban troops could leave that country.[69] The most dramatic example of Soviet-U.S. cooperation followed the Iraqi invasion of Kuwait in August 1990. Presidents Bush and Gorbachev hastily arranged a summit meeting in Helsinki, Finland, and jointly condemned Saddam Hussein's aggression. More important, the two cooperated in passing U.N. resolutions demonstrating the global community's resolve to reverse the aggression.

Solving the German Puzzle.   The revolutionary changes that finally brought an end to the Cold War began with German reunification and communism's collapse in Eastern Europe and, ultimately, in the Soviet Union itself. Poland led the way. By the end of 1989, a noncommunist government had come to power in that country, and the Soviet Union did nothing to reverse the verdict. When it was clear that the U.S.S.R. would not intervene as it had in the past, the challenge to communist power quickly spread. Moscow seemed to have adopted the "Sinatra Doctrine," allowing its neighbors to pursue their "own way."[70] Within the year, Czechoslovakia, Hungary, East Germany, and other Eastern European countries had abandoned communist rule. All these states held democratic elections. The promise of Yalta had finally been fulfilled.

Internationally, the key to the Cold War lay in Germany. If dividing Germany had kindled the Cold War, reunifying the two Germanys was a prerequisite for ending it. But the German Democratic Republic (GDR), long regarded as the keystone in Moscow's empire, must disappear.[71] Political fissures in the GDR became apparent in spring 1989, when many young East Germans took advantage as barriers were dismantled between Austria and Hungary to travel to Hungary as tourists and then flee to West Germany. By August, a trickle had become a deluge of 5,000 emigrants a week. Unlike 1961, when the U.S.S.R. had prodded East Germany to build the Berlin Wall to halt a similar flight, Soviet leaders did nothing to stop this massive emigration. Taking silence as consent, more and more East Germans fled to Hungary, Poland, and Czechoslovakia. Mass demonstrations broke out in East German cities, notably Leipzig.

As demonstrations continued into autumn and opposition political parties formed, the East German communist leadership sought to save itself. The aged hard-line leader, Erich Honecker, was ousted; competitive elections were scheduled; and, on November 9, 1989, the Berlin Wall was opened, with unmistakable symbolism: The Wall was the final piece of the Iron Curtain separating the "Free World" from the "Socialist Bloc."

German reunification, which had seemed unthinkable until then, suddenly looked possible, and, in November 1989, West German Chancellor Helmut Kohl presented a plan for reunification. Six months later, free elections brought to power Kohl's conservative allies in East Germany who were committed to his plan. In summer 1990, Gorbachev agreed to a reunified Germany that would remain within NATO. In October 1990, the two Germanys were officially reunited, and an all-German democratic government was elected in December. A major step was the September 1990 agreement among the World War II victors formally renouncing further claims on Germany and turning Berlin back to the Germans. The German question had been formally and finally resolved.

A final step in resolving the Cold War was ending Soviet-U.S. ideological hostility. At the Malta Summit (December 1989) and the Washington Summit (June 1990), the Cold War was formally ended with commitments between the two states for future cooperation. Two agreements reached late in 1990 clarified the new superpower relationship. The first was a treaty drastically reducing and limiting conventional weapons in Europe, and the second was a nonaggression pact between NATO and the Warsaw Treaty Organization.[72] The nonaggression treaty included a formal declaration that the two sides were no longer adversaries.[73]

Three events in the Soviet Union in 1991 provided a footnote to the end of the Cold War. An attempted coup, led by hard-liners who wanted to restore centralized communist control, collapsed in days in mid-August 1991, and Gorbachev was subsequently forced to renounce the communist party. Even more dramatic, the multinational Soviet state was formally dissolved on December 25, 1991, and replaced by a loose federation of republics known as the Commonwealth of Independent States (CIS). Two years later Boris N. Yeltsin disbanded Russia's Communist Party, and this was accompanied by symbolic gestures including removal of the guards from Lenin's tomb in Red Square.[74]

Interpreting the End

The Power-Politics Lens. When interpreting the end of the Cold War through the lens of power politics, we must focus on changing power relationships in the global system. America's containment strategy had been designed to place sufficient pressure on the Soviet Union to change its internal structure and its global conduct. A power theorist might affirm that these efforts had succeeded. The massive arms buildup by both states had placed heavy burdens on their economies, but the Soviet system proved less able to bear them. Also, because the United States stymied repeated and expensive Soviet efforts to expand influence in the less-developed countries, the Soviet ability to project power was blunted. As viewed through a power-politics lens, U.S. power was instrumental in forcing the Soviet Union to end the Cold War. The power-politics lens pays scant attention to domestic politics, yet it appears that domestic politics played an important role in changing perceptions in both superpowers.

The Domestic-Politics Lens. As Gorbachev undertook to transform and revitalize Soviet society, organizational inertia and the resistance of the many *apparatchiks* (communist bureaucrats) whose careers were endangered transformed his original goal of reform into something more fundamental. Whatever Gorbachev's original objectives, his policies of *perestroika, glasnost,* and democracy set off bureaucratic battles over which he ultimately lost control. The abortive 1991 coup attempt was made by Soviet bureaucrats who wished to turn back the clock, and its failure accelerated the end of the old order and the Cold War.

Within the Soviet party and government bureaucracy, some flatly opposed the 1985 and 1986 Gorbachev reforms. Yegor K. Ligachev, the Communist Party secretary for agriculture, condemned Gorbachev's party reform as "thoughtless radicalism." Others, led by future Russian president Boris Yeltsin, wanted more rapid and radical party reform, and Yeltsin, along with others, quit the Communist Party when Gorbachev seemed to vacillate. Communist members of Russia's parliament continued to sabotage reform efforts.

An important illustration of bureaucratic pulling and hauling in the Soviet government occurred late in 1990 when Gorbachev's economic advisers presented the "Shatalin Plan," outlining the transformation from a command to a market economy within 500 days. The plan met with a firestorm of opposition from a number of quarters. The KGB (secret police) and the military opposed it because it loosened central control too much for their liking and devolved too much power to the constituent republics. Others opposed the plan because they believed it would lead to high unemployment and inflation. Ultimately, Gorbachev presented a compromise. Neither the original proposal nor the compromise was satisfactory, and confusion spread through the Soviet hierarchy. These reform plans, moreover, challenged many old assumptions, such as supremacy of heavy industry over consumer goods, and questioned whether one of the Cold War's pillars—competing conceptions of how societies ought to be organized—was about to fall.

The failed coup attempt against Gorbachev in August 1991 took place as he was about to sign a treaty to enhance the authority of the constituent republics at the expense of the center. The plotters, antireform members of the Communist Party and disaffected government officials, placed Gorbachev under house arrest at his summer dacha and vowed to turn the clock back in the Soviet Union. Aided by massive popular protests in Moscow and other cities and failure by plotters and army to use force to support the takeover, reformers faced down the coup leaders and the coup collapsed in three days (August 19–21). A politically enfeebled Gorbachev was restored to power, his days as head of the Soviet Union numbered.

Ironically, the coup that sought to halt the reform movement accelerated it. The Communist Party was soon disbanded; Gorbachev surrendered power; and the fifteen constituent republics seized the opportunity to declare their independence. Most of the new states quickly abandoned communism. With these stunning domestic events, the Cold War no longer had a raison d'être.

The Transnational Lens.   It is also possible to interpret the end of the Cold War as a process in which one transnational socioeconomic system, capitalism, triumphed over another, socialism. After more than seventy years, communism had shown itself to be a bankrupt system. Anticipating communism's demise, Zbigniew Brzèzinski, President Carter's national security adviser, argued that "communism will be remembered largely as the twentieth century's most extraordinary political and intellectual aberration."[75] In his judgment, communism had failed, not just in the U.S.S.R., but wherever it had been tried.

Nowhere were the failure of transnational ideology and the reassertion of nationalism more dramatic than in Poland. Early in the 1980s, the trade union Solidarity challenged Poland's stagnating socialist system. Led by the charismatic electrician (and future president), Lech Walesa, and supported by Poland's historically nationalist Catholic Church,[76] Solidarity called for massive reform and power-sharing. The government responded by imposing martial law in December 1981 and arresting many of the union's leaders. These acts fueled popular resentment against the Soviet-imposed system. This feeling was translated into "the rebirth of an alternative political elite, potentially capable of replacing . . . the existing Communist rulers."[77] In 1989 Solidarity was again legalized, and Poland's communist authorities capitulated peacefully to the rising tide of Polish nationalism.

Similar resentment spread to Hungary, Czechoslovakia, and East Germany through the informal and underground networks of political opposition in those states. Elites wished to escape their socialist isolation on the eastern fringe of Europe and reassert their traditional identity as "Central" Europeans in the heart of the continent. "Traditional nationalism" within these states was reborn, and "Marxist internationalism was dead."[78]

The political consequences of rising discontent and reasserted national identity gained full expression sooner than expected. In the end, all the former socialist states took steps to institute political democracy and market economies. The ideological struggle between capitalism and communism was over. Marxism-Leninism had been defeated, not so much by capitalism, but by the nationalist forces it had suppressed in the Soviet Union and Eastern Europe.

A memorial service held for Tsar Nicholas II and his family in the Church of the Resurrection in Yekaterinburg. *(Reuters/Sergei Karpukhin/Archive Photos)*

The final acts in the drama took place in August 1991, immediately after the failed coup, when Yeltsin suspended all activities of the Communist Party in Russia. Within the week the party's last general secretary, Mikhail Sergeivich Gorbachev, called upon the central committee to dissolve itself, and shortly thereafter nationalism reigned triumphant as one Soviet republic after another declared its independence. Adam Ulam describes this momentous transition:

> What for seventy years had been hailed as ... "the vanguard of the proletariat"—the celebrated and mighty Communist party of the Soviet Union—for all practical purposes ceased to exist....All over the vast land crowds were dismantling statues of Lenin.... Communism had drawn its strengths and appeal from the claim that it was the only ideology and movement that could rise above nationalism and establish a peaceful and stable state....[79]

And, in a final act of repentance for the excesses of the communist era in Russia's history, in 1998 the remains of Tsar Nicholas II and most of his family who had been murdered in 1917 were ceremonially reinterred in St. Petersburg (formerly Leningrad).[80]

U.S.-Russian Relations After the Cold War

The Cold War over, it seemed that an era of Russo-American harmony was at hand. Casting a shadow over relations was the rise of political extremism in Russia—including communists on the left and nationalists on the right—and the possibility that economic collapse would overthrow Russia's fragile democracy. Following Yeltsin's introduction of free-market reforms in October 1991, the bottom dropped out of Russia's economy. Real incomes plummeted by 50 percent in six months, and production fell by 24 percent in 1992 alone. In 1992, hyperinflation of more than 2,000 percent gripped Russia.[81] Official production fell an additional 29 percent between April 1993 and April 1994, and the country's health system rapidly eroded.[82] Following Yeltsin's call for new parliamentary elections in December 1993, Yeltsin's parliamentary foes tried to seize power and overthrow him. The revolt was crushed early in October 1993 when Yeltsin declared a state of emergency and summoned army units to Moscow to shell the "White House," Russia's parliament building.[83]

Russia's internal politics plays a critical role in shaping foreign policy, especially Russia's relations with its neighbors and the West. Many Russians recall with nostalgia the era when the U.S.S.R. was a superpower,[84] and almost half the population concluded early in 1994 that Russia's political situation "is out of control."[85] President Yeltsin's orders were repeatedly disobeyed by Russian military personnel in Chechnya, the Russian army was on the verge of collapse, and Yeltsin was apparently not informed by the ministry of nuclear energy of details of Russia's proposed sale of nuclear technology to Iran.[86] Domestic opinion, especially in the military, forced Yeltsin to demand that the West heed Russia's views on Bosnia.[87] Yeltsin sought to persuade Washington to support his government lest others less friendly to the West take power.[88] One result of the problems facing Russia and other former East-bloc members has been growing nostalgia for communism. Former communists have been elected to power in Lithuania, Poland, Hungary, and Slovakia,[89] and in December 1995 Russian voters gave communists under Gennadi Zyuganov a plurality in parliamentary elections.[90] Nevertheless, Yeltsin was reelected in July 1996.

Russia and Reform   Reform in Russia has been so slow and intermittent that one elderly lady remarked, "The Russian won't budge until the roasted rooster pecks him in the rear."[91] Integrating Russia and other members of the former East bloc into the global economic system meant educating Russians in the basics of capitalism[92] and transforming state-owned enterprises into private companies. Another aim was to create a stable currency by providing loans and creating a fund to stabilize the ruble. At a 1992 economic summit, Western leaders pledged aid to Russia as a first step in this direction.[93] However, the West and the International Monetary Fund (IMF) declared that additional aid depended on progress toward reform in Russia. This reform should include cutting its budget deficit and reducing runaway inflation. To bolster Yeltsin's reelection prospects, the IMF loaned Russia $10 billion in 1996.

Economic reform has come only slowly in Russia. It poses a dilemma for Russia's leadership because austerity accompanied by unemployment, rising prices and taxes, and falling production increase the popularity of political extremists.[94] By the end of 1993, some 81,000 of Russia's 196,000 state-owned enterprises had been privatized, though many had been sold at bargain prices to political insiders.[95] By 1994, the private sector was producing 60 percent of Russia's income, as well as employing 86 percent of Russia's industrial work force,[96] and by 1996 land could again be privately bought and sold.[97] Conversion of military industries to peaceful uses was also under way.[98] By late 1995, inflation was down, the budget deficit was under control, the value of the ruble was stabilized, and economic growth had resumed.

Yet within a few years, Russia's economy fell victim to fallout from Asia's economic crisis. As foreign investors fled emerging markets, including Russia's, the ruble was placed under intense downward pressure, Russia's stock market plummeted, interest rates skyrocketed, and bank transactions were halted. In addition, unpaid wages provoked labor unrest and occasional violence.[99] By mid-1998, Russia was in dreadful economic shape.[100]

To fend off imminent economic collapse, the IMF, under American pressure, agreed to loan Russia $17 billion. Once again stringent conditions were attached, including spending cuts and tax reform. With the Duma's refusal to enact these reforms or to approve Yeltsin's selection of Victor Chernomyrdin as prime minister, the value of the ruble collapsed.[101] Between 1989 and 1998, Russia's gross national product had declined by 42.5 percent,[102] and in the first week of September 1998 alone prices rose by 36 percent.[103] By the end of 1998, Russia's economic reformers were out of power, and the country was declared to be in default on about $20 billion of its debt.[104]

Russia's economic distress has been accompanied by political and social turmoil. For one thing, the economic crisis has placed strains on the country's unity.[105] The free market led to growing gaps between rich and poor and an explosion in organized crime to such an extent that the Russian system is called *"gangster capitalism."* Economic reform is impeded by "the hydra-headed Russian mafia" that "has openly penetrated virtually every level of local business."[106] The relatively small number of newly rich businessmen have acquired great political influence, and President Yeltsin and his inner circle are as "secretive and corrupt" as their Soviet predecessors.[107] A key reason for Russia's failure to enact meaningful economic reform has been the stalemate between Yeltsin and the communist-dominated Duma. Yeltsin's repeated reshuffling of cabinet ministers and his poor health have left something of a political void at the top. This weakness at the top has enabled provinces to go their own way and follow different policies than those demanded by Moscow.

U.S.-Russian Frictions

High expectations existed for U.S.-Soviet relations in the heady days immediately after the Cold War's end. Among the signs of cooperation were agreements for joint peacekeeping exercises for U.S. and Soviet troops,[108] joint construction of a permanent space station,[109] and American investment in Russia's oil industry.[110] But time has placed strains on the relationship. Nowhere are these more evident than in Russia's support of former Soviet friend Saddam Hussein and its opposition both to economic sanctions and the use of force against Iraq.[111]

The Near Abroad.   One source of friction is Russia's assertion of traditional interests such as support of "fellow Slavs" like the Serbs[112] and involvement in what

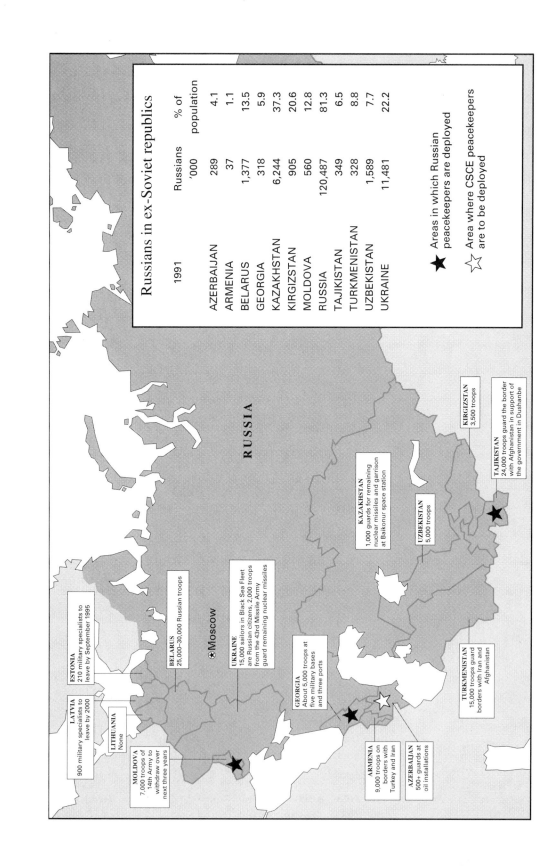

Russians in ex-Soviet republics

1991	Russians '000	% of population
AZERBAIJAN	289	4.1
ARMENIA	37	1.1
BELARUS	1,377	13.5
GEORGIA	318	5.9
KAZAKHSTAN	6,244	37.3
KIRGIZSTAN	905	20.6
MOLDOVA	560	12.8
RUSSIA	120,487	81.3
TAJIKISTAN	349	6.5
TURKMENISTAN	328	8.8
UZBEKISTAN	1,589	7.7
UKRAINE	11,481	22.2

★ Areas in which Russian peacekeepers are deployed

☆ Area where CSCE peacekeepers are to be deployed

LATVIA
900 military specialists to leave by 2000

ESTONIA
210 military specialists to leave by September 1995

LITHUANIA
None

MOLDOVA
7,000 troops of 14th Army to withdraw over next three years

BELARUS
25,000–30,000 Russian troops

UKRAINE
15,000 sailors in Black Sea Fleet are Russian citizens, 2,000 troops from the 43rd Missile Army guard remaining nuclear missiles

GEORGIA
About 5,000 troops at five military bases and three ports

ARMENIA
9,000 troops on borders with Turkey and Iran

AZERBAIJAN
500+ guards at oil installations

TURKMENISTAN
15,000 troops guard borders with Iran and Afghanistan

KAZAKHSTAN
1,000 guards for remaining nuclear missiles and garrison at Baikonur space station

UZBEKISTAN
5,000 troops

KIRGIZSTAN
3,500 troops

TAJIKISTAN
24,000 troops guard the border with Afghanistan in support of the government in Dushanbe

RUSSIA

★ Moscow

ACTORS SPEAK

As Russia and the West increasingly diverge over issues such as the U.S.-British bombing of Iraq, NATO's effort to constrain Serbian actions in Kosovo, and Russia's assistance for Iran's missile program, the question of whether or not Western-Russian cooperation can continue becomes more and more pressing. In the first selection, U.S. Deputy Secretary of State Strobe Talbott argues that Russia is a victim of a bad image and that we can and must continue to cooperate with Moscow. The second selection treats the possibility of Western-Russian cooperation with great caution.

The image of Russia in the mind of the West is increasingly ugly. It has become a cliché of Hollywood to depict Russia not just as a failed state but a criminal one, where the powers that be are mafiosi, renegade generals and former KBGniks, usually trafficking in loose nucks and dirty money....This invidious stereotyping is mirrored in a tendency . . . to see only the darkest side of the picture and therefore to propose a return to the old policy of containing or quarantining Russia. That would be a mistake, every bit as dangerous as those that the Russians themselves are currently making. (Strobe Talbott, "Dealing with Russia in a Time of Troubles," *The Economist,* November 21-27, 1998, p. 56)

A sense of distance has relieved Russia of any strong incentive to model its international relations on those of the West. . . . [I]t hates the current reality of American world leadership. . . . Russia has been reaffirming cordial relations with Soviet-era friends, including such rogue states as Iraq and Iran, and looking at every turn for ways to challenge or outflank American diplomacy. ("Still Most Awkward Partners," *The Economist,* May 9-15, 1998, p. 21)

Figure 4.1
Russians in the Near Abroad

SOURCE: *The Economist,* December 10–16, 1994, p. 55. © 1994 The Economist Newspaper Group, Inc. Reprinted with permission.

Russians call the *"near abroad"*—the lost regions of the Soviet Union. Some 25 million Russians live in these areas (see Figure 4.1), many of whom claim that they are discriminated against, and pressure from old-line communists and newly emboldened nationalists forces Moscow to look after their interests.[113] Russian influence is again spreading in these areas, and Russia is reasserting its traditional regional hegemony.[114] In 1996, Russia formed a common market with Kazakhstan, Kyrgyzstan, and Belarus, and two years later agreed to merge its economy with than of Belarus.[115] Russia also seeks to increase its share of the rich oil and gas reserves of the Caspian Sea, which means augmenting its influence over Azerbaijan, Kazakhstan, and Turkmenistan.[116]

Still, Russian leaders recognize the need for peace and stability in these areas, lest they be torn by the sort of ethnic conflict that could engulf Russia itself.[117] Such concern is heightened by instability along Russia's periphery (e.g., in Georgia, Armenia, Tajikistan, and Azerbaijan). Fear of such instability led Russia to violate the 1990 Conventional Forces in Europe (CFE) treaty that limits Russian forces in the Caucasus in order to ensure stability on its flanks.[118] "The interests of Russia's security and integrity," said the commander of Russian ground forces, "must come above the provisions set in this treaty."[119]

Russian leaders demand that the West recognize Russia's right to act as peace-keeper for its neighbors.[120] Russian troops helped Moldovan rebels in Transdniestria and aided Abkhazia to secede from Georgia, then entered Georgia to restore peace, and Russian troops fought in Tajikistan against Muslim forces seeking to overthrow the government. Despite the presence of 25,000 Russian troops in Tajikistan, civil war continues among regional clans, who trade in opium, arms, and aluminum. Declared a Western diplomat: "You still don't have a real state here. It is a collection of various forces fighting for power."[121] Russo-Ukrainian tensions have fluctuated because of disputes over dividing the Soviet Union's Black Sea fleet, the secessionist efforts of Russians in the Crimea, and Ukrainian hesitation about surrendering to Russia the nuclear arsenal it inherited when the U.S.S.R. collapsed (in return for forgiveness of debts).[122]

Chechnya.   Russia's intervention in secessionist Chechnya late in 1994 and its brutal military campaign there were condemned in the West and drew criticism from antireformers at home. Yeltsin may have reasoned that tiny Chechnya, which had declared independence in 1991, would quickly capitulate and that other potentially rebellious regions would be deterred from following Chechnya's path.[123] Russia consists of eighty-nine political subunits, including twenty-one "ethnic republics," and their governors are increasingly acting with little regard for Moscow; many of them are antidemocratic.[124]

Before the Russian invasion that left Chechnya's capital, Grozny, a smoldering ruin, Chechnya had a reputation "not as a gallant little nation struggling against Kremlin imperialism, but as a tin pot dictatorship bursting with gun-mad gangsters prone to vendettas and shiny sports cars"; "you could be forgiven for thinking that Chechnya is not a country but a rather eccentric gun club."[125] However, the violations of human rights and the brutality of Russia's armed intervention turned world public opinion against Moscow; Russia's failure to bring a quick end to hostilities made it evident that the country's armed forces had seriously deteriorated since the end of the Cold War[126] and stirred dissatisfaction with President Yeltsin at home.[127] In the end, under an agreement negotiated by General Lebed, Chechnya was given de facto independence in 1997, though the decision regarding legal independence was postponed.[128]

NATO Expansion.   Another source of friction was the prospect of Russia's former satellites—Poland, Hungary, and the Czech Republic—joining NATO. President Yeltsin strongly protested NATO's expansion, declaring that Russia does not want to "live in isolation."[129] That expansion would mean a redivision of Europe and, declared Yeltsin, "a conflagration of war throughout Europe for sure."[130] In January 1994, NATO proposed an interim relationship called Partnership for Peace

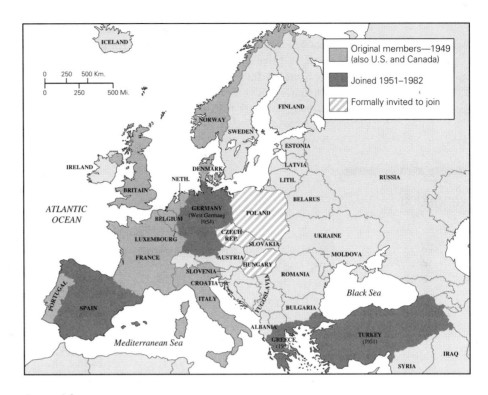

Figure 4.2
The New NATO

With the addition of Poland, Hungary, and the Czech Republic, NATO has extended eastward to the borders of the former Soviet Union. SOURCE: *New York Times,* July 9, 1997, p. A7. Copyright © 1997 by *The New York Times.* Reprinted by permission.

between it, Russia, and some of the new applicants for NATO membership; Russia accepted the offer despite opposing NATO enlargement.[131]

Despite its bellicose rhetoric, Russia accepted NATO expansion relatively quietly. "Russia," declared Foreign Minister Yevgeny Primakov, "while still against enlargement, does realize that NATO is an important organization in Europe and being pragmatists, we are certainly going to base ourselves on that."[132] To reduce the trauma of NATO expansion for Russia, the West made a number of concessions, most importantly the creation of a NATO-Russian consultative council—giving Moscow a voice in NATO policy, but not a veto—and pledges that NATO has no "current" intention to base nuclear weapons or foreign combat troops on the territory of its new members (see Figure 4.2).[133]

Nuclear Sales.   Finally, the United States sought to make Russia cease exporting nuclear technology in violation of the 1992 "suppliers agreement," which forbids exports of nuclear technology to aspiring nuclear powers. Washington urged Moscow to cancel its sale of nuclear reactors and missile technology to Iran and India because of concern about those countries' efforts to acquire nuclear weapons.[134]

President Yeltsin insisted that Moscow had the right to sell such reactors, especially since the United States had offered the same technology to North Korea. He also acidly observed that the United States remained the world's largest arms supplier.

None of this portends a revival of the Cold War, but rather means that the U.S.-Russian honeymoon has come to an end. Despite enormous domestic problems, Russia remains a major factor in global politics. "Our government's policy," declared an adviser to Russia's prime minister, "is the gradual restoration of old Soviet power in any form—economic, military and diplomatic."[135]

Conclusion

In this chapter we have reviewed the stages of the Cold War that shaped global politics for over forty years. With its end, the old world of global politics yielded pride of place to a new world. The case shows how useful it is to examine global events through different theoretical lenses.

History did not end with the resolution of the Cold War. Russia remains a major player, and U.S.-Russian relations remain the world's single most important relationship. The collapse or fragmentation of Russia would likely produce large-scale conflict and might witness the emergence of ultranationalist leaders. No more than one-quarter of Russia's citizens are positive about reform at home; about one-third want a return to communism, and one-tenth a return to tsardom.[136] The dissolution of the Soviet Union and the fall of communism produced great optimism for future U.S.-Russian cooperation, but as power theorists would argue, the two countries have different interests that produce disagreement. In addition, each retains the military capability to devastate the other. Russia's President Yeltsin has spoken of a possible "cold peace" between his country and the West.[137] Only the future will tell if the relationship will be dominated by conflict or cooperation.

Key Terms

Berlin blockade
Berlin Wall
capitalism
Cold War
Cold War consensus
containment
Cuban missile crisis
détente
end of history
gangster capitalism
glasnost
global agenda
iron curtain

issue crisis
issue cycle
issue genesis
issue resolution
issue ritualization
Korean War
Long Telegram
Marshall Plan
mirror image
near abroad
new thinking
Novikov Telegram
NSC-68

peaceful coexistence
perestroika
Potsdam Conference
power vacuum
Riga Axioms
socialism
spheres of influence
Truman Doctrine
Versailles Conference
Vietnam War
Yalta Axioms
Yalta Conference

End Notes

[1]During the U.S.-Soviet détente in the 1970s, the Cold War had prematurely been declared over, only to flare again late in the 1970s and early in the 1980s.

[2]Francis Fukuyama, "The End of History?" *National Interest* (Summer 1989), pp. 3-18.

[3]See Richard W. Mansbach and John A. Vasquez, *In Search of Theory: A New Paradigm for Global Politics* (New York: Columbia University Press, 1981), pp. 87-142. Issues do not always pass through all stages of the cycle.

[4]This section draws on ibid., pp. 87-142.

[5]Cited in Alan Riding, "Paris Meeting Supports U.N. Plan to Combat AIDS," *New York Times,* December 2, 1994, p. A3.

[6]Tim Weiner, "Guatemalan Agent of the C.I.A. Linked to Killing of American," *New York Times,* March 25, 1995, p. A1.

[7]See Charles F. Hermann, *Crises in Foreign Policy* (Indianapolis: Bobbs-Merrill, 1969), pp. 21-29.

[8]The term is intended to convey the sort of conflict in animal species with much sound and fury but little physical harm.

[9]The Bolsheviks ("majority faction") were Lenin's followers in Russia's social democratic movement, in contrast to the Mensheviks ("minority faction").

[10]John Lewis Gaddis, *Russia, the Soviet Union, and the United States* (New York: Wiley, 1978), p. 76.

[11]India was partitioned and, along with its Muslim foe, Pakistan, was granted independence under chaotic circumstances in 1947.

[12]Although inhabitants of such European colonies as Malaya, Indochina, and Indonesia were victims of brutal occupation, the Japanese defeat of the European powers destroyed the myth of European invincibility and energized national independence movements.

[13]Stephen E. Ambrose, *Rise to Globalism: American Foreign Policy 1938-1976* (New York: Peguin Books, 1976), p. 16.

[14]"No End of Lessons," *The Economist,* May 6-May 12, 1995, p. 21.

[15]John Lewis Gaddis, *The Long Peace* (New York: Oxford University Press, 1987) p. 50.

[16]Cited in ibid., p. 48.

[17]On the Yalta agreements see Robert H. Ferrell, *American Diplomacy: A History* (New York: Norton, 1975), pp. 594-603.

[18]Although Roosevelt has been accused of allowing himself to be duped by Stalin, he recognized the realities of power politics both before and after Yalta. In January 1945, he pointed out to a group of senators that "the occupying forces had the power in the areas where their arms were present and each knew that the others could not force things to an issue. The Russians had the power in Eastern Europe." Shortly after Yalta, he made the same point: "Obviously the Russians are going to do things their own way in the areas they occupy." Cited in Daniel Yergin, *Shattered Peace* (Boston: Houghton Mifflin, 1977), pp. 58, 66.

[19]The U.S.S.R. fulfilled this pledge, in the process seizing several small islands in the Kurile chain.

[20]Ferrell, *American Diplomacy,* p. 623. In a bid to maintain cooperation with the U.S.S.R. at Potsdam, the United States had withdrawn its forces from territory outside the occupation zones negotiated at Yalta.

[21]Yergin, *Shattered Peace,* pp. 42-68.

[22]Gaddis, *Russia, the Soviet Union, and the United States,* p. 181.

[23]Gaddis, *The Long Peace,* p. 54.

[24]Yergin, *Shattered Peace,* pp. 17-41. "Riga" refers to the Latvian city of that name, where the first American Soviet watchers were posted after the U.S.S.R. was established.

[25]Ibid., p. 35.

[26]George F. Kennan, *Memoirs 1925-1950* (Boston: Little, Brown, 1967), p. 557.

[27]Ibid.

[28]Ibid., pp. 555-556.

[29]The Novikov Telegram was released to Soviet and American historians in July 1990 at a meeting at the U.S. Peace Institute in Washington, DC. See John Lewis Gaddis, "The Soviet Side of the Cold War: A Symposium," *Diplomatic History* 15:4 (Fall, 1991), p. 525.

[30]"The Novikov Telegram, Washington, September 27, 1946," reprinted in *Diplomatic History* 15:4 (Fall 1991), pp. 529, 530.

[31]Ibid., pp. 535, 537.

[32]William A. Gamson and André Modigliani, *Untangling the Cold War* (Boston: Little, Brown, 1971), p. 109.

[33]Cited in B. Thomas Trout, "Rhetoric Revisited: Political Legitimation and the Cold War," *International Studies Quarterly* 19:3 (September 1975), p. 264.

[34]Deborah Welch Larson, *Origins of Containment* (Princeton: Princeton University Press, 1985), pp. 252-253; and Trout, "Rhetoric Revisited," p. 269.

[35]Robert Rhodes James, ed., *Wintson S. Churchill: His Complete Speeches 1897-1963,* vol. 7: 1943-1949 (New York: Chelsea House, 1974), p. 7290.

[36]Ibid., pp. 7289, 7293.

[37]Gaddis points out that, despite their isolationist heritage, by the early 1940s Americans had begun to think that "primary American

interest in postwar international affairs would be to ensure that no single state dominates Europe." *The Long Peace,* p. 49.

[38]From a power-politics perspective, there is little difference between Soviet behavior in Eastern Europe after World War II and the French design to create a *cordon sanitaire* in the same region after World War I.

[39]Kenneth W. Thompson, *Cold War Theories,* vol. 1 (Baton Rouge: Louisiana State University Press, 1981), pp. 44–45.

[40]Ibid., p. 46.

[41]Adam B. Ulam, *The Communists: The Story of Power and Lost Illusions: 1948–1991* (New York: Scribner's, 1992), pp. 1–2. Emphasis in original.

[42]A Report to the National Security Council, April 14, 1950, p. 5. Declassified February 27, 1975.

[43]Congressional Record, vol. 93, pt. 2, March 12, 1947, pp. 1980–1981.

[44]The parenthetical passages are from Mr. X (George Kennan), "The Sources of Soviet Conduct," *Foreign Affairs* (July 1947), pp. 566–582.

[45]NSC-68 made it a high U.S. priority to alert other countries and the American public to the dangers of communism. Making recommendations for policy abroad, it also called for higher defense budgets at home, protecting U.S. institutions from subversion, rallying public opinion against the Soviet Union, and proceeding with the H-bomb.

[46]The U.S.S.R. prevented Poland and Czechoslovakia from accepting Marshall Plan aid.

[47]The 1949 U.S. Export Control Act, which was not revoked until 1969, gave the president authority to prevent exports to the Soviet Union.

[48]See Dennis L. Bark, *Agreement on Berlin: A Study of the 1970–1972 Quadripartite Negotiations* (Washington, DC, and Stanford: American Enterprise Institute for Public Policy Research and Hoover Institution on War, Revolution and Peace, 1974).

[49]Peter Calvocoressi, *World Politics Since 1945,* 6th ed. (New York: Longman, 1991), p. 19.

[50]Rapid intervention was possible because U.S. occupation troops were in Japan.

[51]Robert Jervis, "The Impact of the Korean War on the Cold War," *Journal of Conflict Resolution* 24:4 (December 1980), p. 563. See John Lewis Gaddis, "Was the Truman Doctrine a Real Turning Point? *Foreign Affairs* 52:2 (January 1974), pp. 386–402, on dating the origins of the Cold War.

[52]These figures are for total national defense rather than only Department of Defense data. See Alice C. Moroni, *The Fiscal Year 1984 Defense Budget Request: Data Summary* (Washington, DC: Congressional Research Service, 1983), p. 13.

[53]Andrew M. Scott, *The Revolution in Statecraft: Informal Penetration* (New York: Random House, 1965). Throughout

the 1980s, "the U.S. government made scores of clandestine purchases of advanced Soviet weapons from Warsaw Pact countries." (Benjamin Weiser, "A Secret Warsaw Pact with the U.S. in the Cold War," *Washington Post National Weekly Edition,* February 21–27, 1994, p. 18). Revelations that Aldrich Ames, head of CIA counterintelligence, spied for Russia indicate that the end of the Cold War did not end Russian espionage against the United States. See James J. Fialka and Thomas E. Ricks, "Espionage Case Against CIA Official and Wife Indicates Spirit of KGB Survived Soviet Breakup," *Wall Street Journal,* February 23, 1994, p. A22.

[54]A possible exception was Chinese intervention in the Korean conflict in 1950 as U.S. forces approached the Yalu River on China's border. The Soviets were largely uninvolved in Beijing's decision to intervene.

[55]Covert assistance, including Stinger antiaircraft missiles, was channeled to the Afghan rebels early, and overt aid was provided by 1986.

[56]Kenneth N. Waltz, "The Stability of a Bipolar World," *Daedalus* 93:3 (Summer 1964), p. 883.

[57]Joseph S. Nye, Jr., "Nuclear Learning and U.S.-Soviet Security Regime," *International Organization* 41:3 (Summer 1987), p. 394.

[58]Eugene R. Wittkopf and James M. McCormick, "The Cold War Consensus: Did It Exist?" *Polity* (Summer 1990), pp. 627–653.

[59]Paul Marantz, "Prelude to Détente: Doctrinal Change Under Khrushchev," *International Studies Quarterly* 19:4 (December 1975), pp. 501–528; and Gordon B. Smith, *Soviet Politics: Struggling with Change,* 2nd ed. (New York: St. Martin's Press, 1992), p. 80.

[60]Smith, *Soviet Politics,* pp. 80–81.

[61]Alexander Haig, "Opening Statement at Confirmation Hearings" (Washington, DC: Bureau of Public Affairs, Department of State, January 9, 1981), p. 2. This was Current Policy Statement No. 257.

[62]Ronald Reagan, "Address to Members of the British Parliament, June 8, 1982," in James M. McCormick, ed., *A Reader in American Foreign Policy* (Itasca, IL: Peacock, 1986), p. 181.

[63] "Excerpts from President's Speech to National Association of Evangelicals," *New York Times,* March 9, 1983, p. A18.

[64]Mary McAuley, *Soviet Politics 1917–1991* (New York: Oxford University Press, 1992), pp. 40–41.

[65]Ibid., p. 78.

[66]Bill Keller, "Soviet Economy: A Shattered Dream," *New York Times,* May 13, 1990, pp. 1, 13; and Keller, "How Gorbachev Rejected Plan to 'Shock Treat' the Economy," *New York Times,* May 14, 1990, pp. A1, A6.

[67]Goods that were available were shoddy, and the Soviet media were filled with stories of exploding television sets and boots that fell apart.

[68]On the changes in the Soviet Union, see Michael Mandelbaum, "Coup de Grace: The End of the Soviet Union," *Foreign Affairs* 71:1 (1992), pp. 164–183. Mandelbaum argues that Gorbachev was a communist reformer and "not a Western-style democrat" (p. 172) who lost control of the reform movement he had begun. Domestic reforms took on a life of their own, and, after the abortive August 1991 coup, "there was nothing left to reform" (p. 173).

[69]The agreement reached between warring factions in Angola broke down in 1993, but did not affect U.S.-Russian relations.

[70]American singer Frank Sinatra popularized a song entitled "My Way."

[71]Soviet control over East Germany, the Soviets had argued, prevented revival of a strong Germany similar to that which had almost conquered Russia in World Wars I and II. For many years after 1945 the East German communists were regarded as among the most loyal to Moscow and the most rigidly authoritarian in Eastern Europe.

[72]This treaty followed a Soviet-American agreement in principle (February 1990) for each to reduce troop strength in Central Europe to 195,000. In fact, for economic reasons, both sides were reducing troop strength below that figure. Indeed, U.S. forces in Germany were rapidly sent to Saudi Arabia as part of the force to liberate Kuwait. The first treaty consisted largely of unilateral Soviet concessions in which Moscow surrendered its massive advantage in numbers of tanks, armored vehicles, artillery, helicopters, and combat aircraft.

[73]Alan Riding, "The New Europe," *New York Times,* November 20, 1990, p. A4.

[74]Steven Erlanger, "Yeltsin Suspends the Communist Party and Other Foes," *New York Times,* October 9, 1993, p. A3.

[75]Zbigniew K. Brzezinski, *The Grand Failure: The Birth and Death of Communism in the Twentieth Century* (New York: Scribner's, 1989), p. 1.

[76]For over three decades, the Polish Church adamantly opposed the communist regime, and the "Polish Pope," John Paul, strongly supported his Polish brethren.

[77]Brzezinski, *Grand Failure,* p. 123.

[78]Ibid., p. 135. The emphasis on Central European identity connoted "a repudiation of the Soviet-sponsored notion of a shared 'socialist' culture" (p. 139).

[79]Ulam, *The Communists,* pp. 490, 494. The Communist Party was later restored in Russia and became increasingly popular as economic conditions deteriorated in 1995 and 1996.

[80]Michael Wines, "Yeltsin in Reversal, Will Attend Rite for Czar and Family," *New York Times,* July 17, 1998, p. A3.

[81]Peter Reddaway, "Russia Comes Apart," *New York Times,* January 10, 1993, sec. 4, p. 3.

[82]"Bleak statistics, bleak politics," *The Economist,* May 8–14, 1994, p. 52. Michael Specter, "Onrush of AIDS is Driving an Infirm Russia to Its Knees," *New York Times,* May 18, 1997, sec. 1, pp. 1, 4.

[83]Serge Schmemann, "Army Ousts Yeltsin Foes from Parliament; President Takes Steps to Solidify Power," *New York Times,* October 5, 1993, pp. A1, A4.

[84]One popular alternative to Yeltsin is General Aleksandr I. Lebed, an authoritarian war hero who argues that the Russian empire must be restored. Alessandra Stanley, "Russia General Woos Votes for Old-Time Soviet Values," *New York Times,* October 13, 1995, pp. A1, A6. During the presidential campaign of 1996, Lebel joined Yeltsin's government but left shortly afterward.

[85]"The Road to Ruin," *The Economist,* January 29–February 5, 1994, p. 25.

[86]"Reliability Moscow-style," *The Economist,* May 13–19, 1995, p. 53.

[87]See "Russia, Bosnia and the West," *The Economist,* September 16–22, 1995, p. 58.

[88]Michael Dobbs, "Telling the Good Guys from the Bad Guys," *Washington Post National Weekly Edition,* May 8–14, 1995, p. 17. Steven Erlanger, "Russian Chief Stays in the Saddle," *New York Times,* March 23, 1997, sec. 1, p. 4.

[89]Jane Perlez, "Welcome Back, Lenin," *New York Times,* May 3, 1994, pp. A1, A5; "Ex-Communists are Back in the Saddle Again," *Washington Post National Weekly Edition*, November 7–13, 1994, p. 7.

[90]Alessandra Stanley, "Communists Lead the Ruling Party by 2 to 1 in Russia," *New York Times,* December 19, 1995, pp. A1, A8. The large communist bloc in the Duma is a major impediment to political and economic reform.

[91]Cited in Serge Schmemann, "Russia Lurches into Reform but Old Ways are Tenacious," *New York Times,* February 20, 1994, p. 6.

[92]See, for example, Adi Ignatius and Neela Banerjee, "Russian Bankers Bring Tricks of the Trade Home After U.S. Visit," *Wall Street Journal,* May 23, 1994, pp. A1, A6.

[93]Stephen Kinzer, "7 Leaders Promise $1 Billion for Russia," *New York Times,* July 9, 1992, p. A4.

[94]For a time the most feared ultranationalist was Vladimir Zhironovsky, whose far-right party received a large protest vote in Russia's December 1993 parliamentary elections. Since then Zhironovsky's star has waned. See "Could It Lead to Fascism?" *The Economist,* July 11–17, 1998, pp. 19–21.

[95]Craig R. Whitney, "Russia Opens Up Market, but Few Have the Money," *New York Times,* November 18, 1993, p. A3; "Counterrevolution," *The Economist,* December 3–9, 1994, pp. 23, 24, 27.

[96]"Call That a Reshuffle, Boris?" *The Economist,* November 12–18, 1995, p. 63.

[97]Michael Specter, "With Land Sale Edict, Yeltsin Opens Way to Longed-for Era," *New York Times,* March 17, 1996, sec. 1, pp. 1, 8.

[98]See, for example, Steve Liesman, "United Technologies to Market Russian Rocket Engines in U.S.," *Wall Street Journal,* July 19, 1995, p. A9.

[99]See, for example Michael Specter, "Protesting Privation, a Million Russian Workers Strike," *New York Times,* March 28,

1997, p. A3; Celestine Bohlen, "After Moscow's Binge, It's Hangover Time," *New York Times,* September 9, 1998, pp. A1, A10. In May 1999, Primakov was fired.

[100]"Russia's Crisis Isn't Over," *The Economist,* June 27-July 3, 1998, p. 49.

[101]Russian foreign minister Yevgeny Primakov was appointed prime minister and seemed to restore some political and economic stability to the battered country. Betsy McKay, "Primakov Surprises Western Investors by Keeping Russia from Splitting Apart," *Wall Street Journal,* December 31, 1998, p. A6. In May 1999, Primakov was fired.

[102]Celestine Bohlen, "Facing Oblivion, Rust-Belt Giants Top Russian List of Vexing Crises," *New York Times,* November 8, 1998, sec. 1, p. 1.

[103]"Russia Shipwrecked," *The Economist,* September 12-18, 1998, p. 55.

[104]Betsy McKay and Carol Redmond, "Moscow Is Declared in Default on Debt," *Wall Street Journal,* December 31, 1998, p. A6. For a review of the events leading up to Russia's economic collapse, see Steve Liesman and Andrew Higgins, "The Crunch Points: How Russia Staggered from There to Here," *Wall Street Journal,* September 23, 1998, pp. A1, A12.

[105]See, for example, Andrew Higgins, "Odd Borders Appear in Russia as Regions Face Poor Harvests," *Wall Street Journal,* October 16, 1998, pp. A1, A11.

[106]Michael Specter, "U.S. Business and the Russian Mob," *New York Times,* July 8, 1994, p. C1. Yeltsin reported that 80 percent of private enterprises in Russia were paying tribute to the "mafia." Cited in Schmemann, "Russia Lurches into Reform," p. 6.

[107]Alessandra Stanley, "Russia's New Rulers Govern, and Live, in Neo-Soviet Style," *New York Times,* May 23, 1995, p. A1.

[108]Michael R. Gordon, "U.S. and Russia Sign Peacekeeper Training Pact," *New York Times,* September 9, 1993, p. A8.

[109]Russia's budget problems delayed the schedule for this project and raised reservations about the project in the U.S. Congress. Warren E. Leary, "Aid to Russia to Complete Space Station Is Defended," *New York Times,* October 8, 1998, p. A24.

[110]Claudia Rossett and Allanna Sullivan, "Conoco Tests the Tundra for Oil Profits," *Wall Street Journal,* September 1, 1994, p. A8.

[111]Michael R. Gordon, "Moscow Orders U.S. Envoy Home to Protest Air Strikes," *New York Times,* December 18, 1998, p. A2.

[112] See, for example, Celestine Bohlen, "Russia Vows to Block the U.N. from Backing Attack on Serbs," *New York Times,* October 7, 1998, p. A8. Russia vigorously protested the 1999 NATO bombing of Serbia.

[113]See, for example, Steven Erlanger, "Russians in Central Asia, Once Welcome, Now Flee," *New York Times,* February 7, 1995, pp. A1, A5. Ethnic Russians account for 37 percent of the population of Kazakhstan, 34 percent of Latvia's, 31 percent of Estonia's, 22 percent of Ukraine's, 21 percent of Kyrgyzstan's, and 13 percent of Moldova's. "Touchy bears," *The Economist,* May 21-26, 1994, p. 56.

[114] See, for example, "The Empire Strikes Back," *The Economist,* August 7-13, 1993, p. 36.

[115]Michael R. Gordon, "Russia Agrees to Closer Links with Three Ex-Soviet Lands," *New York Times,* March 30, 1996, p. 4; Michael Wines, "Yeltsin Agrees to Close Ties with Belarus," *New York Times,* December 26, 1998, pp. A1, A4.

[116]"The Combustible Caspian," *The Economist,* January 11-17, 1997, p. 45.

[117]See, for example, "Losing Control?" *The Economist,* July 18-24, 1998. Ultranationalist Vladimir Zhironovsky has called on Russia to achieve the "quieting of peoples—from Kabul to Istanbul." Cited in "Russia's Overfriendly Squeeze," *The Economist,* April 16-23, 1994, p. 37.

[118]"Manoeuvres," *The Economist,* July 22-28, 1995, p. 50. Russia retains military bases in Georgia and Armenia. "Russia Eyes the World," *The Economist,* November 23-29, 1996, p. 52.

[119]Cited in "Moscow Reportedly to Maintain Large Armed Forces in Caucasus," *New York Times,* April 27, 1995, p. A5. The United States agreed to permit Russia to keep heavy weapons in its southern region, thereby amending the CFE. Eric Schmitt, "U.S. Senate Votes to Let the Russians Shift Troops," *New York Times,* May 15, 1997, p. A9.

[120]See, for example, Steven Greenhouse, "Armenia Says It Would Welcome Russian Peacekeeping Force," *New York Times,* August 12, 1994, p. A3; "A Teddy Bear After All?" *The Economist,* December 10-16, 1994, p. 49. A U.S. draft document, Presidential Decision Directive 13, which proposed the use of U.S. troops for peacekeeping in the former Soviet Union, angered Moscow. Steven Erlanger, "U.S. Peacekeeping Policy Debate Angers Russians," *New York Times,* August 29, 1993, sec. 1, p. 3.

[121]Cited in Steve Levine, "Tajiks Talks of Peace Between Battles," *New York Times,* January 6, 1997, p. A4. See also Hugh Pope, "Helter-Smelter: Why Tajikistan Has an Aluminum Plant," *Wall Street Journal,* July 2, 1998, pp. A1, A10; "Under pressure," *The Economist,* February 3-9, 1996, pp. 30-31.

[122]See Jane Perlez, "Fear of Russia Is a Way of Life for Ukraine," *New York Times,* January 16, 1994, sec. 4, p. 3; Claudia Rosett, "Yearnings in Crimea Threaten to Set Off Ukrainian Powder Keg," *Wall Street Journal,* February 14, 1994, pp. A4, A6. The dispute over the Black Sea fleet was resolved in June 1995. Steve Erlanger, "Russia and Ukraine Settle Dispute over Black Sea Fleet," *New York Times,* June 10, 1995, p. 1.

[123]For ethnic problems elsewhere in Russia, see "How Many Other Chechnyas?" *The Economist,* January 14-20, 1995, pp. 43-45; and "Losing Control?" *The Economist,* July 18-24, 1998, pp. 45-46.

[124]"Fiefs and Chiefs," *The Economist,* January 25-31, 1997; "Naughty Little Tsars," *The Economist,* June 20-26, 1998, p. 60.

[125]"Chechens of the Wild East," *The Economist,* September 24-30, 1994, p. 54.

[126]Michael Specter, "Killed in Chechnya: An Army's Pride," *New York Times,* May 21, 1995, sec. 4, p. 3; Michael Specter, "10 Days That Shook Russia: Siege in the Caucasus," *New York Times,*

January 22, 1996, pp. A1, A4; Michael Specter, "Rebels Overrun Russian Troops in Chechen City," *New York Times*, August 8, 1996, pp. A1, A5; Lee Hockstader, "A Nurse's Own War in Chechnya," *Washington Post National Weekly Edition*, September 23-29, 1996, pp. 16-17.

[127]Michael Specter, "Angry Russian Parliament Votes to Rebuke Yeltsin Government," *New York Times*, June 22, 1995, pp. A1, A7.

[128]"Taiwan on the Caucasus," *The Economist*, February 22-28, 1997, p. 59.

[129]Cited in Charles A. Kupchan, "The Runaway NATO Train," *Washington Post National Weekly Edition*, May 22-28, 1995, p. 23. See also Elaine Sciolino, "Yeltsin Says NATO Is Trying to Split Continent Again," *New York Times*, December 6, 1994, pp. A1, A4; Steven Erlanger, "U.S. Pushes Big NATO Despite Qualms on Russia," *New York Times*, October 10, 1996, p. A4.

[130]Cited in Steven Erlanger, "In a New Attack on NATO, Yeltsin Raises the Specter of War," *New York Times*, September 9, 1995, p. 3.

[131]Elaine Sciolino, "NATO Rejects Russian Role in Decision-Making," *New York Times*, June 10, 1994, p. A4. Russia refused to let its troops in the Bosnia peace force serve under NATO command but agreed to let them serve under U.S. command. Craig R. Whitney, "Russia and U.S. Agree to Have Moscow Troops in Bosnia Serve in U.S. Unit," *New York Times*, November 9, 1995, p. A4.

[132]Cited in Steve Liesman, "Russia Demonstrates New Pragmatism in Accepting NATO's Inevitable Growth," *Wall Street Journal*, December 16, 1996, p. A1. See also Michael R. Gordon, "Russia Agrees to NATO Plan Pushed by Clinton to Admit Nations from Eastern Bloc," *New York Times*, May 15, 1997, pp. A1, A8; "A New European Order," *The Economist*, May 17-23, 1997, pp. 55-56.

[133]These understandings were formalized in a Russian-NATO agreement called "the Founding Act." Craig R. Whitney, "Russia and West Sign Cooperation Pact," *New York Times*, May 28, 1997, pp. A1, A8. See also Steven Erlanger, "U.S. Will Propose Arms Reductions in Central Europe," *New York Times*, February 19, 1997, pp. A1, A6; Michael R. Gordon, "Russia Accepts Eastward Growth of NATO, but Only Inch by Inch," *New York Times*, March 4, 1997, pp. A1, A6; "For NATO, Eastward Ho!" *The Economist*, March 1-7, 1997, pp. 49-51; Craig R. Whitney, "NATO, in Concession to Russia, Won't Base New Forces in East," *New York Times*, March 15, 1997, pp. 1, 5.

[134]Craig R. Whitney, "Albright Presses Russia to Limit Aid to Iran," *New York Times*, December 10, 1998, p. A15; Michael R. Gordon, "Russia Selling Atomic Plants to India; U.S. Protests Deal," *New York Times*, February 6, 1997, p. A3. In an effort to reduce Russian incentives to export enriched uranium derived from nuclear warheads, the United States in 1992 agreed to purchase 500 metric tons, which would be resold to electric utilities. Suspicions have arisen, however, that the Russians may be cheating. William J. Broad, "Uranium Disarmament Deal: Is Russia Delivering?" *New York Times*, January 29, 1996, p. A6.

[135]Cited in "Imperial Nostalgia," *The Economist*, July 2-8, 1994, p. 47.

[136]Eastern Europeans are significantly more optimistic than Russians. See "Feeling Perkier," *The Economist*, March 2-8, 1996, pp. 48-49.

[137]See Andrei Kozyrev, "Partnership or Cold Peace?" *Foreign Policy* no. 99 (Summer 1995), pp. 3-14.

Part Two

Actors and Issues in the Postinternational World

Part Two introduces the different levels of analysis and types of actors in global politics—the global system, the weakening state, and nonstate actors. Chapter 5 looks at the "big picture" of the global system and examines the role its structure plays in shaping political behavior, especially the importance of resource and attitude distribution. Chapter 6 illustrates how the wall between international and domestic politics is collapsing and examines a variety of ways to explain foreign policy. Chapter 7 examines the variety of actors other than states that have prominent roles in global politics, and Chapter 8 examines the proliferation of international organizations, as states seek to maintain their dominance of global politics by cooperating with one another.

Chapter 5

The Global System

T he global political system is the most comprehensive level at which to ana-
lyze global politics; it allows us to see all the pieces of the global puzzle and
how they fit together. Having looked at the forest, we can turn to the trees in
later chapters. Since a system assumes interdependence among its parts, the
concept captures the idea that the preferences of one actor, however strong, cannot be realized in isolation from the preferences and choices of others.

Our ancestors were nomadic hunters and gatherers who lived in small groups.
Individuals might help each other, but these groups had little impact on one another.
They had no organized warfare or commerce.[1] Improvements in agriculture gradually provided food to support larger populations, including concentrations in
cities—which were first established in Mesopotamia (modern Iraq). People living
in towns manufactured tools and clothes that they traded for food and raw materials with those in the country. Some, specializing in violence, became soldiers
organized by local rulers to protect cities and trade routes and raid others' cities
and farms. In this way, groups began to specialize and depend on each other. Some
began to travel great distances to sell their wares.

Nevertheless, until recent centuries, people living in one part of the globe had
few links with those elsewhere. Contacts among Chinese, Europeans, and Arabs,
for example, were episodic, limited to intrepid travelers like the Venetian Marco
Polo (1254–1324), who returned to Europe with tales of the great Mongol Kublai
Khan and the recipe for pasta. Although Chinese explorers sailed the Indian Ocean
and beyond before the birth of Christ and Viking Norsemen traveled to North
America, it was not until European explorers like the Portuguese Vasco da Gama
(1460–1524) and the Italian Christopher Columbus (1446–1506) sailed on their
epic voyages of discovery that regular contact became possible between Africans
and Americans, on the one hand, and Europeans, on the other.

Today, the decisions and actions of Americans, Asians, Europeans, and Africans
enhance one another's opportunities for happiness or deprive them of those
opportunities. Whether people realize it or not, the fates of human beings, even
those remote from and unaware of each other, are linked. Farmers in one country
may have a large harvest, driving down the world price of grain and reducing profits for farmers on the other side of the earth. Wealthy consumers in North America
use vast amounts of oil to drive cars, making it more expensive for the poor in
Africa to obtain petroleum-based fertilizers to grow food and contributing to global environmental problems. In the aggregate, individuals' decisions about which
car to buy or where to travel can enhance or harm the prospects of others living

thousands of miles away whom they have never met. Links such as these create political systems.

Attributes of the Global System

The concept of a political system is intended to convey the reality that people everywhere, wittingly or unwittingly, affect people everywhere else and that the way in which global resources and attitudes are distributed determines the kind of world in which we live.

System Defined: Parts and Wholes

The abstraction *system,* which came to political science from the natural sciences, expresses the idea of sustained and predictable patterns of action and reaction among interdependent individuals or groups—the parts of the system. In a system, the welfare of any one depends on the others' actions and vice versa. The interaction of a system's parts determines the characteristics of the system as a whole. The outcomes of such interactions cannot be predicted with knowledge of separate parts alone. Just as when one combines two atoms of hydrogen and one of oxygen to get water, the outcome of interaction may be *qualitatively* different than the behavior that produces it. Imagine a number of peaceful countries, each developing an army solely for defense. Will the system *as a whole* be peaceful? That depends on how the individual countries—the parts—interact. If each perceives its neighbor's army as threatening, the system may be warlike even though no one seeks war. In this example, war is an *emergent property;* that is, it is an unpredictable consequence of interaction among the parts of the system.

The system idea helps explain why outcomes in global politics are often unexpected. Consider world trade. Leaders recognize that an open trading system, without impediments to free movement of goods and services, benefits everyone. And when one country tries to aid a domestic industry, it may set off a chain reaction, unwittingly producing an economic disaster that no one seeks (see Figure 5.1). American leaders may try to protect U.S. auto manufacturers or farmers by limiting imports of Japanese autos or subsidizing U.S. grain exports. Such actions may harm Japanese auto manufacturers and European farmers, who will pressure their leaders to retaliate against vulnerable U.S. enterprises. A sequence of tit-for-tat actions may ensue which can threaten a trade war that no one wants and in which all will suffer as fewer people around the world buy each other's products.

The consequences of the initial action provide information that conditions the response of those at whom the initial action was directed. Responses are neither random nor mechanical; instead they are purposeful reactions to others' initiatives. Such information is called *feedback.*

Information that reinforces or intensifies existing policies is *positive* or *amplifying feedback.* Escalation and panic reflect positive feedback. *Escalation* is a policy of intensified military action like that adopted by the United States in Vietnam after 1964 in the belief that more of the same will achieve one's goals. Sometimes, as in panics, positive feedback can be pathological. In the Great Depression of

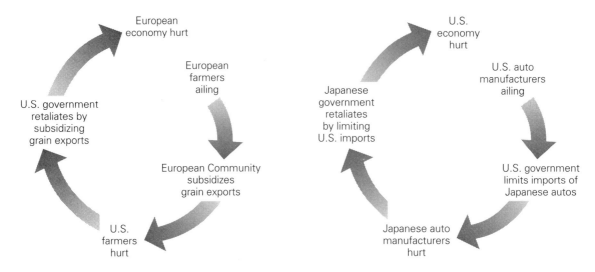

FIGURE 5.1
Parts and Wholes: Domestic Pressures and Global Consequences

In today's world, domestic pressures may produce domestic political decisions with serious international consequences, and foreign-policy decisions will affect the domestic arena in other societies. This is illustrated by hypothetical policies fashioned to aid European farmers and U.S. auto manufacturers.

1929, massive selling in the stock market led to further selling of stock, inducing a stock-market collapse. Those who panicked also sought to get their money out of banks and triggered a run on the banks and a collapse of the U.S. banking system. As rumors spread that people were withdrawing money, others sought to do the same until the banks ran out of cash. Financial crises such as those that have struck Mexico and Asia in recent years are like large-scale runs on the bank.

Information that changes the direction of policy is *negative* or *corrective feedback*. Leaders who recognize that policy has failed may take steps to change ("correct") those policies. Thus, as it became clear that escalation could not achieve Soviet objectives in Afghanistan in 1986, Gorbachev took steps to reduce the military effort. If genuine learning leads to change in goals rather than simply change in policies, we may speak of *second-order feedback*.[2]

Issues, Actors, and Systems

Issues.   Historically, issues expanded geographically to link persons and places far apart. Local and regional trading networks expanded to become global trading networks, and local security issues acquired global scope. It then became possible to speak of a truly global political system. Today, the economic health of a corporation like General Motors (and the millions of Americans and foreigners who directly or indirectly depend on GM for prosperity) is related to such factors as petroleum production and prices in the Middle East; security in the Persian Gulf; labor union decisions in the United States, Canada, Mexico, and Japan that determine labor productivity in those countries; and the budget deficit in Washington, which helps set interest rates at which people borrow money to pay for GM products. In other words, the fate of GM is determined by the global system of which it is a small part.

Subsystems.   Within the global system, selected actors interact especially intensely with one another over specific issues. We designate these very intense relationships *subsystems.* Such interaction is not always friendly and may feature high levels of hostile, even violent, action and reaction. The patterned interaction that sustains subsystems, then, may be either hostile or cooperative.

Many of the most significant subsystems seem to be geographically based, and we give them regional names, such as the Middle East subsystem. But few subsystems are based on geography alone. The problems of peace and war between Arabs and Israel involve many actors that are geographically proximate but others, such as the United States, that are geographically remote. Also, many Arab and Islamic governments and groups, like Algeria, are just peripherally involved in Arab-Israeli quarrels. And, if one thinks about access to energy and oil prices, corporations like EXXON and consumers in the United States could be considered within the subsystem.

System Boundaries.   By identifying which actors are in a subsystem and which are not, we are demarcating the subsystem's *boundaries,* but as our example suggests, this is no simple task. The decision is essentially subjective, determined by the original definition of the issue. Just as no signs hang in space to demarcate the heavenly bodies in our solar system, so there are no objective criteria for determining which actors are part of a subsystem and which are not. The concept is an intellectual tool intended to focus attention and facilitate analysis. It is not an objective reality.

In sum, geography can facilitate or inhibit formation of a system. Throughout history, people have interacted with those they were geographically near to, and so systems often reflect geographic realities. Geographic barriers such as mountain ranges and oceans typically limited the possibilities for systems and still do somewhat. War and trade are possible only if people are physically accessible to each other. Isolation has saved from invasion island countries like Great Britain and Japan, as well as the North American and Australian continents, which have fostered isolationist policies for lengthy periods.

Growing Interdependence of the Global Political System

Technological changes are producing greater interaction than ever before and allowing greater specialization around the world. Interaction and specialization, in turn, have produced interdependence among actors. People can, massively and almost instantly, alter the lives of those living on the other side of the globe. Ideas and images travel at the speed of light, and weapons of mass destruction can span oceans in minutes. Indeed, growing interdependence, perhaps more than any other development, is what provoked political scientists to borrow the system idea from the biologists who originally conceived it.

Systems and subsystems vary significantly in the tightness of their weave. Sometimes interdependence is modest. Each actor's behavior affects others, but only after much time and then marginally. In other systems, each actor's initiative instantly affects others and does so profoundly. Thus, when financial crisis engulfed Mexico in late 1994 because of the depreciation of the peso and the rapid flight of capital, the Clinton administration quickly put together an aid package.

Undersecretary of the Treasury Lawrence H. Summers justified the effort by arguing that "we've recognized the central importance of Mexico to the United States because it is our second-largest trading partner, because we share a 2,000-mile border and because our societies are so closely intertwined."[3] U.S. officials feared that the crisis would spread to financial markets throughout Latin America, endanger the prosperity of American investors, undermine support for NAFTA, and increase illegal Mexican immigration into the United States.

Actors' interdependence extends beyond single subsystems. Actors interact over various issues, some of which overlap, and they participate together in various subsystems. The same actors may find themselves tightly linked in some subsystems and loosely connected in others. Where issues overlap, interdependent actors can bargain across system boundaries, surrendering something on one issue in return for a concession on another. Interaction in one subsystem often has consequences—intended or unintended—in others. The global economy illustrates interdependence of issues across subsystems. If the Federal Reserve Board increases U.S. interest rates to dampen the domestic economy by reducing consumer spending and borrowing, wealthy Japanese investors may be more inclined to invest in U.S. securities. Yet those are the funds that Japan needs to end recession at home. Here, as on other issues, an action taken for one reason in one policy realm has consequences in another.

Sometimes we are unaware how closely our fates are linked. All of us are involved in a global ecosystem, yet only in recent decades have we been made aware of such a system. When Brazilians burn and clear their Amazon jungle, they increase levels of carbon dioxide that contributes to global warming and reduces the oxygen we breathe; when Americans drive automobiles, they exacerbate acid rain and the greenhouse effect.

Leaders' success depends on recognizing interdependence. Russian leaders cannot reform Russia's economy without the capital and expertise of Western governments and corporations. Without economic progress, Russian resistance to their leaders' efforts to impose a free market will intensify. Already inflation, unemployment, and a decline in production have encouraged former communists and nationalist extremists who are unhappy that the Soviet empire and its centralized system have collapsed. But, just as Russian leaders need the West to accomplish reform, so Western leaders need Russia's cooperation to accomplish their aims, especially ending the arms race and preventing nuclear proliferation. Nuclear disarmament imposes financial and technological burdens on Russia, however. No country has ever undertaken nuclear disarmament, and disposing of nuclear wastes is complex. Russia could not accomplish this task without infusions of Western aid and advice, and the West could not reduce the nuclear threat or prevent nuclear proliferation without Russian cooperation. Without economic assistance from the West, Russia might sell sophisticated weapons to others, including America's adversaries, for hard currency.

System interdependence makes it imperative that leaders see the world through the eyes of those with whom they must deal. If they assume that others think as they do, their policies are likely to fail. President Lyndon Johnson's efforts to force North Vietnam to capitulate between 1965 and 1968 failed partly because he believed the Vietnamese perceived the world in the same way as Texans did. He thus wrongly concluded that they would compromise to protect their country's infrastructure from destruction. Japan's recent efforts to gain higher political status have been

TABLE 5.1
*Characteristics of a
Political System:
Key Concepts*

Defining Characteristics	
Parts	Basic components of a system.
Wholes	Result of interaction among the system's parts.
Interaction	Sequence of actions in which one actor's behavior elicits a response from others.
Interdependence	Linked fates in which any unit's welfare depends on decisions by other units.
Feedback	"Information" from previous interaction that structures responses to future actions.
Political Features	
Actors	Individuals, groups, states, international organizations that act jointly toward the same ends.
Political issues	Matters of common interest and concern over which political actors contend and bargain.
Political system	Issues that link actors.
Subsystems	Extensive interaction over specific issues among actors within a larger system.

undermined by its failure to appreciate Asians' sensitivity to anything that smacks of World War II. Japanese decisions to send troops to Cambodia to aid the United Nations in that country, transport enriched nuclear fuel by ship from France, and increase economic cooperation with the Association of Southeast Asian Nations (ASEAN), however innocent, heightened Asian fears of resurgent Japanese ambitions.

Table 5.1 summarizes our discussion so far. We began by focusing on the factors that define a political system (parts, wholes, interaction, interdependence, and feedback), then explained how issues and actors constitute the building blocks of systems and the subsystems within them. The manner in which parts are arranged mainly defines a political system, and that arrangement constitutes *system structure—* the distribution of resources and attitudes.

Structural Properties of Global Systems

All systems have a framework within which actors behave, and understanding that structure provides valuable clues about why actors act as they do. Leaders, for example, often explain their policy toward the Middle East as an effort to maintain a balance of power between Israel and the Arab states. This explanation implies a system structure that determines what is possible and what is probable in that system. Unquestionably, the most important structural property of the global system is the absence of any central government or authority that can prevent conflict or enforce agreements. This condition is what theorists refer to when they speak of *anarchy.*

Anarchy and Absence of Trust

The power-politics tradition sees conflict resulting from the equal status of acquisitive actors and the absence of a central authority to regulate their behavior, arbitrate their quarrels, or enforce agreements among them. Actors can make treaties or reach understandings, but there is no way to enforce them. In other words, anarchy leads to an *absence of trust.* A state can rely on no one but itself and its own capabilities. Some power-politics theorists go farther, arguing that "the fundamental goal of states in any relationship is to prevent others from achieving advances in their relative capabilities."[4] Thus the absence of trust is only part of the problem; states are preoccupied by relative gains and will not cooperate if others gain more than they do.

The absence of trust is a structural problem—the absence of central authority—and it matters little whether people are good or evil by nature. French political philosopher Jean-Jacques Rousseau illustrated this problem with a simple story of five men in the "state of nature"—the *stag-hare parable.* These men recognize that they can satisfy their hunger by cooperating to capture a stag. But, asks Rousseau, what if "a hare happened to pass within reach of one of them"? His answer is that "it must not be doubted that he pursued it without scruple, and that, having caught his prey, he troubled himself very little about having caused his companions to miss theirs."[5]

Unlike theorists who argue that the human propensity to engage in conflict arises from their evil nature,[6] Rousseau believed that human beings were by nature benign. He reasoned that each of the five hunters "certainly felt strongly that for this purpose he ought to remain faithfully at his post."[7] The problem arises from the logic of a situation in which there is no way for the hunter to assure himself that his comrades have not seen the hare and no way to be certain that they will not desert their post to take it and satisfy their hunger. The hunter also recognizes that if he cannot trust the others, then they cannot trust him, and so on ad infinitum.

In seizing the hare, the hunter is pursuing his immediate interest at the expense of his long-term interest and is endangering the well-being of the group as a whole. His four comrades will no longer be able to catch the stag and are unlikely to cooperate with him again. And if they catch him, they will surely avenge themselves. A paradox is described by Kenneth Waltz: "Reason could have told him [the hunter who catches the hare] that his long-run interest depends on establishing, through experience, the conviction that cooperative action will benefit all of the participants. But reason also tells him that if he foregoes the hare, the man next to him might leave his post to chase it, leaving the first man with nothing but food for thought on the folly of being loyal."[8]

The absence of trust and the resulting pressure to pursue immediate individual interests at the expense of long-term collective ones lie at the heart of the *security dilemma.* This metaphor suggests that, without reliable enforcement, actors can trust one another only at their own peril, but efforts by each to augment its own security will be seen as threatening by other actors and so increase their security.

It reflects too how interaction can produce an outcome that actors neither sought nor predicted.

The dilemma can be illustrated by an analogy borrowed from game theory.[9] Two suspects are arrested for robbery. They are placed in separate cells, unable to communicate with each other, and interrogated separately. Each is informed that if neither confesses both will receive a light sentence: one year in prison. If both confess, they will get heavy sentences of eight years in prison. If only one confesses and the other does not, the first will be released, and the second will receive the heaviest possible sentence: ten years. In this situation, an absence of trust prevents players from cooperating.

Figure 5.2 depicts the choices for both prisoners, and the numbers ("values") in the boxes of the matrix represent the joint payoffs that each can receive from available strategies ("no confession" or "confession"). The best joint solution is for neither to confess (outcome 1:1). In doing so, however, each risks that the other may turn state's evidence and confess, in which case the one who does not confess will receive a ten-year sentence, and the "defector" will get off scot-free. Neither prisoner can trust the other, and each must confess to avoid the possibility that the other will do so. By confessing, each guarantees his best payoff under the potentially worst conditions. This is known as a *maximin strategy* because it assures each a maximum minimum. The paradox is that their joint payoff (outcome 2:2) is worse for both than the payoff for joint cooperation (outcome 1:1).[10]

The maximin "solution" in the *prisoner's dilemma*—confession—reflects the participants' aversion to situations in which their well-being depends on someone else's goodwill. With no enforcement mechanism, each player has an incentive to cheat, not for gain but as protection against cheating by the other player. The problem of trust is even greater in global politics because the penalty for error may be national extinction.

Various real-world situations resemble the prisoner's dilemma. In international trade, one state may place obstacles to importing goods from others—quotas, inspection requirements, and so on[11]—because it believes that they will do the same. Each may seek to protect its industries from the *possibility* that others will seek to protect theirs. If one state fails to protect local industries while others do so, it may wake up to discover that its industries have lost markets and are no longer competitive. This is precisely the argument made by American leaders when they threatened to impose high tariffs on imported Japanese luxury cars in May 1995.

Arms control also resembles the prisoner's dilemma. Figure 5.3 depicts the general problem facing an actor that is deciding whether or not to agree to disarm. If both actors continue to arm (outcome 2:2), they will pay a price in continued arms expenditures and political tension. By contrast, mutual disarmament (outcome 1:1) eliminates economic and political costs and is the most advantageous mutual outcome. If actors agree to disarm, however, each runs the risk that the other will cheat by either hiding weapons or building new ones surreptitiously. Then the disarmed actor might find itself at a real, even life-threatening disadvantage.

The incentive is strong to avoid the risks associated with outcomes 1:2 and 2:1.[12] The possibility that one of the parties to an arms-control agreement might cheat is frightening. As in the prisoner's dilemma, those involved in negotiating arms-control agreements ask themselves whether they can trust each other; they

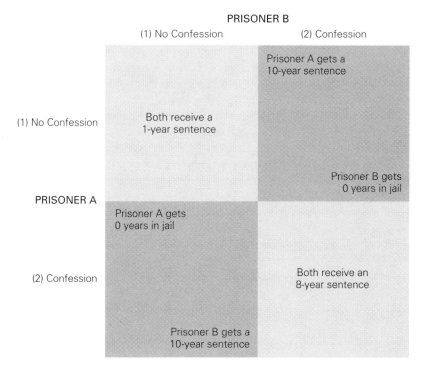

PRISONER B

(1) No Confession   (2) Confession

Prisoner A gets a
10-year sentence

(1) No Confession   Both receive a
1-year sentence

Prisoner B gets
0 years in jail

PRISONER A

Prisoner A gets
0 years in jail

(2) Confession   Both receive an
8-year sentence

Prisoner B gets a
10-year sentence

FIGURE 5.2
Prisoner's Dilemma

The prisoner's dilemma depicts a situation in which players cannot achieve
the *mutually* best outcome ("no confession") because each fears that the
other will confess to get off scot free. Both confess because they cannot trust
each other and receive 8-year sentences. The game illustrates the security
dilemma in global politics under conditions of anarchy.

are, in the words of one observer, "trapped in the double-defection box of a prisoner's dilemma."[13] One can imagine the consequences of a situation in which the
United States and Russia signed an agreement to destroy all nuclear weapons that
one did not honor. If the United States carries out its end of the bargain but Russia
hides 100 missiles, Washington would be at a terrible disadvantage. Trust requires
something to back up the mutual pledge and provide both sides with confidence
in the agreement. That is why means of verification—ability to monitor compliance with an arms-control agreement—has a vital role in arms-control negotiations.

Anarchy in global politics reflects a distribution of power and authority among
a variety of actors, and the way in which capabilities and attitudes are distributed
has a major impact on global politics.

**The Importance of
Distribution**

When neorealists refer to the absence of an authority above states, they are making
a statement about the distribution of power in the system. If power were concentrated in a world government, for example, it could prevent wars from breaking

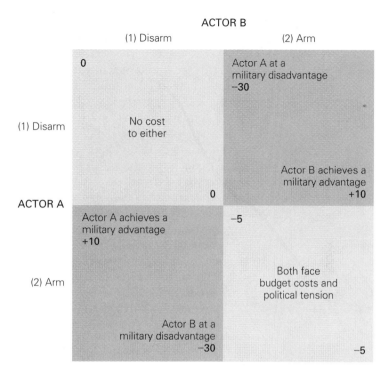

FIGURE 5.3
The Disarmament Game

Efforts to achieve disarmament are a form of the prisoner's dilemma game. Although players could benefit by disarming, each fears the other might "cheat." As a result, both may continue to arm and face budget costs and continued political tension.

out. Without such a government, power is distributed widely, and it is this condition that they believe permits war to occur.

In describing the structure of the global system, we start by outlining how military resources are distributed, including the number of army divisions each actor has, the relative strengths of their air forces, how modern their equipment is, how good their training and mobilization plans are, and so on. We also examine how strong the actors' economies are, how high the quality of their education systems is, how easily available critical raw materials are, and other data that can tell us how resources are distributed. From such data, we can paint a preliminary picture of the global system. But the picture would be incomplete, lacking color and tone. Knowing about resources tells us little until we learn about the intentions, loyalties, and historical memories of actors.

Resources are created to serve actors' objectives, and their attitudes tell us how those resources are likely to be used. What do people think of each other? Do they like or trust each other? What are their memories of each other, what do they intend to do to one another, and what do they expect others to do to them? In the

Middle East, for example, Arab-Israeli expectations are changing, and, as a result, the framework of Middle East politics is dramatically different than it was in 1948, 1967, or even 1990.

How resources are distributed and redistributed affects the distribution and redistribution of attitudes and vice versa. Publics and leaders in less-developed countries are often jealous of Western wealth, and such jealousy produces hostility. Economic assistance rarely inspires gratitude. Instead, beneficiaries may resent those on whom they depend. As societies grow wealthier, citizens may turn more conservative in outlook, seeking to guard what they have from have-nots. Consequently, once we have examined how resources and attitudes are distributed, we must learn how they are related to each other.

The structure of a political system tells us what is possible and what is probable in that system. Specifically, its distribution of resources tells us what *can happen,* and its distribution of attitudes tells us what *is likely to happen* within the possible. Before defining *resources* and *attitudes,* let us consider why we pay attention to distribution and redistribution rather than absolute level. The absolute level of India's resources matters less in understanding politics on the Indian subcontinent than recognizing that Indian capabilities are greater than those of others in the region, including Pakistan, Sri Lanka, Nepal, Afghanistan, and Burma. The fact that India's territory is four times Pakistan's and that India has a population over seven times Pakistan's and an economy five times larger than Pakistan's helps explain Pakistan's fear of India and hostility when India throws its weight around.

Weapons of mass destruction—nuclear, chemical, and biological—also illustrate how distribution matters more than absolute level. Such weapons enable their possesser to annihilate adversaries. But that information alone tells us little until we know how these weapons are distributed. One reason neither the United States nor the Soviet Union used nuclear weapons against the other is that both had them. Knowing that two governments controlled incomparably large and sophisticated nuclear arsenals explains a remarkable and nonobvious paradox: The two actors that held the greatest potential military threat over each other were unlikely to attack each other. The Cold War did *not* become hot partly because of the distribution of weapons of mass destruction.

Peace between the United States and the Soviet Union was an emergent property—that is, peace emerged from the interaction of two hostile actors that were deterred from attacking each other by their possessing nuclear weapons. The outcome—peace—was a surprise to many observers who feared that the Cold War would sooner or later explode into World War III. Although neither superpower was inherently peace-loving, the system's structure, particularly the nuclear stalemate, prevented either from initiating war against the other. And as the distribution of such weapons changes, we expect the probability of peace will also change. As more actors acquire nuclear weapons, complexity and uncertainty make it difficult for any actor to plan a rational defense budget or strategy.

Now the question is, What would be the emergent properties of a system in which nuclear weapons were widely held? One possibility is that an actor might try to prepare itself against all possible enemies. If it did so, the rest would see that actor as a grave threat, and, in turn, seek to add to their armaments (or ally with each other). A frightening arms race would be on, and the risk of war between some or all of the actors would increase. In this example, the arms race and war would be emergent properties. Alternatively, the spread of nuclear weapons might make those possessing them feel more secure, increasing the general feeling of security and the probability of peace, a very different set of emergent properties.

An actor arms against those it fears, and here the distribution of attitudes comes into play. If Pakistanis were to wake up to the news that one of their military bases had been destroyed in a nuclear attack, perpetrator unknown, many would conclude that India was the attacker. After all, Pakistan and India possess nuclear weapons, have gone to war repeatedly since their partition and independence in August 1947, and heatedly dispute the status of Kashmir. By contrast, few Pakistanis could imagine that the attack might have been carried out by the United States or China (though both have the capability to do so) because both have been Pakistan's friends and allies.[14]

Attitude distribution is the key. If Pakistanis knew about nothing more than *distribution of resources*—nuclear weapons—they would have no reason to suspect India more than any other nuclear power. Judging by distribution of resources, it would have been *possible* for any of them to carry out the attack. Knowing attitudes is critical in converting knowledge about what is *possible* into conclusions about what is *probable*. For the observer of global politics, understanding how attitudes are distributed provides useful clues just as understanding motives is critical to a detective trying to solve a crime.

Systems have other emergent properties besides their propensity to conflict. *Distribution of influence* is one such property, and it is the consequence of interaction, the redistribution of resources and attitudes, and other systemic factors such as changes in technology. Another property is *compatibility of goals,* which reflects how the actors perceive their interests, others' interests, and their own experience. Goals in less-developed countries are incompatible with those of Western societies to the extent that have-nots and haves pursue different ends. The former seek change that will redistribute wealth in their favor, and the latter seek stability to safeguard their prosperity.

Another emergent property in a system is *alliances* and *alignments*—actors cooperating by pooling their strength to achieve objectives. Alliances are conditioned by expectations, affect, and identities. Thus the British-American relationship is facilitated by a history of cordial relations, shared traits like language, shared interests and common enemies, and expectations of continued amicable relations in the future.

System stability, a final emergent property, is *the ability of other structural features of a system to maintain themselves over time.* A system is stable to the extent that redistributing resources and attitudes does not trigger massive and rapid changes in the distribution of influence, compatibility of goals, or alliances. Stability is thus a propensity—systems are more or less stable, not stable or unstable. The bipolar system after 1945—the Cold War system—was relatively stable. Influence remained more or less evenly divided between the two poles, Soviet-U.S. goals remained in competition, and alliance systems remained intact despite arms races, regional conflicts, several large wars, and major technological and economic change. By contrast, global politics was less stable after 1918 when the German, Austro-Hungarian, Russian, and Ottoman empires collapsed; new states appeared in Central Europe; the British and French empires were enfeebled; and waves of nationalism were unleashed, climaxing in World War II. One worry today is declining stability in a number of regions since the Cold War ended.

We now examine in greater detail how resources are distributed, emphasizing differences among types of resources, the problem of harnessing them to goals, and limitations on ways of using them. Thereafter, we will look more closely at attitudes to see how they are related to resources.

Distribution of Resources in Global Politics

The only resources that matter in global politics are those that actors can use to achieve goals and objectives or prevent others from doing so. Guns and plutonium count more than stamps. Resources can be either tangible, like precious metals, or intangible, like citizens' morale. The list of vital resources endlessly changes to keep pace with technological, economic, and other innovations. For centuries, territory was the major source of wealth, and population was indispensable to military victory. Today, technological skills and entrepreneurship contribute more to wealth than territory and more to military capability than manpower. Indeed, this shift was essential in transforming international politics into postinternational politics.

Tangible and Intangible Resources

Tangible resources such as population and land are easy to see and measure, and they get more attention from officials than such elusive *intangible resources* as popular satisfaction, citizens' morale, and diplomatic skill. Because dependable and accurate information about intangible resources is difficult to get, decision-makers may disregard them in their calculations or resort to wishful thinking in estimating them.

Soviet dictator Josef Stalin did not recognize how important intangible resources were. He did not understand the barrier that Catholicism posed to communist rule in Eastern Europe, and asked sarcastically, "How many divisions has the pope got?" Since the pope had no armies at his disposal, Stalin believed that the pope could not resist Soviet power. As Stalin and other Soviet leaders discovered, the pope's intangible resources—prestige and moral authority—enabled him to mold Catholic opinion in Eastern Europe.

As a rule, leaders overestimate friends' and allies' intangible resources and underestimate their enemies' intangible resources. They may assume that those who lead friendly countries are popular and that public morale in those countries is high. Thus U.S. leaders consistently overestimated popular support for Jiang Jieshi (Chiang Kai-shek)—"their man"—during the Chinese civil war that pitted Jiang's Guomintang (Nationalist Party) against Mao Zedong's communists. Soviet leaders erred similarly in steadfastly supporting Dr. Sayid Mohammed Najibullah as president of Afghanistan between 1986 to 1991. The opposite tendency was evident in the U.S. belief that Cubans were itching to overthrow Fidel Castro after his revolution toppled an American-supported regime in 1959. As a result, the U.S.-sponsored Cuban émigré invasion of the Bay of Pigs in 1961 was doomed to failure.

Failure to appreciate intangible factors can have unexpected consequences. For example, Hitler decided to launch a bombing blitz against British cities in 1940, believing that it would undermine British morale. In fact, it had the opposite effect. The communist hard-liners' coup d'état to overthrow Gorbachev in August 1991 reflected a similar ignorance of intangible resources. Assuming that many Soviet citizens and officials, especially Soviet military leaders, yearned for the good old days, the hard-liners discovered too late that they were wrong. Their plot collapsed and hastened the demise of the Communist Party and dismemberment of the Soviet Union—precisely the outcome they had sought to prevent.

Knowing how global resources are distributed, we have some idea about what actors *can* do to each other—their *capability*—but not what they *will* do. Most governments ferret out information about others' capabilities. Intelligence agencies use spies, informants, radio intercepts, and sophisticated space satellites to collect such data. Although some information about capabilities is hard to get, it is more difficult to fathom an adversary's *intentions*. To do so with confidence may require a mole in the adversary's inner councils.[15]

Because it is almost impossible to be sure about an adversary's intentions, leaders infer them from known capabilities. They assume the worst and, too often, prepare for it. Late in 1992, it was revealed that Iran was purchasing modern submarines from Russia. The Iranians may have meant them for defending oil-loading platforms in the Persian Gulf if hostilities reignited with Iraq, or the submarines may have had no mission but were purchased because Russia was selling them at bargain rates. United States military leaders, however, dispatched nuclear-attack submarines to the Persian Gulf because Iran's new submarines enabled that country to wreak havoc on Western oil tankers, perhaps even closing the narrow Strait of Hormuz through which ships leaving the gulf must pass.[16] Nevertheless, Iranian acquisition of modern weapons meant that the country's Muslim fundamentalist leaders *might* have sinister intentions toward the West and Arab oil producers in the region. Because certainty was impossible, the Pentagon made a conservative assessment and took steps to prevent Iran from carrying out its worst-case objectives. In all likelihood, Teheran saw Washington's decision to send nuclear submarines as provocative and threatening.

Putting Resources to Work

Merely possessing resources does not mean that an actor can or will achieve its objectives and goals. Resources are "things" that may be helpful in pursuing objectives but that the actor may not use or may use inefficiently. When wealth is employed to provide assistance to others, it is being used directly for foreign-policy ends, but it may be used for purposes that are irrelevant to global politics. Thus, prior to Iraq's invasion in August 1990, Kuwait's ruling emir had spent the country's huge wealth on raising citizens' standard of living. Much had also been squandered on luxuries or invested overseas, but little had been spent to develop Kuwait's military capability. Kuwaiti displays of wealth merely goaded the neighboring Iraqis to jealousy. Where the Kuwaitis had expended wealth in pursuing foreign-policy objectives, they had done so foolishly, trying to bribe Iraq by granting it huge loans during its war with Iran (1980–1988). The wealthy may have great potential for achieving foreign-policy objectives, but wealth alone does not ensure that they will do so.

Resources are not equally useful for all objectives; political leaders tend to overlook this limitation, assuming that if resources are useful in some cases, they are useful in all.[17] This error may have tragic consequences. Humbling experiences in Vietnam and Afghanistan made it clear to American and Soviet leaders that military force has limited value if the objective is to win the local population's hearts and minds and thereby prop up friendly governments. The lesson is difficult for politicians to learn, and the United States continues to use its military resources to achieve objectives for which such resources may be ill suited, such as suppressing cocaine production and export in Peru and Colombia. Russia made the same error in its effort to crush Chechnya. In all likelihood, military resources will mean less in a postinternational world that is more absorbed by economic, environmental, and even gender cleavages than by territorial quarrels.

Resources are effective only for a limited number of people and types of behavior.[18] A medical doctor's resources consist mostly of knowledge and experience, and the doctor's influence is limited to patients (number of people) and health issues (type of behavior). Wealth, experience, and expertise make such giant banks as Citibank or Barclays major players in settling the problem of how debtor countries like Russia will repay their enormous debts, but the banks have little leverage in other global issues.

Barriers to mobilizing resources and applying them effectively and efficiently are numerous, as we see in the trade-off between guns and butter. It is difficult to convert consumer industries to a "war effort" or military resources to serve civilian needs. Automobile factories may be used to produce tanks, hosiery companies may make parachutes, and chemical industries may turn out poison gas. Some industries, however, can serve few military purposes and have to go out of business until the war is over.

The opposite problem—going from military to civilian use—is even trickier, as the United States and Russia discover as they reduce armaments. Retraining and housing hundreds of thousands of unemployed troops withdrawn from Eastern Europe and the Baltic republics posed a threat to Russia's political stability.[19] Few novel uses can be found for nuclear warheads, though some of the material can be reprocessed and used for civilian energy, and there is concern that fissionable material from Russia is being stolen. In the United States, converting resources from military to civilian purposes caused economic dislocation and unemployment in states such as California and was a controversial issue in the 1992 presidential campaign. The Clinton administration appropriated funding to help regions adjust to defense conversion and also sought to cushion Russia's effort to do so. It also decided to close down military bases inside and outside the United States despite local resistance.

Geographic Location

Location may be an important resource. Before the present century, location could give actors advantages or disadvantages. Relative isolation from continental power in Europe and Asia gave Britain and Japan security, whereas Poland, lying between Germany and Russia, and Korea, between China and Russia, had reason to feel insecure.

Geopolitics involves analyzing the relationship between politics and geography.[20] This discipline was in vogue during the nineteenth-century heyday of imperialism when ambitions began to collide at the fringes of Europe and beyond. Among the most celebrated geopolitical analysts was a studious U.S. naval officer, Alfred Thayer Mahan, who argued that global influence is determined by control of the seas, especially strategic chokepoints astride the sea-lanes of global commerce. These included the Straits of Gibraltar[21] between Europe and Africa at the Atlantic entrance to the Mediterranean; the Strait of Malacca between Sumatra and the Malay Peninsula (connecting the Pacific and Indian Oceans and dominated by the British naval base in Singapore); the Dardanelles (guarding the mouth of the Black Sea and dominated by the Turkish fortresses at Gallipoli); the English Channel between the British and French coasts (linking the Atlantic Ocean and the North Sea); the Skaggerak between Denmark and Norway (providing an outlet from the Baltic into the North Sea); and the Suez Canal (linking the Mediterranean and Red Seas). Mahan believed that to become a world power the United States had to acquire and protect a canal across the Isthmus of Panama and the Hawaiian Islands.[22]

Just before World War I, a British student of geopolitics, Sir Halford J. Mackinder, fearful of German land power, expressed doubt that naval power alone could ensure British security. Mackinder's nightmare was an alliance between Germany and Russia, because their geographic position would give them control of the "world island"—Europe, Asia, and Africa—and therefore global supremacy. Mackinder's view of geopolitics was summed up in an aphorism:

> Who rules East Europe commands the Heartland;
> Who rules the Heartland commands the World Island;
> Who rules the World Island commands the World.[23]

Both Mahan and Mackinder saw geography as determining global influence, but we should not conclude that geography is destiny. A country needs access to the sea to become a sea power, but only a few countries with such access do so. Although Great Britain became a maritime power, Japan left its isolation to do so only late in the nineteenth century. Nor does a long, shared border necessarily produce conflict, as U.S.-Canadian relations and postwar Franco-German relations show.

Moreover, advances in technology now enable people to interact at almost any distance, reducing the significance of geography. With jet bombers and intercontinental ballistic missiles, countries can destroy each other at vast distances. Modern computers, facsimile printers, and telephones provide instant communication around the world, and corporations can move billions of dollars across oceans in seconds.

Size and Development

The absolute level of resources controlled by an actor or to which it has access reflects its *size* and indicates its potential oomph or clout in global politics. The average citizen's possession of resources reflects an actor's *social and economic development* and indicates how effectively it can use the resources it has. Neither indicator alone adequately measures an actor's capabilities or its likely success in pursuing objectives. "Big states act differently than small states. Rich states behave in ways that poor states cannot."[24]

Some years ago Bruce M. Russett, using factor analysis, a statistical technique, concluded that combining an actor's *total population, total gross national product,* and *total land area* yielded a measure for size.[25] A large population is the raw material for big armies and plentiful labor; total GNP reflects the overall size of an actor's economy; and total land area is the space it has for everything from agriculture to homes and cities. Of course Russia and China rank high on all three and are "big players" in the game of world politics. Others that are big include India, Brazil, Indonesia, and Iran. When such countries act, everyone, at least in their region, notices, and many are affected by their action. As the role of trade grows and that of territory declines, the cast of "big" actors will shift.

Russia, China, and the other big actors mentioned above are not economically advanced, and poverty and inadequate technology limit how effectively their leaders can use their size to achieve what they want. Although the former Soviet Union created an immense military machine, it could not provide its citizens with basic consumer goods, including food and housing, or compete with other modern societies in such high-technology fields as computers. The communist regime collapsed because it failed to deal with the country's economic crises, as the tsarist system had failed seven decades earlier.

Social and economic development is reflected by other indicators: number of people per physician, number of radios per capita, gross national product per capita, number of students in higher education per capita, literacy rate, ratio of population living in cities, and percentage of labor force in agriculture.[26] Combined, these indicators reveal that some small countries—Canada, Belgium, New Zealand, the Netherlands, Sweden, Switzerland, Israel, and Denmark—are highly "developed." With exceptions such as the United States, Japan, and Germany, those that rank highest on one scale are different from those on the other, as seen in Table 5.2

As in football, often the biggest players are not the most skilled. Size alone tells us little about relative wealth and modernity. People in small countries like Switzerland and Sweden enjoy a far higher standard of living than do people in China and India, and a number of small countries are significant in global politics because they provide vital technical services to others—in effect, exporting skills. Singapore, little more than a city-state, has achieved influence throughout Southeast Asia because it provides varied skills, from medicine to business training, to its larger neighbors.

Modernity is neither inherently superior nor inferior. Some praise it because they equate it with physical comfort and leisure; others decry its accompanying pollution and erosion of spiritual values. Undeniably, societies increasingly need *brains* rather than *muscle* to satisfy human needs. Good health requires doctors; high technology requires knowledge and therefore education; supplying adequate food and clothing for growing populations depends on know-how. Military security and economic competitiveness also depend on science and technology. Populations that are well educated have the skills to provide products and services that are in demand around the world. Today wealth is increasingly the product of skills, and wealth, in turn, is necessary to gain such skills.

Such data are important to observers of global politics because they tell us how effectively a society can apply the resources that make "size" to achieve society's objectives. Education is needed to use technology effectively, and highly skilled soldiers are needed for modern weaponry. Literacy and education are critical for managing complex government, military, and corporate bureaucracies, and such

TABLE 5.2
Top Twenty-five Countries 1996

Per capita GNP (development)	Total GNP (size)
1. Switzerland	1. United States
2. Japan	2. Japan
3. Norway	3. Germany
4. Denmark	4. France
5. Singapore	5. United Kingdom
6. Germany	6. Italy
7. Austria	7. China
8. United States	8. Brazil
9. Belgium	9. Canada
10. France	10. Spain
11. Netherlands	11. South Korea
12. Sweden	12. Netherlands
13. Hong Kong (China)	13. Australia
14. Finland	14. India
15. Australia	15. Russia
16. Italy	16. Mexico
17. United Kingdom	17. Switzerland
18. Canada	18. Argentina
19. Ireland	19. Belgium
20. Israel	20. Sweden
21. New Zealand	21. Austria
22. Spain	22. Indonesia
23. Greece	23. Turkey
24. South Korea	24. Thailand
25. Portugal	25. Denmark

SOURCE: *World Development Indicators 1995,* Table 1.1, pp. 12–14 and Table 3, pp. 166–167.

bureaucracies—international, transnational, national, and even local—are crucial in dealing with the complex issues that confront societies. When the United Nations sought to ferry food supplies to end famine in Somalia, supervise a peaceful transition in Cambodia, or oversee elections in Angola and Mozambique, it recruited highly trained civil and military administrators.

Modernity also means a scientific and secular outlook or way of looking at the world. Citizens in modern societies believe problems can be overcome by applying science and technology rather than accepting them fatalistically as divinely ordained. Such citizens build dams to deal with floods and spend huge sums to build laboratories like the National Institutes of Health in Washington, D.C., to deal with diseases like AIDS. They are also trained to think and behave independently and to use individual initiative in coping with challenges.

Modern military personnel are trained to assume command and continue to fight effectively after losing senior officers. By contrast, soldiers in traditional societies, however brave, are ill prepared to fight effectively if their leaders are out of action.[27] Recognizing this dependence facilitated the British conquest of South Africa and Europe's expansion in the New World. The indigenous Zulus of South Africa, the Aztecs of Mexico, and other American Indians showed ingenuity and courage in defending their lands, but their well-armed enemy could reduce their military effectiveness by intentionally killing their chiefs. During this century, too, those with traditional values have found it difficult to fight effectively against modern foes. The Russian army's catastrophic defeats at the hands of the Germans in 1914 owed much to the Russian peasant soldiers' inability to use effectively the modern equipment they were given—field radios, trains, and so on.[28]

Education, technological training, and social change are necessary for citizens of traditional societies to overcome overpopulation and poverty. Traditional value systems provide spiritual and psychological sustenance but do not foster an outlook conducive to economic growth or scientific discovery. They encourage identification with family and locality but discourage participation in economic markets and social systems. Finally, they emphasize collective rather than individual behavior and rewards.

Capability and Status in Global Politics

The distribution of resources in the global system is highly skewed. Almost three-fifths of 130 countries for which data were available in 1996 had a per capita gross national product (GNP) of less than $2,000 a year, and only nineteen enjoyed per capita GNP in excess of $10,000 a year.[29] It is a world with few top dogs in which the cleavage between rich and poor is exacerbated by regional and racial differences. Of the twenty-five top dogs, over four-fifths are European or populated by those of European descent. By contrast, twenty-three of the poorest thirty-one countries are sub-Saharan African and seven are Asian.[30]

And the growing diffusion of television, radio, motion pictures, glossy magazines, and tourism makes underdogs aware of their relative deprivation. As a result, the many are envious of the few but unable to do much about it except try to migrate. Amid this frustration, the poor may resort to violence and seek the means, even weapons of mass destruction, to force redistribution of resources and get a more equitable share of the world's wealth. The gap and resulting frustration will grow because the world's poorest societies also have the world's highest birth rates.

Inequality *within* poor societies is also sharp.[31] In Latin America, for example, enormous concentrations of land and wealth are held by tiny elites, while many people live in poverty in urban shanties or on small rural plots. Cycles of chronic instability and spasms of political violence, crime, extremism, and military authoritarianism are the companions of inequality. Such a cycle has plagued Latin America, as in the civil war that engulfed El Salvador throughout the 1980s until the peace agreement of 1992 and in the violence in Haiti that persisted even after the restoration to power of the country's popularly elected president, the Rev. Jean-Bertrand Aristide, in late 1994. The main causes were economic inequality, intensified by a growing population of landless peasants, and resistance by elites to change.

The *status* or *prestige* of an actor may be thought of as the rank it is accorded by others in the global hierarchy. Actors thought to be important are treated accordingly. The marks of status are many. One is permanent membership on the U.N. Security Council, and this is why Germany and Japan have expressed interest in such membership. Other marks of status include visits by major leaders,[32] media coverage, and invitations to participate in major conferences. Leaders of high-status actors are routinely consulted by other leaders and have a big part in global decisions. We pay attention to actors that have clout because they can affect our lives. By contrast, we pay little attention to the poor or weak because, with few resources, they seem unable to affect us greatly.

In earlier centuries, diplomatic missions were carefully graded to reflect the relative status accorded states. Ambassadors were assigned only to countries regarded as great powers. Even today, governments, especially those that cannot afford to maintain embassies everywhere, maintain them in high-status countries like the United States (just as major corporations have branch offices in wealthy countries). By carefully observing ambassadorial appointments and the size of embassy staffs, we can get an idea about which actors enjoy high status. United States presidents appoint political donors to plum posts like Tokyo, Paris, and London, and the largest U.S. embassies are in Japan and Germany. Other countries appoint their most experienced diplomats to the United States, as befits the world's remaining superpower.

Leaders—whether prime ministers or CEOs—are sensitive to the status they are accorded. When they are guests at state dinners, they hope to get prestigious seats near their host, and when something significant arises they wish to be consulted. Former French President Charles de Gaulle was prickly on matters of protocol and was sensitive to his role as representative of France. Aware of de Gaulle's sensitivity, President John F. Kennedy sent former U.S. Secretary of State Dean Acheson to speak with the French leader at the height of the 1962 Cuban missile crisis. In one account of their meeting, "De Gaulle raised his hand in a delaying gesture that the long-departed Kings of France might have envied. 'May we be clear before you start,' he said. 'Are you consulting or informing me?' Acheson confessed that he was there to inform, not consult."[33] Countries demand respect and may even go to war over perceived insults.

Actors with many resources usually enjoy high status, so that status and resources are in balance. Sometimes, however, an imbalance may arise. Actors may lose resources yet continue to enjoy high status for some time. Two world wars and decolonization reduced Great Britain from being the center of a great empire and an industrial giant to modest circumstances. Nevertheless, after 1945, London continued to participate in global decision making at the highest levels and to enjoy a "special relationship" with the United States. In the same period, Japan and Germany emerged as economic giants,[34] yet because of the shadow cast by their superpower ally they have only recently begun to receive the attention that their economic muscle merits.

Such imbalance is called *status inconsistency,* and it can be dangerous.[35] Like an aging gunfighter in the Old West, a high-status actor with a declining share of resources may be challenged by upstarts, and, like Austria-Hungary in 1914, it may behave rashly to reverse its growing weakness. Repeatedly challenged by adversaries in the Balkans and elsewhere, the creaking empire sought to avoid its fate with one throw of the dice. When the heir to the imperial throne, Archduke Francis Ferdinand, was assassinated, Austria-Hungary took the opportunity to humiliate upstart Serbia. The result was World War I and the dissolution of the Hapsburg empire. More recently, the 1982 Argentine challenge to British rule of the Falkland Islands (known to Argentina as the Islas Malvinas) seemed an upstart's effort to challenge a declining but still prestigious actor. When a declining actor is challenged, what Robert Gilpin calls hegemonic war ("a war to determine which state or states will be dominant")[36] is always a risk.

Actors that are accorded lower status than they think they deserve may rock the boat until attention is paid them. Germany behaved this way between 1890 and 1914, repeatedly causing crises over such issues as the fate of Morocco. Soviet behavior after 1945 can be explained at least partly as an effort to force others to treat Moscow as a superpower, the status Stalin believed it merited, especially after its sacrifices first to industrialize and then to win World War II. The Soviet leader's desire for respect illustrates how crucial attitudes are in global structure, the topic to which we now turn.

Distribution of Attitudes in Global Politics

If the distribution of resources in world politics tells us what is possible, the *distribution of attitudes* informs us of what is likely to take place. Significant attitudes include *identities, expectations, beliefs,* and *goals.* These attitudes condition how actors will use resources toward each other. Answers to questions such as whether actors like each other, expect friendly acts from each other, and share goals are crucial if we are to make sense of why they behave as they do.

Identities   Identities help determine whom people consider to be friends or foes. People have loyalties to numerous groups and identify with them—government, gender, employer,[37] church, ethnicity, and so on. A person in France might identify with a feminist group seeking gender equality, a farm association trying to hold on to agricultural subsidies, a consumer who would like to reduce such subsidies and so lower food prices, the Catholic Church seeking state funds for parochial schools, or even a right-wing political party seeking to expel France's immigrant population. In complex societies, multiple identities are common.

It is important to discern how people rank their loyalties and whether or not they are compatible. Do we think of ourselves as Americans first or as something else, and do our loyalties clash? Shared identities produce psychological affinity, and conflicting identities produce psychological distance; and the presence or absence of such affinity will reinforce or undermine geographic distance. Thus the major conflicts in global politics are anchored more in attitudes than in geography. Yugoslavs are located in a small geographic area but are separated by an abyss, the product of incompatible self-identities as Serbs, Croats, Albanians, and Muslim Bosnians.

One identity that was believed to defy geography was economic class. In 1848, Karl Marx and Friedrich Engels brought the Communist Manifesto to a stirring conclusion:

The communists disdain to conceal their view and aims. They openly declare that their ends can be attained only by the forcible overthrow of all existing social conditions. Let the ruling classes tremble at a communistic revolution. The proletarians have nothing to lose but their chains. They have a world to win. Workingmen of all countries, unite![38]

Marxists interpreted history as a struggle among classes and tried to ignite a world revolution that would overthrow the bourgeoisie. Repeatedly, however, they overestimated the strength of class identities. In 1914, the Russian revolutionary leader Vladimir Ilych Lenin mistakenly believed that workers would identify with their class rather than with their country and would refuse to fight in World War I. In 1917, when the Bolsheviks seized power in Russia, they believed world revolution was imminent. So confident of this was Leon Trotsky that when he took control of Russia's Foreign Office, he declared: "I will issue some revolutionary proclamations and then close up the joint."[39] The Bolsheviks were wrong, and in the 1920s there ensued a struggle between Trotsky, who wished to pursue the goal of world revolution, and Stalin, who sought to build a power base in the U.S.S.R. before exporting revolution.

Countries are able to act in a unified way only if citizens view them as the ultimate repository of loyalty. When citizens identify with other actors, the state may be torn by conflict. At one extreme is a relatively homogeneous country like Sweden with few rivals for citizens' loyalties. Belgium, on the other hand, is split into rival language groups: Flemish-speaking citizens in the north and French-speaking citizens in the south. Although Belgians are divided over education and other issues, they have contained language-based conflicts by a variety of ingenious political devices.

Things are not so simple in former colonial territories in the less-developed countries, and even Canada, where Europeans imposed boundaries that did not reflect identities. Even today their citizens identify more intensely with entities other than their country, and the result is civil strife. Nigerians think of themselves as Hausa, Ibo, and Yoruba, not Nigerian; these tribal loyalties exploded into bloody civil war between 1967 and 1970, and they remain powerful factors in contemporary Nigeria.[40] Even where civil war is avoided, governments may provide ways for one tribal, language, or religious group to repress or exploit others. In Kenya, for example, members of the Kikuyu and Kalenjin tribes have enjoyed political power at the expense of the Luo since national independence in 1963.

Fortunately, citizens do not usually have to make hard choices among the groups with which they identify. One can be a good American and also be loyal to other groups at home and abroad. There is nothing disloyal about an American whose views on reproductive issues are influenced by loyalty to the Catholic Church or whose views on the Middle East are influenced by identity with Israel and Judaism. The efforts of the church and Israel to influence the American political process are legitimate, and myriad actors participate directly or indirectly, often by employing lobbyists to look after their interests. Sometimes, however, issues force individuals to make difficult choices among deep loyalties. The American Civil War forced people to choose between the United States and the Confederacy, a regional loyalty. This choice was especially painful for the many southerners who had attended the U.S. Military Academy at West Point and were officers in the U.S. Army. One such, Robert E. Lee, became commander of the Confederate Army.

Governments sometimes fear that divided loyalties may engender treason. In the Middle East and North Africa, the governments of Egypt, Syria, Tunisia, Algeria, and Morocco fear fundamentalist Muslims, whose loyalty they suspect. In Asia, the governments of Malaysia and Indonesia look with suspicion on communities of "overseas" Chinese, whose loyalties, they suspect, lie elsewhere, and the Indian government is constantly alert for Sikh, Muslim, and fundamentalist Hindu loyalties that might undermine the fragile unity of the multilingual Indian state.

Like individuals, collective actors identify, feel kinship, and sympathize with each other's goals. Group identities may result from shared historical experience (fighting a war against the same foe) or such traits as language, religion, political ideology, type of political system, and political values.

During the French Revolution and subsequent wars between republican France and the monarchical states of Europe, republican America sympathized with the French cause. Partly this was in gratitude for French help to the colonies during the war for independence and sympathy for another people with similar political institutions. Thomas Jefferson and Alexander Hamilton disputed whether or not the United States should side with France. Jefferson argued that bonds of friendship and ideology required the United States to assist France. Hamilton cited the principle of balance of power to disagree, arguing that the United States was too weak to provide effective assistance and would merely invite British attacks on American commerce.[41] The dispute divided Jefferson's partisans (the Democratic Party) from Hamilton's (the Federalist Party).

In recent decades, British-U.S. ties have been reinforced by the shared experience in World Wars I and II, their common language, and their common heritage. United States–British identities have been strengthened by generations of Americans, like President Bill Clinton, former Justice Byron White, Senator Richard Luger (Ind.), and former Senator Bill Bradley (N.J.), who studied at British universities, and by other forms of people-to-people contact. When the Falklands war began between Britain and Argentina, a debate erupted in the United States about which country to support. One prominent group of Americans led by U.N. Ambassador Jeanne Kirkpatrick favored supporting Argentina because it was in the Western Hemisphere and was a growing power. At first, the Reagan administration tried to take a neutral position, but most Americans identified more closely with the British and the United States finally supported the successful British war effort.

Expectations   What actors expect of each other is a consequence of identities and previous interaction, and such expectations can inspire suspicion or trust. Americans do not expect British hostility but are not surprised by Libyan or Iranian attacks on U.S. interests. Americans identify with the British, and the two peoples have long been friendly. In contrast, most Americans have little in common with the Iran shaped by the Ayatollah Khomeini or Libya under Muammar Qaddafi, and the hostility of these two societies toward the United States readies Americans to expect the worst from them.

When Pan American flight 103 blew up over Lockerbie, Scotland, in December 1988, Americans suspected that Iranian agents were responsible. The Iranian government not only had a reputation for supporting international terrorism but had specifically vowed to avenge the U.S. Navy downing of an Iranian civilian jetliner over the Persian Gulf earlier that year. As the Lockerbie investigation continued, suspicion fell on Libya. Colonel Qaddafi had repeatedly aided international terrorists and had reason to avenge himself for U.S. air raids in April 1986 against Tripoli and Benghazi that had killed one of his children.[42] Cycles of violence are fueled by negative expectations.

In general, people expect the future to resemble the past. Actors that have been in conflict expect such conflict to recur, and those that have had good relations may be surprised if relations sour. Between 1870 and 1913, Europe experienced repeated crises and limited wars. The climate of tension, fear, and frustration these incidents produced made many believe war was inevitable. Ultimately, this "psychology of inevitability" as much as anything else was responsible for the great conflagration of 1914.

Beliefs   What people believe and especially what they regard as right and wrong powerfully shape behavior. Closed sets of beliefs—ideologies—resist change and may produce durable conflicts like the Cold War. Ideological conflicts are especially difficult to compromise and inspire fervor in their adherents. Unlike land and money, ideas cannot be divided fairly. One may depersonalize ideological enemies and declare them anathema, and enemies may seek to extirpate ideological foes. Abraham Lincoln feared the threatened clash between incompatible ideologies when he declared that no nation could exist "half slave and half free." Today, "isms" like Islamic fundamentalism make it difficult for adversaries to find common ground and solve disputes.

At the same time, ideology makes potent new energies available to rulers. With Nazi armies at the gates of Moscow and Leningrad in 1941, Stalin abandoned appeals to Marxist ideology for the more powerful Russian nationalism, and when Mao Zedong took power in China in 1949, he used Marxism-Leninism to mobilize the masses more effectively than previous leaders of the country had done.

Indeed, since the French Revolution, *nationalism*—exclusive attachment to a national or ethnic group—has probably been the most intensely felt "ism" in global politics. Nationalism can be benign, encouraging interest in history, language, and literature, or it can be malignant. It has contributed to starting wars and to the ferocity with which they are fought. Repeatedly, politicians whip up popular fervor for their policies by posing as defenders of the nation. Napoleon almost succeeded in conquering Europe by stirring up French nationalism, and, late in the nineteenth century, Germany's Iron Chancellor, Otto von Bismarck, used nationalism as a cover for repressing opponents at home and carrying out German unification abroad.

Nationalist passions reduce the diplomat's independence and the flexibility of the government's policy. Politicians find it difficult to compromise with adversaries lest they be accused at home of selling out the nation. And during the hard times when flexible policy is needed, nationalism may intensify and grow ugly. Thus, during the 1920s and 1930s, extreme nationalists ended democratic experiments in Italy, Germany, and Japan as people sought simple solutions to social and economic ills. Indeed, part of nationalism's potency as an ideology is its simplicity. It does not depend on complex economic or social theories but merely identifies a heritage (often mythical) shared by a group of people that distinguishes them from others.

Nationalism has resisted challenges by Marxism and liberalism and has survived the Cold War. It remains potent in many parts of the world and has been used to

The yearning for democracy with the end of the Cold War was contagious, even reaching Beijing, capital of the last major communist state. The statue of liberty in Tiananmen Square revealed Chinese aspirations to achieve American-style democracy, but their aspirations were crushed beneath the treads of tanks. *(Reuters/Corbis)*

justify violence by the peoples of the former Yugoslavia, the successor nations to the U.S.S.R., and xenophobic right-wingers in Europe and America. Indeed, political scientist John Mearsheimer triggered a lively debate by arguing that the revival of nationalism might make conflict more likely in Europe than it was during the Cold War. He denies that with the end of the Cold War "harmony can reign among the states and peoples of Europe." Instead, "the decline in nationalism in Europe since 1945 has contributed to the peacefulness of the postwar world."[43] Withdrawing U.S. and Russian troops, ending the nuclear threat, reunifying Germany, and ending communism may all revive dangerous nationalism.

In recent years, democracy has proved a powerful ideological symbol in countries as diverse as China, Indonesia, South Korea, and Nigeria. Young people in particular have increasingly pressured authoritarian leaders to institute democratic practices and institutions.

On the whole, it is unclear whether ideological divisions cause war or whether leaders use such divisions to justify war. The answer is probably a bit of both. Many conflicts (for example, between Catholics and Protestants in Northern Ireland) are clothed in the language of ideology. Leaders can also use ideology to depersonalize an enemy and justify atrocities.[44] The enemy is not a person like us but is a communist, a heretic, or a member of some other hated category.

Goals   Actors' beliefs help determine what they wish to accomplish—their *goals*. If goals are compatible, actors can cooperate; if not, they may find themselves in conflict.

ACTORS SPEAK

Some scholars believe that global outcomes, including war, can be largely explained by features of the global system, especially anarchy. Others argue that explanation must be sought at the level of the individuals or actors that constitute the system rather than the system itself. In the first selection, Kenneth Waltz makes the case for anarchy, and in the second Sigmund Freud argues that human nature is the source of war.

In anarchy, there is no automatic harmony. . . . Because each state is the final judge of its own cause, any state may at any time use force to implement its policies. Because any state may at any time use force, all states must constantly be ready either to counter force with force or to pay the cost of weakness. The requirements of state action are, in this view, imposed by the circumstances in which all states exist. (Kenneth N. Waltz, *Man, the State and War* [New York: Columbia University Press, 1959], p. 160)

We assume that human instincts are of two kinds: those that conserve and unify . . . , and, secondly, the instincts to destroy and kill. . . . With the least of speculative efforts we are led to conclude that this instinct functions in every living being, striving to work its ruin and reduce life to its primal state of inert matter. Indeed, it might well be called the 'death instinct.' (Sigmund Freud, "The Urge to Destruction as the Source of War," in Evan Luard, ed., *Basic Texts in International Relations* [New York: St. Martin's, 1992], pp. 84, 85)

The French revolutionary ideology after 1789 led them to seek the overthrow of the conservative monarchies of Europe, and the Soviet leaders' communist ideology after 1917 led them to help communists elsewhere overthrow capitalism.

In the abstract, goals are efforts to increase human satisfaction—prosperity and peace—and reduce deprivation—poverty, disease, and insecurity. As a rule, people who feel they lack things that they need to survive and be happy make demands on leaders and others in the global system to satisfy those needs. People who are satisfied with their lot try to keep what they have. Conflicts between haves and have-nots are common in global politics, both past and present. In the 1970s, many of these demands were aggregated under pressure exerted in the United Nations for a New International Economic Order (NIEO). In this contest, wealthy states sought to preserve their privileged position, and the poor sought redistribution of resources.

Disputes between haves and have-nots are one example of a larger problem: incompatible goals. Actors assign different priorities to objects that they value. People who are satisfied with their lives rank peace highly, but for those who are starving or are enslaved, peace may be a luxury they cannot afford. Those who sought to appease Hitler in the 1930s were accused of wanting "peace at any price." Every day desperate Kurds, Palestinians, and others say by their deeds that they are willing to sacrifice peace for equality and independence. The patriot Patrick Henry eloquently proposed a similar trade, challenging his fellow Virginians to cast off British rule: "Give me liberty, or give me death!"

Different ordering of what people think is important produces misunderstanding. People who do not share our sense of what is important in similar situations are not necessarily irrational. If we cannot make sense of the values they cherish, we must recognize the cultural and psychological distance that may separate us from them. For Shi'ite Muslims, unlike Americans, ensuring the purity of Islam matters most; for Israelis it may be secure borders; for others it may be a loaf of bread. Value priorities do change, however, driving people's goals further apart or bringing them closer together. North Americans and Europeans, many of whom have not only satisfied basic material needs but enjoy a high standard of living, are increasingly interested in "post-material" goals, including a clean and healthful global environment. The poor inhabitants of the less-developed countries, though, hope to achieve prosperity by industrialization, exacerbating by their determination a number of environmental crises. Inevitably, such differences in value hierarchies lead to disagreements over such issues as deforestation, conservation of energy, and disposal of hazardous wastes.

Conclusion

The belief that the system's structure largely determines behavior is probably misleading as well as dangerous. Frederick the Great of Prussia, an exponent of and participant in balance-of-power politics, recalled ruefully in his Political Testament (1768) the importance of chance in human affairs, which he illustrated by reference to the young King of Denmark:

> How can one foresee all the ideas that might pass through that young head? The favorites, mistresses and ministers, who will take hold of his mind. . . . A similar uncertainty, although every time in another form, dominates all operations of foreign policy.[45]

By studying systems, we look at the big picture to see how the parts of the global puzzle fit together. The system's structure, though mostly invisible to us, conditions what is possible and probable in global politics. The most important characteristic of that structure is anarchy—the absence of any central authority above actors—which makes it difficult for actors to trust each other. The possible is circumscribed by resources, and the probable is conditioned by attitudes. Their distribution and redistribution are critical to understanding the behavior of actors.

Defining and measuring resources and attitudes is neither simple nor easy. Only some resources may be directed toward achieving political goals, and these may or may not be appropriate for attaining objectives. Some resources contribute to overall clout, and others help us use what we have effectively. Too often we study resources and ignore attitudes. Ultimately, the relationship between them is reciprocal.

Having focused on the global system as the setting in which global politics takes place, we shall now turn to some of its parts to enquire about the factors that contribute to foreign policy.

Key Terms

alliances	goals	social and economic development
anarchy	identities	stag-hare parable
beliefs	intangible resources	status
capability	intentions	status inconsistency
compatibility of goals	maximin strategy	subsystem
distribution of attitudes	modernity	system
distribution of influence	nationalism	system boundaries
distribution of resources	negative feedback	system stability
emergent property	positive feedback	system structure
escalation	prisoner's dilemma	tangible resources
expectations	second-order feedback	
feedback	security dilemma	
geopolitics	size	

End Notes

[1]Allen W. Johnson and Timothy Earle, *The Evolution of Human Societies: From Foraging Group to Agrarian State* (Stanford: Stanford University Press, 1987), pp. 19–20.

[2]Karl W. Deutsch, *The Nerves of Government* (New York: Free Press, 1963), pp. 92–93.

[3]Cited in Keith Bradsher, "U.S. Is Readying Further Billions to Rescue Mexico," *New York Times,* December 29, 1994, p. A1.

[4]Joseph M. Grieco, "Anarchy and the Limits of Cooperation: A Realist Critique of the Newest Liberal Institutionalism," *International Organization* 42:3 (Summer 1988), p. 498.

[5]Jean-Jacques Rousseau, *Discourse on Inequality,* in Alan Ritter and Julia Conaway Bondanella, eds., *Rousseau's Political Writings,* trans. Julia Conaway Bondanella (New York: Norton, 1988), p. 36.

[6]See Hans J. Morgenthau, *Politics Among Nations,* 6th ed., rev. Kenneth W. Thompson (New York: Knopf, 1985), p. 4. The English political philosopher Thomas Hobbes argued that human beings have a "perpetuall and restlesse desire of Power after power, that ceaseth only in Death." *Leviathan* (New York: Dutton, 1950), pt. 1, chap. 11, p. 79. Some theologians, for example Reinhold Niebuhr, argue that original sin leads human beings to be wicked. See *Moral Man and Immoral Society* (New York: Scribner's, 1947). The founder of modern psychology, Sigmund Freud, hypothesized an instinct for aggression or "death wish" in human beings. See *Beyond the Pleasure Principle* (New York: Bantam, 1958). Some animal biologists have suggested that aggression is instinctive behavior that enhances evolutionary survival. See Konrad Lorenz, *On Aggression,* trans. Marjorie Kerr Wilson (New York: Bantam, 1966) and Robert Ardrey, *The Territorial Imperative* (New York: Atheneum, 1966).

[7]Rousseau, *Discourse on Inequality,* p. 36.

[8]Kenneth N. Waltz, *Man, the State and War* (New York: Columbia University Press, 1959), p. 169.

[9]The two-by-two game is purely illustrative. The world is not so simple or rational as game theorists would like.

[10]In reality, the widespread norm against squealing or ratting might lead to revenge against one who confessed. This norm serves for enforcement, reducing "anarchy" in the situation.

[11]The incentive to pose obstacles grows as long as it is believed that they can be hidden or disguised.

[12]That incentive varies depending on the values of the double-defection box (2:2) outcome. If that outcome is just slightly better than the worst case in outcomes 1:2 and 2:1, players may be willing to take greater risks to get 1:1; this is a "weak" prisoner's dilemma. If the "worst case" is significantly worse than double-defection—as in the disarmament game—it is a "strong" prisoner's dilemma, and players will be risk-averse.

[13]Glenn H. Snyder, "'Prisoners' Dilemma' and 'Chicken' Models in International Politics," *International Studies Quarterly* 15:1 (March 1971), p. 69.

[14]When a federal building in Oklahoma City was bombed in April 1995, initial speculation centered on Muslim extremists because they had been involved in similar attacks elsewhere and were known to be hostile to the United States.

[15]A mole is a spy who spends years working into an enemy's confidence.

[16]Iran's military occupation of a small island near the Strait of Hormuz reinforced U.S. suspicions.

[17]This is the problem of "fungibility." See David A. Baldwin, "Neoliberalism, Neorealism, and World Politics," in Baldwin, ed., *Neorealism and Neoliberalism* (New York: Columbia University Press, 1993), pp. 20–22.

[18]Baldwin, "Neoliberalism, Neorealism, and World Politics," pp. 16–18.

[19]As part of the agreement that reunified Germany, the German government agreed to underwrite some of the cost of resettling withdrawn Soviet troops.

[20]See Saul B. Cohen, "Geopolitics," in Lawrence Freedman, ed., *War* (New York: Oxford University Press, 1994), pp. 81–85.

[21]Antiquity knew that this narrow strait was critical, and the promontories on either side of this waterway—the Rock of Gibraltar in Europe and the Jebel Musa in Africa—were known as the Pillars of Hercules.

[22]Philip A. Crowl, "Alfred Thayer Mahan: The Naval Historian," in Peter Paret, ed., *Makers of Modern Strategy from Machiavelli to the Nuclear Age* (Princeton: Princeton University Press, 1986), pp. 444–477.

[23]Cited in Harold Sprout and Margaret Sprout, *The Foundations of National Power* (Princeton: Van Nostrand, 1951), p. 155.

[24]Charles Lewis Taylor and Michael C. Hudson, *World Handbook of Political and Social Indicators,* 2nd ed. (New Haven: Yale University Press, 1972), p. 283.

[25]Bruce M. Russett, *International Regions and the International System: A Study in Political Ecology* (Chicago: Rand McNally, 1967), pp. 16–17, 41–46.

[26]Ibid.

[27]Marxist-Leninist regimes sought to uproot traditional value systems, and, in doing so, they were able to improve their soldiers' fighting capacity. The military success of communist guerrilla forces in China and later in Vietnam attests to this.

[28]See Alexander Solzhenitsyn, *August 1914* (New York: Farrar, Straus and Giroux, 1978).

[29]*World Development Indicators 1998* (Washington, DC: World Bank, 1998), Table 1.1, pp. 12–14.

[30]The other is Haiti.

[31]Two useful measures of income inequality are the Lorenz curve and the Gini coefficient. The first combines income distribution and population to measure the shares of income enjoyed by sectors of the population. The second is an arithmetic measure of the area between absolute income equality and the Lorenz curve. Using these tools, one study concludes that income inequality between countries is considerably greater than inequality within most countries. Reuben P. Mendez, *International Public Finance: A New Perspective on Global Relations* (New York: Oxford University Press, 1992), p. 96.

[32]When a new U.S. president takes office, foreign leaders compete to be the first to visit Washington and persuade the new president to visit their country.

[33]Elie Abel, *The Missile Crisis* (New York: Bantam Books, 1966), p. 96.

[34]In 1987, for the first time, Japan's national assets were valued higher than those of the United States. *New York Times,* August 22, 1989, p. 43.

[35]For a summary of research on the relationship between status inconsistency and war, see Michael P. Sullivan, *Power in Contemporary International Politics* (Columbia, SC: University of South Carolina Press, 1990), p. 134. For a theoretical analysis of the importance of a balance between status and resources in a system, which the author calls systemic equilibrium, see Charles F. Doran, *Systems in Crisis* (New York: Cambridge University Press, 1991), pp. 117–140.

[36]Robert Gilpin, *War and Change in World Politics* (New York: Cambridge University Press, 1981), p. 15.

[37]Candidly expressing such loyalty, Charles Wilson, chairman of General Motors, declared, during a Senate hearing on his nomination to become secretary of defense under President Eisenhower, that "what is good for our country is good for General Motors, and vice versa." *Hearings before the Committee on Armed Services, U.S. Senate, 83rd Congress, 1st Session, January 15–16, 1953* (Washington, DC: Government Printing Office, 1953), p. 15.

[38]Karl Marx and Friedrich Engels, "Manifesto of the Communist Party," in Lewis S. Feuer, ed., *Marx and Engels: Basic Writings on Politics and Philosophy* (Garden City, NY: Doubleday, 1959), p. 41.

[39]Cited in Theodore H. Von Laue, "Soviet Diplomacy: G. V. Chicherin, People's Commissar for Foreign Affairs, 1918-1930," in Gordon A. Craig and Felix Gilbert, eds., *The Diplomats 1919-1939*, vol. 1, *The Twenties* (New York: Atheneum, 1965), p. 235.

[40]R.W. Apple, Jr., "Jailed Nigerian Dies Amid Envoys' Visit," *New York Times*, July 8, 1998, pp. A1, A8.

[41]Fearing that U.S. interference in Europe would harm U.S. trade and shipping, President George Washington issued the Neutrality Proclamation of 1793.

[42]The U.S. raids followed terrorist attacks by Palestinians at the Rome and Vienna airports in December 1985 in which Libyan involvement was suspected.

[43]John Mearsheimer, "Back to the Future: Instability in Europe After the Cold War," *International Security* 15:1 (Summer 1990), pp. 5, 7.

[44]The power of ideology as justifying leaders' behavior is portrayed by George Orwell in his novel *1984*.

[45]Cited in Hans J. Morgenthau, *Politics Among Nations*, p. 225.

Chapter 6

The Janus Faces of Foreign Policy

N ation-states are still among the most important parts of the global system. Their governments, as well as other groups within states, account for much of the interaction that takes place in the global system. In this chapter, we look at the sources of state behavior and review some perspectives that focus on different aspects of foreign policy.

Invoking *Janus*,[1] the two-faced Roman god, we suggest that it is necessary to look simultaneously at events inside and outside state boundaries to understand the sources of foreign policy. Foreign policy is made at the nexus of intrastate and interstate politics, and only by evaluating both arenas *together* can we paint a comprehensive picture. The challenge is to disentangle the political games simultaneously played among and within foreign-policy actors—governmental, nongovernmental, and transnational—and to uncover both faces of foreign-policy issues in a postinternational world. The boundary demarcating the foreign and domestic policy arenas virtually disappears as governments and the bureaucracies of which they are constituted interact freely with one another at home and abroad, as well as with the rich galaxy of nonstate actors that form global civil society. Each issue induces action from a different cast of actors and produces different alliances and conflicts.

What Is Foreign Policy?

First, we must specify what we mean by *foreign policy.* At least three conceptions have been suggested. The phrase denotes behavior that is external or foreign to the state, leading to the first version: "the general tendencies and principles that underlie the conduct of states." This definition focuses on the interests and goals of states but largely ignores their actual *behavior* or *actions.* A second definition describes foreign policy as "the concrete plans and commitments" that leaders devise. But, though this definition anticipates purposive action, it fails to include the behavior itself. A third definition brings in behavior by defining foreign policy as "the concrete steps that officials of a state take with respect to events and situations abroad." Foreign policy is now more than an orientation, more than a tendency, and even more than an action program; it is "what individuals representing the state do or do not do in their interactions with individuals, groups, or officials elsewhere in the world."[2]

This last definition is more inclusive, but it too is incomplete. It leaves the impression, first, that sovereign states and their surrogates are the only actors involved; foreign policy is "public policy," in contrast to the activities of nonsovereign actors, which constitute "private policy." Second, the definition implies that only behavior external to the state is involved. In reality, the cast of actors involved in foreign policy depends on the issue at hand. Some issues—for example, those involving trade and immigration—inevitably attract more domestic attention than others. Also, individuals and groups inside and outside the state affect foreign policy more generally, as do institutions above or beyond the state's control. Indeed, in the postinternational world, which features fragmentation of some states and the integration of others into larger systems of authority, the notion of "foreign" policy is becoming increasingly anomalous, and the distinction between "public" and "private" policy tends to vanish.

Consider Pope John Paul II's condemnation of the destruction of the Amazon rain forest or the rich countries' material excesses. The moral impact of such behavior matters more for global politics than actions by such sovereign states as Nauru or Palau. Similarly, the European Union's collective decision to achieve greater economic and political unity by the beginning of the twenty-first century is far more consequential than individual foreign-policy decisions made by some states in that organization. In short, foreign policy is influenced and carried out by a diverse cast of actors, not just by states.

Descriptions of foreign policy are often incomplete because they only look at external sources and consequences of behavior. Many apparent domestic-policy decisions have dramatic external consequences. Failure to appreciate how "foreign" and "domestic" are two sides of the same coin can be costly. For example, Japanese auto companies purchase auto parts mainly from Japanese suppliers because of what is described as a "cartel-like structure that ties Japanese parts makers, auto companies and dealers together in networks that are hard for outsiders to penetrate, no matter how attractive their products are."[3] The Japanese government is unwilling to cajole the automakers partly because they are big sources of political contributions.[4] Yet these policies reduce U.S. exports to Japan and strain U.S.–Japanese relations, especially when, as in the 1996 American presidential race, they become entangled in political campaigns.[5]

A more subtle illustration is Saudi Arabia's way of deciding how much oil to pump from its vast resources. On the one hand, this decision involves domestic economic considerations, but foreign-policy consequences can be enormous. Increasing Saudi oil production reduces world prices, harming economies in other oil-producing states, including those of some Saudi rivals, and enhancing prosperity in industrialized societies, including those of Saudi friends like the United States. The foreign-policy objective may even be more specific. The high level of Saudi oil production in 1991–1992 may have reflected a conscious decision to assist President George Bush's bid for reelection. Following Bill Clinton's election, the Saudis announced they were in favor of reducing production.

The distinction between domestic and foreign policy is blurred not just in economic matters but also in political, military, and environmental issues. For instance, an Israeli decision to expel Palestinian activists from the occupied West Bank and Gaza early in 1992, for reasons of internal security, temporarily delayed the peace talks between Israel and its neighbors and intensified suspicion between the Bush administration and Israel's Likud government. An Israeli decision later that year to expel more than four hundred Islamic fundamentalists further strained U.S.-Israeli relations. In sum, the separation between the domestic and foreign spheres is artificial.

The First Janus Face: The External Face of the State-Centric Tradition

The world has changed and become more complex, but *state-centric explanations*—those with unitary states at the center of analysis—of foreign-policy behavior remain influential. Recently, however, other theories have appeared that try to account for increased complexity.

States, Billiard Balls, and Global Politics

The state-centric tradition holds that global power distribution determines actors' interests and that foreign policy is a rational power-maximizing response to this distribution. State-centric theorists largely ignore what goes on *within* the state; it is *black-boxed.* One scholar says, "We see what comes out but not much of what happens inside."[6] Another metaphor describes states in this model as a game of *billiards* (see Figure 6.1), in which states—all similar entities—are analogous to billiard balls, their behavior unaffected by anything other than competition for power.[7] Just as one would not explain a game of billiards by referring to anything other than Newtonian principles—action, reaction, balance, and equilibrium—so theorists in this tradition see global politics as an activity in which, in Arnold Wolfer's classic exposition, "the stage is preempted by a set of states, each in full control of all territory, men, and resources within its boundaries. Every state represents a closed, impermeable, and sovereign unit, completely separated from all other states."[8] Looking outward, this approach deals with only one of the Janus faces.

Seen thus, unitary states are the only important actors in global politics. One state acts toward another (much as one billiard ball hits another), which, in turn, compels a second state to respond either by changing the direction of policy or deflecting the action of the first state (much as one billiard ball would do to another). Whether one state will be affected by another's action, in this perspective, depends on their respective geographic and political location (just as a billiard ball's movement partly depends on its position on the billiard table). As the force and angle with which one billiard ball hits another determine the outcome, so the amount of power one state brings to bear on another will determine the magnitude and kind of response and outcome.

The analogy between billiard balls and states breaks down when we recognize that, whereas billiard balls have the same size and weight, states vary significantly in size and capability. Any differences among billiard balls pale in comparison with the difference between a superpower like the United States and microsovereignties like Tonga. And factors such as size are crucial in explaining differences in foreign-policy behavior; small states act differently than large ones, and developed states differently than developing ones.[9]

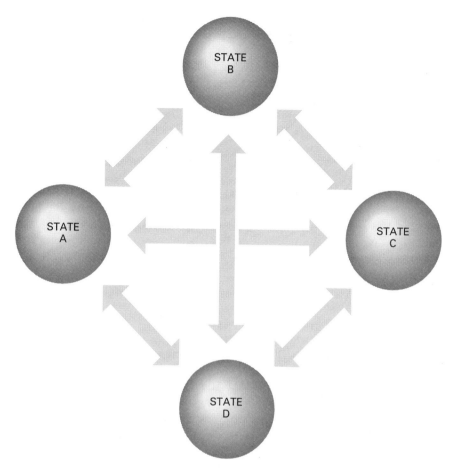

FIGURE 6.1
The Billiard Model

The billiard-ball model of global politics captures the realist view of foreign policy as little more than action-reaction.

A more sophisticated version of the state-centric tradition has recently evolved in which "the metaphor of *tectonic plates*"—the folds in the earth's crust whose movement causes earthquakes—is used to represent foreign policy. This model places somewhat less emphasis on conflict and recognizes intervening factors between the distribution of power and outcomes. Stephen Krasner writes:

> The second realist tradition envisions a more complicated universe. Here the issue is the impact of the distribution of state power on some external environment. The interaction of states may, for instance, structure the pattern of world trade, the distribution of radio frequencies, the use of outer space, or the rules governing the exploitation of deep seabed nodules. Conflict is not ignored, but the world is not zero-sum.[10]

Despite its greater sophistication, this approach ignores domestic factors and assumes rational behavior.

State-Centric Theory and the Rational-Actor Model

Although metaphors like billiard balls and tectonic plates oversimplify states' conduct, like models in general, they highlight what theorists think are the important attributes of reality. The metaphors we have described reflect the state-centric claim that foreign policy is really an *action-reaction* or *stimulus-response* process between two or more states. The underlying assumption is that a state's internal decision processes are mostly the same (and hence irrelevant) in the sense that foreign-policy decisions everywhere are motivated by the desire to realize the national interest. Power-politics theorists regard the pursuit of national interest, as determined by the distribution of power, as the essence of a rational, value-maximizing process.[11] Such logic suggests, among other things, that a weaker state will not attack a stronger one unless it has enough allies to ensure victory and that weak states will seek allies to protect them from the strong.

Power-politics theorists explain U.S. and Soviet behavior during the Cold War as a function of their being superpowers. Possessing great power presumably explains U.S. intervention in such diverse places as Vietnam (1961–1973), the Dominican Republic (1965), Grenada (1983), Panama (1989), Somalia (1992), and Haiti (1994), as well as Soviet intervention in Hungary (1956), Czechoslovakia (1968), and Afghanistan (1979). From this perspective, it does not matter that the United States was democratic and capitalist or that the Soviet Union was authoritarian and Marxist. Instead, U.S. and Soviet policies are seen to have been rational responses to a national interest that was shaped by their relative capabilities.[12] Superpowers have more far-ranging interests than small states and a greater capacity to realize or defend those interests. Regional powers—India, China, Brazil, Egypt, South Africa—may have ambitious regional interests and aspirations, and small powers have limited interests and capacity.

In the state-centric tradition, then, foreign policy is not Janus-faced, but single-faced, looking only at actions taken by states toward each other and the resulting power configurations. The sources of each state's foreign-policy behavior are other states' actions and their relative power in the global system. Although recent power-politics theorists have relaxed some of their predecessors' assumptions, recognizing the role of international organizations and the importance of economics in global politics, they too treat the state as a black box. As scholars recognized the limitations of state-centric theories, however, they began to look inside the black box, thereby taking cognizance of the second Janus face, processes internal to states.

The Second Janus Face: Factors Inside the State

In 1956, economist Kenneth Boulding hinted at a new approach in arguing the simple but powerful proposition that "behavior *is dependent upon image*."[13] In other words, each of us perceives the world differently, and our behavior depends on our version of reality. Our *image* of the world is not the same as reality; instead, it is subjective knowledge, or what we *believe* to be true. For example, Americans' ways of perceiving the U.S.S.R.'s reality, *not reality as defined by some objective standard,* determined U.S. foreign policy toward the Soviet Union. Although most Americans held a negative image of the Soviet Union during the Cold War, contrasting with the benign image of that country during World War II, the Soviet system was much the same in both periods.

Internal Processes and Foreign Policy

At the heart of a second, competing approach to explaining foreign policy is the assumption that *perceptions* are critical. This approach claims that policy-makers in different states perceive reality differently because of differing "belief systems." Hence, the *decision-making approach,* as it came to be called, serves as a counterpoint to state-centric theory because it sees foreign policy as the result of decisions reached *within* states following interaction among them.[14] This model equates the state with its decision-makers and sees foreign policy as a product of domestic processes that intervene between state action and reaction. The goal is to explain how decision-makers view the world and predict how they are likely to act in specific situations. In this view, the perceptions and actions of policy-makers are *not* determined by system structure. Instead, policies flow from the ways in which policy-makers "construct" reality.

Two concepts are at the heart of this approach—*key decision-makers* and their *definition of the situation.* First, the analyst must identify the primary decision-makers in a state and describe their motivations, information, and perceptions. Second, the analyst must define the international situation that conditions the decision-makers' perceptions of the world—"a set of images possessed by an individual, representing his view of what other nations are like, what relevance they have to the goals of his own nation, and what behavior toward them would be appropriate for his own nation."[15] In the original formulation, many factors were identified as shaping this definition for an individual policy-maker: the internal setting, the nature of the social structure within the nation, and the external setting.

The *internal setting* and the nature of the *social structure* refer to the domestic political and social environments facing policy-makers. Such factors condition the way in which policy-makers in each state define the same situation. Policy-makers in democratic societies may have different policy options and constraints than those in authoritarian societies and, as a result, may define the same situation differently. Leaders in democratic states generally need to calculate the domestic political costs of policy more than do leaders of authoritarian states. Thus Boris Yeltsin, who had served on the Politburo of the Communist Party prior to the collapse of the Soviet Union, discovered that domestic factors mattered in the new Russia when he had to confront harsh criticism of his policy after he ordered the invasion of Chechnya. Similarly, the Israeli government under Shimon Peres found that, after a series of suicide attacks against Israelis in early 1996, Israeli public opinion began to turn against the Middle East peace process and forced Peres to look "tough."

Leaders in societies composed of several ethnic or religious groups or political parties will define a situation differently than those in a society dominated by a single ethnic group or political party. In a country like India, which is divided between Muslims and Hindus, the government has a more difficult time defining the situation in the Middle East than the government of Saudi Arabia, dominated by one religion—Islam—and one ruling family—the House of Saud.

American foreign-policy leaders keep at least one eye on changing domestic conditions. President George Bush, criticized late in 1991 for spending too much time on foreign policy, was forced to postpone a long-scheduled trip to Asia. When he finally made the trip early in 1992, he shifted its main purpose from bolstering alliances in Asia to opening markets for U.S. exports and creating jobs back home. Bush thus defined the situation differently and acted differently under pressure from domestic politics and an impending presidential election. Similarly, President Bill Clinton's 1995 decision unilaterally to impose sanctions on Japanese imports—only a year after supporting creation of the World Trade Organization to prevent trade wars—was taken with an eye to improving his 1996 electoral prospects, especially in Michigan, Missouri, and Ohio. "While the U.S. action is not without some merit," declared former National Security Adviser Zbigniew Brzezinski, "it's the absence of a larger foreign policy design and the catering to domestic political considerations that is troublesome."[16]

The *external setting* is the global system's influence on decision-makers' perceptions. In the decision-making approach, the external setting's effect is not direct but is filtered through decision-makers' perceptions. External events are relevant only after decision-makers notice and interpret them. When China sells ballistic missiles to Iran, Argentine leaders may not notice, but Iraqi leaders will, because Iraq and Iran are traditional foes. Thus there is a difference between a decision-maker's "*psychological environment* (with reference to which an individual defines choices and takes decisions) and the *operational environment* (which set limits to what can happen when the decision is executed)."[17] In this perspective, the impact of global events on foreign policy is mediated through the perceptual screens of decision-makers.

The distinction among types of situations that decision-makers face was subsequently added to the originally formulated definition of the situation. *Crises* that surprise leaders, threaten core values, and leave decision-makers only a short time to act challenge policy-makers more than anticipated, routine events that unfold slowly and have low stakes. Situations that share only some of these traits will elicit still other decision-making processes, definitions of the situation, and foreign-policy responses.[18]

Individuals and Foreign Policy

Foreign-policy observers, facing the many factors that affect the definition of a situation, have devised decision-making theories that, for simplicity, can be grouped into two general categories: One emphasizes decision-makers' cognitive processes and the other their affective processes. The *cognitive approach* involves assessing distortions in perception due "to the difficulties a careful and logical person would have in making inferences from an ambiguous environment under trying conditions," and the *affective approach* examines distortions in perception "due to personal emotions, such as insecurity, hostility, and humiliations."[19] Examples of studies in both traditions illustrate how they have been applied to foreign policy.

Cognitive Processes and Foreign Policy.[20]   Political scientist Ole R. Holsti's study of Secretary of State John Foster Dulles—a principal architect of U.S. foreign policy in the 1950s—shows how cognitive processes are assessed to understand foreign policy.[21] After examining what Dulles wrote and said, Holsti concluded that Dulles had a closed belief system about the Soviet Union. Dulles's personality, background, and negative experiences with the U.S.S.R. predisposed him to view that country in terms of "atheism, totalitarianism, and communism," and little could be done to alter that image. Holsti showed that, seeking *cognitive consistency* between this negative image and Soviet behavior that seemed to contradict it, Dulles reinterpreted that behavior so that the Soviets appeared sinister. When Soviet leaders proposed the Austrian State Treaty in 1955, under which Austria would be neutral, Dulles interpreted it, not as a conciliatory act, but as a sign that the Soviet system was weakening. Whenever he perceived a thaw in the Cold War, Dulles explained it away as a trick or as evidence that the U.S.S.R. was failing. Throughout his secretaryship (1953–1959), Dulles varied little in his evaluation of the Soviet Union, always seeking the most negative interpretation of events in that country.

The Dulles study tells us two things about decision making in foreign policy. First, it shows how important individual decision-makers are in shaping foreign policy. Dulles was at the center of U.S. foreign policy, and his image of the Soviet Union predicted how the United States would behave toward Moscow. Second, we see that decision-makers' cognitions mediate between state action and reaction. Despite the ebb and flow of Soviet behavior—from conciliation to hostility— Dulles was unable or unwilling to alter his image of the Soviet Union. Little wonder that U.S. policy toward the U.S.S.R. changed only minimally during the Dulles years.

Since Holsti, others have tried to study decision-makers' cognitive processes to account for foreign-policy decisions. Much has been said about how perceptions affect decisions in interstate crises. One project sought to determine how much leaders' perceptions had to do with starting World War I. The results demonstrated how misperceptions shaped policy responses by both alliance systems. One conclusion was that "the leaders of the Dual Alliance [Germany and Austria-Hungary] consistently overperceived the level of violence in the actions of the Triple Entente [Great Britain, Russia, and France]. On the other hand, the Triple Entente tended to underperceive the actions of the other coalitions."[22] In a subsequent study of the Cuban missile crisis, the same researchers showed how perceptions differed then from 1914: "Unlike some of the key decision-makers in the 1914 crisis, those in October 1962 thought in terms of linked interactions—closely tied reciprocations—rather than two sides, each acting independently, *in vacuo.*"[23] That outcomes differ in similar situations shows how powerful images and perceptions are in shaping policy.

Affective Processes and Foreign Policy.   Decision-makers' affective characteristics may also distort perceptions. Political psychologist Margaret Hermann examined various personality characteristics: degree of nationalism, belief in one's ability to control events, need for power, need for affiliation, conceptual complexity, and distrust of others. She also considered the relationship of leaders' traits to types of foreign policy decisions: professed orientation to change, independence or interdependence of action, commitment, affect, and environmental feedback.[24] Her findings suggest that leaders who strongly need affiliation are more likely to follow change-oriented policies; those who need power are more likely to follow an independent foreign-policy course; and those who distrust others are less likely to make foreign-policy commitments. Hermann also reports that personal characteristics were more important in leaders with little foreign-policy training than in those with foreign-policy experience. Lyndon Johnson, who had little experience in foreign affairs prior to becoming president, greatly needed power, and this, Hermann suggests, led him doggedly to increase U.S. involvement in Vietnam despite doubts among those around him and among U.S. allies.

Lloyd Etheredge did a similar affective analysis of a group of U.S. policy-makers in office between 1898 and 1968.[25] Etheredge focused on two personality traits—dominance over subordinates and extroversion—of thirty-six U.S. presidents, secretaries of state, and advisers to discover if personality differences predicted variations in their foreign policies. He found that officials who score high on dominance are more likely to favor force and those who are extroverts are more likely to pursue cooperative foreign policies.

Evaluating the Decision-Making Approach

Despite the interest generated by the decision-making approach, it has proved less useful than proponents hoped. First, the approach is largely directed at domestic factors. Whereas state-centric theorists attend exclusively to the external environment, the opposite criticism can be made of the decision-making approach, which mainly omits external factors. Second, in some ways the approach is little more than a collection of diverse internal factors that are rarely easy to evaluate. Decision-makers' perceptions are especially difficult to fathom. Third, the approach is more applicable to large states with complex bureaucracies than in settings where decision-making structures are smaller and less complex.

Nonetheless, decision-making studies, and especially the cognitive and affective approaches, raise questions about two core assumptions of state-centric theorists: the capacity for rationality in the underlying process and the role of objective national interest in shaping outcomes. Even if we demonstrate that two individuals act in the same way under similar conditions, one (or both) may be misperceiving reality and reaching "inappropriate decisions."[26] Or individuals may see reality in different ways and act appropriately, though differently. Either way, the factors that shape individual perception explain policy outcomes better than a rational cost-benefit calculus. As a result, it is difficult to identify an objective national interest because definitions of it are mostly subject to cognitive and affective factors.

Bureaucratic and Organizational Models of Foreign Policy

Early in the 1970s, theorists proposed moving beyond examination of just a few key decision-makers—as early practitioners of the decision-making approach had done—to focus on the broader decision-making environment in which policy-makers operate. They argued that the domestic decision-making environment should be viewed as an agglomeration of bureaucratic and organizational structures that shape policy choices.

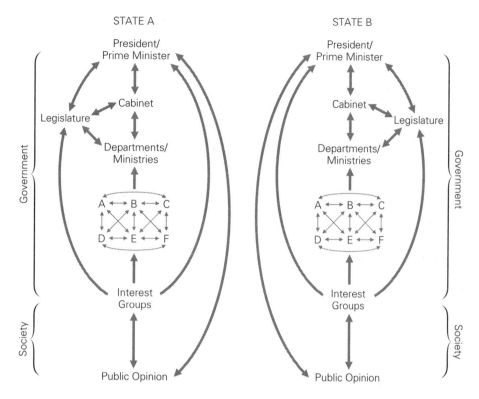

FIGURE 6.2
The Bureaucratic-Politics Model

The bureacratic-politics model describes a world in which the foreign policies of states are produced by pulling and hauling among bureaucracies, between bureaucracies and legislatures, and among bureaucracies, legislatures, and organized social interests.

Two complementary models eventually emerged from this reassessment of decision making: the *bureaucratic-politics* (see Figure 6.2) and *organizational-process models.*[27] Although both models continued to assume that foreign policy resulted mostly from domestic politics, they emphasized different aspects of that environment and abandoned assumptions of a unitary state and an objective national interest.

The Bureaucratic-Politics Model

Foreign-policy decisions, according to the bureaucratic-politics model, result from bargaining games among competing domestic "players" (groups). Decisions are reached less by the rational choices of individual decision-makers than by "the pulling and hauling that is politics" among groups of policy-makers.[28] To understand foreign-policy decisions from this perspective, one must untangle this web of participants, their interests, their relative influence, and the bargaining that occurs among them prior to a decision. Even though a top decision-maker like the U.S. president may be offered a range of alternatives, his choices will be narrowed by bureaucratic interests. Those powerful bureaucratic interests will have eliminated some options before the president is asked to make a decision and will have structured those that remain to make some appear more attractive than others. Thus at the height of the Cold War, U.S. intelligence agencies stressed different aspects of the Soviet threat because of their implications for pieces of the military budget.[29]

With these premises, policy analyst Morton Halperin sought to understand why the Johnson administration decided late in the 1960s to deploy an antiballistic missile (ABM) system against China, when in fact the Chinese had not acquired a ballistic-missile capability. Halperin argues that that decision resulted from competition among organizations and individuals with a stake in it. On the side favoring ABM deployment were a group of powerful bureaucracies—Army, Navy, Air Force—and several prominent individuals, including John S. Foster, Director of Defense Research and Engineering, Senators Richard Russell (chairman of the Senate Armed Services Committee), John Stennis, and Henry Jackson. Opposed to ABM deployment were two Department of Defense offices—Office of Systems Analysis and Office of International Security Affairs—and several individuals, including Secretary of Defense Robert McNamara. President Johnson was somewhere in the middle.[30] The president cared about the issue mostly because of the intense feelings it produced in other participants with whom he had good relations. Hence, his decision was a compromise—a small ABM deployment (not a large-scale deployment across the country) directed against China (not the Soviet Union). The president's decision was "qualitatively different," and he was "not simply a very powerful player among less powerful players"; but his actions were shaped by the environment in which he made the decision.[31] The decision was not rational as most of us define the term, and it was not responsive to any objective national interest.

Another study of bureaucratic politics is Graham Allison's analysis of decision making during the 1962 Cuban missile crisis. Allison argues that members of the Executive Committee of the U.S. National Security Council "whistled many different tunes" as the decision-making process began over what to do about the Soviet missiles discovered in Cuba. By the end, however, a consensus had formed to impose a naval quarantine around Cuba. "The process by which this happened is a story of the most subtle and intricate probing, pulling, and hauling, leading, guiding, and spurring" among the participants.[32]

Public opinion, though amorphous, is another important factor in democratic societies. It may encourage presidents to take certain steps or prevent them from doing so. Thus the public's painful memories of 58,000 American deaths in the Vietnam War prevented the restoration of U.S.–Vietnamese economic ties for almost two decades.[33] An enormous number of interest groups lobby the U.S. government, especially Congress, on issues of importance to them. Most represent domestic interests, but some are transnational, and others represent foreign groups. Thus President Clinton received significant campaign contributions from Chinese and Indonesian groups, and some observers feared that foreigners had been able to influence U.S. foreign policy toward their country. The impact that interest groups have on U.S. foreign policy is mixed. They are most effective on issues that do not attract large-scale public attention. Even here, however, the activity of interest groups on one side of an issue often calls forth other groups with antithetical views that can balance the influence of its opponents.

The largest number of domestic interest groups are economic in nature. Business groups like the National Association of Manufacturers and labor unions like the United Auto Workers are very active, especially regarding trade issues. Other lobbyists active in foreign policy represent agricultural, religious, and veterans groups. Other important players are ethnic and racial-interest groups. Cuban Americans in Florida and elsewhere lobby the government to keep pressure on Fidel Castro.[34] African Americans helped reshape U.S. policy toward Haiti.[35] Jewish Americans advocate U.S. support of Israel, and Greek and Armenian Americans lobby against Turkey.[36]

All fifty states try to get as much federal money as possible while preventing the federal government from adopting policies that are unpopular with voters, such as storing or transporting hazardous nuclear waste.[37] In recent years, the issue of immigration has engaged a number of states because voters believe it places a burden on state finances, leading one observer to comment that "Florida in recent years has tried to have its own foreign policy."[38] On one occasion Florida Governor Lawton Chiles threatened to order state officials to detain Cuban boat people, and his position was popular, especially outside Miami, where there are few Cuban exiles.[39] In California, illegal immigration was an issue in the 1994 gubernatorial campaign, with Governor Pete Wilson supporting a referendum that would strip such immigrants of the right to welfare, health care, and schooling,[40] suggesting that Californians have official identity cards.[41] California also sued the federal government for state costs in imprisoning illegal immigrants. In addition to California, Texas, Arizona, Florida, and New Jersey have sought federal funding to compensate for costs associated with illegal immigrants.[42] Texans, however, are far less truculent about Mexican immigrants than Californians because about 40 percent of their exports, worth about $24 billion, went to Mexico in 1995.[43]

Even New York's Mayor Rudolph W. Giuliani, mindful of the city's large Jewish constituency, took foreign-policy matters into his own hands by having Palestinian leader Yasir Arafat ejected from a concert for world leaders during the U.N.'s fiftieth anniversary celebrations. One U.S. official denounced the mayor's action as "an embarrassment to everyone associated with diplomacy,"[44] and a New York official observed: "It's a long and noble tradition of New York City mayors to exercise independent foreign policy judgments. It goes with the turf. The city has the world's most diverse population, and the people of New York expect the mayor to represent their interests."[45]

On some issues, Congress is a key player and can be a problem for a president, especially if it is controlled by the opposition party. Rarely, however, has a president's foreign policy been so vigorously attacked as Bill Clinton's after Republican majorities took control of both houses of Congress in January 1995.[46] On some issues, Republicans staked out positions with an eye toward key domestic constituencies.[47] Republicans opposed U.S. aid to Mexico after it appeared that the country was on the verge of financial collapse, forcing President Clinton to give up his initial aid plan for one that did not require congressional approval;[48] in turn the president used another hot issue—fear of growing foreign immigration—to justify aiding Mexico.[49] Republicans also demanded NATO bombing of Bosnian Serbs and a unilateral end to the arms embargo on Bosnia.[50] They sought, too, to slash funding for the United Nations and for population-control programs, demanded that greater pressure be applied to get Russia to alter its policies,[51] and opposed an agreement with North Korea aimed at stopping that country's nuclear arms program.[52] Their special target, however, was foreign aid, which North Carolina's conservative Senator Jesse Helms, chairman of the Senate Foreign Relations Committee, described as "going down foreign rat-holes, to countries that constantly oppose us in the United Nations. . . ."[53] For months Senator Helms also prevented congressional action on vital treaties such as the Strategic Arms Reduction Treaty and the Chemical Weapons Convention and on many ambassadorial appointments in order to force President Clinton to end the independence of the U.S. Information Agency and the Arms Control and Disarmament Agency. This prompted a State Department official to declare that the "nation's security interests are being held hostage."[54]

The bureaucratic-politics model is especially applicable to countries like Japan because of the relative weakness of short-lived ministers, sometimes in coalition cabinets, in contrast to bureaucrats who serve for many years unexposed to the glare of publicity and partisan politics. Thus Japan's powerful Finance Ministry undermined the impact of tax cuts intended to stimulate Japan's economy by forcing the government to make up lost revenues in other ways. This led a former Finance Ministry official to observe: "These policy decisions are made by the bureaucrats, that is clear. If you had a stronger government in power it is very unlikely this would have happened."[55] The Ministry of International Trade and Industry (MITI) is among the most powerful Japanese bureaucracies and plays a key role in Japan's trade policies. MITI's influence makes it difficult for Japanese politicians to carry out promises of opening the country to foreign goods and services or to make trade concessions to the United States.

The idea that bureaucrats compete with each other to get policies adopted that benefit them contrasts with the idea that bureaucracies function in routine, almost compulsive ways and that foreign policy is the unplanned result of "normal" bureaucratic routines and procedures. We now turn to this model.

The Organizational-Process Model

The organizational-process model also sees foreign policy as driven primarily by internal processes, but less from bargaining among bureaucracies than by *standard operating procedures (SOPs)* that large organizations follow. These procedures are policies designed for *classes* of situations, and are efficient ways for organizations to deal with complex but similar and repetitive issues. They provide guidelines in responding to problems without having to reach a new decision in each case, and they help an organization draw upon expertise from all its divisions. Immigration authorities require prospective immigrants to fill out standardized forms and answer standard questions, regardless of who the prospective immigrants are and what their personal situations are. The steps are standard operating procedures, and violations of those are "exceptions to the rule."

Such procedures exist in any large organization, and we need to decipher how they operate in order to understand the organizational-process model. The theoretical source of that model is the work of organizational theorists like Herbert Simon. Taking exception to the *"comprehensive rationality"* assumption of economists, Simon claims that organizational decision making is based on *"bounded rationality."*[56] This principle recognizes human limitations that make it impossible for decision-makers to consider *all* possible alternatives. Instead of evaluating each and making a decision based on comprehensive rationality, decision-makers *"satisfice";* that is, they search among available options and seek the first that provides minimal satisfaction, even though it may not be the best of all possible choices. In making a selection, decision-makers try to avoid uncertainty, focusing on alternatives with assured outcomes rather than trying to estimate the probabilities in different choices. They also follow institutional repertoires—plans for dealing with categories of situations—to reduce time and uncertainty.

These insights into organizational behavior are integrated into the *cybernetic model* of foreign-policy decision making. According to the cybernetic model, bureaucrats try to limit uncertainty by relying on a simplified procedure, in which only information relevant to the issue, combined with established responses, is used to guide decisions. Rather than seeking to maximize value outcomes, decision-makers seek to preserve existing values. The cybernetic decision-maker acts like Simon's "satisficer."[57] The cybernetic model advances the organizational-process model by showing that bureaucratic organizations have the capacity to change internally to deal with complex problems. Such problems attract attention from more individuals in the organization, and subgroups are formed to cope with them.[58]

These approaches apply to policy-making in many societies. States are often confronted with complex decisions, in situations fraught with uncertainty. The norm for dealing with such complexity is collective, not individual, decision making. The organizational-process model points to ready routines to knit together the collective process and manage complexity and uncertainty. At the same time, these routines provide the basis for an *incremental bias,* which means that policy evolves slowly through a series of small (incremental) decisions. Graham Allison writes: "The best explanation of an organization's behavior at t is t-1; the best prediction of what will happen at $t + 1$ is t."[59] In other words, large organizations are risk-averse and are likely to support policy changes only at the margin. Thus, despite promised reductions, President Clinton's 1993 "post–Cold War" defense budget strongly resembled President Bush's last Cold War budget. Even dramatic external disturbances may fail to produce change in organizational routines.

Evaluating the Models　In the U.S. foreign-policy establishment, a number of *senior interagency groups (SIGs)* and *interagency groups (IGs)* address foreign-policy issues. These structures are hierarchic, in that they are created by the president and the National Security Council (NSC)[60] and in turn are responsible to the president and NSC. They also incorporate expertise from the various foreign-policy bureaucracies and, at any time, may be composed of representatives from the State Department, the Defense Department, the CIA, the Treasury Department, or the National Security Council. Their composition can change as necessary. (If an agricultural-aid issue arises, the Department of Agriculture and the Agency for International Development might have representatives on an IG.) After an IG reviews and develops policy options, it passes its recommendations on to the SIG, where the process is repeated. The SIG's recommendations are forwarded to the National Security Council, and ultimately to the president.

Using an organizational model, Graham Allison was able to explain apparent anomalies in the sequence of events for both superpowers during the Cuban missile

ACTORS SPEAK

Among competing models of foreign policy, the state-centric tradition remains the most popular. It assumes that states have national interests, based on their relative power, that determine their policies and that leaders evaluate those interests and act accordingly. In the first passage, Hans Morgenthau illustrates the way this model works. Others contend that national interests are perceived differently in different government bureaucracies and that policy is the outcome of bargaining among the bureaucracies. The second passage reflects this view of the sources of foreign policy.

We assume that statesmen think and act in terms of interest defined as power.... That assumption allows us to retrace and anticipate, as it were, the steps a statesman—past, present, or future—has taken or will take on the political scene. We look over his shoulder when he writes his dispatches; we listen in on his conversation with other statesmen; we read and anticipate his very thoughts. Thinking in terms of interest defined as power, we think as he does, and as disinterested observers we understand his thoughts and actions perhaps better than he, the actor on the political scene, does himself. (Hans J. Morgenthau, *Politics Among Nations: The Struggle for Power and Peace,* 6th ed., rev. by Kenneth W. Thompson [New York: Knopf, 1985], p. 5)

The apparatus of each national government constitutes a complex arena for the intranational game. Political leaders at the top of the apparatus are joined by officials who occupy positions on top of major organizations to form a circle of central players.... The nature of foreign policy problems permits fundamental disagreement among reasonable people about how to solve them.... Because their preferences and beliefs are related to the different organizations they represent, their analyses yield conflicting recommendations. Separate responsibilities laid on the shoulders of distinct individuals encourage differences in what each sees and judges to be important. (Graham Allison and Philip Zelikow, *Essence of Decision: Explaining the Cuban Missile Crisis,* 2nd ed., [New York: Longman, 1999], pp. 255–256)

crisis. Organizational complexities seem to explain why Soviet surface-to-air missile (SAM) defenses were not operational in Cuba before their medium-range ballistic missiles (MRBMs) were functional and thus why the MRBMs were vulnerable to a potential U.S. air strike. The Soviet Air Defense Forces were responsible for constructing the SAM sites, but the Soviet Strategic Rocket Forces were responsible for constructing the MRBM sites.[61] The different organizations had different schedules and, in this case, lacked coordinating mechanisms. Similarly, President

Kennedy's public warnings to Soviet leaders not to install offensive missiles in Cuba "were too late; the Soviet decision to deploy had been made months before, and the relevant machinery had been set in gear."[62]

Organizational routines also seem to have dictated U.S. decisions connected with the quarantine around Cuba. To give the Soviet Union more time to contemplate its responses to U.S. actions, President Kennedy decided within a day of ordering the blockade to pull it closer to Cuba. Orders went out to the U.S. Navy to make this change, and specific rules for engaging Soviet vessels were issued. However, it appears that naval officials resisted these rules because they did not correspond to standard navy doctrine.[63] Standard operating procedures in the U.S. Navy proved more compelling than the commander-in-chief's directives.

Both the organizational-process and bureaucratic-politics models move beyond the model of a unitary rational state with an objective national interest to guide it. Many actors with multiple, and often competing, interests shape foreign-policy outcomes though the "pulling and hauling" of bureaucratic competition or the routines and programs of organizations' structures. Appealing though these approaches are, they too have generated questions and criticisms.

One question is how applicable these models are in other settings. They seem most applicable to developed states with complex bureaucracies and democratic institutions. Are they really useful outside this context? At least one critic has doubts: "The characteristics that make bureaucratic politics an important feature of foreign policy-making in the United States are not to the same extent or degree in other national systems."[64] Parliamentary systems in Europe, Canada, and Australia have some of the same characteristics as the U.S. political system that might encourage struggles among "players in positions." All face foreign-policy issues that cut across ministries; they have agencies with different responsibilities that try to coordinate policy; and some—Canada and Australia—have a federal structure like that of the United States. Yet research on Canada suggests that these models do not work well in these settings because "in parliamentary systems the concentration of political authority in cabinet allows the political executive to impose constraints on legitimate conflict between policy-makers at lower levels in the decision-making process."[65]

The criticism that these models are not widely applicable is even sharper when looking at countries that are either less developed or nondemocratic. Developing countries have small bureaucracies. Some countries cannot even afford representation abroad and depend on their U.N. representative in New York or the good offices of larger countries to keep them informed about global developments. In such cases, bureaucratic competition and organizational routines can hardly explain policy. In nondemocratic societies the problem is different. The views of dominant individuals or elites are likely to shape foreign policy, and the bureaucracy is left to implement the leadership's wishes.[66]

The models have been criticized even in the U.S. context. One critic argues that presidential preferences and domestic politics are more pivotal than bureaucratic politics, especially in such major decisions as using military force. Only in decisions affecting "institutionally grounded issues," which rarely are critical, does bureaucratic politics explain the outcome.[67] It is also argued that, despite claims by bureaucratic theorists, it is unlikely that a U.S. president can be captured by

Washington's bureaucracies.[68] A president is accountable to the electorate for his actions and is likely to ensure that foreign policy reflects his wishes. As a result, the president is likely to select foreign-policy advisers who are dedicated to his interests and use agencies only if he believes they will operate in a way compatible with those interests. Finally, despite bureaucratic-politics theorists' assumption that *role*—behavior associated with the official position one holds—determines outlook, bureaucrats can adopt positions divorced from the role they occupy. They are influenced by general culture and values in arriving at their views and are susceptible to presidential influence. These considerations lead some critics to argue that foreign policy is more likely to be explained by top decision-makers' values than by the parochial values of lower-level bureaucrats:

> Neither organizational necessity nor bureaucratic interests are the fundamental determinants of policy. The limits imposed by standard operating procedures as well as the direction of policy are a function of the values of decision-makers. . . . The failure of the American government to take decisive action in a number of critical areas reflects not so much the inertia of a large bureaucratic machine as a confusion over values which afflicts the society in general and its leaders in particular.[69]

The Janus Faces of Foreign Policy: The Transnational-Politics Model

The various criticisms of the models we have been examining suggest a need for a more comprehensive approach that can account for more of the realities of postinternational politics—simultaneously accounting for both Janus faces. Integrating insights from transnational politics allows us to account for the increasingly porous nature of state boundaries and the ideas, people, and things that flow across.

The state-centric and decision-making approaches focus on the state and fail to capture the influence of international institutions and nonstate actors on foreign policy. By contrast, transnational and complex-interdependence theorists[70] argue that foreign policy emerges from many sources. Many actors, or "multiple channels," flow among societies beyond governments' formal relations, and contacts between state and nonstate elites and masses and among nonstate groups also shape foreign policy. Actors such as transnational corporations, revolutionary movements, intergovernmental and nongovernmental organizations, and even individuals also shape foreign affairs.

Transnationalism theorists offer several reasons for enlarging the galaxy of actors to understand foreign policy. First, foreign affairs is not confined to issues of military power. The global agenda has expanded to take in economic and social issues as well. Second, leaders have more ways of influencing each other today than even a few decades ago. Third, because capabilities are not easily converted from one use to another, different issues have different casts of actors, which enjoy varying degrees and types of influence in each issue.[71]

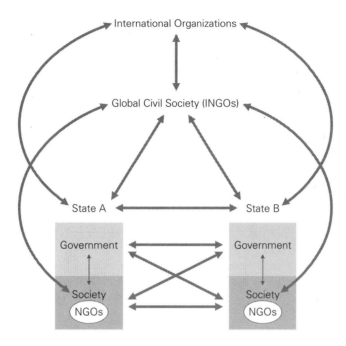

FIGURE 6.3
The Transnational-Politics Model

The transnational-politics model captures the complexity of the postinternational world in which governments and societies interact with one another, as well as with the international organizations and transnational groups that constitute global civil society. This is a world in which transnational links are forged among bureaucracies and nonstate groups that have common or congruent interests.

The *transnational model* (see Figure 6.3) moves us beyond the unitary state, just as the bureaucratic-politics and organizational-process models did. But it also forces us to look to actors outside the state's government apparatus. The number of these actors is growing and their importance has yet to be fully assessed.

International Organizations and Foreign Policy

International organizations have been around for centuries but were usually assumed to be subservient to states and to have a small role as independent actors. Now, however, we find a more nuanced view of international organizations and can identify at least three foreign-policy roles: (1) as instruments of foreign policy by states or groups, (2) as intermediaries in global politics that can modify states' actions, and (3) as autonomous global actors.[72]

States use international organizations as instruments of national policy as the West used NATO as a means to police the Bosnian peace agreement.[73] Relatively few studies have explained how states use international organizations for their own ends.[74] Foreign-policy analysts need to study how extensively states rely on international institutions to carry out their obligations and achieve their goals.

International organizations also serve as intermediaries between actors and may modify foreign-policy actions undertaken by states. Institutions like the United Nations and the European Union restrain and facilitate members' foreign-policy behavior. After the Persian Gulf War, Iraq had to agree to U.N.-authorized inspection of its nuclear facilities as a condition for ending hostilities. After the collapse of the Warsaw Pact, the European Union (EU), the Conference on Security and Cooperation in Europe (CSCE), and NATO became important in shaping relations between Western Europe and the newly democratic states of Central Europe; one new task that NATO has assumed involves maintaining peace and stability beyond the territory of its members. To this end, NATO initiated the bombing of Yugoslavia in the spring of 1999 in an effort to force Belgrade to accept an agreement that would grant additional rights to the Albanian majority in Kosovo (a province of Serbia).

International organizations are vital intermediaries for small states. Using the United Nations as a forum, they can bring issues to the attention of the world community and try to shape the policies of large states. These states used U.N. agencies to focus world attention on such issues as global poverty and economic inequality, racial discrimination in Rhodesia and South Africa, and independence for Namibia. Regionally, such organizations as the Organization of African Unity (OAU) serve a similar function for small states. The fifty-two African states together may adopt a unified (or nearly so) position on issues and wield more influence than their individual size might predict.

International economic institutions also serve as foreign-policy intermediaries. The International Monetary Fund (IMF) and the World Bank often provide aid to developing countries only on condition that they adopt specified economic and political reforms. States may have to reduce imports, devalue currency, or undertake other reforms, such as reducing the number of state-run industries. Such conditions can be intrusive. Between 1969 and 1972, World Bank and IMF officials subjected Ghana to so many requirements as conditions of economic aid that the government in Accra lost domestic support and was overthrown.[75] In this case, international organizations undermined the state's internal stability.

But in return, poor states have relied on international organizations to influence the policies of wealthy states. In the 1960s, when many developing states were dissatisfied with trading arrangements made through the General Agreement on Tariffs and Trade (GATT), they pressured the United Nations to establish the U.N. Conference on Trade and Development (UNCTAD) as an institutional counterweight to GATT. UNCTAD sought to reduce barriers to trade between the developed and developing worlds, and earned the title of "trade union of the poor against the rich."[76] The appeal of such an organization is that it gives weak states, acting in concert, the chance to place pressure on powerful states.

In other ways too, poor states get help from international organizations. Some countries, such as the Sudan, rely on U.N. agencies like the Food and Agricultural Organization (FAO) and the World Food Council to avoid famine.

Nonstate Actors and Foreign Policy

Some theorists also point to the role of private individuals and groups in foreign policy. Among these are private individuals (such as former President Jimmy Carter, who was involved in negotiating agreements with Haiti, North Korea, and

Bosnia),[77] organized interest groups (business, labor, and agriculture), political parties, terrorists, and humanitarian groups. Such groups may affect foreign policy in two ways: They may exercise indirect influence by lobbying their governments, or they may interact directly with foreign actors. Many contemporary issues—global warming, AIDS, nuclear proliferation, international trade—defy state frontiers and elicit transnational responses. Private actors recognize that such issues affect their interests and organize themselves to influence them. Not surprisingly, such issues may produce alliances among groups in several societies, and some of these may integrate institutionally to the point that they become genuinely transnational. This is most evident in the case of giant corporate enterprises, but it is equally the case with the National Rifle Association,[78] Amnesty International, and the host of environmental, humanitarian, and feminist groups that routinely lobby governments and international organizations.

When the French government announced in 1995 that it would conduct nuclear tests in the South Pacific, Greenpeace tried to disrupt them.[79] And widespread civil strife in the postinternational world and the presence of between 80 and 110 million antipersonnel mines in sixty-four countries led America's Roman Catholic bishops to denounce U.S. involvement in the global arms trade and, along with a coalition of humanitarian groups, to ask for a ban on land mines, which kill or maim 500 people a week, mainly civilians.[80] When a treaty banning mines was adopted despite American opposition, observers conceded that it was nonstate actors that were largely responsible.

Trade issues attract numerous interest groups. Former U.S. Trade Representative and Ambassador to Russia Robert Strauss was struck by the number of groups active on trade issues and the complications they caused in interstate negotiations. "I spent as much time negotiating with domestic constituents (both industry and labor) and members of the U.S. Congress as I did negotiating with our foreign trade partners."[81] The influence of agricultural interest groups was evident, following the imposition of economic sanctions, as required by law, on India and Pakistan following their nuclear tests in 1998. Within days, Congress and the president agreed to revoke the sanctions that affected agricultural exports. "The timing could not be worse," declared a Republican congressman from the Midwest, because farmers in other countries "will exploit this lucrative wheat export market at a time when American wheat prices are at their lowest price in decades and we desperately need to hold on to those export markets." "Clearly," argued a Democratic congressman from California, "it is in the interests of U.S. workers and U.S. companies to eliminate sanctions that penalize our working men and women. . . ."[82]

In addition to trade, several other issues attract especially widespread domestic attention in the United States. These include human rights, drugs, and birth control. Human-rights groups in the United States try to cajole the government to adopt a confrontational attitude toward China, while corporations seek to uncouple commerce and human rights.[83]

Birth control and abortion are highly contentious issues in the United States. Thus, in 1988, when the French pharmaceutical company Roussel-UCLAF (a subsidiary of a German corporation) began to market an "abortion pill" (RU-486) in France, those on both sides of the abortion issue in the United States were mobilized. Abortion opponents successfully lobbied the Bush administration to keep

(Copyright 1996. Distributed by the Los Angeles Times Syndicate. Reprinted by permission.)

the pill out of the U.S. market, and the company, fearing a boycott, did not try to market it in the United States. After the 1992 election, President Clinton called for a review of the ban, partly in response to groups on the other side of the issue, and in 1994 clinical trials were begun to make the pill available to Americans.[84] Responding to conservative efforts to ban any U.S. aid for international birth-control efforts that involve abortion or abortion counseling, the Clinton administration argued that, in the words of Secretary of State Madeleine K. Albright: "Our voluntary family-planning programs serve our broader interests by elevating the status of women, reducing the flow of refugees, protecting the environment and promoting economic growth."[85]

Finally, the drug issue, especially the role of Mexicans in the transnational drug trade, evokes anger on the part of Americans, who demand greater American cooperation in halting the flow of drugs northward, and Mexicans, who claim American antidrug efforts violate their country's sovereignty.[86]

In light of the United States' importance in global politics, it is hardly surprising that foreign governments and interests try to influence the American debate on foreign policy. For many years, the Israeli lobby in the United States has effectively fostered American support for Israel. Another influential foreign lobby is that of Taiwan, of which President Reagan's national security adviser Richard V. Allen said: "They're either tied with or second only to the Israelis in their effectiveness."[87]

Indeed, while he was governor of Arkansas, Bill Clinton was invited on four journeys to Taiwan. It was apparently Taiwan's success in lobbying influential Americans that, according to a report of the National Security Administration (NSA), induced Chinese officials to funnel money illegally to American politicians during the 1996 American election campaign.[88]

Foreign-Policy Analysis and the Persian Gulf War

The approaches we have discussed illustrate how many types of actors contribute to understanding foreign policy. The last two of the three models—bureaucratic organizations and transnational processes—moved us far from looking only at undifferentiated rational states. Each added complexity to foreign-policy analysis.

What is the best model for understanding foreign policy? The question merits two responses. One is that the best model depends on the questions you ask. For crises that threaten war, the state-centric perspective may be adequate, but for ecological issues, a transnational perspective provides the richest picture. In the end, each model contributes something.

The case of the Persian Gulf War shows how these models can be combined to enrich our understanding. Each helps us fit another piece of the global puzzle.

Persian Gulf War: The Background

With improved East-West relations and the Cold War over, President Bush enthusiastically spoke of the coming new world order. Within months, however, the United States was at war with Iraq over Saddam Hussein's invasion of Kuwait. Although Iraq had been a client of the Soviet Union and had received large amounts of Soviet military assistance, by early 1991 the Soviet Union was on the verge of collapse, and Soviet leaders were disenchanted with Saddam. Warming U.S.-Soviet relations meant that Baghdad could no longer depend on its patron for protection.

This dramatic shift in Soviet-Iraqi relations had another effect: The United Nations could respond to Iraqi aggression in the manner intended by its founders yet almost unprecedented since its establishment. Because the Soviet Union no longer automatically vetoed U.S.-supported initiatives, it proved to be a helpful, if cautious, partner in steering resolutions through the U.N. Security Council demanding Iraqi withdrawal from Kuwait. Soviet-American cooperation ultimately led to a U.N. resolution late in November 1990 calling on members to use force against Iraq.

Behind the response to Iraqi aggression lay recognition of a feature of the new world—economic interdependence. Saddam Hussein's control of Kuwait not only threatened the territorial integrity of neighboring states but also appeared about to give him a stranglehold on the global economy. Were one leader in a position to determine oil production and therefore oil prices, the rest of the world could be bullied to carry out his political agenda.[89] Arrangements governing oil production and pricing, already under stress from different sources, would be in danger of collapse, and rapid changes in oil prices could throw the world economy into chaos.[90] Recognizing this face of the crisis, the members of the allied coalition were determined to end this threat to the stability of the global economic system.

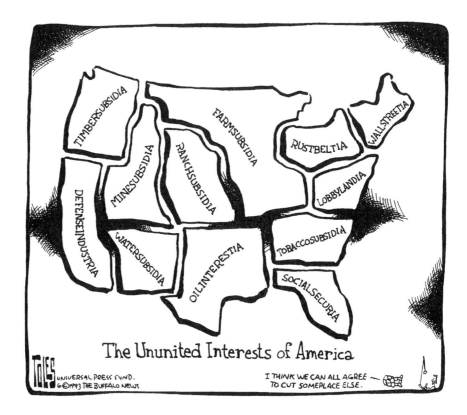

The idea that states have a coherent and identifiable national interest is a fiction—instead, groups identify their interest with the interest of the state and seek to justify policies that they prefer. *(Toles, The Buffalo News, copyright 1993. Dist. by Universal Press Syndicate. Reprinted with permission. All rights reserved.)*

Saddam Hussein himself appreciated some of the new global interdependencies when he caused a giant oil spill to foul the Persian Gulf in January 1991. Whatever the military purpose in this act (perhaps to shut down desalinization plants in Saudi Arabia that provided fresh water to coalition forces), he must have known that eco-terrorism would frighten the world and conjure up visions of environmental catastrophes to come.

The Iraq crisis showed the Janus face of foreign policy. In the United States, attitudes toward the conflict were shaped by an economic recession, memories of the Vietnam quagmire, and calculations of partisan political gain. Conventional wisdom about foreign policy stopping at the water's edge proved untrue. Among the domestic groups that became involved were defense contractors,[91] oil corporations, military reservists, peace activists, and others who recognized their stake in events taking place thousands of miles away. The sensitivity of the issue at home was reflected in the importance attached to the positive vote by both houses of Congress authorizing the president to use military force.

The Persian Gulf War illustrates that we may be in a transition in global politics. Some of the elements of the old world—force, the role of states, balance of power—were visible. Yet some of the elements of the new world—great-power cooperation, global interdependence, the Janus face of politics, and the enhanced role of nonstate actors—were also apparent. Let us see how each of the three foreign-policy models informs our understanding of the issue.

The State-Centric Perspective

One incentive behind opposition to Iraq was fear that an aggressor was threatening an existing regional balance of power. The allied coalition was determined to prevent a major change in the Middle East balance of power and show that such a violation of state sovereignty would not be tolerated. In all, twenty-eight allied states took the field against Iraq.

From a state-centric perspective, the Persian Gulf War might be explained by the challenge that Iraq's seizure of Kuwait posed to the system of state actors and the security of its leading members. Iraq's challenge to the stability of the global system could not go unanswered. Iraq's actions threatened the principles of sovereignty and national interest for states both in the region and elsewhere and threatened Western interest in keeping unimpeded the oil flowing from the region. Although Kuwait was the immediate victim of Iraqi aggression, many feared that Iraqi domination of the Persian Gulf would give it immense oil-rich leverage over Saudi Arabia. The allies were protecting their national interests by trying to safeguard their oil supply.

From Iraq's vantage, Kuwait's actions caused the invasion. Iraqis argued that Kuwait had violated Iraq's sovereignty by claiming border areas rich in oil and by engaging in "slant drilling" to tap Iraq's reserves. Kuwait did not seize Iraqi territory, but its actions had the same effect. Iraq also had a historical claim to Kuwait, whose borders had been drawn by British colonial authorities.[92] Beyond these territorial quarrels, Iraq sought to defend its economic interests. Baghdad was vexed by Kuwait's refusal to cancel debts incurred in Iraq's eight-year war against Iran, in which the Iraqis felt they were protecting the "Arab nation" against "Persian aggression." Baghdad also sought to force an increase in global oil prices, which the Iraqis believed were being kept artificially low by Kuwaiti and Saudi overproduction. Negotiations between Iraq and Kuwait failed, and Iraq felt compelled to force a resolution to these questions and, when it saw an excuse, did so.

The Decision-Making Perspective

Another explanation for Iraq's decision to invade Kuwait and for the U.S. response to it is based on the radically differing perceptions held by Presidents George Bush and Saddam Hussein and their advisers. Their perceptions about the Middle East situation and the events that led up to the conflict were so at odds that their decisions set them on a collision course.

We can summarize President Bush's foreign-policy values and beliefs as pragmatic and prudent, labels that are closely associated with power politics, the approach that informed the president's view of the world. His administration was generally cautious in foreign policy, carefully watching changes in power and threats to the global status quo. Within days of the invasion, President Bush's definition of the situation compelled him to make a decisive response. He saw Kuwait as a close U.S. ally and was sensitive to growing Saudi fears that they might be the next victims. First, Bush believed that Saddam Hussein had deceived him: "This aggression came just hours after Saddam Hussein specifically assured numerous countries in the area that there would be no invasion. . . . Only 14 days ago, Saddam Hussein promised his friends he would not invade Kuwait. And 4 days ago, he promised the world he would withdraw. And twice we have seen what his promises mean. His promises mean nothing." Second, recalling his own experience in World War II and the bitter fruit of Western appeasement of Hitler (to whom he compared Saddam), Bush concluded that aggression must be answered. "There is no justification whatsoever," he declared, "for this outrageous and brutal act of aggression." Third, for the president, much more than Kuwait was at stake: "This is not an American problem or a European problem or a Middle East problem."[93] These perceptions led the president to order an embargo on U.S. trade with Iraq, freeze Iraqi assets in the United States, and deploy a military force to Saudi Arabia to protect that country.

Saddam Hussein's definition of the situation was crucial in Iraq's decision to seize Kuwait. He believed that the United States would not react; indeed, he saw the United States as indifferent to his disputes with Kuwait over territorial boundaries and oil prices. This perception was encouraged by American actions throughout the 1980s and immediately before the crisis in August 1990. After 1984, when U.S.-Iraqi ties were restored after having been severed during the 1967 Six-Day War, the United States sought to improve relations with Iraq. During the Iran-Iraq War (1981–1988), Washington tilted toward Iraq and shared with Baghdad intelligence information about Iran. Even when Iraqi jets, perhaps by error, attacked the USS *Stark* in May 1987 in the Persian Gulf, killing thirty-seven American sailors, the Reagan administration accepted the explanation that the attack was a mistake. Further, although the Reagan administration chided Iraq for using chemical weapons against Kurdish villages, it did little more. Indeed, both the Reagan and Bush administrations worked to forestall congressional economic sanctions against Iraq from 1988 through summer 1990 by removing Iraq from the list of states that supported international terrorism.[94]

Saddam's perception of the United States was reinforced by reassurances of American friendship offered by the U.S. ambassador to Iraq, April Glaspie. About a week before the invasion, Ambassador Glaspie told Saddam Hussein, "I have direct instructions from President Bush to seek better relations with Iraq" and added that the United States had "no opinion on the Arab-Arab conflict, like your border disagreement with Kuwait."[95] In congressional testimony only days before the invasion, U.S. officials failed to issue a warning to Saddam. Saddam Hussein undoubtedly held President Bush personally responsible for Iraq's subsequent expulsion from Kuwait. In revenge, he apparently organized an unsuccessful assassination attempt against Bush when the former president visited Kuwait early in 1993.[96]

Organizational and Bureaucratic Perspectives

Theories of bureaucratic and organizational politics are helpful in explaining allied and Iraqi actions as the Gulf crisis deepened between August 1990 and mid-January 1991. As the allies sought to strengthen their forces in the Persian Gulf and deter Iraqi aggression against Saudi Arabia, standard operating procedures were followed to determine the mix of naval, air force, and army units dispatched to the area. Initially, General Norman Schwarzkopf, allied commander in the Gulf, had insufficient forces to deter Saddam. As the crisis began, Schwarzkopf estimated that it would take seventeen weeks to build up an effective deterrent force.[97] Thus at first the allies were trying to bluff the Iraqis about the allied armies' strength to make deterrence credible.

Coordination and bureaucratic bargaining among the allies was an important requisite for action. Crucial bargains had to be struck among Europeans, Japan, and the United States on funding the military effort. The United States wanted Europe and Japan to foot more of the bill, and it wanted the Europeans to provide more forces. In the end, Japan provided about $11 billion and Germany about $6.5 billion to support the operation, and the Europeans (principally the British and French) provided large military contingents.[98]

We can glean more about the Persian Gulf events by applying the bureaucratic-politics approach to the U.S. decision to use force. Congress and the public supported President Bush's decision to impose an economic embargo and send forces to the Persian Gulf, but agreement was less solid on the actual use of force.[99] The administration sought an adequate rationale for initiating the use of force and trumpeted Saddam's development of weapons of mass destruction and allegations about Iraqi atrocities in Kuwait to set the stage for offensive operations. As the president took steps to double U.S. forces in Saudi Arabia early in November 1990 to give the allies an "offensive capability," Congress felt its constitutional prerogative to declare war was being infringed upon. Some members of Congress wanted to vote on the question promptly; others wanted to wait until the new Congress was seated in January 1991 and the president made a formal request. Still others believed the president had the authority to go forward if he wished.[100]

Thus, pulling and hauling started between the two branches of government with all the features of the bureaucratic-politics model evident. Congressional foreign-affairs and armed-services committees launched public hearings to assess the wisdom of continuing economic sanctions versus authorizing the use of force. The president argued that he did not need congressional authorization and had authority as chief executive to use force if necessary.[101] Fifty-four members of Congress even filed a legal challenge to the president in a U.S. district court. The case was dismissed, pending a decision by Congress itself. By January 8, 1991, however, President Bush had changed his mind and requested authorization from Congress to carry out U.N. Resolution 678 to use force to end Iraq's occupation of Kuwait.[102] After three days of debate in both chambers, Congress approved the president's request by narrow margins (205–183 in the House and 52–47 in the Senate). The fate of American policy in the Middle East was bound up in bargaining between the two branches of government. To this extent, the bureaucratic-politics model provides a useful guide to events.

The Transnational Perspective

The transnational perspective on the Gulf War focuses on the global system, a broader range of actors, and the links among them to explain what transpired. The issue involved a variety of actors. Among them were private arms suppliers and defense industries—"merchants of death"—in Germany, France, Sweden, and elsewhere who had provided Iraq with information and material necessary for producing chemical, biological, and even nuclear weapons. A number of terrorist groups were sheltered by the Iraqi dictator and offered him their services. Transnational corporations, especially oil firms like Aramco and Exxon, saw their profits soar as the price of crude oil jumped after Iraq occupied Kuwait. The International Red Cross encouraged both sides to observe international law, including humane treatment of prisoners of war.

From the beginning, the United Nations was involved. Within hours of Iraq's invasion, the U.N. Security Council passed a resolution condemning the act and calling for swift Iraqi withdrawal. Through eleven other resolutions from August to November 1990, the Security Council imposed air, sea, and land sanctions against Iraq to compel it to leave Kuwait. The last of these resolutions, passed on November 29, 1990, took the step of authorizing member states "to use all necessary means to uphold and implement" the previous resolutions.[103] The only reservation was that Iraq be given until January 15, 1991, to leave Kuwait before force would be used.

These resolutions enjoyed broad support, and no more than two states voted against any of the twelve resolutions the Council passed. Hence, they signified consensus in the global community about Iraq's actions. It might be argued that these resolutions served only as instruments for implementing the policy desired by one country—the United States—but the resolutions also played an intermediary role in many states' foreign-policy calculations. Some states were undoubtedly more likely to accept using force against Iraq because the global community voiced approval by the Security Council's action. This approval was absolutely essential to obtain compliance from Arab states such as Egypt and Syria.

Conclusion

In this chapter, we have examined factors internal and external to states that influence foreign policy, thereby exposing the Janus faces of the process. We looked at the state-centric and decision-making approaches, in which the unitary state or its primary decision-makers are considered sufficient to explain foreign policy. These perspectives provide competing explanations that focus respectively on action-reaction among states and on perceptions and interests of decision-makers within states. Each adds to the mosaic that explains foreign policy, but each also omits important factors.

The organizational-process, bureaucratic-politics, and transnational models of foreign policy provide increasingly richer detail. The first two enable the analyst to appreciate the complexity of decision making within a state. These approaches also move us away from the unitary rational-state actor. Instead, they suggest a process that is more competitive (the bureaucratic-politics model) or more cybernetic and routinized (the organizational-process model) than the state-centric model allows. The transnational perspective prompts us to look at actors other than the state to make sense of foreign policy. Both international organizations and nonstate actors have interests that transcend state frontiers and the capacity to act autonomously. As we move from one model to the next, we get a more complete picture of the sources of foreign policy.

To illustrate how these several perspectives can be applied to enrich our understanding of foreign policy, we examined the Persian Gulf War. Each perspective depicts somewhat differently the events that led up to the war because each points to different factors. By combining those perspectives, we come to comprehend the Janus faces of foreign policy.

Having seen that states are not the only actors on the global stage, the next chapter focuses on some of these other entities—nonstate actors. It will describe the origins and evolution of some of these and assess their changing role in global politics.

Key Terms

action-reaction model
affective approach
billiard-ball model
black-boxing
bounded rationality
bureaucratic-politics model
cognitive approach
cognitive consistency
comprehensive rationality
crisis
cybernetic model

decision-makers
decision-making approach
definition of the situation
external setting
foreign policy
image
incremental bias
interagency group (IG)
internal setting
Janus faces of foreign policy
organizational-process model

perceptions
role
satisficing
senior interagency group (SIG)
social structure
standard operating procedures
  (SOPs)
state-centric theory
stimulus-response
tectonic-plates model
transnational model

End Notes

[1] In Roman tradition, Janus is depicted as looking both to the future and to the past.

[2] These distinctions are drawn from James N. Rosenau, "The Study of Foreign Policy," in Rosenau, Kenneth W. Thompson, and Gavin Boyd, eds., *World Politics: An Introduction* (New York: Free Press, 1976), p. 16.

[3] Lawrence Chimerine and James Fallows, "Japan Deserves a Tariff," *New York Times,* June 9, 1995, p. A29.

[4] David E. Sanger, "U.S. Plans to Threaten Japan with Tariffs in Trade Dispute," *New York Times,* April 13, 1995, p. C5.

[5] See Alison Mitchell, "Clinton Meets Japan's Premier as Trade Heats Up Campaign," *New York Times,* February 25, 1996, sec. 1, p. 4.

[6] Charles W. Kegley, Jr., "Decision Regimes and the Comparative Study of Foreign Policy," in Charles F. Hermann, Charles W. Kegley, Jr., and James N. Rosenau, eds., *New Directions in the Study of Foreign Policy* (Boston: Allen & Unwin, 1987), p. 248.

[7] Stephen D. Krasner, "Regimes and the Limits of Realism: Regimes as Autonomous Variables," *International Organization* 36:2 (Spring 1982), p. 498.

[8] Arnold Wolfers, *Discord and Collaboration* (Baltimore: Johns Hopkins University Press, 1962), p. 19.

[9] James N. Rosenau, "Pre-Theories and Theories of Foreign Policy," in R. Barry Farrell, ed., *Approaches to Comparative and International Politics* (Evanston, IL: Northwestern University Press, 1966), pp. 27–92.

[10] Krasner, "Regimes and the Limits of Realism," p. 498.

[11] An ideally "rational" process assumes agreement on underlying values, perfect information about alternatives, and unfettered capacity to take advantage of that information.

[12] The classic treatment of national interest and foreign policy is Hans J. Morgenthau, *Politics Among Nations* (New York: Knopf, 1948). More recent treatments of national interest and

[13]Kenneth E. Boulding, *The Image* (Ann Arbor: University of Michigan Press, 1956), p. 6. Emphasis in original. Also see Harold and Margaret Sprout, "Environmental Factors in the Study of International Politics," in James N. Rosenau, ed., *International Politics and Foreign Policy,* rev. ed. (New York: Free Press, 1969), pp. 41-56. For the sort of research that this insight inspired, see Herbert C. Kelman, ed., *International Behavior* (New York: Holt, Rinehart and Winston, 1965.)

[14]Richard C. Snyder, H.W. Bruck, and Burton Sapin, "The Decision-Making Approach to the Study of International Politics," in Rosenau, ed., *International Politics and Foreign Policy,* pp. 199-206.

[15]Dean G. Pruitt, "Definition of the Situation as a Determinant of International Action," in Kelman, ed., *International Behavior,* p. 394.

[16]Cited in Bob Davis and Michael Williams, "U.S.-Japan Trade Flap Intensifies as U.S. Sets Early Date for Tariffs," *Wall Street Journal,* May 17, 1995, p. A1. Clinton's strong stand against Fidel Castro's Cuba also reflected electoral imperatives in the United States, especially in Florida. Thus in 1996 Clinton signed the Helms-Burton bill even though it required taking steps against Canadian and European companies with business in Cuba.

[17]Harold and Margaret Sprout, "Environmental Factors in the Study of International Politics," p. 45. Emphasis in original.

[18]For an analysis of different situations and their effect on policy, see Charles F. Hermann, "International Crisis as a Situational Variable," in Rosenau, ed., *International Politics and Foreign Policy,* pp. 409-421.

[19]Robert Mandel, "Psychological Approaches to International Relations," in Margaret G. Hermann, ed., *Political Psychology* (San Francisco: Jossey-Bass, 1986), p. 253.

[20]For more on cognitive approaches, see Christer Jonsson, ed., *Cognitive Dynamics and International Politics* (New York: St. Martin's Press, 1982); and Donald A. Sylvan and Steve Chan, eds., *Foreign Policy Decision Making: Perception, Cognition, and Artificial Intelligence* (New York: Praeger, 1984).

[21]Ole R. Holsti, "The Belief System and National Images: A Case Study," *Journal of Conflict Resolution* 6:3 (September 1962), pp. 244-252.

[22]Ole R. Holsti, Robert C. North, and Richard A. Brody, "Perception and Action in the 1914 Crisis," in J. David Singer, ed., *Quantitative International Politics* (New York: Free Press, 1968), p. 154. Also Dina A. Zinnes, "The Expression and Perception of Hostility in Prewar Crisis: 1914," in ibid., pp. 85-119.

[23]Ole R. Holsti, Robert C. North, and Richard A. Brody, "Measuring Affect and Action in International Reactions Models: Empirical Materials from the 1962 Crisis," in Rosenau, ed., *International Politics and Foreign Policy,* p. 694.

[24]Margaret G. Hermann, "Explaining Foreign Policy Behavior Using the Personal Characteristics of Political Leaders," *International Studies Quarterly* 24:1 (March 1980), pp. 7-46. Also see Robert Mandel, "Psychological Approaches to International Relations," p. 256.

[25]Lloyd S. Etheredge, "Personality Effects on American Foreign Policy, 1898-1968: A Test of Interpersonal Generalization Theory," *American Political Science Review* 72:2 (June 1978), pp. 434-451. Also see Etheredge, *A World of Men: The Private Sources of American Foreign Policy* (Cambridge: MIT Press, 1978).

[26]See Robert Jervis, *Perception and Misperception in International Politics* (Princeton: Princeton University Press, 1976), pp. 28-31 for a two-step perceptual model. The phrase is at p. 29.

[27]The most accessible exposition of these models is in Graham Allison and Philip Zelikow, *Essence of Decision,* 2nd ed. (New York: Longman, 1999). Allison labels his bureaucratic-politics model "governmental politics." Nevertheless, the former label is more widely applied to this approach in the literature. For penetrating critiques of the bureaucratic-politics approach, see Jonathan Bendor and Thomas H. Hammond, "Rethinking Allison's Models," *American Political Science Review* 86:2 (June 1992), pp. 301-322, and Edward Rhodes, "Do Bureaucratic Politics Matter? Some Disconfirming Findings from the Case of the U.S. Navy," *World Politics* 47:1 (October 1994), pp. 1-41.

[28]Allison and Zelikow, *Essence of Decision,* p. 255.

[29]Michael Cooper, "Once Secret, 80 Reports Illuminate the Cold War," *New York Times,* December 4, 1994, sec. 1, p. 16.

[30]Some foreign-policy bureaucracies are typically left out of the decision making. For the ABM, the Arms Control and Disarmament Agency, State Department, and President's Science Advisory Committee did not have "a major role in the decisions." Morton H. Halperin. "The Decision to Deploy the ABM: Bureaucratic and Domestic Politics in the Johnson Administration," *World Politics* 25:1 (October 1972), p. 72.

[31]Ibid., p. 91.

[32]Allison and Zelikow, *Essence of Decision,* p. 346.

[33]Douglas Jehl, "Clinton Drops 19-Year Ban on U.S. Trade with Vietnam: Cites Hanoi's Help on M.I.A.'s," *New York Times,* February 4, 1994, pp. A1, A6.

[34]José de Cordoba, "Politics vs. the Heart: New U.S. Policy Toward Cuban Refugees Receives Little Heat—So Far," *Wall Street Journal,* August 29, 1994, p. A12.

[35]Steven A. Holmes, "With Persuasion and Muscle: Black Caucus Reshapes Haiti Policy," *New York Times,* July 14, 1994, p. A6.

[36]Raymond Bonner, "U.S. Helicopter Sale to Turkey Hits Snag," *New York Times,* March 29, 1996, p. A4.

[37]See "Agreement on Nuclear Fuel Prompts South Carolina Suit," *New York Times,* September 11, 1994, sec. 1, p. 15.

[38]Larry Rohter, "Foreign Policy: Florida Has One," *New York Times,* May 22, 1994, sec. 4, p. 1. See also Eric Schmitt, "Debate

on Immigration Bill Yields Deep Division and Unusual Allies," *New York Times,* February 26, 1996, pp. A1, A7.

[39]Steven Greenhouse, "Untidy Policy Pays Off in Cuba Crisis," *New York Times,* September 11, 1994, sec. 1, p. 4; Richard L. Berke, "Gov. Chiles Seizes the Refugee Issue," *New York Times,* September 11, 1994, sec. 1, p. 12.

[40]"To the Rescue," *The Economist,* September 3-9, 1994, p. 35; "California, Here We Still Come," *The Economist,* November 12-18, 1994, pp. 53-54. Mexicans were angered at this referendum. "Protesters in Mexico City Ransack a McDonald's," *New York Times,* October 9, 1994, p. A3.

[41]B. Drummond Ayres, Jr., "California Governor Suggests Requiring Citizenship Cards," *New York Times,* October 27, 1994, pp. A1, A11.

[42]Deborah Sontage, "3 Governors Take Pleas on Aliens to the Senate," *New York Times,* June 23, 1994, p. A10; Sam Howe Verhover, "Texas and California," *New York Times,* June 26, 1994, sec. 1, p. 8; "Congressional Commission Calls for Crackdown on Illegal Aliens," *New York Times,* October 1, 1994, p. 8. Concern about the harsh rhetoric about immigrants was reflected in Pope John Paul II's call to the United States "to be a hospitable society, a welcoming culture." Cited in Celestine Bohlen, "Pope Urges Nations to Confront Crises," *New York Times,* October 6, 1995, p. A1.

[43]Mexico ranked only fourth, behind Japan, Canada, and South Korea, as a market for California's exports. "Two States of Mind About Those Southern Neighbours," *The Economist,* July 13-19, 1996, pp. 25-27.

[44]Cited in David Firestone, "White House Condemns Giuliani for Ejecting Arafat from Concert," *New York Times,* October 25, 1995, p. A1. In May 1996, Arafat was hosted by President Clinton at the White House.

[45]Cited in David Firestone, "Behind Giuliani's Snub of Arafat Lies Strategy," *New York Times,* October 26, 1995, p. B9.

[46]See Steven Greenhouse, "A G.O.P. House Leader Presses Attack on Clinton Foreign Policy," *New York Times,* December 9, 1994, p. A7.

[47]One example was Republican demands to move the U.S. Embassy in Israel from Tel Aviv to Jerusalem even at the risk of disrupting Israeli-Palestinian peace negotiations.

[48]Anthony dePalma, "Economy Reeling, Mexicans Prepare Tough New Steps," *New York Times,* February 26, 1995, sec. 1, p. 1. In turn, Mexican domestic interests pressed President Ernesto Zedillo to resist steps surrendering Mexican sovereignty "for a sack full of American dollars." Anthony dePalma, "Dollar Duress?" *New York Times,* February 22, 1995, pp. A1, C16.

[49]David E. Sanger, "Mexico Crisis Seen Spurring Flow of Aliens," *New York Times,* January 18, 1995, p. A3.

[50]Elaine Sciolino, "New Dole Bills Seeking to Steer Foreign Policy," *New York Times,* January 5, 1995, pp. A1, A3; Alison Mitchell, "White House Seeks to Halt Bosnia Bill," *New York Times,* July 19, 1995, p. A4.

[51]Steven Greenhouse, "White House Urges Senate to Maintain U.S. Global Role," *New York Times,* February 27, 1995, p. A4; Eric Schmitt, "Republicans Say Nuclear Deal with Iran Imperils Aid to Russia," *New York Times,* May 8, 1995, p. A4.

[52]Steven Greenhouse, "Republicans Seek to Derail Accord with North Korea," *New York Times,* November 27, 1994, sec. 1, pp. 1, 11.

[53]Cited in Steven Greenhouse, "Republicans Plan to Guide Foreign Policy by Purse String," *New York Times,* November 13, 1994, sec. 1, p. 8. The Clinton administration pointed out that foreign aid was at its lowest level since World War II. Steven Greenhouse, "Foreign Aid and G.O.P.: Deep Cuts," *New York Times,* December 21, 1994, p. A4.

[54]Cited in Elaine Sciolino, "Awaiting Call, Helms Puts Foreign Policy on Hold," *New York Times,* September 24, 1995, sec. 1, p. 6.

[55]Cited in James Sterngold, "Japanese Tax Cuts Are Thwarted," *New York Times,* April 27, 1994, p. C9.

[56]Herbert A. Simon, *Models of Man* (New York: Wiley, 1957), p. 198.

[57]John D. Steinbruner, *The Cybernetic Theory of Decision* (Princeton: Princeton University Press, 1974), pp. 66-67.

[58]Ibid., p. 69.

[59]Allison and Zelikow, *Essence of Decision,* p. 175.

[60]Established by the 1947 National Security Act, the NSC consists of the president, vice president, secretary of state, secretary of defense, and others that the president may name, and it is "to advise the president with respect to the integration of domestic, foreign, and military policies. . . ." P.L. 253, in United States Statutes At Large, vol. 61, p. 1, 80th Cong., 1st Sess., p. 496.

[61]Allison and Zelikow, *Essence of Decision,* pp. 210-217.

[62]James G. Blight, Joseph S. Nye, Jr., and David A. Welch, "The Cuban Missile Crisis Revisited," *Foreign Affairs* 66:1 (Fall 1987), p. 181. This article gives a taste of information that became available about the crisis when the Cold War ended. See also David A. Welch and James G. Blight, "The Eleventh Hour of the Cuban Missile Crisis: An Introduction to the ExComm Transcripts," *International Security* 12:3 (Winter 1987/88), pp. 5-29.

[63]Allison and Zelikow, *Essence of Decision,* pp. 235-236.

[64]Kim Richard Nossal, "Bureaucratic Politics and the Westminster Model," in Robert O. Matthews, Arthur G. Rubinoff, and Janice Gross Stein, eds., *International Conflict and Conflict Management* (Scarborough, Ont.: Prentice-Hall of Canada, 1984), p. 122.

[65]Ibid., p. 125.

[66]There are exceptions. Allison was able to use his models to explain Soviet actions in the Cuban case. Another scholar who has used this approach effectively to explain Soviet policy is Jiri Valenti. See "The Bureaucratic Politics Paradigm and the

Soviet Invasion of Czechoslovakia," *Political Science Quarterly* 94: 1 (Spring 1979), pp. 55-76.

[67]Robert J. Art, "Bureaucratic Politics and American Foreign Policy: A Critique," *Policy Sciences* 4 (1973), pp. 467-490.

[68]Stephen D. Krasner, "Are Bureaucracies Important? (Or Allison Wonderland)," *Foreign Policy* 7 (Summer 1972), pp. 159-179.

[69]Ibid., pp. 169, 179.

[70]Robert O. Keohane and Joseph S. Nye, Jr., *Power and Interdependence,* 2nd ed. (Glenview, IL: Scott, Foresman, 1989). Also Richard W. Mansbach, Yale H. Ferguson, and Donald E. Lampert, *The Web of World Politics* (Englewood Cliffs, NJ: Prentice Hall, 1976).

[71]Keohane and Nye, *Power and Interdependence,* pp. 29-37; and Joseph S. Nye, Jr., *Bound to Lead* (New York: Basic Books, 1990), pp. 174-201.

[72]See James M. McCormick, "Alternate Approaches to Evaluating International Organizations: Some Research Directions," *Polity* 14, 3 (Spring 1982), p. 532; and Charles Pentland, "International Organizations," in Rosenau, Thompson, and Boyd, eds., *World Politics,* pp. 621-659.

[73]"A New NATO," *The Economist,* December 9-15, 1995, p. 51. The NATO force was called the Implementation Force (Ifor).

[74]See John G. Stoessinger, *The United Nations and the Superpowers,* 4th ed. (New York: Random House, 1977), and Alexander Dallin, *The Soviet Union at the United Nations* (New York: Praeger, 1962).

[75]Ronald T. Libby, "External Co-Optation of a Less Developed Country's Policy Making: The Case of Ghana, 1969-1972," *World Politics* 29:1 (October 1976), pp. 67-89.

[76]Robert L. Rothstein, *The Weak in the World of the Strong: The Developing Countries in the International System* (New York: Columbia University Press, 1977), p. 145.

[77]Douglas Jehl, "Carter, His Own Emissary, Outpaces White House," *New York Times,* June 20, 1994, p. A3.

[78]Katherine Q. Seelye, "National Rifle Association Is Turning to World Stage to Fight Gun Control," *New York Times,* April 2, 1997, p. A12.

[79]Philip Shenon, "French Plans for Nuclear Tests Incite Anger in Pacific Nations," *New York Times,* June 18, 1995, sec. 1, p. 4.

[80]Gustav Niebuhr, "U.S. Bishops Urge Curb on Global Arms Trade and Ban on Land Mines," *New York Times,* June 17, 1995, p. 8.

[81]Cited in Robert D. Putnam, "Diplomacy and Domestic Politics: The Logic of Two-Level Games," *International Organization* 42:3 (Summer 1988), p. 433. See also Putnam, "Diplomacy and Domestic Politics: The Impact of Domestic Politics on Transatlantic Bargaining," in Helga Haftendorn and Christian Tuschhoff, eds., *America and Europe in an Era of Change* (Boulder, CO: Westview, 1993), pp. 69-83.

[82]Cited in "House Passes Bill to Lift Nuclear Sanctions on Food for India and Pakistan," *New York Times,* July 15, 1998, p. A9.

[83]See, for example, Steven Erlanger, "China Policy: Politics Rules," *New York Times,* April 29, 1997, pp. A1, A6; David E. Sanger, "Boeing and Other Concerns Lobby Congress for China," *New York Times,* April 29, 1998, p. A6.

[84]Katherine Q. Seelye, "Accord Opens Way for Abortion Pill in U.S. in Two Years," *New York Times,* May 17, 1994, pp. A1, A8; Philip J. Hilts, "Trials of French Abortion Pill Begin in U.S.," *New York Times,* October 28, 1994, p. A8.

[85]Cited in Katherine Q. Seelye, "Family Planning and Foreign Policy Are Linked, Albright Tells House Panel," *New York Times,* February 12, 1997, p. A12. See also Steven A. Holmes, "U.S. Assistance to International Birth-Control Programs Faces Further Cuts," *New York Times,* September 12, 1996, p. A6.

[86]See Sam Dillon, "Mexico and Drugs," *New York Times,* March 8, 1997, p. 5.

[87]Cited in Elaine Sciolino, "Taiwan's Lobbying: Friendship Plus Hardball," *New York Times,* April 9, 1996, p. A6.

[88]David Johnston, "U.S. Agency Secretly Monitored Chinese in '96 on Political Gifts," *New York Times,* March 13, 1997, pp. A1, A12. See also Robert Pear, "F.B.I. Warned of Donations from China, Senator Says," *New York Times,* March 10, 1997, p. A11; Elaine Sciolino, "Campaign Finance Complicates China Policy," *New York Times,* March 10, 1997, pp. A1, A7. Other effective ethnic lobbies in the United States include those of India, Pakistan, Greece, and Armenia. See Dan Morgan and Kevin Merida, "When Foreign Concerns Invade Our Politics," *Washington Post National Weekly Edition,* March 31, 1997, pp. 11-12.

[89]Such a scenario recognizes that manipulation of prices would prove costly to the bully as well as to its victims but assumes that the bully is prepared to bear those costs for political ends.

[90]Much of the world's agriculture depends on petroleum-based fertilizers. Modern agricultural techniques also rely on combines and other vehicles that consume large amounts of oil. In consequence, agrarian societies in Africa and Asia are as sensitive to shifts in oil prices as are industrialized regions.

[91]The apparent success of U.S. high-tech weapons, such as Patriot missiles, enhanced the value of the stock of corporations like Raytheon that built them. The use of such weapons in the war renewed calls for investment in the moribund Star Wars program and for protecting the defense budget from further cuts.

[92]Three decades earlier, Iraqi claims to Kuwait had been rebuffed by the British.

[93]The cited passages are from President Bush's speech to the nation, "The Arabian Peninsula: U.S. Principles," delivered on August 8, 1990.

[94]During this period Baghdad hosted and assisted some of the world's most notorious terrorists.

[95]The first passage is cited in Tom Matthews, "The Road to War," *Newsweek,* January 28, 1991, p. 56. The second is from

Elaine Sciolino with Michael R. Gordon, "U.S. Gave Iraq Little Reason Not to Mount Assault," *New York Times,* September 23, 1990, p. 1.

[96]In retaliation, President Clinton ordered a cruise-missile attack against Iraqi intelligence headquarters in central Baghdad.

[97]Bob Woodward, *The Commanders* (New York: Simon & Schuster, 1991), p. 252.

[98]Others making major financial commitments to the war effort were Saudi Arabia, Kuwait, the United Arab Emirates, and South Korea. Statement of Charles A. Bowsher, Comptroller General of the United States, before the Committee on Budget, U.S. House of Representatives, February 27, 1991 (Washington, DC: U.S. General Accounting Office, n.d.), p. 12.

[99]As a rule, the American public rallies in support of the president when force is actually used.

[100]Adam Clymer, "Congress in Step," *New York Times,* January 14, 1991, p. A11.

[101]President Clinton took the same position on America's intervention in Haiti. Neil A. Lewis, "Aides Say Clinton Doesn't Need Vote in Congress to Invade Haiti," *New York Times,* September 12, 1994, pp. A1, A8.

[102]Clymer, "Congress in Step," p. A11.

[103]U.N. Security Council Resolution 678 (1990), reprinted in Marjorie Ann Browne, "Iraq-Kuwait: U.N. Security Council Resolutions—Texts and Votes." Washington, DC: Congressional Research Service, the Library of Congress, December 4, 1990.

Chapter 7

Beyond the Nation-State: A World of Many Actors

W e live in a world in which numerous actors compete for loyalties and resources.[1] The global system is no longer dominated only by sovereign states, and global politics features extensive interaction among "qualitatively different types of actors,"[2] from global international organizations (to which we shall turn in the next chapter) to tiny bands of mercenaries.[3]

In this chapter we survey *nonstate actors* (sometimes called *nongovernmental organizations* or *NGOs*) in world politics. NGOs are composed of private individuals or groups. They include *subnational groups* like most political parties located within a single state and *transnational actors* like corporations or religious groups that operate across national frontiers. Depending on the issue, these actors may challenge the prerogatives of states in different ways. Giant corporations challenge states' economic independence; terrorists challenge the security of their citizens; and dissatisfied ethnic groups challenge their territorial integrity. In other words, there is an enormous variety of nonstate actors performing a variety of tasks and participating in global *governance* in a variety of ways. Governance, declares political scientist James Rosenau, "encompasses the activities of governments, but it also includes any actors who resort to command mechanisms to make demands, frame goals, issue directives, and pursue policies."[4] Some, especially transnational corporations, knit together peoples from around the world. Others, especially humanitarian groups like the International Red Cross and Doctors Without Borders, help people survive when states have collapsed.[5] Still others, like terrorists, ethnic groups, and religious fundamentalists, are among the most important sources of fragmentation in our postinternational world. Even individuals, for example, Pope John Paul II or the American tycoon Ted Turner, who has promised $1 billion to the United Nations, may be autonomous actors.

Together, nonstate actors produce, in the words of Rosenau, a *"multicentric" world,* in contrast to the *"state-centric" world* of "sovereignty-bound" nation-states.[6] Nonstate actors collectively constitute *global civic society*—an arena "in which people engage in spontaneous, customary, and nonlegalistic forms of association."[7] "The idea of world civic politics," writes Paul Wapner, "signifies that embedded in the activities" of nonstate actors "is an understanding that states do not hold a monopoly over the instruments that govern human affairs but rather that nonstate forms of governance exist and can be used to effect widespread change."[8]

Almost no area of human activity is untouched by nonstate actors. To illustrate the range and significance of these actors, we survey a few key types. Keep in mind three considerations. First, similar groups have existed historically. Second, such actors are being asked to do more and more in the post–Cold War era. Third, some integrate disparate peoples in different states and so further globalization, whereas others fragment states, creating ever smaller and more parochial polities in the process.

Transnational Corporations

A useful place to begin is with *transnational corporations (TNCs)*.[9] These corporations—economic enterprises that engage in foreign direct investment and conduct business in more than one country[10]—are engines of globalization, knitting peoples together in a vast system of economic exchange.

There are about 37,000 TNCs, with more than 200,000 foreign affiliates,[11] and, in 1995 alone, they invested a record $325 billion to buy out or set up new subsidiaries.[12] TNCs span the globe and control immense economic resources, and their names are household words. General Motors, for example, has revenues in excess of $178 billion and has almost 700,000 employees.[13] Table 7.1 depicts the sixty wealthiest economic entities in the world as measured by gross domestic product and total corporate revenue.[14] It shows how transnational corporations like General Motors, Ford, and Mitsui rank ahead of most states and account for over one-third of the world's sixty largest economic entities. Indeed, there is growing fear that some corporations may become global monopolies, and it was this concern that led the European Union initially to oppose the merger of Boeing Corporation with McDonnell Douglas.[15] Such concentrations of economic power can be used for political ends in a variety of ways, from contributing to political campaigns and bribing government officials to providing or withholding investments on which national prosperity depends. As we shall see in Chapter 12, TNCs seek to operate in politically favorable environments with a minimum of government supervision.

Although there are historical examples of transnational corporations and trading groups—for instance, the English and Dutch East India companies[16] and the Hanseatic League[17]—the role of such corporations has greatly expanded in recent decades. With proliferating links among national economies and revolutions in communication, transportation, and computer technologies, TNCs have become global actors, and global trade increasingly takes place among these corporations or their subsidiaries rather than among nation-states. TNCs enjoy more flexibility than most states. Says one observer:

> While multinational companies can invest or disinvest, merge with others or go it alone, rise from nothing or disappear in bankruptcy, the state seems stodgy and stuck in comparison. The state is glued more or less to one piece of territory, fighting off entropy and budget crises, the national community usually assessing the latest foreign attacks upon a condition of declining competitiveness and the vulnerability in its domestic markets.[18]

Country*	U.S. dollars (billions)	Country	U.S. dollars (billions)
1. United States	7,433.5	31. South Africa	132.5
2. Japan	5,149.2	**32. Mitsubishi**	**128.9**
3. Germany	2,364.6	**33. Royal Dutch/Shell**	**128.1**
4. France	1,533.6	**34. Itochu**	**126.6**
5. United Kingdom	1,152.1	35. Poland	124.7
6. Italy	1,140.5	**36. Exxon**	**122.4**
7. China	906.1	37. Greece	120.0
8. Brazil	709.6	**38. Wal-Mart Stores**	**119.3**
9. Canada	569.9	39. Finland	119.1
10. Spain	563.2	**40. Maruben**	**111.1**
11. South Korea	483.1	**41. Sumitomo**	**102.4**
12. Netherlands	402.6	42. Portugal	100.9
13. Australia	367.8	**43. Toyota Motor**	**95.1**
14. India	357.8	44. Singapore	93.0
15. Russia	356.0	**45. General Electric**	**90.8**
16. Mexico	341.7	46. Israel	90.3
17. Switzerland	313.7	47. Malaysia	89.8
18. Argentina	295.1	48. Philippines	83.3
19. Belgium	268.6	**49. Nissho Iwai**	**81.9**
20. Sweden	227.3	50. Colombia	80.2
21. Austria	226.5	**51. International Business Machines**	**78.5**
22. Indonesia	213.4	**52. Nippon Telegraph & Telephone**	**77.0**
23. General Motors	**178.2**	**53. Axa**	**76.9**
24. Turkey	177.5	**54. Daimler-Benz**	**71.6**
25. Thailand	177.5	**55. Daewoo**	**71.5**
26. Denmark	168.9	**56. Nippon Life Insurance**	**71.4**
27. Ford	**153.6**	**57. British Petroleum**	**71.2**
28. Hong Kong	153.3	58. Chile	70.1
29. Norway	151.2	**59. Hitachi**	**68.6**
30. Mitsui	**142.7**	60. Venezuela	67.3

*The economies of states are measured by GNP—those of TNCs by revenue.

TABLE 7.1
The World's Top Sixty Economic Entities

SOURCES: States' total GNP are from Table 1.1 of the *World Development Indicators 1998,* pp. 12–14. Corporate revenues are from *Fortune* (138:3), August 1998.

Global Reach of the TNC   A transnational corporation is centrally organized but has no home. Whatever its national origin, it pursues its own interests rather than those of any country. TNCs now span the globe and operate in all sectors in both developed and developing countries. Whatever their national origins, these become less and less significant as Ford buys out Mazda, Daimler-Benz buys out Chrysler, and Cadbury Schweppes buys out Dr. Pepper/Seven-Up. "What's emerging," declares one CEO, "is truly a global economy."[19] Sophisticated TNCs like McDonalds tailor products to local tastes and use local management. "You don't have 2,000 stores in Japan," declared one company executive, "by being seen as an American company."[20] Although many TNCs originate in developed countries, some are now appearing in newly industrializing countries, such as Samsung and Hyundai in Korea and Pemex in Mexico.

Corporations have several motives for expanding overseas. First, they seek access to new markets. By establishing subsidiaries in a region, they can avoid import barriers. Second, corporations may expand to get access to local capital markets, raw materials, or low-cost labor. American corporations have established facilities in countries like Mexico to keep down the cost of labor and maintain a competitive edge. Since 1965, U.S. firms have established some 1,700 plants called *maquiladoras* (mills) just across the border in Mexico, which employ some 500,000 Mexicans at wages about 40 percent as high as those in the United States.[21] Third, corporations may move "offshore" to escape a strong currency that makes their products expensive overseas. Japanese firms have expanded significantly into Southeast Asia in recent years, especially because of the strength of the yen. Fourth, corporations may leave a country and settle elsewhere because of a poor local business climate or labor unrest. Whatever their motivation, the flexibility of corporations helps them to play off states against each other.

Corporations become transnational in varying degrees. Some remain ethnocentric, reflecting the values and interests of their home country. Such corporations organize to maximize control by managers at home. Although they have worldwide operations, they remain national in spirit. Other corporations—akin to holding companies—are organized more loosely, giving local affiliates latitude to make decisions and allowing local managers to exercise authority. Subsidiaries are managed locally but receive assistance from the center. Like franchise operations, such corporations benefit by marketing products of local firms. Such arrangements help corporations mobilize local support and evade national restrictions. Combining the advantages of being transnational with sensitivity to local tastes and customs has been called *"multilocalism."*[22]

Escalating foreign investment has globalized production. Today, products like automobiles usually include parts made in several countries, and Ford is producing a "world car" that is much the same no matter where it is sold.[23] As a result, many corporations have progressively fewer ties to their home country. When America's automobile manufacturers invoke patriotism in urging Americans to forsake Japanese cars and "come home," they do not publicize the fact that "American" cars are assembled in many countries and are made from parts produced all over the world. In some respects, "domestic" corporations such as Ford are no more American than Nissan, Toyota, Honda, or Hyundai, which have subsidiaries in the United States and employ large numbers of American workers and managers.

TNC Influence Worldwide

Although states have a variety of weapons they can use against TNCs, among them taxation, capital controls, regulation, and nationalization, they rarely do so because they need corporate investment. When states and TNCs collide, both may be losers. TNC influence differs from country to country, depending on the kind of industry and the skill of local governments. TNCs in extractive industries—tin, silver, coal—are more easily subject to local control because they cannot move away, whereas TNCs in semiskilled manufacturing can pull up stakes and go elsewhere.

Corporations see national impediments to trade or investment and do not want "politics" to interrupt the smooth transaction of business. This makes tension between governments and corporations inevitable and has led to repeated quarrels between the United States and American-based TNCs.[24] Some TNCs fiercely opposed the U.S. policy in 1974 linking Soviet willingness to permit Jewish emigration to granting that country most-favored-nation trade status. They opposed President Jimmy Carter's imposing sanctions on the U.S.S.R. after the 1979 Afghanistan invasion, and President Reagan's efforts to limit Western high-technology exports to the Soviet Union after martial law was declared in Poland in 1981. Although the U.S. government had its way in the first two cases, it incurred political costs in doing so and was forced to reverse its policy in the third.

More recently, as a result of U.S. economic embargoes on Iran, Iraq, and Libya, U.S. oil companies have been unable to compete with European competitors in those countries such as the French Elf Aquitaine and Total SA. In 1995, the Clinton administration forced Conoco to cancel a deal to develop an oil field in Iran.[25] Conoco was quickly replaced by Royal Dutch Shell and Total.[26] Such issues cause friction between the United States and U.S. oil companies because they create "an uneven playing field for U.S. companies and could lead to a major power shift away from the U.S. oil industry."[27] Arguments that economic sanctions rarely work and merely harm U.S. businesses have produced greater reluctance on the part of the U.S. government to use them.[28]

In the main, however, the influence of TNCs has met with little resistance from economically advanced states. Americans consider their growth benign, partly because many of them have American roots and are seen as global engines of free enterprise. It is a different story in less-developed countries (LDCs). Transnational corporations enjoy great economic and political leverage in LDCs, and their presence has generated great debate there. A desperate need for capital, technology, skilled management, and employment opportunities may dissuade governments in LDCs from limiting corporate freedom of operation. Corporations are sometimes able to enlist political aid from home countries, and their influence is increased by control over assets like technology and global marketing and distribution networks. Competition among governments for investment and corporate threats to move operations elsewhere provide added corporate leverage.

A number of cases illustrate how TNCs exert political influence. International Telephone & Telegraph (ITT) was recalled for efforts to prevent the election in Chile of a leftist government headed by Salvador Allende Gossens and for then supporting his overthrow in 1973 by General Augusto Pinochet. ITT memos "give us a picture of ITT operatives and executives, CIA leaders, and State Department people scurrying around in a strenuous 'effort' to stop Allende's assumption of power."[29] The corporation was consumed by fear that its Chilean subsidiary would be nationalized and aligned itself with Allende's internal and external foes. At the time of Allende's election in Chile, more than a hundred U.S.-based firms, including twenty-four of the largest U.S. TNCs, had operations in that country. TNCs such as Phelps Dodge, General Motors, General Cable, RCA, and Xerox controlled much of Chile's economy.[30] Such economic power brings with it political power and ambition.

TNC political influence is also illustrated by the controversial role of seven oil corporations, known collectively as the *"seven sisters."*[31] Shortly after the Standard Oil Trust was broken up in the United States in 1909, Standard Oil of New Jersey began to operate overseas, especially in Venezuela and the Middle East. It was followed by European giants like Royal Dutch/Shell. By the late 1920s, they had formed an oligopoly over oil production, refining, and distribution. For years the companies influenced regional politics directly and indirectly. In 1948, they sought to prevent the U.S. from recognizing Israel so as to avoid antagonizing Arab oil-producing states. In 1953, the Anglo-Iranian Oil Company persuaded the United States and Britain to overthrow Iranian premier Muhammad Mossadegh and, thereafter, formed a consortium to develop Iran's oil resources.

The corporate oligopoly was broken in the 1960s and 1970s by new firms entering the market and the growing power of the oil-producing states. The newer firms produced oil-price reductions in 1959 that triggered the creation of the Organization of Petroleum Exporting Countries (OPEC), an interstate cartel consisting of most of the world's leading oil-producing countries. Nevertheless, petroleum corporations remained in the global corporate elite, constituting the single largest group in the "billion-dollar club" (corporations with sales exceeding $1 billion).[32] And, in recent years, Unocol and Royal Dutch/Shell have been accused of propping up dictators in Myanmar (Burma) and Nigeria, respectively,[33] and mergers such as that of Exxon and Mobil threaten to rebuild the earlier corporate oligopoly.[34]

Some TNCs have used bribery, campaign contributions to favored political candidates, or other corrupt practices, especially when they compete for contracts. Following the discovery that Lockheed Corporation had bribed Japanese officials, the United States passed the 1977 Foreign Corrupt Practices Act, which forbids U.S. companies from paying bribes to win business.

Although some U.S. companies such as Goodyear Tire & Rubber and Napco International have been caught violating this law, most have developed legal practices that help them compete, such as using middlemen or making small "facilitation" payments that they claim are not bribes.[35] A 1998 survey of businessmen and journalists conducted by the NGO Transparency International ranked Cameroon, Paraguay, Honduras, Tanzania, Nigeria, Indonesia, Colombia, Venezuela, Ecuador, Russia, and Vietnam and Kenya (in a tie) as the most corrupt countries in which to do business, and Denmark, Finland, Sweden, and New Zealand as the least corrupt.[36] In 1997, an agreement was reached among the twenty-nine member states in the Organization for Economic Cooperation and Development (OECD) to ban bribery on the part of corporations seeking contracts.[37]

Even when they have no political intent, corporate decisions may have important political consequences, over which governments have limited control. IBM, for example, illegally exported advanced computers to a Russian nuclear weapons laboratory, causing one observer to declare: "This shows that one of America's leading corporations has been undermining national security because it was willing to take risks in entering the Russian market."[38] Swiss, British, French, Italian, American, and, most important, German firms aided Iraq's and Libya's[39] efforts to make weapons of mass destruction. German companies such as Karl Kolb, Rhein Bayern Fahrzeugbau, Thyssen GmbH, Gildemeista Projecta, Inwako, and Messerschmitt-Boelkow-Blohn are accused of providing Iraq with lathes and presses to enrich uranium, plants and equipment to produce poison gas, equipment to make botulin toxin and myco-toxin weapons, and equipment for improving Scud missiles.[40]

A variety of criticisms are directed at TNCs operating in the less-developed countries. One is that that they are lax about the environment. The chemical giant Union Carbide was involved in an environmental disaster in India in which over 2,500 people died quickly and thousands more perished in ensuing weeks or suf-fered debilitating illness. In December 1984, the highly toxic chemical methyl iso-cyanate leaked from a Union Carbide pesticide factory in the city of Bhopal. According to one terrifying description:

> The vapor passed first over the shanty-towns of Jaiprakash and Chhola, just outside the walls of the plant, leaving hundreds dead as they slept. The gas quickly enveloped the city's railway station, where beggars were huddled against the chill. . . . Through temples and shops, over streets and lakes . . . the cloud continued to spread, noiselessly and lethally. . . . As word of the cloud of poison began to spread, hundreds then thousands took to the road in flight from the fumes. . . . As in some eerie science-fiction night-mare people blinded by the gas groped vainly toward uncontaminated air. . . .[41]

More recently, RTZ-CRA, the world's biggest mining group, and ABB Asea Brown Boveri, a Swiss-based TNC, were accused of environmental carelessness.[42] These cases illustrate how developing countries, needing jobs and capital, may be unable to enforce standards that the corporation has to observe at home.

Another charge is that TNCs make unjustifiable profits that they do not share with host countries. It is also argued that relatively few citizens in host countries benefit from the operations of these corporations. The wealthy who spend their money on imports create enclaves of conspicuous consumption in poor societies. TNCs are also accused of overcharging for imported and often obsolete technology. The corporations, it is argued, also make products for export rather than products that would be useful to local populations of poor peasants and residents of teem-ing urban slums. Far from providing capital for local growth, the TNCs compete for local capital, driving up rates for local enterprises. In sum, there are three types of complaints: first, that TNCs do not serve the interests of host states; second, that parent states exercise influence through corporations; and third, that TNCs can take advantage of economic interdependence among states without being subject to international regulation.[43]

Although the growing number of TNCs looking for worldwide opportunities has provided bargaining leverage for a few countries, the bargaining position of LDCs has been further eroded by a shift in corporate investment away from "emerging markets" in the LDCs to the more secure environment of the developed countries. One result has been an improved climate for TNCs in the LDCs. After all, TNCs provide a variety of benefits for host countries. Corporations bring capital investment, train local managers, provide jobs, develop new products (which can be substituted for imports), and infuse new technology. They tend to be export-oriented and sources of needed hard currency. Most important, TNCs link relatively isolated societies to the global economy through global networks of production and distribution. From this perspective, they are capitalism's engines of modernity.

International Terrorists

The simultaneous and bloody bombing of the U.S. embassies in Nairobi, Kenya, and Dar es Salaam, Tanzania, and America's retaliation with cruise missile attacks against terrorist camps in Afghanistan and against a Sudanese factory that was suspected of producing the ingredients for toxic gas remind us of the growing importance of terrorist groups.[44] International terrorists are those who commit acts of violence in several countries or who cross state frontiers to carry out terrorism. Such groups impinge on global politics very differently than TNCs. Whether seeking weapons of mass destruction or bombing trains,[45] terrorists threaten our sense of well-being. Shortly after assuming office in 1981, U.S. Secretary of State Alexander Haig declared that the "ultimate abuse of human rights" was international terrorism,[46] and almost fifteen years later Secretary of State Warren Christopher spoke of how terrorist attacks "have brought home the ruthless persistence of evil, cowardice and intolerance in the world—and the frightening ease with which terrorists can obtain destructive technology."[47] Those who employ terrorism care little for human life and believe that the ends justify the means. *Terrorism* uses violence, often against innocent civilians, to publicize a cause, force a state to change some policy, tempt a state to overreact, frighten citizens into aiding the terrorists, and even make a profit.[48]

The proliferation of terrorist groups has reduced the sense of security of citizens around the world. Authorities everywhere find themselves under siege and threatened by terrorism. Despite vigorous efforts to control skyjacking or to increase security in public buildings, the global community cannot entirely prevent such incidents. And whether we find ourselves in long lines at airports or prevented from traveling as freely as in the past, we are all affected in some way by global terrorism.

Governments and their opponents can become enmeshed in a vicious cycle of terrorism and counterterrorism. The Russian armed forces used indiscriminate shelling and bombing to level the city of Grozny and end Chechnya's independence, and atrocities were committed by Russian soldiers against Chechens suspected of aiding rebels. The Chechens swore revenge, and in June 1995 a group of Chechen rebels fell upon the Russian provincial city of Budyonnovsk, shooting civilians and taking many civilians in a hospital as hostages to force Russia to declare a cease-fire in Chechnya.[49] These actions provoked President Yeltsin to denounce Chechnya as "the center of world terrorism, of bribery and corruption and mafia."[50] When governments fail to respect human rights, their adversaries are unlikely to do so.

Political terrorism and common criminality may merge. Profits from international drug trafficking sometimes help purchase weapons for revolutionaries like Colombia's Revolutionary Armed Forces (FARC).[51] And the drug barons themselves—the Sicilian Mafia and the drug "families" in the Colombian cities of Cali and Medellín—use terrorist violence to produce political unrest and inhibit opponents.

The *narcotraficantes* of Peru and Colombia have used terror without scruple to keep control of the coca industry and to undermine local- and national-government challenges to them. They extend their violence overseas, where their drugs are distributed and sold. Sometimes alliances between drug traffickers and political terrorists are overt, as in Peru, where the *narcotraficantes* and Sendero Luminoso (Shining Path) were aligned in a sinister symbiosis. Shining Path, a Maoist group, needed a haven from which to strike and chose the Upper Huallanga Valley, also home to *narcotraficantes*.[52] In the resulting collaboration, the group provided protection for the drug traffickers in return for financial support. In Burma too, an alliance exists between Shan separatists and a "heroin warlord."[53] Indeed, transnational criminals have become such a problem that a 1994 U.N. conference was held on the topic.[54]

Although some states use terrorism,[55] we are interested here in the nonstate terrorist groups that have proliferated in recent decades and whose behavior violates the international laws and customs established to protect states and to justify their claim to a monopoly of the means of coercion.

The Global Expanse of International Terrorism

Terrorist violence has been used for political purposes throughout history. Writing of the terrorist campaign of Jewish zealots against Roman control of Palestine at the time of Christ's birth, Roman historian Flavius Josephus declared that tactics included "assassinations and guerrilla attacks on Roman personnel and installations."[56] The anti-Roman campaign continued more than a century, culminating in mass suicide by Jewish zealots at Masada. In this century, the most notorious act of terrorism was the assassination of Archduke Francis Ferdinand, heir to the Austro-Hungarian throne, by Gavrilo Princip, a member of the Serbian terrorist Black Hand group, which triggered World War I. The potential danger of terrorism in modern society was clearly shown in the April 1995 bombing of a federal office building in Oklahoma City that killed 168 people and in a religious cult's nerve gas attack on the Tokyo subway system that killed 12 and injured 5,500 on March 20, 1995.[57]

We have some idea about how widespread terrorism has become. During the 1980s, incidents of international terrorism—incidents involving the citizens or territory of more than one country—rose sharply, reaching 665 in 1987.[58] Counterterrorist measures, especially cooperation among states, has reduced the overall level of international terrorism in recent years. In 1996, the number of international terrorist acts was the lowest since 1971, but casualties from those acts, the bloodiest of which was a car-bombing of a Jewish center in Buenos Aires, rose from the previous year[59] and remained high the following year (see Figure 7.1).

Today, terrorism touches every corner of the world. Latin America, Western Europe, and the Middle East have been the most frequent sites for international terrorism. Even China has been victimized by terrorists in recent years.[60] Overall, U.S. citizens and property have been frequent targets of terrorist acts (40 percent). Until recently, U.S. territory has been spared the terrorism frequent elsewhere, but the bombing of New York's World Trade Center in March 1993 by Muslim radicals and three months later the FBI's disruption of a plot to set off car bombs in the highway tunnels under New York's Hudson River and to bomb buildings in New York, including the United Nations, are omens of worse things to come. One of the accused declared in a taped conversation: "The water will be going everywhere—everything will be

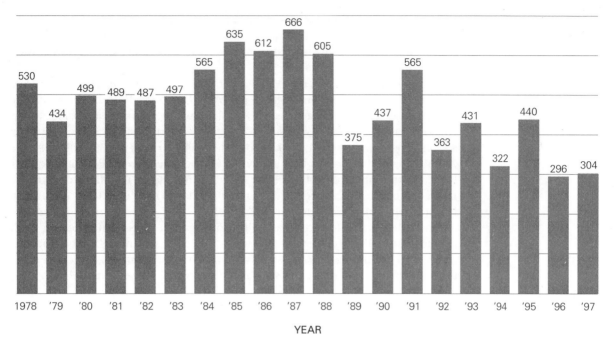

FIGURE 7.1

International Terrorist Incidents, 1978–1997

The total number of international terrorist incidents soared in the early 1970s and mid-1980s and in recent years has begun to decline. SOURCE: U.S. Department of State, *Patterns of Global Terrorism: 1997* (Washington, DC: U.S. Department of State, April 1998).

broken into smithereens, everything. The World Trade Center, compared with this, will be like a dwarf."[61] Lax immigration procedures and growing numbers of political refugees are bringing the United States into the front lines of global terrorism. As a major power involved in trouble spots all around the world, the United States and its citizens are targeted by many terrorists. In 1997, about one-third of the attacks were against American targets, and the 1998 attacks on the U.S. embassies in Kenya and Tanzania were a grim reminder of this trend.

Terrorist groups may form wherever there is intense dissatisfaction with the political status quo. Among the reasons for increased international terrorism are the growing accessibility of weapons and explosives and the revolutions in global travel and communication that facilitate their movement across frontiers. State support for terrorist groups and the propensity of terrorists to copy each other's behavior—the *demonstration effect*—have also contributed to the trend.

Terrorism and the Middle East: A Case

Repeatedly, the Middle East peace process between Israel and the Palestinians has been hostage to terrorism by both Arabs and Jews. In recent years, suicide bombings by the Islamic Resistance Movement (also known as Hamas) against Israeli civilians triggered Israeli reprisals and gave Israel's former hawkish Likud-dominated government under Prime Minister Binyamin Netanyahu plausible reasons not to stick to the 1993 Israeli-Palestinian Declaration of Principles reached between Israeli Prime Minister Yitzhak Rabin and Palestine Liberation Organization (PLO) Chairman Yasser Arafat.

A brief description of a few Middle East terrorist groups suggests how varied they are. The Abu Nidal group, which split from the PLO in 1974, has been responsible for more than ninety attacks in more than twenty countries. Hizballah[62] operates in Lebanon and was responsible for seizing Western hostages in the 1980s and a suicide bombing of the U.S. Marine barracks in Beirut in 1983 that killed over 200 Marines. Other groups (Popular Front for the Liberation of Palestine, Popular Front for the Liberation of Palestine–General Command, Popular Front for the Liberation of Palestine–Special Command, and Hamas) have used terrorism against Israeli targets and those viewed as pro-Israeli.

Much Middle East terrorism, though by no means all, has been associated with Palestinian or Islamic extremists. When possible, their violence is directed against Israel,[63] but the difficulty terrorists have in striking Israel directly has encouraged them to strike at "softer" targets, especially the interests of Americans and Europeans whom the terrorists accuse of being pro-Israeli.

Motives and Tactics of Terrorists

International terrorists act from a variety of motives.[64] One powerful motivation is to gain independence for an ethnic group. Palestinian groups like Hamas justify their behavior in this way. Perhaps the most prominent European national-liberation group is the Provisional Irish Republican Army (PIRA). Known as the Provos, this group, heir to earlier efforts to unite Ireland, carried out terrorist acts in England,[65] Northern Ireland, Belgium, and elsewhere for over two decades to force Britain out of Northern Ireland, until a truce was declared in 1995 to allow direct British-Irish-PIRA negotiations. By 1999 these negotiations seemed to have brought Northern Ireland to the verge of peace at last.

Other groups are motivated by ideologies, sometimes obscure. Two notorious examples in the 1970s were the Italian Red Brigades and the West German Baader-Meinhof Gang (later called the Red Army Faction) that staged attacks against corporations, businessmen, and prominent politicians to demonstrate their dislike for Western materialism. Other widely feared terrorist groups motivated by ideology are Hizballah (Party of God), Sendero Luminoso (Shining Path), and Túpac Amaru. Hizballah, an Iranian-supported Shi'ite Muslim group, promotes Islamic fundamentalism and seeks to rid the Middle East of Western influence.[66] Shining Path's objective is described as vaguely Maoist (after the ideas of Chinese communist leader Mao Zedong). Its aim is to transform Peru into a communist society led by ethnic Indians. The group "announced itself in May 1980 by hanging dead dogs from lamp-posts in Lima."[67] Another Peruvian terrorist group, Túpac Amaru, with a vaguely Marxist ideology, was founded by a college roommate of former Peruvian President Alan Garcia. The group's occupation of the Japanese ambassador's residence in Lima, during which Peru's foreign and agricultural ministers and other Peruvian and foreign dignitaries were made hostage, made headlines until Peruvian troops stormed the building four months later.[68] Escalating violence in Peru made large areas of the country ungovernable until President Alberto Fujimori suspended Peru's constitution in April 1992.

Middle East terrorists pursue various objectives. Some seek to punish Israel directly for its "crimes" against the Palestinians. Others seek to punish those who assist Israel. Still others use terrorism to poison the atmosphere and rouse popular passions, hoping to sabotage peace efforts by triggering a spiral of violence and counterviolence. To this end, Hizballah has attacked Israelis in south Lebanon and northern Israel and overseas,[69] and Hamas[70] has used suicide bombings to anger Israelis and undermine the authority of Arafat and the PLO.[71] Speaking of Hamas, one captured terrorist declared: "They thought that the military operations would work to the benefit of the Likud and against the left. They wanted to destroy the political process, and they thought that if the right succeeded, the political process would stop."[72] Such terrorism has not always originated among Arabs. Israeli extremists like Baruch Goldstein, who slaughtered Arab worshipers in a Hebron mosque, also have tried to undermine the peace process.[73]

Osama bin Laden and his followers (to whom we shall return later in this chapter) reflect an upsurge in terrorism justified by "religious or pseudo-religious reasons."[74] Bin Laden's effort to acquire weapons of mass destruction and the large number of casualties caused by the attacks on American embassies have led to speculation about a new and more deadly kind of terrorism: "It used to be said of terrorists that 'they want a lot of people watching and not a lot of people dead'; but the new variety of killers apparently see destruction as an end in itself. Where old terrorism sought to change the world—however misguidedly—the new sort is often practised by those who believe the world is beyond redemption."[75] "In the past," declared an FBI official about the terrorist who organized the bombing of the World Trade Center,

> we were fighting terrorists with an organizational structure and some attainable goal like land or the release of political prisoners. But Ramzi Yousef, one of the perpetrators of the New York's World Trade Center bombing in 1993, is the new breed, who are more hazardous. They want nothing less than the overthrow of the West, and since that's not going to happen, they just want to punish—the more casualties the better.[76]

International terrorists use many forms of violence and intimidation. Skyjacking, accompanied by demands for release of passengers, was popular in the 1970s but declined as airline security improved. The Palestine Liberation Front (PLF) pioneered in hijacking ships when Muhammad Abu al Abbas along with other terrorists took control of the Italian cruise ship *Achille Lauro* in October 1985.[77] During the operation, a U.S. tourist was murdered in his wheelchair, and his body was thrown overboard. In another notorious operation, Pan American Flight 103 was blown out of the sky over Lockerbie, Scotland, in December 1988, killing 259 passengers and 11 local residents.

Some groups specialize in kidnapping those whom they view as symbols of their enemy, and others carry out suicide missions or random shooting and bombings to dramatize their views. The Red Brigades used kidnapping extensively. In one incident, they kidnapped U.S. general James Dozier and held him for five days until his rescue by Italian counterterrorist forces. In another, they kidnapped former Italian prime minister Aldo Moro, murdered him, and left his body in a truck on a street in Rome. Other groups try to stir fear by machine-gun or grenade

The bombing of New York's World Trade Center in 1993 indicated that international terrorism could threaten Americans at home. The U.S. government offered a reward for the capture of the alleged "mastermind" of the bombing, and he was subsequently caught by the FBI in Pakistan and returned to the United States to be tried. *(AP/Wide World Photo)*

attacks against innocent civilians. The Provos repeatedly launched bombing campaigns in central London and elsewhere in Britain and used bombs to murder Louis, Earl Mountbatten, a war hero, last viceroy of India and a member of the British royal family (August 1979) and to try to assassinate British prime minister Margaret Thatcher in Brighton (October 1984).

Ethnic and Tribal Actors

Ethnic and *tribal actors* are also prominent in global politics.[78] A shared ethnic or tribal heritage can be a source of unity for a state, but its absence can be a major challenge to a state's integrity. In much of the world, ethnic and tribal loyalties collide

ACTORS SPEAK

Even as those who commit terrorist acts claim they do so for high-minded motives, the threat of new and more destructive forms of terrorism is growing. In the first passage Ramzi Ahmed Yousef, one of the organizers of the World Trade Center bombing, explains his actions as patriotic, and in the second President Bill Clinton describes the emerging terrorist threat.

If "terrorist" means that I regain my land and fight whoever assaults me and my people, then I have no objection to being called a terrorist. (Ramzi Ahmed Yousef, cited in David Kocieniewski, "An Enigma with a Goal: Punish the United States," *New York Times*, September 6, 1996, p. A16)

All of you know the fight against terrorism is far from over, and now terrorists seek new tools of destruction. The enemies of peace realize they cannot defeat us with traditional military means, so they are working on two new forms of assault which you've heard about today: cyberattacks on our critical computer systems and attacks with weapons of mass destruction—chemical, biological, potentially even nuclear weapons. (President Bill Clinton, cited in John M. Broder, "President Steps Up War on New Terrorism," *New York Times*, January 23, 1999, p. A12)

with rather than reinforce nationalism. Bloody examples in Rwanda, Burundi, and the former Yugoslavia illustrate how politicians "from Belgrade to Armenia to Kashmir and beyond have been playing upon long-simmering ethnic divisions to a remarkable degree in recent years."[79] Not only did the U.S.S.R. split into quarreling nationalities, but several are at each other's throats—Armenians and Azeris and Russians and Moldovans.

Perhaps more than other actors, ethnic and tribal actors have deep historical roots.[80] As Europeans established their colonial empires, state frontiers were imposed on top of ethnic and tribal loyalties that were ignored by colonial authorities. The Spanish conquest of the Aztecs and Mayans in Mexico and Guatemala[81] and the Incas in Peru and the European conquest of native Indians all across North America reflect this process. Seldom were earlier identities forgotten, and in some cases, like that of the Mayans in Chiapas, Mexico, and in Guatemala, discrimination, (and in the case of Guatemala even attempted genocide) against native Indians have provoked rebellions against the state.

Colonial boundaries had little in common with tribal realities in Africa. Some African states consist of tribal entities that continue to battle for power. Elsewhere, tribes were divided by state boundaries. Regardless of the situation, many Africans continue to have greater loyalty to a tribe than to their state, and African governments are often controlled by tribal groups. Therein lies one source of weakness in many African states and the endemic violence that has convulsed much of the continent.[82] Democracy in Africa is threatened by political parties based on tribe, language, and region. Declared a Kenyan scholar about Nigeria:"In Nigeria, although there is apparent ethnic balance between the north, the east and the west, the three major ethnic entities of the country see the game of politics as a means of capturing power to the exclusion of the others. The state does not really exist, because its elites cannot agree to submit to it."[83]

Middle Eastern politics is also "tribal," featuring conflicts between peoples who reside in artificial states created by colonial masters and who either are persecuted minorities in those states or separated from their brethren by state boundaries. A great deal of conflict in the Middle East is rooted in ethnic tension. Figure 7.2 illustrates the ethnic and religious diversity of the region.

Israel's founding—the final chapter in a displaced people's search for a permanent home—was an expression of ethnic aspiration. The country was established by European Jews who believed that they could find safety only by gathering in the lands of their Biblical forefathers. Early Zionist settlers brought to Palestine a vibrant culture and sophisticated technology and science. Their arrival and prosperity were viewed as threatening by traditional Arab leaders, who had been handed power by the British and French. That threat perception increased when, after 1945, Jewish survivors of the Holocaust poured into Palestine.

The Palestinians' search for a national home in recent decades is reminiscent of the earlier story of the Jews. The Palestinian Liberation Organization (PLO), founded in Cairo in 1964, is an expression of Palestinian aspirations and has become the Palestinian Authority, governing the Gaza Strip and those areas of the West Bank that Israel has surrendered to the Palestinians. Palestine became a volatile issue after the 1967 Six-Day War, during which almost one million additional Palestinians in the West Bank and Gaza came under Israeli rule. Throughout its existence, the Palestinian movement has faced two main problems: where to establish a state and where to operate until its establishment. Although some extremists still dream of driving Israelis into the sea and reclaiming all of Palestine, for most this goal is no longer realistic. For the residents of the West Bank and Gaza and for Palestinian refugees living in squalid camps in Lebanon and Syria or cities such as Amman and Cairo, the question is acquiring an independent existence for the Palestinian "nation."

By the early 1990s, Palestinian aspirations seemed nearer to fulfillment than ever before. After secret negotiations in Norway, Israel and the PLO reached an agreement by which both sides formally recognized each other as legitimate representatives of their respective people. Justifying his government's shift in policy, Prime Minister Rabin declared, "Peace is not made with friends. Peace is made with enemies, some of whom . . . I loathe very much."[84] In a ceremony hosted in the White House Rose Garden by President Bill Clinton on September 13, 1993, the world saw Rabin and Arafat shake hands. The parties agreed that self-rule would gradually extend throughout the West Bank over a period of five years. Israel would retain external security responsibilities, and a Palestinian Authority would police the territories. The agreement included formation of a Joint Israeli-Palestinian Liaison

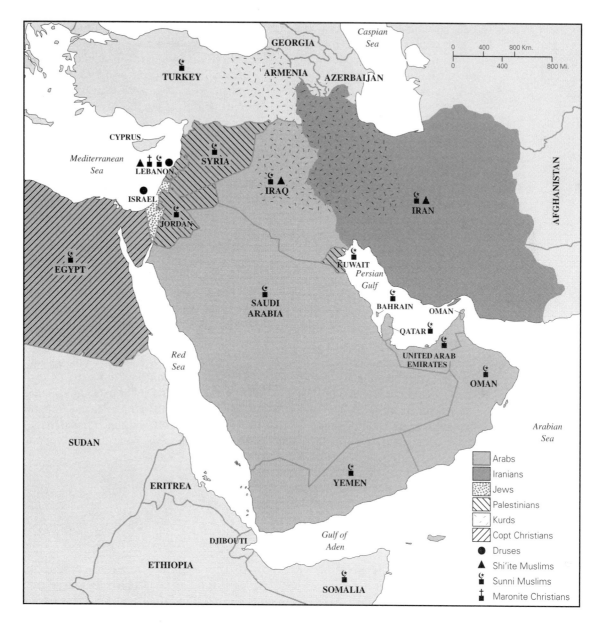

FIGURE 7.2
Ethnicity and the Middle East

The Middle East—site of the origins of three of the world's great religions—also is home to a rich variety of ethnic and national groups.

Committee and an Israeli-Palestinian Economic Cooperation Committee to plan regional economic development, and elections for a Palestinian Council.[85] All agreed that Palestinians had to see swift improvement in living conditions if self-rule was to succeed, and pledges of foreign aid were made by more than three dozen countries, including the United States and Israel.[86]

The ink was not dry when extremists on both sides attacked the agreement.[87] It was as though Israeli and Arab hard-liners were conspiring to draw out the Palestinian-Israeli quarrel, and by 1997 the peace process had ground to a virtual halt. Some Palestinians and Israelis believed the peace process was "dead."

Jews and Palestinians are not the only significant ethnic groups in the Middle East. The Kurds, an Islamic people who speak their own language and live as minorities mainly in Turkey, Iraq, Syria, and Iran,[88] have been engaged for decades in a struggle for an independent "Kurdistan." Under the Ottomans, the Kurds enjoyed local autonomy, and many served in the imperial military forces. Kurdish minorities have missed out on the economic and social progress in their countries and have been targets of efforts at forced assimilation. Kurdish unrest is endemic in the countries in which they live, and Kurdish aspirations have been repeatedly manipulated to serve others' interests. The Shah of Iran and the mullahs who came after aided Kurdish resistance against Iraq. Saddam Hussein has aided Kurdish rebels in Turkey and Iran even while murderously repressing the Kurds in his own country.[89] And, since 1991, the Turks have allowed the United States to aid Iraq's Kurds while attacking rebels in the Kurdistan Workers' Party (PKK) who seek sanctuary in Iraq.[90]

Although many of the most serious ethnic conflicts are in the developing world, there are ethnic strains in the developed world as well. In Canada, many French-speaking Quebecois seek independence.[91] In the Balkans, Albanians in Kosovo seek independence from Serbia,[92] in Spain, Basque and Catalan nationalists seek autonomy,[93] and in France Corsican separatists demand their independence.[94]

Religious Actors

Among the most influential nonstate actors are fundamentalist religious movements and groups that believe that societies should be governed in accordance with religious precepts and law. Islamic fundamentalists have received the greatest attention because of their global visibility and their association with terrorism, but Jewish, Hindu, and Christian fundamentalists have also become politically influential. The growing political activism of fundamentalists in global politics and the support they enjoy are partly a consequence of the fear that globalization is eroding traditional values, morals, and customs and partly of opposition to the consequences of modernity.[95]

Israel is deeply divided between those who are secular and those who are ultra-Orthodox, especially in Jerusalem, and violence has broken out between these groups over such issues as whether or not streets and stores should remain open on the Sabbath.[96] The small political parties that represent the ultra-Orthodox enjoy political influence because they often hold the balance of power in forming a government.[97]

The ultra-Orthodox constitute most of Israel's 147,000 West Bank settlers, and their presence constitutes a major obstacle to a final Israeli-Palestinian peace. They believe this area is part of Biblical Israel, to which they give its Biblical name of Judea and Samaria. "These are true believers," declared an Israeli religious student. "They believe it was God, not so much the Israeli Army, but the hand of God that gave them back these lands in 1967."[98] An agreement to transfer extensive authority in parts of the West Bank to an elected Palestinian Council[99] triggered the assassination of Yitzak Rabin by a religious nationalist and a West-Bank settler, Yigal Amir, who was described by a former fellow soldier as "a real fanatic, even the religious guys in the platoon got sick of his zeal and his nitpicking. . . . In matters of religion he was a real nudge. Stubborn as a mule, wouldn't let us breathe."[100]

Hindu fundamentalism is largely an Indian phenomenon. When India was granted independence, it was a secular state. Some Hindus, who constitute a majority in the country, wanted India to be governed according to Hindu principles, and they objected to granting equality to India's Muslim minority. One of them assassinated Mahatma Gandhi, the leader of India's independence movement and a passionate advocate of pacifism. In recent years, Hindu nationalism has gained greater influence,[101] and by 1998 a coalition government headed by a Hindu nationalist party held power in New Delhi.

Most global attention, however, has been focused on the upsurge in *Islamic fundamentalism*—the belief that Muslims should be governed in strict accordance with the Koran. The issue received global attention when Iran's shah was overthrown in 1979 by followers of Ayatollah Ruhollah Khomeini. Shi'ism became Iran's official religion, and power was placed in the hands of the Shi'ite clergy, the mullahs. The Ayatollah and his followers embarked on an effort to "purify" Islam and bring to power in other countries those who would rule according to these principles.

The issue has two aspects: The first is divisions within Islam itself, and the second is the struggle between secular leaders and those who would restore a state to Islamic "purity." The main division in Islam dates from the seventh century A.D. Following Muhammad's death, the Islamic community remained in the throes of a succession crisis. The fourth caliph, Ali (656–661), a cousin and friend of Muhammad who was married to the Prophet's daughter, was assassinated. Subsequent caliphs and their supporters were known as *Sunni Muslims.* Most Arabs were Sunni and permitted tribal ways to dominate politics. A minority of Muslims, however, declared the caliphs after Ali to be illegitimate, claiming that only his male heirs could govern the Islamic community. Known as *Shi'a Muslims,* they advocated adhering to the original precepts of Islam and believed that the word of Allah was sufficient to govern Muslims.

Sunni-Shi'ite antipathy was a factor in the Iraq-Iran war (1980–1988) as Iran tried to oust Saddam Hussein's Sunni regime. Saddam repeatedly brutalized Iraq's Shi'ites, most recently after the 1991 Gulf War. Because Shi'ites are the poorest group in Arab countries like Lebanon, many were receptive to Iranian efforts to mobilize them. Sunni-Shi'ite suspicion has produced conflict in several countries, including Pakistan,[102] and was a factor in bringing Iran and the Sunni fundamentalist Taliban in Afghanistan to the brink of war in 1998.

The second aspect of the issue involves fundamentalists' efforts to overthrow secular governments and rid their societies of Western influences. If they would succeed, these countries would grow increasingly anti-Western.[103] Islamic fundamentalists hold power in Iran, the Sudan,[104] Somalia, and Afghanistan[105] and are engaged in sometimes violent struggle with governments in Algeria,[106] Egypt,[107] Pakistan,[108] Saudi Arabia,[109] and even China.[110] Islamists have made inroads in a variety of other countries, including Indonesia[111] and Tanzania,[112] and Muslim militants are battling Russian troops in Tajikistan.[113]

Even the secular Turkish state has been challenged by politicians who embrace the principles of Islamic fundamentalism as the path to a Muslim revival. Thus, in the shantytowns of Istanbul, Turkey's secular tradition was assailed by fundamentalists who were "trying to segregate buses by sex, attacking ballet as a degenerate art form."[114] In 1996 the leader of Turkey's Islamist party, Necmettin Erbakan, became Turkey's prime minister in a coalition government, producing anxiety among secular Turks and the Turkish military, which declared that "no steps away from the contemporary values of the Turkish Republic" would be tolerated and that "destructive and separatist groups are seeking to weaken our democracy and legal system by blurring the distinction between the secular and anti-secular."[115]

Some of the most extreme Islamic fundamentalists are members of the Taliban, a rural Islamic religious movement made up of religious students, which, with aid from Pakistan,[116] defeated its rivals for power in Afghanistan.[117] Taliban supporters argue that society should be governed strictly according to the Will of Allah, as revealed in the Koran and in Muhammad's life. The zealots are anti-Israeli and anti-Western. They wish to return their people to simpler and more austere lives and values, including forcing women back into the home and making them subject to their father's and husband's will.

No sooner had the Taliban taken power in Kabul, Afghanistan's capital, in September 1996 than it shut down movie theaters and the television station; closed girls' schools; ordered women to stay at home, give up their jobs, and be fully covered from head to toe when outside the home; and established a ruling council of Muslim clerics and a Department for the Propagation of Virtue and the Prohibition of Vice.[118] Men were ordered to wear beards, and citizens were ordered to get rid of televisions, videocassette recorders, videotapes, and satellite dishes or see them destroyed.[119] A common wisecrack in Kabul was: "It's not 1996, it's 1375."[120] "The people of Afghanistan," declared one mullah, "had deviated from the past of Islam, and all these miseries that befell us were a punishment that was imposed on us by Allah for our sins."[121] By the autumn of 1998, the Taliban had conquered virtually all of Afghanistan.[122]

Islamic fundamentalism is a backlash to modernity and bitterly opposes many of its features, including equality for women, sexual freedom, political individualism, religious tolerance, and economic globalism. Governments have sought to combat fundamentalism in a variety of ways, ranging from military repression to co-optation in the existing political order. None have succeeded for any length of time, and, as technology accelerates the linking of societies, we can expect to see fanatics like Ramzi Ahmed Yousef, who tried to begin "a worldwide terrorist campaign involving high-profile bombings and assassinations, including a plan to kill Pope John Paul II . . . and crash a light plane packed with explosives into the Central Intelligence Agency headquarters in Virginia."[123]

Individuals

Even individuals can behave as independent actors in global politics. Political leaders, good and bad, like Napoleon, Hitler, Stalin, and Franklin Roosevelt have had an impact on history far beyond that inherent in the political positions they occupied. Others, from Mother Theresa to Albert Einstein, have enjoyed enormous influence because of their deeds and accomplishments. Individual charisma has always been important. Moses, Jesus, and Muhammad, like many political leaders, moved their followers by force of personality and ideas.

The case of Osama bin Laden, the son of a wealthy Saudi Arabian family, illustrates the potential impact of individuals on global politics. The bombings of an American military barracks in Saudi Arabia in 1996 and of the U.S. embassies in Africa two years later are alleged to have been planned and financed by bin Laden and his followers.[124] The U.S. missile attack on Afghanistan following the embassy bombings was aimed at training camps set up by bin Laden, and the Sudanese factory that was struck was owned by an alleged associate of his.

Bin Laden originally made common cause with the United States against the Soviet occupation of Afghanistan in 1979, but the presence of U.S. troops in Saudi Arabia during and after the 1991 Persian Gulf War was, according to one observer, regarded by him "as an occupation of the Islamic holy places by the United States."[125] A wealthy man, bin Laden has used the fortune he inherited from his father to form what one U.S. intelligence official called "a multinational organization for jihad (holy war) to purge the world of Western corrupters and their Arab friends" and thereby realize his goal of "a stateless, global jihad without borders."[126] "He has networks on every continent almost," declared a senior U.S. intelligence officer. "He has an infrastructure that's very, very replete with capability, people, money."[127] Bin Laden has funded a variety of Muslim terrorists in Aden, Egypt, Algeria, Yemen, the Sudan, Lebanon, the Philippines, and possibly those who bombed the World Trade Center and the U.S. military barracks in Saudi Arabia in 1996.[128] Officials also believe that bin Laden has sought to obtain materials to develop nuclear weapons.[129]

The mobility of terrorists like bin Laden and his followers and their ability to operate transnationally have forced states to respond in kind, but this is not easy to do. Referring to bin Laden, a former State Department counterterrorism official noted: "The ability of extremely wealthy individuals to bankroll mercenaries for their own end is a relatively new development and one we're not well equipped to deal with from an intelligence standpoint."[130] In the case of bin Laden, the United States orchestrated an international effort in Europe and Africa, as well as in the United States itself, to weaken his terrorist networks.[131] In addition, the FBI, which in the past did not operate outside of American borders, participated in the investigation of the embassy and barracks bombings.[132] In another case, U.S. and Pakistani officials captured the mastermind of the World Trade Center bombing in Islamabad and spirited him back to the United States to stand trial.[133] A State Department official described American policy as follows: "The policy is that no nation should offer itself as a refuge or safe haven for terrorists. They have an obligation to extradite or prosecute them...."[134] The United States has over one hundred

Osama bin Laden, a wealthy
Saudi Arabian, is believed to
be responsible for the terrorist
bombings of U.S. embassies
in Kenya and Tanzania.
(AP/Wide World Photo)

bilateral extradition treaties with other countries and is a party to ten international treaties that require the extradition or trial of alleged terrorists, and in 1984 the U.S. Congress enacted a law making it a crime to attack Americans anywhere in the world.[135]

Despite such efforts, concern about terrorism in the United States has grown. Indeed, such concern has prompted the Pentagon to ask President Clinton to appoint a military commander for the continental United States who could take charge of emergency efforts in the event of a major terrorist attack.[136]

Conclusion

In sum, states are neither alone nor unchallenged as objects of human loyalties. Few generalizations can do justice to the variety of nonstate actors in contemporary global politics. "Embracing a bewildering array of beliefs, interests, and agendas, they have the potential to do as much harm as good."[137] However, the growing importance of politically relevant religious and ethnic identities and loyalties has persuaded one prominent political scientist, Samuel Huntington, that interstate conflicts are being replaced by "the clash of civilizations."[138]

Important nonstate actors not only help compensate for weak states' reduced capacity but, in some cases, knit together peoples around the world. The evolution of the global economic system may provide clues for the future. The growing role of transnational corporations has accompanied declining national economic autonomy, growing economic interdependence, and globalization. In other cases, however, such as that of ethnic separatists or religious fundamentalists, nonstate actors play a major role in fragmenting and polarizing peoples. Which tendency, integration or fragmentation, will dominate the future?

Probably both tendencies will continue simultaneously. Even as a globalized world economy evolves and as the elements of a homogenized world culture emerge, fragmentation of states is likely to continue, especially, but not only, in the developing world. In the words of one observer, we are simultaneously witnessing a "retribalization of large swaths of humankind" and "an onrush of economic and ecological forces that demand integration and uniformity. . . . The planet is falling precipitately apart and coming reluctantly together at the very same moment."[139]

Key Terms

demonstration effect
ethnic actors
global civic society
governance
Islamic fundamentalism
multicentric world
multilocalism

nongovernmental organizations
  (NGOs)
nonstate actors
seven sisters
Shi'a or Shi'te Muslims
state-centric world

subnational groups
Sunni Muslims
terrorism
transnational corporations
  (TNCs)
tribal actors

End Notes

[1]The title is from Ernst B. Haas, *Beyond the Nation-State: Functionalism and International Organization* (Stanford, CA: Stanford University Press, 1964).

[2]Oran R. Young, "The Actors in World Politics," in James N. Rosenau, Vincent Davis, and Maurice A. East, eds., *The Analysis of International Politics* (New York: Free Press, 1972), p. 139.

[3]David Shearer, "Outsourcing War," *Foreign Policy* 112 (Fall 1998), pp. 68–80. In contemporary Colombia, foreign oil companies have begun to pay the Colombian military to deploy its best units for their protection in what one political scientist calls "the privatization of the Colombian Army." Diana Jean

Schemo, "Oil Companies Buy an Army to Tame Colombia's Rebels," *New York Times,* August 22, 1996, pp. A1, A8.

[4]James N. Rosenau, *Along the Domestic-Foreign Frontier: Exploring Governance in a Turbulent World* (Cambridge, UK: Cambridge University Press, 1997), p. 145. See also James N. Rosenau and Ernst-Otto Czempiel, eds., *Governance Without Government: Order and Change in World Politics* (Cambridge, UK: Cambridge University Press, 1992).

[5]Such work can be dangerous. See, for example, "Red Cross Halts Tajik Mission as Rebels Kidnap 4 Workers," *New York Times,* February 7, 1997, p. A7. Groups such as these were

instrumental in drawing attention to the human effects of land mines and small arms in global politics and in advocating the establishment of a permanent international court to try those accused of war crimes. See, for example, Alessandra Stanley, "U.S. Presses Allies to Rein in Proposed War Crimes Court," *New York Times,* July 18, 1998, p. A8; and Raymond Bonner, "U.S. Joins 20 Nations in Urging Controls on Spread of Small Arms," *New York Times,* July 15, 1998, p. A5.

[6]James N. Rosenau, *Turbulence in World Politics* (Princeton: Princeton University Press, 1990), pp. 11, 36.

[7]Paul Wapner, *Environmental Activism and World Civic Politics* (Albany, NY: State University of New York Press, 1996), p. 5.

[8]Ibid., p. 7.

[9]We regard transnational and multinational corporations as equivalent but prefer the former term because it conveys the sense of mobility characteristic of many corporations.

[10]Joan E. Spero and Jeffrey A. Hart, *The Politics of International Economic Relations,* 5th ed. (New York: St. Martin's Press, 1997), p. 96.

[11]"Globe-Trotting," *The Economist,* September 3-9, 1994, p. 62.

[12]Fred R. Bleakley, "Multinational Firms Spent $325 Billion in 1995 on Foreign Direct Investment," *Wall Street Journal,* June 5, 1996, p. A2.

[13]Keith Bradsher, "Forget Microsoft. G.M. Is Still the Biggest Kid on the Block," *New York Times,* July 26, 1998, sec. 4, p. 4.

[14]This measure inflates states' relative ranking because GNP includes corporate sales.

[15]Edmund L. Andrews, "Europeans Take Boeing to Brink," *New York Times,* July 24, 1997, pp. A1, C5.

[16]These trading companies "were not only authorized to use violence but were endowed with nearly all the powers of sovereignty." Janice E. Thomson, *Mercenaries, Pirates, and Sovereigns* (Princeton: Princeton University Press, 1994), p. 32. Founded in 1600, the English East India Company at its height administered large areas of India and at its peak could boast an army of 150,000 troops. Shearer, "Outsourcing War," p. 70.

[17]The Hanseatic League was a consortium of 200 northern European trading towns. See Hendrik Spruyt, *The Sovereign State and Its Competitors* (Princeton: Princeton University Press, 1994), pp. 109-129.

[18]Robert A. Isaak, *Managing World Economic Change,* 2nd ed. (Englewood Cliffs, NJ: Prentice-Hall, 1995), p. 264.

[19]Cited in Fred R. Bleakley, "Foreign Investment by Multinationals Grew 40% in 1995, Lifted by Mergers," *Wall Street Journal,* September 25, 1996, p. A12. Transnational mergers sometimes find it difficult to overcome cultural differences. See Robert Frank and Thomas M. Burton, "Cross-Border Merger Results in Headaches for a Drug Company," *Wall Street Journal,* February 4, 1997, pp. A1, A12.

[20]Cited in Thomas L. Friedman, "Big Mac II," *New York Times,* December 11, 1996, p. A21.

[21]"Hi, Amigo," *The Economist,* December 12-18, 1992, p. 21.

[22]Friedman, "Big Mac II."

[23]Richard W. Stevenson, "Ford Sets Its Sights on a 'World Car'," *New York Times,* September 2, 1993, pp. C1, C4.

[24]The legal power of the government to make U.S. corporations obey its policies was established by the Supreme Court's decision in *U.S. v. Curtiss-Wright Export Corporation et al.* (1936). The Court upheld the enforcement of an embargo declared against arms exports to belligerents in the Chaco War.

[25]Robert S. Greenberger and Allanna Sullivan, "Clinton Bars Conoco's Plan for Iran Project," *Wall Street Journal,* March 15, 1995, p. A3.

[26]Youssef M. Ibrahim, "Teheran Finds Other Buyers for Its Oil After U.S. Sales Are Ended," *New York Times,* June 21, 1995, p. A6.

[27]Anne Reifenberg and James Tanner, "U.S. Oil Companies Fret over Losing Out on Any Jobs in Iraq," *Wall Street Journal,* April 17, 1995, p. A1.

[28]Eric Schmitt, "U.S. Backs Off Sanctions, Seeing Poor Effect Abroad," *New York Times,* July 21, 1998, pp. A1, A6.

[29]Elizabeth Farnsworth, "More Than Admitted," *Foreign Policy* 16 (Fall 1974), p. 130. For a contrary view, see Paul E. Sigmund, "Less Than Charged," *Foreign Policy* 16 (Fall 1974), pp. 142-156.

[30]Dale L. Johnson, *The Chilean Road to Socialism* (Garden City, NY: Doubleday, 1973).

[31]The seven were Exxon, Shell, British Petroleum, Gulf, Texaco, Chevron, and Mobil.

[32]U.N. Centre on Transnational Corporations, *Transnational Corporations in World Development* (New York: United Nations, 1988), p. 34.

[33]Shell was accused of supporting Nigeria's former military strongman, General Sani Abacha, and of persuading the Nigerian Army to crush the Ogoni people, who were complaining that Shell was damaging their environment. Paul Lewis, "Nigeria's Deadly Oil War: Shell Defends Its Record," *New York Times,* February 13, 1996, pp. A1, A4.

[34]Allen R. Myerson, "Exxon and Mobil Announce $80 Billion Deal to Create World's Largest Company," *New York Times,* December 2, 1998, pp. A1, C3.

[35]Dana Milbank and Marcus W. Brauchli, "How U.S. Concerns Compete in Countries Where Bribes Flourish," *Wall Street Journal,* September 29, 1995, pp. A1, A14.

[36]Barbara Crossette, "Europe Dominates Survey's Top 10 Least-Corrupt-Countries List," *New York Times,* October 4, 1998, sec. 1, p. 5. See also Raymond Bonner, "The Worldly Business of Bribes: Quiet Battle Is Joined," *New York Times,* July 8, 1996, p. A3.

[37]Nicholas Bray, "OECD Ministers Agree to Ban Bribery As Means for Companies to Win Business," *Wall Street Journal,* May 27, 1997, p. A2.

[38]Cited in Jeff Gerth, "I.B.M. Guilty of Illegal Sales to Russian Lab," *New York Times,* August 1, 1998, p. A1.

[39]Raymond Bonner, "Germany's Search for Libya Suspect Finds Ties to Its Own Spies," *New York Times,* August 22, 1996, p. A9.

[40]R. Jeffrey Smith and Marc Fisher, "Saddam Hussein's German Connection: Exports of Nuclear Knowledge," *Washington Post National Weekly Edition,* August 3-9, 1992, pp. 8-9.

[41]"India's Night of Death," *Time,* December 17, 1984, p. 22.

[42]"The Fun of Being a Multinational," *The Economist,* July 20-26, 1996, pp. 51, 52.

[43]Robert S. Walters and David H. Blake, *The Politics of Global Economic Relations,* 4th ed. (Englewood Cliffs, NJ: Prentice-Hall, 1992), p.111.

[44]James C. McKinley, Jr., "Bombs Rip Apart 2 U.S. Embassies in Africa; Scores Killed; No Firm Motive or Suspects," *New York Times,* August 8, 1998, pp. A1, A7; James Bennet, "U.S. Cruise Missiles Strike Sudan and Afghan Targets Tied to Terrorist Network," *New York Times,* August 21, 1998, pp. A1, A10; "After the Bomb," *The Economist,* August 22-28, 1998, p. 36.

[45]Christopher Drew, "Japanese Sect Tried to Buy U.S. Arms Technology, Senator Says," *New York Times,* October 31, 1995, p. A5; Marlise Simons, "French Police Search for Train Bombers; Death Toll at 7," *New York Times,* July 27, 1995, A3.

[46]Alexander Haig, "News Conference" (Washington, DC: Bureau of Public Affairs, Department of State, January 28, 1981), p. 5.

[47]Cited in "Terrorist Attacks Declined in '94 but Death Toll Rose, U.S. Reports," *New York Times,* April 29, 1995, p. 5.

[48]Brian Jenkins, "International Terrorism: The Other World War," in Charles W. Kegley, Jr., ed., *International Terrorism* (New York: St. Martin's Press, 1990), p. 28. See also "What Is Terrorism?" *The Economist,* March 2-8, 1995, pp. 23-25.

[49]Steven Erlanger, "Moscow Accepts Chechnya Talks," *New York Times,* June 19, 1995, pp. A1, A4; "Yeltsin's Vietnam?" *The Economist,* February 10-16, 1996, pp. 51-52.

[50]Cited in David E. Sanger, "Seeking an Embrace, Yeltsin Is Rebuffed at Talks," *New York Times,* June 18, 1995, sec. 1, p. 1.

[51]James Brooke, "Colombia's Rebels Grow Rich from Banditry," *New York Times,* July 2, 1995, sec. 1, pp. 1, 4; "Next-Door to Guerrilla War," *The Economist,* September 7-13, 1997, p. 40. The ten largest drug dealers in Colombia are estimated to have assets of about $76 billion, ranking them among the largest global corporations. Diana Jean Schemo, "Colombia Peasants to Get Stake from Drug Assets," *New York Times,* December 18, 1996, p. A9.

[52]Donald M. Snow, *Distant Thunder* (New York: St. Martin's Press, 1993), pp. 169-178.

[53]"The Golden Triangle's New King," *The Economist,* February 4-10, 1995, pp. 35-36.

[54]Alan Cowell, "138 Nations Confer on Rise in Global Crime," *New York Times,* November 22, 1994, p. A4.

[55]Some states aid terrorist groups, and the U.S. government keeps a list of "state sponsors of terrorism." Those listed in 1998 were Cuba, Iran, Iraq, Libya, North Korea, Sudan, and Syria.

[56]Donna M. Schlagheck, *International Terrorism* (Lexington, MA: Lexington Books, 1988), p. 15.

[57]"Japanese Arrest Leader of Cult Linked to Gas Attack," *New York Times,* May 16, 1995, pp. A1, A6. Fearing terrorists armed with chemical, biological, or nuclear weapons, the United States is trying to train local officials how to respond to a terrorist attack involving such weapons and to provide them with resources for such an eventuality. Judith Miller, "U.S. to Reduce Bureaucracy in Responding to Terrorism," *New York Times,* October 8, 1998, p. A19.

[58]Walter Enders, Gerald F. Parise, and Todd Sandler, "A Time-Series Analysis of Transnational Terrorism: Trends and Cycles," *Defence Economics* 3 (1992), p. 306.

[59]"Terrorist Attacks Declined in '94," p. 5.

[60]"China's Rebellious West," *The Economist,* February 15-21, 1997, pp. 33-34; Patrick E. Tyler, "Ethnic Strain in China's Far West Flares with Bombs and Rioting," *New York Times,* February 28, 1997, pp. A1, A7; Ian Johnson, "China's Recent Bombings Push Beijing to Greater Role in Fighting Terrorism," *Wall Street Journal,* March 10, 1997, p. A15; "A Bomb in Beijing," *The Economist,* March 15-21, 1997, pp. 37-38.

[61]Cited in Joseph P. Fried, "Tapes Indicate Plan to 'Stall' Bomb-Laden Cars in Tunnels," *New York Times,* June 18, 1995, sec. 1, p. 6.

[62]Douglas Jehl, "Lebanon Fighters Gain Stature, but for How Long?" *New York Times,* April 21, 1996, sec. 1, p. 4.

[63]Palestinian leaders also have frequently been targets of terrorist attacks by rivals in the struggle for power that characterizes Palestinian politics.

[64]Schlagheck, *International Terrorism,* pp. 5-8.

[65]See, for example, Richard W. Stevenson, "100 Are Wounded By London Bomb; IRA Is Suspected," *New York Times,* February 10, 1996, pp. 1, 5.

[66]See, for example, "Two Eyes for an Eye," *The Economist,* April 20-26, 1996, pp. 15-16, 18; Barton Gellman, "Teaching the Craft of Irregular War," *Washington Post National Weekly Review,* December 9-15, 1996, pp.14-15; Anthony dePalma, "Canada Links Pro-Iranian Group to Saudi Attack at U.S. Barracks," *New York Times,* March 28, 1997, pp. A1, A6; Anthony dePalma, "Saudi Case Casting a Light on How Militants Infiltrate and Exploit Canada," *New York Times,* March 4, 1997, sec. 1, p. 6; Douglas Jehl, "Saudi Opposition Group Suspected in Other Attacks," *New York Times,* March 29, 1997, p. 5; David B. Ottaway and Brian Duffy, "A Trail That Points to Tehran," *Washington Post National Weekly Edition,* April 21, 1997, p. 18.

[67]Gabriel Escobar, "Facing Down the Enemies of National Security," *Washington Post National Weekly Edition,* May 8-14, 1995, p. 14.

[68]Calvin Sims, "Guerrillas in Peru Threaten to Kill Hostages," *New York Times*, December 19, 1996, pp. A1, A8; Clifford Krauss, "Peru Troops Rescue Hostages; Rebels Slain As Standoff Ends," *New York Times*, April 23, 1997, pp. A1, A8.

[69]James Brooke, "Argentina's Jews Cry for Their Shattered Heart," *New York Times*, July 21, 1994, pp. A1, A6; "Car Bomb Outside the Israeli Embassy in London Wounds 13," *New York Times*, July 27, 1994, p. A8; Douglas Jehl, "With Iran's Aid, Guerrillas Gain Against Israelis," *New York Times*, February 26, 1997, p. A4.

[70]Increasingly Palestinians have turned away from violence, and Hamas's popularity has suffered. Barton Gellman, "Hamas Seems to Be Bowing to the Palestinian Inevitable," *Washington Post National Weekly Edition*, October 23-29, 1995, pp. 16-17.

[71]"Bombs, Blood and Fences," *The Economist*, January 28-February 3, 1995, p. 39; Youssef M. Ibrahim, "Palestinians Seize 100 Militants Who Oppose Talks with Israel," *New York Times*, April 11, 1995, pp. A1, A4; "Divided," *The Economist*, May 13-19, 1995, p. 40; Serge Schmemann, "Target Was Israeli Government, Says Arab Linked to 3 Bombings," *New York Times*, March 7, 1996, pp. A1, A6.

[72]Cited in Schmemann, "Target Was Israeli Government," p. A1.

[73]Chris Hedges and Joel Greenberg, "A Seething Hate, a Gun, and 40 Muslims Died," *New York Times*, February 28, 1994, pp. A1, A6.

[74]Cited in Stephen Engelberg, "Terrorism's New (and Very Old) Face," *New York Times*, September 12, 1998, p. A16. Sheik Omar Abdel Rahman, an Egyptian fundamentalist convicted of plotting a series of bombings, is an example of a terrorist who was motivated by religion. See Joseph P. Fried, "Sheik Draws Life in Plot to Bomb Public Buildings," *New York Times*, January 18, 1996, pp. A1, A16; Philip Shenon, "Holy War Is Home to Haunt the Saudis," *New York Times*, July 14, 1996, sec. 4, p. 3.

[75]"Coming Soon to a City Near You," *The Economist*, August 15-21, 1998, p. 17.

[76]Cited in David Kocieniewski, "An Enigma with a Goal: Punish the United States," *New York Times*, September 6, 1996, p. A16.

[77]In 1996, Chechen separatists highjacked a ferry in Turkey and threatened to kill the passengers unless Russia ceased its military campaign in Chechnya. Stephen Kinzer, "Ferry Episode Increases Turkish-Russian Tensions," *New York Times*, January 21, 1996, sec. 1, p. 4. Islam is a rallying cry for Chechens. Alessandra Stanley, "Islam Gets the Law and Order Vote," *New York Times*, January 26, 1997, sec. 4, p. 4.

[78]A *tribe* is an entity whose members claim a common ancestry. For an empirical analysis of ethnically based conflict, see Ted Robert Gurr, *Minorities at Risk* (Washington, DC: U.S. Institute of Peace Press, 1993).

[79]Donatella Lorch, "Hate Returns to Haunt Those Who Cradled It," *New York Times*, July 17, 1994, sec. 4, p. 1.

[80]See, for example, Steve LeVine, "After Karl Marx, a 1,000-Year-Old Superman," *New York Times*, August 31, 1995, p. A4, which tells of efforts in Kyrgyzstan to reawaken cultural identity.

[81]Larry Rohter, "Maya Renaissance in Guatemala Turns Political," *New York Times*, August 12, 1996, pp. A1, A5; Larry Rohter, "Maya Dress Tells a New Story, and It's Not Pretty," *New York Times*, June 13, 1997, p. A4.

[82]The Ethiopian government took the unusual step of offering the country's many peoples the option of independence. "The Caravan Passes On," *The Economist*, May 6-12, 1995.

[83]Cited in Howard W. French, "Can African Democracy Survive Ethnic Voting?" *New York Times*, March 17, 1996, sec. 4, p. 4. Asia also has acute interethnic tensions. Overseas Chinese in Indonesia, for example, are frequently the target of violence. See Seth Mydans, "Rioting Aimed at Minorities Is Setting Indonesia on Edge," *New York Times*, April 8, 1997, pp. A1, A7.

[84]Cited in Thomas L. Friedman, "Israel and the Palestinians See a Way to Co-exist," *New York Times*, September 5, 1993, sec. 4, p. 1.

[85]"The Accord: What Comes Next," *New York Times*, September 14, 1993, p. A7.

[86]Steven Greenhouse, "Group of Nations to Offer $2 Billion for Palestinians," *New York Times*, September 30, 1993, pp. A1, A6.

[87]Serge Schmemann, "'My Enemy's Enemy . . .,'" *New York Times*, August 23, 1995, pp. A1, A12.

[88]As many as 12 million Kurds live in Turkey (about 24 percent of the population) and 2.6 million in Iraq (15.5 percent). The number in Iran, though large, is unknown. See also Amy Dockser Marcus, "Mideast Minorities: Kurds Aren't Alone," *Wall Street Journal*, September 5, 1996, p. A12.

[89]Stephen Kinzer, "Iraqi Attack on Kurdish Region Was a Part of a Larger Campaign That Is Aimed at Iran," *New York Times*, September 3, 1996, p. A6.

[90]"The Stateless Nation," *The Economist*, June 25-July 1, 1994, p. 15; "Springtime Means Wartime," *The Economist*, May 11-17, 1996, pp. 51-52; Stephen Kinzer, "Kurdish Rebels in Turkey Are Down but Not Out," *New York Times*, March 8, 1997, p. 6; "Down but Far from Out," *The Economist*, August 1-7, 1998, pp. 44-45.

[91]Christopher J. Chipello, "English-Rights Militant Galls Quebec's Francophones," *Wall Street Journal*, July 13, 1998, p. A10.

[92]Chris Hedges, "Resistance to Serbia Turns Violent in Kosovo," *New York Times*, February 17, 1997, p. 3; "The Descent into Another Balkan War," *The Economist*, June 13-19, 1998, pp. 47-48.

[93]"Will the Basques Relent?" *The Economist*, July 20-26, 1996, pp. 41-42; "Basque Bind," *The Economist*, February 22-28, 1997, p. 57.

[94]Craig R. Whitney, "Corsica Rebels Fight the French, and One Another," *New York Times*, June 2, 1996, sec. 1, p. 3; Craig R. Whitney, "Corsicans Say They Set Weekend Bomb on French Mainland," *New York Times*, October 8, 1996, p. A4.

[95]See, for example, Douglas Jehl, "Iran Militants Are Attacking Influences from the West," *New York Times*, May 9, 1996, p. A6.

[96]See, for example, Judith Miller, "Israel's Fundamentalist Thing," *New York Times,* June 9, 1996, sec. 4, p. 5; Joel Greenberg, "Jerusalem Road Is Secular-Religious Battleground," *New York Times,* July 15, 1996, p. A3; "Culture war," *The Economist,* August 20-26, 1996, p. 34; Serge Schmemann, "Israeli Court Voids Closing of a Street on Sabbath," *New York Times,* April 14, 1997, p. A6; Serge Schmemann, "Orthodox Israelis Assault Jews Praying at Western Wall," *New York Times,* June 13, 1997, p. A3.

[97]Joel Greenberg, "Orthodoxy and Politics Mix in Israel," *New York Times,* June 14, 1996, p. A5; Joel Greenberg, "New Israel Premier Accepts Religious Party Terms," *New York Times,* June 18, 1996, p. A3; Gustav Niebuhr, "U.S. Jewish Leader Opposes Push for Control by Orthodox in Israel," *New York Times,* April 17, 1997, pp. A1, A10.

[98]Cited in John Kifner, "Zeal of Rabin's Assassin Springs from Rabbis of Religious Right," *New York Times,* November 12, 1995, sec. 1, p. 6.

[99]Serge Schmemann, "Israel and P.L.O. Reach Accord to Transfer West Bank Areas," *New York Times,* September 25, 1995.

[100]Cited in John Kifner, "With a Handshake, Rabin's Fate Was Sealed," *New York Times,* November 19, 1995, sec. 1, p. 10.

[101]See, for example, John F. Burns, "Hindu Die-Hards Seizing Their Day in the India Sun," *New York Times,* May 20, 1996, pp. A1, A4; "King of Mumbai," *The Economist,* February 3-9, 1996, p. 28. Caste constitutes another cleavage in Indian politics. John F. Burns, "Lower Castes Hold the Key As India Gets Ready to Vote," *New York Times,* April 10, 1996, pp. A1, A5; Miriam Jordan and Peter Waldman, "With Congress Party Battered, Others Gain Greater Clout in India," *Wall Street Journal,* May 10, 1996, pp. A1, A7.

[102]"Guns and God," *The Economist,* May 10-16, 1997, p. 34.

[103]See Edward G. Shirley, "Is Iran's Present Algeria's Future?" *Foreign Affairs* 74:3 (May-June 1995), pp. 28-44.

[104]The Sudan has promoted Islamic zealotry in Ethiopia, Eritrea, and Uganda, and was involved in an attempt to assassinate Egypt's president Hosni Mubarak.

[105]Veterans of the Islamic resistance to the Soviet invasion of that country have aided Muslim causes elsewhere, including Bosnia, where they were thought to pose a threat to U.S. forces sent to the region to police the Dayton peace accords. Chris Hedges, "Foreign Islamic Fighters in Bosnia Pose a Potential Threat for G.I.'s," *New York Times,* December 3, 1995, sec. 1, pp. 1, 4.

[106]In February 1992 the army canceled Algeria's first multiparty elections rather than permit the Islamic Salvation Front to take power. Bloody war then ensued that has spilled over into France, where many Algerians live. Algeria's Muslim militants have targeted for assassination foreigners, journalists, and professional women. "One-Way Road," *The Economist,* February 17-23, 1996, pp. 39-40; Roger Cohen, "A Chance to End an Agony," *New York Times,* February 2, 1997, sec. 4, p. 4; "Wanted: An Algerian Policy," *The Economist,* March 22-28, 1997, pp. 47-48.

[107]Egypt's President Anwar Sadat was assassinated by fundamentalists in 1981, and fundamentalists in Egypt have attacked foreign tourists and Egypt's Coptic Christians.

[108]"As You Sow," *The Economist,* November 25-December 1, 1995, pp. 35-36. There are about five times the number of militants—including veterans of the Afghan war—as policemen in Pakistan. "Holy War," *The Economist,* January 28-February 3, 1995, p. 37.

[109]Youssef M. Ibrahim, "West's Uneasy Presence: Infidels or Protectors?" *New York Times,* June 28, 1996, p. A6.

[110]"10 Die as Muslims Battle Chinese in Border Zone," *New York Times,* February 11, 1997, p. A4.

[111]Jay Solomon, "New Muslim Political Parties Sow Unease Among Some Indonesians," *Wall Street Journal,* August 13, 1998, p. A10.

[112]Robert Frank, "Amid Bombings, A Muslim Holy War Brews in Tanzania," *Wall Street Journal,* August 14, 1998, pp. A1, A8.

[113]"Russian Confusion," *The Economist,* September 24-30, 1994, p. 39. Russia fears the spread of militant Islam to the Islamic ex-Soviet republics on its southern flank. "The Crusade Against the Wahhabis," *The Economist,* July 4-10, 1998, pp. 36-37.

[114]John Darnton, "Discontent Seethes in Once-Stable Turkey," *New York Times,* March 2, 1995, p. A6. The European Union's agreement to form a customs union with Turkey may strengthen the hand of secularists in that country. Celestine Bohlen, "European Parliament Admits Turkey to Its New Customs Union," *New York Times,* December 14, 1995, p. A11. Turkish-European relations are complicated by the country's poor human rights record and by tension with Greece over Cyprus and conflicting claims in the Aegean Sea.

[115]Cited in Stephen Kinzer, "Turkey's Military Gives Islamic Leaders a Warning in Defense of Secularism," *New York Times,* March 2, 1997, sec. 1, p.6. See also "Crumbling Castle," *The Economist,* December 7-13, 1996, pp. 49-50; Stephen Kinzer, "Secular Turks Alarmed by Resurgence of Religion," *New York Times,* February 13, 1997, pp. A1, A8; Stephen Kinzer, "Turks March Against Move to Establish Islamic Rule," *New York Times,* February 16, 1997, sec. 1, p. 6; Stephen Kinzer, "With Possibly Fateful Results, Turkey Debates Islamic Schools," *New York Times,* May 19, 1997, p. A6. The Turkish Army finally forced the Islamic government to step down, and the Islamist Welfare Party was banned. It has reemerged as the Virtue Party. Stephen Kinzer, "Mayor Guilty of Godliness: What Next for Turkey?" *New York Times,* October 7, 1998, p. A4.

[116]John F. Burns, "Pakistan Is Rethinking Its Support for an Afghan Muslim Group," *New York Times,* March 27, 1996, p. A8.

[117]"The Road to Koranistan," *The Economist,* October 5-11, 1996, pp. 21-22, 24; John F. Burns, "A Village Dies at the Hands of Afghanistan's Zealots," *New York Times,* October 27, 1996, pp. 1, 8; John F. Burns and Steve LeVine, "How Afghans' Stern Rulers Took Hold," December 31, 1996, pp. A1, A6.

[118]John F. Burns, "Kabul's Victors Impose Harsh Islamic Mores," *New York Times,* October 1, 1996, pp. A1, A7; John F. Burns, "Walled In, Shrouded and Angry in Afghanistan," *New York Times,* October 4, 1996, p. A3; John F. Burns, "Afghanistan's Professional Class Flees Rule by Ultra-Strict Clerics," *New York Times,* October 7, 1996, pp. A1, A6; John F. Burns, "An Afghan Execution: It's Swift and Personal," *New York Times,* December 19, 1996, pp. A1, A4.

[119]Barbara Crossette, "Afghan Rulers Planning to Smash TV Sets," *New York Times,* July 10, 1998, p. A7.

[120]Cited in John F. Burns, "Kabul's Rulers Face Rivals and Popular Unrest," *New York Times,* October 22, 1996, p. A6.

[121]Cited in John F. Burns, "With Sugared Tea and Caustic Rules, An Afghan Leader Explains Himself," *New York Times,* November 24, 1996, sec. 4, p. 9.

[122]John F. Burns, "For Afghans, Full Circle," *New York Times,* August 13, 1998, pp. A1, A9.

[123]Keith B. Richburg, "Peace Is Not on Their Agenda," *Washington Post National Weekly Edition,* May 29–June 4, 1995, p. 19.

[124]The attack in Kenya was led by a former student of the Koran from the Comoro Islands. Donald G. McNeil, Jr., "Assets of a Bombing Suspect: Keen Wit, Religious Soul, Angry Temper," *New York Times,* October 6, 1998, p. A6.

[125]Cited in Tim Weiner, "Man with Mission Uses Whole World to Attack the U.S.," *New York Times,* August 21, 1998, p. A11. See also Youssef M. Ibrahim, "Saudi Exile Warns West New Attacks Are Planned," *New York Times,* July 11, 1996, p. A6; James Risen, "New Evidence Ties Sudanese to Bin Laden, U.S. Asserts," *New York Times,* October 4, 1998, sec. 1, p. 7; Benjamin Weiser, "U.S. Says It Can Tie Bin Laden to Embassy Bombings," *New York Times,* October 8, 1998, p. A3.

[126]Cited in Weiner, "Man with Mission," p. A11. Bin Laden's network is called Al Qaeda, and it was established in 1989.

[127]Ibid.

[128]"Today's New Cult Hero," *The Economist,* August 29–September 4, 1998, p. 44.

[129]Benjamin Weiser, "U.S. Says Bin Laden Aide Tried to Get Nuclear Weapons," *New York Times,* September 26, 1998, p. A3.

[130]Cited in Jeff Gerth and Judith Miller, "Funds for Terrorists Traced to Persian Gulf Businessmen," *New York Times,* August 14, 1996, p. A4.

[131]James Risen, "U.S. Directs International Drive on Bin Laden Networks," *New York Times,* September 25, 1998, p. A3.

[132]See Tim Weiner, "Out of the Spotlight, Intelligence Services Weigh an Alliance Against Terror," *New York Times,* March 13, 1996, p. 8; Tim Weiner, "Sophisticated Terrorists Pose Daunting Obstacle," *New York Times,* August 13, 1998, p. A8.

[133]Christopher S. Wren, "U.S. Jury Convicts 3 in a Conspiracy to Bomb Airliners," *New York Times,* September 6, 1996, pp. A1, A16.

[134]Cited in Christopher S. Wren, "Long Arm of U.S. Law Gets Longer," *New York Times,* July 7, 1996, sec. 4, p. 4. Libya's refusal to hand over the suspected perpetrators of the bombing of a Pan Am plane over Lockerbie, Scotland, led to the imposition of a partial trade embargo on the country. The embargo was lifted when Libya turned the suspects over in April 1999 for trial before a Scottish court sitting in the Netherlands.

[135]Ibid.

[136]William J. Broad and Judith Miller, "Pentagon Seeks Command for Emergencies in the U.S.," *New York Times,* January 28, 1999, p. A19.

[137]P. J. Simmons, "Learning to Live with NGOs," *Foreign Policy* 112 (Fall 1998), p. 83.

[138]Samuel P. Huntington, "The Clash of Civilizations?" *Foreign Affairs* 72:3 (Summer 1993), pp. 29–35. For an alternate view, see "Living with Islam," *The Economist,* March 18–24, 1995, pp. 13–14. Those who agree with Huntington can point to Bosnia, Kosovo, and Chechnya as evidence of the clash. See Roger Thurow, "Muslims from Bosnia Find Refuge in Islam While Adrift in Europe," *Wall Street Journal,* September 6, 1994, pp. A1, A5; Michael Specter, "Faith Reinforces Hate in the Caucasus," *New York Times,* January 15, 1995, sec. 4, p. 5.

[139]Benjamin R. Barber, "Jihad vs. McWorld," *Atlantic Monthly,* No. 269 (March 1992), p. 53.

Chapter 8

Interstate Organizations: Responses to the Erosion of State Sovereignty

his chapter examines the evolution and variety of *intergovernmental orga-nizations (IGOs)*—organizations whose members are states—in global poli-tics. These organizations exist in large measure as the responses of states to problems and issues with which they cannot cope on their own. Increasingly, IGOs serve as the means by which states confront the forces of fragmentation in global politics—ethnic violence, human poverty, contagious diseases, monetary volatility, international terrorism, and so forth. There are also a few *supranational organizations* that have authority *over* states.

The number of IGOs has grown dramatically in this century. In 1909, there were 37. By 1994, that number had increased to 263. About three-quarters are regional organizations with membership confined to a particular part of the world. The other 25 percent are universal or intercontinental in membership.[1]

Almost no area of human activity is untouched by IGOs. To illustrate the range and significance of these actors, we survey a few key types. Keep in mind three considerations. First, similar groups have existed historically. Second, such actors are being asked to do more and more in the post–Cold War era. Third, some are regional and others global, and some specialize and others are multipurpose. Along with states, IGOs and nongovernmental organizations (NGOs) create the mosaic of actors that constitute today's global society.

Just as nongovernmental organizations take varied forms, so do intergovern-mental organizations (often called international organizations). Some IGOs enjoy large responsibilities and are relatively autonomous. Others merely carry out states' commands. And still others try to influence states to change policy.

The Seeds of International Organization

Various proposals have been aimed at overcoming conflict in global politics. Some theorists have called for different kinds of states that they believe are naturally more peace-loving, and others have advocated building international institutions to obviate the need for self-help.

Kant, Rousseau, and Woodrow Wilson

Two eighteenth-century political philosophers, Immanuel Kant and Jean-Jacques Rousseau, prescribed how states could reduce conflict. Born into Europe's Age of Enlightenment, they believed in the power of rationality and thought that people would pursue their rational self-interest if they knew what it was. Their proposals touched on the perfectibility of human beings and states and on the means for overcoming the system's anarchic properties.

Kant argued that human beings exist in two worlds—the world of the senses (the phenomenal) and the world of reason (the noumenal).[2] Although both worlds guide and shape human conduct, the world of the senses often prevails over that of reason. For reason to prevail, human beings must enter civil society and create the civil state "in which," Kenneth Waltz says, "rights are secured, and with them the possibility of moral behavior."[3] But, thought Kant, only one kind of state can foster individual moral development and international peace: a republic with representative institutions. Kant held that, unlike authoritarian states, republics enhance cooperation because they act in their citizens' interests, and cooperation and peace serve those interests.

Kant believed that states and their relationships were analogous to individuals in a state of nature. How could states escape anarchy? He had two answers. First, states should seek to improve internally and become republics so that "perpetual peace" is possible. Second, republics should combine into a "voluntary combination of different States that would be *dissoluble* at any time"[4] so that reason can govern passion and ambition. Why Kant's preference for a voluntary rather than a supranational arrangement? Waltz argues that Kant had two reasons:

> States already have a legal constitution; it would be illogical to place them under another. . . . One suspects that his second reason . . . is more important. He fears that such a state, once achieved, would be a greater evil than the wars it is designed to eliminate. It could so easily become a terrible despotism, stifle liberty, kill initiative, and in the end lapse into anarchy.[5]

Rousseau's analysis parallels Kant's, though he reached a different conclusion. Like Kant, Rousseau saw the condition of states as analogous to that of individuals in a state of nature. He also argued for the need to escape from that state into civil society and called for establishing republics. But, whereas Kant thought that the existence of "good" states—republics—and a voluntary confederation would be sufficient to ensure peace, Rousseau proposed a world state that "shall unite nations by bonds similar to those which already unite their individual members, and place the one no less than the other under the authority of the Law." "It must have a coercive force capable of compelling every State to obey its common resolves . . . and . . . it must be strong and firm enough to make it impossible for any member to withdraw at his own pleasure the moment he conceives his private interest to clash with that of the whole body."[6] The reason for this difference is that Rousseau believed conflict arose from the structure of the international system itself, whereas Kant believed conflict was a result of defects within states.

President Woodrow Wilson's proposals for collective security and a League of Nations showed the enduring influence of Kant and Rousseau on the liberal tradition in global politics. Wilson proposed a *collective-security* system in reaction to World War I, which he believed had been caused by balance-of-power policies and authoritarianism in Germany, Austria-Hungary, and Russia.[7] With Kant and Rousseau, he believed war was caused by *both* the imperfection of states and the international system's structure.

Aggressive autocracy, according to Wilson, could be overcome by national self-determination and the spread of democracy. Whereas authoritarian leaders go to war for personal profit and glory, democracy prevents leaders from doing so without good cause. And if some states still behaved aggressively, the remedy would be a new security structure to replace the balance of power. As the last of his *Fourteen Points* (a statement of war aims made on January 8, 1918), Wilson proposed "a general association of nations . . . formed under specific covenants for the purpose of affording mutual guarantees of political independence and territorial integrity to great and small states alike."[8]

A collective-security system, thought Wilson, would treat all nations as interdependent members of one community. Like the Three Musketeers, whose motto was "one for all and all for one," all states would help any state that was threatened by aggression. Aggressors would be deterred by knowing that punishment would be swift and effective.[9] Collective security, Wilson believed, could not rely only on the deterrent effect of one for all; it had to carry moral force. "Moral force is a great deal more powerful than physical."[10] Peace would be assured only when leaders recognized that aggression was morally wrong.

Wilson was hardly naive, though some of his critics have argued he was, and he did not dismiss the role of power in confronting power. In a speech in South Dakota on September 8, 1919, he declared: "You have either got to have the old system . . . or you have got to have a new system," and "you cannot establish freedom . . . without force, and the only force you can substitute for an armed mankind is the concerted force of the combined action of mankind."[11]

Functionalism and Neofunctionalism

After World War II, other ideas were advanced to bind people together and bring down the walls of state sovereignty. Like Kant's federalism, some of these entailed moving beyond the state system by creating structures above states. Two of the most durable ideas were *functionalism* and *neofunctionalism,* both arising from the idea that societies have "functional needs," such as feeding and housing citizens, that states may not successfully meet.

The origin of functionalism is associated with David Mitrany.[12] Appalled by war's carnage, he called for new global arrangements to meet peoples' unsatisfied needs for economic and social welfare, which he thought led to conflict. With those new structures, the response to global needs would be relatively spontaneous, involving the "binding together [of] those interests which are common, where they are common, and to the extent . . . they are common."[13] Mitrany's premise was optimistic: Individuals are able to recognize their functional needs and will organize themselves to satisfy them.

Functionalists believed a snowballing effect would occur once successful functional organizations had been built. Success would breed success, and new institutions would be created to meet other needs. Global efforts to address one demand (such as monitoring global food production) would stimulate additional demands to satisfy others (such as monitoring global weather). Functional agencies would be like "stones cast into a pond," each producing ever-widening ripples into new functional areas. According to functionalist theory, states would more readily surrender nonpolitical technical and economic responsibilities than security tasks. Nevertheless, sovereignty would gradually erode, and a new global community would emerge. Mitrany's goal was clear: to create "a complex, interwoven network of cross-national organizations performing all the traditional welfare functions of the nation-state at the same time rendering war impossible."[14]

Functional organizations date from the International Telegraphic Union in 1865 and the Universal Postal Union in 1874. The Central Commission for the Navigation of the Rhine River, created after the Congress of Vienna in 1815, antedates both and is regarded as the first modern international functional organization. However, proliferating functional organizations have not eroded state sovereignty as functionalists believed they would, and states have not surrendered significant powers to them. Even technical tasks are highly political, and there is little evidence of an automatic extension of functional organization to meet human needs. However, such organizations have reduced the effects of anarchy.

Some refinement in functionalist theory was called for, and it took the form of neofunctionalism. In neofunctionalism, expanding global cooperation is no longer taken for granted. Instead, governments are pressured to cooperate by domestic interest groups and lobbyists who see an advantage to themselves in such cooperation. Genuine progress required simultaneously extending supranational authority to new issues and deepening that authority. And if this spillover went far enough, it would lead to a shift in loyalties and political activities from states to a new political community.[15]

Business groups in several countries may believe that eliminating interstate trade barriers will benefit them by stimulating greater sales, and they may lobby governments to form a common market. Thereafter, corporations may organize internationally to take advantage of the new opportunities and lobby for additional standardization of policy in taxes and welfare. This initiative may induce national labor unions to join one another to bargain effectively with the corporations. Because many economic policies are linked, creating a supranational agency to foster cooperation on one issue may produce pressures for cooperation on others. Thus negotiations for a North American Free Trade Agreement could not be limited to reducing tariffs because wage and tax policies, environmental regulations, and labor laws all influence the distribution of costs and benefits.

In sum, neofunctionalism shares features with functionalism, but it also differs. Like functionalists, neofunctionalists rely on common welfare needs to stimulate cooperation, and they depend on technocrats to facilitate this cooperation. Both approaches assume that cooperation confers more benefits than going it alone. On the other hand, neofunctionalists are more aware of how controversial economic and technical issues can be. They advocate selecting issues that are technical but also important to governments, and they are conscious that political institutions must be built to facilitate cooperation. Finally, neofunctionalists select areas with a potential for spillover into other sectors that can increase overall authority for supranational institutions.

The League of Nations

The *League of Nations* and the *United Nations,* both *multipurpose intergovernmental organizations,* were established at the end of the world wars and had similar goals—maintaining peace, mobilizing the collective will of member states to do so, and addressing social and economic needs.

The League: Origins and Characteristics

Among League predecessors were the Hague Conferences in 1899 and 1907, whose achievements included a convention specifying peaceful ways to settle disputes and a Permanent Court of Arbitration. The League idea evolved during World War I. In 1915, a group of idealistic Americans who belonged to the Century Club in New York and British pacifists who formed the Bryce Group in London offered alternate plans for a League of Nations.[16] These plans were brought to President Wilson's attention, and he embraced the idea of a "general association of nations" as the last of his Fourteen Points.

Wilson saw the League as a way of enforcing collective security, but disputes erupted at Versailles about the form the organization should take.[17] The British and Americans argued about how much the League should encourage change, the Americans hoping the organization would become a means for altering the status quo. Small states were unhappy with their proposed representation in the organization. The French wanted the *League Covenant* to provide a stronger role for force with an eye toward preventing restoration of German power. Finally, the Japanese sought to have a statement on racial equality added to the Covenant but failed before American and Australian opposition. Despite these controversies, the Covenant was ratified at Versailles in April 1919.

The League consisted of a Council, an Assembly, and a Secretariat, with a Permanent Court of Justice added in 1921. The Council consisted of the "Principal Allied or Associated Powers" and four additional members selected by the Assembly. The Assembly, composed of all League members with equal voting rights, could deal with any issue "within the sphere of action of the League or affecting the peace of the world." The Secretariat would serve as the League's executive.

The Council was to be the principal mechanism for dealing with threats to peace. Among its options if a dispute arose were arbitration, judicial settlement, and investigation. If the Council became involved, it was obligated to investigate and issue a report. If a state still resorted to war, the Covenant specified members' collective obligations. The offender would "be deemed to have committed an act of war against all other Members of the League" and be subject to "severance of all trade or financial relations" by other states. If necessary, says Article 16, "it shall be the duty of the Council . . . to recommend . . . what effective military, naval or air force the Members of the League shall severally contribute . . . to be used to protect the covenants of the League." Aggression would be met by collective sanctions and, if necessary, by collective force.

Evaluating the League's Effectiveness

The obligations outlined in the Covenant were voluntary and limited, ultimately undermining collective security. States could join or leave the League as they wished, and universal membership was never achieved. Seventeen states withdrew or were expelled, including Germany, Italy, Japan, and the Soviet Union. Some never joined, most important the United States, where the Senate, dominated by a Republican majority, refused to confirm the Treaty of Versailles because they feared a loss of state sovereignty. Indeed, the U.S. policy of isolationism during the 1920s weakened the collective-security principle, and that fact is still cited to justify U.S. activism in global politics. Another source of weakness was institutional: Most League decisions required unanimity, and even then they were only recommendations. Procedures for moving from recommending to implementing were not fully spelled out. Finally, and most important, when challenges arose, major members acted unilaterally and failed to meet their collective-security obligations.

In the temperate 1920s political climate, the League seemed to work. It eased disputes between Turkey and Iraq, Greece and Bulgaria, and Poland and Lithuania. The Greek-Bulgarian question showed the League at its best. A border conflict between the two broke out in October 1925. Within days, Bulgaria asked for the League's help. The Council met, called for a ceasefire, sent observers, and started a formal inquiry. By December, a report was made to the Council, and an indemnity was awarded to Bulgaria. Yet even at this time the League's failure to grapple with issues such as Poland's seizure of Vilna from Lithuania (1920), France's occupation of the Ruhr (1923), and Italy's bombardment of the Greek island of Corfu (1923) boded ill for its future. *The League could only succeed in relatively minor quarrels in which great powers were not directly involved.*

In the 1930s, the League was helpless in coping with conflicts in which great powers were major players. Four episodes spelled the League's doom as a collective-security organization—the Japanese seizure of Manchuria (1931), the Italian invasion of Ethiopia (1935), and the German occupation of Austria and Czechoslovakia (1938). After the Japanese invasion, China appealed to the League. After a delay, the Council passed resolutions requesting Japan's withdrawal and establishing a commission of inquiry. It took a year before the commission's report was adopted. Known as the Lytton Report, it supported China's claims against Japan but suggested that Japan had been provoked. Its recommendations—that China and Japan sign trade and nonaggression treaties and set up a joint "special administration" over Manchuria—were "well-intentioned daydreaming."[18] Japan refused to accept even these timid recommendations and withdrew from the League.

The League had failed to meet its first big challenge, and the reasons for failure showed how difficult it is to elicit cooperation among powerful states with competing interests. First, Manchuria was geographically and psychologically remote. Second, Britain and France were ill prepared to challenge Japan militarily, and the United States preferred to invoke moral suasion against Japan's aggression. Third, the Great Depression reduced any interest in vigorous international action. Finally, the League's leading members preferred conciliation to sanctions in dealing with fellow members.

Italy's invasion of Ethiopia in October 1935 was an even clearer challenge. The Haitian representative to the League declared: "Great or small, strong or weak, near or far, white or coloured, let us never forget that one day we may be somebody's Ethiopia."[19] Italy's use of poison gas and high-level bombing against Ethiopians horrified observers. Economic sanctions were applied, but with little effect. Although Britain supported sanctions, it refused to close the Suez Canal to Italian shipping or halt the flow of oil that was necessary for the fascist war machine to function. When it was clear sanctions did not work, the League refused to go further.

The Ethiopian case revealed a fundamental difficulty in applying collective security. Britain and France were less interested in stopping Italian dictator Benito Mussolini than in making him an ally against Hitler. These biases became stronger when Hitler announced in March 1936 that he was reneging on the Locarno Treaty of 1925 and remilitarizing the Rhineland. Of British Prime Minister Stanley Baldwin, Winston Churchill wrote, "The Prime Minister had declared that sanctions meant war; secondly, he was resolved that there must be no war; and, thirdly, he decided upon sanctions."[20] In their eagerness to avoid war with Italy, British Foreign Secretary Sir Samuel Hoare and French Foreign Minister Pierre Laval secretly offered Mussolini a deal in December 1935 giving him most of what he demanded.[21] Both countries were absorbed by events in Europe, not Africa, contradicting the collective-security assumption that aggression against anyone was important. Competing issues divided actors' attention, and they decided to sacrifice principle in one to strengthen their hand in another. The requirements of collective security and the demands of European politics could not be reconciled.

The bankruptcy of collective security showed in the League's failure to resist Hitler's aggression against Austria and Czechoslovakia in 1938. Amid these crises, the League Assembly debated whether to weaken the obligation of states to resist aggression.[22] In a last act of folly, the League expelled the U.S.S.R. in 1939 for invading Finland at the moment when Hitler mortally threatened the rest of Europe. The Assembly held a final session in April 1946 before formally ending its existence. The world's first experiment with collective security had failed. In constructing a successor, efforts were made to avoid the League's mistakes.

The United Nations

The idea for a new international organization was again born in wartime—in a 1942 declaration by twenty-six nations (the "United Nations"). These discussions led the United States to invite representatives from Great Britain, Russia, and China to meet at Dumbarton Oaks in Washington in August 1944, where they drafted proposals that became the basis for the *U.N. Charter*.[23] The U.N. Charter was signed in April 1945 in San Francisco. Since then the U.N. has become "an enormous body that, among other things, buys half the world's children's vaccines, protects 22m refugees, is host to 7,500 meetings in Geneva alone and is the world's biggest purchaser of condoms."[24]

The United Nations Structure

The goals and structure of the new organization resembled those of the League, but the U.N. Charter also had provisions to address deficiencies in the League Covenant. For example, the U.N., more than the League, emphasized global economic and social needs. In this, the U.N. more fully reflected the functionalist belief that conflict arises from poverty.

The number and responsibilities of U.N. organs reflected these ideas (see Figure 8.1). The Charter established six organs: a General Assembly, a Security Council, an Economic and Social Council, a Trusteeship Council, a Secretariat, and an International Court of Justice. Three of these—the Security Council, the Secretariat, and the International Court—were intended to address peace and security; two others—the Economic and Social Council and the Trusteeship Council—were responsible for functional activities; and the sixth—the General Assembly—dealt with both types of activity.

The General Assembly.   The *General Assembly* was to shoulder responsibilities in both areas (Articles 10, 12, 13). Every member was represented in the Assembly, and each was given one vote. The Assembly could take up any issue and could discuss any issue relating to the maintenance of peace and security (Article 12). However, it was not to take up a matter that was before the Security Council, and its resolutions were only nonmandatory recommendations. In addition, the Assembly had to approve the U.N. budget (Article 17) and was to receive regular reports from other U.N. organs, including the Security Council (Article 15). General Assembly debates rarely resolve issues. Instead, because of the public nature of such debates, often issues only reach the floor of the Assembly after quiet negotiation has failed and they have become stalemated.

Unlike the League, the United Nations did become a genuinely universal body. Fifty-one states were charter members, and thereafter membership expanded dramatically, fueled by incoming independent states in the 1960s and 1970s and, more recently, by the breakup of the U.S.S.R. and Yugoslavia. With the admission of Eritrea and Palau, membership reached 185 in 1995.

During the early years of the U.N., membership consisted largely of American allies and friends from Europe and Latin America, but, as membership grew, largely because of decolonization, the United States found itself less and less able to command voting majorities in the General Assembly. Figure 8.2 depicts how the United States progressively found itself voting in the minority there. After 1960, U.N. majorities coalesced around the less-developed countries (LDCs), which had strong interests in redistributing global resources and were supported by members of the Soviet bloc.

The Security Council.   Though analogous to the League Council, the *Security Council* differs from its predecessor in several ways. In matters of peaceful settlement and peacekeeping, the Security Council's authority is greater than that of the League Council. Under the Charter, the Security Council enjoys "primary responsibility for the maintenance of international peace and security" and has authority to "investigate any dispute, or any situation which might lead to international friction or give rise to a dispute." Unlike the League Council, it does not have to wait for a dispute to be brought before it. Under Chapters Six and Seven (Articles 33–51)[25] of the Charter, the Council may order a spectrum of actions to end a threat to peace. These range from inquiry, mediation, and conciliation to "complete or partial interruption of economic relations and of rail, sea, air, postal, telegraphic, radio, and other means of communication." In recent years the Council has imposed sanctions against South Africa, Iraq, Serbia, and Libya. If sanctions prove

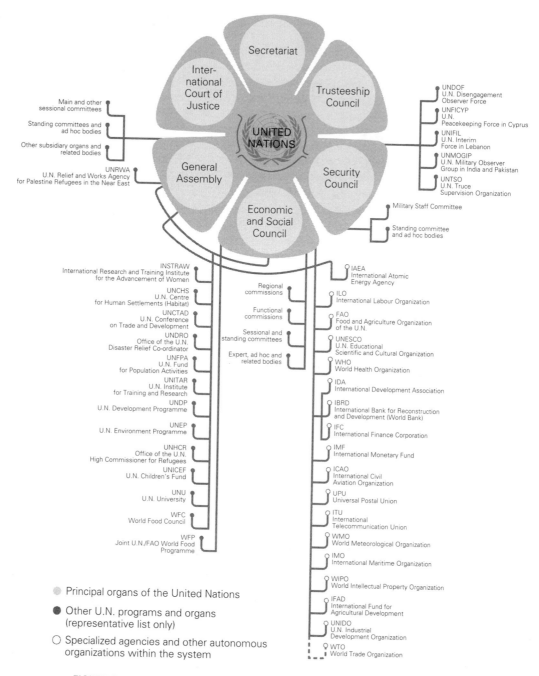

Main and other sessional committees

Standing committees and ad hoc bodies

Other subsidiary organs and related bodies

UNRWA U.N. Relief and Works Agency for Palestine Refugees in the Near East

Secretariat

International Court of Justice

Trusteeship Council

General Assembly

UNITED NATIONS

Security Council

Economic and Social Council

UNDOF U.N. Disengagement Observer Force

UNFICYP U.N. Peacekeeping Force in Cyprus

UNIFIL U.N. Interim Force in Lebanon

UNMOGIP U.N. Military Observer Group in India and Pakistan

UNTSO U.N. Truce Supervision Organization

Military Staff Committee

Standing committee and ad hoc bodies

INSTRAW International Research and Training Institute for the Advancement of Women

UNCHS U.N. Centre for Human Settlements (Habitat)

UNCTAD U.N. Conference on Trade and Development

UNDRO Office of the U.N. Disaster Relief Co-ordinator

UNFPA U.N. Fund for Population Activities

UNITAR U.N. Institute for Training and Research

UNDP U.N. Development Programme

UNEP U.N. Environment Programme

UNHCR Office of the U.N. High Commissioner for Refugees

UNICEF U.N. Children's Fund

UNU U.N. University

WFC World Food Council

WFP Joint U.N./FAO World Food Programme

Regional commissions

Functional commissions

Sessional and standing committees

Expert, ad hoc and related bodies

IAEA International Atomic Energy Agency

ILO International Labour Organization

FAO Food and Agriculture Organization of the U.N.

UNESCO U.N. Educational, Scientific and Cultural Organization

WHO World Health Organization

IDA International Development Association

IBRD International Bank for Reconstruction and Development (World Bank)

IFC International Finance Corporation

IMF International Monetary Fund

ICAO International Civil Aviation Organization

UPU Universal Postal Union

ITU International Telecommunication Union

WMO World Meteorological Organization

IMO International Maritime Organization

WIPO World Intellectual Property Organization

IFAD International Fund for Agricultural Development

UNIDO U.N. Industrial Development Organization

WTO World Trade Organization

● Principal organs of the United Nations

● Other U.N. programs and organs (representative list only)

○ Specialized agencies and other autonomous organizations within the system

FIGURE 8.1
The United Nations System

The United Nations system consists of six principal organs and a variety of specialized agencies and groups.

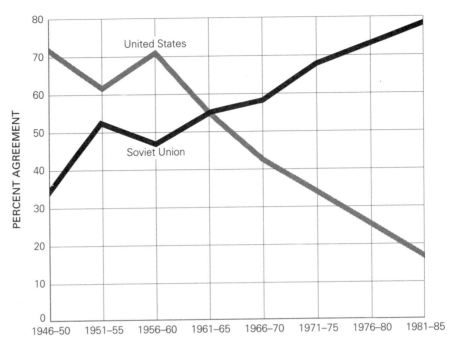

FIGURE 8.2
U.S. and Soviet Union Percentage Agreement with the Majority

Until the mid-1960s, the United States found itself in the majority on most issues while the Soviet Union was in the minority. The growth in the U.N. membership, especially of less-developed countries, accompanied the progressive isolation of the United States in the General Assembly after 1970. SOURCE: *The United Nations: International Organization and World Politics* by Robert E. Riggs and Jack C. Plano. Copyright © 1988 by Harcourt, Inc. Reprinted by permission of the publisher.

inadequate, the Council "may take such action by air, sea, or land forces as may be necessary to maintain or restore international peace and security."

Two big differences between the Charter and Covenant merit attention here. First, the Charter strengthened all states' obligations to carry out Security Council decisions. Chapter Seven states categorically that all members "shall join in affording mutual assistance in carrying out the measures decided upon by the Security Council." Second, the Charter provides a stronger statement about the possible use of force. In the end, however, despite the Charter's strong language, compliance remains voluntary, and the Council, like its predecessor, depends on members' willingness to provide resources.

The structure of the League and U.N. Councils also differs. Membership in the League Council was divided between the permanent "Principal Allied and Associated Powers" and several appointed states. Each had one vote, and most decisions required unanimity. The Security Council also has permanent and temporary members, but with a difference in voting. Under the Charter, the United States, the Soviet Union, China, France, and Britain were designated permanent members and six (later ten) elected states were to serve in rotation as nonpermanent members.[26]

Voting on procedural matters requires a majority of nine of fifteen, but votes on substantive actions (which includes deciding when matters are procedural) require that the majority include *all* permanent members, giving each a veto on Council action. Japan and Germany want to become permanent Council members, but the developing world opposes this, demanding the addition of permanent members from its ranks.[27] Under a recent proposal, the Security Council would be enlarged from fifteen to twenty-four members. And of the nine additional members, five would be permanent (though without the veto power), and four would rotate in two-year terms. Under the plan, two of the new permanent members would come from the industrial world (probably Germany and Japan), and three from the developing world.[28]

The limit on the veto power became clear when the Soviet representative's absence from the Council when the Korean War began was not considered a veto. Previously, it had been thought that Council action required positive votes by all permanent members. The Korean precedent meant that absence or abstention implied neither consent nor disagreement. Permanent members could disassociate themselves from a Council action without being obstructionist.

Following China's intervention in Korea, the General Assembly took additional action to circumvent the veto. It adopted a *Uniting for Peace Resolution* permitting it to meet in emergency session within twenty-four hours to make "recommendations to Members for collective measures" if the Security Council was unable to act. At the time the U.S.S.R. protested, but it invoked the provisions of this resolution during the 1967 Six-Day War.

The veto has advantages and disadvantages. Its main advantage is ensuring that Council recommendations will have support from the principal powers. One lesson from the 1930s was that the pivotal powers must provide support if collective action is to work. The disadvantage of the veto is that one permanent member can frustrate the Council. In a sense, the veto was an admission that collective security was not workable and that there was no point in trying to run roughshod over major powers' objections. A superpower can thwart the Security Council, with or without a formal veto, by withholding resources or opposing Council action. Such actors enjoy a tacit veto. During the early decades, the Council was dominated by the United States and its allies. For that reason, the Soviet Union cast many vetoes. Between 1946 and 1990, the U.S.S.R. was responsible for about half (116 out of 238),[29] many to prevent admission of new pro-Western members (until an agreement was reached on joint admission for both East- and West-bloc members in the mid-1950s). The United States cast its first veto in 1970, but thereafter, Washington used the veto more frequently.[30] The initial U.S. vetoes were used to prevent U.N. action against the white-minority government of Rhodesia and to stop resolutions condemning Israel and U.S. control of the Panama Canal. Between 1970 and 1990, the United States used its veto sixty-nine times, and the Soviet Union cast none after 1984.[31] In 1997, China cast a veto for the first time in twenty-six years on an issue other than the selection of a Secretary-General.[32]

The Secretariat.   The *Secretariat* is the U.N. executive organ and is directed by a Secretary-General, the highest U.N. "civil servant." The Secretariat manages the organization's bureaucracy and finances and oversees the operation of all organs and personnel, from technicians and policemen to doctors and soldiers. Initially, the United Nations had 1,500 permanent employees; by 1993 it had close to 52,000. The Secretary-General is appointed by the General Assembly after a recommendation by the Security Council and serves for a renewable five-year term. Because the Secretary-General has the power to "bring to the attention of the Security Council any matter which in his opinion may threaten the maintenance of international peace and security," his selection involves delicate negotiations among members to ensure that their interests are looked after. The Secretary-General is also charged with carrying out the Council's recommendations. The United Nations has had only seven Secretaries-General—Trygve Lie of Norway, Dag Hammarskjöld of Sweden, U Thant of Burma, Kurt Waldheim of Austria, Javier Pérez de Cuellar of Peru, Boutros Boutros-Ghali of Egypt, and Kofi Annan of Ghana. Their varied personalities and skill have determined the U.N.'s effectiveness. Hammarskjöld became a target of Soviet wrath for his activism and pro-Western bias. By contrast, Waldheim and Pérez de Cuellar were accused of being anti-Western. Boutros-Ghali was an active spokesman for the interests of the less-developed countries.[33] He became a target of American anger because of his abrupt manner and his alleged inability to reform the world organization as quickly as Washington wished. Despite the opposition of its allies, the United States vetoed Boutros-Ghali's effort to serve a second term.[34]

The International Court of Justice.   The fourth organ, the *International Court of Justice (ICJ)*, was the successor to the League's Permanent Court of Justice. The fifteen justices, appointed for nine-year terms, reflect geographic and political diversity. By the Charter, the Court is authorized to decide cases brought to it or provide advisory opinions when asked by the Council or Assembly. Few states have accepted the Court's "compulsory jurisdiction," and most have decided, case by case, whether to allow the ICJ to render a binding decision. In 1984, the United States refused to accept the ICJ's judgment in a case brought against it by Nicaragua's Sandinista government because of U.S. support for the contras.[35] As of 1995, fourteen cases were before the ICJ, including the issue of French nuclear tests in the South Pacific (brought by New Zealand) and the American downing of an Iranian passenger plane in 1988.[36]

The Economic and Social Council and the Trusteeship Council.   The remaining organs are the *Economic and Social Council (ECOSOC)* and the *Trusteeship Council.* Both were intended to carry out U.N. functional responsibilities. ECOSOC's principal task is reporting on global "economic, social, cultural, educational, health and related matters," about which it may make recommendations to the Assembly and the specialized agencies. Associated with but largely independent of the League and United Nations are *specialized agencies* that have specific functional responsibilities to cope with the challenges posed by specific issues. Their tasks range from activities such as delivering the mail (Universal Postal Union), regulating airplane traffic (International Civil Aviation Organization), and monitoring global weather (World Meteorological Organization) to increasing nutrition for the world's hungry (World Food Program), improving global health (World Health Organization), and improving the global environment (U.N. Environment Program).

The Trusteeship Council was established to monitor the progress of former colonial territories placed under U.N. trust as a result of World War II, previous League mandates, or voluntary actions. With the independence of Palau, administered by the United States since 1947, the last trust territory became independent, and the Trusteeship Council is out of business.[37] Some suggest, however, that the agency be given new responsibilities for countries in which government has broken down.

U.N. Effectiveness in Maintaining Peace and Security

Although its record is mixed, the United Nations has been more successful than the League of Nations. In the course of over fifty years, it has used many mechanisms to manage tensions, including nonbinding resolutions, fact-finding missions, observers, economic and military sanctions, peacekeeping forces, and, on a few occasions, peace enforcement in which military force is mobilized to combat aggression. By one count, the United Nations took up more than two hundred disputes between 1946 and December 1992.[38] Most U.N. activity involved identifying, debating, and trying to end disputes by negotiation and mediation. Relatively few cases have entailed more extensive measures, and the U.N.'s inability to resolve some of the most intransigent disputes and its failure to deal with others (especially at the height of the Cold War) also point to its limitations.

The veto is one reason the Security Council has authorized the use of force to stop aggression only twice—first in Korea in 1950 and then in 1990 when members were authorized to use force to end Iraqi occupation of Kuwait.[39] On both occasions, unusual circumstances prevailed. When the Council authorized force in Korea, the Soviet representative was boycotting its sessions. Forty years later, the U.N. authorization to use force against Iraq coincided with the end of the Cold War. Both cases exemplify *peace enforcement* in which an aggressor is identified and labeled and large-scale military force is mobilized to defeat the aggressor.

Unable to enforce peace except on these two occasions, the U.N. early on devised the less-demanding techniques of *peacekeeping* and *preventive diplomacy*. Unlike peace enforcement in Korea and the Persian Gulf, peacekeeping does not label an aggressor, nor does it require that the United Nations take sides, as when forces were mobilized against North Korea and Iraq. The objective of peacekeeping is not to stop aggression but to separate warring parties, contain violence by interposing U.N. forces, and cool off adversaries. Unlike the forces mobilized under peace enforcement, peacekeepers are only lightly armed and are not to initiate conflict. Since peacekeeping could prevent local disputes from expanding, it was called preventive diplomacy. In the words of Secretary-General Dag Hammarskjöld, who coined the expression,

> Preventive action . . . must, in the first place, aim at filling the vacuum so that it will not provoke action from any of the major parties, the initiative from which might be taken for preventive purposes but might in turn lead to a counter action from the other side. . . . Temporarily . . . the United Nations enters the picture on the basis of its non-commitment to any power bloc. . . .[40]

One example of preventive diplomacy occurred in the former Belgian Congo (first renamed Zaire and, more recently, the Democratic Republic of Congo) in

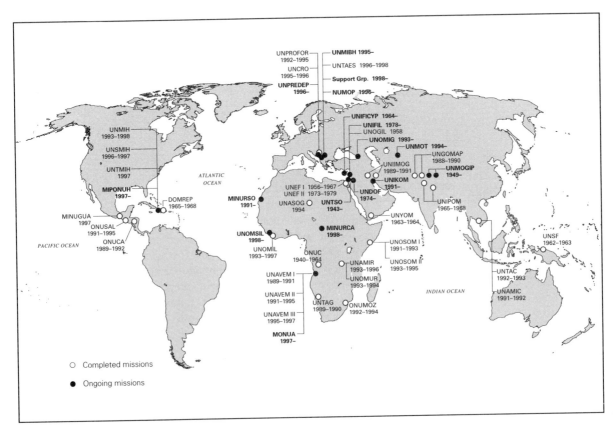

FIGURE 8.3
Completed and Ongoing Peacekeeping Missions

SOURCE: U.N. Department of Public Information, www.un.org/Depts/dpko

1960, where it was feared that a breakdown in law and order would embroil the United States and the Soviet Union in a dangerous confrontation.

United Nations peacekeepers come from many countries and, as shown in Figure 8.3, have been sent to every continent,[41] and their distribution reflects the world's trouble spots. Thus, as Table 8.1 shows, current threats to peace and security are concentrated in Africa, the former Yugoslavia, and the Middle East. Between 1948 and 1998, almost 1,600 U.N. personnel died in peacekeeping operations. At its peak in July 1993, the U.N. employed 78,744 soldiers and observers. Because of financial exigency, by the end of 1998 this number had declined to 14,347 (in 16 countries), including soldiers from 76 countries.[42] The first peacekeeping force was the U.N. Emergency Force (UNEF), which was sent to the Middle East in 1956 following the Anglo-French seizure of the Suez Canal and Israel's invasion of Egypt's Sinai Peninsula.[43] Operations range from a few peacekeepers—twenty to monitor the Greek border in 1947—to large-scale military exercises—the 1992–1994 Somali

TABLE 8.1
Current Peacekeeping Operations (1999)

Africa

1. Angola—MONUA
   United Nations Observer Mission in Angola
   July 1997 to present
2. Central African Republic—MINURCA
   United Nations Mission in the Central African Republic
   April 1998 to present
3. Sierra Leone—UNOMSIL
   United Nations Mission of Observers in Sierra Leone
   July 1998
4. Western Sahara—MINURSO
   United Nations Mission for the Referendum in Western Sahara
   April 1991 to present

Americas

5. Haiti—MIPONUH
   United Nations Civilian Police Mission in Haiti
   December 1997 to present

Asia

6. India/Pakistan—UNMOGIP
   United Nations Military Observer Group in India and Pakistan
   January 1949 to present
7. Tajikistan-UNMOT
   United Nations Mission of Observers in Tajikistan
   December 1994 to present

Europe

8. Bosnia & Herzegovina—UNMIBH
   United Nations Mission in Bosnia and Herzegovina
   December 1995 to present
9. Croatia-UNMOP
   United Nations Mission of Observers in Prevlaka
   January 1996 to present
10. Cyprus—UNFICYP
    United Nations Peacekeeping Force in Cyprus
    March 1964 to present
11. Former Yugoslav Republic of Macedonia—UNPREDEP
    United Nations Preventive Deployment Force
    March 1995 to present
12. Georgia—UNOMIG
    United Nations Observer Mission in Georgia
    August 1993 to present

Middle East

13. Golan Heights—UNDOF
    United Nations Disengagement Observer Force
    June 1974 to present

(continued)

TABLE 8.1
(continued)

14. Iraq/Kuwait—UNIKOM
    United Nations Iraq-Kuwait Observation Mission
    April 1991 to present
15. Lebanon—UNIFIL
    United Nations Interim Force in Lebanon
    March 1978 to present
16. Middle East—UNTSO
    United Nations Truce Supervision Organization
    June 1948 to present

SOURCE: U.N. Department of Public Information, www.un.org/Depts/dpko, October 1998

relief operation carried out by more than 30,000 U.S., French, Pakistani, Italian, and other troops. Although peacekeepers cannot address underlying disputes, they demonstrate that a relatively small U.N. presence can defuse tensions among adversaries. Their presence helps states extricate themselves from difficult situations without losing face. These forces remain at the pleasure of the combatants. When they are no longer welcome, they can do little except leave. In 1967 UNEF left the Sinai when ordered to do so by Egypt's President Nasser. Shortly afterwards, the Six-Day War erupted, leaving Israel in control of the Sinai, Jerusalem, the Left Bank of the Jordan River, and the Golan Heights in Syria. Thus, because peacekeepers cannot solve underlying disputes, peacekeeping alone is not enough.

Following UNEF in 1956, peacekeeping efforts were directed at some of the most intractable problems in global politics. In 1960, the U.N. Congo Operation (ONUC) was sent to pacify the former Belgian Congo. ONUC was controversial because it sought to impose a particular solution in a civil war. In 1964, the Security Council approved establishing the U.N. Force in Cyprus (UNFICYP) to separate the warring Turkish and Greek communities on that island. Additional operations took place in the Middle East—UNEF II and U.N. Interim Force in Lebanon (UNIFIL).

A variant of peacekeeping is the unarmed observer team sent to monitor agreements and verify that they are faithfully carried out. One of the earliest was the U.N. Truce Supervision Organization in Palestine (UNTSO), sent to oversee the cease-fires between Israel and its Arab enemies after 1948. Since then, similar teams have served in Lebanon, the Sinai Peninsula, and the Golan Heights. Following the Persian Gulf War, U.N. observers were sent to monitor Iraq's compliance with U.N. resolutions on treatment of the Kurds and on destruction of weapons of mass destruction. The latter met with repeated resistance from Iraq's Saddam Hussein.

In Asia, too, observer teams have been valuable. In 1949, a U.N. Military Observer Group in India and Pakistan (UNMOGIP) was set up to monitor a cease-fire between those two nations in their dispute over Kashmir.[44] United Nations observers have been in Korea since 1953 to monitor the armistice that ended the war there, and a team of U.N. observers—the U.N. Transitional Authority in Cambodia (UNTAC)—was sent to Cambodia in 1992 to monitor the cease-fire among the warring parties in that country, demobilize the combatants, operate

International peacekeeping missions are highly complex, requiring cooperation among participants using different languages, tactics, and operating procedures. *(Peters for the Dayton Daily News, Ohio. © Tribune Media Services, Inc. All rights reserved. Reprinted with permission.)*

important domestic ministries, and supervise elections.[45] The Cambodian operation was the most ambitious effort to rebuild a nation up to that time, but, following withdrawal of U.N. personnel, the country again began to come apart.[46]

Africa, Latin America, and Europe have also hosted U.N. observer missions. Two, the U.N. Observer Group in Central America (ONUCA) and the U.N. Observer Mission in El Salvador (UNONVSAL), were sent to monitor peace arrangements in Nicaragua and El Salvador early in the 1990s. In October 1993, a U.N. force (UNMIH) was sent to Haiti to oversee that country's return to democracy under President Jean-Bertrand Aristide. In southern Africa, the U.N. Transition Group (UNTAG) was responsible for supervising elections in Namibia. And following genocidic civil strife in Rwanda in 1994, U.N. peacekeepers were sent to join military observers already there.[47] In the former Yugoslavia, an observer team was sent in March 1992 to monitor cease-fires among the factions in Bosnia-Herzegovina. Another U.N. observer team including American soldiers was sent to the Serbian border with Macedonia to prevent the spread of war to that country, and yet another arrived to monitor Croatia's borders with Serbia and Bosnia.

The Functional Side of the United Nations

Following World War II, greater attention was paid to the economic and social sources of conflict. The U.N. and other international organizations reflected the assumption that violence arises from poverty, illiteracy, and disease. Although initial post–Cold War hopes for expanding the U.N. role in maintaining peace and security have been tempered, its functional agencies continue to enjoy quiet successes, such as persuading governments to take simple steps that can save the lives of children in poor countries—immunization, provision of vitamins and iodized salt, rehydration for victims of dysentery, and mosquito nets treated with insecticide to fight malaria.[48]

ECOSOC coordinates its activities with the sixteen semiautonomous specialized agencies described in Table 8.2. Much of ECOSOC's work is carried on by six functional and five regional commissions. It has functional commissions for Human Rights, Narcotic Drugs, Social Development, the Status of Women, and Population. The sixth—the Statistical Commission—is responsible for maintaining data collections for economic and social development. The regional commissions for Africa, Europe, Latin America and the Caribbean, Asia and the Pacific, and Western Asia try to stimulate economic activity. Each is autonomous and has its own customs and procedures. The Economic Commission for Africa (ECA) emphasizes food production and agricultural self-sufficiency to reduce the specter of famine that haunts many African countries, and the Economic Commission for Europe (ECE) focuses on environmental protection and on coordinating policies on transportation and energy. Usually these commissions try to uphold the nonpolitical spirit of functionalism, but sometimes, as in the 1977 decision by the Economic and Social Commission for Western Asia to grant membership to the Palestine Liberation Organization, they dabble in charged political issues.

ECOSOC works and consults with more than three hundred interest-based international nongovernmental organizations (INGOs). Some thirty-five INGOs known as Category I enjoy special privileges, such as adding items to ECOSOC's formal agenda. An additional three hundred INGOs in Category II may submit statements to ECOSOC and its commissions. Finally, about five hundred additional INGOs are on the ECOSOC roster and can attend Council meetings as observers. In some instances such as at the 1992 Earth Summit in Rio de Janeiro, INGOs have a significant impact on those in the U.N. whom they are lobbying.[49]

In addition to ECOSOC, several forums have been created in the U.N. framework to deal with functional issues. Some of the most important are the U.N. Conference on Trade and Development (UNCTAD), created in 1964 to address developing countries' concerns about trade; the United Nations Children's Fund (UNICEF), which tends to children's needs worldwide; and the United Nations Environmental Program (UNEP).

U.N. Prospects   In October 1995, the United Nations marked its fiftieth anniversary with six days of speeches and festivities. The end of the Cold War was accompanied by a wave of optimism about expanding the U.N. peace enforcement and peacekeeping roles. Security Council cooperation during the Persian Gulf War and U.N. sanctions against Serbia and Libya (for its unwillingness to surrender those accused of the bombing of Pan Am flight 103 over Lockerbie, Scotland) generated optimism for the organization's future. In this mood, Secretary-General Boutros-Ghali asked the Security Council to consider establishing a permanent U.N. peacekeeping contingent. Under his proposal, as many countries as possible would each make available to the United Nations a force of about one thousand, available on twenty-four hours' notice, for peacekeeping.[50] The U.N. also worked out arrangements with NATO and the Organization for Security and Cooperation in Europe (OSCE)[51] by which those organizations could assist in peacekeeping.

TABLE 8.2

Functionalism in Action: Specialized Agencies Affiliated with the United Nations

1. Food and Agricultural Organization (FAO)
   Seeks to increase food production, raise rural standards of living, and help cope with emergency food situations.
2. International Civil Aviation Organization (ICAO)
   Facilitates and promotes safe international air transport by setting binding international standards.
3. International Fund for Agricultural Development (IFAD)
   Lends money on concessionary terms for agricultural development projects, primarily to increase food production for poor rural populations.
4. International Labor Organization (ILO)
   Formulates international labor standards and provides technical-assistance training to governments.
5. International Maritime Organization (IMO)
   Promotes cooperation on shipping and provides a forum for discussing and adopting conventions and recommendations on such matters as safety at sea and control of pollution.
6. International Monetary Fund (IMF)
   Provides technical assistance and financing to countries experiencing difficulty in balance of payments.
7. International Telecommunication Union (ITU)
   Promotes global cooperation in telecommunications, allocates bands in the radio frequency spectrum, and collects and disseminates telecommunications information.
8. United Nations Educational, Scientific and Cultural Organization (UNESCO)
   Coordinates cooperation in education, science, culture, and communications.
9. United Nations Industrial Development Organization (UNIDO)
   Serves as an intermediary between developing and developed countries in industry and as a forum for consultations and negotiations to further industrialization.
10. Universal Postal Union (UPU)
    Sets international postal standards and provides technical assistance to developing countries.
11. International Bank for Reconstruction and Development (IBRD)
    Along with the IFC and IDA, forms the World Bank. Lends funds to governments and some private enterprises (with government guarantees) for specific projects.
12. International Finance Corporation (IFC)
    Lends funds to private corporations in developing countries that do not have government guarantees.
13. International Development Association (IDA)
    Provides interest-free credits to the world's poorest countries for fifty years, with a ten-year grace period.
14. World Health Organization (WHO)
    Conducts immunization campaigns, promotes and coordinates research, and provides technical assistance to improve public-health services.
15. World Intellectual Property Organization (WIPO)
    Promotes protection of intellectual property rights (e.g., patents and copyrights). Encourages adherence to relevant treaties, provides legal and technical assistance to developing countries, encourages technology transfers, and administers the International Union for the Protection of Intellectual Property and the International Union for the Protection of Literary and Aristic Works.

(continued)

TABLE 8.2
(continued)

16. World Meteorological Organization (WMO)
    Promotes exchange of meteorological information through its World Weather
    Watch and conducts research and training programs.

SOURCE: *The United Nations at a Glance,* (New York: United Nations Association of the United
States of America, n.d.).

The end of the Cold War broke the logjam that had prevented the United Nations from becoming an effective factor in global politics, and nowhere was this more evident than in the upsurge in U.N. peacekeeping activities around the world: Angola,[52] Namibia, Cambodia, Kuwait, Iraq, Croatia, Bosnia, Central America, Mozambique,[53] Haiti, and Somalia. In 1993 alone six new U.N. missions were begun,[54] and, by late 1995, nearly 60,000 troops were deployed in sixteen operations.[55] As of 1993, U.N. tasks included the following:

1. Election observation (Eritrea and Liberia) and organization (Cambodia)
2. Humanitarian assistance and securing of safe conditions for its delivery (Bosnia and Herzegovina, Somalia and Kurdish areas of Iraq)
3. Observation and separation of combatants along a more or less demarcated boundary (Croatia, southern Lebanon, Cyprus, India-Pakistan, Kuwait-Iraq, Israel-Syria, and Israel-Egypt)
4. Disarmament of military and paramilitary forces (Cambodia and Haiti)[56]
5. Promotion and protection of human rights (Cambodia and El Salvador)
6. Mine clearance, training, and mine awareness (Afghanistan and Cambodia)
7. Military and police training (Haiti)
8. Boundary demarcation (Kuwait-Iraq border)
9. Civil administration (Cambodia)
10. Provision of assistance to and repatriation of refugees (the former Yugoslavia, Cambodia and Somalia)
11. Reconstruction and development (Cambodia and Somalia)[57]

The U.N. missions in Somalia and in the former Yugoslavia at first seemed to augur a new role for U.N. forces—*humanitarian intervention* intended to save civilian lives endangered by civil strife. But it soon became clear that such operations pose complex problems, including the need to serve as a de facto government for countries without law and order.[58] In both cases, the U.N. ran the same risk of appearing to tilt to one side as it had in the earlier Congo operation, and the Secretary-General was the target of hostile demonstrations in Mogadishu and Sarajevo in January 1993 by groups that claimed that the United Nations was favoring their adversaries.[59] In both cases, U.N. missions mixed peacekeeping with peace enforcement, trying to impose peace by military means without sufficient forces to do so: "In Bosnia, its policemen are accused of doing too little; in Somalia of doing too much."[60]

As violence between U.N. forces and Somali warlords increased and U.N. objectives expanded, it became clear that large-scale combat forces would be needed to unify the country and restore peace. Neither the United States nor the United

Nations was willing to make such a commitment and, instead, chose to end the operation without achieving their aims. The U.N. Protection Force (UNPROFOR) was created to supervise cease-fires among Serbian, Croatian, and Bosnian factions in Bosnia and to monitor U.N. economic sanctions on Serbia. The multinational force, with contingents from France, Britain, Bangladesh, Russia, Ukraine, the Netherlands, and Turkey, also tried to get relief supplies to besieged Bosnian communities and to establish safe havens for Bosnian Muslims. Only when combat units from NATO were dispatched to Bosnia was peace restored. In contrast to these cases, when the United Nations did not try to do too much—for example, in monitoring the peace accord between adversaries in Guatemala—it has enjoyed great success.[61]

Peacekeeping, with its requirements for large-scale combat units, and peace enforcement, with its requirement for impartial and lightly armed noncombatants, are partly incompatible. Unlike peacekeeping, peace enforcement requires a warfighting capacity. As Madeleine K. Albright, then America's U.N. representative, argued, "The U.N. has not yet demonstrated the ability to respond effectively when the risk of combat is high and the level of local cooperation is low."[62] "The concept of peacekeeping," argued Boutros-Ghali, "was turned on its head, and worsened by the serious gap between mandates and resources."[63] According to political scientist Paul Diehl, we should be cautious about peacekeeping. It can only succeed when (1) there are only two adversaries; (2) disputes are interstate rather than intrastate; (3) there is cooperation from combatants; (4) other major actors in the region are supportive; (5) peacekeepers are relatively invulnerable to attack and can detect violations easily; (6) operations are along a clearly defined international border; and, most important, (7) peacekeepers are perceived to be impartial.[64] *None of these conditions were present in Somalia or Bosnia.*

From the beginning, UNPROFOR seemed to tilt toward Bosnian Muslims, who were victims of rape, ethnic cleansing, and indiscriminate shelling. United Nations humanitarian relief (including food convoys), the setting up of U.N. safe havens, and declaring exclusion zones for heavy weapons and aircraft largely benefited isolated Muslim communities such as Gorazde, Zepa, Srebrenica, and Bihac and placed limits on the Bosnian Serbs. United Nations efforts could not save the country from being carved into three ethnically based areas, with the Muslims receiving the least desirable piece of the pie. By 1995 UNPROFOR was close to siding with the Muslim-led Bosnian government, thereby crossing the *Mogadishu line,* a term derived from the intervention in Somalia when U.S. soldiers shifted from behaving as peacekeepers to peace enforcers against one Somali faction.[65] In the words of one observer: "Where the peacekeepers, egged on by do-gooders everywhere, turned out to have over-reached themselves was in thinking they could progress from saving lives to remodeling them."[66] The televised image of a dead U.S. marine being dragged around Mogadishu hastened U.S. withdrawal from Somalia and persuaded the Clinton administration to limit situations in which U.S. troops would serve under U.N. command.[67] American disillusionment was reflected in the words of one U.S. congressman: "Recapture in your mind the unbelievable scene we saw on our televisions over the weekend. Somalis rejoicing with glee over the remains of our destroyed United States helicopter and downed United States servicemen, our aircraft blasted out of the sky by those we came to aid."[68]

Tension between UNPROFOR and the Bosnian Serbs exploded in mid-1995 when, at U.S. urging, NATO air strikes against Bosnian Serb installations followed the latter's violation of the exclusion zone around Sarajevo.[69] In retaliation, Bosnian Serbs took U.N. soldiers hostage, chaining some to possible bombing targets.[70] UNPROFOR had little choice but to back down, agreeing that it would "abide strictly by peacekeeping principles until further notice"[71] in return for release of its peacekeepers.[72] UNPRO-FOR had used more force than required by peacekeeping, but its limited capabilities and the absence of U.S. forces meant that it could not enforce peace. Renewed NATO bombing at the end of August 1995[73] virtually transformed the mission in Bosnia into peace enforcement and helped create the conditions under which first a truce was declared and then a peace treaty was negotiated in Dayton, Ohio, in November and signed in Paris the following month.[74] Shortly after, the Security Council formally ended its peacekeeping role in Bosnia, turning over authority to NATO.

When, four years later, the Serbian government refused to accept an agreement that would have brought an end to conflict between it and Albanians living in the Serb province of Kosovo, NATO began to bomb Serbia. On this occasion, U.N. approval was not sought because it was widely believed that Russia and China would cast vetos in the Security Council. Following Serbian capitulation, a U.N.-authorized and heavily armed NATO and Russian force occupied Kosovo.

The important U.N. role in promoting peace and security should not be allowed to obscure growing U.N. activity in other areas, especially in postinternational issues. This is reflected by the variety of U.N.-sponsored conferences held in recent years. In 1992, the Earth Summit on the environment met in Rio de Janeiro. In 1993 the World Conference on Human Rights met in Vienna, and the following year the International Conference on Population and Development was held in Cairo. In 1995, a World Summit for Social Development convened in Copenhagen and the Fourth World Conference on Women was held in Beijing. The following year Istanbul was the site of the Second U.N. Conference on Human Settlements (Habitat II).

All this requires funding, and the United Nations relies on members' goodwill and financial backing. United Nations expenditures had passed $1 billion by 1979 and continued to grow (see Figure 8.4). Peacekeeping costs grew from $1.4 billion in 1992 to $3.6 billion in 1993,[75] declining to $1.3 billion in 1997 because of financial stringency. With members already in arrears in October 1998 by $2.5 billion ($1.8 billion for peacekeeping, $683 million for the regular budget, and $22 million for international tribunals), the U.N. was staving off bankruptcy by raiding its peacekeeping budget and deferring payments to countries contributing peacekeeping troops and commercial suppliers.[76]

Between 1946 and 1992, the United States contributed more than $20.3 billion to the United Nations. Washington is assessed 31 percent of peacekeeping costs (under a complex formula based on gross national product) and 25 percent of regular costs, in contrast to almost half the member states, which pay the minimum of one one-hundredth of 1 percent. Unhappy with this state of affairs, the U.S. Congress unilaterally reduced the American share of peacekeeping costs to 25 percent.[77] Although it paid off $1.2 billion in debt to the U.N. in 1994, the U.S. was still in arrears by $1.5 billion (combined regular dues and peacekeeping costs) in September 1998, and, because of U.S. refusal to meet its obligations, Japan had

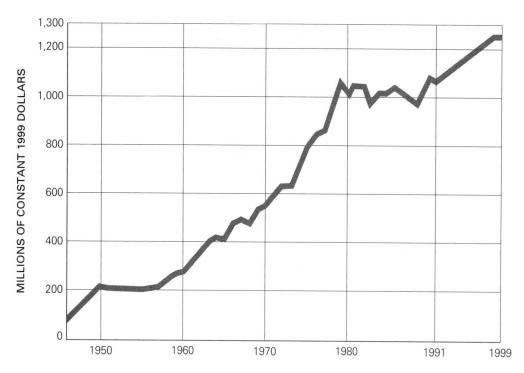

FIGURE 8.4

U.N. Secretariat Expenditures

U.N. expenditures began to rise dramatically in the 1960s and now exceed one billion dollars. SOURCE: © 1992, *The Washington Post*. Reprinted with permission. Updated by author.

become the largest contributor to the U.N.[78] "Calls for ever greater United Nations effectiveness under conditions of financial penury," declared Secretary-General Boutros-Ghali, "make no sense. It is as though the town fire department were being dispatched to put out fires raging in several places at once while a collection was being taken to raise money for the fire-fighting equipment."[79]

Under Article 19 of the U.N. Charter, the United States could be deprived of its vote in the General Assembly because its debt exceeded what it had paid in the previous two years, and one U.S. official at the U.N. declared that "our influence is plummeting through the floor every day."[80] The Clinton administration had little success in persuading the Republican-dominated Congress to pay U.S. arrears, as Republicans demanded a number of reforms, including reducing America's annual dues and slashing the expense accounts of U.N. officials.[81] Other delinquents included Russia ($266 million) and the Ukraine ($252 million).[82] Indeed, as of 1995, only forty-eight members had fully paid their regular budget contributions, and thirty-nine had paid nothing the previous year.[83] Even the international tribunals established to try alleged war criminals from the Balkans and Rwanda were endangered by U.N. financial woes.[84]

American congressmen link their refusal to vote in favor of additional funds for the U.N. to inefficiency,[85] mismanagement,[86] and corruption[87] in the organization. Another contributory factor is the apparent failure of U.N. peacekeeping efforts in a variety of trouble spots—for example, Angola,[88] Rwanda,[89] and Cambodia[90]—where it had been believed that the U.N. had succeeded. Many believed that Secretary-General Boutros Boutros-Ghali was incapable of imposing reform on and streamlining the organization, and they opposed his reelection to a second term.[91] He in turn blamed the United States for the U.N.'s financial crisis: "We know what causes it and what is needed to end it. It is not the result of mismanagement. It is the refusal to fulfill a treaty obligation. Now that a new Secretary General is being appointed, all arrears should be paid at once, as has been promised so often in the past few months."[92]

Mismanagement and incompetence also undermined specific operations. Negligence by U.N. personnel caused deaths from starvation among refugees in Africa, and abuses were covered up. In addition, the U.N. ignored reports of massacres of Hutus in the Congo (formerly Zaire)[93] and was unable to protect a former president of Afghanistan from being murdered by Islamic zealots in Kabul.[94] The organization, its peacekeeping operations, and even its international tribunals and narcotics control program were afflicted by nepotism, fraud,[95] waste, and poor management, and some U.N. agencies are staffed by poorly qualified bureaucrats, subject to little oversight, who use resources lavishly for things that do little for those in need. Referring to widespread nepotism, then U.S. Ambassador Albright likened the U.N. to "a business with 185 members; all of them with strong and contradictory opinions, coming from every conceivable culture, speaking every conceivable language—and each with a brother-in-law who is unemployed."[96] Efforts to reform the giant U.N. bureaucracy are met with resistance. One report says:

> Abuses within the organization persist and often go unpunished. Chiefs of some autonomous U.N. agencies rule their fiefdoms like autocrats, . . . Regional mafias of bureaucrats have consolidated their power through favoritism in hiring and promotions. Recipient governments routinely plunder U.N. programs, diverting aid from intended beneficiaries.[97]

Although U.N. officials are instituting fiscal reforms, including cutting the Secretariat's staff and filling the posts of Under Secretary-General for Administration and Management and Under Secretary-General for Internal Oversight Services (created on June 30, 1995),[98] some members continue to withhold funding to pressure the organization to improve its management and auditing practices. These countries are frustrated because they pay most of the U.N.'s budget but have the same vote as others that pay little (see Table 8.3). Some are also disturbed about the organization's alleged bias, toward less-developed countries, while paying less attention to the bloodier policies of dictators in Africa and the Middle East.

Boutros-Ghali's successor, Kofi Annan—the first person from sub-Saharan Africa to serve as Secretary-General—promised reforms and sought to appease the U.N.'s American critics. Shortly after assuming office, Annan promised to change the U.N.'s management

TABLE 8.3

*U.N. Assessments,
1998–2000, Selected
Countries*

Rank by Contribution	U.N. Regular Budget %	GDP 1996 % of World	U.S.$ per Person
1 United States	25.0	20.8	28,020
2 Japan	18.0	8.3	23,420
3 Germany	9.6	4.8	21,110
4 France	6.5	3.5	21,510
5 Italy	5.4	3.2	19,980
6 Britain	5.1	3.3	19,960
7 Russia	2.9	1.7	4,190
8 Canada	2.8	1.8	21,380
16 Mexico	0.9	2.0	7,660
18 China	0.9	11.3	3,330
23 Saudi Arabia	0.6	0.5	9,700
38 Malaysia	0.2	0.6	10,390
39 Singapore	0.2	0.2	26,910

SOURCE: Data from "Pope Kofi's Unruly Flock," *The Economist*, August 8–14, 1998, p. 20.

system and restructure the organization's administration.[99] U.N officials also promised to cut expenditures.[100] Since 1994, the numbers of U.N. central bureaucrats has been reduced by 14 percent, and Annan has reorganized the central U.N. bureaucracies into five "executive groups," bringing their executives together in a sort of U.N. cabinet.[101] But Annan's pledges to institute reform while refusing to reduce dramatically the U.N. payroll did not assuage the U.N.'s critics.[102]

Thus the optimism of the early 1990s has given way to pessimism, even cynicism, about the United Nations. In a poll of Americans taken in October 1991, after the Gulf War, 67 percent (the highest in U.N. history) said the United Nations was doing "a good job." By June 1995 only 42 percent of Americans thought this, and 46 percent thought the U.N. was doing a bad job.[103] Republican congressional majorities elected in November 1994 sought to reduce U.S. contributions to and participation in U.N. activities, and Senator Jesse Helms, chairman of the Foreign Relations Committee, bluntly said: "United States participation in most United Nations programs should be terminated."[104] Nevertheless, most Americans (72 percent) still think that it is "very important" for the United States to be an active member of the U.N. and 73 percent think that the U.S. should pay its dues. Indeed, partly because of Secretary-General Annan's efforts, by late 1998 most Americans (60 percent) again believed that the U.N. was doing a good job.[105]

The U.N.'s future is murky. Initial post–Cold War euphoria has passed, and a number of institutional reforms have been suggested. These include enlarging the Security Council, creating earmarked contingents of trained peacekeepers,[106] simplifying the General Assembly committee structure, consolidating the work of the specialized agencies, eliminating or reviving ECOSOC and the Trusteeship Council, revising selection and recruitment procedures for the Secretary-General and other U.N. civil servants, and eliminating waste and fraud.[107]

ACTORS SPEAK

In recent years, support for the United Nations among Americans has declined, and the organization has experienced a serious financial crisis. Some observers blame the failure of the U.S. Congress to meet America's financial obligations for the crisis in the U.N. Others argue that the U.N. itself is at fault and that the United States should withhold financial support until the organization is reformed.

The severest financial crisis in the history of the United Nations casts a dark shadow over the 50th anniversary. The failure of particularly one major member state to meet its obligations by withholding legally obligated contributions is not only contrary to Article 17 of the Charter, but has also driven the organization to the very brink of insolvency. (Indonesian Foreign Minister Ali Alatas, cited in Barbara Crossette, "Even Its Allies Castigate U.S. Over Failure to Pay U.N. Dues," *New York Times,* October 3, 1995, p. A3)

As it currently operates, the United Nations does not deserve continued American support. Its bureaucracy is proliferating, its costs are spiraling, and its mission is constantly expanding beyond its mandate—and beyond its capabilities. Worse, with the steady growth in the size and scope of its activities, the United Nations is being transformed from an institution of sovereign nations into a quasi-sovereign entity in itself. That transformation represents an obvious threat to U.S. national interests. (Senator Jesse Helms, Chairman of the U.S. Senate Committee on Foreign Relations, "Saving the U.N.," *Foreign Affairs* 75:5 (September–October 1996, p. 2)

Regional Intergovernmental Organizations

On every continent, *regional IGOs* are at work. Some regional IGOs are *multipurpose,* and some are *specialized.*

Types of Regional IGOs   Figure 8.5, which maps the extent of several regional IGOs, suggests how varied these organizations are. Almost every country is a member of at least one such organization, and many are members of several. The Organization of African Unity (OAU), the Organization of American States (OAS), and the Association of Southeast Asian Nations (ASEAN) are among the most prominent regional IGOs. The OAU has with considerable success prevented changes in postcolonial frontiers in Africa because of fear that the legitimacy of all African frontiers would then be open to question. The OAS has occasionally balanced the influence of the "Colossus of the North," and at other times has helped the United States organize its friends in the Western Hemisphere against threats like the Soviet installation of nuclear missiles in Cuba in 1962. The ASEAN group, started initially to stimulate trade in Southeast Asia, has expanded into a multipurpose institution that coordinates economic, social, and political activities.

There are also many specialized regional IGOs. NATO was the West's bulwark against the U.S.S.R. during the Cold War. With that conflict ended, the purpose of this organization has come under scrutiny. Can it remain useful in coming years? Should it assume a new role in Europe to put out brushfire wars along its periphery and dampen ethnic rivalries arising from communism's collapse?[108] Will the admission to NATO of former members of the Soviet bloc—Poland, the Czech Republic, and Hungary—alienate Russia? NATO illustrates how IGOs must adapt to new conditions.

New IGOs have sprung up in post–Cold War Europe, and old ones have been revived. The Conference on Security and Cooperation in Europe (CSCE), which has changed its name to the Organization for Security and Cooperation in Europe (OSCE) and which was originally established in 1975 among states of Central Europe and North America to provide a forum for adversaries, now emphasizes preventive diplomacy and conflict management. In 1995 alone, it operated ten missions in a variety of settings, including Bosnia, Kosovo, Macedonia, Georgia, Moldova, Estonia, Latvia, Chechnya, Ukraine, and Tajikistan.[109] Finally, as we shall see shortly, the most important aspect in the growth of specialized IGOs has been the regional economic organization.

Regional Organizations and Neofunctionalism

The neofunctionalism ideal of expanding interstate cooperation through lobbying by domestic interest groups is best reflected in the *European Union* (EU), made up of a group of countries in Western Europe that have turned over significant authority for economic policy to this organization, headquartered in Brussels, Belgium. We discuss the EU in greater detail in Chapter 13 but suggest an outline here.

In line with neofunctionalist expectations, the EU has evolved since several specialized arrangements were merged. Its membership has grown, and it has assumed an expanding array of functional tasks. It originated in the European Coal and Steel Community (ECSC) in 1951. Encouraging German industrial reconstruction in a European rather than a national context, ECSC stimulated cooperation among Europeans and reduced the prospects of regional conflict. A remarkable feature of the ECSC was a supranational "government" known as the Higher Authority, which was authorized to make decisions about producing and distributing coal and steel.

Prodded by advocates of functional integration, the ECSC became a launching pad for extending functional cooperation to other areas, notably trade and peaceful nuclear energy. In 1965, these tasks were placed in one institutional context called the European Community. In recent years, an effort has begun to complete the economic integration of Western Europe, including instituting a single European currency (the euro), and also transform the EU into a political union. It is now possible to travel among the member states of the EU without a passport, and customs barriers and other impediments to free movement have virtually disappeared.

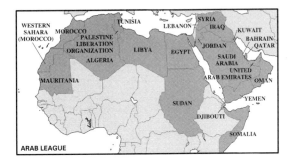

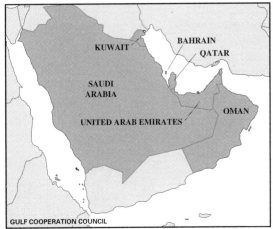

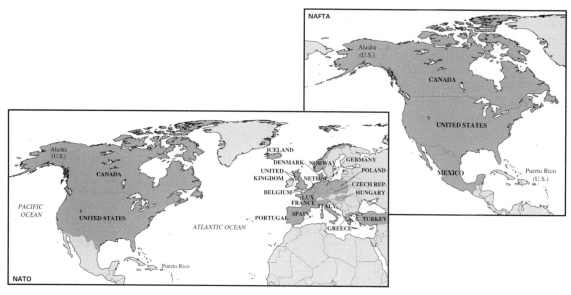

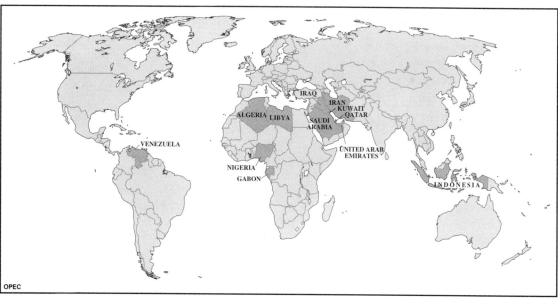

FIGURE 8.5

International Organizations: A Sample

Intergovernmental organizations that perform a wide variety of functions exist in every region of the world. They include economic groupings (ASEAN, EU, NAFTA, and OPEC), security arrangements (Gulf Cooperation Council and NATO), and political forums (Arab League, OAU, and OAS). Some countries are members of several organizations.

The EU is an increasingly important factor in the lives of most Europeans. Its executive body employs almost 14,000 bureaucrats in Brussels and is trying to harmonize and standardize the regulations of member states. These efforts have created fears among European publics that national customs will be eroded, national culture threatened, and people's fate placed in the hands of "faceless bureaucrats." One satirical evaluation of events summarizes matters thus:

> Brussels is, if you would believe the press, about to take away British prawn-cocktail crisps, German beer, French cheese, Danish apples, the Spanish tilde (the squiggle over the 'n') and Italian pasta.... Take the question of foam-filled furniture.... For some reason, Britons are particularly apt to be killed by the fumes from flaming sofas. Britain now has laws requiring fire-retardant chemicals in furniture foam, and fears the import of dangerous foreign foam.... The British government says it will ban the import of foreign foam-filled furniture; and so, in one area, the single market will not exist.... The Germans will resist. Although they do not seem to get killed by their sofas, they are worried by the idea of pumping chemicals into their furniture which—who knows?—could do dreadful things to their babies' health.[110]

The difficulties the EU has faced reflect the barriers to regional integration. "Low politics," as social and economic issues are described, elicit strong national passions, and efforts to move into the realm of "high politics"—foreign and defense policy— generate stiffer national resistance. Spillover is neither as automatic nor as rapid as neofunctionalists had hoped. The experience of two other regional groups, the Central American Common Market (CACM) and the East African Common Market (EACM), suggests that the success of the EU may be more the exception than the rule. CACM was established in 1960 and by 1963 had five members: Guatemala, Nicaragua, El Salvador, Honduras, and Costa Rica. CACM's initial goal was to create a free market and a customs union. At first the experiment was successful, and trade among members rose dramatically between 1960 and 1968. By then, however, some members were benefiting more than others, and the elimination of tariffs had reduced government revenues in some member countries.[111]

Friction between Honduras and El Salvador turned violent in June 1969 after soccer matches in both countries. The Soccer War had less to do with sport than with population growth and economic and social rivalries brought on partly by CACM. Hondurans believed El Salvador was flooding their market with products and encouraging its poor to emigrate to their country. Salvadorans argued that Hondurans discriminated against Salvadorans who sought to settle in Honduras. These frustrations led to a military clash that required the OAS to send a fact-finding mission. Following the Soccer War, in the course of which invading Salvadoran forces inflicted heavy casualties on the Honduran defenders, CACM limped along, and, by the late 1970s, local elites were unwilling to go beyond commitments already made.

Originally formed among Kenya, Tanzania, and Uganda in 1963, EACM met with a similar fate. Efforts to kindle integration were stymied by political and economic rivalries among members.[112] Kenya, with a more highly developed market economy than its partners, was better able to benefit from EACM, and Tanzania and Uganda grew envious of their neighbor. This jealousy led Tanzania to close its border with Kenya, and economic friction was worsened by political differences among elites in the three countries and personal animosity between Uganda's Idi Amin and Tanzania's Julius Nyerere.[113] As these cases show, economic integration requires a high level of economic and political compatibility among members.

Nevertheless, regional economic groupings, especially free-trade areas, have proliferated. Africa has an Economic Community of West African States (ECOWAS) and the Southern African Development Community (SADC).[114] Asia has ASEAN and the recent Asian Pacific Economic Cooperation (APEC).[115]

President Clinton has failed both to make progress toward achieving the Free-Trade Agreement of the Americas (FTAA) proposed by President George Bush in 1990 or to win fast-track trade-negotiating authority from Congress that would allow the president to negotiate trade agreements that Congress would have to approve or disapprove as a whole without amendments. This failure has produced doubts among Latin Americans that the U.S. is serious about increasing trade with its Latin American partners. Such doubts have provided an incentive for deepening regional economic cooperation.[116] Central and South America are home to CACM (Guatemala, Honduras, El Salvador, Costa Rica, and Nicaragua), the Andean Group (Venezuela, Colombia, Ecuador, Peru, and Bolivia), Group of Three (Mexico, Colombia, and Venezuela), and Mercosur or Southern Common Market (Brazil, Argentina, Paraguay, and Uruguay).[117] To the North, the North American Free Trade Agreement (NAFTA) binds the United States, Canada, and Mexico; and in Oceania a free-trade zone exists between Australia and New Zealand. Others have been promised: a South Asian Preferential Trade Area (consisting of the seven members of ASEAN), a Central European Free Trade Area (Slovenia, the Czech Republic, Hungary, Poland, and Slovakia), and, most ambitious of all, a free-trade area linking North America and the EU.[118] The influence of these groups differs from region to region, but their pervasiveness is impressive.

Commodity Cartels: The Case of OPEC

Like organizations that promote economic integration, commodity cartels also represent the efforts of states to cooperate for economic reasons. There, however, the similarity ends. *Commodity cartels* are organizations consisting of the major producers of particular commodities and raw materials such as coffee and rubber. Their aim is to reduce competition among commodity producers and maintain higher prices for their products by controlling production.

The *Organization of Petroleum Exporting Countries (OPEC)* is one such commodity cartel. In the 1970s, the "OPEC cartel" looked like an oligopoly that could determine oil prices, and it enjoyed leverage over both industrialized states and developing countries in which cheap oil is critical for industrialization and agriculture. Two observers commented: "The dramatic success of OPEC between 1973 and the early 1980s is one of those seismic events in world affairs that directly affects virtually all dimensions of international political activity." [119]

Oil is essentially an economic issue—oil-producing states wish to control their commodity and earn as much as possible while it lasts, and industrialized societies want access to plentiful oil at stable prices—but it can assume a political complexion too. Arab oil producers, wishing to show solidarity with the Palestinians and fellow Arabs, have tried to use oil as a weapon and the profits from its sale as a means of aiding fellow Arabs.

Libya was the first country to force companies to renegotiate previous arrangements. Threatening to seize company assets, Muammar Qaddafi in 1970 demanded that they raise the price of Libyan crude and reduce the amount being pumped. The companies' bid to defy Libya collapsed when Occidental Petroleum broke ranks and raised prices. Libyan success led other oil-producing states to demand similar increases, and, trying to stabilize prices, the oil companies tried to involve oil-producing states in multilateral negotiations to set a common price. Although agreement was reached in 1971, several factors in the following years conspired to create an upward price spiral: global demand, devaluation of the dollar, and the 1973 Yom Kippur War and subsequent Arab oil embargo. Between 1970 and 1973 crude oil prices jumped from $1.80 to $11.67 a barrel. In the same period, oil-producing states seized control of price and production levels from the companies and assumed ownership of company concessions within their borders, while continuing to rely on the companies for technology, capital, and marketing.[120]

Declining American oil production and growing consumption made the United States more dependent on foreign oil. Oil prices began to edge up as OPEC presented a united front toward the oil companies and limited supply by assigning production quotas to members. Dollar devaluations in 1971 and 1973, however, diluted profits because industrialized societies paid for oil in dollars. Although OPEC members had more dollars, they were worth less.

After the 1973 Yom Kippur War, the Arabs tried to use the oil weapon to make industrialized countries change their policies and pressure Israel to make concessions. A selective oil embargo was imposed on the United States, the Netherlands, and Portugal, and, although the oil weapon failed to change policies in any major state, it did induce some to use caution. Politics and economics combined to boost the price of oil (the first "oil shock"), the profits of the oil-producing states, and the costs to oil consumers. In 1972, America paid $4.8 billion for oil imports; in 1980, it paid $80 billion.[121]

Between 1973 and 1980, supplies remained tight; OPEC discipline held; and prices continued to soar. In 1979–1980, oil prices again shot up (the second "oil shock"). They peaked in 1981 and then began to fall because of global economic recession, conservation in the industrialized world, broken discipline in the oil-producing cartel, and resulting overproduction. Non-OPEC countries—Norway, Mexico, Great Britain, Oman, and Russia[122]—also began to account for a greater share of production and export. By April 1994, oil prices had dropped to under $14 a barrel, about where they were in 1973 when adjusted for inflation,[123] and even Saudi Arabia was finding it hard to make ends meet.[124] Although the price of oil began to rise in subsequent years, it dropped precipitously between 1997 and 1998 from $22 a barrel to $12 a barrel.[125]

The decline in oil revenues and in the political leverage that oil provided was a factor behind events leading to Iraq's occupation of Kuwait. Kuwait tried to get Iraq to repay the huge debts incurred during Baghdad's war with Iran, and Iraq charged that Kuwait was profiting by exceeding its OPEC production quota. Iraq also claimed that Kuwait was pumping more than its share of oil from an oil field that straddled their common border. Control of Iraq and Kuwait gave Saddam 20 percent of the world's oil reserves. More important, it placed the Iraqi war machine at the Saudi border, endangering an additional 25 percent.

A number of factors have robbed OPEC of much of its former influence. The biggest is non-oil-related conflicts among its members—Iran versus Iraq, and Iraq versus Kuwait and Saudi Arabia. These are exacerbated by oversupply and falling prices for oil. A third factor is a textbook example of the problem of collective goods: the failure of leading members to remain within the production quotas set by OPEC. "After many years of widespread cheating on production quotas by its members," declares an observer, "the once-mighty OPEC has become virtually powerless to influence the oil markets by itself." [126] And prices may plummet further when Iraq is permitted to sell its oil and when new Iraqi and Iranian oil fields are developed. [127]

The growing importance of non-OPEC oil producers led leading OPEC producers to initiate negotiations with some of them in 1998, leading to an agreement among Saudi Arabia, Mexico, and Venezuela (the Riyadh Pact) to reduce world oil production. [128] It appeared that a new informal arrangement among leading OPEC and non-OPEC producers was a serious possibility. Although prices remain low, growing demand globally and rising U.S. oil imports (up from 30 percent in 1984 to 45 percent in 1994) and decreasing U.S. oil production may augur growing OPEC political leverage in future years. [129] Nevertheless, as reflected by the growing conflict for control of the vast oil and gas reserves in and near the Caspian Sea, the oil issue will not disappear. [130]

Conclusion

In this chapter we have reviewed the role of international organizations in global politics. We have also looked at various proposals for international organization and for improving interstate cooperation, including functionalism and neofunctionalism. Finally, we addressed several organizational efforts to reduce interstate conflict and integrate and link people in different countries and parts of the world: the League of Nations, the United Nations, the specialized agencies, and the European Union.

We can offer some tentative observations here about IGOs' effects on world politics. First, international organizations may reduce the chaotic consequences of fragmenting states. Second, the evolving web of IGOs, and the interlocking memberships of states in them, have left states less free to act on some issues while providing them with additional capabilities for other issues. To date, the effect of regional IGOs has been in the more prosperous regions of the world. Some argue that IGOs have already transformed global life, whereas others remain skeptical, believing that this network "has not yet radically transformed this [global political] system" but admitting that "the radical transformation may yet come."

> The complexity of modern life creates many pressures for states to establish additional IGOs. What has happened so far demonstrates the overwhelming sense of governments throughout the world that states no longer provide enough frameworks for tackling pressing problems. [131]

Key Terms

collective security
commodity cartels
Economic and Social Council
European Union (EU)
Fourteen Points
functionalism
General Assembly
humanitarian intervention
intergovernmental organizations
International Court of Justice

League Covenant
League of Nations
Mogadishu line
multipurpose regional IGOs
neofunctionalism
Organization of Petroleum
  Exporting Countries (OPEC)
peace enforcement
peacekeeping
preventive diplomacy

Secretariat
Security Council
specialized agencies
specialized IGOs
supranational organizations
Trusteeship Council
U.N. Charter
United Nations
Uniting for Peace Resolution

End Notes

[1]*Yearbook of International Organizations 1994/95,* vol. 3 (Munchen: K.G. Saur, 1994), pp. 1738-1739.

[2]Kenneth N. Waltz, "Kant, Liberalism, and War," *American Political Science Review* 56:2 (June 1962), p. 332.

[3]Ibid.

[4]Kant, as cited in ibid., p. 337. Emphasis in original.

[5]Ibid.

[6]Rousseau, *A Lasting Peace,* as cited in Kenneth N. Waltz, *Man, the State, and War* (New York: Columbia University Press, 1959), p. 185.

[7]The collective-security idea dates back at least to the seventeenth century. Inis L. Claude, Jr., *Power and International Relations* (New York: Random House, 1962), pp. 106-107.

[8]A speech by Woodrow Wilson to a joint session of the U.S. Congress, *Congressional Record,* January 8, 1918, p. 691.

[9]Claude, *Power and International Relations,* p. 114.

[10]Woodrow Wilson, "Collective Security vs. Balance of Power," in Frederick H. Hartmann, ed., *World in Crisis,* 4th ed. (New York: Macmillan, 1973), p. 233.

[11]Ibid., pp. 232, 233.

[12]David Mitrany, *A Working Peace System* (London: Oxford University Press, 1943).

[13]Mitrany, cited in James P. Sewell, *Functionalism and World Politics* (Princeton: Princeton University Press, 1966), p. 9.

[14]Charles Pentland, *International Theory and European Integration* (New York: Free Press, 1973), p. 70.

[15]See Ernst B. Haas, *The Uniting of Europe* (Stanford, CA: Stanford University Press, 1958), p. 16.

[16]F. S. Northedge, *The League of Nations: Its Life and Times, 1920-1946* (Leicester, UK: Leicester University Press, 1986), pp. 26-27.

[17]Ibid., pp. 43-46.

[18]Ibid., p. 159.

[19]Cited in F. P. Walters, *A History of the League of Nations,* vol. 2 (London: Oxford University Press, 1952), p. 653.

[20]Winston S. Churchill, *The Gathering Storm* (Boston: Houghton Mifflin, 1948), p. 7.

[21]The deal leaked, and in the ensuing public outcry Hoare was dismissed and the French cabinet was replaced.

[22]Walters, *A History of the League,* vol. 2, pp. 780-782.

[23]Evan Luard, *A History of the United Nations,* vol. 1, *The Years of Western Domination, 1945-1955* (London: Macmillan, 1982), pp. 17-32.

[24]"Pope Kofi's Unruly Flock," *The Economist,* August 8-14, 1998, p. 19.

[25]Chapter Six deals with "Pacific Settlement of Disputes" and is meant for conflicts caused by misunderstanding. Chapter Seven—"Action with Respect to Threats to the Peace, Breaches of the Peace, and Acts of Aggression"—deals with premeditated aggression.

[26]After the U.S.S.R. collapsed, Russia was given the permanent seat on the Council.

[27]"To Bury or to Praise," *The Economist,* October 21-27, 1995, p. 27.

[28]Paul Lewis, "U.N. Panel Proposes Expanding Security Council to 24 Members," *New York Times,* March 21, 1997, p. A5.

[29]See John G. Stoessinger, *The United Nations and the Superpowers: China, Russia, and America,* 4th ed. (New York: Random House, 1977), p. 6, for Soviet vetoes through 1975. For the veto record through 1990, see U.S. Department of State, *Report to Congress on Voting Practices in the United Nations, 1990* (Washington, D.C: Bureau of International Organization Affairs, March 1991), p. 78.

[30]Stoessinger, *United Nations and Superpowers,* pp. 16-17.

[31]*Report to Congress on Voting Practices in the United Nations, 1990,* p. 78. For a different scoring, see Anjali V. Patil, *The UN Veto in World Affairs, 1946-1990* (London: Mansell, 1992). Before 1970, Britain and France cast vetoes to save the United States from having to use its veto power. China's only veto came in 1955 on the issue of Mongolia's membership. In 1993, Russia vetoed a resolution to make funding for peace-keeping contributions mandatory.

[32]Paul Lewis, "China Lifts U.N. Veto It Aimed At Guatemala," *New York Times,* January 21, 1997, p. A5. To protest Guatemala's policy toward Taiwan, China vetoed the dispatch of U.N. observers to verify a cease-fire between Guatemala's government and leftist rebels. The veto was lifted in a matter of days after it became clear that the issue would be transferred to the General Assembly under the Uniting for Peace Resolution.

[33]Julia Preston, "Boutros-Ghali Rushes In . . .," *Washington Post National Weekly Edition,* January 10-16, 1994, pp. 10-11.

[34]Barbara Crossette, "Ghanaian Chosen To Head The U.N., Ending Standoff," *New York Times,* December 14, 1996, pp. 1, 5; Steven Lee Myers, "New U.N. Chief in Washington, Finds the Climate Much Warmer," *New York Times,* January 24, 1997, pp. A1, A6.

[35]See Table 8.1 in A. Leroy Bennett, *International Organizations,* 6th ed. (Englewood Cliffs, NJ: Prentice-Hall, 1995), pp. 189-194, for a list of ICJ cases and advisory opinions between 1947 and 1992.

[36]*SIPRI Yearbook 1996* (Oxford, UK: Oxford University Press, 1996), Table 2.1, p. 43.

[37]Richard D. Lyons, "U.N. Spares Trustee Council," *New York Times,* November 6, 1994, sec. 1, p. 10.

[38]See Table 6.1 in Bennett, *International Organizations,* pp. 110-122.

[39]Korea was not a case of collective security because U.N. forces were largely American and South Korean. The operation against Iraq came closer to the collective-security ideal, though again few states sent troops.

[40]*Introduction to the Annual Report of the Secretary-General on the Work of the Organization,* June 16, 1959, to June 15, 1960, General Assembly, Official Records, 15th sess., supp. no. 1A, p. 4.

[41]See Ann Florini and Nina Tannenwald, *On the Front Lines: The United Nations' Role in Preventing and Containing Conflict* (New York: U.N. Association of the United States of America, 1984). See also William J. Durch, ed., *The Evolution of UN Peacekeeping* (New York: St. Martin's, 1993).

[42]U.N. Department of Peacekeeping Operations, Military Adviser's Office, December 11, 1998, www.un.org/Depts/dpko.

[43]UNEF was authorized under the Uniting for Peace Resolution because of British and French threats to veto Security Council action.

[44]British India was given independence in 1947 after a long struggle waged by Mahatma Gandhi and the Indian Congress Party. Rioting between Hindus and Muslims forced partition of the subcontinent into mainly Hindu India and Muslim Pakistan. Kashmir was one of the princely states of India that were allowed to choose which country to join. Although most of its inhabitants were Muslim, the local prince chose to join India, and the two countries have contested the region ever since.

[45]Henry Kamm, "Despite U.N.'s Effort, Cambodia Is Chaotic," *New York Times,* July 4, 1994, p. 1.

[46]Barbara Crossette, "Outsiders Gone, Cambodia Unravels," *New York Times,* December 3, 1995, sec. 4, p. 1.

[47]Declaring that it needed economic aid more than peacekeepers, the Rwandan government demanded their departure. Barbara Crossette, "Send the Peacekeepers Home, A Ravaged Rwanda Tells U.N.," *New York Times,* June 8, 1995, p. A6. Nevertheless, the U.N. decided to extend its mission in Rwanda by three months at the end of 1995. Barbara Crossette, "U.N. to Extend Its Force in Rwanda for 3 Months," *New York Times,* December 13, 1995, p. A5.

[48]"Staying Alive," *The Economist,* December 17-23, 1994, p. 46; Warren E. Leary, "With One Disease Defeated, Another Is Attacked," *New York Times,* December 6, 1995, p. A10; Barbara Crossette, "U.N. and World Bank United To Wage War on Malaria," *New York Times,* October 3, 1996, p. A4. Even the specialized agencies have felt the U.N. financial pinch. Barbara Crossette, "As U.S. Payments Lag, U.N. Agencies Feel Pain," *New York Times,* March 11, 1996, p. A4.

[49]Barbara Crossette, "Private Groups Show Strength at U.N. Events," *New York Times,* March 13, 1995, sec. 1, p. 9.

[50]Paul Lewis, "UN Chief Asks for 1,000-Troop Units," *New York Times,* June 20, 1992, p. 5, and "Excerpts from U.N. Report," *New York Times,* June 20, 1992, p. 5. Canada proposed the creation of a standing force of 5,000 peacekeepers. Christopher S. Wren, "Canada Offers Plan for United Nations Rapid Reaction Force," *New York Times,* September 29, 1995, p. A4.

[51]With authorization from the U.N. Security Council to mount a three-month operation, a multinational force with 6,000 troops from eight countries under Italian command was dispatched in April 1997 to ensure humanitarian relief to Albania when anarchy gripped that country. Paul Lewis, "U.N. Backs Sending Troops to Restore Order in Albania," *New York Times,* March 29, 1997, p. 4; Celestine Bohlen, "First Troops In Peace Force Get a Fanfare From Albania," *New York Times,* April 16, 1997, p. A5.

[52]This was the second time U.N. peacekeepers were sent to Angola; "U.N. Peacekeeping Troops Arrive for Duty in Angola," *New York Times,* June 1, 1995, p. A4.

[53]This proved a successful operation. "After the Homecoming," *The Economist,* August 5-11, 1995, p. 45.

[54]Trevor Findlay, "Multilateral conflict prevention, management and resolution," *SIPRI Yearbook 1994,* (New York: Oxford University Press, 1994), p. 26.

[55]Wren, "Canada Offers Plan," p. A4.

[56]In 1998 in the case of Albania, the United Nations for the first time undertook to help disarm a civilian population. Barbara Crossette, "U.N. Agrees to Help Albanian Government Disarm Civilians," *New York Times,* July 14, 1998, p. A3.

[57]Findlay, "Multilateral conflict prevention," p. 27.

[58]See Paul Lewis, "Painting Nations Blue," *New York Times,* December 9, 1992, p. A17.

[59]Douglas Jehl, "U.N. Leader's Visit To Somalia Is Met By Angry Protests," *New York Times,* October 23, 1993, pp. 1, 5.

[60]"Dial Emergency," *The Economist,* August 14-20, 1993, p. 17. Secretary-General Boutros-Ghali tried to clarify the distinction between peacekeeping and peace enforcement. Barbara Crossette, "U.N. Chief Ponders Future of Peacekeepers," *New York Times,* March 3, 1995, p. A3.

[61]Julia Preston, "In a U.N. Success Story, Guatemalan Abuses Fall," *New York Times,* March 27, 1996, p. A5.

[62]Cited in Elaine Sciolino, "New U.S. Peacekeeping Policy De-emphasizes Role of the U.N.," *New York Times,* May 6, 1994, p. A1.

[63]Cited in Barbara Crossette, "As Torch Passes, U.N. Chief Scolds U.S. For Arrears," New York Times, December 18, 1996, p. A9.

[64]Paul F. Diehl, *International Peacekeeping* (Baltimore: Johns Hopkins, 1993), pp. 167-175.

[65]John Darnton, "U.N. Buildup in Bosnia Eyes 'Mogadishu Line'," *New York Times,* June 7, 1995, p. A6. For details on U.S./U.N. failure in Somalia, see Donatella Lorch, "Rising Violence in Somalia Throws U.N.'s Role into Question," *New York Times,* January 10, 1994, p. A3; "Closing-Down Sale," *The Economist,* September 24-30, 1994, p. 43.

[66]"The Somali Spectre," *The Economist,* October 1-7, 1994, p. 20.

[67]Elaine Sciolino, "U.S. Narrows Terms for Its Peacekeepers," *New York Times,* September 23, 1993, p. A4.

[68]Cited in Clifford Krauss, "House Vote Urges Clinton To Limit U.S. Somalia Role, *New York Times,* September 29, 1993, p. A4.

[69]"The U.N.'s Last Chance in Bosnia," *The Economist,* June 10-16, 1995, p. 43.

[70]An American F-16 was shot down, and the rescue of pilot Scott O'Grady caused a public sensation back home.

[71]Cited in Roger Cohen, "U.N. Captives Linked to Bosnia Debate," *New York Times,* June 13, 1995, p. A6.

[72]Roger Cohen, "Captives Free, U.N. Gives Up Effort to Shield Sarajevo," *New York Times,* June 19, 1995, pp. A1, A5.

[73]R. W. Apple, Jr., "Bombers Goal: The Bargaining Table," *New York Times,* August 31, 1995, pp. A1, A6.

[74]Craig R. Whitney, "Balkan Foes Sign Peace Pact, Dividing An Unpacified Bosnia," *New York Times,* December 15, 1995, pp. A1, A8. Under the agreement U.N. forces were replaced by a multinational force under NATO command. Chris Hedges, "Vanguard Forces Arriving in Balkans," *New York Times,* December 5, 1995, p. A8.

[75]Findlay, "Multilateral conflict prevention," p. 26. Of this total 60 percent were accounted for by Bosnia. The U.N. pays about $1,000 a month per soldier, thus helping some poor states pay for their armed forces. Raymond Bonner, "Job Done, U.N. Troops Stay On In Croatia," *New York Times,* August 25, 1995, p. A5.

[76]Christopher S. Wren, "Unpaid Dues Could Cost the U.S. Its U.N. Vote," *New York Times,* June 28, 1998, sec. 1, p. 9. As of 1999, the U.N. owed some 70 countries about $864 million for troops and equipment.

[77]The U.N. has recommended reducing the U.S. percentage. Some rapidly developing countries such as South Korea and Singapore are underassessed, as are others like Saudi Arabia. Barbara Crossette, "Facing Cuts, U.N. Tries to Rejuggle Its Books," *New York Times,* June 4, 1995, sec. 1, p. 8.

[78]Wren, "Unpaid Dues Could Cost the U.S. Its U.N. Vote," sec. 1, p. 9; Barbara Crossette, "Darkest Hour at U.N. For Richest Deadbeat," *New York Times,* September 21, 1998, p. A6. The United States argues that it owes only $1 billion based on its rejection of expanded assessment for peacekeeping. The U.S. owed an additional $300 million to other U.N. agencies, including the World Health Organization and the International Labor Organization. Ted Turner, the founder of CNN, has promised to donate $1 billion of his own money to the U.N.

[79]Cited in Christopher S. Wren, "Boutros-Ghali Says U.N.'s Worsening Finances Hurt Its Role," *New York Times,* September 12, 1995, p. A5.

[80]Cited in ibid. See also "The United Nations Heads for Bankruptcy," *The Economist,* February 10-16, 1996. Eighteen other countries, mainly impoverished less-developed countries, could lose their General Assembly vote under Article 19.

[81]Steven Lee Myers, "Plan To Pay Off U.N. Dues Stalls," *New York Times,* May 21, 1997, pp. A1, A7; Steven Lee Myers, "U.S. May Pay Some Arrears to the U.N.," *New York Times,* June 11, 1997, p. A11.

[82]Steven Lee Myers, "Administration Proposes Paying U.N. Debt, but Congress Resists," *New York Times,* December 30, 1996, p. A5.

[83]Barbara Crossette, "To Pay Some Debts, U.N. Will Try Borrowing From World Bank," *New York Times,* September 27, 1995, p. A4.

[84]Raymond Bonner, "U.N. Fiscal Woes Are Said to Threaten War Crime Tribunals," *New York Times,* October 4, 1995, p. A4.

[85]Barbara Crossette, "Is the U.N. Inefficient? U.S. Critics Draw Retort," *New York Times,* July 7, 1996, sec. 1, p. 6. One U.N.

agency that has been praised for instituting reform is the United Nations Children's Fund (Unicef). Paul Lewis, "A Reengineered Unicef Wins Points, and Rights for Children," *New York Times,* April 27, 1997, p. 9.

[86]Barbara Crossette, "U.N. Meeting on Urban Crises Draws Criticism on Financing," *New York Times,* February 11, 1996, sec. 1, p. 6; Raymond Bonner, "Reform Message to U.N. Weakening a Development Agency," *New York Times,* September 15, 1996, p. 11.

[87]William Branigin, "United Frustrations: The U.N. Is Tripping Over Its Own Bloat and Corruption," *Washington Post National Weekly Edition,* November 30-December 6, 1992, pp. 6-7.

[88]"Angola on the Way to War," *The Economist,* July 25-31, 1998, pp. 43-44.

[89]"Rwanda After the UN," *The Economist,* March 23-29, 1996, pp. 37-38.

[90]Seth Mydans, "Fighting Erupts Between Rivals Ruling Cambodia," *New York Times,* July 6, 1997, sec. 1, pp. 1, 4; Barbara Crossette, "Cambodian Government Tries to Bully Voters, U.N. Is Told," *New York Times,* July 15, 1998, p. A4.

[91]Barbara Crossette, "U.S. Stands Alone Against U.N. Chief," *New York Times,* November 19, 1996, pp. A1, A5. Boutros-Ghali is not the only U.N. official that the Clinton administration sought to remove from office. Another was the director general of the World Health Organization, Dr. Hiroshi Nakajima. Barbara Crossette, "U.N. Official To Drop Bid For New Term In Health Post," *New York Times,* May 1, 1997, p. A5.

[92]Cited in Crossette, "As Torch Passes, U.N. Chief Scolds U.S. For Arrears," p. A9.

[93]Barbara Crossette, "Agencies Say U.N. Ignored Pleas on Hutu," *New York Times,* May 28, 1997, p. A3.

[94]Barbara Crossette, "Afghan Hanging Fans Debate on Asylum Role of U.N.," *New York Times,* October 22, 1996, p. A6.

[95]See Barbara Crossette, "U.N. Pays Twice to Start Aid Programs," *New York Times,* December 15, 1994, p. A6; Christopher S. Wren, "Unicef Says Fraud Cost $10 Million," *New York Times,* May 26, 1995, p. A1; Barbara Crossette, "New U.N. Chief Gives Support To Reforms, but Not Job Cuts," *New York Times,* January 10, 1997, p. A9. Allegations of fraud have also been leveled against World Bank officials. William Murray, "World Bank Investigating Possible Embezzlement," *Wall Street Journal,* July 17, 1998, p. A12.

[96]Cited in Christopher S. Wren, "Mismanagement and Waste Erode U.N.'s Best Intentions," *New York Times,* June 23, 1995, p. A6.

[97]Julia Preston, "A Bloated World Body," *Washington Post National Weekly Edition,* January 30-February 5, 1995, p. 6. The United States left the U.N. Educational, Scientific, and Cultural Organization (Unesco) in 1984, charging it with mismanagement and anti-Western bias, and has not rejoined even though the organization made the changes that were demanded. Barbara Crossette, "White House Backs Away From Plan to Rejoin Unesco," *New York Times,* January 1, 1995, sec. 1, p. 6.

[98]Christopher S. Wren, "Surprise! New U.N. Auditors Find Waste in Peacekeeping Missions," *New York Times,* October 29, 1995, sec. 1, p. 4.

[99]Paul Lewis, "New U.N. Chief Proposes Plans To Slash Waste," *New York Times,* March 18, 1997, pp. A1, A6; Barbara Crossette, "U.N. Chief Promises to Overhaul Organization From the Top Down," *New York Times,* July 17, 1997, pp. A1, A7.

[100]Barbara Crossette, "U.N. Plans Deep Cuts In Budget For First Time," *New York Times,* April 2, 1996, p. A6; Barbara Crossette, "U.N. Plans to Hold Spending And Cut Staff by 30 Percent," *New York Times,* August 17, 1996, p. 5; Paul Lewis, "U.N. Finance Officer Says Costs Are Leveling Off," *New York Times,* March 5, 1997, p. A6.

[101]"Pope Kofi's Unruly Flock," p. 20.

[102]Crossette, "New U.N. Chief Gives Support To Reforms, but Not Job Cuts," p. A9.; Elaine Sciolino, "Under Pressure, New U.N. Chief Defends His Style," *New York Times,* February 9, 1997, sec. 1, pp. 1, 4.

[103]Barbara Crossette, "U.N. Finds That Its Reputation Has Slumped for Many in U.S.," *New York Times,* June 25, 1995, sec. 1, pp. 1, 4. An earlier peak in positive U.S. attitudes toward the United Nations (58 percent) was in 1954, after the Korean War.

[104]Cited in Ibid., p. 4.

[105]Crossette, "Darkest Hour at U.N. For Richest Deadbeat," p. A6.

[106]Seven European countries agreed to set up a 4,000-soldier force in Denmark—the United Nations Standby High Readiness Brigade—for rapid deployment in peacekeeping. "7 European States Set Up Rapid Intervention Force," *New York Times,* December 16, 1996, p. A5.

[107]Barbara Crossette, "As Leaders Gather to Celebrate, Problems Are Increasing," *New York Times,* October 22, 1995, sec. 1, pp. 1, 8.

[108]NATO interventions in Bosnia and Kosovo have exemplified this role. "The Balkan End-Game," *The Economist,* January 20-26, 1996, pp. 19-21. NATO's new tasks are summarized in "A New Kind of Alliance?" *The Economist,* June 1-7, 1996, pp. 19-21.

[109]*SIPRI Yearbook 1996,* p. 297, footnote 86.

[110]"Why Brussels Sprouts," *The Economist,* December 26-January 8, 1993, pp. 70, 72.

[111]See Royce Q. Shaw, *Central America: Regional Integration and National Political Development* (Boulder, CO.: Westview Press, 1978), pp. 6-9.

[112]Domenico Mazzeo, "The Experience of the East African Community: Implications for the Theory and Practice of Regional Cooperation in Africa," in Mazzeo, ed., *African Regional Organizations* (Cambridge, UK.: Cambridge University Press, 1984), pp. 150-170.

[113]In 1979, Tanzanian troops invaded Uganda and helped the Uganda National Liberation Army (UNLA) overthrow Amin, who fled to Libya. The three countries have agreed to recreate EACM. Donatella Lorch, "Where Uganda and Kenya Collide," *New York Times,* April 2, 1994, p. 4.

[114]"Southern Africa Dreams of Unity," *The Economist,* September 2–8, 1995, p. 35.

[115]ASEAN has expanded rapidly, recently adding Burma, Laos, and Cambodia. The members resist any temptation to interfere in one another's internal affairs despite widespread human-rights abuses in several countries, the Asian economic melt-down that began in 1997, and the growing problem of region-wide pollution owing to fires in Indonesia's rain forests. "Never Mind the Quality," *The Economist,* March 1–7, 1997, pp. 39, 41.

[116]Larry Rohter, "Free Trade Goes South With or Without U.S.," *New York Times,* January 6, 1996, p. A4; "The Road from Santiago," *The Economist,* April 11–17, 1998, p. 43.

[117]"Getting Together," *The Economist,* June 29–July 5, 1996, pp. 42–43; "Now They are Six," *The Economist,* December 21, 1996–January 3, 1997, pp. 52–53. Chile and Bolivia have become associate members of Mercosur.

[118]"The Right Direction?" *The Economist,* September 16–22, 1995, pp. 23–27.

[119]Robert S. Walters and David H. Blake, *The Politics of Global Economic Relations* (Englewood Cliffs, NJ: Prentice-Hall, 1992), p. 205.

[120]Ibid., pp. 199–203. Today, 22 of the 50 largest oil companies are state-owned. James Tanner, "State-Owned Oil Firms Are Seeking Expansion In Refining, Marketing," *Wall Street Journal,* August 29, 1994, p. A4.

[121]Walters and Blake, *Politics of Global Economic Relations,* p. 204.

[122]James Tanner and Bhushan Bahree, "Rise in Russian Oil Exports Is Likely To Attract Attention at OPEC Parley," *Wall Street Journal,* June 13, 1994, p. A2.

[123]Thomas L. Friedman, "OPEC's Lonely at the Tap, But China's Getting Thirsty," *New York Times,* April 3, 1994, sec. 4, p. 3.

[124]"The Cracks in the Kingdom," *The Economist,* March 18–24, 1995, pp. 21, 22, 25.

[125]Youssef M. Ibrahim, "Falling Oil Prices Pinch Several Producing Nations," *New York Times,* June 23, 1998, p. A6; "The Suffering Gulf," *The Economist,* October 24–30, 1998, pp. 41–42.

[126]Agis Salpukas, "Challenges Inside and Out Confront OPEC," *New York Times,* June 23, 1998, p. A8.

[127]Daniel Southerland, "Opportunity's Knocking for Someone," *Washington Post National Weekly Edition,* May 15–21, 1995, p. 20.

[128]Steve Liesman and Bhushan Bahree, "'Big 3' Exporters' Pact To Cut Oil Output Signals Seismic Shifts," *Wall Street Journal,* June 23, 1998, pp. A1, A10.

[129]James Tanner, "U.S. Oil Imports Are Rising Rapidly, As Consumption Grows, Output Declines," *Wall Street Journal,* October 20, 1994, p. A2; Agis Salpukas, "Still Looking to the Persian Gulf," *New York Times,* March 26, 1995, sec. 4, p. 5. Efforts by oil companies to drill for oil to unprecedented depths in the Gulf of Mexico and develop new oil fields in the Caspian Sea off Azerbaijan may delay OPEC's revival. Agis Salpukas, "Oil Companies Drawn to the Deep," *New York Times,* December 7, 1994, pp. C1, C5; and Agis Salpukas, "Huge-Scale Caspian Oil Deal Signed," *New York Times,* September 21, 1994, p. C2.

[130]Stephen Kinzer, "A New Big-Power Race Starts on a Sea of Crude," *New York Times,* January 24, 1999, sec. 4, p. 4.

[131]Harold K. Jacobson, William M. Reisinger, and Todd Mathers, "National Entanglements in International Governmental Organizations," in Paul F. Diehl, ed., *The Politics of International Organizations* (Chicago: Dorsey Press, 1989), p. 79–80.

Part Three

Cooperation and Conflict: A Changing Balance

Part Three examines the changing balances of order and disorder and conflict and cooperation in global politics, paying special attention to changes in the military and economic realms. Chapter 9 focuses on the implications of anarchy in global politics, arguing that, even in the absence of world government, informal rules, international law, and international regimes foster cooperation and provide the bases for global society. Chapters 10 and 11 evaluate the changing nature and role of war in global politics. Chapters 12 and 13 focus on the growing role of economic factors in global politics, especially in promoting globalization, and examine relations among the United States, Japan, China, and the European Union to illustrate the pressure that a globalized economy exerts on actors to coordinate goals and policies.

Chapter 9

Going It Alone or Working Together in Global Politics?

Is global politics unbridled conflict, or does it have enough cooperation and common interests to make it resemble a society?[1] Traditionally, the conflictual elements of global politics have been the focus of attention, and cooperative elements have been ignored or given short shrift. In as much as the postinternational world features issues with which individual states cannot cope, it is more necessary than ever to identify those factors that facilitate cooperation. What, in fact, is the balance between force and cooperation in the postinternational world? These are questions to which we now turn.

A World of Conflict and Cooperation

Many classic theorists of global politics—Thucydides, Machiavelli, and Hobbes—focused on conflict.[2] They rarely paid attention to situations featuring common interests or *cooperation*—coordination of policy even in the face of divergent interests to achieve outcomes that a single actor could not achieve on its own.[3] Although most interaction is cooperative,[4] many theorists reason that independent actors with incompatible interests must clash, and, in consequence, there can be no natural harmony of interests.[5]

Mixed Motives   Some actors, such as the United States and Canada, enjoy a history of trust and friendly relations and usually cooperate. Others, such as the Hutus and Tutsis in Rwanda and Burundi, have a history of disagreement, mistrust, and animosity and usually are in conflict with each other. However, some issues—for example, fishing quotas in the Pacific Ocean off the state of Washington and the province of British Columbia—produce conflict between the United States and Canada, just as some issues—for example, technology transfer from the developed to the developing world—find India and Pakistan on the same side. In fact, virtually all issues and relationships feature elements of both conflict and cooperation, although some issues, like global trade, encourage cooperation more than others—for example, incompatible claims to the same territory.

To be sure, a few observers have analyzed cooperation, especially after wars, when thinkers propose schemes to prevent wars from recurring or to outlaw barbarous practices. The Abbé de Saint-Pierre (1658-1743) outlined a scheme for a federal union among European states after the War of the Spanish Succession (1701-1714). Jean-Jacques Rousseau (1712-1778) and Immanuel Kant (1724-1804), reacting to warfare in their time, proposed schemes for interstate cooperation. After World War I, Woodrow Wilson, with his proposal for collective security, ushered in a period of interest in international law and organization. This trend peaked in the interwar period (1919-1939), when many proposals were advanced for altering the structure of global affairs. Perhaps the most famous, the Kellogg-Briand Pact of 1928, sought to outlaw war. Such efforts, collectively labeled idealism or utopianism,[6] were short-lived.

Rousseau recognized that cooperative and conflictual attributes coexist uneasily in global politics. He described eighteenth-century Europe as "a real community with a religion and a moral code, with customs and even laws of its own."[7] He also captured the other side of the equation. "Observe the perpetual quarrels, the robberies, the usurpations, the revolts, the wars, the murders, which bring daily desolation to this venerable home of philosophy."[8] He concludes that such "glaring contradictions" are made possible because "every community without laws and without rulers, every union formed and maintained by nothing better than chance, must inevitably fall into quarrels and dissensions at the first change that comes about."[9]

Cooperation sometimes exists simply because it entails few risks. Situations such as economic coordination among industrial democracies may elicit cooperation because the difference in gains and losses between going it alone and cooperating are small. Other situations, such as engaging in an expensive arms race with a neighbor, provide less scope for coordinating policies because of the penalty that may be incurred if other players do not cooperate. As we shall see, cooperative strategies are encouraged if actors recognize the long-term effects of their behavior. Finally, the more numerous the players, the greater the opportunities for cooperation. More players provide the possibility of trade-offs and coalitions among like-minded actors.

Sometimes a mix of "stick" and "carrot" is needed to induce cooperation. During the Persian Gulf crisis, Jordan, fearing Iraqi power and loss of Iraqi markets for its goods, did not cooperate in enforcing U.N.-mandated sanctions against Saddam Hussein. Others sought to force Jordanian compliance by raising the costs for not doing so. The United States condemned Jordan's noncompliance, and Saudi Arabia cut off oil shipments to Jordan. Positive incentives were also used in the crisis to maintain cooperation against Iraq. Japan and Germany provided financial aid to Arab countries whose economies were harmed by upholding economic sanctions, and the United States promised to forgive $7 billion in debt owed it by Egypt to keep that pivotal state in the coalition.

The most important cause of cooperation, however, lies in the mutual dependence of actors in global politics. Most actors cannot achieve their objectives without the aid or at least consent of others. Game theory is useful for illustrating this interdependence.

Linked Fates and the Metaphor of Games

Simple game theory and the metaphor of *games* helps us understand how every actor's well-being depends on decisions made by others as well as by itself and how global politics is a dynamic interplay of competition and cooperation involving risky choices.

Briefly, what elements of game theory do we need to begin our analysis? All games have *players, payoffs, rules,* and *strategies.* We assume that players are unitary actors rationally seeking to maximize their gains and minimize their losses—the payoffs. These assumptions, of course, are often inappropriate in the real world. Rules describe the structure and procedures governing how games are played (such as the time allowed for moves), and strategies are the set of moves that guide the players' actions. A game's structure helps to determine players' strategies. For instance, strategies differ in games limited to two players from those with many (where alliances can form), or in games that do not permit communication among players from those that do.

Few games are *zero-sum*—that is, one player's gains are equal to the other's losses so that they have no incentive to cooperate or compromise.[10] Most games are *variable-sum* (or non-zero-sum) contests. Players can gain or lose more or less depending on the strategies they select. Since one player's gain is not equal to another's loss, the players have incentives to cooperate—avoiding serious losses or gaining more for everyone.[11] In variable-sum games, compromise is possible even in the teeth of hostility. Once we recognize the variable-sum quality of most issues, it becomes clearer why cooperation is possible.

As in real games, actors in global politics select among strategies and calculate others' probable responses. An actor's fate depends as much on what other players do as on its own behavior. Like all games, global politics has rules that determine who wins. In some games (such as war), winning requires one player to defeat others. Other games require that actors coordinate behavior to win (as in economic sanctions).[12]

Sometimes it may appear that actors are engaged in a zero-sum game when in reality they have common or compatible interests. Consider the Middle East peace process between Israel and the Palestine Liberation Organization (PLO). Israeli hard-liners, especially in the Likud Party, oppose the process because they fear that turning over the West Bank to the PLO, which they claim is still a terrorist organization, will endanger Israel's security. On the other side, Palestinian hard-liners in groups such as Hamas and the Popular Front for the Liberation of Palestine (PFLP) also oppose the peace process because they think Israel is insincere in claiming to want peace and because they fear that any deal with Israel will leave the Palestinians at Israel's mercy in the future. Although on the surface the hard-liners on both sides appear to be bitter enemies, they share the common aim of undermining the process. Every terrorist act by Hamas seems to justify the arguments of Likud militants that Palestinians cannot be trusted or that the PLO will not control the terrorists, and every Israeli concession to its hard-liners, such as building new Israeli settlements on the West Bank, undermines the PLO and increases Hamas's popularity. Thus the hard-liners help one another and undermine moderates on both sides.

Many apparently disparate global or regional games are so tightly linked that gains or losses in one affect resources available for others.[13] Thus Arab-Israeli hostility between 1948 and the Cold War's end reflected regional games that were played against the backdrop of the global contest between the United States and the Soviet Union. Finally, the prospects for cooperation or conflict depend on the strategies available to players and the nature of the stakes for which they are competing.

The Conflictual Side of Global Politics

Those who believe that conflict is the dominant feature of global politics reason that, without central power, actors must rely on themselves for security *(self-help)*. In such conditions, conflict is inevitable, and each actor must prepare to defend itself. Because conflict is inevitable, human ingenuity can do little other than limit its scope and consequences. This is the world depicted by Thomas Hobbes in *Leviathan:*

> Hereby it is manifest that, during the time men live without a common power to keep them all in awe, they are in that condition called war, and such a war as is of every man against every man.... In such condition there is no place for industry, because the fruit thereof is uncertain: and consequently no culture of the earth; no navigation nor use of the commodities that may be imported by sea ...; no arts; no letters; no society; and, which is worst of all, continual fear and danger of violent death....[14]

In a Hobbesian world, actors cannot trust each other, must depend only on themselves, and must prepare for the worst possible contingencies. This is *worst-case analysis.*

Consequences of Assuming the Worst

In a Hobbesian world, it would be rational for practitioners to exercise prudence and avoid risks. If actors cannot trust each other, then leaders have little choice but to select risk-averse strategies that minimize the mischief that others can do to them.

One reason for selecting risk-averse strategies is the paucity of reliable information in global politics. If leaders do not know what their adversaries are planning, they may assume the worst. In many *intelligence failures,* victims have had information that an adversary was able to carry out an attack but lacked specific intelligence about its intentions. Some illustrations are the U.S. failure to predict the Japanese attack on Pearl Harbor in 1941, Soviet surprise at the Nazi attack in 1941, and Israeli failure to predict Egypt's surprise attack in 1973. To avoid such disasters, actors prepare for the worst, assuming that, because they cannot get accurate information about intentions, this is their safest course.

However, *worst-case analysis* produces conservative thinking that resists change. Resulting policies may intensify the security dilemma and produce the fear and suspicion they were supposed to counter. Actors may build new weapons systems or conclude alliances in reaction to adversaries' capabilities—actions with defensive purposes—but a weapons system or alliance that can be used for defense can also be used aggressively. Because an opponent also is likely to use worst-case analysis, it may reciprocate, triggering an arms race. Over time, such interaction will make both sides feel less rather than more secure. As in the prisoner's dilemma, adversaries may find that prudence produces poor outcomes for both. By trying to assure itself of minimal security that does not depend on trusting the adversary, each actor frightens and alienates the other and provokes it to respond in kind.

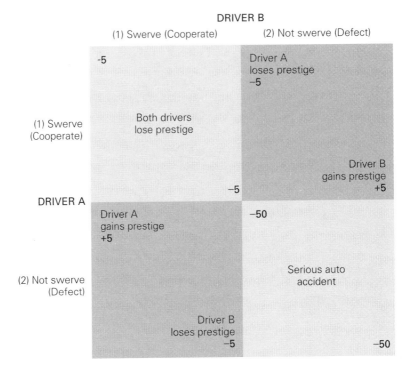

FIGURE 9.1
Chicken

By contrast with prisoner's dilemma, the game of chicken reflects conflict spirals in global politics in which players fear that each will carry out its threats. In the game, two cars speed toward one another; whoever swerves first loses, but if neither do so catastrophe will ensue. There is great pressure for both to "bluff" but ultimately to swerve. The situation is analogous to crises in global politics in which actors engage in brinkmanship.

Such a hostile spiral resembles the *game of chicken* (see Figure 9.1).[15] This is a game in which two cars speed toward each other, straddling the road's center line. The object is to see which driver will "chicken out" and swerve first. If both drivers swerve (outcome 1:1), both suffer loss of reputation. If only one swerves, there is a loser and a winner (outcomes 1:2 and 2:1). If neither swerves, both are big losers in the inevitable collision (outcome 2:2). In global politics, flaming crises like that of the Soviet missiles in Cuba in 1962 resemble games of chicken. And sometimes disaster does occur, and both players lose. Thus, in 1914, European leaders sought to force each other to make concessions to avoid collision. No one swerved, and all were losers.

Disaster occurs in chicken when both players believe the other is *bluffing,* and neither can be persuaded to swerve. Disaster can be avoided only when one player believes that the other will not swerve, thereby causing a life-threatening crash. *Fear forces the players to cooperate.* The way one wins a game of chicken is by making the adversary believe one is sufficiently irrational to risk mutual disaster. This is the heart of the general problem of making credible commitments that underlies the strategies of deterrence and coercive diplomacy. A number of tactics are available to a hot-rodder (or a leader) in a chicken game. For example, you might throw the steering wheel out the window, making it impossible to swerve. This action makes your commitment not to chicken out, however irrational, quite credible.[16]

In global politics, the willingness of actors to behave in apparently irrational ways—take risks with the prospect of little gain—is based on a belief that such behavior will affect their overall *bargaining reputation.* In other words, actions and outcomes in one case affect actions and outcomes in others. As in poker, players who get a reputation for bluffing will have their bluff called. As Robert Jervis explains, "The state must often go to extremes because moderation and conciliation are apt to be taken for weakness."[17] Sometimes, however, the result of a chicken game can be catastrophic, as it was in U.S.-Japanese relations leading up to World War II.

Japanese-U.S. Relations Before World War II: "Chicken" and the Conflict Spiral

Relations between the United States and Japan in the 1930s went into a negative spiral that culminated in Japan's attack on Pearl Harbor on December 7, 1941. Disagreement over major issues intensified hostility, which became intermingled with racial, economic, religious, cultural, and other differences. Disagreement and hostility set the stage for a cycle of reciprocally provocative acts in the months before war broke out.[18]

Japan was a latecomer among the major powers. The country was dragged out of isolation in 1853 by a U.S. fleet under Commodore Matthew Perry. A treaty of friendship and trade relations between the two countries was followed in the next decades by rapid industrialization of Japan. Japan's leaders decided that the country should acquire an empire and achieve military and political equality with the Western powers. One consequence of rapid development was Japan's growing dependence on imported food and raw materials. In 1895, Japan went to war with China and acquired the island of Formosa (Taiwan). Ten years later, in the first military victory of an Asian country over a European power, Japan defeated Russia and acquired new influence in Korea (which it annexed in 1910), South Sakhalin, and the Chinese province of Manchuria.[19] Manchuria was especially important because of its industries and such natural resources as iron and coal and because it served as a buffer zone between Japan and Russia. Japan also benefited from Germany's defeat in World War I by acquiring German concessions in China and Germany's territories in the Pacific.

Despite these triumphs, the Japanese felt they were being treated unequally by the West. One reason was a residue of racial animosity. Japanese efforts to include a clause affirming racial equality in the 1919 Versailles Treaty was blocked by U.S. President Woodrow Wilson, who feared that it would invalidate U.S. immigration laws, which excluded most Asians from America's shores. Japan's failure to gain tangible benefits from its policy of cooperation with the West during the 1920s and economic difficulties at home during the 1930s frustrated Japanese nationalists and military officers. Among these groups, admiration was growing for Benito Mussolini and the fascists, who had seized power in Italy in 1923. In September 1931, Japanese armed forces in Manchuria (the Kwantung Army), threatened by growing Chinese nationalism, occupied the province.[20] Japan's conquest of Manchuria

CHICKEN!

The game of chicken describes the relationship of adversaries that seek to force each other to give way to their demands. Each tries to make the other believe that it will take enormous risks in order to "win" the confrontation. This cartoon describes the repeated U.S.-Japanese trade confrontations as a chicken game which could lead to a dangerous trade war if neither country swerves. *(Reprinted with special permission of Kings Feature Syndicate.)*

and the creation of a puppet state called Manchukuo in 1932[21] deepened U.S. suspicions about Japanese intentions.[22] Japanese militarists viewed Western opposition to their penetration of China as an effort to deny Tokyo an imperial destiny already enjoyed by Western states. Mutual suspicion was transformed into open antagonism after Japan's invasion of China in 1937 and the barbarous atrocities its army committed in Shanghai and Nanking.

Tokyo viewed U.S. assistance to China as an effort to hamstring Japan and feared the U.S. Pacific fleet as a threat to Japan's national survival. American opposition to Japanese expansionism in China and the Japanese belief that this opposition was an effort to prevent Japan from realizing its destiny led to tit-for-tat behavior that produced a spiral of mutual insecurity. Japan needed secure access to raw materials, especially oil and iron, to bring the war in China to a successful conclusion. This problem was part of a more general one: Japan lacked most natural resources, and if cut off from external resources, its industrial economy would shrivel and die. Raw materials whetted Japan's interest in Southeast Asia, placing it on a collision course with the colonial powers that still ruled the area.[23]

In June 1940, Japanese military observers were sent to Tonking in northern Indochina, and additional troops followed in September. That month Japan entered into a military alliance—the Tripartite Pact—with fascist Italy and Nazi Germany. Japanese expansion into Southeast Asia engaged public attention in the United States, convincing observers that Tokyo was aggressive and a threat to U.S. interests. In response, the U.S. government halted sales of aviation gasoline to Japan in July 1940 and in September placed an embargo on steel and scrap iron.

Just as Japan's actions had antagonized rather than cowed the United States, so the U.S. response fueled anti-Americanism in Japan, creating fear that additional U.S. actions might be forthcoming and producing determination to secure raw-material sources and to close down the southern supply routes to China. The lure of oil, rubber, and other resources needed by Japan grew. In July 1941, the die was cast as Japanese troops occupied southern Indochina. In response, the U.S., British, and Dutch[24] governments embargoed oil exports to Japan, cutting off 90 percent of Japan's oil imports. By late 1941, U.S.-Japanese relations had become a game of chicken. Each side blustered, threatened, and took steps to convince the other that it was willing to go to war rather than back down. Concern for Japan's bargaining reputation was evident when Japanese Prime Minister Hideki Tojo argued in September 1941 that "the real purpose of the United States [is] the domination of the Far East. Consequently, to yield on one matter would be to encourage other demands, until there would be no end to the concessions required of Japan."[25]

Japan's leaders were under mounting pressure. Oil reserves were limited, and, in time, Japan's capacity to wage war would decline. Yet an effort to seize Southeast Asia's oil wealth had to take into account the U.S. Pacific fleet. On September 3, Japanese leaders decided to attack the United States if the oil issue remained unresolved by October. Tokyo simultaneously intensified diplomatic efforts and began to plan a sneak attack on America's giant naval base at Pearl Harbor in Hawaii. On Sunday, December 7, a day President Roosevelt declared "would live in infamy," the escalating spiral of U.S.-Japanese hostility exploded in the attack on Pearl Harbor.

United States-Japanese relations before World War II were a case of two actors with incompatible interests using the threat of force to increase their security and finding themselves embroiled in a conflict spiral that climaxed in war. But, as we shall see, conflict is only one side of the coin.

The Social Side of Global Politics

There are a number of ways of creating trust even under anarchy and of escaping the security dilemma. Some of the factors that promote cooperation include the following:

1. Long time horizons
2. Regularity of stakes
3. Reliability of information about the other's actions
4. Quick feedback about changes in the other's actions[26]

Where such factors are present, even actors that are adversaries on some issues can work together on others.

In the remainder of the chapter we address the question of cooperation in the absence of overarching authority. First, we will look at the role of *reciprocity,* which helps explain why it is expedient for actors to cooperate. Second, we consider how *history of rewarding cooperation and shared values* encourage cooperation. Third, we examine how *concern about the future* also encourages cooperation. Fourth, we look at how *learning* occurs in global politics. Such learning is a prerequisite for *norms and rules of behavior* that are necessary if cooperation is to become habitual. Where there is such cooperation, global politics resembles what Hedley Bull calls a *society of states.* In such a society, "a group of states, conscious of certain common interests and common values . . . conceive themselves to be bound by a common set of rules in their relations with one another, and share in the working of common institutions."[27]

Reciprocity   When an actor behaves cooperatively over time, it will elicit cooperation from others. Describing U.S.-Russian relations, Joshua Goldstein and John Freeman argue that beginning in 1985 Soviet leaders "launched a series of . . . cooperative initiatives toward both the United States and China," including a moratorium on nuclear tests, concessions on Asian security, withdrawal from Afghanistan, and promises of additional unilateral military cuts.[28] This case suggests that the absence of a higher authority to enforce cooperation does not prevent it from taking place.

For this reason, Rousseau's stag-hare parable, described in Chapter 5, is deeply flawed. Rousseau's state of nature differs from the real world in that its inhabitants interact only episodically. Rousseau's hunter is like a fly-by-night salesman or con artist who cheats customers and then flees with the profits, hoping never to see them again. In the real world, most actors, like reputable business leaders, keep faith with each other, not only from ethical considerations, but because their interests are served by the golden rule—do unto others as you would have them do unto you. Despite the absence of central authority, most promises are kept and most treaties are observed.[29]

The golden rule reflects reciprocity—an exchange in which each actor's behavior emulates that of the other "in such a way that good is returned for good, and bad for bad."[30] Rousseau's stag-hare parable describes an *end-of-the-world* or *one-shot game,* which does not permit reciprocity. By acknowledging that reciprocity is indispensable in creating common interest in not cheating, we acknowledge that global politics is not an end-of-the-world game but is continuing interaction in which each actor's behavior conditions others' expectations for the future. Unlike the hunters in Rousseau's state of nature, who presumably never expect to meet again, Israelis and Palestinians must consider the eventual consequences of what they do to each other. An actor that regularly cheats will not be trusted. If it plays by the rules, it will probably receive the same treatment in return.

If actors have an eye to the future, they may be willing to take risks to achieve large long-term gains; unlike the stag-hare hunter, they can compare short-term and long-term interests. Whether cooperation evolves depends on the context in which actors find themselves and on how they respond to initiatives intended to promote trust. As Robert Axelrod and Robert Keohane observe, "Effective reciprocity depends on three conditions: (1) players can identify defectors; (2) they are able to focus retaliation on defectors; and (3) they have sufficient long-run incentives to punish defectors."[31] Where many actors are involved it may be difficult to recognize cheating or know who the culprits are. Actors may also lack the will to retaliate, hoping that someone else will do it for them.

The most important factor in achieving cooperation, however, is recognizing long-term interests. "The more future payoffs are valued relative to current payoffs," observe Axelrod and Keohane, "the less incentive to defect today—since the other side is likely to retaliate tomorrow."[32] They illustrate this with the example of relations between international banks and Latin American governments that are in debt to them:

> Negotiations among banks, and between banks and debtor countries, are heavily affected by the shadow of the future....[T]he banks know that they will be dealing ...with the debtor countries...again and again....Continuing relations between banks and debtor countries give the banks incentives to cooperate with the debtor countries, not merely in order to facilitate debt servicing on loans already made, but to stay in their good graces—looking toward a more prosperous future.[33]

This example also shows that past interactions and expectations for the future condition the present.

Weight of the Past and Future

For better or worse, leaders are influenced by both the past and "the shadow of the future." By "past," we mean both the history of actors' relations and the personal experiences of the leaders themselves. By "future," we mean expectations and aspirations of the collectivities and of individual leaders.

A people's *historical experience* is relevant to the present in several ways. History is the basis of "myths" that are necessary for group solidarity and values.[34] In the United States, stories about the revolution against British rule in 1776 and the subsequent Constitutional Convention; the Civil War (1860–1865) that ended slavery; and the "conquest" of the West are invoked to define American values— individualism, pragmatism, equality, tolerance, and hard work. The stories may be only partly accurate, but accuracy is not the point. They serve the purpose of providing a shared past and shared experiences to deepen unity, and, like Biblical parables, they help define what each society regards as ethical.[35]

The past is relevant in another way. If actors have enjoyed warm relations in the past, leaders assume they will continue to do so. They react sympathetically and are sensitive to each other's needs, thereby confirming the original assumption, and if they are in disagreement, they will try to find common ground.[36] Thus a history of cooperation facilitates future cooperation. The *special relationship* between the United States and Britain shows how a long history of good relations influences the present. When the Argentine army seized the Falkland (Malvinas) Islands in the South Atlantic from Britain in 1982, there should have been little doubt that, once Washington failed to negotiate a peaceful resolution to the conflict, it would tilt toward London. The British government showed similar sensitivity to U.S. interests in 1986 when it permitted U.S. bombers to use British air bases to bomb targets in Libya in retaliation for Libyan support of international terrorism and again in 1990 when the British government sent troops to stand alongside their American allies in Kuwait.

Because the past is assumed to be a reliable predictor of the future, leaders may be caught by surprise when change does occur. Events like Iraq's invasion of Kuwait in 1990 following U.S. aid to that country during the Iraq-Iran war came as a surprise despite evidence of its imminence. The event was not expected because it did not fit past patterns.

Leaders are also prone to interpret the present through the lens of personal experience. The problem, as one historian explains, "is that framers of foreign policy are often influenced by beliefs about what history teaches or portends. Sometimes, they perceive problems in terms of analogies from the past. Sometimes, they envision the future either as foreshadowed by historical parallels or as following a straight line from what has recently gone before."[37] However, *analogies from the past* can be dangerous.[38] Though inappropriate, such analogies may guide or rationalize policy and substitute for more relevant information, as happened in the years prior to World War II.

Those who remembered the senseless carnage of World War I, like British Prime Minister Neville Chamberlain, tried to appease Hitler and Mussolini in the 1930s in order to prevent the carnage from being repeated. Contemplating another war with Germany, Chamberlain declared in a radio broadcast: "How horrible, fantastic, incredible it is that we should be digging trenches and trying on gas-masks here because of a quarrel in a far-away country between people of whom we know nothing."[39] Chamberlain, declares one historian, "was so deeply, so desperately, anxious to avoid war that he could not conceive of its being inevitable."[40]

Expectations of and concerns for the future can exercise as powerful an influence on present behavior as memories of the past. An actor's concern for reputation is one way in which the future influences the present. If a leader is worried about his reputation for keeping commitments in the future, he may be more pugnacious in the present. This is why actors may become embroiled in serious crises over what appear to be minor issues.

On two occasions (1954 and 1958), the United States seemed willing to risk war with China over the tiny Taiwanese-occupied islands of Quemoy and Matsu in order to maintain a reputation for toughness. During the crises over these two specks off the coast of China, "[President] Eisenhower actually brought the country to the 'nuclear brink,' far closer to war than a distraught public feared in 1955, closer than Eisenhower acknowledged in his own memoirs, and closer than most historians have heretofore even suspected."[41] As in these cases, the costs of maintaining a reputation for toughness may become disproportionate to the ends sought. Another was U.S. intervention in Vietnam—"70 percent" of the aim of which, according to Assistant Secretary of Defense John T. McNaughton, was "to avoid humiliating U.S. defeat (to our reputation as a guarantor)."[42]

Learning by Doing

As our discussion of reciprocity suggests, *learning* does take place in global politics so that the way in which actors perceive the world and the way in which they behave can change. In the language of game theory, the way in which one game is played affects the values attached to other games.[43] It is this assumption that underlies leaders' willingness to forego immediate gain for long-term interests. Let us use two cases to illustrate learning by doing. The first shows how Western leaders learned in the 1930s that the leaders of Germany, Japan, and Italy were not traditional statesmen who could be wooed to the path of peace with concessions. The second case illustrates the process by which the leaders of East and West learned how to overcome years of hostility and bring the Cold War to an end.

Learning the Hard Way: The 1930s

The steps leading up to World War II show one way in which leaders learn. Western leaders in the 1930s repeatedly chose to appease the dictators of Germany, Japan, and Italy rather than risk war. None of the violations of international law and decency—the Japanese invasion of Manchuria (1931) and China (1937), Italian aggression against Ethiopia (1935), German repudiation of the Treaty of Versailles (1935),[44] and occupation of the Rhineland (1936),[45] Austria (1938),[46] the Czech Sudetenland (1938), and the remainder of "rump" Czechoslovakia (1939)—triggered military resistance from the Western democracies. Why did this happen and why, in the end, was appeasement discarded?

The reasons for Western passivity in the face of provocation were complex—memories of trench-warfare horrors in World War I, fear of airpower, public opposition to defense expenditures during economic hard times, and lack of military preparedness, among others. Perhaps most important was that Western leaders were convinced that the dictators' demands were limited. The feeling was widespread that the Versailles Treaty, imposed on defeated Germany, was unfair and that, as British economist John Maynard Keynes wrote, "little has been overlooked which might impoverish Germany now or obstruct her development in future."[47] Many observers believed German efforts to regain equality with the other Europeans were justified.

Consequently, when Hitler claimed that his aims were limited—to restore German dignity and afford German-speaking peoples national self-determination by uniting them in one state—Western leaders took him at his word.[48] Because they had supported the rights of other nationalities to have their own state, it seemed unfair for them to oppose Hitler's stated objective. They believed the costs of war outweighed the value of stakes such as the Rhineland or the Sudetenland. This attitude changed dramatically, however, when Hitler occupied the ancient Czech provinces of Bohemia and Moravia, where, unlike the Sudetenland, few Germans lived. Clearly, the German leader was after more than national self-determination for Germans; now his earlier actions seemed more sinister, part of a larger plot to give Germany control of Europe. His previous actions now looked like *salami tactics,* in which an actor makes small demands (like thin slices of a salami) that collectively add up to something more significant (the whole salami). Thomas Schelling writes:

> "Salami tactics," we can be sure, were invented by a child; whoever first expounded the adult version had already understood the principle when he was small. Tell a child not to go in the water and he'll sit on the bank and submerge his bare feet; he is not yet "in" the water. Acquiesce, and he'll stand up; no more of him is in the water than before. Think it over, and he'll start wading, not going any deeper; take a moment to decide whether this is different and he'll go a little deeper, arguing that since he goes back and forth it all averages out. Pretty soon we are calling to him not to swim out of sight, wondering whatever happened to all our discipline.[49]

On September 1, 1939, the Nazis attacked Poland. Within hours, Great Britain and France declared war on Germany, and World War II began. In some ways, their decision made little sense. A year before, they had abandoned Czechoslovakia even though France and the Soviet Union had an alliance with that country and even though it was a democracy. Czechoslovakia also had an excellent army and enjoyed strong natural defenses. By contrast, neither Britain nor France was allied to the authoritarian Polish government. The Polish army was mostly obsolete, and Poland's flat terrain was ideal for mechanized warfare of the sort Germany waged. It seemed as though Western leaders had chosen to fight in the wrong place and at the wrong time. Their decision makes sense only because events in 1938 had so greatly altered their perceptions of Hitler. They had learned he was a radical with unlimited aims.[50]

Learning was also apparent in the sequence of events leading up to the end of the Cold War. After Mikhail Gorbachev came to power in the Soviet Union in 1985, a benign spiral took place during which each side came to reevaluate the other.

Learning How to Cooperate: The Cold War Ends

Gorbachev realized that Soviet policies were leading to economic and political bankruptcy. The Cold War had to end to enable the Soviet Union to free up resources for consumers and for modernizing its society and economy. As a result, Gorbachev initiated a series of unilateral and *entirely unexpected* concessions to the West on arms control and regional conflicts.[51] These initiatives were initially greeted with skepticism,[52] which was understandable in view of Gorbachev's background as a loyal communist functionary. Gradually, however, Western leaders accepted Gorbachev's "new thinking" as genuine and made reciprocal concessions as "partners in peace." In time, Western leaders came to regard Gorbachev as someone with whom they could do business.[53]

Gorbachev's strategy was apparent in negotiations leading to the Intermediate-Range Nuclear Forces (INF) Treaty that he signed with President Ronald Reagan on December 8, 1987. A brief history of the case is instructive. After 1979, Western leaders sought to deploy a new generation of missiles in Western Europe that could strike at targets in Eastern Europe and the U.S.S.R. This initiative was a response to Soviet deployment of an accurate new mobile missile equipped with multiple warheads—the SS-20. A comparable system of Western missiles seemed imperative to convey to Moscow a credible NATO commitment on nuclear deterrence. NATO's plan was called the *dual-track decision* because it committed the West to negotiate with the U.S.S.R. at the same time that missiles were being deployed.[54] Such negotiation was regarded as mostly cosmetic, to win public opinion, and few expected the negotiations to bear fruit.

To the chagrin of Western leaders, the planned deployment was confronted by massive opposition among Europeans and Americans. Soviet leaders launched an effective propaganda campaign against deployment of INF missiles, seeking to abet Europe's "peace movement." In the end, the missiles were deployed, but Europe's publics had to be shown that NATO was seriously negotiating with the Warsaw Treaty Organization. The Reagan administration had little interest in an arms-control agreement with Moscow, but it had a serious public-relations problem.

To allay public fears about nuclear war, the administration in 1981 proposed a *zero option*—worldwide elimination of INF missiles. The administration believed this simple proposal would find public favor in the West but would be unacceptable to Moscow because it required the U.S.S.R. to eliminate the many missiles that had already been deployed while merely requiring NATO not to deploy the proposed missiles. At first, the ploy worked, but in 1986, "when Gorbachev offered to eliminate all SS-20s in Europe, the West was trapped."[55] The offer was attractive to Western publics and satisfied Western demands for verification by permitting on-site inspections. Most important, it was a concession by Gorbachev because it committed the U.S.S.R. to eliminate far more weapons than the West. The Reagan administration was forced to go along or else pay a price in public support.

After the INF Treaty, new arms-control initiatives got under way. Each step was encouraged by unilateral initiatives on the part of the Soviet leader. Sensing the need for a U.S. initiative and prodded by the abortive coup against Gorbachev by hard-liners in the U.S.S.R., President Bush announced in September 1991 that the United States would unilaterally eliminate its vast arsenal of short-range nuclear weapons.[56] A few days later, Gorbachev announced that the U.S.S.R. would reciprocate and, in some arms categories, go even further.[57]

Once learning has gone sufficiently far to create stable expectations on the part of actors, coherent norms may begin to govern their relations. In time, these may make behavior sufficiently predictable to prevent misperception and reduce the likelihood of conflict due to misunderstanding.

Global Norms and Rules of the Game

Learning is reflected in norms that evolve to shape expectations and define what behavior is proper. Despite those who believe that global politics is unchangeable— an anarchic universe dominated by conflict—different eras and settings have different norms. During the twelfth century, it was acceptable for a conqueror like Genghis Khan to burn and loot cities and sell captives into slavery. By the nineteenth century, however, such behavior was regarded as depraved. The 1864 Geneva Convention reflected this change by establishing rules for the humane treatment of prisoners of war and of the sick and those wounded in battle. During World War II, Hitler violated international law and other global norms, and the *Nuremberg trials* of captured Nazis after the war were an effort to outlaw such behavior. As this example suggests, international law, to which we shall shortly turn, is one way in which norms become publicized and institutionalized, but many norms never achieve the status of law.

Norms, in the sense used here, apply to behavior that is regarded as appropriate by actors. When such norms are widely accepted, they provide *rules of the game* that actors follow out of habit and self-interest. They provide coherence even without central authority, thereby reducing anarchy. Norms can be surmised from reasoning such as the following:

"Under conditions A and B, actors expect us to do X."

"Under conditions A and B, action Y will violate other actors' expectations and produce unpredictable reactions."

"If we wish to avoid mutual harm, we should do X."

Actions communicate intent. If actors follow the rules of the game, initiatives will be met by standard responses that have evolved for such situations and are anticipated by all. When actors limit themselves to standard repertoires of behavior, the probability is reduced that fear and uncertainty will trigger spiraling conflict. Mutual interests encourage actors to develop repertoires of cooperative actions covering diverse issues. Norms that define for participants what is permissible and what is improper under different conditions underlie these cooperative endeavors. They permit activities that, like trade and travel, are critical to maintaining the fabric of global society. If all goes well, these activities are conducted routinely and quietly and go unnoticed.

Clear norms are important in regulating the behavior of adversaries. Under the best of conditions adversaries find it difficult to maintain control over events. Only if norms indicate what they can and cannot do is it possible to avoid catastrophe. Actor A may start an action that it knows will anger B but *only* so much that B will issue a protest. If norms are clear, B, although unhappy with A's action, will recognize that A's objectives are limited. Actor B can then "retaliate" in the manner expected by A, thereby avoiding an uncontrollable conflict spiral. If norms are murky and A's action seems to violate the rules of the game, B may feel threatened. Such fear can trigger extreme, even unthinking, responses.

When norms are clear, global life is predictable and safe. But when norms decay or change rapidly or major actors persistently violate them, the resulting unpredictability makes global life perilous. In some instances, major wars may result. Indeed, the assassination of the archduke and heir to the Austro-Hungarian throne in 1914 seemed as contrary to the norms of decency in that era as the release of poison gas in the Tokyo subway or the bombing of a federal building in Oklahoma City do today.

The French Revolution of 1789 illustrates the impact of rapidly changing norms. The Revolution brought new norms of equality and democracy, which revolutionaries tried to export. The revolutionaries set out to eliminate all vestiges of Europe's feudal past, dramatically altering laws, property rights, and social customs. In a word, they refused to play by the old rules of the game. Other European rulers saw revolutionary norms as dangerous to their security, and their fears were intensified by French efforts to imbue others with the new ideologies of nationalism and republicanism. French actions at home and abroad violated the accepted rules of the time, notably balance-of-power politics and nonintervention in the domestic affairs of sovereign states. At home the king and his family were executed in January 1793, and a reign of terror ensued, featuring "Madame Guillotine," who stood "grim and gaunt, with long thin arms stretched out towards the sky, the last glimmer of waning light striking the triangular knife . . . where it was not rusty with stains of blood."[58] Abroad, French armies occupied Belgium and the Rhineland, annexed neighboring territories, and declared war on England and Holland. Even France's way of waging war, with a huge army of conscripted citizens, was terrifyingly new.

English political philosopher Edmund Burke reflected the widespread loathing that greeted the French Revolution, which "doubled the licence, of a ferocious dissoluteness in manners, and of an insolent irreligion in opinions and practices," "utterly disgraced the tone of lenient council in the cabinets of princes," "sanctified the dark suspicious maxims of tyrannous distrust," and gave rise to "treasons, robberies, rapes, assassinations, slaughters, and burnings throughout their harassed land." Burke added with disgust that "in the groves of *their* academy, at the end of every vista, you see nothing but gallows," and he predicted that "learning will be cast into the mire, and trodden down under the hoofs of a swinish multitude."[59]

Conservative monarchs reacted with alarm to this mortal threat against the old order, and Europe remained at war until the final defeat of the French Emperor Napoleon Bonaparte in 1815. The victors sought to restore the old rules of the game at the Congress of Vienna.[60] They tried to prevent a similar catastrophe by agreeing to restore the balance of power in Europe and, if necessary in the future, to intervene in each other's domestic affairs to prevent another revolutionary outburst like that which had engulfed France.[61]

World War II had as dramatic an impact on global norms as the French Revolution. The leading players—Germany, Great Britain, France, and Japan—were swept aside and replaced by two inexperienced superpowers, the United States and the Soviet Union, without clear norms to guide their behavior toward each other. All of a sudden, two countries towered over the rest of the world like two Gullivers amid a host of Lilliputians. The superpowers found themselves in confrontation, each with only a vague understanding of the other's intentions. Lacking shared norms, each tried to impose its norms on the other, and the sequence of moves and countermoves produced mistrust and fear. The summit conferences at Yalta and Potsdam produced misunderstandings because the superpowers found themselves in command of a strange new world, facing new challenges they did not understand. Fortunately, war did not result, and the two sides evolved rules for surviving together in a nuclear world—"basic rules of prudence."[62]

When global norms are sufficiently clear and durable they may be codified as international law. Such law reflects norms that have become highly institutionalized.

International Law

The rule of law as reflected in *international law*—"the body of rules and principles of action which are binding upon civilized states in their relations with one another"[63]—is the clearest evidence that social bonds exist in global politics.

International Law and the State System

Writing in 1628 in the midst of the Thirty Years' War, Hugo Grotius, the "father of international law," declared:

> Throughout the Christian world I observed a lack of restraint in relation to war, such as even barbarous races should be ashamed of; I observed that men rush to arms for slight causes, or no cause at all, and that when arms have once been taken up there is no longer any respect for law, divine or human; it is as if . . . frenzy had openly been let loose for the committing of all crimes.[64]

Grotius argued that wars were just when fought to defend oneself or one's property, enforce rights, or punish violations of law. While arguing that some international law derived from nature, he regarded agreements reached by states as more important. Finally, he saw war as a contest between states, not individuals, so that noncombatants should not be mistreated. Thus Grotius dealt with the justice of war *(jus ad bellum)* and justice in war *(jus in bello).*

Efforts to codify the law of war have been episodic, with most activity immediately after bloody wars. A few efforts have been made to outlaw war, for example, the Kellogg-Briand Pact of 1928—but more energy has been invested in limiting the effects of war or outlawing especially repugnant practices. Thus the treatment of prisoners of war and civilians has been the subject of many treaties, notably the Hague Regulations of 1907, the Geneva Convention of 1949, and the 1977 Geneva Conference on Humanitarian Law.

International law is studied less frequently today than in the past. Several reasons account for its decline as a focus of attention (except in law schools). First, international law evolved with the European state system; it was, as Hans Morgenthau argued, "the result of the great political transformation of the feudal system into the territorial state."[65] It dealt extensively with the rights and duties of sovereign states to each other and evolved to protect and legitimate state sovereignty. As a result, international law is built on principles such as territorial integrity and nonintervention in states' domestic affairs, which are increasingly irrelevant. According to one observer, nine principles "summarize years of thought about the proper relations between sovereign entities."

1. The sovereign equality of states
2. The territorial integrity and political independence of states
3. Equal rights and self-determination of peoples
4. Nonintervention in the internal affairs of states
5. Peaceful settlement of disputes between states
6. No threat or use of force
7. Fulfillment in good faith of international obligations
8. Cooperation with other states
9. Respect for human rights and fundamental freedoms[66]

Second, most international law is of European origin and is viewed by non-Europeans as serving the interest of the West. Whether or not that is the case, international law, like law generally, favors continuity and stability—the status quo—over change. Third, a good deal of international law has been overtaken by technological change that dilutes the importance of state frontiers. For example, space satellites make obsolete states' "complete and exclusive sovereignty" of airspace over their territory as guaranteed by the 1944 Chicago Convention on International Civil Aviation.[67] Fourth, in a world featuring vastly different cultures, legal systems, and ideas of right and wrong, there will necessarily be different definitions of even basic concepts—peace, aggression, justice, rights, and so forth—essential for building a community of law in a world no longer dominated by Europeans. In consequence, as fragmenting tendencies overtake large areas of the world, the difficulties of achieving consensus about international law and thereby knitting disparate peoples together increase.

Even in the heyday of international law, questions were raised about whether it was true law. Morgenthau argues that international law, unlike domestic law, is "a primitive type of law resembling the kind of law that prevails in certain preliterate societies."[68] In the absence of a world government, international law requires the consent of major actors and regulates only those issues in which they have a common interest. In contrast to domestic law, international law lacks a binding arbiter who can interpret and judge the law, and it cannot be enforced except by those who are subject to it. Finally, international law is based mainly on custom, precedent, and treaties, rather than on legislation.[69]

International law, as it developed in the West, applied only to states because applying it to individuals seemed to violate state sovereignty. However, to deal with instances in which states themselves violate human rights, efforts have been made to give individuals—both victims and criminals—legal standing under international law. An important precedent was set when a U.S. federal appeals court ruled that two women could use American courts to enforce international human-rights standards and sue Bosnian Serb leader Radovan Karadzic for war crimes committed against the women in Bosnia.[70]

International Law and Individuals: The Nuremberg Precedent

Against a background of atrocities committed against civilians and prisoners of war in World War II, German and Japanese leaders were made to stand trial. The only precedent was a provision in the Versailles Treaty for trying Kaiser Wilhelm after World War I, which he avoided by seeking asylum in Holland. The trials after World War II were unique in that they were conducted before international tribunals. The best known consisted of jurists from the United States, U.S.S.R., France, and Great Britain and was set up at Nuremberg. Defendants were accused of three types of crimes: *war crimes, crimes against peace,* and *crimes against humanity.* The traditional defenses of superior orders and reason of state were not accepted, and twelve of twenty-two defendants were sentenced to be hanged.

The most controversial of the allegations were crimes against peace, defined as conspiracy to wage war or actual waging of aggressive war. International law traditionally had sanctioned the right of states to go to war, and defining aggression or identifying aggressors is so complex as to defy consensus. Even Grotius had failed to define aggression, and the problem has grown more perplexing since the seventeenth century. Thus some observers felt that charges of crimes against peace lacked legitimacy and represented "victors' justice."

No one was convicted only for crimes against peace. Crimes against humanity included genocide, murder, deportation, and enslavement of civilian populations for racial or political reasons, either before or during war. The attempt to convict the accused for acts committed *before* the war was also novel and seemed to many to violate due process. Most convictions were for war crimes, the category with the clearest precedents.

The postwar trials established the principle that individuals are responsible for their acts in times of war and departed from the tradition of treating only sovereign states as subjects of international law. However, until recently, the Nuremberg precedent stood alone. Then, as conflict in Bosnia grew increasingly brutal and allegations of ethnic cleansing—the forced movement of members of an ethnic group from an area—surfaced, acting U.S. Secretary of State Lawrence

Eagleburger said in December 1992 that war-crimes investigations of Serbian leaders were justified. Some months later the International Court of Justice (ICJ) warned Serbia that its leaders might be charged with genocide.[71]

In May 1996, the first international war-crimes trial since the trails of Nuremberg began in the Hague. Called the International Criminal Tribunal for the former Yugoslavia, the tribunal had to contend with inadequate funding and the ambiguous attitude of several key states, including Russia and the United States.[72] Pressure for action had grown as confirmation of charges of ethnic cleansing became available.[73]

The tribunal had handed down its first indictment in early 1995, charging a Serbian concentration-camp commander with "genocide and crimes against humanity,"[74] and documentary evidence had surfaced of the direct complicity in war crimes of Serbia's President Slobodan Milosevic, Bosnian Serb leader Radovan Karadzic, and Bosnian Serb army commander General Ratko Mladic.[75] Karadzic and Mladic, along with others, had been indicted in July 1995 for genocide, war crimes, and crimes against humanity.[76] In November 1995 new charges of genocide were brought against Karadzic and Mladic for acts committed after the fall of the Muslim enclave of Srebenica in July, and their fate became entangled in the Bosnian peace negotiations in Dayton, Ohio.[77] It is difficult to bring them to trial because Serbian leaders do not wish to let them give testimony that might incriminate Belgrade. Although all signatories to the Dayton accords promised to cooperate with the U.N. tribunal, no one wished to do anything that would upset the fragile agreement. Nevertheless, in June 1996, the Hague Tribunal issued international arrest warrants for Karadzic and Mladic. However, fearing that arresting them would trigger renewed violence, plans to seize them were abandoned. By that time, sixty-two persons had been indicted, and nearly half were in custody.[78] Three years later, in the midst of the Serbian ethnic cleansing of ethnic Albanians from Kosovo, the United States and its NATO allies warned Milosevic and his followers that they would be held legally accountable for atrocities against the Albanians.

The United Nations also set up an international tribunal to deal with Rwandans charged with genocide in the 1994 massacres in that country.[79] That tribunal opened in Arusha, Tanzania, in December 1995, indicting eight unnamed defendants.[80] Most of the senior perpetrators of the Rwandan genocide fled the country and sought asylum in neighboring countries.[81] Rwanda's Tutsi-dominated government jailed as many as 85,000 alleged Hutu murderers under primitive conditions and has brought a number of them to trial.[82]

These cases reflect the tension between the demand for justice represented by the tribunals and international law more generally and the practical necessity of bringing an end to conflict and bloodshed.[83] "The court," said one observer of the Hague Tribunal, "has the apparently impossible task of trying people still engaged in a war."[84] November 21, 1995 marked the fiftieth anniversary of the opening of the Nuremberg trials. Only time will tell whether the precedent set there, described by a law professor as "the idea that peace without justice is an incomplete peace,"[85] can be applied where there are no clear victors and alleged criminals are not in custody.

One important step, however, is the U.N. effort to create a permanent court to try individuals accused of genocide, war crimes, or crimes against humanity. After four years of negotiations, representatives from 120 countries met in Rome, Italy,

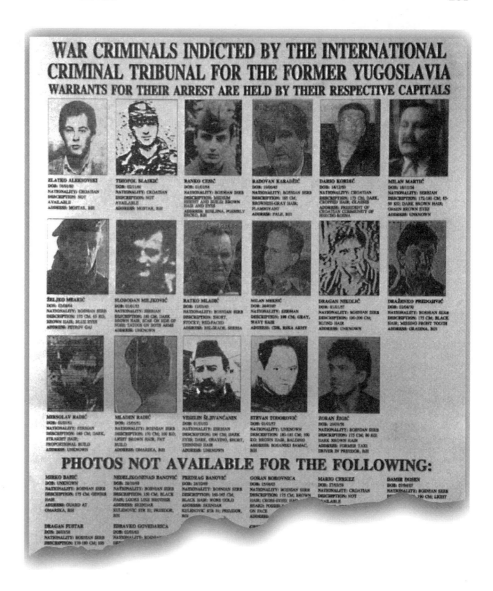

This wanted poster released by NATO in 1996 was intended to help troops in Bosnia identify fifty-one suspected war criminals. *(AP/Wide World Photo)*

in the summer of 1998 to conclude a treaty establishing the *International Criminal Court (ICC)*. The key dispute, not surprisingly, was over the degree to which the court could defy state sovereignty in taking up cases.[86] Most disappointing from the perspective of human-rights advocates was the vigorous opposition of the United States to a strong, independent court. Fearing that American soldiers overseas might be charged with crimes by foes of U.S. policies and confronted with strong Republican opposition in Congress, the Clinton administration

ACTORS SPEAK

There is strong disagreement about the powers that should be vested in the new International Criminal Court that was established to try individuals charged with genocide, war crimes, or crimes against humanity.

We must not turn an International Criminal Court—or its prosecutors—into a human rights ombudsman open to, and responsible for, responding to any and all complaints from any source. . . . [W]e are not here to create a court that exists to sit in judgment on national systems, to second guess each action and intervene if it disagrees. (Former U.S. Ambassador to the United Nations, Bill Richardson, as cited in Paul Taylor, "U.S. Demands Limits on World Criminal Court," *Yahoo News,* http: www.yahoo.com/h, June 17, 1998)

American negotiators seem to want to set up a court, but only over whose investigations and prosecutions the American government would have a veto. In particular, they seem to be seeking a guarantee that no American citizen would ever be subject to the court's jurisdiction. Supporters of a strong court argue, rightly, that such a politicised institution would be worse than no court at all. ("A New World Court," *The Economist,* June 13–19, 1998, p. 17)

took the position that, except for genocide, the court's jurisdiction should be automatic only in those countries that had signed the treaty. In the end, the United States voted against the treaty, along with China, Iraq, Libya, Qatar, Yemen, and Israel.[87] Declared Amnesty International Secretary-General Pierre Sane: "To have a weak and ineffective court will not solve the problem."[88]

International Regimes

In recent decades, some of the ideas involved in international law have resurfaced in descriptions of international regimes. An *international regime* exists when norms governing an issue become so systematic, habitual, and rulelike that behavior and outcomes become predictable.[89] Such norms—understandings of how actors should behave—grow out of the mutual interests of actors and are learned from experience. Regimes are a prominent example of governance in the postinternational world and provide an important way for states and other actors to cooperate in coping with transnational issues that none of them can deal with on its own. Such norms evolve out of the common interests of participants and are learned by trial-and-error experience. Although a regime is not a full-fledged government, law, or international organization, it is more formal, legitimate, and institutionalized than simple habit, something stronger and more durable than "temporary arrangements that change with every shift in power or interests."[90] And the creation and maintenance of regimes have been facilitated in recent years by the telecommunications revolution and the resulting upsurge in the exchange and dissemination of information.

Although treaties may be part of a regime—as the Nuclear Nonproliferation Treaty is of the nonproliferation regime—they are not necessary for it to exist. Sometimes an international organization may become part of a regime, as is the World Trade Organization in the case of the international trade regime, but such an organization may play only a small role or no role at all. Commonly regimes include a variety of actor types. For example, humanitarian and human rights groups play a key role in the human rights regime, as do international organizations, especially the United Nations, and, as we shall see, U.N.-sponsored treaties are essential elements in this regime. In sum, an international regime mixes "multilateral systems of rules and procedures"[91] and "norms, rules, and procedures agreed to in order to regulate an issue-area."[92] Regimes, then, help overcome geographic distance and promote global integration.

Types of Regimes   Regimes have been identified for issues as varied as food assistance, trade, whaling, ozone depletion, drug trafficking, telecommunications, banking, human rights, and piracy.[93] Egoistic actors have not only learned to cooperate in these issues but have come to see their interests as served by binding norms and rules.[94] Security regimes have even been identified where one would least expect to find them because of actors' reluctance to entrust their survival to others. Writing in 1987, Joseph Nye defined U.S.-Soviet relations "as a patchwork quilt, or a mosaic of subissues in the security area, some characterized by rules and institutions we would call regimes and others not."[95]

Regimes vary in several ways.[96] In some, norms and rules are binding; others allow actors to opt out under special circumstances; and still others are merely hortatory, not binding at all. Thus the prohibition against nuclear proliferation is regarded as binding on all who subscribe to the Nuclear Nonproliferation Treaty. In contrast, the European Union allows individual members to veto actions they regard as contrary to their essential interests.

Another distinction is between regimes that can enforce obedience to rules and those that only monitor compliance. As Iraq discovered after invading Kuwait, the U.N. Security Council can enforce its decisions if it elects to do so. But the International Atomic Energy Agency (IAEA) mostly monitors compliance with international norms and rules, as illustrated by North Korea's ability to get around or prevent IAEA inspections. Still weaker are regimes that can only bring participants together and facilitate cooperation without monitoring or enforcing, or that can only provide information about the content of norms and rules.

Regimes reduce anarchy and facilitate cooperation among independent actors by compensating for "institutional deficiencies,"[97] such as absence of information and a framework of conventional law. Robert Keohane writes:

> Regimes . . . enhance the likelihood of cooperation by reducing the costs of making transactions that are consistent with the principles of the regime. They create the conditions for orderly multilateral negotiations. . . . They . . . improve the quality of the information that governments receive. . . . [T]hey help to bring governments into continuing interaction with one another, reducing incentives to cheat and enhancing the value of reputation. By establishing legitimate standards of behavior for states to follow and by providing ways to monitor compliance, they create the basis for decentralized enforcement founded on the principle of reciprocity.[98]

Imagine how much easier it would be for prisoner's dilemma players to cooperate if they could freely communicate their intentions and had some way of penalizing each other for squealing. That is what an effective regime does for participants. Without a regime, reciprocity is difficult with more than two actors because of the difficulty in assigning responsibility when conflict occurs and coordinating sanctions against a defector. Regimes help overcome these difficulties by providing "information about actors' compliance; they facilitate the development and maintenance of reputations; they can be incorporated into actors' rules of thumb for responding to others' actions; and they may even apportion responsibility for decentralized enforcement of rules."[99] In sum, an international regime governs an issue without a government. When the regime functions well, an issue features clear and consensual norms and is regulated by binding rules that, though perhaps not legislated by actors, exist by virtue of actual practice.

In international trade, for example, rules are clear on what individual actors are permitted to do to assist their exporters and protect home industries. Sometimes these rules are violated or tested to their limits. Nevertheless, they are observed surprisingly often by governments, when we consider the intense pressures placed on them by domestic industries and labor. Governments are constantly tempted to cheat but are discouraged from doing so because of the advantages they would forego by not participating in the trade regime and because of the probable retaliation of trading partners. Indeed, the recently created World Trade Organization (WTO) has rules that stipulate how victims of cheating may retaliate against cheaters, making the costs of cheating clear and, if those costs are high enough, reducing the temptation to do so.

Some argue that international regimes take root because actors are rational enough to recognize a long-term advantage in following rules and the costs in not doing so. Others argue that regimes are created and survive only in the presence of a superior power, a *hegemon* whose interests the regime serves and by whom it can be enforced. Finally, some claim that the real key to regime formation lies in hard bargaining among independent actors.[100] Related to the debate about how a regime is created is disagreement about how institutionalized rules and norms must be for a regime to exist. Some think that a regime exists only when norms and rules are incorporated in formal international organizations or legal documents like treaties. In this view, a regime requires formal consent by those who are part of it, and power has more to do with creating it than rationality. Others claim that a regime is virtually identical with any system of interdependent actors, so that "a regime exists in every substantive issue-area where there is discernibly patterned behavior."[101]

In this perspective, a regime requires no formal arrangements or agreements; custom and habit are sufficient. For those who hold this view, the rational pursuit of interest is sufficient to explain why actors form and maintain regimes; power has a smaller role.

In all likelihood, power, rationality, and bargaining all take part in creating and maintaining a regime. Power is involved because some actor or actors must provide leadership. But power, in the sense that one actor is able to enforce obedience to regime norms, is probably not sufficient to maintain a regime in the long run unless it is perceived to serve common interests. Finally, bargaining is essential if rules are to be sufficiently clear and consensual for a regime to endure and adapt to changing conditions.

This debate matters because some of the most important regimes in global politics, especially those of an economic variety, were created with U.S. leadership immediately after World War II. At that moment, the United States sat alone atop the global hierarchy and was able to create and enforce the rules and norms it wished. Under U.S. leadership, agencies like the International Monetary Fund and the World Bank were created, and a liberal international economic order based on free trade was instituted. The system was hegemonic—a system "in which one state is able and willing to determine and maintain the essential rules by which relations among states are governed. The hegemonical state not only can abrogate existing rules or prevent the adoption of rules that it opposes but can also play the dominant role in constructing new rules."[102]

In recent decades, the U.S. hegemony has receded. What does this portend for the future of regimes? If they require powerful hegemons to survive, then the complex norms that provide coordination for issues like international trade, nuclear proliferation, and pollution may decline, and the world will be a more dangerous place. By contrast, if hegemonic leadership is unnecessary, then we can expect arrangements that are useful to continue to flourish and new regimes to come into existence. The world is grappling with a host of complex problems, ranging from trade negotiations to whaling quotas, that will test these divergent views. Only time will tell which perspective is correct.

Nuclear Proliferation and the Environment

A brief discussion of two regimes—one that has existed for some time and another only now forming—illustrates how regimes produce cooperation in the face of common global problems. An international regime to limit the spread of nuclear weapons (horizontal nuclear proliferation) has evolved slowly in the past thirty years. The first step was an agreement to outlaw atmospheric testing of nuclear weapons (the Limited Test Ban Treaty), later extended to outlaw all nuclear testing (the Comprehensive Test Ban Treaty of 1996). This limitation restricted the number of states permitted to test weapons and therefore develop their own. The next step was to create several nuclear-free regions or zones where nuclear weapons could not be deployed. Nuclear weapons were prohibited in the Antarctic (the Antarctic Treaty of 1959), Latin America (the Latin American Nuclear Free Zone Treaty of 1967), outer space (the Outer Space Treaty of 1967), and the seabed (Seabed Arms Control Treaty of 1971). The most important step was a treaty prohibiting transfer of nuclear-weapons technology by the nuclear haves to states that do not have nuclear weapons and calling for international inspection of peaceful nuclear facilities to ensure that they are not being used surreptitiously to produce nuclear weapons (the Nuclear Nonproliferation Treaty of 1968 and its 1995 renewal). Finally, agreement was reached to ban chemical weapons, and several understandings, agreements, and prohibitions were placed on transferring of nuclear-energy and missile technology and nuclear fuels among states.

Collectively, these agreements and understandings have established a broad global norm against nuclear proliferation. Although agreements are voluntary, the regime has largely worked. Only two states (India and Pakistan) have publicly joined the nuclear club since the regime was established, and one (South Africa) has publicly given up nuclear ambitions. Nevertheless, the regime has not been strong enough to prevent nuclear competition between such adversaries as India and Pakistan. That North Korea and Iraq were able to divert nuclear fuel from peaceful purposes to develop nuclear weapons suggests that the inspection system operated by the IAEA is far from foolproof, and North Korea's defiance of the IAEA was a challenge to the future of the regime.

More recently, a regime has emerged to protect and promote global ecology. The U.N. Conference on the Environment and Development (UNCED), also known as the Earth Summit, held in Rio de Janeiro, Brazil, in June 1992 was a major step toward creating such a regime. The results of the conference were encouraging, though hardly decisive. Two conventions were signed, and the conferees published three declarations. However, the norms they include may signal the beginning of an important international regime.[103]

The first agreement was a Declaration on Environment and Development stating twenty-seven principles that link efforts to protect the environment with the promotion of global economic development. The declaration recognized that less-developed countries must bear a special burden in protecting their fragile ecosystems while developing economically. A second declaration, entitled Agenda 21, was even broader, articulating a commitment to clean up the environment and leave it in better condition in the coming century. A third declaration was more specific and dealt with principles to protect forests worldwide. It called upon countries to evaluate the effect of economic development on forests and act to protect that valuable resource for the future. Although these declarations are nonbinding, they establish norms and expectations toward which countries must strive and which, if flagrantly flouted, will elicit widespread disapproval.

The two conventions, a biodiversity treaty and a global-warming treaty, entail more binding commitments for signatories, but they also leave room for extension and expansion in the future. The biodiversity treaty calls for assembling a world inventory of plants and animals and for making plans to protect endangered species. Under the agreement, the signatories must share "research, profits, and technology with nations whose genetic resources they use," a clause that the Bush administration invoked to explain America's initial refusal to sign the treaty.[104] The Clinton administration reversed this stand, and the treaty took effect in 1994. The global-warming treaty recommends, but does not explicitly require, curbing the various "greenhouse gases"—carbon dioxide, methane, and chlorofluorocarbons—and follow-up conferences to specify national goals for reducing emission of these gases have been held. Again, not all countries signed the treaty, agreed on the target dates for reducing these gases, or accepted the targets for specific emissions reductions. Other environmental agreements include ending the production and use of chemicals responsible for harming the ozone layer and fighting desertification.

At best, the ecology regime is growing by fits and starts. Meeting two years after the Rio conference, the U.N. Commission on Sustainable Development concluded that the global community was providing insufficient funds and expertise to foster environmental reforms in the developing world.[105] Nor has substantial progress been made in reducing global carbon dioxide emissions that cause global warming.[106] Four years after the Rio conference, the U.N. Commission on Sustainable Development met in New York to prepare for a review of progress since 1992. Although fear was expressed that other issues were diverting attention from the environment, the British Secretary of the Environment captured the essence of the young regime when he said: "We are accepting as a world community that there are to be world rules."[107]

Conclusion

The claim that global politics is conflict-ridden is only half true. Conflict and cooperation are both common features of global politics. Cooperation requires only a mix of common and divergent interests in which such factors as reciprocity and bargaining help actors identify what they have in common and overcome that which separates them. When these conditions are present, processes of integration dominate those of fragmentation in global politics. Although global politics lacks a central authority that can monopolize coercion and coordinate behavior, much of what goes on in the global arena features cooperation and coordination. Large areas of global interaction are so routinized and function so smoothly that they are regarded as humdrum and make the front pages or the evening news only when something goes wrong.

Much of global politics is governed by norms that define what is proper and that create stable expectations. Such expectations are crucial to cooperation and trust. At one extreme are epochs and issues governed by international law and international regimes. At the other, where norms are absent, we encounter dark ages of peril and violence. For this reason we explore in Chapters 10 and 11 the changing role of force in global politics. Force is the hallmark of conflict and self-help, the negation of community and trust, and a major symptom of fragmentation in global politics.

Key Terms

analogies from the past
bargaining reputation
bluffing

chicken game
concern about the future
cooperation

crimes against humanity
crimes against peace
dual-track decision

end-of-the-world game

games

global norms

hegemon

historical experience

history of rewarding cooperation

intelligence failures

International Criminal Court
(ICC)

international law

international regime

learning

Nuremberg trials

one-shot game

payoffs

players

reciprocity

rules of the game

salami tactics

self-help

society of states

special relationship

strategies

variable-sum game

war crimes

worst-case analysis

zero option

zero-sum game

End Notes

[1]See Adam Watson, *The Evolution of International Society* (New York: Routledge, 1992), pp. 311–318.

[2]K. J. Holsti, *The Dividing Discipline* (Boston: Allen & Unwin, 1985), pp. 8–9.

[3]Those who believe in the possibility of cooperation under anarchy are sometimes labeled *liberals*. For a summary of liberal theory, see Mark W. Zacher and Richard A. Matthews, "Liberal International Theory: Common Threads, Divergent Strands," in Charles W. Kegley, Jr., ed., *Controversies in International Relations Theory* (New York: St. Martin's Press, 1995), pp. 107–150.

[4]See James M. McCormick, "Intergovernmental Organization and Cooperation Among Nations," *International Studies Quarterly* 24:1 (March 1980), pp. 75–98.

[5]According to the liberal economic tradition associated with Adam Smith, the pursuit by individuals of selfish interests in a free market is transformed into general prosperity by an "invisible hand." The liberal tradition in economics and politics in which Smith was so influential stresses the individual and the primacy of private enterprise, and is optimistic about the prospect for progress.

[6]See E. H. Carr, *The Twenty Years' Crisis 1919-1939* (New York: St. Martin's Press, 1962).

[7]Jean-Jacques Rousseau, "Abstract of the Abbé de Saint-Pierre's Project for Perpetual Peace," in M.G. Forsyth, H.M.A. Keens-Soper, P. Savigear, eds., *The Theory of International Relations* (New York: Atherton Press, 1970), p. 135.

[8]Ibid.

[9]Ibid., p. 136.

[10]Zero-sum means that the total of gains and losses equals zero.

[11]There are many kinds of variable-sum games. In some, all players win (positive-sum games), and in others all lose (negative-sum games). In most, some players lose and others win.

[12]The U.S. role in building a coalition against Iraq in 1990 reflects the claim of theorists that cooperation among actors is made possible by "dominant, hegemonic, or core powers" because "would-be cooperators can elect to cooperate secure in the knowledge that the dominant power will prevent their exploitation; would-be defectors are deterred by the expectation that the dominant power will sanction defection." Joanne Gowa, "Anarchy, Egoism, and Third Images: The Evolution of Cooperation in International Relations," *International Organization* 40:1 (Winter 1986), p. 174.

[13]For a cogent analysis of the "congruence and discontinuity" between regional and global systems, see Oran R. Young, "Political Discontinuities in the International System," *World Politics* 20:3 (April 1968), pp. 369–392.

[14]Thomas Hobbes, *Leviathan, Parts I and II* (Indianapolis: Bobbs-Merrill, 1958), pp. 106–107.

[15]See Thomas C. Schelling, *Arms and Influence* (New Haven: Yale University Press, 1966), pp. 116–125; and Glenn H. Snyder and Paul Diesing, *Conflict Among Nations* (Princeton: Princeton University Press, 1977), pp. 107–122.

[16]A hot-rodder who uses this tactic had better do so before his adversary. If he waits to throw away his steering wheel until after the other driver does so, he will commit suicide. Thomas Schelling refers to the principle of "last clear chance." He writes: "In strategy when both parties abhor collision the advantage goes often to the one who arranges the status quo in his favor and leaves to the other the 'last clear chance' to stop or turn aside" (*Arms and Influence*, pp. 44–45).

[17]Robert Jervis, *Perception and Misperception in International Politics* (Princeton: Princeton University Press, 1976), p. 59.

[18]See Richard W. Mansbach and John A. Vasquez, *In Search of Theory: A New Paradigm for Global Politics* (New York: Columbia University Press, 1981), pp. 234–240.

[19]The Russo-Japanese War was a disaster for Russia's Tsarist

government and triggered revolutionary currents in 1905 that were a foretaste of 1917.

[20]The Japanese were agreed about the need to maintain influence in Manchuria against the forces of Chinese nationalism that had rallied around Jiang Jieshi, but Japan's civilian cabinet sought to use peaceful means to do so.

[21]The puppet ruler of Manchukuo was Pu-yi, the "last emperor" of China, who is depicted in a film with that name. The United States refused to recognize Manchukuo.

[22]Suspicion grew so strong that U.S. Secretary of State Cordell Hull described Japan's Foreign Minister Matsuoka Yosuke as "crooked as a basket of fishhooks." Cited in John K. Fairbank, Edwin O. Reischauer, and Albert M. Craig, *East Asia: The Modern Transformation* (Boston: Houghton Mifflin, 1965), p. 608.

[23]The colonial powers in Asia were Britain (Singapore, Hong Kong, India, Burma, Ceylon), France (Indochina), Holland (Indonesia), and the United States (the Philippines). Other than Japan, Thailand was the only major Asian society that escaped Western colonization.

[24]By this time Holland had been occupied by the Germans, but Dutch administrators continued to govern the Dutch East Indies (Indonesia).

[25]Cited in Robert Butow, *Tojo and the Coming of War* (Princeton: Princeton University Press, 1961), p. 280.

[26]Robert Axelrod and Robert O. Keohane, "Achieving Cooperation Under Anarchy: Strategies and Institutions," *World Politics* 38:1 (October 1985), p. 232.

[27]Hedley Bull, *The Anarchical Society: A Study of Order in World Politics* (New York: Columbia University Press, 1977), p. 13.

[28]Joshua Goldstein and John Freeman, *Three-Way Street: Strategic Reciprocity in World Politics* (Chicago: University of Chicago Press, 1990), p. 154.

[29]If agreements are imposed rather than voluntary, the rate of defection will be higher.

[30]Robert O. Keohane, "Reciprocity in International Relations," *International Organization* 40:1 (Winter 1986), p. 8. Emphasis omitted. Empirical support for the power of reciprocity is extensive. See, for example, Russell J. Leng, "Influence Techniques in Militarized Crises: Realpolitik versus Reciprocity," in Frank W. Wayman and Paul F. Diehl, eds., *Reconstructing Realpolitik* (Ann Arbor: University of Michigan Press, 1994), pp. 125-160.

[31]Axelrod and Keohane, "Achieving Cooperation," p. 235.

[32]Ibid., p. 232.

[33]Ibid., p. 233. See also Charles Lipson, "Bankers' Dilemmas: Private Cooperation in Rescheduling Sovereign Debts," *World Politics* 38:1 (October 1985), pp. 200-225.

[34]If people cease believing such myths, unity will suffer. The debate over "multiculturalism" in U.S. education reveals growing doubts about America's myths; the collapse of the U.S.S.R. followed a long period in which the "heroes" of Bolshevism were shown to have feet of clay.

[35]With an eye to how history will treat them, statesmen try to show that they remain faithful to their society's values. Attorney General Robert Kennedy may have had this in mind when, in discussing the possibility of attacking Soviet installations in Cuba during the 1962 missile crisis, he passed his brother, the president, a note reading: "I now know how Tojo felt when he was planning Pearl Harbor." Robert F. Kennedy, *Thirteen Days* (New York: Norton, 1968), p. 9.

[36]If they fail to do so, however, the resulting schism may be more serious because of a mutual sense of betrayal by a long-time friend. Sino-Soviet relations in the late 1960s and 1970s saw such a sense of betrayal following their falling out after two decades of Marxist-Leninist "fraternal" cooperation.

[37]Ernest R. May, *"Lessons" of the Past: The Use and Misuse of History in American Foreign Policy* (New York: Oxford University Press, 1973), p. ix.

[38]See Richard E. Neustadt and Ernest R. May, *Thinking in Time: The Uses of History for Decision Makers* (New York: Free Press, 1986).

[39]Cited in Francis L. Loewenheim, ed., *Peace or Appeasement?* (Boston: Houghton Mifflin, 1965), p. 55. Hitler intuitively knew how to take advantage of this longing for peace. See Alan Bullock, *Hitler and Stalin: Parallel Lives* (New York: Knopf, 1991), p. 524.

[40]John W. Wheeler-Bennett, *Munich: Prologue to Tragedy* (New York: Viking Press, 1964), p. 269.

[41]Gordon H. Chang, "To the Nuclear Brink: Eisenhower, Dulles, and the Quemoy-Matsu Crisis," *International Security* 12:4 (Spring 1988), p. 97.

[42]Neil Sheehan, ed., *The Pentagon Papers* (New York: Bantam Books, 1971), p. 432.

[43]See Kenneth A. Oye, "Explaining Cooperation Under Anarchy: Hypotheses and Strategies," *World Politics* 38:1 (October 1985), p. 9, for a discussion of "strategies to alter the payoff structure."

[44]This repudiation included the limitation on the size of military forces that the treaty had imposed on Germany after 1919.

[45]The Rhineland, on the west bank of the Rhine River, was demilitarized to prevent Germany from posing another threat to France.

[46]The union of Austria and Germany—called *Anschluss*—was forbidden by the Versailles Treaty.

[47]John Maynard Keynes, *The Economic Consequences of the Peace* (New York: Harper & Row, 1971), pp. 111-112.

[48]Hitler's pose as an enemy of Bolshevism also appealed to some Western leaders. For an analysis of the development of Hitler's ideas, see Ian Kershaw, *Hitler 1898-1936: Hubris* (New York: Norton, 1999).

[49]Schelling, *Arms and Influence*, pp. 66-67.

[50]Hitler's views, virulent with racism, were available for anyone to read. During the year (1923-1924) when he was in prison

for seeking to overthrow the German government, he wrote *Mein Kampf (My Struggle)*. Few of his opponents chose to take him seriously, perhaps because, as one historian writes, his ideas were "written in a verbose style which is both difficult and dull to read." Alan Bullock, *Hitler, A Study in Tyranny,* rev. ed. (New York: Harper & Row, 1964), p. 121.

[51]When Gorbachev took power, the United States and Soviet Union were supporting rival political factions in Nicaragua, El Salvador, Afghanistan, Angola, Ethiopia, and Cambodia. By the early 1990s, all these conflicts had been resolved or muted.

[52]See James Schlesinger, "Reykjavik and Revelations: A Turn of the Tide?" *Foreign Affairs* 65:3 (1987), pp. 426–446.

[53]The series of reciprocal concessions after 1985 resembles the proposal advanced by psychologist Charles Osgood: graduated reduction in tension (GRIT). Osgood, *An Alternative to War or Surrender* (Urbana: University of Illinois Press, 1962).

[54]NATO planned to deploy 572 Pershing 2 and ground-launched cruise missiles (GLCMs) in West Germany, Britain, Italy, Belgium, and the Netherlands. Even after their deployment, the U.S.S.R. would still have enjoyed a numerical advantage in intermediate-range missiles.

[55]Lynn E. Davis, "Lessons of the INF Treaty," *Foreign Affairs* 66:4 (Spring 1988), p. 727.

[56]As the U.S.S.R. was engulfed by domestic conflict in 1991, the Bush administration worried that short-range nuclear weapons stationed by the Soviet military on land and sea in the Soviet republics might fall into the wrong hands. The U.S. offer, it was believed, would make it possible for the Soviet Union to withdraw these weapons and eliminate this danger.

[57]Serge Schmemann, "Gorbachev Matches U.S. on Nuclear Cuts and Goes Further on Strategic Warheads," *New York Times,* October 6, 1991, sec. 1, p. 1.

[58]Baroness Orczy, *The Elusive Pimpernel* (New York: Buccaneer Books, 1984), p. 245. Charles Dickens in *A Tale of Two Cities* (New York: Harper & Brothers, n.d.) wrote: "Above all, one hideous figure as familiar as if it had been before the general gaze from the foundations of the world—the figure of the sharp female called La Guillotine" (p. 289).

[59]Edmund Burke, *Reflections on the Revolution in France* (Garden City, NY: Doubleday, 1961), pp. 50, 52, 91, 92. Emphasis in original.

[60]The Congress began in September 1814 but was interrupted by Napoleon's escape from exile on the island of Elba. After his final defeat at the Battle of Waterloo, Napoleon was removed to the remote Atlantic island of St. Helena, where he died.

[61]René Albrecht-Carrié, *The Concert of Europe* (New York: Harper & Row, 1968), p. 4.

[62]Joseph S. Nye, "Nuclear Learning and U.S.-Soviet Security Regime," *International Organization* 41:3 (Summer 1987), p. 392.

[63]J. L. Brierly, *The Law of Nations,* 5th ed. (New York: Oxford University Press, 1954), p. 1.

[64]Hugo Grotius, *Prolegomena to the Law of War and Peace* (New York: Bobbs-Merrill, 1957), p. 21.

[65]Hans J. Morgenthau, *Politics Among Nations: The Struggle for Power and Peace,* 6th ed., rev. Kenneth W. Thompson (New York: Knopf, 1985), p. 293.

[66]Dorothy V. Jones, "The Declaratory Tradition in Modern International Law," in Terry Nardin and David R. Mapel, eds., *Traditions of International Ethics* (Cambridge: Cambridge University Press, 1992), pp. 44–45.

[67]Hans Kelsen, *Principles of International Law,* 2nd ed., rev. Robert W. Tucker (New York: Holt, Rinehart and Winston, 1966), p. 340.

[68]Morgenthau, *Politics Among Nations,* p. 295.

[69]International law regards treaties as binding *(pacta sunt servanda)* but only as long as conditions do not change significantly *(rebus sic stantibus)*.

[70]Neil A. Lewis, "U.S. Backs War-Crimes Lawsuit Against Bosnian Serb Leader," *New York Times,* September 27, 1995, p. A8; "U.S. Court Allows Suit Against Bosnia Serbs," *New York Times,* October 14, 1995, p. 4.

[71]Stephen Kinzer, "Belgrade Warned on Genocide Issue," *New York Times,* September 14, 1993, p. A4.

[72]Jane Perlez, "Problems Hamper the Crime Inquiry in Bosnia Conflict," *New York Times,* January 28, 1996, sec. 1, pp. 1, 5. South African Supreme Court judge Richard J. Goldstone was finally chosen as chief prosecutor.

[73]Roger Cohen, "Ex-Guard for Serbs Tells of Grisley 'Cleansing' Camp," *New York Times,* August 1, 1994, pp. A1, A4; Roger Cohen, "C.I.A. Report Finds Serbs Guilty in Majority of Bosnia War Crimes," *New York Times,* March 9, 1995, pp. A1, A6.

[74]Its first conviction, a year later, was of a Croat who fought in the Bosnian Serb army. "Croat is First to Be Convicted by Balkan War Crimes Panel," *New York Times,* June 1, 1996, p. 6.

[75]Suspicion of Milosevic's complicity in atrocities grew with the indictment of three senior officers in the Serbian Army. Roger Cohen, "Tribunal Indicts 3 Serbia Officers," *New York Times,* November 10, 1995, pp. A1, A7; Stephen Engelberg, "Tribunal Asks U.S. for Pledge on War Crimes," *New York Times,* November 3, 1995, pp. A1, A5. By May 1996, 57 suspects had been indicted (46 Serbs, 8 Croats, and 3 Muslims), but only 3 were in custody. Chris Hedges, "First Hague Trial for Bosnia Crimes Opens on Tuesday," *New York Times,* May 6, 1996, pp. A1, A5.

[76]Marlise Simons, "U.N. Tribunal Indicts Bosnian Serb Chief," *New York Times,* July 26, 1995, p. A7.

[77]Elaine Sciolino, "Fate of 2 Bosnian Serb Leaders, Facing New Charges, Snags Talks," *New York Times,* November 17, 1995, pp. A1, A3. Initially, NATO forces in Bosnia made little effort to capture alleged war criminals. Chris Hedges, "Bosnia Limits War-Crimes Arrests After NATO Delivers 2 Suspects," *New York Times,* February 13, 1996, pp. A1, A6. A year later NATO did employ force in seeking to arrest a suspect. Chris Hedges,

"NATO Troops Kill a Serbian Suspect in War Atrocities," *New York Times*, July 11, 1997, pp. A1, A6.

[78]Tim Weiner, "U.S. Drops Plan to Raid Bosnia to Get 2 Serbs," *New York Times*, July 26, 1998, sec. 1, pp. 1, 8. Some of the accused had been arrested elsewhere in Europe. Alan Cowell, "A Croat, a Muslim and a Serb Are Held in Balkan War-Crimes Case," *New York Times*, March 20, 1996, p. A8.

[79]Richard D. Lyons, "U.N. Approves Tribunal for Rwandan Atrocities," *New York Times*, November 9, 1994, p. A6.

[80]Barbara Crossette, "U.N. to Extend Its Force in Rwanda for 3 Months," *New York Times*, December 13, 1995, p. A5. Some months later, two additional men jailed in Zambia were also indicted. James C. McKinley Jr., "Rwanda War Crimes Tribunal Indicts 2 Men in Jail in Zambia," *New York Times*, February 26, 1996, p. A5; "Rwanda Genocide Tribunal Hears First Two Defendants," *New York Times*, May 31, 1996, p. A4.

[81]Initially, Kenya did not cooperate with the tribunal, but foreign pressure made the Kenyan government more willing to help. Donatella Lorch, "Kenya Refuses to Hand Over Suspects in Rwanda Slayings," *New York Times*, October 6, 1995, p. A3; James C. McKinley Jr., "Kenya Arrests 7 Suspects in '94 Killings of Rwandans," *New York Times*, July 19, 1997, p. 4.

[82]"Rwanda to Execute 2 Hutu; First Verdict in '94 Killings," *New York Times*, January 4, 1997, p. 5; Stephen Buckley, "Trial and Error in Rwanda's Massacres," *Washington Post National Weekly Edition*, February 3, 1997, p. 18.

[83]"The World Tries Again," *The Economist*, March 11-17, 1995, pp. 21-23; Roger Cohen, "Tribunal to Cite Bosnia Serb Chief as War Criminal," *New York Times*, April 24, 1995, pp. A1, A6; Roger Cohen, "Bosnia Plight for the U.N.," *New York Times*, April 25, 1995, pp. A1, A3.

[84]Cited in Roger Cohen, "In the Dock: Balkan Nationalism," *New York Times*, April 30, 1995, p. 5.

[85]Cited in Neil A. Lewis, "Nuremberg Isn't Repeating Itself," *New York Times*, November 19, 1995, sec. 4, p. 5.

[86]"How Strong a Court?" *The Economist*, June 13-19, 1998, p. 46; "A New World Court," *The Economist*, June 13-19, 1998, pp. 16-17.

[87]Alessandra Stanley, "U.S. Specifies Terms for War Crimes Court," *New York Times*, July 10, 1998, p. A7.

[88]Cited in Jude Webber, "Annan calls for strong world court," *Yahoo News*, http:www.yahoo.com/h, July 15, 1998.

[89]The best-known formulation of an international regime is that of Stephen D. Krasner: "principles, norms, rules, and decision-making procedures" that are sufficiently clear to enable actors' expectations to "converge in a given issue-area." "Structural Causes and Regime Consequences: Regimes as Intervening Variables," *International Organization* 36:2 (Spring 1982), p. 185.

[90]Robert O. Keohane, *After Hegemony* (Princeton: Princeton University Press, 1984), p. 64. Some scholars argue that the concept of the international regime is wooly, hardly distinct from international law and organization. See Susan Strange, *"Cave! Hic dragones:* A Critique of Regime Analysis," *International Organization* 36:2 (Spring 1982), pp. 484-486. Those called constructivists believe that the identities and practices of actors based on intersubjective understanding are the bases of the norms associated with regimes. See Ted Hopf, "The Promise of Constructivism in International Relations Theory," *International Security* 23:1 (Summer 1998), pp. 188-191.

[91]Vinod K. Aggarwal, "The Unraveling of the Multifiber Agreement, 1981: An Examination of International Regime Change," *International Organization* 37:4 (Autumn 1983), p. 618.

[92]Ernst B. Haas, "Why Collaborate? Issue-Linkage and International Regimes," *World Politics* 32:3 (April 1980), p. 358.

[93]The literature on specific regimes has become huge. See, for example, Peter F. Cowhey, "The International Telecommunications Regime: The Political Roots of Regimes for High Technology," *International Organization* 44:2 (Spring 1990), pp. 169-199; Ethan A. Nadelmann, "Global Prohibition Regimes: The Evolution of Norms in International Society," *International Organization* 44:4 (Autumn 1990), pp. 479-526; Robert H. Bates, Philip Brock, and Jill Tiefenthaler, "Risk and Trade Regimes: Another Exploration," *International Organization* 45:1 (Winter 1991), pp. 1-18; Raymond F. Hopkins, "Reform in the International Food Aid Regime: The Role of Consensual Knowledge," *International Organization* 46:1 (Winter 1992), pp. 225-264.

[94]See Alexander Wendt, "Anarchy Is What States Make of It: The Social Construction of Power Politics," *International Organization* 46:2 (Spring 1992), p. 417. In this view, the structured features of a system, for example, the absence of world government, does *not* determine how actors behave.

[95]Nye, "Nuclear Learning," p. 376.

[96]For more on these distinctions, see Jack Donnelly, "International Human Rights: A Regime Analysis," *International Organization* 40:3 (Summer 1986), pp. 603-605.

[97]Keohane, *After Hegemony*, p. 85.

[98]Ibid., pp. 244-245.

[99]Axelrod and Keohane, "Achieving Cooperation," *World Politics* 38:1 (October 1985), p. 237.

[100]Oran R. Young, "The Politics of International Regime Formation: Managing Natural Resources and the Environment," *International Organization* 43:3 (Summer 1989), pp. 349-375.

[101]Donald J. Puchala and Raymond F. Hopkins, "International Regimes: Lessons from Inductive Analysis," *International Organization* 36:2 (Spring 1982), p. 247.

[102]C. Fred Bergsten, Robert O. Keohane, and Joseph S. Nye, "International Economics and International Politics: A Framework for Analysis," *International Organization* 29:1 (Winter 1975), p. 14.

[103]The summary of the Rio summit accords is from "Accords for Nature's Sake," *New York Times,* June 15, 1992, p. A5.

[104]The Bush administration feared that the clause would undermine the exclusive patents held by U.S. pharmaceutical companies.

[105]Paul Lewis, "U.N. Panel Finds Action on Environment Lagging," *New York Times,* May 29, 1994, p. 6.

[106]"Global Warming and Cooling Enthusiasm," *The Economist,* April 1-7, 1995, pp. 33-34.

[107]Cited in Barbara Crossette, "Other Issues Edging Out Environment," *New York Times,* May 5, 1996, sec. 1, p. 6.

Chapter 10

Force in Global Politics: A Changing Role

The study of war has occupied students of global politics for centuries. This is a consequence of the widespread belief that war is inevitable in a system lacking central authority. In this view, force is to be regretted but must be expected as a consequence of the right of self-help. Because independent actors can depend on no one but themselves to survive, they must be armed and alert. Wrote Machiavelli: "The main foundations of every state ... are good laws and good arms."[1]

> A prince, therefore, should have no other object or thought, nor acquire skill in anything, except war, its organization, and its discipline. ... The first way to lose your state is to neglect the art of war; the first way to win a state is to be skilled in the art of war.[2]

Even political economist Adam Smith acknowledged that "the one thing more important than opulence is defense."[3]

In the next two chapters we examine force in global politics, how its use has changed, and its influence on the human condition. In this chapter we look at changes in the frequency, intensity, and nature of war; factors that contribute to war's outbreak; how technology affects the frequency and conduct of war; and some of the consequences for society of preparing for war. In the next chapter, we address how warfare has changed with nuclear weapons. Let us begin by seeing whether there have been changes in the number and magnitude of wars and by sampling several explanations for the outbreak of war.

The Nature of War

Rarely has the world been free of *war*—organized violence between armed groups—though the sort of global conflict that shatters a political order and remakes world politics has, thankfully, been infrequent. Examples of such conflicts over the past four centuries include the Thirty Years' War (1618-1648), the wars of the French Revolution and Napoleon (1792-1815), World War I (1914-1918), and World War II (1939-1945). Despite the ideological competition that engulfed the

TABLE 10.1
*Frequency of
International Wars*

Period	Number of years	Number of wars
1816–1849	34	21
1850–1870	21	20
1871–1890	20	12
1891–1914	24	20
1917–1940	24	16
1945–1965	20	14
1966–1980	14	16

SOURCE: The number of wars in each period is calculated from Melvin Small and J. David Singer, "Patterns in International Warfare, 1816-1980," in Small and Singer, eds., *International War: An Anthology* (Chicago: Dorsey Press, 1989), Table 1, pp. 28–30. Copyright 1982 Sage Publications. Reprinted with permission of Sage Publications, Inc.

world during the Cold War, we have been spared a similar cataclysm since, but recent decades have been neither peaceful nor bloodless. Although recent years have witnessed few interstate wars, there have been many bloody civil wars, for example, in the former Yugoslavia and Rwanda.

**Frequency of War:
The Historical Record**

To put the current period in perspective, we review briefly the frequency and magnitude of wars in recent centuries. The best-known compilation of war-related data was developed by the Correlates of War (COW) Project directed by political scientist J. David Singer. Singer and historian Melvin Small collected and coded data on civil and international wars from 1816 to 1980. These data allow us to generalize about changes in war during this period.

Table 10.1 summarizes the number of wars during seven historical eras. The first—1816-1849—demarcates the era after the Congress of Vienna and prior to the era of revolutionary change that began in 1848. The second—1850-1870—was a period of flux in world affairs during which Italy and Germany were united. The third—1871-1890—saw the ascendancy of Bismarckian Germany in world politics. The fourth—1891-1914—witnessed a hardening of alliance systems in Europe, culminating in World War I. The fifth—1919-1940—saw the ascent of Hitler and Mussolini, and the final period—1966-1980—was the height of the Cold War.[4]

Although Table 10.1 indicates a slight decline in wars, Singer and Small report that "no trend, either upward or downward, is evident. . . . [W]e do not find appreciably more or less war in any of the sub-epochs covered."[5] Although more people died from wars in the twentieth century than in the nineteenth, in a relative sense—considering population growth—the apparently greater severity of recent warfare disappears. What about civil wars during the same time period? Again, Singer and Small provide systematic evidence, and as Table 10.2 shows, they conclude that such wars have neither increased nor decreased significantly during the period. Although the years after 1945 saw a growing number of civil wars, especially as part of decolonization, their absolute growth is not as great as it appears because more states were entering global politics and the opportunity for civil strife was greater.[6]

By extending our time horizon beyond the two centuries that Singer and Small consider, we reach a different conclusion. Over five centuries, the frequency of

TABLE 10.2
Frequency of Civil Wars, 1816–1977

Period	Number of years	Number of wars
1816–1849	34	12
1850–1870	21	15
1871–1890	20	6
1891–1914	24	17
1919–1939	21	11
1946–1965	20	26
1966–1977	12	11

SOURCE: From Table 4 in Melvin Small and J. David Singer, "Conflict in the International System, 1816–1977: Historical Trends and Policy Futures," in Charles W. Kegley, Jr., and Patrick J. McGowan, *Challenges to America: United States Foreign Policy in the 1980s.* Copyright © 1979 by Sage Publications. Used with permission.

war has declined. And if we count only wars involving great powers, the decline is even more pronounced. "The number of Great Power wars," declares Jack Levy, "declined continuously from the sixteenth to the nineteenth centuries, with a very slight increase in the twentieth century." The number of such wars "has been only one-fourth as frequent in the twentieth century as in the sixteenth century."[7] According to Levy's analysis, the sixteenth and seventeenth centuries were the most warlike, the eighteenth the least, and the nineteenth and twentieth centuries roughly the same in war frequency.[8] Although these data suggest a decline in the frequency of war, their severity (measured by war deaths) has remained about the same. Great-power wars, though less frequent, have become more severe (see Table 10.3). Levy concludes that the frequency of war has declined somewhat but the human costs of war have remained much the same. The two world wars in this century embroiled entire societies, and with nuclear, chemical, and biological weapons, future wars could threaten our survival.

War Since 1945

A closer look at the period since World War II provides more clues about changing warfare. Between 1945 and 1990, 140 wars took 25 million lives.[9] Unlike earlier eras, war since 1945 has been almost absent from developed regions like Europe and North America but has become endemic in the less-developed countries. "War today . . .," one observer writes, "is a phenomenon generally limited to the non-European (non-white) peoples of this planet."[10] Table 10.4 shows that Asia has been the bloodiest region, including major wars in Korea and Vietnam. The Middle East, North Africa, and Muslim regions in South Asia have been almost as war-prone, with major conflicts involving the Arab states, Pakistan, and Afghanistan.

Although the number of interstate wars is declining, the frequency of civil strife is growing.[11] *Since 1993, most major armed conflicts taking place around the world have been "intrastate."*[12] Indeed, as state boundaries erode, the distinction between civil and interstate wars is blurring. As the conflicts between Hutu and Tutsi in Central Africa suggest, we are beginning to witness *transnational wars* in which adversaries who are citizens of the same state(s) fight one another in the territories of several countries and move across frontiers with ease. Civil wars are also becoming bloodier as citizens use modern arms that were originally acquired

TABLE 10.3
The Bloodiest Interstate Wars, 1816–1988

War and dates	Estimated battle deaths
1. World War II (1939–1945)	15,000,000
2. World War I (1914–1918)	9,000,000
3. Korean War (1950–1953)	2,900,000
4. Vietnam War (1965–1973)	2,058,000
5. Iran-Iraq (1980–1988)	1,500,000
6. Sino-Japanese War (1937–1941)	1,000,000
7. Russo-Turkish War (1877–1878)	285,000
8. Crimean War (1853–1856)	264,200
9. Franco-Prussian War (1870–1871)	187,500
10. Chaco War (1932–1935)	130,000
10. Russo-Japanese War (1904–1905)	130,000
10. Russo-Turkish War (1828–1829)	130,000

SOURCE: J. David Singer and Melvin Small, *The Wages of War 1816–1965: A Statistical Handbook* (New York: Wiley, 1972), Table 4.2., pp. 60–69; and Michael J. Sullivan III, *Measuring Global Values: The Ranking of 162 Countries* (New York: Greenwood Press, 1991), Table VI.1a, pp. 35–38.

TABLE 10.4
Wars Since 1945

Zone[a]	Wars	Interstate	Colonial	Civil	Deaths
Europe	5	3	0	2	0.0 million
Islamic	37	10	4	23	5.3 million
Africa	26	2	7	17	4.5 million
Asia	46	14	5	27	17.0 million
Latin America	27	6	0	21	0.6 million
Totals	141	35	16	90	27.6 million

[a]The five zones, taken from Sullivan, correspond to continental divisions with the exception of "Islamic," which includes the Arab Middle East (including Israel and Cyprus), northern Africa (including Chad, Sudan, Djibouti, and Somalia), and west Asia (including Iran, Afghanistan, and Pakistan).

SOURCE: From *Measuring Global Values* by Michael J. Sullivan III, pp. 35–38, Greenwood Press, an imprint of Greenwood Publishing Group, Inc., Westport, CT. Reprinted with permission.

to fight other armies. Civil war in the former Yugoslavia after 1992 epitomized the destructiveness of modern weaponry in urban settings by devastating cities like Sarajevo, Mostar, and Dubrovnik. Cities such as Mogadishu in Somalia and Grozny in Chechnya were also all but leveled. In President Bill Clinton's words, "The end of Communism . . . lifted the lid on age-old conflicts rooted in ethnic, racial and religious hatreds. These forces can be all the more destructive today because they have access to modern technology."[13]

Civil war has always been less restrained than interstate war. International law, embodied in instruments like the Geneva Conventions, applies only to interstate wars and places no limits on combatants in civil wars. Atrocities like those in Kosovo would be unthinkable in wars between most states. The Nigerian civil war between 1967 and 1970 and the civil war in Cambodia between 1975 and 1978 (portrayed in the movie *Killing Fields*) are among the most savage conflicts since 1945. The first is estimated to have cost 2 million lives and the second 1 to 1.5 million (of a population of 8 million).[14]

Causes of War

For social scientists, explaining why wars occur is as elusive as the search for a cure to cancer is for medical researchers. There is probably more than one cause, and their impact is likely to vary depending on such factors as type of war, place, and era. Thus no single explanation is likely to prove adequate for all cases. Recognizing that war has multiple causes, our review is not intended to be exhaustive. Rather, the aim is to give readers the flavor of the varied theorizing that goes on in global politics about this issue. For the sake of clarity, we organize these theories into three clusters—those emphasizing the behavior of individuals, those dealing with societies and governments, and those focusing on the global system as a whole.[15] In practice, insights from all three are probably necessary to understand war. Thus John A. Vasquez combines variables from the second and third clusters when he concludes: "In the modern state system one of the main sets of factors that brings about war among equals is the rise of territorial disputes, particularly between neighbors, that in the absence or failure of a global institutional network to resolve the issue politically makes actors resort to the unilateral solutions provided by power politics."[16]

Individuals and Aggression

The contention that the causes of war must be sought in individuals rather than in states or whole systems is not new. Political theorists long ago identified *human nature* as the source of violence in human affairs, and some religious thinkers like St. Augustine maintain that "man's fallen nature," along with original sin, also contributes. More recently, biologists and psychologists have focused on aggressive behavior. Sigmund Freud, in a pessimistic letter to Albert Einstein in 1932, posited a *thanatos* or *death instinct:*

> We assume the human instincts are of two kinds: those that conserve and unify . . . and . . . the instincts to destroy and kill. . . . [T]his latter instinct functions in every living being, striving to work its ruin and reduce life to its primal state of inert matter.[17]

Others have focused on the relationship between *aggression* and *frustration.* Aggressive behavior, one team of psychologists argues, "always presupposes the existence of frustration and . . . the existence of frustration always leads to some form of aggression."[18] A number of studies suggest that the aggression produced by frustration may be "displaced" onto innocent victims or scapegoats, such as minorities or foreigners.[19] Much of this thinking seems remote from war but is not. Soldiers can be encouraged by war propaganda to displace aggressive feelings onto an enemy who is depersonalized, and they do not hesitate to commit acts in wartime that they might regard as repugnant in peacetime. Thus the most decorated American soldier in World War I, Sergeant Alvin C. York, had been a conscientious objector.

Most people do not question authority and are willing to obey orders. Experiments conducted by Stanley Milgram to find out whether individuals would obey orders requiring them to inflict pain revealed that most were prepared to do so. Although willingness varied, depending on a variety of factors, those who were tested routinely gave electric shocks to victims when ordered to do so. This result disappoints those who believe "it can't happen here" because the United States is a democracy in which individual liberties have legal protection. Milgram says,

> With numbing regularity good people were seen to knuckle under to the demands of authority.... If in this study an anonymous experimenter could successfully command adults to subdue a fifty-year-old man, and force on him painful electric shocks against his protests, one can only wonder what government, with its vastly greater authority and prestige, can command of its subjects.[20]

Still others are convinced that aggression, whether of leaders or followers, is related to gender. Most societies are controlled by males, and males are typically more aggressive than females. The roots of this difference may lie in early conditioning or in brain and hormonal factors. Dr. Helen Caldicott sums up this perspective:

> Men and women are psychologically and physiologically different.... Typically,... men are always sure of themselves;... above all, they are always tough and strong.... A typical woman ... innately understands the basic principles of conflict resolution.... Women are nurturers. Their bodies are built anatomically and physiologically to nurture life.... [M]ost women care deeply about the preservation of life.[21]

Theorists like Caldicott point out that much of the vocabulary of nuclear deterrence reflects male sexuality—"spasm war," "penetration aids," and so forth. When all is said and done, soldiers fight for a variety of motives—adventure, comradeship, patriotism, ideology, professional satisfaction, religion, and honor.[22]

Perhaps we should look less at "followers" than at "leaders," who give orders. After all, politics involves struggles for status, and those who succeed may be more aggressive than those who do not. In recent years, greater use has been made of individual and social psychology to understand political elites.[23] Using Freudian insights, psychobiographies have been written delineating leaders' unique personality attributes. A psychobiography of President Woodrow Wilson concludes that he was unwilling to compromise with political foes because of his childhood competition with his father. As a child, the authors argue, Wilson was forced to repress his rebelliousness; consequently, as an adult, he "could brook no interference.... He bristled at the slightest challenge to his authority."[24]

Much research on leaders and their relationship to war has focused on impediments to rationality. As we noted in Chapter 6, scholars have identified cognitive and affective sources of perceptual distortion that reduce rational capacity. Cognitive analysis focuses on the way in which leaders obtain and process information, and affective analysis emphasizes emotional factors like hostility in decisions.[25] Among scholars seeking the sources of cognitive distortion, some have studied ethnocentrism—belief that one's own group is superior—as a factor behind misunderstanding.[26] Others emphasize the need for *cognitive consistency*—balance between feelings about and attitudes toward a phenomenon and the information that is received about it.

Psychological discomfort ensues when facts seem to deny the validity of those feelings, and leaders may skew the facts to make them compatible with affect. As Robert Jervis writes, "Evidence is being ignored, misremembered, or twisted to preserve old ideas."[27]

Although many observers believe that leaders' personality attributes influence the outbreak of war, little systematic research has been conducted on these factors. Margaret G. Hermann's research on forty-five leaders, including France's Charles De Gaulle, Cuba's Fidel Castro, and China's Chou En-Lai, suggests that "aggressive leaders are high in need for power, low in conceptual complexity, distrustful of others, nationalistic, and likely to believe that they have some control over the events in which they are involved. . . . [C]onciliatory leaders are high in the need for affiliation, high in conceptual complexity, trusting in others, low in nationalism, and likely to exhibit little belief in their own ability to control the event in which they are involved."[28] Hermann's research reveals links between personality attributes and types of foreign-policy behavior, illustrating that those attributes have an impact on state actions and ultimately war and peace.

In contrast to Hermann's work, much effort has been spent applying the assumption of *individual rationality* to decisions to go to war. Political scientist Bruce Bueno de Mesquita developed an *"expected-utility" theory* of war that "is predicated on the belief that national leaders behave as if they are rational expected-utility maximizers. The broadest . . . generalization that emerges from the theory is the expectation that wars . . . will be initiated only when the initiator believes the war will yield positive expected utility."[29] In Bueno de Mesquita's view, war results less from irrationality than from rational decisions by policy-makers. According to prospect theory, individual rationality, though imperfect owing to such tendencies as preference for preventing loss rather than assuring gain, still dominates behavior.[30]

Societies, Governments, and War

Aggressive behavior and war occur more frequently in some cultures than in others, leading some to suspect that human nature and individual psychology are not the whole story. Little evidence appears of organized violence among prehistoric hunter-gatherers. Warfare may be a relatively recent phenomenon, dating from about 6500 B.C. in communities of herdsmen who found that "violent seizures of someone else's animals or pasture grounds was the easiest and speediest way to wealth and might be the only means of survival in a year of scant vegetation."[31]

Indeed, warfare may still not exist in some cultures. Anthropologist Margaret Mead describes societies that apparently neither know war nor have language to describe it. "Warfare is an invention like any other of the inventions in terms of which we order our lives, such as writing, marriage, cooking our food instead of eating it raw, trial by jury, or burial of the dead." She continues: "There are people even today who have no warfare. Of these the Eskimos are perhaps the most conspicuous examples, but the Lepchas of Sikkim . . . are as good."[32]

Why should some societies be prone to war and others not? One answer was provided by Marxists, who believe that acquisitive capitalist societies are inherently more violent than socialist ones. Karl Marx (1818–1883) in his theory of class struggle between the proletariat and bourgeoisie had little to say directly about global politics, but he did predict revolutions that would sweep away capitalist society. It was left to others to explain the link between class struggle and global politics. How was it that, despite Marx's predictions of world revolution, the late nineteenth century proved to be an era of political stability in the capitalist states of Europe and North America where Marx had expected the fires of revolution to burn first? An English economist, John A. Hobson (1858–1940), sought the answer in the growth of European and American *imperialism* in the less-developed countries.[33] Hobson argued that a small wealthy minority and a large impoverished majority created a situation in which capitalist economies produced more than citizens could afford to consume. To deal with this *crisis of overproduction*, capitalists, he claimed, invested overseas (where overproduction at home could be absorbed). Imperialism and wars among imperialists were the result.

Hobson's work influenced Vladimir Ilyich Lenin. Leader of the 1917 Bolshevik Revolution in Russia, Lenin declared that world revolution had been delayed by imperialism, which allowed capitalists in advanced societies to exploit poor societies. This exploitation provided capitalists with resources to "buy off" workers at home with an improved standard of living and vicarious national glory. Imperialism was "the highest stage of capitalism,"[34] the result of the merger of banking and industrial monopolies and their quest overseas for raw materials and markets for surplus production. War was a result of clashes between expanding imperialists seeking exclusive control over overseas markets, cheap labor, and sources of raw materials. Only by eliminating capitalism, Lenin concluded, could the practice of war be ended.

Some theorists claim that type of government is the key to explaining war. Liberals believe that democracies with limited government are less likely to go to war than authoritarian states because the people, not the rulers, have to pay war's price. By contrast, authoritarian rulers can benefit from war, while not having to fear personal risk or hardship. As Kenneth Waltz writes, "The transitory interests of royal houses may be advanced in war; the real interests of all peoples are furthered by peace. Most men suffer because some men are in positions that permit them to indulge their kingly ambitions."[35] Thus Woodrow Wilson believed that peace could be secured only if governments were democratically elected. Empirical analysis yields mixed results: It appears that "liberal states have . . . established a separate peace,"[36] but "promoting democracy may not promote peace because states are especially war-prone during the transition toward democracy."[37]

Finally, some scholars think differences in propensity to war are related to conflict *within* societies. It is widely believed that domestic unity increases during external crises and that leaders may provoke external tension to increase their popularity at home. Stalin, for example, sought to rally support at home by pointing to "capitalist encirclement" of the U.S.S.R. Typical of this perspective is Richard Rosecrance's claims of "a correlation between international instability and the domestic insecurity of elites."[38]

Systemic Theories of War

Perhaps it is not the parts of systems—individuals and states—that produce war but the system itself. Neorealists (or structural realists), as we saw earlier, focus their attention on the system, especially its distribution of power, as the principal source of war in global politics.[39] From this perspective, war is a property of interaction among actors, and the characteristics of leaders or groups are less important. War does not necessarily arise when states are belligerent, because a balance of power or nuclear parity may prevent war from taking place. By contrast, war may ensue even where no actor wishes it to happen. In sum, system-level theorists believe that the *whole* (system) is greater than the sum of its *parts* (actors), a view similar to that of classical economists like Adam Smith, who believed that, under free-market conditions, an "invisible hand" transforms the acquisitive behavior of individuals into a productive and benevolent economic system.

Neorealists consider absence of central authority and distribution of power as structural sources of war. As Waltz declares, "Wars occur because there is nothing to prevent them," and, though this condition might suggest a need for world government, he dismisses this as impractical—"unassailable in logic" but "unattainable in practice."[40] Considerable research has been done on how the distribution of power affects the probability of war. Does a system in which power is equally distributed produce more war than one in which power is unequally distributed? One view is that as the global system moves toward equality, the likelihood of war is reduced because equality increases uncertainty about the outcome of war and uncertainty produces caution on the part of actors.[41] Would the United States have initiated war to free Kuwait in 1991 if U.S. leaders believed they had a 50–50 chance of losing?

Others believe that *power preponderance* or *hegemony* ensures peace and that movement toward power equality is dangerous. In a hegemonic system, the hegemon fears no one and has no reason to go to war, and the weak powers do not dare resort to war because of the certainty that they will face defeat. As a system moves toward equal distribution of power, however, the former hegemon grows more fearful for its security, and weak powers grow more daring. The likelihood of war is thus enhanced.[42]

These arguments have been refined by introducing *polarity*—the number of power centers in a system—as a key factor in producing or preventing war.[43] "It is to a great extent due to its bipolar structure," says Waltz, "that the world since the war has enjoyed a stability seldom known where three or more powers have sought to cooperate with each other or have competed for existence."[44] Unlike the balance-of-power system, he argues, the superpowers were so much more powerful than anyone else that they could ignore all but the most important power shifts. Waltz thought the periodic crises that punctuated U.S.-Soviet relations were healthy signs of bilateral attention and believed (correctly as it turned out) that leaders would work out procedures for resolving crises peacefully. Two superpowers "supreme in their power have to use force less often" and are "able to moderate other's use of violence and to absorb possibly destabilizing changes that emanate from uses of violence that they do not or cannot control."[45]

Political scientists Karl W. Deutsch and J. David Singer make the opposite argument, claiming that, as predicted by theorists of political pluralism, a system of many power centers—multipolarity—produces crosscutting cleavages that attenuate any single conflict. Adversaries in one issue can look to one another for support in another issue, and their attention will be divided among several opponents rather than in a single enemy.[46] Efforts to test these conflicting propositions have been inconclusive, and it is difficult to know whether "decision makers act as if they were significantly constrained by variations in the structural attributes."[47]

Whatever the role of structural features in war, we must recognize that identifying causes of war that cannot be altered (such as human nature) are of little use to policy-makers or theorists. If the factors that trigger war cannot be changed, then policies cannot be fashioned to prevent its outbreak. We might as well shrug our shoulders, accept the idea that sooner or later we will find ourselves in another war, and turn our energy to a more rewarding pursuit.

Some suspect that structural configurations like polarity matter less in triggering war than do the rate and magnitude of change from one configuration to another. Unequal distribution of power may create envy in the weak and determination to overcome their inferiority; their temptation to avenge past grievances may grow as power distribution is equalized. In this view, "war is caused by differences in rates of growth among the great powers and, of particular importance, the differences in rates between the dominant nation and the challenger that permit the latter to overtake the former."[48] Some scholars posit a *power cycle* in which the danger of war is greatest at "critical points," when the power and role of key states are changing rapidly.[49] States with growing power demand a greater role in the system, and declining states are reluctant to surrender their prerogatives.

The belief that changes in power distribution are important have interested scholars in *arms races* as factors in the outbreak of war. Shortly after World War I, British physicist Lewis Fry Richardson, a pioneer in mathematical modeling, argued that war was related to arms races and the fear that accompanies them. Richardson used differential equations to depict the manner in which the level of arms in two countries interact with variables like threat perception to produce war. He did not view his equations as genuine models of reality but as illustrations of "what people would do if they did not stop to think."[50] More recently, Michael D. Wallace found arms races to be associated with alliance formation (itself related to status inconsistency) and onset of war.[51] He found that in twenty-eight cases between 1816 and 1965 in which there were arms races *and* serious disputes, twenty-three ended in war.[52]

Many arms races grow out of changing technology. Such changes alter global distribution of power, and that is one reason the relationship between technology and war has received close attention.

Changing Technology and the Evolution of War[53]

Actors' ability to adapt changing technology to achieve objectives has been a great factor in their rise and fall. Advances from the humble horse-drawn chariot of ancient civilizations, archers' use of stirrups in the fifth century A.D., and pikes and longbows early in the fourteenth century to the splitting of the atom have allowed some actors and even some regions of the world to dominate others. Technological advances that enabled the West to dominate global politics by the eighteenth and nineteenth centuries continued into the twentieth. In this section, we briefly review the evolution of technology, examining its relation to changes in warfare. It is remarkable how often statesmen have misunderstood the implications of technological change and planned for the future as though it were the same as the past.

Arms, Politics, and the End of Chivalry

Innovations in military technology between A.D. 1000 and 1500 brought great changes to global politics. The feudal system of medieval Europe depended on military domination exercised by a class of mounted knights who could afford armor and horses. With the rise in commerce and expansion of commercial cities in Italy and Holland starting in the eleventh century, a middle class appeared that could afford to hire mercenary armies and equip them with armor-penetrating crossbows. The results were changes in warfare that ended the dominance by aristocratic knights.[54]

The political and military revolution was completed by improvements in guns and artillery and by emerging kings with a capacity to tax subjects sufficiently to pay for such innovations. By the middle of the fifteenth century, heavy artillery could reduce the walls of castles or cities to rubble in hours. On one occasion, a fortress in southern Italy, famous because it had withstood an earlier siege for seven years, was destroyed in eight hours.[55] Artillery made defensive fortifications in general less effective, and facilitated territorial expansion. Historian William McNeill writes:

> Wherever the new artillery [of mobile siege guns] appeared, existing fortifications became useless. The power of any ruler who was able to afford the high cost of the new weapons was . . . enhanced at the expense of neighbors and subjects who were unable to avail themselves of the new technology of war.[56]

These changes, along with improvements in naval warfare and growth in commerce, ushered in the era of the large territorial state.

War in Eighteenth-Century Europe

As the sovereign state became the principal unit of social organization in the seventeenth and eighteenth centuries, global politics became more stable. One reason was the state of military technology. Weapons and tactics provided few advantages for adopting offensive strategies. Armies lacked the logistical capacity to move quickly and could not get far ahead of their baggage trains. Muskets were inaccurate, could only fire a short distance, and were effective only when fired in volleys by highly trained soldiers who stood in mass formations. Warfare was a costly, bloody, and indecisive enterprise.

The new technology was compatible with the economic, political, and social conditions of the time. Rulers did not wish to levy high taxes on subjects or interfere with economic activities that were the basis of their wealth and power. Dependent on professional soldiers recruited or impressed into service from the lowest rungs of society, officers devised tactics meant as much to prevent desertion as to gain victory. Brightly colored uniforms so that officers could keep an eye on soldiers, and rigidly disciplined mass formations kept armies together better than winning decisive victories. The low status of the military profession in Europe at the time was reflected in signs in cafés that read: "No dogs, lackeys, prostitutes or soldiers."[57] Because professional armies were expensive, neither commanders nor employers wanted needless bloodletting. All this fit an age of dynastic wars in which kings were conservative and had no wish for unrestrained war like the Thirty Years' War of 1618–1648 that might endanger their thrones. Most kings were related to one another by marriage or blood, and none wished to do *too* much harm to a son-in-law or uncle.

Prussia's Frederick the Great was the most successful commander of this era—improving logistics and organizing his army into self-sufficient divisions—and his approach to war, described by a historian, gives the flavor of the period:

> Battle . . . was a methodical affair. Opposing armies were arrayed according to pattern, almost as regularly as chessmen at the beginning of a game. . . . Frederick . . . was not fond of full-size battles. . . . So Frederician war became increasingly a war of position, the war of complex maneuver and subtle accumulation of small gains; leisurely and slow in its main outlines. . . . He was a dynast, not a revolutionary or an adventurer.[58]

Napoleonic Revolution in Warfare

Much changed with the French Revolution and the Napoleonic Wars. Awakened nationalism went hand in hand with new tactics and larger armies of aroused citizens. Artillery improved in accuracy and mobility. Technology and organization allowed large armies with greater firepower to move farther and faster than before. Popular fervor enlarged the objectives that leaders pursued, even as it allowed more of the population to become involved in the war effort. France's proclamation of the *levée en masse* in August 1793 forecast the mobilization of entire populations for war:

> From this moment until our enemies have been driven from the territory of the Republic, all Frenchmen are permanently requisitioned for military service. Young men will go forth to battle; married men will forge weapons and transport munitions; women will make tents and clothing; children will make bandages from old linen; and old men will be brought to the public squares to arouse the courage of the soldiers, while preaching the unity of the Republic and hatred against kings.[59]

Napoleon was able to send huge armies—more than a million in a population of twenty-five million[60]—into the field, and they were able to win crushing one-punch victories between 1800 and 1806 at Marengo, Ulm, Jena, Auerstadt, and Austerlitz. A visitor to Paris can get a sense of these battles at a monument in the center of the Place Vendôme that was constructed from cannon captured by Napoleon.

The lessons of the French Revolution and the power of the new nationalism were not lost on the greatest military intellectual of the age, the Prussian general Karl Maria von Clausewitz. Clausewitz was the military theorist of the age of sovereign states. He had fought against Napoleon for his native Prussia and then for the Russian Tsar, and was struck by the ferocity of the Napoleonic Wars. Unlike wars in the previous century, they seemed to bear little relation to aims other than destroying the enemy. Such wars could get out of hand, escalating until the political objectives for which they had been initiated were forgotten and replaced by blind hatred.

Clausewitz could imagine no political end to justify total war, and he wrote his unfinished masterpiece *On War (Von Kriege)* "to iron out the creases in the heads" of generals he feared might dictate the way wars were fought. As a professional soldier, Clausewitz believed that war was a science, but recoiled at the prospect of its being waged solely by military professionals according to technical principles.[61] Just as no battle should be undertaken without recognizing its implications for the overall war effort, so no war should be waged without a clear understanding of its implications for the long-term political situation. NATO's bombing of Serbia in 1999 was criticized precisely because such understanding was lacking.

Clausewitz held that the military requirements of war should be subordinated to civilian leaders' political needs. Wars, he reasoned, were not mindless outbreaks of violence. Rather, they were like games in which chance and probability determine the outcome. And, though a general seeks to destroy his enemy's forces and will to fight, that is not the true objective of war. "Force . . . is . . . the *means;* to impose our will upon the enemy is the *object.*"[62] The aim was not to hurt the enemy but to coerce him to accede to political demands.

Because wars begin for political reasons, such reasons should be kept in mind even as the fighting rages. "Now if we reflect that war has its origins in a political object, we see that this first motive, which called it into existence, naturally remains the first and highest consideration to be regarded in its conduct."[63] If the original reasons were forgotten, means and ends would become confused. The amount of violence should be commensurate with the political objectives. If objectives are limited, war too should be limited. "This explains how . . . there can be wars of all degrees of importance and energy, from a war of extermination down to a mere state of armed observation."[64] For Clausewitz, war, like diplomacy or trade, was a political instrument, albeit a violent one, "not merely a political act but a real political instrument."[65]

Clausewitz's influence on modern strategy is evident in the work of theorists like Thomas Schelling, who writes: "The power to hurt is bargaining power. To exploit it is diplomacy—vicious diplomacy, but diplomacy."[66] The idea of war as an extension of policy to coerce an adversary without escalating out of control was seen in the lengths to which American leaders went in Korea (1950–1953) to limit the conflict. The Americans neither invaded nor bombed China and eschewed nuclear weapons. Following Clausewitz's advice that generals must not take over the direction of war, President Truman fired his field commander, General Douglas MacArthur, in 1951 when the general pressed publicly to widen the war.[67] MacArthur was a war hero, and Truman had to pay a steep political price at home for asserting his authority.[68] A recent use of armed forces to send a political message was President Clinton's dispatch of 36,000 troops to the Persian Gulf to counter a buildup of Iraqi troops near the Kuwait border in October 1994.

Technology and World War I

Clausewitz's nightmare came to life in World War I (1914–1918). The war was sparked by a conflict between Austria-Hungary and Serbia,[69] and, with the major countries of Europe linked by alliances,[70] it spread rapidly. Though remaining mostly European, the war spread to Africa, Asia, and the Middle East, and before it ended, one in every 28 Frenchmen, every 32 Germans, every 57 Englishmen, and every 107 Russians had been killed.[71] But statistics fail to convey the suicidal violence of trench warfare or how vast areas of Europe were turned into barren seas of mud. War was no longer an affair of honor or individual valor. English poet Wilfred Owen captured this change in describing a gas attack:

> Bent double, like old beggars under sacks,
> Knock-kneed, coughing like hags, we cursed through sludge,
> Till on the haunting flares we turned our backs,
> And towards our distant rest began to trudge.
> Men marched asleep. Many had lost their boots,
> But limped on, blood-shod. All went lame, all blind;

Drunk with fatigue; deaf even to the hoots
Of gas-shells dropping softly behind.

Gas! Gas! Quick boys!—An ecstasy of fumbling,
Fitting the clumsy helmets just in time,
But someone still was yelling out and stumbling
And floundering like a man in fire or lime.
Dim though the misty panes and thick green* light
As under a green sea, I saw him drowning.

In all my dreams before my helpless sight
He plunges at me, guttering, choking, drowning.

If in some smothering dreams, you too could pace
Behind the wagon that we flung him in,
And watch the white eyes writhing in his face,
His hanging face, like a devil's sick of sin;
If you could hear, at every jolt, the blood
Come gargling from the froth-corrupted lungs,
Bitter as the cud
Of vile, incurable sores on innocent tongues,
My friend, you would not tell with such high zest
To children ardent for some desperate glory,
The old Lie: Dulce et decorum est
Pro patria mori.†[72]

*Green was the color of mustard gas—$(ClCH_2CH_2)_2S$—which burns, blinds, and kills.

†"How sweet and fitting it is to die for one's homeland."

Incomprehension of how military technology had altered the relationship between the offense and the defense—and military plans reflecting these errors—were partly responsible for a war no one wanted.[73] Indeed, it is still not clear whether statesmen simply ignored the implications of technological change or misunderstood them.[74] Politicians and generals planned for a quick offensive war but instead found themselves in a defensive war of attrition.

Leaders were influenced by Germany's wars of unification against Denmark (1863), Austria (1866), and France (1870), which became models for planning future wars. The unification wars were rapid affairs in which the outcome was settled in one decisive battle. At least two technological innovations contributed to these decisive victories. The first was the railroad, enabling actors to assemble large armies quickly at one location from which they could attack; the second was heavy artillery that could send huge projectiles twenty miles and more and reduce defensive strong points.[75]

Other cases, if understood, might have led to different conclusions. The American Civil War (1860-1865) cost 500,000 lives in a deadly war of attrition, but was dismissed with contempt by the chief of the German general staff as "movements of armed mobs."[76] The enormous toll in lives from frontal attacks on fixed positions during the Russo-Japanese War of 1904-1905 showed how technology had improved defensive prospects. Barbed wire and machine guns, combined with rows of trenches, made mincemeat of horse cavalry and frontal infantry assault. Massed attacks were vulnerable to the greater accuracy and range of artillery and small arms that used high explosives rather than gunpowder as propellant. Long-range artillery was as deadly to concentrations of troops preparing to attack as to fortresses.[77]

Instead, European observers concluded that the "real lesson of the Russo-Japanese War . . . was not technology but *morale*. . . ."[78] If soldiers were imbued with the right spirit, they could overcome concentrated fire: mind over matter.[79] Thus French regulations in 1894 demanded that infantry advance "elbow to elbow in mass formations, to the sound of bugles and drums."[80] In short, the problem was not merely failure to recognize new technology, but lack of imagination in exploiting this technology.[81]

The *cult of the offensive* reached a peak in Germany's *Schlieffen Plan*, conceived in 1897.[82] It assumed that Germany would face a war on two fronts and would be outnumbered. German survival therefore depended on rapidly mobilizing and striking before Russian mobilization was completed. German forces would mass on the western front with only a screening force remaining in the east. The main German blow would fall on the French left flank, avoiding the French frontier fortresses, seizing French and Belgian ports to prevent British intervention, and sweeping behind French lines to rupture communications and smash the French army against the Alps. Then, taking advantage of Germany's internal lines of communication, forces would rush eastward to meet the Russian advance.[83] The plan's success depended on avoiding delay (including lengthy political negotiations) and on ruthlessly violating Belgian neutrality. Contrary to Clausewitz's dictum, military considerations came to dominate political decisions. In one illustrative episode, the Russian foreign minister informed the chief of staff that he should "smash" his telephone so that Tsar Nicholas II could not postpone declaring war in order to seek a political solution.[84]

Reality soon intruded in the plans of the general staffs, revealing that technology favored the defense. The German attack on France, the Russian advance against Germany, the Austro-Hungarian offensive against Russian Poland, and the French invasion of Alsace-Lorraine[85] all failed, with huge losses of life. Of the 1,500,000 French troops who marched off to war in August 1914, one in four were casualties within six weeks, and 110,000 were dead.[86] Rather than forcing a change in tactics, the toll hardened the resolve of generals on both sides to prove they had been right in the first place. Time after time, following deafening artillery barrages, masses of troops went "over the top" to be mowed down by an entrenched enemy. Michael Howard captures the futility and carnage of the war in describing the British offensive on the Somme in summer 1916:

> By the end of June 1, 437 guns had been assembled along an eighteen-mile front, and in a week-long bombardment they fired over 1,500,000 shells. . . . So the infantry went over the top on July 1 . . . expecting at worst to have to mop up a few dazed survivors. The result was one of the most terrible days in the history of the war. The barrage had not been heavy enough to reach the dugouts that the Germans had excavated deep in the chalk hills above the Somme. Appalling as the experience they suffered was, the German infantry were still able to set up their machine guns and mow down the advancing waves of British infantry. . . . Of the 120,000 men who assaulted, nearly half were casualties, and 20,000 were dead. The

attacks continued until November, by which time the British and French armies engaged had lost nearly 500,000 men.[87]

Technology and World War II

Unlike World War I, fascination with the defensive dominated planning for World War II, at least among the British and the French. After World War I, French "security policies and doctrines," observe two historians, "naturally became defensive, and the 1920s witnessed a return to the traditional military credo of the Third Republic: faith in the trinity of a fortified eastern border, foreign alliances, and universal conscription."[88] This was reflected in a line of fixed fortifications from Switzerland to Luxembourg—the Maginot Line.[89]

Germany and Japan proved more imaginative in adapting new military technologies.[90] To avenge the defeat of 1918, the Germans developed tactics that could exploit the new weapons, especially tanks and aircraft. Unlike the French and British, who thought of tanks as providing support for infantry, German planners had the idea of creating separate tank formations closely supported by aircraft that could move rapidly and break through enemy weak points, creating havoc in the rear.[91] The German doctrine—*blitzkrieg* (lightning war)—was different in another way: It wedded political indoctrination and ideology to mechanized warfare.[92] Prior to attack, the enemy was softened up by unconventional tactics aimed at lowering morale and undermining the will to resist. Before their invasion of France, for example, the Germans established a news agency in that country to spread Nazi propaganda.[93] Nazi techniques included forging economic ties to increase dependency on Germany and recruiting local Germans to carry out assassinations and espionage.[94] Since World War II, these tactics have been emulated by others, and political warfare has become standard fare in world politics.

Hitler intuitively understood Clausewitz's idea of war as an extension of politics, and he used the threat of war to bully his adversaries into making concessions, leaving them room to retreat and promising that he had no further ambitions. In 1936, against the advice of his generals, he bluffed his enemies by reoccupying the Rhineland. Historian Alan Bullock writes:

> German rearmament was only beginning and the first conscripts had only been taken into the Army a few months before. France, together with her Polish and Czech allies, could immediately mobilize ninety divisions, with a further hundred in reserve. . . . Hitler did not dispute these facts; he based his decision on the belief that the French would not march—and he was right.[95]

But in the end, Hitler forgot Clausewitz and waged war indiscriminately against civilians and soldiers in "a war in which the expanding torrent of destruction became the main operational and tactical rationale. Its main and only operational goal was to inflict damage and destruction, to destroy the enemy state and to batter enemy societies and their armed forces into submission."[96] *The link between war and politics had been severed.* Nazi policies of conquest and genocide cause revulsion among civilized peoples and brought into being the most powerful coalition in history—the United States, Britain, and the Soviet Union.[97]

The Japanese also used tactical ingenuity to exploit technology. The attack on Pearl Harbor was a tactical masterpiece, revealing for the first time how useful the aircraft carrier was. Only the absence of America's carriers from Pearl Harbor at the time of the attack forced the United States into the carrier age.[98] On the other hand, like their German allies, the Japanese failed to understand Clausewitz. The Japanese plan was to put the American fleet out of commission, seize Southeast Asia and its raw materials, and then sit tight behind a barrier of island fortresses. In time, they believed, the Americans would become frustrated and give up the war. They did not appreciate the implications of America's enormous industrial might and population and their own vulnerability to U.S. carrier forces. This vulnerability was brought home to them sooner than anyone expected when a U.S. air raid was launched against Tokyo led by General James H. Doolittle in April 1942.

Once again warfare technologies are rapidly changing, especially information technologies. Missile ships may replace carriers,[99] and new computers and satellites will provide detailed intelligence about enemies and integrate complex battlefield systems. "Think of it," says one observer, "as information logistics" in which control of "the electromagnetic dimension" and "information supremacy—of knowing, or being able to know, everything about the battlespace" determine victory.[100] Indeed, future war may be "cyberwar" as foes seek to destroy each other's computers by unleashing destructive "worms" and "viruses," thereby "blinding" and "deafening" the enemy. However, as these pages show, technology is only a means to political ends, and failure to learn that lesson can have dire consequences.

Postmodern War

The British military historian John Keegan opens his history of war by starkly denying Clausewitz: "War is not the continuation of policy by other means." Keegan argues that Clausewitz's idea "implies the existence of states, of state interests and of rational calculation about how they may be achieved," and observes that war antedates the state and "reaches into the most secret places of the human heart, places where self dissolves rational purpose, where pride reigns, where emotion is paramount, where instinct is king."[101] In many respects war in the world today resembles Keegan's description more than Clausewitz's. Ethnic, tribal, and ideological conflicts in Angola, Mozambique, the Sudan, Cambodia, and Guatemala[102] had little in common with interstate war as envisioned by Clausewitz and resembled the Thirty Years' War that Clausewitz so disliked. Clausewitz is even less relevant to the endemic violence that afflicts failed states and many of the densely populated cities of the developing world.[103]

Postmodern wars are not rational, nor do they arise from clear political objectives. Thus the distinction between legitimate violence and crime breaks down in such conflicts. They are not fought by states or for state interests, and they reveal that many states no longer control even a significant part of the means of coercion in their territory.[104] Ours is "an epoch of themeless juxtapositions, in which the classificatory grid of nation-states is going to be replaced by a jagged-glass pattern of city-states, shanty-states, nebulous and anarchic regionalisms."[105] As this quote suggests, postmodern war is a symptom of global fragmentation in the postinternational world.

The twentieth century has witnessed some of the cruelest wars in history, wars in which unspeakable atrocities have been committed against innocent civilians. In this cartoon participants in these conflicts are toasting the civil war in Bosnia. (The Philadelphia Inquirer, *Copyright 1995. Dist. by Universal Press Syndicate. Reprinted with permission. All rights reserved.*)

These wars are fought "by militias or other informal—often tribal—groupings whose ability to use sophisticated weaponry is very limited."[106] Civilians are the chief victims in these wars, especially children, who are often forced to fight. So much concern was raised about the use of children in these wars that in 1998 the issue was taken up by the U.N. Security Council, and a U.N. Special Representative on Children and Armed Conflict was appointed. "The moral center is no longer holding," he declared. "In so many conflicts today, anything goes. Children, women, the elderly, granary stores, crops, livestock—are all fair game in the single-minded struggle for power."[107] And a coalition of six nonstate organizations, including Amnesty International and Human Rights Watch, was formed to halt the use of child soldiers.[108] Between 1985 and 1995 as many as two million children died in these wars; four to five million were disabled; and twelve million were made homeless.[109] Iran used children as "human minesweepers" in its 1980–1988 war with Iraq.

Sixty thousand Afghan children need artificial limbs because of land mines; and as many as 80,000—one per 140 people—are amputees in Angola. It is estimated that there are ten million uncleared mines in Afghanistan and nine million in Angola alone, and an organization of former British soldiers, the Halo Trust, was formed solely to clear mines in the developing world.[110] Such data explain why there is growing concern about the availability of such weapons as antipersonnel land mines. Such mines

TABLE 10.5
Nations with the Most Uncleared Mines

Country	Uncleared Mines (millions)
Afghanistan	9–10
Angola	9
Iraq	5–10
Kuwait	5–7
Cambodia	4–7
Mozambique	2
Bosnia	1–1.7
Somalia	1–1.5
Croatia	1
Sudan	0.5–2
Serbia	0.5–1
Ethiopia/Eritrea	0.3–1

SOURCE: Data from the U.S. State Department, 1996.

kill or maim 20,000 civilians each year, and there are as many as 110 million mines sown in sixty-four countries, especially Egypt, Iran, Angola, Afghanistan, Cambodia, China, Iraq, and Bosnia (where there are about 152 mines per square mile).[111] An additional 1.5 to 2.0 million mines are sown each year.[112] Although the 1996 Geneva Conference on Conventional Weapons agreed that use of "nondetectable" (plastic) mines and "dumb" mines that do not self-destruct should be curtailed, little progress had been made up to that time in outlawing what the French called this "humanitarian catastrophe."[113] Table 10.5 lists the nations with the most uncleared land mines.

However, following a media blitz orchestrated by a coalition of humanitarian nongovernmental organizations showing the effects of antipersonnel land mines on civilians, more than one hundred countries signed a treaty in Ottawa, Canada, in December 1997 banning such mines. Under pressure from the Pentagon, which argued that such mines were still necessary to help defend South Korea, the Clinton administration found itself in the company of Russia and China in refusing to sign the treaty.[114]

Enthused by their success in mobilizing support for the ban on mines, humanitarian nonstate organizations began a campaign in 1998 to stop the spread of such readily available small arms as assault rifles, pistols, hand grenades, and mortars, all of which are widely used in postmodern wars. Since World War II such weapons have caused far more casualties than weapons of mass destruction, which receive much more attention. Although the U.S. government was prepared to join an agreement dealing with illicit trafficking in such arms, concern about the domestic gun lobby contributed to U.S. reluctance to limit the legal trade in such weapons.[115]

In postmodern wars, it is difficult to know who is in command of rival armies or what their objectives are other than killing for its own sake. Why the slaughter of Tutsi by Hutu in Rwanda? According to one report: "Tutsis and Hutus may look different—Tutsis are a taller, Nilotic people, while Hutus are darker and stockier—but they have for centuries shared a common language and culture in Rwanda. . . . Yet now they have turned on each other not with impersonal mortars or long-range rifles but with machetes, hoes, clubs and bare hands. Neighbors have killed neighbors, even old childhood friends. . . .Why? No one seems able to say."[116] No one knows why such wars start, and they are hard to end. And, according to Russia's former foreign minister, they are "no less serious than the threat of nuclear war was yesterday."[117]

Those who try to end such wars must be prepared for threats such as terrorism, sniping, and mines and need equipment such as that sent with U.S. forces into Bosnia—drones for surveillance, body armor, special plows for mine clearing, rifles with thermal sights for dealing with snipers, and special panels for vehicles to prevent allied troops from shooting each other accidentally.[118] Let us look briefly at a few cases that illuminate the features of postmodern war.

Liberia   Events in Liberia illustrate the combination of an absence of political objectives with the ferocity of postmodern war. In 1980, a coup led by army sergeant Samuel K. Doe overthrew a government dominated by the Americo-Liberian descendants of American slaves. In 1990, Doe was murdered, and Liberia descended into anarchy, as civil war pitted Doe's Krahn tribal supporters against rebel military units led by U.S.-educated Charles Taylor and principally drawn from other tribal groups. As violence continued, the various factions splintered into "vague and shifting fronts and alliances"[119] with meaningless names like the United Liberation Movement, the Liberian Peace Council, the Armed Forces of Liberia, and the National Patriotic Front of Liberia. According to one report, "the Liberian Peace Council uses cannibalism the same way the Bosnian Serbs use rape—as a means of ethnic cleansing."

> Cannibalism used to be held in check by tribal chiefs and by the zoes, priests of the secret societies that have long regulated life in Liberia's interior. But the war has destroyed the old order. The gerontocracy has melted away, and now witchcraft, like the AK-47, is in the hands of teen-age fighters, who have run amok.[120]

Fighters are "adolescents high on marijuana and cane juice" who give themselves "comic-book names: General Jungle King, Colonel Evil Killer, General Monster."[121]

A West African force led by Nigeria intervened in 1990 but failed to restore peace outside the capital city.[122] By 1995, 150,000 Liberians, mainly civilians, had been killed, and almost one million, 80 percent of the country's population, had fled to refugee camps.[123] National frontiers became meaningless as refugees fled to Guinea, the Ivory Coast, and even Mali, and as violence engulfed neighboring Sierra Leone, where the Revolutionary United Front fed children drugs and "forced them to witness or even take part in public rituals of torture and execution of elders, even their own relatives."[124] Referring to the violence in Liberia and Sierra Leone, one observer wrote: "In both countries rebellions . . . began in the bush. War enables young people to live by the gun, and live better: looting is far more profitable than waiting, half-educated for a job that will never come. . . . Beyond the appalling massacres and brutality, autonomous war-gangs began to establish mini-states. . . .And the state, in both countries, died, its authority, physical and moral destroyed. . . ."[125]

In September 1995 an agreement was declared to end Liberia's civil war as exhaustion gripped all parties. "Man," declared one teenage soldier, "this war has got to come to an end now. We have no schools, no homes and no money, and if it doesn't stop now, we will all die just like this, with nothing."[126] Fighting resumed in January 1996, and Liberia was plunged back into anarchy. Westerners in Monrovia, the country's capital, were evacuated by U.S. Marines, and "young men, armed with AK-47 assault rifles and in many cases addled by drugs and moonshine, roamed the streets killing and plundering."[127]

"The Great Lakes Region" of Africa

No conflict reveals the breakdown of state frontiers imposed by colonial authorities more vividly than that which began in Rwanda, then spilled over into the Congo (formerly Zaire), and involved Burundi, Uganda, Kenya, Angola, and the Congo Republic. So irrelevant were state designations to the violence that observers began to speak of "the Great Lakes Region of Central Africa" (regions adjacent to Lakes Kivu and Victoria) instead of Rwanda, the Congo, and so forth.

Formerly a Belgian colony, the Republic of Rwanda became independent in 1962. Since then it has experienced continual tribal conflict. Rwanda's population is 90 percent Hutu, 9 percent Tutsi, and 1 percent Twa (or pygmies). Before the European arrival, Rwanda had been a feudal monarchy ruled by the Tutsi minority, and Tutsi dominance persisted during the colonial era and afterward. Hutu resistance grew in the 1950s, and a bloody rebellion in 1959 overthrew the monarchy. In the early 1960s, civil war slaughtered thousands of Tutsis and forced many others to flee.[128] But it was nothing compared to what lay ahead.

As an émigré army of Tutsis from neighboring Uganda invaded Rwanda to restore Tutsi dominance, an airplane carrying the presidents of Rwanda and Burundi was shot down on April 6, 1994. This event triggered a genocidic slaughter[129] of Tutsis by Hutu extremists and the Hutu-dominated Rwandan army.[130] No Tutsi was safe—women, children, or priests—and no quarter was given. Before it was over at least 500,000, or roughly half of all Rwandan Tutsis, were killed. Sheer numbers fail to convey the ferocity of the violence. One report noted: "Cloaking the countryside with the stench of death, the bodies—as many as 100 an hour—are being washed ashore in . . . southern Uganda or onto islands in Lake Victoria."[131]

However, the Tutsi invaders—the Rwandan Patriotic Front—triumphed, and as many as two million Hutus fled their homes to escape Tutsi revenge. The refugee camps in Goma, Mugunga, and Bukavu in the Congo sheltered not only the innocent but also the Hutu extremists who had managed the campaign of murder, and they terrorized the refugees, preventing them from returning home and launching guerrilla attacks back into Rwanda with at least the tacit collusion of the Congo army.[132]

Aided by Rwanda's Tutsi government, which sought to drive the Hutu refugees from territory adjacent to Rwanda, Congo Tutsis known as the Banyamulenge began to attack Congolese soldiers and Hutu refugee camps.[133] Thereafter, the Congo army, always more adept at pillaging than genuine warfare, rapidly collapsed despite the aid of Belgian and Serbian mercenaries.[134] The Congo's central government under its longtime authoritarian president, Mobutu Sese Seko, already unable to exercise authority over most of the huge country beyond the capital Kinshasa, was helpless in the face of a Tutsi army reinforced with Rwandan soldiers. With Mobutu ill with terminal cancer,[135] Tutsi rebels, calling themselves the Alliance of Democratic Forces for the Liberation of Congo-Zaire under Laurent Kabila, moved swiftly to overthrow Mobutu and seize control for themselves. In the course of their rapid advance, Kabila's forces committed numerous atrocities against the Hutu refugees who fled before them, and

Kabila, no more committed to democracy than had been Mobutu, made it impossible for U.N. personnel to investigate the charges of war crimes leveled against his troops. Kabila's failure to end Hutu raids into Rwanda and his efforts to distance himself from his Tutsi supporters triggered a Ugandan- and Rwandan-supported Tutsi insurrection against him a year later which evolved into a full-scale regional conflict as troops from Angola, Zimbabwe, and Namibia hastened to assist Kabila.[136]

Sri Lanka

In no conflict have children been more deeply involved than in that which pits Sri Lanka's government and majority Sinhalese community against its Tamil minority led by the Liberation Tigers of Tamil Eelam, located largely in the north. Between 1983 and 1998, at least 54,000 people were killed, and efforts by India first to intercede between the combatants and then to suppress the Tamil rebellion (1987–1990) failed.[137] The Tigers used suicide bombings, often carried out by women known as Freedom Birds, to assassinate opponents such as India's Prime Minister Rajiv Gandhi and Sri Lankan political leaders.[138] But what is unique about them is "their reliance on what amounts to a children's army. Tiger leaders have recruited boys and girls as young as 11, sending them into battle equipped with 'suicide capsules,' glass vials of potassium cyanide on cords around their necks to be taken if they are threatened with capture."[139] A cease-fire was negotiated in early 1995, but the conflict continues.[140]

The wars we have been describing are fueled by the sale or transfer of arms from state and private sources, legal and illegal, and it is to that topic we now turn.

Global Arms Trade

Defense remains a big industry, and arms manufacturers employ many people in many countries. A standard theme of Marxist analysis is that arms manufacturers' search for profits is a cause of war. A U.S. Senate committee looking into the causes of World War I concluded that a small group of profit-minded industrialists, referred to as "merchants of death," were responsible for the conflict. Arms companies such as Vickers in Britain, Krupp in Germany, Schneider-Creusot in France, and Skoda in Austria-Hungary reaped great profits by selling arms to anyone who would buy them before 1914, and, more recently, U.S. and European defense contractors sold Iraq weapons it used in the Persian Gulf War, as well as components for nuclear and chemical weapons.

The global traffic in arms among governments is a huge business, peaking at about $74 billion (constant 1993 dollars) in 1987 before dropping to $22 billion in 1993. For some countries, like Czechoslovakia before the overthrow of communism and Bulgaria today, arms sales are a key source of hard currency. From 1985 to 1989, the U.S.S.R. was responsible for more than two-fifths of world arms exports, selling to almost anyone who could pay in hard currency, including Libya and Iraq, which then made those arms available to terrorist groups they supported. By 1991 Russia still accounted for 26 percent of the world's total, but this figure declined dramatically to less than 12 percent in 1993.[141] Others, including the United States, France, and China, were only marginally more scrupulous about whom they sold arms to. Arms exports fuel regional conflicts, and some of the world's largest importers are regional adversaries such as India and Pakistan.

For the West, especially the United States, which sold $53.4 billion in arms to the developing world between 1990 and 1997, arms are a major export industry and keep local defense manufacturers busy. In 1997, the United States sold $15.2 billion in weapons or 44 percent of a shrinking global arms market. Far behind were Britain ($5.9 billion), France ($4.9 billion), and Russia ($2.4 billion). By far the largest purchasers of arms between 1994 and 1997 were in the Middle East: Saudi Arabia ($36.4 billion), Taiwan ($9.1 billion), Egypt ($5.9 billion), and Kuwait ($4.5 billion).[142] Rivalry to sell arms is fierce, even among allies, because jobs at home are at stake.[143] For ambitious countries like China, Israel, Brazil, and Spain, selling arms is a source of influence and provides funds to maintain a home defense industry. The sale of arms to the less-developed countries, open and covert, is still big business.[144] Little wonder that during the wars between foes such as India and Pakistan, commentators wryly report whether U.S., British, Soviet, or French tanks and planes perform better. Perhaps there are merchants of death after all.

Recognizing that arms exports often aid repressive or aggressive governments, a group of Nobel Peace Prize winners headed by the former Costa Rican president, Oscar Arias Sánchez, drafted a proposed "code of conduct" to prohibit arms export to countries that do not hold free elections or respect human rights or that are engaged in armed aggression.[145] And, in July 1996, thirty countries reached an agreement called the Wassenaar Arrangement on Export Controls for Conventional Weapons and Dual-Use Goods and Technologies to control sales of technologies like sophisticated computers that can be used to develop new weapons.[146]

Costs and Consequences of Military Security

As the foregoing suggests, reliance on military force entails significant costs and consequences for actors. Three related consequences are especially important: (1) the burden in military expenditures and forces, (2) the growth of military influence in politics, and (3) the militarization of societies.

Trends in Military Expenditures and Force Levels

The costs of security pose heavy economic and social burdens. Although blood and treasure have always been consumed in the pursuit of security, costs ballooned in the decades after World War II. By spending a large portion of scarce resources on the military, actors have less to spend on education and welfare, and economic growth is delayed. Thus, in 1993, Angola spent $475 million for the military, $18.5 million for health, and $12 million for education.[147] With the end of the Cold War, people worldwide hoped for a generous *peace dividend,* some of which has been forthcoming.

Global military spending peaked at $1.36 trillion in 1987 and thereafter declined each succeeding year until it fell to $864 billion in 1995 (see Figure 10.1) and $811 billion in 1996 (as measured in constant dollars; that is, taking account of inflation)—the lowest since 1966 and 40 percent below 1987.[148] Most of this reduction was accounted for by the former members of the Warsaw Treaty Organization (WTO). In 1989, members of NATO and and the WTO accounted for 80 percent of global military expenditures. Although such expenditures were a burden on the West, they were even more onerous for the smaller economies in the former Soviet bloc.[149] In 1980 that bloc accounted for close to two-fifths of global military expenditures, and by the end of the decade it was still responsible for more than 35 percent. As Figure 10.2 and

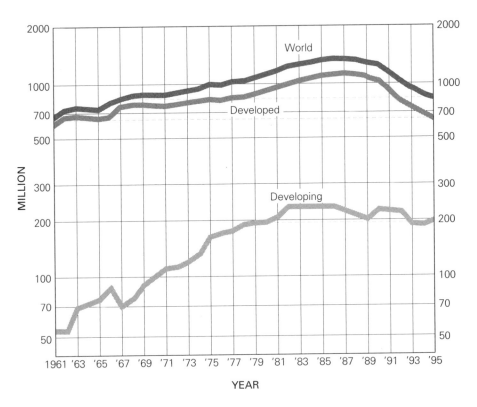

FIGURE 10.1
World Military Expenditures: 1961–1995 (in billions of constant 1995 dollars)
Worldwide military expenditures grew steadily from the 1960s until it peaked in 1987 and began to decline as the Cold War came to an end. The decline has been greater in the developed than developing world. SOURCE: U.S. Arms Control and Disarmament Agency, *World Military Expenditures and Arms Transfers, 1995–1996.*

Table 10.6 show, between 1983 and 1993 that burden declined from $423 billion to $134 billion for Eastern Europe and Russia, dropping almost 10 percent in the decade and almost 23 percent between 1988 and 1993.

As shown by the regional breakdown in Figure 10.2 and the growth rates in spending in Table 10.6, the defense burden is widespread. The dramatic decline in defense spending in Russia and Eastern Europe is accompanied by declines in the Middle East, owing to reduced oil prices, and in Central America, reflecting the end of civil wars in El Salvador and Nicaragua. By contrast, the increase in U.S. defense expenditures during the Reagan years (1980–1988) was followed by only a modest reduction.

The numbers of persons under arms reflect regional rivalries as well as changes in global politics at the end of the Cold War. The world's armed forces declined from a 1986 peak of 28.9 million to 22.8 million in 1995.[150] Five countries had armies of

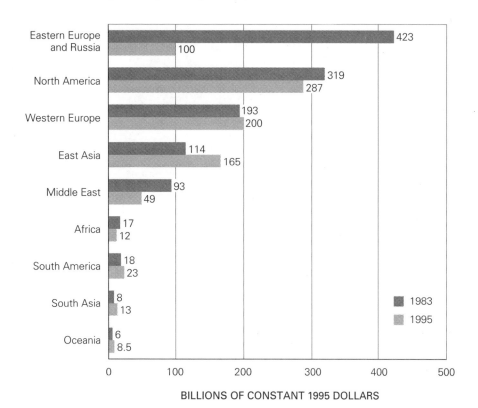

FIGURE 10.2

Military Expenditure by Region, 1983 and 1995

Since the Cold War ended, Eastern Europe (including Russia) and the Middle East have seen dramatic declines in military spending. SOURCE: U.S. Arms Control and Disarmament Agency, *World Military Expenditures and Arms Transfers, 1993–1994*, pp. 43–48, Table 1, and *World Military Expenditures and Arms Transfers, 1995–1996*, pp. 2–4.

more than one million in 1995—China, Russia, the United States, India, and North Korea—with Russia's down from the Cold War peak of 4.2 million.[151] The Middle East had far and away the highest proportion of labor force under arms, and Israel, Syria, Jordan, Oman, and Iraq—all in the Middle East—were among the world's five leaders in terms of proportion of labor force under arms.[152]

The Military in Politics
When defense is economically important and perceptions of insecurity are great, military officials may acquire popularity, prestige, and political influence, sometimes at a cost to citizens' liberties. Political dominance by military leaders may undermine or distort civilian control of government and society. This phenomenon has deep historical roots.

The Greek city-state Sparta, under constant military threat from within and without for much of its history, organized its whole society according to military precepts. France, in the midst of revolution and at war with much of Europe in 1799, turned the country over to a young military hero named Napoleon Bonaparte, and Bonapartism is still used to describe a military hero who seizes or is given political power often at

TABLE 10.6
*Military Expenditures:
Shares and Growth
(in percent)*

	World Share		Real Growth Rate*	
	1985	**1995**	**Decade 85–95**	**2nd Half 91–95**
World	100.0	100.0	−4.9	−7.1
Developed	82.7	77.3	−5.6	−8.0
Developing	17.3	22.7	−1.7	−3.8
Region				
North America	27.4	33.4	−2.7	−3.0
Western Europe	17.3	23.2	−1.3	−3.3
East Asia	9.8	19.1	2.3	3.3
Eastern Europe	34.1	11.5	−15.5	−24.1
Middle East	7.0	5.6	−5.3	−18.0
South America	1.4	2.7	.2	5.2
South Asia	.8	1.5	2.2	3.6
Oceania	.6	1.1	2.1	3.4
North Africa	.6	.6	−5.8	−.6
Subsaharan Africa	.4	.4	−2.3	−6.4
Central Asia & Cauc.	—	.4	—	—
Central Amer. & Car.	.2	.1	−9.6	−11.9
Europe, all	51.4	34.7	−9.0	−13.2
Africa, all	1.3	1.4	−4.3	−5.0
Organization / Reference Group				
OECD	48.2	63.5	−1.7	−2.7
OPEC	5.8	4.3	−6.1	−21.7
NATO, all	43.4	54.5	−2.2	−3.3
Warsaw Pact (fmr)	33.7	11.4	−15.6	−24.5
NATO Europe	16.0	21.3	−1.4	−3.5
Latin America	1.8	3.1	−.5	4.6
CIS	—	9.7	—	—

*Average annual rate, calculated as a compound rate curve fitted to all points.

SOURCE: U.S. Arms Control and Disarmament Agency, *World Military Expenditures and Arms Transfers 1995-1996*, p.3.

the expense of democracy. Eighteenth-century Prussia, threatened on all sides by larger powers, transformed itself under Frederick the Great into a modern Sparta. And, in 1917, in the midst of World War I, the German government turned over the country to two senior military officers, Field Marshals Erich Ludendorff and Paul von Hindenburg.

In this century, the military's takeover of Japan in the 1930s set the stage for World War II. For centuries, the military caste—the *samurai*—had been admired in Japan and honored by Japan's official religion, Shinto. Although Japan's political system in the 1920s was a multiparty parliamentary democracy, the armed forces remained independent of civilian control, and military officers without party affiliation were appointed ministers of the army and navy. Dissatisfaction with civilian rule was fueled by the world economic depression, Japanese dependence on imported raw materials, and Japanese perceptions of discrimination by the West. On September 18,

1931, Japanese army officers in China staged an "incident" in Mukden, without the civilian government's permission, and used that episode as an excuse to conquer all of Manchuria. Historian Edwin Reischauer describes what happened next:

> The . . . change of mood within Japan soon brought an end to party cabinets. Small bodies of ultra-rightists among military officers and civilians had for some time been agitating for a military coup. The prime minister . . . was shot by a fanatic. . . . Other leaders were assassinated early in 1932. . . . Young army officers almost brought off a *coup d'état* on February 26, 1936 . . . , and in 1937 all party participation in the cabinet was eliminated under a prime minister who was an army general.[153]

It was this military-dominated government that launched a full-scale invasion of China in 1937 and planned the attack on Pearl Harbor.

Following Japan's defeat, an effort was made to eliminate the militarist spirit that had cost the country and the world so much, and the new Japanese constitution that took effect in May 1947 renounced war forever. To this day, Japan continues to limit itself to "self-defense" forces, and is reluctant to provide combat forces even for multilateral operations like U.N. peacekeeping.

Many of the world's governments are dominated by authoritarian military officers—*"leaders in mufti."* In some countries, the military's main purpose is maintaining domestic peace and keeping authoritarian regimes in power rather than providing security from external aggression. Armies in Latin America rarely fight wars. Instead, they function as political arbiters, deciding who should or should not remain in power, occasionally overthrowing civilian politicians and ruling directly, and forcing governments to pursue conservative policies at home. Although recent years have witnessed the military's retreat from politics in Latin America—Chile, Venezuela, Argentina, and Uruguay—military corruption remains widespread and civilian leaders remain in the soldiers' shadow.

Notorious military strongmen in recent years include Libya's Colonel Muammar Qaddhafi (1969-), Major-General Idi Amin of Uganda (1971-1979), Major-General Joseph D. Mobutu of Zaire (1965-1997), General Alfredo Stroessner of Paraguay (1954-1989), General Muhammad Zia ul-Haq of Pakistan (1978-1988), Chile's General Augusto Pinochet (1974-1990), and Panamanian leaders Omar Torrijos (1969-1981) and Manuel Noriega (1983-1989). Not all military leaders who seize power come from the higher ranks. Mobutu was a sergeant when he took control of the former Belgian Congo, and the governments of Ghana and Liberia were overthrown by Flight Lt. Jerry Rawlings (1979) and Sergeant Samuel Doe (1980), respectively. The military routinely intervenes in political life in Africa and Asia and even in Europe where military leaders used to govern Spain, Portugal, and Greece. A strong tradition of civilian supremacy in politics exists in relatively few countries.

Militarizing Society: The U.S. Experience

Even where the military is barred from directly participating in governing, its influence can become pervasive. Influenced by the militarization of German society in World Wars I and II and the military takeover of Japan in the 1930s, political scientist Harold D. Lasswell feared that a rise in tension among the major powers would thrust military leaders into power. "Specialists in violence" might, he believed, seek to maintain global tension to preserve their status and privileges. Such societies Lasswell described as *garrison states.*[154] Despite the Cold War, the United States did not become a garrison state. Instead, it became what one observer has called a *contract state,* which "extracted money and manpower for military purposes" but "at levels lower than Lasswell had anticipated."[155]

As the Cold War triggered an explosive expansion of American defense budgets, interest groups proliferated, with the object of maintaining and even enlarging military spending. Even today, the Pentagon seeks to maintain spending not only to ensure U.S. security but also to provide status and promotions for its personnel. Defense industries,[156] labor unions in which members' jobs depend on defense spending, and congressmen from districts where such industries and/or military bases are located are natural allies of the Pentagon.[157] Other allies include local districts with soldiers and dependents, which receive special government grants for schools and where military spending aids the economy. The influence of such interests is one reason the peace dividend has been disappointing.

Although reducing the defense budget to free up funds for pressing civilian needs may seem desirable,[158] such reductions entail wrenching dislocations as corporations lose business, jobs disappear, and communities find themselves losing business and government money.[159] As outlays tumble, communities and corporations compete for what remains.[160] The Pentagon is providing funds to such regions to ease the impact of reduced defense spending. Communities like Groton, Connecticut, where the Electric Boat Division of the General Dynamics Corporation builds U.S. nuclear submarines, and their representatives in Congress have counterattacked to stave off painful cuts.[161] Thus, in 1995, President Clinton and Congress decided to build another Seawolf nuclear attack submarine at a cost of $2.5 billion even though there is no military need for it.[162]

The cozy relationship among private defense interests, Congress, and the Pentagon gave rise to the idea of a *military-industrial complex.* This idea was described by sociologist C. Wright Mills, who argued that key political decisions in U.S. society are made by a small *power elite* held together by economic, social, and psychological factors. According to Mills,

> There is no longer, on the one hand, an economy, and, on the other, a political order, containing a military establishment unimportant to politics and to money-making. There is a political economy numerously linked with military order and decision.[163]

The warming uttered by President Dwight D. Eisenhower to the American public when he retired in 1961 reflects these concerns:

> This conjunction of an immense military establishment and a large arms industry is new in the American experience. The total influence—economic, political, even spiritual—is felt in every city, every state house, every office of the Federal Government. . . . In the councils of Government, we must guard against the acquisition of unwarranted influence . . . by the military-industrial complex. The potential for the disastrous rise of misplaced power exists and will persist.[164]

Military contractors in the United States are among the country's largest industrial corporations and, as shown in Table 10.7, even after significant reductions in U.S.

TABLE 10.7

Leading U.S. Defense Contractors and the Value of Their Contract Work (1997)

Defense contract rank	Company	Value of prime contract awards (in $ billions)
1	Lockheed Martin	11.6
2	Boeing/McDonnell Douglas	9.6
3	Northrop Grumman	3.5
4	General Dynamics	3.0
5	Raytheon	2.9
6	General Motors	2.8
7	United Technologies	1.8
8	General Electric	1.7
9	Litton Industries	1.6
10	Textron, Inc.	1.4

SOURCE: "Lockheed #1 in 1997," ABCNEWS.COM, http:www.abcnews.com, March 25, 1998. Reprinted with permission of the American Broadcasting Companies, Inc.

defense spending in recent years. Thus as shown in Table 10.8, 11 of the largest defense companies in the world are American, including the top 3. Is it coincidental that of 234 high-ranking officeholders Gabriel Kolko identified in the Departments of States, Defense, Treasury, and Commerce between 1944 and 1960, 60 percent were "men who came from big business, investment, and law" so that "at every level of the administration of the American state, domestically and internationally, business serves as the fount of critical assumptions or goals and strategically placed personnel"?[165] Despite massive deficits and tight budgets, the Pentagon continues to spend millions to send weapons and personnel to trade shows around the world to help U.S. defense contractors hawk their wares.[166]

With government encouragement, America's leading defense companies have merged with one another in order to remain financially healthy in an era of declining defense budgets. Thus Lockheed and Martin Marietta merged to become the world's largest defense contractor,[167] and in 1997 Raytheon purchased Hughes Electronics from General Motors and the defense assets of Texas Instruments to become the world's largest supplier of military electronics.[168]

Some theorists fear that long periods of war or insecurity may undermine democracy. Thucydides described how democratic institutions in ancient Athens were eroded by the Peloponnesian War and how demagogues ultimately brought Athens to disaster. The perversion of Athenian democracy has been cited as an example of arrogance of power. Writing of U.S. intervention in Vietnam, Senator J. William Fulbright of Arkansas recalled Athen's fate: "Other great nations . . . have aspired to too much, and by overextension of effort have declined and then fallen."[169] During the Vietnam War, intolerance of dissent at home, abuses of individual rights by the FBI and CIA in the name of national security, and a pattern of government disregard for democratic traditions climaxed in the Watergate scandal and the resignation of President Richard M. Nixon in 1974. During the 1980s, fear of Soviet influence led to U.S. support of covert operations worldwide, sometimes in violation of congressional prohibitions. In Nicaragua, support for the anti-Sandinista rebels resulted in the illegal transfer of arms to Iran with profits used to fund the rebels. Lasswell feared precisely such challenges to the rule of law when he wrote of the garrison state.

TABLE 10.8
World's Top Defense Companies*

Company	Country	Defense revenues $bn
Lockheed Martin	United States	19.39
Boeing/McDonnell Douglas	United States	17.90
Raytheon/Hughes/ Texas Instruments	United States	11.67
British Aerospace	Britain	6.47
Northrop Grumman	United States	5.70
Thomson	France	4.68
Aérospatiale/Dassault	France	4.15
GEC	Britain	4.12
United Technologies	United States	3.65
Lagardère Groupe	France	3.29
Daimler-Benz Aerospace	Germany	3.25
Direction des Constructions Navales	France	3.07
General Dynamics	United States	2.90
Finmeccanica	Italy	2.59
Litton Industries	United States	2.40
Mitsubishi Heavy Industries	Japan	2.22
General Electric	United States	2.15
Tenneco	United States	1.80
TRW	United States	1.71
ITT Industries	United States	1.56

*Based on 1995 figures

SOURCE: "Linking Arms," *The Economist,* special report, June 14–20, 1997, p. 4. © 1997 The Economist Newspaper Group, Inc. Reprinted with permission. Further reproduction prohibited. www.economist.com.

Defense Conversion

One of the challenges of reduced defense outlays is how to convert defense industries to civilian uses. Otherwise, military facilities will go unused, large numbers of workers will be unemployed,[170] and defense corporations may go out of business. Thus nearly 80 percent of all industry in the Russian city of Novosibirsk was defense-related, and some companies have no orders to fill. And between 1987 and 1995, Americans employed by the armaments industry declined from 17.5 million to 11.1 million.[171] Some efforts at *defense conversion* are highly original.

Thus the U.S. Energy Department is building a giant laser machine at California's Lawrence Livermore National Laboratory—"a cold-war bastion set adrift with the demise of its old job of designing nuclear warheads"—to study how stars shine, how to generate electric power from nuclear fire, and how to maintain the reliability of hydrogen bombs without underground testing.[172] The U.S. Navy is letting civilian scientists use its nuclear attack submarines to study the Arctic Ocean as well as its undersea microphones to study seaquakes, undersea volcanoes, and whale migrations.[173] The Defense Department will allow its orbiting satellites to be used for such civilian tasks as tracking truck fleets and guiding hikers,[174] and old missiles may be used to launch commercial satellites.[175]

ACTORS SPEAK

As part of the conversion of military technology to civilian use, the U.S. government is permitting companies such as Earthwatch Inc. and Space Imaging Inc. to launch once highly classified spy satellites for commercial purposes. Those companies are enthused about the commercial possibilities, but others fear the consequences of declassifying their technology.

The possibilities are endless. Vacationers will plan exotic sailing cruises along foreign coasts. Small retail businesses will have a better understanding of demographics. (From a brochure of Earthwatch Inc. of Longmont, Colorado, as cited in William J. Broad, "Private Ventures Hope for Profits on Spy Satellites," *New York Times,* February 10, 1997, p. A1)

The biggest market for this information is going to be foreign governments that can't afford their own reconnaissance systems. The issue is going to heat up the first time we get a real crunch between two friends, like Pakistan and India. (Albert D. Wheelon, former CIA official, as cited in William J. Broad, "Private Ventures Hope for Profits on Spy Satellites," *New York Times,* February 10, 1997, p. A1)

Elsewhere, similar efforts are under way. The United States is providing funds for U.S. companies proposing joint ventures with Russia's defense industries.[176] The Chinese army already runs a business empire for profit.[177] The World Bank is experimenting in Uganda with a plan to provide funding for severance packages for soldiers to reduce the size and costs of armies in the less-developed countries.[178]

Conclusion

Actors' willingness to go to war and the manner in which wars are waged differ by time and place. The probability and nature of war at any moment reflect the underlying global politics of the era. Changing technology is a large factor in determining political tension and providing opportunities and setting limits on warfare. War, as one historian observes, "is completely permeated by technology and governed by it."[179] Memories of the past and expectations of the future condition leaders' willingness to use force and influence the types of wars they prepare to fight. In this chapter we have reviewed the nature of war over the past six centuries. Disentangling the causes of those wars is very complex. Although there are numerous theories of war, evidence is insufficient to decide which are best. However, analyses of interstate wars are perhaps less germane than in the international era of state relations. The postinternational epoch features violence within and across states that is not relevant to theories of interstate relations, or to Clausewitz's theory of the relationship of war and politics.

The world wars profoundly affected a generation of leaders who found themselves at the helm during the Cold War. One additional factor intervened, however, altering everyone's calculations of the future. Nuclear weapons, introduced in 1945, forever changed warfare and global politics generally. In Chapter 11, we complete the story of war by examining the implications of these weapons of mass destruction.

Key Terms

aggression
arms races
blitzkrieg (lightning war)
cognitive consistency
contract state
crisis of overproduction
cult of the offensive
death instinct
defense conversion
expected-utility theory

frustration
garrison state
human nature
imperialism
individual rationality
leaders in mufti
levée en masse
military-industrial complex
peace dividend

polarity
postmodern war
power cycle
power elite
power preponderance
samurai
Schlieffen Plan
transnational war
war

End Notes

[1]Niccolò Machiavelli, *The Prince,* trans. George Bull (Baltimore: Penguin Books, 1961), chap. 12, p. 77.

[2]Ibid, chap. 14, p. 87.

[3]Cited in Martin van Creveld, *Technology and War: From 2000 B.C. to the Present* (New York: Free Press, 1989), p. v.

[4]These breakpoints are based on Melvin Small and J. David Singer, "Conflict in the International System, 1816–1977: Historical Trends and Policy Futures," in Charles W. Kegley, Jr., and Patrick J. McGowan, eds., *Challenges to America: United States Foreign Policy in the 1980s* (Beverly Hills: Sage, 1979), pp. 94–95.

[5]Melvin Small and J. David Singer, "Patterns in International Warfare, 1816–1980," in Small and Singer, eds., *International War,* 2nd ed. (Chicago: Dorsey Press, 1989), p. 31.

[6]Small and Singer, "Conflict in the International System," pp. 100–101.

[7]Jack S. Levy, *War in the Modern Great Power System, 1495–1975* (Lexington: University Press of Kentucky, 1983), p. 117.

[8]Ibid., pp. 116 and 139–140.

[9]Michael J. Sullivan III, *Measuring Global Values: The Ranking of 162 Countries* (New York: Greenwood Press, 1991), p. 27. Different sources provide different data depending on their definition of war. As Sullivan (p. 25) notes: "It is difficult to identify clearly examples of belligerent states in this era of undeclared wars, revolutions without borders, military aid for probes by proxies, and other blurred distinctions between domestic and international conflict."

[10]Ibid. War in the former Yugoslavia since 1990 is the example that proves the rule.

[11]With European empires gone, colonial wars—frequent between 1945 and 1975—have ceased. A few colonial hotspots still remain, including East Timor's war to free itself from Indonesia.

[12]Margareta Sollenberg and Peter Wallensteen, "Major armed conflicts," in *SIPRI Yearbook 1996* (New York: Oxford University Press, 1996), p. 15. The bloody war between

Ethiopia and Eritrea that was fought in 1999 over worthless territory suggests that interstate wars have not disappeared.

[13]"Clinton Speaks: Battling Forces of Disintegration," *New York Times,* June 1, 1995, p. A6.

[14]Sullivan, *Measuring Global Values,* pp. 36, 37.

[15]This corresponds to the three "images" Kenneth N. Waltz employs in *Man, the State and War* (New York: Columbia University Press, 1959).

[16]John A. Vasquez, *The War Puzzle* (New York: Cambridge University Press, 1993). This is a thoughtful synthesis of empirical research on the causes of war.

[17]Sigmund Freud, "Why War?" in Leon Bramson and George W. Goethals, eds., *War,* rev. ed. (New York: Basic Books, 1968), pp. 76, 77. Other early psychologists, including William James and William McDougall, thought that human instinct lay behind aggressive behavior.

[18]John Dollard, Leonard W. Doob, Neal E. Miller, et al., *Frustration and Aggression* (New Haven: Yale University Press, 1939), p. 1.

[19]Bernard Berelson and Gary A. Steiner, *Human Behavior: An Inventory of Scientific Findings* (New York: Harcourt Brace Jovanovich, 1964), pp. 267-269. The authors describe an earlier investigation that found that lynchings in the American South increased when the price of cotton declined! In recent years, high unemployment in Europe has been accompanied by violence against both legal and illegal immigrants from the less-developed countries.

[20]Cited in Roy L. Prosterman, *Surviving to 3000* (Belmont, CA: Duxbury Press, 1972), p. 101. Military forces all over the world use similar methods to ensure obedience and conformity—drills, uniforms, ranks, and so on.

[21]Helen Caldicott, *Missile Envy* (New York: Bantam Books, 1985), pp. 235-237.

[22]Richard Holmes, *Acts of War: The Behavior of Men in Battle* (New York: Free Press, 1985), pp. 270-315.

[23]See Robert Mandel, "Psychological Approaches to International Relations," in Margaret G. Hermann, ed., *Political Psychology* (San Francisco: Jossey-Bass, 1986), pp. 251-278; and Charles A. Powell, James W. Dyson, and Helen E. Purkitt, "Opening the 'Black Box': Cognitive Processing and Optimal Choice in Foreign Policy Decision Making," in Charles F. Hermann, Charles W. Kegley, Jr., and James N. Rosenau, eds., *New Directions in the Study of Foreign Policy* (Boston: Allen & Unwin, 1987), pp. 203-220.

[24]Alexander George and Juliette George, *Woodrow Wilson and Colonel House* (New York: Day, 1956), p. 11.

[25]Mandel, "Psychological Approaches to International Relations," p. 253.

[26]See Albert F. Eldridge, *Images of Conflict* (New York: St. Martin's Press, 1979), pp. 41-45.

[27]Robert Jervis, *Perception and Misperception in International Politics* (Princeton: Princeton University Press, 1976), p. 154.

[28]Margaret G. Hermann, "Explaining Foreign Policy Behavior Using the Personal Characteristics of Political Leaders," *International Studies Quarterly* 24:1 (March 1980), p. 8.

[29]Bruce Bueno de Mesquita, *The War Trap* (New Haven: Yale University Press, 1981), p. 127. Also, Bruce Bueno de Mesquita and David Lalman, "Reason and War," *American Political Science Review* 80:4 (December 1986), pp. 1113-1129.

[30]See Jack S. Levy, "Prospect Theory, Rational Choice, and International Relations," *International Studies Quarterly* 41:1 (March 1997), pp. 87-112.

[31]William H. McNeill, *The Rise of the West* (Chicago: University of Chicago Press, 1963), p. 28.

[32]Cited in Roy Prosterman, *Surviving to 3000,* p. 149. Mead, along with anthropologists Franz Boas and Ruth Benedict, are known as cultural determinists. John Keegan, *A History of Warfare* (New York: Knopf, 1993), pp. 86-89.

[33]John A. Hobson, *Imperialism* (Ann Arbor: University of Michigan Press, 1965).

[34]V. I. Lenin, "Imperialism, the Highest State of Capitalism," in Robert C. Tucker, ed., *The Lenin Anthology* (New York: Norton, 1975), pp. 204-274.

[35]Waltz, *Man, the State and War,* p. 98. The most influential of the liberal thinkers were political philosophers Immanuel Kant and John Stuart Mill and political economist Adam Smith.

[36]Michael W. Doyle, "Liberalism and World Politics," *American Political Science Review* 80:4 (December 1986), p. 1156. Between 1816 and 1980, only 12 of 416 wars were between democracies. "The politics of peace," *The Economist,* April 1-7, 1995, p. 17.

[37]Edward D. Mansfield and Jack Snyder, "Democratization and War," *Foreign Affairs* 74:3 (May/June 1995), p. 94.

[38]Richard N. Rosecrance, *Action and Reaction in World Politics* (Boston: Little, Brown, 1963), p. 304. For a contrasting view, see Geoffrey Blainey, *The Causes of War,* 3rd ed. (New York: Free Press, 1988), pp. 71-86. The most ambitious effort to test the relationship between domestic instability and interstate conflict is the Dimensionality of Nations (DON) project. Its results have been inconclusive. See R. J. Rummel, *The Dimensions of Nations* (Beverly Hills, CA: Sage, 1972), and Rummel, *Field Theory Evolving* (Beverly Hills, CA: Sage, 1977).

[39]For an excellent summary of alternate systemic approaches, see John A. Vasquez, "The Steps to War: Toward a Scientific Explanation of Correlates of War Findings," *World Politics* 40:1 (October 1987), pp. 108-145.

[40]Waltz, *Man, the State, and War,* pp. 232, 238.

[41]For a summary of the following two arguments, see Bruce Bueno de Mesquita and David Lalman, "Empirical Support for Systemic and Dyadic Explanations of International Conflict," *World Politics* 41:1 (October 1988), especially pp. 3-4.

[42]The preponderance argument can be found in A.F.K. Organski, *World Politics* (New York: Knopf, 1968). For a more recent version, see A.F.K. Organski and Jacek Kugler, *The War Ledger* (Chicago: University of Chicago Press, 1980).

[43]Polarity is a vague concept. Some use it to mean the number of blocs or alliances in a system, and for others it is synonymous with distribution of power.

[44]Kenneth N. Waltz, "The Stability of a Bipolar World," in David Edwards, ed., *International Political Analysis* (New York: Holt, Rinehart and Winston, 1970), p. 340.

[45]Kenneth N. Waltz, "International Structure, National Force, and the Balance of World Power," *Journal of International Affairs* 21:2 (1967), pp. 220, 223.

[46]Karl W. Deutsch and J. David Singer, "Multipolar Power Systems and International Stability," in James N. Rosenau, ed., *International Politics and Foreign Policy,* rev. ed. (New York: Free Press, 1969), pp. 315-324. Richard N. Rosecrance criticized both Waltz and Deutsch/Singer, reasoning that a system with features from both ("bimultipolarity") would be the safest. Rosecrance, "Biopolarity, Multipolarity, and the Future," in ibid., pp. 325-335.

[47]De Mesquita and Lalman, "Empirical Support," p. 20. See also Ned Sabrosky, ed., *Polarity and War* (Boulder, CO: Westview Press, 1985). Distribution of economic power is at the heart of the world-systems argument of Immanuel Wallerstein, and is the basis of "long cycle theory," which sees war as related to the domination of world politics by leading trading states. George Modelski, "The Long Cycle of Global Politics and the Nation-State," *Comparative Studies in Society and History* 20:2 (April 1978), pp. 214-235; and Joshua Goldstein, *Long Cycles: Prosperity and War in the Modern Age* (New Haven: Yale University Press, 1988). Long cycle theory owes much to the Kondratieff theory of technological change and economic growth and contraction.

[48]Organski and Kugler, *War Ledger,* p. 61.

[49]Charles F. Doran, *Systems in Crisis* (New York: Cambridge University Press, 1991).

[50]Lewis F. Richardson, *Arms and Insecurity* (Chicago: Quadrangle, 1960), p. 12.

[51]Michael D. Wallace, "Status, Formal Organization, and Arms Levels as Factors Leading to the Onset of War, 1820-1964," in Bruce M. Russett, ed., *Peace, War, and Numbers* (Beverly Hills, CA: Sage, 1972), pp. 49-71.

[52]Michael D. Wallace, "Arms Races and Escalation: Some New Evidence," *Journal of Conflict Resolution* 23:1 (March 1979), p. 14-15. See Wallace, "Armaments and Escalation," *International Studies Quarterly* 26:1 (March 1982), pp. 37-56, in which the author shows that the relationship of arms races to war remains no matter who is winning the race.

[53]For an excellent one-volume review, see Archer Jones, *The Art of War in the Western World* (Urbana, IL: University of Illinois Press, 1987).

[54]William H. McNeill, *The Pursuit of Power* (Chicago: University of Chicago Press, 1982), p. 68.

[55]Ibid., p. 89.

[56]Ibid.

[57]Cited in R. R. Palmer, "Frederick the Great, Guibert, Bulow: From Dynastic to National War," in Peter Paret, ed., *Makers of Modern Strategy* (Princeton: Princeton University Press, 1986), p. 93.

[58]Ibid., pp. 99, 103, 104, 105.

[59]Cited in John Shy, "Jomini," in Paret, ed., *Makers of Modern Strategy,* pp. 144-145.

[60]Ibid., p. 145. For the first time in history, armies were too large for a single commander to follow visually.

[61]Military leaders did not appreciate this prescription. Thus Helmuth von Moltke, chief of staff of the Prussian Army from 1857 to 1887, idealized Clausewitz but argued, "In no case must the leader allow his operations to be influenced by politics *alone.*" Moltke, "Doctrines of War," in Lawrence Freedman, ed., *War* (New York: Oxford University Press, 1994), p. 219. Emphasis in original.

[62]Karl von Clausewitz, *On War,* trans. O. J. Matthijs Jolles (New York: Random House, Modern Library, 1943), Book I, chap. 1, p. 3. Emphasis in original.

[63]Ibid., Book I, chap. 1, p. 16.

[64]Ibid., Book I, chap. 1, p. 10.

[65]Ibid., Book I, chap. 1, p. 16.

[66]Thomas C. Schelling, *Arms and Influence* (New Haven: Yale University Press, 1966), p. 2. See also Schelling, *The Strategy of Conflict* (Cambridge: Harvard University Press, 1960).

[67]At MacArthur's urging, U.S. forces had marched north of the 38th parallel and were sweeping toward the Yalu River border with China when Chinese forces intervened. The temptation to expand the war beyond its original objectives almost led to military disaster.

[68]As voter dissatisfaction with American failure to "win" in Korea mounted, the Republican Party chose another war hero, General Dwight D. Eisenhower, to run for the presidency in 1952. Eisenhower, vowing to visit Korea, defeated his Democratic opponent, Adlai E. Stevenson, in a landslide.

[69]The trigger was the assassination on June 28 of the heir to the Hapsburg throne by a Serbian nationalist during a state visit to Sarajevo, capital of Bosnia-Herzegovina.

[70]On one side was the Triple Entente of Britain, France, and Russia (Serbia's protector). On the other was the Triple Alliance of Germany, Austria-Hungary, and Italy (which backed out of its obligation and later joined the other side).

[71]Barbara Tuchman, *The Guns of August* (New York: Macmillan, 1962), p. 488 n.

[72]Wilfred Owen, "Dulce Et Decorum Est," in John Heath-Stubbs and David Wright, eds., *The Faber Book of Twentieth Century Verse* (London: Faber and Faber, 1953), p. 253. The title of the poem—"How Sweet and Fitting It Is"—is taken from an ode by the ancient Roman poet Horace lauding patriotism.

[73]See Jack S. Levy, "Preferences, Constraints, and Choices in July 1914," *International Security* 15:3 (Winter 1990/91), pp. 151–186.

[74]One unresolved issue is whether the state of technology determined the actors' tactical preferences. Jonathan Shimshoni, "Technology, Military Advantage, and World War I: A Case for Military Entrepreneurship," *International Security* 15:3 (Winter 1990/91), pp. 187–215.

[75]One long-range German artillery piece that was used in 1914 with great effect against Belgian and French fortresses was known as Big Bertha after the daughter of the head of Krupp armaments, which made the guns.

[76]Cited in Sigmund Neumann and Mark von Hagen, "Engels and Marx on Revolution, War, and the Army in Society," in Paret, ed., *Makers of Modern Strategy*, p. 274.

[77]Michael Howard, "Men Against Fire: The Doctrine of the Offensive in 1914," in Paret, ed., *Makers of Modern Strategy*, pp. 517–518.

[78]Ibid., p. 519. Emphasis in original.

[79]Ardant du Picq, "Moral Elements in Battle," in Freedman, *War*, pp. 222–225.

[80]Cited in Howard, "Men Against Fire," p. 514.

[81]This failure of comprehension is nowhere captured better than in Alexander Solzhenitsyn's fictional account of Russia's disastrous advance into East Prussia in 1914. The author describes how Russian troops were made to march all the way to the front, where they arrived exhausted, while horses were transported by rail, and how the Russians failed to encode radio messages, assuming the Germans would not be listening. *August 1914*, trans. Michael Glenny (New York: Farrar, Straus & Giroux, 1971).

[82]See Richard Ned Lebow, *Nuclear Crisis Management* (Ithaca, NY: Cornell University Press, 1987), pp. 109–112. On the cult of the offensive, see Stephen Van Evera, "Why Cooperation Failed in 1914," *World Politics* 38:1 (October 1985), especially pp. 83–84; Jack Snyder, *The Ideology of the Offensive: Military Decision Making and the Disasters of 1914* (Ithaca, NY: Cornell University Press, 1984). The plan was the brainchild of Alfred von Schlieffen, chief of the German general staff (1891–1906). Other countries had similar plans.

[83]Ironically, Germany's greatest triumphs of 1914 came against the Russians in the battles of Tannenberg and the Masurian Lakes. In a panic, German forces that might have brought victory in France were hurriedly sent east but arrived too late to play a role. Deprived of the forces envisioned in the Schlieffen Plan, the German offensive in the west came up short at the gates of Paris. Following the battle of the Marne, the war in the west became a defensive slugfest.

[84]Lawrence Lafore, *The Long Fuse*, 2nd ed. (New York: Lippincott, 1971), p. 257.

[85]Alsace-Lorraine had been severed from France by Germany after the 1870 Franco-Prussian War. It became a symbol of French nationalism, and, in 1880, French leader Léon Gambetta said of the "lost" province, "Think of it always, speak of it never." Cited in René Albrecht-Carrié, *A Diplomatic History of Europe Since the Congress of Vienna* (New York: Harper & Row, 1958), p. 167. Visitors to Paris may observe that the Place de la Concorde at the city's center is encircled by statues of women representing the country's different cities. From 1870 until return of the province, the statues representing the Alsatian cities of Metz and Strasbourg were draped in black crepe.

[86]Howard, "Men Against Fire," p. 523.

[87]Ibid., p. 525. The ineptitude of officers on both sides and the slaughter of their troops are captured in Lyn Macdonald, *1915: The Death of Innocence* (New York: Henry Holt, 1993).

[88]Brian Bond and Martin Alexander, "Liddell Hart and De Gaulle: The Doctrines of Limited Liability and Mobile Defense," in Paret, ed., *Makers of Modern Strategy*, p. 598.

[89]It was named after André Maginot, the war minister who oversaw its construction. The Germans having outflanked the line in 1940, the fortifications were used to grow mushrooms during the war.

[90]Some of the most imaginative tactics did not require high technology at all. The Japanese used bicycles to move down through the Malay jungles to spring from the rear upon the British naval fortress at Singapore in 1942. Believing that Singapore could be attacked only from the sea, British guns pointed seaward, and defenders made little effort to fortify the Straits of Johore separating the city from the Malay peninsula.

[91]A number of young British and French strategists, including Charles de Gaulle, understood the implications of the new weapons but were ignored by their superiors. Bond and Alexander, "Liddell Hart and de Gaulle," pp. 600 ff.

[92]Andrew M. Scott, *The Revolution in Statecraft: Informal Penetration* (New York: Random House, 1965), p. 32.

[93]Ibid., p. 36.

[94]In 1934, Nazi sympathizers murdered the Austrian chancellor, and four years later Hitler contemplated ordering the assassination of his own ambassador to Austria to justify the Nazi takeover of that country.

[95]Alan Bullock, *Hitler, A Study in Tyranny*, rev. ed. (New York: Harper & Row, 1962), p. 343.

[96]Michael Geyer, "German Strategy in the Age of Machine Welfare, 1914–1945," in Paret, ed., *Makers of Modern Strategy*, p. 593.

[97]Hitler repeatedly made the error of confronting new foes before defeating old ones, invading the U.S.S.R. ("Operation Barbarossa") in June 1941 before Britain had been defeated, and declaring war against the United States shortly after Pearl Harbor.

[98]In World War I, airplanes had served primarily for observation. Nevertheless, a number of far-sighted strategists understood the potential of airpower. In the United States, General Billy Mitchell was the leading exponent of tactical airpower, especially its

potential effectiveness against surface ships. Edward Warner, "Douhet, Mitchell, Seversky: Theories of Air Warfare," in Edward Mead Earle, ed., *Makers of Modern Strategy*, 1st ed. (New York: Atheneum, 1967), pp. 497–501. Also David MacIsaac, "Voices from the Central Blue: The Air Power Theorists," in Paret, ed., *Makers of Modern Strategy*, pp. 624–647.

[99] Eric Schmitt, "Aircraft Carrier May Give Way to Missile Ship," *New York Times*, September 3, 1995, sec. 1, pp. 1, 11.

[100] "Defense Technology," special survey, *The Economist*, June 10–16, 1995, pp. 8, 10.

[101] Keegan, *A History of Warfare*, p. 3. See Susan Ehrenreich, *Blood Rites* (New York: Henry Holt, 1997).

[102] The civil war in Guatemala lasted 36 years. Larry Rohter, "Guatemalans Formally End Their 36-Year Civil War," *New York Times*, December 30, 1996, p. A4.

[103] See, for example, Seth Mydans, "In Lush Tropics, a Flowering of Murderous Gangs," *New York Times*, May 1, 1997, p. A4.

[104] In some of these wars, mercenaries play a key role. For example, a company of South African mercenaries called Executive Outcomes aided the Angolan government to defeat its foes. Howard W. French, "Now for Hire: South Africa's Out-of-Work Commandos," *New York Times*, May 24, 1995, p. A3. See also "French Mercenary Gives up in Comoros Coup Attempt," *New York Times*, October 6, 1995, p. A7.

[105] Robert D. Kaplan, "The Coming Anarchy," *Atlantic Monthly*, February 1994, p. 72. A world such as Kaplan describes will surely feature an explosion in "private" security to protect the well-to-do from violence. Already, there are about ten times as many private security guards in Russia and South Africa as there are "public" police. "Welcome to the New World of Private Security," *The Economist*, April 19–25, 1997, pp. 21–24.

[106] Roger Cohen, "In Sarajevo, Victims of a 'Postmodern' War," *New York Times*, May 4, 1995, sec. 1, pp. 1, 8.

[107] Cited in Barbara Crossette, "U.N. Council Looks at Rise in Number of Children in Combat," *New York Times*, June 30, 1998, p. A3.

[108] The United States is resisting the effort of this coalition to make 18 the minimum age for soldiers.

[109] Barbara Crossette, "Unicef Report See Children as Major Victims of Wars," *New York Times*, December 11, 1995, p. A7.

[110] Molly Moore and John Ward Anderson, "War's Young Victims," *Washington Post National Weekly Edition*, May 8–14, 1995, pp. 6–7; "Hidden Horrors Without End," *The Economist*, September 16–22, 1995, p. 50.

[111] Christopher S. Wren, "Everywhere Weapons That Keep on Killing," *New York Times*, October 8, 1995, sec. 4, p. 3.

[112] John J. Fialka, "Land Mines Prove to Be Even Harder to Detect Than They Are to Ban," *Wall Street Journal*, May 17, 1996, p. A1.

[113] Cited in "France to Halt Production of Some Land Mines," *New York Times*, September 27, 1995, p. A4. See also Barbara

Crossette, "Pact on Land Mines Stops Short of Total Ban," *New York Times*, May 4, 1996, p. 4; "Treading gingerly," *The Economist*, April 27–May 3, 1996.

[114] Some 64,000 U.S. troops were killed or injured by mines (often of U.S. make or design) in the Vietnam War. Philip Shenon, "U.S.-Made Land Mines Killed or Injured 64,000 Americans, Report Says," *New York Times*, July 29, 1997, p. A9. See also "Dual track," *The Economist*, January 25–31, 1997, p. 42; "Ban mines now," *The Economist*, May 24–30, 1997, p. 16.

[115] Raymond Bonner, "21 Nations Seek to Limit the Traffic in Light Weapons," *New York Times*, July 13, 1998, p. A3. See also Raymond Bonner, "The Murky Life of an International Gun Dealer," *New York Times*, July 14, 1998, p. A3, which describes the illegal shipment of small arms from Europe to a militant Hindu fundamentalist group in Calcutta, India. Bulgaria is a leading source of light arms for regional conflicts. Raymond Bonner, "Bulgaria Becomes a Weapons Bazaar," *New York Times*, August 3, 1998, p. A3. The small arms issue was a topic at the West's annual economic summit meeting in Birmingham, UK, in May 1998. "Hey, Anybody Want a Gun?" *The Economist*, May 16–22, 1998, pp. 47–48.

[116] "Genocide in Rwanda," *The Economist*, May 21–27, 1994, p. 45.

[117] Cited in Paul Lewis, "At U.N., Russian Compares Peril of Ethnic Strife to Nuclear War," *New York Times*, September 29, 1993, p. A4.

[118] Eric Schmitt, "American Arsenal Honed for Bosnia," *New York Times*, December 5, 1995, pp. A1, A8.

[119] Howard W. French, "As Violence Mounts, Liberians Hope for Foreign Help," *New York Times*, May 3, 1995, p. A3.

[120] Jeffrey Goldberg, "A War Without Purpose in a Country Without Identity," *New York Times Magazine*, January 22, 1995, p. 38.

[121] Ibid.

[122] Howard W. French, "War Engulfs Liberia, Humbling Peacekeepers," *New York Times*, October 7, 1994, p. A7. The peacekeepers themselves indulged in plundering and smuggling. Howard W. French, "Warlords Ascend in Liberia's Ruins," *New York Times*, April 21, 1996, sec. 4, p. 4.

[123] Howard W. French, "62 Slain in a Liberian Village; Most Are Women and Children," *New York Times*, April 19, 1995, p. A8.

[124] "Out of the Bush," *The Economist*, May 6–12, 1995, p. 42.

[125] "Vote to Nowhere," *The Economist*, March 2–8, 1996, p. 44. See also "Sliding Back to War?" *The Economist*, March 15–21, 1997, p. 43.

[126] Cited in Howard W. French, "After 6 Brutal Years of War, Peace Is Celebrated in Liberia," *New York Times*, September 1, 1995, p. A1.

[127] Phillip van Niekerk, "U.S. Is Set to Rescue Americans from Fighting in Liberia Capital," *New York Times*, April 9, 1996, p. A1. See also "Sharks and Alligators," *The Economist*, April 13–19, 1996, pp. 34–35; "Vacant Possession," *The Economist*, April 19–25, 1997, p. 45.

[128] Neighboring Burundi also has a Tutsi minority and Hutu majority, and ethnic slaughter has taken place there as well.

"Tribal Massacre Toll in Burundi May Top 150,000, Official Says," *New York Times,* November 28, 1993; "Twin Horror," *The Economist,* July 6-12, 1996, p. 42; "The Next Disaster," *The Economist,* October 19-25, 1996, p. 18; "Burundi on the Brink of Peace?" *The Economist,* June 20-26, 1998, pp. 49-50.

[129]Initially the Clinton administration instructed its spokesmen not to describe events in Rwanda as genocide because of the obligations of states, including the United States, under the 1948 Genocide Convention. Douglas Jehl, "Officials Told to Avoid Calling Rwanda Killings 'Genocide'," *New York Times,* June 10, 1994, p. A8. Nevertheless, Rwanda was a clear case of genocide—the eradication of an entire ethnic community. Roger Winter, "Rwanda, Up Close and Horrible," *Washington Post National Weekly Review,* June 13-19, 1994, p. 23.

[130]The massacres had been planned months before. Raymond Bonner, "A Once-Peaceful Village Shows the Roots of Rwanda's Violence," *New York Times,* July 11, 1994, pp. A1, A5.

[131]Donatella Lorch, "Thousands of Rwanda Dead Wash Down to Lake Victoria," *New York Times,* May 21, 1994, pp. 1, 3. See also Donatella Lorch, "Bodies from Rwanda Cast a Pall on Lakeside Villages in Uganda," *New York Times,* May 28, 1994, pp. 1, 5.

[132]Roger Rosenblatt, "The Killers in the Next Tent: The Surreal Horror of the Rwanda Refugees," *New York Times Magazine,* June 5, 1994, pp. 37 ff.; James C. McKinley, Jr., "In Pastoral Land, Rwandans Engage in Murderous Tit for Tat," *New York Times,* October 6, 1996, sec. 1, p. 6; James C. McKinley, Jr., "Rural Rwanda's Uneasy Balance of Fear," *New York Times,* December 26, 1996, pp. A1, A7; Howard W. French, "Zaire's Military Reported to Arm Rwandan Exiles to Fight Rebels," *New York Times,* February 19, 1997, pp. A1, A3.

[133]James C. McKinley, Jr., "220,000 Hutu Flee Fight Between Zaire and Tutsi Settlers," *New York Times,* October 22, 1996, p. A3; Howard W. French, "Robbed of Nationality, a Zairian Tutsi Family Run for Their Lives," *New York Times,* November 17, 1996, sec. 1, p. 4.

[134]Howard W. French, "As Zaire Splits, History Repeats Itself," *New York Times,* November 11, 1996, p. A6; Howard W. French, "Army's Morale Declines as Rebels Gain in Zaire," *New York Times,* February 8, 1997, pp. 1, 4; "The Last Days of Mobutu," *The Economist,* March 22-28, 1997, pp. 21, 22, 27. Luba tribesmen in the Zairian provinces of Kasai and Shaba took advantage of the chaotic situation to wrest greater autonomy for themselves. "A Provincial Gem," *The Economist,* April 27-May 3, 1996, pp. 46-47.

[135]As Mobutu's power waned, Zairians started referring to their new local currency as "prostates," a darkly humorous reference to their leader's illness. Howard W. French, "Hard Times for Zaire: It Can't Give Cash Away," *New York Times,* February 16, 1997, sec. 1, p. 9.

[136]See, for example, Howard W. French, "In a Zaire Forest, Hutu Refugees Near End of Line," *New York Times,* March 13, 1997, pp. A1, A7; Barbara Crossette, "U.N. Team Says Congo Army Killed Hutu," *New York Times,* July 1, 1998, p. A8; For the anti-Kabila insurrection, see Howard W. French, "Congo Replay,"

New York Times, August 5, 1998, pp. A1, A8. For the regional conflict, see Donald G. McNeil, Jr., "A War Turned Free-for-All Tears at Africa's Center," *New York Times,* December 6, 1998, sec. 4, p. 5; Ian Fisher, "Rwanda's Huge Stake in Congo War," *New York Times,* December 27, 1998, p. 8.

[137]"Sri Lanka Vote in Doubt; Tamil Unrest Is Feared," *New York Times,* August 5, 1998, p. A11. In 1995 India set up a naval blockade in the Palk Strait to prevent arms from reaching the Tamil Tigers. John F. Burns, "India Sets Up Blockade to Aid Sri Lanka Against Rebels," *New York Times,* June 14, 1995, p. 13.

[138]John F. Burns, "Asia's Latest Master of Terror," *New York Times,* May 28, 1995, sec. 4, p. 3; "After the Bomb," *The Economist,* January 10-16, 1996, p. 36.

[139]John F. Burns, "A Corner of Sri Lanka Tires of Living Under Siege," *New York Times,* October 16, 1994, sec. 1, p. 3.

[140]John F. Burns, "Rebel Attack Ends a Cease-Fire in Sri Lanka," *New York Times,* April 20, 1995, p. A6.

[141]Russia and other former communist countries still try hard to sell arms for hard currency. See Raymond Bonner, "U.S. Tries to Stem East Europe Arms," *New York Times,* February 13, 1994, p. A1.

[142]Tim Weiner, "Russia and France Gain on U.S. Lead in Arms Sales, Study Says," *New York Times,* August 4, 1998, p. A5.

[143]See Brian Coleman, "In Jets, the U.S. Makes, the World Takes," *Wall Street Journal,* June 13, 1995, p. A14. U.S. arms sales in 1995 earned $29 billion.

[144]See "The Second-Oldest Profession," *The Economist,* February 12-18, 1994, pp. 21-23; "Peddling Death to the Poor," *The Economist,* June 4-10, 1994, p. 43.

[145]Stephen Kinzer, "Nobel Peace Laureates Draft Plan on Arms Trade," *New York Times,* September 1, 1995, p. A6.

[146]"30 Nations Agree to Control Arms Sales," *New York Times,* July 13, 1996, p. 2. The U.S. Congress in 1998 banned joint training exercises with military officers responsible for human-rights abuses. Tim Weiner, "Military Spending Approved With Curbs on Rights Abuses," *New York Times,* August 1, 1998, p. A6.

[147]John Darnton, "Civil War of Nearly Two Decades Exhausts Resource-Rich Angola," *New York Times,* May 9, 1994, p. A6.

[148]U.S. Arms Control and Disarmament Agency, *World Military Expenditures and Arms Transfers 1995-1996* (Washington, DC: U.S. Government Printing Office, 1996), p. 1, and "Linking Arms," special report, *The Economist,* June 14-20, 1997, p. 3.

[149]In 1988, Soviet GNP was about half that of the United States. Sullivan, *Measuring Global Values,* p. 101.

[150]*World Military Expenditures and Arms Transfers 1993-1994,* p. 5; *World Development Indicators 1998,* Table 5.7, p. 280.

[151]Serge Schmemann, "Moscow Outlines 'Doctrine' for Its Military of the Future," *New York Times,* November 3, 1993, p. A6; *World Development Indicators 1998,* Table 5.7, pp. 278-280.

[152]*World Development Indicators 1998,* Table 5.7, pp. 278-280. North Korea ranks second.

[153]Edwin O. Reischauer, *The Japanese* (Cambridge: Harvard University Press, 1977), p. 99.

[154]Harold D. Lasswell, "The Garrison State," *American Journal of Sociology,* 46 (January 1941), pp. 455-468. Lasswell's hypothesis applied in a Cold War setting can be found in Lasswell, "The Garrison State Hypothesis Today," in Samuel P. Huntington, ed., *Changing Patterns of Military Politics* (New York: Free Press, 1962), pp. 51-70.

[155]Aaron L. Friedberg, "Why Didn't the United States Become a Garrison State?" *International Security* 16:4 (Spring 1992), p. 113.

[156]Despite efforts to limit the practice, it is common for retiring military officers to take positions with defense contractors with which they have dealt previously.

[157]Senator Henry "Scoop" Jackson of Washington, who served thirty years in the Senate (1953-1983), was referred to as the "Senator from Boeing" because that giant corporation was in his state and Jackson supported military spending that would benefit Boeing.

[158]It is difficult to show that defense reductions provide funds for other areas. Alex Mintz, "Guns Versus Butter: A Disaggregated Analysis," *American Political Science Review* 83:4 (December 1989), pp. 1285-1293.

[159]Some communities—for example, Los Alamos, New Mexico—were almost entirely dependent on defense funding. James Brooke "Atomic City Ponders Its Future After Bomb," *New York Times,* November 29, 1995, p. A14. Communities in other countries confront the same problem. Thus the mayor of Bourges, France, expressed his fear of declining defense spending, noting: "We live off the Leclerc tank in Bourges." Cited in Craig R. Whitney, "Short of Money, the French Face Cuts in Their Cherished Military," *New York Times,* February 22, 1996, p. A5.

[160]A U.S. Navy decision about whether to award a cruise-missile contract to McDonnell Douglas or Hughes Aircraft pitted Florida against Arizona. Jeff Cole, "GM's Hughes Gets Navy Job for Missiles," *Wall Street Journal,* September 19, 1994, pp. A3, A5.

[161]Thomas E. Ricks, "Military Unveils Plan to Reshape Armed Forces," *Wall Street Journal,* September 2, 1993, p. A3; Eric Schmitt, "2 Submarine Makers Vie for $60 Billion Deal," *New York Times,* May 17, 1995, pp. A1, A13.

[162]Dana Priest and John Mintz, "The Unsinkable Seawolf," *Washington Post National Weekly Edition,* October 23-29, 1995, p. 33. Subcontractors in all but six U.S. states will profit from the submarine's construction.

[163]C. Wright Mills, "The Structure of Power in American Society," in Richard Gillam, ed., *Power in Postwar America* (Boston: Little, Brown, 1971), p. 55. Mills's full argument can be found in *The Power Elite* (New York: Oxford University Press, 1956).

[164]Dwight D. Eisenhower, "The Military-Industrial Complex," in Gillam, ed., *Power in Postwar America,* p. 158.

[165]Gabriel Kolko, *The Roots of American Foreign Policy* (Boston: Beacon Press, 1969), pp. 19, 26.

[166]R. Jeffrey Smith, "Guess Who's Paying to Hawk the Defense Industry Overseas?" *Washington Post National Weekly Edition,* May 18-24, 1992, p. 31.

[167]Lockheed also sought to acquire Northrop Grumman, but antitrust concerns prevented the merger. Leslie Wayne, "Lockheed Cancels Northrop Merger," *New York Times,* July 17, 1998, pp. A1, C17.

[168]Jon G. Auerbach, William M. Bulkeley, and Jeff Cole, "Raytheon's Picard Does It His Way, Pulling Off Deal for Hughes Assets," *Wall Street Journal,* January 17, 1997, pp. A1, A8. See also "Linking Arms," pp. 1-18.

[169]J. William Fulbright, *The Arrogance of Power* (New York: Vintage Books, 1966), p. 3. Belief that military overextension erodes power has been popularized by historian Paul Kennedy in *The Rise and Fall of the Great Powers: Economic Change and Military Conflict from 1500 to 2000* (New York: Random House, 1988).

[170]See, for example, Seth Mydans, "Displaced Aerospace Workers Face Grim Future in California Economy," *New York Times,* May 3, 1995, p. A8.

[171]Steven Erlanger, "Russia's Workers Pay Price as Military Industries Fade," *New York Times,* December 3, 1993, p. A4; and "Linking Arms," p. 3.

[172]William J. Broad, "U.S. Will Build Laser to Create Nuclear Fusion," *New York Times,* October 21, 1994, p. A1.

[173]William J. Broad, "U.S. Navy's Attack Subs to Be Lent for Study for the Arctic Icecap," *New York Times,* February 21, 1995, pp. B5, B10.

[174]Warren E. Leary, "Civilian Uses Are Proposed For Satellites," *New York Times,* June 1, 1995, p. A3.

[175]Edmund L. Andrews, "New Careers for Cold War Relics," *New York Times,* April 15, 1994, pp. C1, C2.

[176]A. Ignatius, "Russians Resent Array of U.S. Partners Chosen to Convert Defense Industry," *Wall Street Journal,* September 19, 1994, p. A1.

[177]Kathy Chen, "Chinese Army Fashions Major Role for Itself as a Business Empire," *Wall Street Journal,* May 24, 1994, pp. A1, A9.

[178]"Army Surplus," *The Economist,* February 11-17, 1995, p. 39.

[179]Martin van Creveld, *Technology and War: From 2000 B.C. to the Present* (New York: Free Press, 1989), p. 1.

Chapter 11

The Special Case of Nuclear Weapons

On August 6, 1945, a lone U.S. B-29 Superfortress, *Enola Gay*, dropped an atom bomb (called "Fat Man") on the Japanese city Hiroshima, and the world would never be the same. Winston Churchill declared: "What was gunpowder? Trivial. What was electricity? Meaningless. This Atomic Bomb is the Second Coming in Wrath!"[1] The bomb, only 12 kilotons, was tiny by contemporary standards,[2] yet it killed between 100,000 and 200,000 human beings.[3] Three days later Nagasaki was struck, and soon World War II was over. Since 1945, nuclear weapons have not again been unleashed, but the threat of nuclear war has hung like the blade threatening Damocles. By one estimate, the United States built 70,000 nuclear weapons and spent $5.48 trillion (in 1996 dollars) on these weapons between 1940 and 1996.[4] The nuclear age once born, global politics was forever changed.

The remarkable aspect of Hiroshima and Nagasaki was not the numbers who died but that so many were killed so quickly by one bomber and one bomb.[5] Thomas Schelling chillingly summarizes the nuclear revolution:

> Japan was defenseless by August 1945. With a combination of bombing and block-
> ade, eventually invasion, and if necessary the deliberate spread of disease, the
> United States could probably have exterminated the population of the Japanese
> islands without nuclear weapons. . . . Against defenseless people there is not much
> that nuclear weapons can do that cannot be done with an icepick.[6]

Since Hiroshima, controversy has raged about whether the United States should have dropped the atom bomb. Although a nuclear device had been tested, no one knew whether the bomb would work in combat. Suggestions that it be dropped on an unpopulated island, inviting Japanese witnesses, were set aside as impractical. President Harry S Truman and his advisers feared that, if invading the Japanese islands proved necessary, the cost in U.S. lives would be astronomical. In the battles for Iwo Jima and Okinawa, Japanese defenders had shown themselves willing to fight to the death. Also, Truman wanted a quick end to the war to minimize the U.S.S.R.'s postwar role in Japan.[7]

In this chapter we examine how nuclear weapons have changed global politics. Has the nuclear weapon's destructive power made war obsolete? Under what conditions can force be conceived of as a political instrument? How have these new weapons changed actors' calculations? What strategies have been designed to use such weapons for political ends, and how do conventional weapons fit? What efforts have been made to control proliferation of weapons of mass destruction?

Needed: A New Military Strategy

The atom bomb grew from the discovery that enormous amounts of energy could be produced by splitting atoms in a chain reaction. The fission of uranium atoms releases neutrons and creates an atomic explosion. Scientists successfully tested this theory first at Alamagordo, New Mexico, July 16, 1945, and for a time, the United States enjoyed a monopoly on atomic knowledge. That ended in September 1949, when the Soviet Union tested its own atomic bomb,[8] earlier than U.S. experts had believed possible.

Vertical proliferation—competition between the United States and the Soviet Union to build more and better weapons—began immediately upon President Truman's decision (January 31, 1950) to develop a hydrogen or fusion bomb.[9] Instead of *nuclear fission*—splitting heavy atoms—the hydrogen bomb is based on *nuclear fusion,* combining isotopes of hydrogen which fuse into larger helium atoms. Enriched uranium is the trigger for igniting the thermonuclear part of fusion weapons. One major difference is that, unlike atom bombs, there is no upper limit on the potential size of hydrogen bombs. In 1952, the United States successfully tested its first hydrogen bomb, and two years later the U.S.S.R. did the same.

In the next years, proliferation was horizontal—weapons spread to additional countries. In 1952, the British tested their first atomic device, and, in 1960, France tested two in the Sahara Desert. Not to lag behind, the People's Republic of China joined the nuclear club in 1964, and, in 1974, India exploded a nuclear device and became the world's sixth nuclear power. With the U.S.S.R. dissolving in 1991, *horizontal proliferation* quickened. Four of the new states inherited Soviet nuclear weapons: Russia, Ukraine, Kazakhstan, and Belarus. As we shall see, other states probably now have nuclear weapons, and still others are seeking nuclear capability.

America's nuclear monopoly after World War II and participation by civilian strategists in military planning made the United States a source of strategic nuclear innovation. The superpowers found a new strategy—nuclear deterrence—on which to build their relations. To convey the flavor of this strategy and its evolution, we consider the late 1940s to the early 1960s, during which time the United States enjoyed military superiority. We then turn to later changes in the deterrence relationship, after Moscow achieved nuclear parity with the United States.

A Munich–Pearl Harbor Complex

Two aspects of America's World War II experience structured leaders' perceptions, deeply influencing their attitudes toward nuclear weapons. First, they believed that prewar appeasement, combined with U.S. isolationism between World War I and II, had whetted the dictators' appetites, encouraging aggression.[10] Second, they feared that a surprise attack, as at Pearl Harbor, might be repeated. For many postwar politicians, the 1930s and the subsequent war formed beliefs that would guide their decisions in the Cold War.

The idea that appeasement had not satisfied but provoked Hitler, Mussolini, and Tojo became axiomatic as the Cold War unfolded. For an American politician to be seen as an appeaser was political suicide. Stalin was another dictator hungering for conquest, and Western leaders were determined not to make the same mistake again.

President Truman recalled how he thought back to the 1930s, as he rushed back from Kansas City to Washington, D.C., after Secretary of State Dean Acheson told him about the invasion of South Korea:

> In my generation, this was not the first occasion when the strong had attacked the weak. I recalled some earlier instances: Manchuria, Ethiopia, Austria. I remembered how each time that the democracies failed to act it had encouraged the aggressors to keep going ahead. Communism was acting in Korea just as Hitler, Mussolini, and the Japanese had acted ten, fifteen, and twenty years earlier. I felt certain that if South Korea was allowed to fall Communist leaders would be emboldened to override nations closer to our own shores. . . .If this was allowed to go unchallenged it would mean a third world war, just as similar incidents had brought on the second world war.[11]

To avoid having to mobilize for war *after* it broke out, as in 1917 and 1941, U.S. leaders devised a strategy built on advance *commitments*[12] and positions of strength. The nuclear-deterrence strategy was meant to avoid war by threatening retaliation. The strategy was anchored by clear commitments[13] and powerful military forces to carry them out.

For Americans, the bolt from the blue at Pearl Harbor was traumatic, a tragedy that must not be permitted to recur. One consequence of Pearl Harbor was the building of an elaborate system of human and technical intelligence organized in an intelligence community—the Central Intelligence Agency (CIA), the National Security Agency (NSA), the Defense Intelligence Agency (DIA), among others—with the task of preventing a surprise attack.[14] A second consequence was the introduction of military technologies and tactics designed either to allow nuclear forces to retaliate before being struck or to survive such a strike and retaliate afterward.

The Doctrine of Massive Retaliation

During the U.S. nuclear monopoly, the American strategy was to use nuclear weapons as heavy bombers had been used in World War II, without recognizing the change nuclear weapons had caused in warfare.[15] In time, however, it became apparent that nuclear weapons posed new problems. Once the Soviet Union exploded an atomic bomb, fears of a *bolt from the blue* focused U.S. attention on preventing an attack on America's homeland. Making a credible threat to retaliate for such an attack seemed simple for two reasons: First, no one doubted that Americans were committed to defending their own homes, and second, the nuclear balance favored the United States.

In 1954, the Eisenhower administration introduced the strategy of *massive retaliation*. The idea behind the strategy—a strategy never actually practiced—was to threaten a possible nuclear first strike against the U.S.S.R. or China if the communists initiated conventional or guerrilla war.[16] Secretary of State John Foster Dulles described massive retaliation as willingness to "retaliate, instantly, by means and at places of our own choosing."[17] The doctrine had two purposes—to provide a credible deterrent to such local probes as the invasion of South Korea and to contain mounting defense costs by finding an inexpensive substitute for the massive conventional forces thought necessary to cope with the U.S.S.R. and China.

The Eisenhower administration talked tougher than it acted,[18] hoping that the mere possibility of retaliation would be sufficient to prevent aggression. In 1954, Dulles wrote:

It should not be stated in advance precisely what would be the scope of military action if new aggression occurred.... That is a matter as to which the aggressor had best remain ignorant. But he can know ... that the choice in this respect is ours and not his.[19]

Discussion of rolling back the Red Army from Eastern Europe reinforced this devil-may-care impression. The strategy's real aim was to prevent a Soviet invasion of Western Europe. In that goal, it succeeded. It was less successful elsewhere.

America's Nuclear Monopoly Ends

Even as massive retaliation was being expounded, the real world was making it obsolete. Growing Soviet nuclear capability heightened the risk to continental America and challenged America's ability to ensure security for allies. Before the U.S.S.R. acquired the ability to strike North America, U.S. nuclear weapons had held Soviet cities hostage for their government's good behavior.[20] In turn, the Red Army's conventional might held U.S. allies hostage for Washington's behavior. Growing Soviet capabilities altered this equation. The U.S. threat to use nuclear weapons first in the event of a Soviet conventional attack on an ally lost *credibility* because it was difficult to believe that Americans would risk their own survival for someone else.

By 1957, North America was vulnerable to attack, and a new military strategy was urgently needed. America's sense of vulnerability was heightened by Soviet deployment of new bombers with the range to strike the United States. More troubling, the Soviet Union successfully tested an intercontinental missile in August 1957 and then launched the first artificial satellite, *Sputnik* ("fellow traveler") I, in October. The United States was no longer invulnerable to a nuclear attack. The alleged missile gap with its claim of Soviet superiority in missile technology became a presidential-election issue in 1960.

These events had three major consequences. First, U.S. strategists began to consider the requirements of a nuclear force with *second-strike capability*—that is, capable of absorbing an initial nuclear attack and retaliating afterward. Second, thought was given to a nuclear war-fighting strategy. What should the targets be? How should nuclear war be fought? Third, attention was paid to the conditions under which nuclear war would be fought. Should nuclear war be an immediate option, as implied by the strategy of massive retaliation; should nuclear weapons be used only as a last resort; or should such weapons be part of a *flexible-response* strategy?

These questions led to a strategy that took account of the superpowers' growing capabilities. Before turning to the details of that strategy—*mutual assured destruction (MAD)*—we must examine more closely the nuclear-deterrence concept on which that strategy was built.

Deterrence in Theory and Practice

The essential claim behind *deterrence* may be stated succinctly: A potential aggressor will not attack if it is persuaded that it will suffer unacceptable punishment from a defender in retaliation. The aggressor is deterred if it believes the defender has the *means* and *will* to carry out its retaliatory threat. Assuming rationality, an actor will refrain from attacking because the expected costs will exceed expected gains.[21] But how do we know that the target of the strategy intended to attack in the first place? It is like the joke about a person who stands on his head at one end of the Brooklyn Bridge. When asked by a policeman why he is behaving so oddly, the person answers that he is "keeping the elephants out of Manhattan." When the policeman chuckles that there are no elephants in Manhattan, the person declares: "See? It works!"

Deterrence also assumes that actors are unitary and ignores differences in cultural norms, propensity to take risks, leaders' psychological stability, or procedures for making decisions. We shall address these assumptions shortly, but let us first bring the weapons themselves into the discussion.

First Strike, Second Strike, and Nuclear Deterrence

We must first define first-strike and second-strike capability. *First-strike capability* is the ability to initiate an attack that will destroy an enemy's capacity to retaliate. When a successful first strike is possible, there is an incentive to attack first and defeat the enemy before being attacked in return. The prospect of actors having a crippling first-strike capability is frightening. In tense conditions, the security dilemma intensifies, and each adversary fears the other may be tempted to strike first, removing the threat to its survival in one fell swoop.

Once an actor gains the means to enable a significant portion of its nuclear forces to survive an enemy's first strike, it has a *second-strike capability*. That capacity is the way to reduce incentives to attack quickly or first, for a first strike would only induce destructive retaliation. Such capability can stabilize a nuclear relationship if adversaries have roughly equivalent capability. If one actor has a second-strike capability and the other does not, the first may still have an incentive for a first strike in a conflict. Once adversaries gain a substantial second-strike capability, though, little incentive remains for either to attack first. The result is a balance of terror, in which stability flows from the condition called mutually assured destruction. That stability is, however, contingent on the absence of technological changes that give either actor a first-strike capability.

Maintaining Successful Deterrence

Successful deterrence depends on the "rationality of irrationality." It is rational to persuade an enemy that you are crazy enough to start a nuclear war, but it is probably crazy to carry out the threat. The problem with nuclear deterrence becomes clearer when it is viewed as what Edward Rhodes calls "a relationship in which the rational and the irrational are inherently linked." He continues:

> On the one hand, nuclear threats create the potential for significant political power.... On the other hand, the mutual vulnerability ... that stems from the existence of capabilities for Mutual Assured Destruction ... threatens to make the actual execution of nuclear threats quite mad, at least for a state that values its own survival.[22]

With this conundrum in mind, Herman Kahn imagined a "Doomsday Machine," a "Doomsday-in-a-Hurry Machine," and a "Homicide Pact Machine," all computers that would enhance credibility by removing from human control the decision about whether to retaliate and automatically trigger nuclear retaliation under stated conditions.[23]

Successful deterrence, then, is a psychological relationship[24] between two or more actors in which each threatens the other(s) with destruction even though it may mean collective suicide. It is rational to be deterred by such a threat if one accepts that the adversary is sufficiently irrational to carry it out. It is also rational to *pretend* either to be irrational enough to use nuclear weapons first or not to care whether the enemy does so. Before the Soviet Union acquired nuclear weapons, Stalin discounted the importance of such weapons in war[25] to convince the West that he could not be blackmailed by them.

Extended Deterrence, Counterface, and Nuclear Weapons

The issue of *extended deterrence*—providing nuclear protection to allies—sharpened the problem of credibility. With America vulnerable to Soviet nuclear attack and such Europeans as French President Charles de Gaulle expressing doubts about U.S. willingness to commit suicide for Europe, strategists in the 1960s began to accept, in Thomas Schelling's words, "that it does not always help to be, or to be believed to be, fully rational, cool-headed, and in control of oneself or of one's country."[26] For extended deterrence to work, it was not necessary for the adversary to be *absolutely* certain that nuclear weapons would be introduced, only that the risk that they would was significant.

Uncertainty was the key to extended deterrence, and as such it could be manipulated by actions that raised the cost of backing down in a crunch. Among such U.S. actions was stationing troops (along with dependents) in Europe where their presence would raise the stakes if war with the U.S.S.R. came. The U.S. garrison in West Berlin was a *tripwire.* Surrounded by the enemy and far from help, the only role for that garrison in a U.S.-Soviet conflict would be to die, raising the stakes of the conflict.

It was not necessary to threaten immediate nuclear retaliation for an attack on Western Europe; it was enough merely to threaten escalation to any level necessary to halt aggression. During the 1960s a version of this strategy, *flexible response,* provided extended deterrence. Beefed up U.S. conventional forces would initially try to defend Europe against a conventional attack, but if they failed, NATO reserved the option of introducing nuclear weapons. Under such conditions, things might get out of control, a condition Schelling described as *brinkmanship:*

> It means exploiting the danger that somebody may inadvertently go over the brink, dragging the other with him. If two climbers are tied together, and one wants to intimidate the other by seeming about to fall over the edge, there has to be some uncertainty or anticipated irrationality or it won't work. . . . With loose ground, gusty winds, and a propensity toward dizziness, there is some danger when a climber approaches the edge; one can credibly threaten to fall off *accidentally* by standing near the brink.[27]

Credibility is high because it is a "threat that leaves something to chance," in which *"the final decision is not altogether under the threatener's control."*[28] Although the details of flexible response changed over time, later NATO strategies were variations on the original theme.

The dilemma posed by extended deterrence cannot be completely overcome, because the guarantor has two audiences—its adversary *and* its allies. On the one hand, the guarantor must be tough and willing to take risks to convince the adversary that its threat is credible. On the other, the guarantor must be judicious and prudent enough to persuade its allies that it will not trigger a war in which they will be embroiled against their will. The appearance of prudence, though reassuring to allies, may reduce an adversary's fear of the guarantor and so weaken deterrence. How to balance the need for a reputation for strength and risk-taking with an image of caution and reasonableness is an unsolved puzzle in the nuclear age.

From time to time strategies that seek to back away from relying on mutual assured destruction of population centers and toward including *counterforce* attacks on military targets have been put forward. These rival strategies, proposed by both U.S. and Soviet leaders at various times, envision controlled conflicts in which escalation leads to nuclear exchanges that can be terminated by political agreement short of all-out war. Such attacks, it was argued, could save lives by reducing an enemy's arsenal and signaling resolve. But counterforce strategies leave a number of unanswered questions: Do not accurate counterforce weapons also provide a first-strike capability? Is it possible during a nuclear exchange for leaders to remain sufficiently cool-headed and in control of their forces to prevent escalation to all-out war?

Problems in Nuclear Deterrence

Such doubts raise further concerns about nuclear weapons and deterrence. *Stability* and *vulnerability* are at the heart of most of these questions. These in turn are related to problems posed by technological change, especially missile and warhead accuracy.[29] A basic ethical question is: What good is a strategy that depends on nuclear threats to prevent war?

Stability and Vulnerability

Strategic stability refers to incentives or disincentives to decide in haste and strike an adversary first. If actors fear that their ability to retaliate is at risk, they may be tempted to use nuclear weapons quickly, especially during crises in which tempers are short and stress is high. Such a relationship is unstable. When conditions are stable, both sides feel that their retaliatory systems are secure and are under no pressure to strike first.

One of the paradoxes in a deterrence relationship is that stability, and therefore safety, actually *increase* if actors lack the means to defend themselves. As long as each side believes it can retaliate against an enemy no matter what that enemy does first, it feels secure. This appears to turn common sense on its head. However, a serious civil-defense effort to construct antimissile missiles or air-raid shelters reduces stability (even though it might save lives if war comes). Although such shelters do not appear offensive in intent, constructing them reduces the deterrent effect of a retaliatory threat. For this reason, in the logic of deterrence, such shelters are highly provocative. If this logic appears convoluted, imagine your thoughts on awakening to a news report that during the night Russian citizens had moved into air-raid shelters.

Vulnerability is related to stability and refers to the survivability of an actor's nuclear forces after an enemy first strike. Vulnerability and stability are inversely related: If nuclear weapons are vulnerable to attack, a deterrence relationship is unstable;

Nuclear proliferation is a major problem in the post–Cold War world, and many observers fear that post-communist Russia's desperate need for hard currency and lax security may encourage Russians to sell some of their vast stockpile of plutonium to pariah countries such as Iran, Libya, or Iraq. *(By permission of Mike Luckovich and Creators Syndicate)*

if such weapons are invulnerable, stability is enhanced. The superpowers took several steps to make their nuclear-weapons systems less vulnerable, including keeping forces on alert, dispersing and hiding weapons, "hardening" weapons, and making forces mobile. Arms-control agreements were reached as part of the effort to stabilize the relationship.

The U.S.-Soviet strategic relationship was most dangerous in the 1950s and early 1960s when the superpowers depended on long-range bombers to deliver nuclear weapons, because airports and aircraft are relatively indefensible targets (as shown at Pearl Harbor). Under such conditions, both sides kept forces in high readiness. Unidentified blips on radar screens, and during the Cuban missile crisis a faulty alarm system, sent crews scurrying to their aircraft.[30] During this period, the Soviet Union depended on its gigantic land area to disperse and hide aircraft and missiles. In May 1960 an American U-2 spy plane, piloted by Francis Gary Powers, was downed near the Soviet city of Sverdlovsk. Soviet Premier Nikita S. Khrushchev, incensed by the incident, canceled a summit conference with Western leaders. One reason for his anger was his recognition that the United States had the means to pinpoint Soviet bases, increasing Soviet forces' vulnerability.

The development of ballistic missiles raised new fears about vulnerability. The new technology meant that cities and weapons were vulnerable to a first strike. The first generation of missiles on both sides sat in the open and had to be filled with liquid fuel before launch. (The fuel was too volatile to be kept on board.) Such weapons were tempting targets. A second generation of missiles soon began to appear, using solid fuel and based in underground concrete silos, making them difficult to destroy and easy to launch quickly. Even more revolutionary were submarine-launched missiles that were made invulnerable by combining concealment and mobility. In time, U.S. and Soviet nuclear-powered submarines with submarine-launched ballistic missiles (SLBMs) would spend months at a time lying silent and undetected under the polar icepack, ready to retaliate if war began.

Part of the effort to reduce vulnerability was maintaining long-range bombers, nuclear submarines, and land-based missiles, called the triad doctrine in the United States. Each leg of the triad provided an independent second-strike capability. The elements in each nation's triad differed: About 70 percent of the Soviet force were land-based missiles, but U.S. nuclear weapons were more evenly divided.

One of the main concerns about the spread of nuclear weapons to additional countries is that, unlike the United States and Russia, other countries will lack the sophisticated and relatively invulnerable delivery systems necessary for deterrence stability. Neither India nor Pakistan, both now openly nuclear powers, has second-strike weapons, and it is not difficult to imagine rapid escalation to the nuclear level in the event of renewed tension or war over the disputed province of Kashmir. Neither has a clear system of command and control that is necessary to prevent matters from getting out of hand. Thus, when asked how prepared India was to be a nuclear power, a retired Indian nuclear strategist answered ominously: "On the record, we are working toward it. . . . Off the record, we are totally unprepared."[31] "I'm sorry to say it," declared one observer, "but South Asia is fundamentally different than the United States and the Soviet Union. If both India and Pakistan deployed nuclear weapons, I think it would almost certainly lead to a nuclear exchange in combat."[32]

Destructiveness, Accuracy, and Stability

Destructiveness and accuracy of nuclear weapons help determine stability and vulnerability. *Destructiveness* is the extent of damage caused by weapons, and *accuracy* is their ability to hit targets. Both superpowers sought to create more destructive and more accurate weapons. The United States was able to deploy more accurate weapons, obviating the need for more destructive power. The Soviet Union built weapons with greater destructive power, partly to compensate for the lower accuracy of some of its missiles.

The link connecting destructiveness, accuracy, and stability is illustrated by the consequences of a Soviet decision to deploy such giant missiles as the SS-8 and SS-9 and later the SS-18 and SS-19. These were thought to threaten U.S. land-based missiles, making one leg of the triad vulnerable to a Soviet first strike. The United States also built new generations of missiles—Minuteman III and later the missile experimental or MX—with improved accuracy that gave it a first-strike potential. The *MIRVed* (multiple independently targetable reentry vehicles) *missile* was a major destabilizing factor. MIRVed missiles have several nuclear warheads that can be programmed to hit different targets, and they, too, can be first-strike weapons. Such technological improvements fueled the arms race and reduced, rather than increased, the rivals' security.

Even as the Cold War wound down, the superpowers continued to upgrade nuclear forces. Early in the 1980s, the Reagan administration committed the United States to modernizing all three triad components—MX missiles for the land-based leg, Trident-D submarines for the sea-based leg, and B-1 and Stealth bombers for the air leg. The Soviets continued to build heavy missiles (the SS-18s and SS-19s) and deployed new ones (SS-24 and SS-25). Both sides also introduced new intermediate-range missiles (under 3,000 miles in range)—the Soviet SS-20 and the American cruise missile and Pershing II. These missiles were accurate and mobile and could launch a first strike against Western Europe or the U.S.S.R., respectively.

Cruise missiles, which are pilotless planes with precision guidance, pose a special problem for stability because it is difficult to verify whether they carry nuclear warheads. They can be launched from bombers, allowing the latter to stand off and fire at targets without penetrating enemy airspace, from naval vessels, and from land.[33] Cruise missiles are slow compared with ICBMs. However, their accuracy and ability to evade radar detection by flying at low altitudes make them potential first-strike weapons. They are also a relatively simple and inexpensive technology that is available to other countries, worsening the prospect of nuclear proliferation.

The most controversial weapon system in the 1980s was President Ronald Reagan's proposal of March 23, 1983, for a *Strategic Defense Initiative (SDI),* also called "Star Wars."[34] The proposal was notable not simply because of the revolutionary technology it required but because it was a giant step away from MAD. Apparently, President Reagan had been horrified to learn that the strategy for mutual survival depended on holding populations hostage and therefore on ensuring that they would be killed in a nuclear war. According to one source, the president "is alleged to have postponed his SIOP [Single Integrated Operations Plan—the list of enemy targets to be struck in the event of war] briefing for three years after assuming office," and that briefing "reportedly left him ashen-faced and speechless."[35] "Wouldn't it be better," Reagan asked, "to save lives than to avenge them?" "What if free people could live secure in the knowledge that their security did not rest upon the threat of instant United States retaliation to deter a Soviet attack, that we could intercept and destroy strategic ballistic missiles before they reached our own soil or that of our allies?" To this end, he called for an antiballistic missile system that "could counter the awesome Soviet threat with measures that are defensive," offering to share research results with the U.S.S.R.[36]

There were several proposed SDI variants, but all depended on generating critical new technologies. Many billions of dollars later SDI seemed an expensive illusion that was unlikely to be realized. We will never know how SDI would have affected the superpower deterrence relationship, but we can tentatively conclude that *if only one side had deployed the system,* it would have been destabilizing, permitting that side to act with impunity. If both sides had deployed such a system simultaneously (an idea implicit in the president's offer to share SDI technology), stability would not have been endangered.

Nuclear Deterrence: Conceptual and Ethical Concerns

Other criticisms of nuclear deterrence focus on doubts about its assumptions and ethics. The strategy assumes that actors are unitary and rational, not that decisions may be made by bureaucratic power struggles or by political pulling and hauling. And we can hardly assume that all leaders will evaluate costs and benefits in the same way

ACTORS SPEAK

In July 1996, the International Court of Justice by a narrow margin rendered an advisory opinion that the use or threat of nuclear weapons would violate international law. The arguments presented to the court during public pleadings reflected very different views on the issue.

The fact remains that the existence of nuclear weapons as a class of weapons threatens the whole of civilization. This is not the case with respect to any other class or classes of conventional weapons. It cannot be consistent with humanity to permit the existence of a weapon which threatens the very survival of humanity. (Australian Foreign Minister M. Gareth Evans, as cited in "Refusing to Learn to Love the Bomb: Nations Take Their Case to Court," *New York Times,* January 14, 1996, sec. 4, p. 7)

We might wish nuclear weapons away, as we might wish away all weapons, indeed the whole concept of war and coercion. But nuclear weapons do exist, and the court, as a court of law, must operate not in some idealized world but in the real world. (British Attorney General Sir Nicholas Lyell, as cited in "Refusing to Learn to Love the Bomb: Nations Take Their Case to Court," *New York Times,* January 14, 1996, sec. 4, p. 7)

or perceive a situation correctly. The quality of information and amount of stress will vary and so, therefore, will perceptions.

Leaders differ in cognitive and cultural predispositions, and their experiences and personalities are different. Some leaders may be victims of wishful thinking, group pressure, or other factors that distort judgment and perceptions of reality.[37] As one observer concludes: "Deterrence is inadequate as an explanatory theory of international relations because the growing body of empirical evidence ... indicates that neither leaders contemplating challenges nor leaders seeking to prevent them necessarily act as the theory predicts."[38]

Ethical objections have also been raised against nuclear deterrence. Is it moral to premise a strategy on possible use of weapons of mass destruction (even for a "just" cause) that by their nature indiscriminately kill noncombatants?[39] Despite the opposition of the nuclear powers, the International Court of Justice in 1996 by a vote of 8 to 7 rendered an advisory opinion that "the threat or use of nuclear weapons would generally be contrary to the rules of international law applicable in armed conflict."[40] To what extent is use of such weapons "thinkable"?[41]

Some scientists argue that nuclear war cannot be waged without catastrophic consequences (see Figure 11.1).[42] The blast and radiation of a single one-megaton weapon, detonated 3,000 feet up, would kill all unprotected people in a nine-square-mile area.[43] An electromagnetic pulse from that weapon might destroy all electrical

98 percent of people are killed by flying debris, thermal radiation and fire storms. Few structures are left standing.

50 percent of people are killed, and 40 percent are injured, half of whom may die. Only the strongest structures survive.

50 percent of people are killed or injured. Most homes are blown out or leveled.

20 percent of people are killed by injuries or burns; people in the open receive second- and third-degree burns or are blinded by flash. Most buildings are damaged.

FIGURE 11.1
Effects of Bomb

The concentric circles illustrate the effect of a one-megaton nuclear bomb at a distance of up to 8 miles from ground zero. SOURCE: From *The ABC's of the Soviet-American Nuclear Arms Race* by Ray Perkins, Jr. Copyright © 1991 by Harcourt, Inc., reproduced by permission of the publisher.

equipment in North America. Thermal radiation (heat and light) would blind anyone looking at it, cause fires out to eight miles, third-degree burns at ten miles, and second-degree burns up to thirteen miles away. A nuclear detonation would produce a blast wave that could destroy dwellings more than eight miles away. Finally, radioactive debris would be dispersed great distances from the blast, some carrying hundreds of miles and contaminating whatever it touched.

A group of American scientists has suggested that the environmental consequences of a nuclear war would be even worse than imagined, perhaps leading to extinction of life itself. They argue that the four major environmental consequences of nuclear war—"obscuring smoke in the troposphere, obscuring dust in the stratosphere, the fallout of radioactive debris, and the partial destruction of the ozone layer"[44]—would cause a period of life-threatening darkness and cold on earth, a *nuclear winter.* Among its consequences, this "winter" might destroy almost all agriculture in the Northern Hemisphere and make water unavailable by freezing and contamination. Others challenge the nuclear-winter description, arguing that the effect would be closer to a "nuclear fall," but few dispute that nuclear war would have severe consequences for the planet.[45]

Debate over the morality of nuclear deterrence reached a crescendo as the "nuclear freeze" movement grew early in the 1980s, and as observers denounced the "immorality of nuclear deterrence," which involves deliberately killing "tens of millions of people" and holding "whole peoples as hostages."[46] A May 1983 pastoral letter of the American National Conference of Catholic Bishops accepted nuclear deterrence, conditioned upon rejecting nuclear war as an acceptable outcome, rejecting the search for nuclear superiority, and viewing deterrence as only a way station on the road to disarmament.[47] They went on to recommend steps that could be taken to move away from this strategy.[48]

Political scientist Joseph Nye argues that "nuclear deterrence is conditionally moral" under three conditions. First, the means one uses and their consequences should be proportionate to the cause of an action. Second, limits should be placed on the means one uses. Third, "a prudent consideration of consequences in both the near term and the indefinite long term" should inform policy. Nye outlines five "maxims of nuclear ethics":

Self-defense is a just but limited cause.

Never treat nuclear weapons as normal weapons.

Minimize harm to innocent people.

Reduce risks of nuclear war in the near term.

Reduce reliance on nuclear weapons over time.[49]

Nye accepts limited extended deterrence but says targeting population centers *(countervalue strategy)* should be avoided. Instead, he proposes targeting "counter-combatants" or a more limited "counter-city targeting approach" to minimize harm to civilians. Some of Nye's concerns were answered by the dramatic arms-control agreements ending the Cold War. Thus, after spending $8 billion on an effort to ensure that the U.S. government could function after a nuclear attack, Washington abandoned the top-secret Doomsday Project in 1994.[50] Issues of nuclear ethics, as well as the morality of other weapons, for example, laser weapons that blind foes, remain.[51]

Vertical Proliferation: Controlling the Arms Race

When unilateral efforts by the superpowers failed to achieve nuclear superiority, mutual efforts to stabilize the arms race became more attractive. Controlling vertical proliferation meant constraining quantitative and qualitative improvements in the nuclear arsenals of states already possessing such weapons. These efforts can take the form of *arms control* or *disarmament.*

Those who favor disarmament argue that weapons themselves cause war and thus reducing the numbers of weapons and even eliminating them is necessary to prevent war. Those who advocate arms control contend that some configurations of weapons are more likely to produce war than others and that the way to avoid war is not simply to eliminate weapons wholesale but to reinforce stability in deterrence relationships. They further argue that conflicting political interests mean that arms-control measures are feasible where disarmament is not and that such measures are a prerequisite for disarmament.

Sometimes the two schools advocate the same policies, but even then they differ over the reasons they give. Disarmers favored eliminating short-range and theater (tactical) nuclear weapons in Europe in the 1980s because it would have reduced nuclear stocks on the continent. Arms-control specialists also advocated eliminating such weapons, but for a different reason; they believed them to be destabilizing because, being vulnerable to enemy attack, they must be used quickly in conflict or be lost.

Sometimes the two schools' recommendations differ radically. Disarmers always advocate fewer weapons, but arms-control theorists can envision situations in which larger numbers of weapons enhance stability. Instability might result, for instance, if both sides depend on only a few weapons for deterrence. Then it would be relatively easy for one side to eliminate the other's forces, and, during a crisis, the temptation to do so would grow. If both sides have many weapons, it is difficult to eliminate the threat of devastating retaliation, and so the incentive to try is reduced.[52] Most superpower negotiations were based on the logic of arms control.

Nuclear Arms-Control Agreements

Efforts to reach agreement on arms control between the United States and the Soviet Union during the Cold War were frustrated by mistrust. Each side made proposals with an eye toward wooing world public opinion rather than achieving substantive agreement. Each advocated positions that it knew in advance would be unacceptable to the other.

By the early 1960s, a number of factors had improved the prospects for arms control. Stalin's death in 1953 reduced Western fears of the U.S.S.R., and his successors communicated more openly with the West. Several dangerous U.S.-Soviet crises, especially the 1962 Cuban missile crisis, brought home to leaders that, however incompatible many of their interests were, they shared an overriding interest in surviving by avoiding nuclear war. Nowhere was this awareness more sharply reflected than in a letter Soviet Premier Khrushchev sent to President Kennedy as the missile crisis peaked. Khrushchev used the metaphor of a "knot" to describe their predicament:

> Mr. President, we and you ought not to pull on the ends of the rope in which you have tied the knot of war, because the more the two of us pull, the tighter the knot will be tied. And a moment may come when that knot will be tied so tight that even he who tied it will not have the strength to untie it, and then it will be necessary to cut that knot, and what that would mean is not for me to explain to you, because you understand perfectly of what terrible forces our countries dispose.[53]

In June 1963, President Kennedy made a dramatic appeal for arms control in a speech at American University, and two months later the first U.S.-Soviet arms-control agreement was signed—the Partial Test Ban Treaty (August 1963).[54] This agreement forbade testing nuclear weapons in the atmosphere, under water, or in outer space. Although the agreement addressed an environmental problem resulting from the release of nuclear materials in the air, it did not significantly alter the arms race. Still, it was an important first step (see Table 11.1).

TABLE 11.1
Major Arms-Control Agreements

Antiproliferation Agreements

Antarctic Treaty (1959): Demilitarizes the Antarctic, prohibiting its use for military purposes.

Outer Space Treaty (1967): Prohibits weapons of mass destruction, military installations, or testing weapons in outer space.

Treaty of Tlatelolco (1967): Prohibits testing, using, manufacturing, or acquiring nuclear weapons in Latin America.

Nuclear Nonproliferation Treaty (1968): Prohibits transfer of nuclear weapons by nuclear countries to nonnuclear countries and forbids nonnuclear countries to acquire such weapons. Requires nuclear countries to seek disarmament. Renewed in 1995.

Seabed Treaty (1971): Prohibits placing nuclear weapons on the sea bottom beyond the twelve-mile limit.

Treaty of Rarotonga (1985): Prohibits testing, manufacture, or acquisition of nuclear devices in the South Pacific.

Confidence-Building Measures

Hot Line Agreement (1963): Creates a direct U.S.-Soviet communications link for use during crises. Link improved in 1971 and 1984.

Nuclear Accidents Agreement (1971): Requires immediate notification of the other signatory in the event of an accident, unauthorized incident, or detonation involving a nuclear weapon.

High Seas Agreement (1972): Establishes rules of conduct to avoid collision among naval vessels and prohibits simulated attacks on each other's ships.

Agreement on Prevention of Nuclear War (1973): Agreement to do everything possible to prevent nuclear war. Revised in 1987 to establish nuclear-risk reduction centers in Washington and Moscow.

Conference on Security and Cooperation in Europe (1975): Agreement to give prior notice of major military exercises in Europe. Updated in 1986 to require advance notice of large troop movements and allow aerial inspection of such movements.

Open Skies Treaty (1992): Agreement among NATO countries, successor states of the former Soviet Union, and former members of the Warsaw Pact to permit surveillance flights over North America, Europe, and the Asian regions of the former Soviet Union to verify arms-control commitments.

Nuclear Testing Limitations

Partial Test Ban Treaty (1963): Prohibits nuclear testing in the atmosphere, outer space, or under water and commits signatories to seek a total test ban.

Threshold Test Ban Treaty (1974): Prohibits underground nuclear tests in excess of 150 kilotons.

Peaceful Nuclear Explosions Treaty (1976): Limits peaceful nuclear explosions to 150 kilotons.

Comprehensive Test Ban Treaty (1996): U.N. General Assembly voted 158 to 3 (India, Libya, Bhutan) in favor. Would end all nuclear testing.

Limitations on Nuclear Weapons

Antiballistic Missile Treaty (1972): Limits U.S. and U.S.S.R. to two ABM sites with 100 interceptors each. Reduced to one site in 1974.

(continued)

TABLE 11.1
*Major Arms-Control
Agreements
(continued)*

Limitations on Nuclear Weapons (continued)

Interim Agreement (1972)*: Froze the total number of ballistic-missile launchers for
    five years. Both sides continued to observe the limit after 1977.

SALT II (1979): Limited missiles and bombers on each side to 2,400, to be reduced to
    2,250 by 1982. Limited MIRVed launchers to 1,320. Limited ICBM warheads to 10
    per missile, SLBM warheads to 14, and cruise missiles on bombers to 20. The treaty
    was not finalized and was breached by the United States in 1986.

Intermediate-Range Nuclear Forces Treaty (1987): Prohibits producing or deploying
    missiles with a range of 300 to 3,400 miles. Required destruction of INF missiles
    within three years and on-site inspections for verification. Some 2,700 missiles elim-
    inated by 1992 in the first agreement to *reduce* nuclear weapons.

START I (1991): Reduces the number of warheads from 11,600 to 8,600 for the U.S. and
    from 10,222 to 6,500 for the U.S.S.R. by the year 2000. After the U.S.S.R. collapse, these
    targets were reaffirmed by the United States, Russia, Ukraine, Belarus, and Kazakhstan.

Short-Range Commitments (1991): Committed the U.S. and U.S.S.R. (now Russia) to
    reduce short-range land, air, and sea-based nuclear warheads by varying numbers
    and take nuclear forces off alert status.

START II (1992): Reduces the number of nuclear warheads on each side in two stages
    to 3,800–4,250 and then to 3,000–3,500 by the year 2003 (extended by one year in
    1997). Not yet ratified.

De-Targeting Agreement (1994): U.S.-Russian and Anglo-Russian agreement no longer
    to target each other's territory with nuclear weapons.

START III (1997): Reduces warheads on each side to no more than 2,000–2,500 by the
    end of the year 2007. Not yet ratified.

Nonnuclear Weapons Limitations

Biological and Toxins Weapons Convention (1972): Prohibits developing, producing,
    and stockpiling biological weapons and requires that stockpiling be eliminated.

Environmental Modification Convention (1977): Prohibits modifying the environ-
    ment for military purposes.

Inhumane Weapons Convention (1981): Prohibits use of specified fragmentation
    bombs as well as using booby traps, incendiary weapons, and mines against civilians.

Missile Technology Control Regime (1987): Bans sale of equipment and technology
    for missiles capable of carrying weapons of mass destruction. 30 signatories.

U.S.-Soviet Agreement on Chemical Arms (1990): Requires that stockpiles of chemical
    arms be cut to 5,000 tons by the year 2002 and bans additional production.

Conventional Armed Forces in Europe Treaty (1990): Limits the number of tanks,
    combat vehicles, aircraft, and helicopters available to NATO and the Warsaw Pact in
    Central Europe, establishing parity in conventional forces. Revised in 1996 to permit
    additional arms on northern and southern flanks.

Chemical Weapons Convention (1993): Prohibits development, production, stockpil-
    ing, and use of chemical weapons and requires destruction of existing stockpiles.

Wassenaar Agreement (1996): Agreement to control the sale of conventional weapons
    and dual-use technology, especially to rogue states.

Antipersonnel Mines Agreement (1997): Bans the production or deployment of
    antipersonnel land mines.

*The Antiballistic Missile Treaty and Interim Agreement together constituted SALT I.

SOURCES: *SIPRI Yearbook 1994;* "The Desperate Efforts to Block the Road to Doomsday," *The
Economist,* June 6–12, 1998, pp. 23–25. © 1998 The Economist Newspaper Group, Inc. Reprinted with
permission. Further reproduction prohibited. www.economist.com.

As appreciation of deterrence stability deepened, and as the Soviet Union came to enjoy greater security, having attained nuclear parity or "essential equivalence" with the United States in the 1970s, serious negotiations became possible. Nuclear superiority was increasingly seen to be illusory. As Henry Kissinger wrote some years later, "What in the name of God is strategic superiority? What is the significance of it, politically, militarily, operationally, at these levels of numbers? What do you do with it?"[55]

The first major negotiation aimed at controlling the nuclear-arms race was the strategic arms limitation talks, or SALT. The negotiations began late in the 1960s and concluded when the *SALT I* accords were signed in Moscow in May 1972. Negotiations were arduous. As in other arms-control negotiations, the participants sought to limit weapons in which they were inferior. The United States sought to limit large land-based intercontinental ballistic missiles with multiple warheads, a Soviet specialty, and the Soviet Union sought to limit long-range bombers, submarine-launched ballistic missiles, and, later, cruise missiles and the Strategic Defense Initiative—all areas of American advantage. American negotiators focused on *throw weight* (the load that can be delivered aboard bombers and missiles) and numbers of *launch vehicles* (missiles and bombers), both areas of Soviet advantage, while Soviet negotiators emphasized the U.S. advantage in numbers of warheads, including bombs.

SALT I consisted of two agreements. The first limited offensive missiles and the second antiballistic missiles. The first agreement stabilized the number of land-based and sea-based delivery vehicles that each side could possess for five years, effectively freezing each side's quota at the number in production by July 1, 1972. The United States accepted the provision for more Soviet than U.S. delivery vehicles because the agreement did not restrict qualitative improvements in nuclear forces or limit long-range bombers (areas of U.S. advantage). The Nixon administration was comfortable signing the agreement because the United States already had MIRVed missiles.

The *Antiballistic Missile (ABM) Treaty* limited development of a weapon system that might degrade the stability of nuclear deterrence. If one side could protect cities against an enemy attack, it might no longer be deterred by fear of retaliation. An ABM system would also invite deployment of additional offensive weapons to evade or defeat that system, intensifying the arms race. The 1972 treaty restricted deployment of ABMs to two sites—one around each nation's capital and the other around one of its land-based missile sites. It was believed that such limitations would discourage ABM development, thereby reinforcing the nuclear stalemate.[56] The ABM controversy was resurrected in the SDI debate a decade later.

Although SALT I was a breakthrough in the effort to institutionalize MAD, it was only a first step. Not all nuclear delivery vehicles were included, and, more important, qualitative improvements were excluded. As a result, a qualitative arms race ensued after SALT I was completed. The Soviet Union developed MIRVed missiles and built larger missiles with more warheads, while the United States began to modernize all legs of its triad.

The *SALT II* treaty, signed in June 1979 in Vienna, addressed quantitative and qualitative issues. The treaty covered all types of delivery vehicles, including long-range bombers, set numerical limits on delivery vehicles, including MIRVed missiles, that each side could have, and placed restrictions on technological improvements that the superpowers could make. President Jimmy Carter withdrew SALT II from Senate consideration after the Soviet invasion of Afghanistan, but both sides adhered to the treaty until 1986, when the Reagan administration exceeded its limits after accusing the Soviet Union of doing so.

Confidence-Building Agreements

Another set of arms-control agreements involve *confidence-building measures (CBMs)*. The aim of such measures is to improve communication between foes to reduce the possibility of misunderstandings that might lead to war. The initial measure, the Moscow-Washington hot line, like the Partial Test Ban Treaty, was a response to the Cuban missile crisis. The original teletype link has been modernized twice, with satellite communication added in 1971 and facsimile ("fax") equipment in 1984.

Additional confidence-building measures followed. In 1973, the superpowers signed the "Agreement Between the United States and the Union of Soviet Socialist Republics on the Prevention of Nuclear War." The pact committed the two to act to prevent the development of situations, either with one another or with third parties, that could cause their relationship to deteriorate. If such a situation did develop, the superpowers were "to enter into urgent consultations with each other."[57] To date, the agreement has worked well.

Other agreements have incorporated confidence-building measures. Political, cultural, scientific, and trade agreements, including provision for a joint Apollo-Soyuz space mission, accompanied SALT I. A few years later, the statement of principles of the *Conference on Security and Cooperation in Europe (CSCE)*, an August 1975 meeting of thirty-five nations in Europe and North America, incorporated additional confidence-building measures. "Baskets" one and two of the Helsinki Accords (after Helsinki, Finland, where the accord was signed) provided for improved East-West cultural exchange, exchange of environmental information, and warning of military maneuvers. The Helsinki initiatives bore fruit at the 1986 Stockholm Conference on Confidence and Security-Building Measures and Disarmament in Europe, at which measures were adopted to reduce the risk of war in Europe. These included prior notification of military maneuvers, invitations to states to observe military maneuvers, exchange of information on future military activities, and the right to demand on-site inspection.[58]

The *Open Skies Treaty* of March 1992, a recent CBM, permits observation flights over countries that are parties to the agreement. The treaty aims "to enhance mutual understanding and confidence" by allowing signatories to gather "information about military activities of concern to them." Making military activities "transparent" plays a major role in reducing regional tension and preventing conflict.[59]

Agreements on Nuclear Disarmament

Although arms-control and confidence-building measures were important, they did not alter the main contours of the arms race. Despite SALT I and II, nuclear arsenals remained large, and loopholes permitted modernizing weapons systems. Ronald Reagan ran for office in 1980 on a commitment to close the "window of vulnerability" that he argued was a result of improvements in the Soviet nuclear arsenal that endangered U.S. land-based missiles. The administration, with its NATO allies, also decided to introduce intermediate-range nuclear weapons in Western Europe to balance Soviet deployment of SS-20s. This decision produced an outcry of opposition among peace movements in Europe, the United States, and the Soviet bloc.[60]

Liberal and pacifist opinion in the United States and Western Europe was roused by reckless rhetoric from the Reagan administration. On one occasion the president jokingly announced in a weekly radio broadcast that he thought had ended that he had ordered a nuclear attack on the U.S.S.R. On another occasion he appeared not to realize that, once launched, a missile could not be recalled. In another gaffe the president suggested that he could imagine a nuclear exchange in Europe that would not escalate to a superpower nuclear exchange, and he frightened observers with colorful phrases like "a nuclear shot across the bow."

More worrisome to some was speculation by experts with influence in the White House about how nuclear war could be fought and won. The United States and Soviet Union enjoyed enormous "overkill" capacity by the mid-1980s.[61] The apparent excess of weapons was based on the premise that no retaliatory force was completely invulnerable and that large forces were needed to discourage an enemy from contemplating a first strike. The superpowers controlled roughly 18,000 strategic nuclear weapons with a yield of about 10,000 megatons. Counting short- and medium-range weapons, the superpowers had between 50,000 to 75,000 warheads between them with a yield of over 15,000 megatons.[62]

The outcry over nuclear weapons subsided with two sets of U.S.-Soviet negotiations in the early 1980s. These differed from talks a decade earlier because the focus shifted from arms control to arms reduction. Negotiations began in November 1981 to limit or eliminate intermediate nuclear forces in Europe, and the strategic arms reduction talks (START) began in June 1982 with the aim of reducing the superpowers' long-range nuclear weapons. When completed, these two negotiations produced the first nuclear arms-reduction agreement in history.

The 1987 *Intermediate-Range Nuclear Force (INF) Treaty* was a major step. It called for the superpowers to eliminate and destroy medium- and intermediate-range weapons within three years. It provided for on-site inspection of the dismantling process and allowed for continued inspections for thirteen years after the treaty came into force to ensure compliance. This treaty was *the most important* single step in disarmament history, eliminating an entire class of nuclear weapons and demonstrating that arms reduction was possible.

The crowning achievement of Soviet-American arms control was the Strategic Arms Reduction Treaty *(START I)* in 1991. The U.S.S.R. agreed to cut 3,722 of its 10,222 nuclear warheads and the United States to reduce its 11,600 warheads by 3,000. Before the treaty could be completed, however, the Soviet Union collapsed, and four of its successor states—Russia, Ukraine, Belarus, and Kazakhstan— retained a share of the Soviet arsenal. Under these conditions the treaty could not come into effect until all four agreed to the terms concluded by Presidents Bush and Gorbachev. In May 1992, the United States and the four former Soviet republics agreed to honor the treaty.[63] Ukraine (1,240 nuclear warheads), Belarus (72 nuclear warheads), and Kazakhstan (934 nuclear warheads) agreed to destroy or turn over all nuclear warheads to Russia and subscribe to the Nuclear Nonproliferation Treaty. The signatories were committed to carrying out the reductions in three stages over a seven-year period, but Ukraine, pressured by nationalists who expressed fear of Russian intentions, delayed carrying out its obligations. In September 1993, as part of a deal by which Russia agreed to buy Ukraine's share of the former Soviet Black Sea fleet, Ukraine agreed to let Russia dismantle nuclear weapons on Ukrainian territory in return for the uranium taken

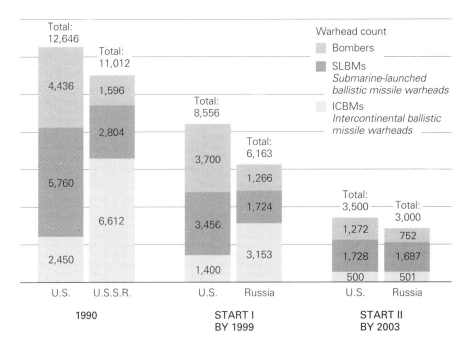

FIGURE 11.2
Reduction in Strategic Warheads Under START I and II

The end of the Cold War has produced an end to the U.S.-Soviet nuclear arms race and a dramatic reduction in nuclear weapons. Between 1990 and 2003, total U.S. and Russian warheads will be reduced from 23,658 to 6,500 weapons. SOURCE: Reprinted with permission of AP/Wide World Photos.

from their warheads.[64] Shortly after, a struggle broke out between President Leonid M. Kravchuk and opponents of surrendering Ukraine's nuclear weapons, and Kravchuk tried to squeeze more economic assistance from the West.[65] Agreement was finally reached at a summit meeting between Presidents Clinton and Kravchuk in Kiev in 1994, and Ukraine's nuclear disarmament was completed two years later.[66] The agreement with Ukraine allowed START I to come into force.[67]

Although START I entailed major reductions in nuclear arsenals, *START II,* which Presidents Bush and Yeltsin completed at the end of 1992, was still more dramatic. It called for a 50 percent reduction in U.S. and Russian nuclear arsenals, including the large MIRVed land-based Russian missiles that U.S. strategists feared were a first-strike threat. By START II, both sides will be allowed only 3,000–3,500 warheads by the year 2003.[68] Figure 11.2 depicts the cuts in strategic warheads under START I and II. START II was ratified by the U.S. Senate in 1996 but still awaits ratification by Russia's legislature.

At their 1997 summit in Helsinki, Presidents Clinton and Yeltsin agreed to *START III.* If ratified, this treaty will reduce long-range warheads on both sides to no more than 2,000 to 2,500 by the end of 2007, a cut of 80 percent from 1990 levels.[69]

Horizontal Proliferation: More Fingers on More Triggers

Despite progress in vertical proliferation, the problem of horizontal proliferation—spreading nuclear-weapons technology to other actors—remains formidable. One reason for worry is sheer probability: the more fingers on nuclear triggers, the higher the probability that someone will use nuclear weapons intentionally or by accident. One observer writes of "new knowledge about bizarre and dangerous incidents within the U.S. nuclear arsenal—like how a bear climbing a fence almost caused nuclear-armed aircraft to be launched" and "serious incidents within the U.S. nuclear arsenal that could have produced an accidental or unauthorized detonation of a nuclear weapon, and potentially even an accidental war. . . ."[70]

Proliferation also greatly complicates deterrence calculations because each nuclear-armed actor has to guess who might be its adversaries and arm accordingly. Does each nuclear-armed actor prepare for *all* possible adversaries or just the most dangerous ones? Actor A might increase its arms to counter Actor B, but this will be destabilizing if Actor C concludes that the increase threatens its security. Finally, new nuclear powers have less sophisticated weaponry than superpowers, and their relative vulnerability to a first strike creates unstable rivalries.

Technological change complicates the proliferation issues. The growing availability of peaceful nuclear reactors that yield plutonium is a danger because that metal can be reprocessed to make nuclear arms,[71] and there is concern about world plutonium production and the construction of nuclear plants that produce excess plutonium.[72] Advances in miniaturization make it possible for nuclear weapons to be carried by hand, and fanatical terrorists straining to grab or set off such ordnance can easily be imagined. In November 1994, a nuclear power plant in Lithuania closed down after threats were made that it would be attacked. In recent years small quantities of plutonium and enriched uranium[73] have been illegally diverted from either military or civilian stockpiles for sale to terrorists or rogue states.[74] A German police agent even speculated about "a nuclear mafia" in Germany with "excellent contacts with the former Soviet Union."[75] Concern about diversion of weapons-grade plutonium and uranium from Russian stockpiles led that country and the United States to install an experimental remote-control monitoring system at the Kurchatov Institute in Russia and the Argonne-West laboratory in Idaho.[76] Another important agreement reached in August 1992 provided for U.S. purchase of 500 metric tons of bomb-grade uranium (enough to build more than 30,000 atom bombs) from scrapped Russian nuclear weapons.[77]

Smuggled nuclear material has turned up in Germany, the Czech Republic, and Slovakia,[78] and Kazakh and U.S. officials were so concerned about the possible theft of nuclear material from a poorly guarded metallurgy plant in Kazakhstan that U.S. aircraft secretly transported half a ton of enriched uranium to Oak Ridge, Tennessee, in November 1994.[79] Fears have been raised about thefts from U.S. nuclear facilities where some 1.5 metric tons of plutonium (enough to make 300 nuclear weapons) remain unaccounted for.[80]

The United States, Russia, Britain, France, and China were nuclear powers by the mid-1990s, and India and Pakistan publicly tested nuclear weapons in 1998 and intermediate-range missiles the following year. Belarus, Kazakhstan, and Ukraine, heirs to Soviet nuclear weapons, agreed to surrender them, after negotiations sweetened by promises of U.S. economic assistance. South Africa is the only country to have acquired nuclear weapons and given them up afterward. Israel probably has nuclear weapons, and several Arab states threatened to oppose renewing the Nuclear Proliferation Treaty until Israel signed the treaty and allowed inspection of its nuclear facilities.[81] Iraq came close to developing nuclear weapons until forced by the United Nations to give up its capacity to do so.[82] North Korea acquired nuclear weapons or a capacity to make them, and others, including Iran, may be trying to develop them.[83]

Nuclear Nonproliferation Treaty

The global community has tried to stop proliferation by means of the *Nuclear Nonproliferation Treaty (NPT)* of 1968. The treaty has four key provisions:

1. No nuclear power that has subscribed to the treaty is to transfer nuclear-weapons technology to nonnuclear states.
2. No nonnuclear-armed state that has agreed to the treaty is to develop nuclear-weapons technology.
3. All nonnuclear states that use nuclear energy are to have safeguards and are to conclude an agreement with the International Atomic Energy Agency (IAEA) for inspecting nuclear facilities.
4. The nuclear-weapons states are to "pursue negotiations in good faith on effective measures relating to the cessation of the nuclear arms race . . . and to nuclear disarmament."[84]

Had this agreement been universally accepted, horizontal proliferation would, at least in theory, have ceased. Although most countries signed the treaty, a number refused to do so. Initially France and China claimed that the NPT violated their sovereignty and only agreed to sign some years later. The NPT's principal shortcoming is that some "near-nuclear" or recent nuclear states did not sign the treaty and others that did agree to it are not in full compliance. Israel, India, and Pakistan are in the first category, and Iraq, Iran, Libya, and North Korea are in the second. In 1993, North Korea threatened to become the first state to withdraw from the NPT, leading President Clinton to declare that "it is pointless for them to try to develop nuclear weapons, because if they ever use them it would be the end of their country." Other countries that had not signed the NPT by mid-1995 were Brazil, Chile, Cuba, Oman, and the United Arab Emirates.

A second problem limiting the NPT's effectiveness has been expansion of nuclear fission as an energy source. Safeguards to prevent transfer of nuclear fuels to nuclear weapons are inadequate. The IAEA has primary responsibility for ensuring that such transfer does not happen, but it is a difficult task for an agency with few inspectors to watch over more and more nuclear reactors. Moreover, countries still retain the right to refuse or restrict inspections, as North Korea did. North Korea apparently used a nuclear reactor and a small reprocessing facility at Yongbyon to convert used fuel rods into plutonium. The North Koreans "were apparently astounded," declared one IAEA official, "about what we could detect with such a tiny amount of samples, and what the Americans could see from the satellites."[85] The United States also suspects Iran of seeking to divert fuel to develop nuclear weapons and has sought to prevent such countries as

Russia, China, Ukraine, and the Czech Republic from providing Iran with nuclear power plants.[86]

These and similar problems were evident in the weeks leading up to the conference on renewing the NPT. The treaty was extended in perpetuity by 174 states in May 1995, but not before a number of divisive issues were raised.[87] Countries such as Mexico, Venezuela, Egypt, Indonesia, and Nigeria preferred to renew the NPT for only a limited period of time, arguing that the treaty gave a few countries a monopoly of nuclear arms. Thus India described the NPT's approval as "the institutionalization of nuclear double standards."[88] The nuclear haves, claimed NPT opponents, had not fulfilled the treaty's requirement to move toward nuclear disarmament, nor had they provided adequate nuclear technology for peaceful uses to developing countries. As part of the effort to gain support for the NPT's renewal, the U.N. Security Council agreed to help countries threatened or attacked by a nuclear power.[89]

Other Nonproliferation Agreements

Several other agreements restrict the spread of nuclear weapons, although none is as comprehensive as the NPT. The 1959 Antarctica Treaty was the first agreement of this kind. It limited use of Antarctica to "peaceful purposes only." No military bases, maneuvers, or "testing of any type of weapons" are permitted there. Moreover, the treaty prohibits "any nuclear explosions in Antarctica and the disposal there of radioactive waste materials."[90] Some years later, the Outer Space Treaty, modeled on the Antarctica Treaty, was signed. This 1967 agreement prohibited placing weapons of mass destruction in orbit around the earth or stationing such weapons in outer space. Finally, the 1971 Seabed Arms Control Treaty prohibits placing nuclear weapons on the ocean floor beyond the twelve-mile territorial limit.

Other agreements have focused on keeping specific regions free of nuclear weapons. The most successful has been the Latin American Nuclear-Free Zone Treaty, known as the Treaty of Tlatelolco (1967).[91] The treaty commits signatories to apply nuclear energy only to peaceful purposes and prohibits use of their territories for manufacturing or storing nuclear weapons. The treaty was accompanied by two protocols. Protocol I calls on states outside Latin America with territories in the area defined by the treaty to commit themselves to regional denuclearization. Thus the United States cannot install nuclear weapons in Puerto Rico or the U.S. Virgin Islands. Protocol II calls on the nuclear powers to respect the nuclear-free status of Latin America and refrain from action that might violate the agreement.

Banning testing is a critical step to preventing nuclear proliferation.[92] The 1963 Partial Test Ban Treaty committed signatories to seek a total test ban, but negotiations for a U.N.-sponsored Comprehensive Test Ban Treaty did not begin until January 1994. Recognizing that U.S. actions would influence the 1995 NPT renewal talks, the Clinton administration, after much internal debate, decided to continue a moratorium on testing begun in July 1993.[93] In October 1994 and June 1996, against U.S. protests, China violated the voluntary moratorium by testing a new generation of missile warheads beneath its western desert at Lop Nor but indicated that it would cooperate in efforts to ban all tests by September 1996.[94] In June 1995, French President Jacques Chirac reversed his predecessor's policy and France too resumed underground testing at Mururoa Atoll in the Pacific, declaring that it would stop once and for all by May 1996.[95]

Despite strong support from the United States and Russia, progress toward agreement on a Comprehensive Test Ban Treaty was slow.[96] The chief impediment was a requirement that the treaty could not go into effect until signed and ratified by the five avowed nuclear powers and three additional countries—India, Pakistan, and Israel—thought to have secret nuclear weapons programs. India's refusal to sign unless the treaty included a requirement for the destruction of existing nuclear weapons within a specified time period seemed to doom the treaty.[97] However, led by Australia, a large number of countries shifted the issue from the 61-member Conference on Disarmament in Geneva, Switzerland, to the U.N. General Assembly, where the treaty's passage only required a simple majority. By an overwhelming vote of 158 to 3 (India, Libya, and Bhutan opposing), with 24 absent or abstaining, the treaty was approved.[98] Because of sophisticated computer modeling and nonnuclear testing, the ban on testing will probably not prevent development of simple "first-generation" nuclear weapons or the maintenance of the major nuclear powers' arsenals, but, if they accede to it, it will impede countries like India and Pakistan from developing more sophisticated nuclear weapons.[99] Declared the director of the U.S. Arms Control and Disarmament Agency: "What this treaty does in practical terms is cut off any new avenues of nuclear weapons development. The opportunity to plumb nuclear technology further to come up with new destructive techniques . . . is ruled out."[100]

As though to signal its contempt for the Comprehensive Test Ban Treaty, India staged a series of underground nuclear tests in May 1998, and Pakistan followed suit shortly thereafter.[101] Rejecting an American demand that India give up developing nuclear weapons, an Indian spokesman declared that his country was concerned, not with Pakistan, but with China and that his country was seeking "a minimum deterrent."[102]

Nuclear Proliferation: A Continuing Problem

Despite efforts to keep nuclear-weapons technology from spreading, the problem remains severe, and the United States has adopted a new military mission called *counterproliferation* to halt the spread of nuclear weapons. Indeed, the Cold War actually slowed proliferation because many states felt comfortable under a superpower's nuclear umbrella and because the superpowers cooperated to discourage proliferation. At least four major developments are ominous.

First, efforts to keep delivery systems such as missiles from spreading have lagged behind efforts to stop disseminating nuclear weapons. Figure 11.3 depicts the upsurge in the sale of nuclear and missile technology after the Cold War ended. Several states have purchased missiles and nuclear reactors, and these purchases raise questions about the future. Some of the sellers are not parties to the NPT (for example, India), and even those that are (such as North Korea) are not strong advocates of this control mechanism. Some of the buyers appear to be interested in acquiring nuclear weapons and the means to deliver them. Beginning in 1986, an effort was made to restrict transfer of missiles, but success was mixed. The *Missile Technology Control Regime (MTCR)* banned the sale of technology for missiles capable of carrying weapons of mass destruction. An attempt to tighten these restrictions began after Iraq used Soviet Scud missiles in the Persian Gulf War.[103] China's aid for a missile factory in Pakistan was a sore point in U.S.-Chinese relations until China took steps toward joining MTCR.[104]

Second, as more states use nuclear power to meet energy needs and as sales of nuclear reactors grow, nuclear materials will become easier to get. Although the NPT does not limit peaceful use of nuclear energy and the International Atomic Energy Agency conducts periodic inspections of nuclear facilities, the success of Iraq and North Korea in fooling the IAEA raises questions about the effectiveness of inspections. Although the IAEA adopted tougher safeguards in 1995,[105] new and more sophisticated systems for monitoring compliance are needed, and the global community must be prepared to act decisively if violators are found. Some observers regarded the outcome of efforts to make North Korea give up its nuclear-weapons program "an early and potentially disturbing test of whether the West, Russia and the United Nations can create effective institutions, systems and principles for a new and much more diffuse post–Cold War era of global nuclear security."[106]

Negotiations with North Korea involved threats of sanctions and even war. The sudden death of North Korea's long-time leader Kim Il Sung in July 1994 slowed the pace of negotiations, even as enough used North Korean nuclear fuel rods to make four or five bombs continued to sit in a "muddy pond."[107] Finally, a U.S.-North Korean deal was hammered out under which (1) North Korea would freeze its nuclear program, would not refuel its Yongbyon reactor, and would allow inspection of its used fuel rods; (2) the United States and North Korea would establish diplomatic and economic relations; (3) North Korea would open its nuclear installations to international inspection within five years; (4) North Korea would replace its graphite nuclear reactors (from which plutonium can be reprocessed relatively easily) with light-water reactors provided by South Korea; (5) North Korea would remain a party to the NPT; (6) the United States would provide free coal and fuel to take care of North Korea's interim energy needs; and (7) ultimately North Korea would dismantle key plants that figured in its nuclear program.[108] After additional delay caused by North Korean insistence that a U.S. company rather than a South Korean one build the new reactors, a compromise was reached in June 1995.[109] North Korea continues to refuse IAEA inspectors full access to nuclear sites, and, in the words of one observer, "The danger is that the North Koreans already have nuclear weapons on the shelf."[110]

Third, the agreements that call for destroying nuclear weapons will make more fissile materials available for use by other actors. With the high levels of existing fissile stockpiles, better safeguard and storage systems are required to prevent illegal and clandestine diversion of nuclear material. And fourth, chemical and biological weapons are also proliferating.

Chemical and Biological Weapons

Nuclear weapons are not the only weapons of mass destruction. Because they are easily hidden, cost little, and are easily manufactured, chemical and biological weapons "may become the terror weapons of choice for outlaw regimes or terrorists."[111] The world was dramatically reminded of this when the Japanese religious cult Aum Shinrikyo unleashed a poison gas attack in the Tokyo subways, killing 10 and injuring 5,000. Police found supplies of the nerve gas sarin and materials to make biological weapons in the cult's compound"[112] (see Figure 11.4).

The 1972 *Biological and Toxins Weapons Convention (BWC)* required the destruction of all biological weapons and prohibited the production of such weapons (their use has been outlawed since 1925), and the 1993 *Chemical Weapons Convention (CWC)* made chemical weapons subject to the same rules. U.S. and Russian stockpiles of chemical weapons were estimated at 33,000 and 40,000 tons, respectively.[113] By June 1998, 130 countries had ratified the BWC, and 168 countries

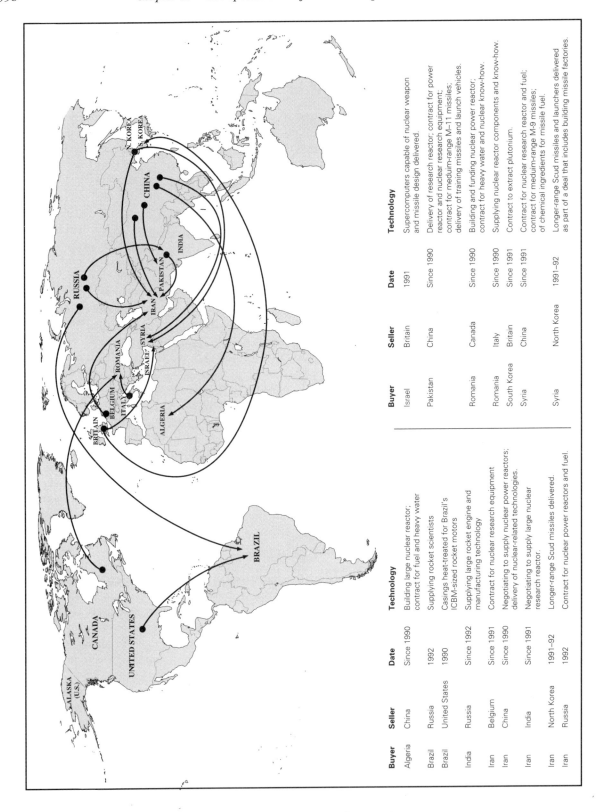

Buyer	Seller	Date	Technology
Algeria	China	Since 1990	Building large nuclear reactor; contract for fuel and heavy water
Brazil	Russia	1992	Supplying rocket scientists
Brazil	United States	1990	Casings heat-treated for Brazil's ICBM-sized rocket motors
India	Russia	Since 1992	Supplying large rocket engine and manufacturing technology
Iran	Belgium	Since 1991	Contract for nuclear research equipment
Iran	China	Since 1990	Negotiating to supply nuclear power reactors; delivery of nuclear-related technologies.
Iran	India	Since 1991	Negotiating to supply large nuclear research reactor.
Iran	North Korea	1991–92	Longer-range Scud missiles delivered.
Iran	Russia	1992	Contract for nuclear power reactors and fuel.

Buyer	Seller	Date	Technology
Israel	Britain	1991	Supercomputers capable of nuclear weapon and missile design delivered.
Pakistan	China	Since 1990	Delivery of research reactor; contract for power reactor and nuclear research equipment; contract for medium-range M–11 missiles; delivery of training missiles and launch vehicles.
Romania	Canada	Since 1990	Building and funding nuclear power reactor; contract for heavy water and nuclear know-how.
Romania	Italy	Since 1990	Supplying nuclear reactor components and know-how.
South Korea	Britain	Since 1991	Contract to extract plutonium.
Syria	China	Since 1991	Contract for nuclear research reactor and fuel; contract for medium-range M-9 missiles; of chemical ingredients for missile fuel.
Syria	North Korea	1991–92	Longer-range Scud missiles and launchers delivered as part of a deal that includes building missile factories.

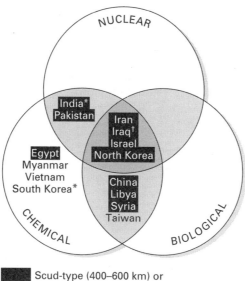

Scud-type (400–600 km) or
longer-range ballistic missiles

FIGURE 11.4
Circles of Fear

Some countries are suspected of developing several types of weapons of mass destruction, while others like Egypt are only developing one. SOURCE:"The Desperate Efforts to Block the Road to Doomsday," *The Economist,* June 6–12, 1998, p. 24. © 1998 The Economist Newspaper Group, Inc. Reprinted with permission. Further reproduction prohibited. www.economist.com.

*Declared chemical weapons, subject to verification
†Subject to special UN inspection regime

FIGURE 11.3
Dangerous Transfers: The Traffic in Nuclear and Missile Technology

The international market in missile and nuclear arms technology has been thriving in the 1990s. This is a list of transactions known to have taken place after Iraq invaded Kuwait, touching off the Persian Gulf War. Any list of important participants in previous years would also have included France, Germany, and Switzerland, which were among the many nations trading in nuclear and missile technology with Iraq before the war; Germany also helped the nuclear programs of India, Pakistan, and South Africa.

had signed the CWC and 110 had ratified it.[114] But most Arab states, including Egypt and Syria, refuse to sign the CWC until Israel signs the NPT, and there are reports that Syria has armed Scud-C missiles with chemical warheads.[115] Indeed, as the discovery of traces of deadly VX nerve gas, as well as anthrax and botulism, on Iraqi missile fragments[116] and the American cruise-missile attack on a suspected Sudanese chemical plant remind us, the entire Middle East features, as one observer puts it, "creeping proliferation."[117] And in 1996, when American troops in Saudi Arabia were rebased in more remote areas, concern about chemical or biological weapons in the hands of terrorists was cited as a key reason.[118]

However, it is difficult to verify controls on biological and chemical weapons, and several countries, possibly including Russia,[119] have continued to develop them. Iraq had an advanced germ warfare program at the time of the Persian Gulf War;[120] China, India, Israel, North Korea, South Africa, and Syria are "possessors" or "potential possessors" of such weapons; Libya is trying to develop them.[121] And both Serbia and the Bosnian Muslims are suspected of having produced chemical weapons.[122] Even more chilling is the fact that nonstate actors such as terrorists are not parties to the international treaties that ban these weapons, thereby further complicating efforts to prevent the proliferation and use of chemical and biological weapons. Thus there is great danger that chemical and biological weapons will proliferate. A U.S. congressional report somberly concluded: "The chemical and biological threat has increased in terms of widespread proliferation, technical diversity, and probability of use. The threat is now truly global . . . and the volatility of the world political environment has probably lowered the threshold and increased the potential use of these weapons."[123]

Limited Force in a Nuclear Age

We have still barely touched on conventional war in the nuclear age. What place has force in a nuclear environment? If we are mired in a nuclear stalemate, how can force be used?

Compellance   Deterrence must be distinguished from what Schelling calls *compellance.* Deterrence seeks to prevent attack by threatening retaliation. It works only if threats do not need to be carried out and force does not have to be used. Compellance, by contrast, entails threatening or using force to make an adversary do something it is unwilling to do or to undo something it has already done.[124] If deterrence works, it is easier and less expensive than compellance. Schelling summarizes the differences between the two:

> Deterrence involves setting the stage . . . and *waiting.* . . . [T]he act that is intrusive, hostile, or provocative is usually the one to be deterred; the deterrent threat only changes the consequences *if* the act in question—the one to be deterred—is then taken. Compellance, in contrast, usually involves *initiating* an action . . . that can cease . . . only if the opponent responds. . . . To deter, one digs in . . . and waits. . . . To compel, one gets up enough momentum . . . to make the other act to avoid collision.[125]

Compellance is linked to deterrence in the sense that an actor may use force on one occasion to bolster a reputation for toughness necessary to make credible deterrent threats, but the two strategies are fundamentally different.

Compellance in Action   American policy during the 1962 Cuban missile crisis typifies a compellant strategy. The Soviet Union had secretly installed offensive missiles in Cuba, where they were being prepared for deployment when the United States became aware of their presence. American leaders had two compellant objectives: (1) to halt further shipments of offensive Soviet weapons to Cuba, and (2) to force the Soviet Union to withdraw the missiles it had already placed on the island.[126] The first objective entailed coercing Moscow to cease an activity that was under way, and the second, forcing Moscow to undo a fait accompli. The first was accomplished by establishing a naval "quarantine" around Cuba with U.S. vessels instructed to interdict Soviet arms shipments. The second and more difficult objective was achieved by a U.S. ultimatum to attack the missile sites in Cuba if they were not dismantled. To make the ultimatum more palatable to the Soviet Union, the United States promised not to invade Cuba and agreed to withdraw missiles from Turkey (which Washington had planned to do anyway).

Five factors favored compellance during the Cuban crisis. American motivation to win was high, and the government had strong domestic support. The United States enjoyed strategic and local military superiority. American objectives were clear and consistent throughout the crisis. The bargaining was simplified because only two actors were involved. Finally, the effect of U.S. coercion was intensified by the speed with which it was applied.

By contrast, the U.S. effort to compel North Vietnam between 1965 and 1973 was unsuccessful. Retrospectively, it is easy to understand America's failure. The United States was divided over the war, and public opposition to it grew after the 1968 Tet offensive.[127] During this period, the United States and Soviet Union were military equals, and U.S. military power in Vietnam, though greater than its enemy's, was unsuited to waging unconventional guerrilla war. American objectives were murky. Were we there to prop up a pro-American government in Saigon, eliminate communism in all of Vietnam, teach the Chinese that guerrilla insurgencies would not weaken America's will, or reinforce America's bargaining reputation? At one time or another, all these reasons were cited to justify the U.S. presence in Vietnam. The bargaining situation was murky, too. The United States was simultaneously trying to influence communist rebels in South Vietnam (the Vietcong), the communist government in North Vietnam, and the governments of China and the Soviet Union. Dealing with each posed different problems. Finally, the conflict escalated so slowly that the enemy was able to adapt to each increment of violence.

The United States also used a compellant strategy against Iraq following its occupation of Kuwait. Initial efforts to force Iraq's retreat by applying economic sanctions were unsuccessful, and so too was threatening to use force. Even overwhelming airpower in the bombing campaign of January and February 1991 did not do the trick. The Iraqis were thrown out of Kuwait only after a massive multinational ground attack was launched from Saudi Arabia.

As in Cuba, U.S. motivation was high, but many feared getting bogged down in a land war. The United States enjoyed strategic military superiority, but achieving local military superiority proved a slow chore. The objective of America's compellant strategy—forcing Iraq to leave Kuwait—was again clear, though it became confused with the desire to overthrow Saddam Hussein. Pressure was applied slowly on Iraq, allowing the Iraqis to adjust to each increment. Part of the reason for the delay was the complicated bargaining to construct and maintain a large and diverse alliance. An added complication was persuading Israel not to intervene despite Iraqi missile attacks against Israeli population centers.

The problems of using compellance were even greater in NATO efforts to compel Serbia to stop its ethnic-cleansing policy in Kosovo. Eschewing the use of ground troops, NATO bombed Serbia, trying to raise the costs for the Serbs to force withdrawal. Serbian capitulation in June 1999 gives new life to the idea of compellance.[128]

Conclusion

Deterrence and compellance as strategies for managing conflict face an uncertain future. Nuclear deterrence must be rethought because of reductions brought about by arms control and growing unease about nuclear proliferation. Although deterrence seems to have been stabilized at lower levels by superpower agreements, new nuclear-armed states with leaders less willing to accept the status quo may try to change the rules of the game. Deterrence is further complicated by the proliferation of chemical and biological weapons and by new generations of highly destructive conventional weapons.

Compellance too may be less usable in the future. As the global community grows more diverse and alliances weaken, the prospect of one actor or group of actors successfully coercing others may become more real. The unity shown by the global community in the Persian Gulf War may prove an aberration. Without stabler institutions and with more nuclear-armed states, the strategy of compellance will be sorely tested.

Although the long night of Soviet-American nuclear confrontation has ended and nuclear arsenals have been reduced, the threat of nuclear war is not over. Horizontal proliferation seriously threatens peace and stability. If the theory of nuclear deterrence is correct, new nuclear powers will be dangerous for several reasons. First, unlike the superpowers, they have little experience with flaming crises and do not yet have repertoires for preventing escalation. Second, like first-generation U.S. and Soviet nuclear weapons, the weapons of new nuclear powers will be vulnerable to a first strike, pressuring decision-makers in crises to "use them or lose them."

Nevertheless, the Cold War's end offers opportunities for cooperation in global politics, especially in global economics, the topic to which we now turn. Until recently, security narrowly defined neglected goals like economic prosperity, social justice, and environmental health. As we enter the twenty-first century, such goals are likely to be as important as more traditional aims like territorial integrity. Finally, exaggerating military factors has the air of a self-fulfilling prophecy; leaders come to believe that force is the alpha and omega of global politics and act accordingly.

Key Terms

ABM Treaty
accuracy of nuclear weapons
arms control
Biological and Toxins Weapons
   Convention (BWC)
bolt from the blue
brinksmanship
Chemical Weapons Convention
   (CWC)

commitments
compellance
Conference on Security and
   Cooperation in Europe (CSCE)
confidence-building measures
   (CBMs)
counterforce strategy
counterproliferation
countervalue strategy

credibility
destructiveness of nuclear
   weapons
deterrence
disarmament
extended deterrence
first-strike capability
fission
flexible response

fusion
horizontal proliferation
Intermediate-Range Nuclear
   Force (INF) Treaty
launch vehicles
massive retaliation
MIRVed missile
Missile Technology Control
   Regime (MTCR)

mutual assured destruction
   (MAD)
Nuclear Nonproliferation Treaty
   (NPT)
nuclear winter
Open Skies Treaty
SALT I
SALT II
second-strike capability

START I
START II
START III
Strategic Defense Initiative (SDI)
strategic stability
throw weight
tripwire
vertical proliferation
vulnerability of nuclear weapons

End Notes

[1]Cited in Herbert Feis, *The Atomic Bomb and the End of World War II* (Princeton: Princeton University Press, 1966), p. 87.

[2]Most U.S. warheads range from .5 to 1 megaton. Russian warheads tend to be larger. The U.S.S.R. tested one device of 58 megatons. A kiloton is equivalent to 1,000 tons of TNT; a megaton to a million tons of TNT.

[3]Similar numbers died in the bombing of Tokyo in March 1945; there, incendiaries were used, not high explosives, because most Japanese lived in homes made of wood and thatch rather than brick. Most deaths were caused by firestorms so intense that people perished from suffocation because oxygen was burned away.

[4]Matthew L. Wald, "Today's Drama: Twilight of the Nukes," *New York Times,* July 16, 1995, sec. 4, p. 5; Matthew L. Wald, "Total Cost of U.S. Nuclear Arms Is Put at $5.48 Trillion," *New York Times,* July 1, 1998, p. A14. This represents about one-third of U.S. military spending and one-tenth of all government spending during that period.

[5]Previously it would have taken 300 planes to have caused such damage. General H. H. Arnold, "Air Force in the Atomic Age," in Dexter Masters and Katherine Way, eds., *One World or None* (New York: McGraw Hill, 1946), pp. 26–29.

[6]Thomas C. Schelling, *Arms and Influence* (New Haven: Yale University Press, 1966), p. 19.

[7]At Yalta, the U.S.S.R.—previously neutral in the Pacific conflict—agreed to enter the war against Japan "two or three months" after Germany's surrender. The U.S.S.R. declared war on Japan on August 8, 1945, the day before Nagasaki was bombed. See Harry S Truman, *Memoirs,* vol. 1, *Year of Decisions* (Garden City, NY: Doubleday, 1955), pp. 415–426.

[8]Peter R. Beckman, Larry Campbell, Paul W. Crumlish, Michael N. Dobkowski, and Steven P. Lee, *The Nuclear Predicament,* 2nd ed. (Englewood Cliffs, NJ: Prentice Hall, 1992), p. 87. Albert Carnesale, Paul Doty, Stanley Hoffmann, Samuel P. Huntington, Joseph S. Nye, Jr., and Scott D. Sagan, *Living with Nuclear Weapons* (New York: Bantam Books, 1983) point out

that the Soviet Union, even after acquiring nuclear weapons, lacked long-range aircraft to deliver them (p. 79), leaving the U.S. with an effective nuclear monopoly.

[9]Richard Smoke, "The Year of Shocks," in Jeffrey Porro with Paul Doty, Carl Kaysen, and Jack Ruina, eds., *The Nuclear Age Reader* (New York: Knopf, 1989), p. 51.

[10]For an effort to reappraise prewar appeasement using new information, see J. L. Richardson, "New Perspectives on Appeasement: Some Implications for International Relations," *World Politics* 40:3 (April 1988), pp. 289–316.

[11]Harry S Truman, *Memoirs,* vol. 2, *Years of Trial and Hope* (Garden City, NY: Doubleday, 1956), pp. 332–333. President Bush was influenced by the same analogy when faced with Iraq's invasion of Kuwait. Lawrence Freedman and Efraim Karsh, *The Gulf Conflict, 1990–91: Diplomacy and War in the New World Order* (London: Faber, 1993), p. 212.

[12]Some empirical analysis suggests that the stuff of which commitments are made—alliances, weapons, and past performance—does *not* contribute to successful deterrence. Paul Huth and Bruce Russett, "What Makes Deterrence Work? Cases from 1900 to 1980," *World Politics* 36:4 (July 1984), pp. 496–526. For criticism of the assumptions and methods Huth and Russett use, see Richard Ned Lebow and Janice Gross Stein, "Rational Deterrence Theory: I Think, Therefore I Deter," *World Politics* 41:2 (January 1989), pp. 208–224; and Lebow and Stein, "Deterrence: The Elusive Dependent Variable," *World Politics* 42:3 (April 1990), pp. 336–369. Lebow and Stein argue for the historical-case method, and Huth and Russett reply that "Lebow and Stein's conceptual imprecision and theoretical misunderstandings cause them to present a misleading critique of our work and to offer an alternative research strategy that fails to meet the standards of rigorous social science." "Testing Deterrence Theory: Rigor Makes a Difference," *World Politics* 42:4 (July 1990), p. 468.

[13]In 1914, Germany may have been deceived by the absence of a clear British commitment to come to the aid of France. This

claim was put about by German Chancellor Bethmann-Hollweg, who sought to excuse his own errors.

[14]The end of the Cold War created a crisis for U.S. intelligence agencies, forcing them to adapt to conditions in which the threat of a Soviet attack was no longer the first priority. The agencies began to focus on such issues as terrorism and economic and ecological trends.

[15]Initial U.S. policy was to limit nuclear sharing and turn nuclear technology over to the U.N. under the Baruch Plan. The British protested against their exclusion from this new technology, and the Soviets rejected the Baruch Plan. See Peter A. Clausen, *Nonproliferation and the National Interest* (New York: HarperCollins, 1993), pp. 9–22.

[16]See Lawrence Freedman, *The Evolution of Nuclear Strategy,* 2nd ed. (New York: St. Martin's Press, 1989), pp. 81–88.

[17]Cited in Beckman, et al., *Nuclear Predicament,* p. 79.

[18]At the same time, U.S. conventional forces in Europe and Asia were equipped with short-range nuclear weapons to compensate for disadvantages in numbers.

[19]Cited in Freedman, *Evolution of Nuclear Strategy,* p. 86.

[20]As early as 1946, President Truman threatened the U.S.S.R. with nuclear weapons if it did not withdraw troops from northern Iran.

[21]For a defense of this assumption, see Christopher H. Achen and Duncan Snidal, "Rational Deterrence Theory and Comparative Case Studies," *World Politics* 41:2 (January 1989), pp. 143–169. Deterrence theory originally evolved as an exercise in deductive logic with little empirical input, and it assumed that leaders are rational.

[22]Edward Rhodes, *Power and MADness: The Logic of Nuclear Coercion* (New York: Columbia University Press, 1989), p. 1.

[23]Herman Kahn, "The Arms Race and Some of Its Hazards," in Donald G. Brennan, ed., *Arms Control, Disarmament, and National Security* (New York: Braziller, 1961), pp. 89–129. In 1993, it was alleged that Russia actually had a computerized system that could automatically fire nuclear weapons if military commanders were dead. William J. Broad, "Russia Has a Nuclear 'Doomsday' Machine, U.S. Expert Says," *New York Times,* October 8, 1993, p. A11.

[24]Robert Jervis, "Introduction: Approach and Assumptions," in Jervis, Richard Ned Lebow, and Janice Gross Stein, eds., *Psychology and Deterrence* (Baltimore: Johns Hopkins University Press, 1985), p. 1.

[25]See H. S. Dinerstein, *War and the Soviet Union* (New York: Praeger, 1959).

[26]Schelling, *Arms and Influence,* p. 37.

[27]Ibid., p. 99. Emphasis in original.

[28]Thomas C. Schelling, *The Strategy of Conflict* (Cambridge: Harvard University Press, 1960), pp. 187, 188. Emphasis in original.

[29]For a summary of such issues, see Ray Perkins, Jr., *The ABCs of the Soviet-American Nuclear Arms Race* (Pacific Grove,

CA: Brooks/Cole, 1991).

[30]Scott D. Sagan, *The Limits of Safety: Organizations, Accidents, and Nuclear Weapons* (Princeton: Princeton University Press, 1993), pp. 99–100. During crises, U.S. bombers took off and flew toward the U.S.S.R. This was the "fail-safe procedure" (ibid., pp. 163–166). The deteriorating condition of Russia's nuclear command system heightens the risk of accidental nuclear war. In one incident a routine U.S. flight in Scandinavia was identified as a possible nuclear attack by Russian forces. See Sam Nunn and Bruce Blair, "From Nuclear Deterrence to Mutual Safety," *Washington Post National Weekly Edition,* June 30, 1997, p. 22; Leslie Gevirtz, "Risk of Accidental Nuclear Attack Said Rising," *Yahoo News,* www.yahoo.com/h, April 29, 1998.

[31]Cited in John F. Burns, "In Nuclear India, Small Stash Does Not a Ready Arsenal Make," *New York Times,* July 26, 1998, sec. 1, p. 3. For the view that even a modest mutual nuclear capability has made India and Pakistan more careful about the Kashmir dispute, see John F. Burns, "Nuclear Fear Helps Enforce the Calm in Kashmir," *New York Times,* June 14, 1998, sec. 1, pp. 1, 8. Bruce Blair, "Whose Finger Is on The Trigger?" *Washington Post National Weekly Review,* October 7–13, 1996, p. 21.

[32]Cited in Steven Erlanger, "India's Arms Race Isn't Safe Like the Cold War," *New York Times,* July 12, 1998, sec. 4, p. 18.

[33]A new generation of acronyms accompanied these missiles: ALCMs (air-launched cruise missiles), SLCMs (sea-launched cruise missiles), and GLCMs (ground-launched cruise missiles). SLCMs with nonnuclear payloads were used against Iraq in the Gulf War and some years later against Bosnian Serb targets. Cruise technology begat a whole generation of precision-guided or "smart" weapons that revolutionized conventional warfare.

[34]The U.S.S.R. deployed a modest antimissile defense system ("Galosh") around Moscow late in the 1960s.

[35]Richard Ned Lebow, *Nuclear Crisis Management: A Dangerous Illusion* (Ithaca, NY: Cornell University Press, 1987), p. 121.

[36]"Peace and Security," President Reagan's Televised Address to the Nation, March 23, 1983," reprinted in *Realism, Strength, Negotiation: Key Foreign Policy Statements of the Reagan Administration* (Washington, DC: Department of State, May 1984).

[37]Extensive research exists on perception and rationality in international crises. See Robert Jervis, *Perception and Misperception in International Politics* (Princeton: Princeton University Press, 1976); Alexander L. George and Richard Smoke, *Deterrence in American Foreign Policy* (New York: Columbia University Press, 1974); Richard Ned Lebow, *Between Peace and War: The Nature of International Crisis* (Baltimore: Johns Hopkins University Press, 1981); Lebow, *Nuclear Crisis Management;* Glenn H. Snyder and Paul Diesing, *Conflict Among Nations: Bargaining, Decision Making, and System Structure in International Crises* (Princeton: Princeton University Press, 1977); and John D. Steinbruner, *The Cybernetic Theory of Decision* (Princeton: Princeton University

Press, 1974). Especially provocative is Irving L. Janis, *Victims of Groupthink* (Boston: Houghton Mifflin, 1972).

[38]Richard Ned Lebow, "Conclusions," in Jervis et al., *Psychology and Deterrence,* p. 203.

[39]Thomas Donaldson, "Kant's Global Rationalism," in Thomas Nardin and David R. Mapel, eds., *Traditions of International Ethics* (New York: Cambridge University Press, 1992), p. 152. Some 22 countries have joined in the World Court Project, which seeks to get the International Court of Justice to rule that any use of nuclear weapons is illegal. "Refusing to Learn to Love the Bomb: Nations Take Their Case to Court," *New York Times,* January 14, 1996, sec. 4, p. 7.

[40]"World Court Condemns Use of A-Weapons," *New York Times,* July 9, 1996, p. A7.

[41]Herman Kahn, *Thinking About the Unthinkable* (New York: Horizon Books, 1962).

[42]Carl Sagan, "Nuclear War and Climatic Catastrophe: Some Policy Implications," *Foreign Affairs* 62:2 (Winter 1983/84), pp. 257-292.

[43]The following is based on Perkins, *ABCs of the Soviet-American Nuclear Arms Race,* pp. 25-31.

[44]Sagan, "Nuclear War and Climatic Catastrophe," pp. 263-264.

[45]See "Comment and Correspondence," *Foreign Affairs* 62:4 (Spring 1984), pp. 995-1002; Starley L. Thompson and Stephen H. Schneider, "Nuclear Winter Reappraised," *Foreign Affairs* 64:5 (Summer 1986), pp. 981-1005; and "Comment and Correspondence," *Foreign Affairs* 65:1 (Fall 1986), pp. 163-178.

[46]James A. Stegenga, "The Immorality of Nuclear Deterrence," *Arms Control* 4 (May 1983), pp. 65, 67, and 69.

[47]See "The Challenge of Peace: God's Promise and Our Response," reprinted as the appendix to Jim Castelli, *The Bishops and the Bomb: Waging Peace in a Nuclear Age* (Garden City, NY: Doubleday, 1983), p. 241. The U.S. bishops were not the only religious leaders to question nuclear deterrence. See Joseph S. Nye, Jr., *Nuclear Ethics* (New York: Free Press, 1986) for a discussion of others; and Perkins, *ABCs of the Soviet-American Nuclear Arms Race,* pp. 146-147.

[48]"The Challenge of Peace: God's Promise and Our Response," pp. 241-242. These proposals are discussed in Nye, *Nuclear Ethics,* pp. 97-98. For a sympathetic critique of the logic used to reach this conclusion, see Susan Moller Okin, "Taking the Bishops Seriously," *World Politics* 36:4 (July 1984), pp. 527-554.

[49]Nye, *Nuclear Ethics,* pp. 98-99.

[50]Tim Weiner, "Pentagon Book for Doomsday to Be Closed," *New York Times,* April 18, 1994, pp. A1, A8.

[51]William M. Arkin, "The Pentagon's Blind Ambition," *New York Times,* May 10, 1995, p. A19.

[52]Hedley Bull, "Disarmament and the Balance of Power," in Lawrence Freedman, ed., *War* (New York: Oxford University Press, 1994), pp. 297-303.

[53]Cited in Robert F. Kennedy, *Thirteen Days* (New York:

Norton, 1969), pp. 67-68. Recent revelations show that the two superpowers were closer to the brink than many had believed, especially because local commanders of nuclear forces in Cuba at the time had been given latitude in making decisions.

[54]The texts of many of the arms agreements discussed in this chapter appear in United States Arms Control and Disarmament Agency, *Arms Control and Disarmament Agreements: Texts and Histories of the Negotiations* (Washington, DC: U.S. Arms Control and Disarmament Agency, 1990).

[55]Cited in Freedman, *Evolution of Nuclear Strategy,* p. 363.

[56]At the time, congressional opposition prevented ABM deployment in the United States. In 1999, claiming a threat existed of a nuclear missile attack from a rogue state like North Korea, Iraq, or Iran, the Clinton administration came out in favor of a modest ABM system. Russia complained bitterly at what it saw as a violation of the 1972 agreement. Steven Lee Myers, "Rethinking a Treaty for a New Kind of Enemy," *New York Times,* January 24, 1999, sec. 4, p. 16; Eric Schmitt, "Missile Defenses Leave Fantasy Behind," *New York Times,* March 21, 1999, sec. 4, p. 1.

[57]*Arms Control and Disarmament Agreements,* p. 180.

[58]Ibid., p. 322.

[59]*Message from the President of the United States* transmitting the Treaty on Open Skies, with Twelve Annexes, Signed at Helsinki on March 24, 1992 (Washington, DC: Government Printing Office, 1992), p. viii.

[60]The weapons proposed for deployment in Western Europe had a range of 300 to 3,400 miles, making them neither short-range nor intercontinental. With strategic parity between the superpowers, it was feared that a Soviet advantage in theater nuclear weapons would allow Moscow to blackmail the Europeans. Many West Europeans reacted negatively to NATO's proposal because they feared their countries would become targets for Soviet nuclear attack.

[61]According to one Russian official, Moscow's nuclear arsenal included some 45,000 nuclear warheads in 1986, twice the number of U.S. warheads at the time and 12,000 more than U.S. estimates. William J. Broad, "Russian Says Atom Arsenal Was Larger Than West Estimated," *New York Times,* September 26, 1993, pp. 1, 7. The U.S. arsenal peaked in 1967 at about 30,000 weapons. Wald, "Today's Drama: Twilight of the Nukes."

[62]A contentious problem, rarely discussed during the Cold War, is how to dispose of nuclear waste produced by reducing stockpiles. Russia has inadequate resources to dismantle and dispose of its weapons safely, and the United States is assisting Moscow in this effort. See, for example, "Russia's Nuclear Nightmare," *The Economist,* January 21–February 2, 1997, p. 43.

[63]Barbara Crossette, "4 Ex-Soviet States and U.S. in Accord on 1991 Arms Pact," *New York Times,* May 24, 1992, pp. 1, 4. Previously, Ukraine, Belarus, and Kazakhstan had turned over short-range nuclear weapons to Russia, which had agreed to destroy them.

[64]Celestine Bohlen, "Ukraine Agrees to Allow Russians to Buy Fleet and Destroy Arsenal," *New York Times,* September 4, 1993, pp. 1, 5.

[65]Elaine Sciolino, "Ukraine Spells Out Tough Terms on Missiles," *New York Times,* October 26, 1993, p. A4.

[66]Douglas Jehl, "Ukrainian Agrees to Dismantle A-Arms," *New York Times,* January 13, 1994, p. A5; Jane Perlez, "Economic Collapse Leaves Ukraine with Little to Trade but Its Weapons," *New York Times,* January 13, 1994. Jane Perlez, "Sunflower Seeds Sown at Ukraine Missile Site," *New York Times,* June 5, 1996, p. A6. For a time, Belarus also was reluctant to carry out its promise. Steven Erlanger, "U.S. Presses Shaky Belarus on Arms Pact," *New York Times,* October 12, 1996, p. 4.

[67]Jane Perlez, "Treaty to Cut A-Weapons Now in Effect," *New York Times,* December 6, 1994, p. A4.

[68]R. W. Apple, Jr., "Clinton and Yeltsin to Speed the Dismantling of A-Arms," *New York Times,* September 29, 1994, p. A5.

[69]Steven Erlanger, "A Clinton-Yeltsin Sidelight: Progress on Arms Control," *New York Times,* March 24, 1997, p. A4.

[70]Sagan, *The Limits of Safety,* pp. 3, 4. See James Brooke, "Shipments of A-Bombs Questioned, as 2 Skid Off Nebraska Road in a Storm," *New York Times,* December 19, 1996, p. A18. Accidents have also occurred with biological agents. The worst known outbreak of anthrax originated in spores released from a Soviet biological-warfare plant in 1979. Philip J. Hilts, "1979 Anthrax Outbreak Traced to Soviet Plant," *New York Times,* November 18, 1994, p. A4.

[71]Japan's program to build fast breeder reactors and use plutonium to generate electricity has drawn protests. Andrew Pollack, "Japan Throws the Switch on Reactor," *New York Times,* August 30, 1995, p. A6. The United States also opposes German plans to build a nuclear reactor that uses highly enriched uranium, claiming that it undermines efforts to halt nuclear proliferation. Alan Cowell, "Germans Rebuff U.S. on Plans for Nuclear Research Reactor," *New York Times,* July 22, 1995, p. A3. Despite fears of proliferation, the U.S. lifted restrictions on exporting high-performance computers that can be used to design nuclear weapons, apparently to help business executives who had supported President Clinton's 1992 campaign. Stephen Engelberg, "Clinton to Ease Computer Sales," *New York Times,* October 2, 1995, pp. A1, A2.

[72]Matthew L. Wald with Michael R. Gordon, "Russia Treasures Plutonium, but U.S. Wants to Destroy It," *New York Times,* August 19, 1994, pp. A1, A6; "To Ban the Bomb," *The Economist,* August 27–September 2, 1994, pp. 10–11. In March 1995 the United States announced it would significantly reduce its stockpiles of plutonium and enriched uranium. Douglas Jehl, "Clinton Orders a Reduction in U.S. Nuclear Stockpiles," *New York Times,* March 2, 1995, p. A7.

[73]Enrichment involves extracting uranium-238 from uranium ore until only uranium-235, which can be used in bombs, remains. Enriched uranium is used to produce nuclear power, during which process plutonium-239 is produced. Spent or used fuel rods can be reprocessed so that the resulting uranium and plutonium can be used in bombs. Jane Perlez, "Tracing a Nuclear Risk: Stolen Enriched Uranium," *New York Times,* February 8, 1995, p. A3. Recently, it has been admitted that less nuclear material is needed to make bombs than previously thought, thus making nuclear smuggling even more dangerous. John J. Fialka, "IAEA Says Its Plutonium Threshold for Making Nuclear Bombs Is Too High," *Wall Street Journal,* August 23, 1994, p. A4. A nuclear bomb needs only 33 pounds of enriched uranium or 11 pounds of plutonium. William C. Potter and Leonard S. Spector, "Nuclear Terrorism—The Next Wave?" *New York Times,* December 19, 1994, p. A15.

[74]Concerned that these materials originated in Russia, the Clinton administration asked Moscow to reveal the location of storage sites and review security procedures. Michael R. Gordon, "U.S. Asks Russia for Data on Nuclear Material Stocks," *New York Times,* May 5, 1994, p. A4. See also Michael R. Gordon, "Russian Says Gangs Try to Steal Atom Matter," *New York Times,* May 26, 1994, p. A10; Ferdinand Protzman, "Germany Reaffirms Origin of Seized Plutonium in Russia," *New York Times,* July 21, 1994, p. A6; Michael R. Gordon with Matthew L. Wald, "Russian Controls on Bomb Material Are Leaky," *New York Times,* August 18, 1994, pp. A1, A8; Steven Erlanger, "Germany and Russia Agree to Combat Nuclear Smuggling," *New York Times,* August 23, 1994, p. A5.

[75]Cited in Craig R. Whitney, "Germans Seize More Weapons Material," *New York Times,* August 17, 1994, p. A4.

[76]"U.S. and Russia Unveil Remote-Control Monitoring System of Nuclear Sites," *New York Times,* April 2, 1995, sec. 1, p. 12.

[77]The agreement threatened to unravel when the federally owned corporation that was to carry out the deal was privatized and the price of uranium declined. Matthew L. Wald, "U.S. Privatization Move Threatens Agreement to Buy Enriched Uranium From Russia," *New York Times,* August 5, 1998, p. A6.

[78]Craig R. Whitney, "A Second 'Sample' of Atomic Material Found in Germany," *New York Times,* August 12, 1994, pp. A1, A6; Craig R. Whitney, "Germans Seize 3d Atom Sample, Smuggled by Plane from Russia," *New York Times,* August 14, 1994, sec. 1, pp. 1, 6; Mark M. Nelson, "Another Seizure of Plutonium Adds to Fears," *Wall Street Journal,* August 17, 1994, p. A8; Rick Atkinson, "A Nuclear Nightmare?" *Washington Post National Weekly Edition,* September 5–11, 1994, pp. 6, 8; Jane Perlez, "Radioactive Material Seized in Slovakia; 9 Under Arrest," *New York Times,* April 22, 1995, p. 4. German intelligence may be behind some of these incidents. Alan Cowell, "Questions Raised on Russian Plutonium Deal," *New York Times,* May 18, 1995, p. A3.

[79]Michael R. Gordon, "U.S. Negotiates Deal to Remove Bomb Fuel in Ex-Soviet Republic," *New York Times,* November 23, 1994, pp. A1, A4. Russia thwarted a U.S. effort to spirit a vulnerable cache of nuclear material out of Thilisi, capital of Georgia. Michael R. Gordon, "Russia Thwarting U.S. Bid to Secure a Nuclear Cache," *New York Times,* January 5, 1997, sec. 1, pp. 1, 4.

[80]William J. Broad, "Experts Say U.S. Fails to Account for Its Plutonium," *New York Times,* May 20, 1994, pp. A1, A8.

[81]Chris Hedges, "Egypt Eases Its Stand on Israel and Nuclear Pact," *New York Times,* March 23, 1995, p. A4.

[82]Iraq had a crash program to develop a nuclear device by April 1991. Barbara Crossette, "Iraqis Set Target of '91 for A-Bomb," *New York Times,* August 26, 1995, pp. 1, 3.

[83]Iran denies it is seeking to become a nuclear power, but U.S. and German intelligence has information that suggests otherwise. Chris Hedges, "Iran May Be Able to Build an Atomic Bomb," *New York Times,* January 5, 1995, p. A5; Elaine Sciolino, "Iran Says It Plans 10 Nuclear Power Plants, but No Atom Arms," *New York Times,* May 14, 1995, sec. 1, pp. 1, 8.

[84]*Arms Control and Disarmament Agreements,* p. 100.

[85]Cited in David E. Sanger, "U.S.-North Korean Atom Accord Expected to Yield Dubious Results," *New York Times,* January 9, 1994, sec. 1, p. 5. Also Michael R. Gordon, "North Korea Is Said to Have Nuclear Fuel," *New York Times,* June 8, 1994, p. A1. With the Korean case in mind, a new IAEA inspection system that involves more sophisticated equipment and sampling and includes monitoring the environment. More information from states being inspected came into existence in 1997. The IAEA is aided by two overlapping groups of nuclear-exporting states—the Zangger Committee and the Nuclear Suppliers Group—that provide it with information.

[86]Stephen Engleberg, "U.S. Asks Czechs to Halt Nuclear Sale to Iran," *New York Times,* December 16, 1993, p. A5; Steven Greenhouse, "U.S. Says Russia Promised Nuclear Gear to Iran," *New York Times,* April 29, 1995, p. 3; Elaine Sciolino, "China Cancels Deal for Selling Iran 2 Reactors," *New York Times,* September 28, 1995, pp. A1, A3; Michael R. Gordon, "Ukraine Decides Not to Supply Key Parts for Iranian Nuclear Reactor," *New York Times,* April 15, 1997, p. A3. China also provided Pakistan with 5,000 ring magnets that can be used to develop nuclear weapons. Steven Erlanger, "U.S. Set to Impose Limited Trade Sanctions on China Administration Says," *New York Times,* February 21, 1996, p. A5; Kathy Chen, "Beijing Admits to Nuciear Deal, Denies Violation," *Wall Street Journal,* April 15, 1996, p. A11.

[87]Barbara Crossette, "Discord over Renewing Pact on Spread of Nuclear Arms," *New York Times,* April 15, 1995, pp. A1, A4; Barbara Crossette, "Treaty Aimed at Halting Spread of Nuclear Weapons Extended," *New York Times,* May 12, 1995, pp. A1, A4.

[88]Cited in Sanjoy Hazarika, "India Assails Pact to Curb Atomic Arms" *New York Times,* May 16, 1995, p. A4.

[89]Barbara Crossette, "U.N. Council Seeks Support to Renew Pact Curbing Spread of Nuclear Arms," *New York Times,* April 6, 1995, p. A7. By 1998, 186 states had signed the NPT, and only five (India, Pakistan, Israel, Brazil, and Cuba) had not. "The Desperate Efforts to Block the Road to Doomsday," *The Economist,* p. 23. India and Pakistan have indicated they might sign once economic sanctions imposed at the time of their nuclear tests are lifted.

[90]*Arms Control and Disarmament Agreements,* pp. 23-24.

[91]Ibid., pp. 64-67.

[92]One Soviet test exposed 45,000 Russians to high radiation levels. Marlise Simons, "Soviet Atomic Bomb Test Exposed 45,000 to High Level of Radiation," *New York Times,* November 7, 1993, pp. 1, 8. American citizens were subjected to radioactivity experiments and were also exposed to radioactivity. Keith Schneider, "Disclosing Radiation Tests Puts Official in Limelight," *New York Times,* January 6, 1994, pp. A1, A14; Michael Janofsky, "Neighbors of Bomb-Test: Unlucky and Embittered," *New York Times,* January 11, 1994, pp. 1, 10.

[93]Steve Coll and David B. Ottaway, "Burying the Nuclear Hatchet," *Washington Post National Weekly Edition,* April 17-23, 1995, pp. 6-9.

[94]Patrick E. Tyler, "Chinese Test Atomic Bomb Underground," *New York Times,* October 8, 1994, p. 3; Patrick E. Tyler, "China Upgrades Nuclear Arsenal as It Re-examines Guns vs. Butter," *New York Times,* October 26, 1994, pp. A1, A4; Barbara Crossette, "In Concession, China Is Ready to Ban A-Tests," *New York Times,* June 7, 1996, pp. A1, A4; "China Stages Nuclear Test and Vows to Join Ban After One More," June 9, 1996, sec. 1, p. 9. Chinese leaders argue the need for "peaceful nuclear explosions" to combat the threat that an asteroid might strike the earth. Patrick E. Tyler, "Chinese Seek Atom Option to Fend Off Asteroids," *New York Times,* April 27, 1996, p. 4.

[95]Philip Shenon, "France, Ignoring Protestors, Conducts Pacific Atom Test," *New York Times,* September 6, 1995, pp. A1, A3. Partly as a protest against French and Chinese tests, the Norwegian Nobel Committee awarded the 1995 Nobel Peace Prize to Joseph Rothblat, a physicist and leading critic of nuclear testing. Richard W. Stevenson, "Peace Prize Goes to A-Bomb Scientist Who Turned Critic," *New York Times,* October 14, 1995, p. 3. France carried out its promise ahead of schedule after conducting six tests. Craig R. Whitney, "Under Pressure, France Is Ending Its Nuclear Tests," *New York Times,* January 30, 1996, pp. A1, A4.

[96]Barbara Crossette, "U.S. Pushes Treaty to Ban Nuclear Tests," *New York Times,* January 22, 1996, p. A5; Seth Mydans, "U.S. and Russia to Seek Approval of Atom Test Pact," *New York Times,* July 24, 1996, pp. A1, A7.

[97]Barbara Crossette, "Nuclear Test Ban Negotiators to End Talks Without Accord," *New York Times,* June 28, 1996, p. A2; Barbara Crossette, "India Deadlocks Nuclear Test-Ban Treaty," *New York Times,* August 15, 1996, p. A4; John F. Burns, "India, Old Foe of Atom Arms, Stops Test Ban," *New York Times,* August 17, 1996, pp. 1, 3; Barbara Crossette, "India Vetoes Pact to Forbid Testing of Nuclear Arms," *New York Times,* August 21, 1996, p. A1.

[98]Barbara Crossette, "U.N. Endorses Treaty to Halt All Nuclear Testing," *New York Times,* September 11, 1996, p. 3. Although the voluntary U.S. moratorium on nuclear tests continues, opposition by the Republican-controlled Senate Foreign Relations Committee and its chairman Jesse Helms has pre-

vented U.S. ratification of the treaty. Indeed, a report warning that Iran and North Korea could develop long-range ballistic missiles within five years has heightened the skepticism of some legislators about arms control in general and has led to renewed calls for developing a national missile-defense system (in violation of the 1972 ABM treaty). Carla Ann Robbins, "Beyond India and Pakistan, Arms Control Is Failing," *Wall Street Journal,* July 16, 1998, p. A20.

[99]R. Jeffrey Smith, "A Treaty Not Quite on Target," *Washington Post National Weekly Edition,* September 30–October 6, 1996, p. 18.

[100]Cited in Barbara Crossette, "Test Ban Debate Goes to Wider Forum Tomorrow," *New York Times,* September 8, 1996, sec. 1, p. 8. Republicans included a rejection of the treaty in their 1996 campaign platform.

[101]"A Bomb in Every Backyard?" *The Economist,* June 6–12, 1998, p. 17. The Hindu-nationalist Bharatiya Janata Party (BJP), which led a coalition government to power shortly before the nuclear tests, had earlier given warning that it favored testing. See Miriam Jordan, "Indian Opposition Party Would Assert Nuclear Capability if It Gains Power," *Wall Street Journal,* April 2, 1996, p. A10.

[102]John F. Burns, "India, Eye on China, Insists It Will Develop Nuclear Deterrent, *New York Times,* July 7, 1998, p. A7. Pakistan rejected India's claim that it had developed nuclear weapons with China in mind. Barbara Crossette, "Pakistan Says India Uses False Threats to Justify Nuclear Arms," *New York Times,* July 8, 1998, p. A7. In accordance with the 1994 Arms Export Control Act, the United States initially imposed economic sanctions on India and Pakistan but removed most in a short time as a result of interest-group pressure at home. Steven Erlanger, "Clinton Seeks Power to Lift India-Pakistan Sanctions," *New York Times,* July 14, 1998, p. A9.

[103]Leonard S. Spector and Virginia Foran, *Preventing Weapons Proliferation: Should the Regimes Be Combined?* A Report of the Thirty-Third Strategy for Peace, U.S. Foreign Policy Conference, October 22–24, 1992, p. 8.

[104]Patrick E. Tyler, "China Raises Nuclear Stakes on the Subcontinent," *New York Times,* August 27, 1996, p. A5; R. Jeffrey Smith, "The Arming of Pakistan," *Washington Post National Weekly Edition,* September 2–8, 1996, p. 16; John M. Broder, "Jiang Held Cards till Final Moment," *New York Times,* June 30, 1998, p. A9.

[105]Christopher S. Wren, "Making It Easier to Uncover Nuclear Arms," *New York Times,* June 16, 1995, p. A6.

[106]Steve Coll, "North Korea at a Nuclear Turning Point," *Washington Post National Weekly Edition,* p. 16. Also see "A Dangerous Game," *The Economist,* May 28–June 3, 1994, pp. 19, 20, 22.

[107]James Sterngold, "On Korea: the Central Nuclear Issue," *New York Times,* July 24, 1994, sec. 1, p. 8.

[108]Alan Riding, "U.S. and North Korea Agree to Build on Nuclear Accord," *New York Times,* October 18, 1994, pp. A1,

A7; Michael R. Gordon, "U.S.-North Korea Accord Has a 10-Year Timetable," *New York Times,* October 22, 1994, p. A4.

[109]The compromise allowed South Korea to build the reactors but publicly referred only to "the advanced version of U.S.-origin design and technology." Andrew Pollack, "South Korea Likely to Build New Reactors," *New York Times,* June 14, 1995, p. A5. The agreement is endangered over a squabble over how the United States, South Korea, and Japan will divide the cost of the reactors.

[110]Cited in Philip Shenon, "North Korea Said to Block Inspection of Nuclear Sites," *New York Times,* July 15, 1998, p. A9.

[111]"Ban the Bug Bomb," *The Economist,* November 23–29, 1996, p. 19.

[112]Andrew Pollack, "Police Find Germ War Material at Japan Site," *New York Times,* March 29, 1995, p. A6. The CIA believes the United States is "very poorly equipped to defend itself against a terrorist group armed with nuclear, biological or chemical weapons." Cited in Tim Weiner, "U.S. Is Called Vulnerable to Terrorist Chemical Arms," *New York Times,* March 21, 1996, p. A4.

[113]"The Desperate Efforts to Block the Road to Doomsday," *The Economist,* June 5–12, 1998, p. 24.

[114]Ibid. U.S. ratification of the CWC in 1997 was only achieved with difficulty, as 26 of 55 Republican senators voted against it. Carla Anne Robbins, "Senate Battle on Arms Control Is Still Far from Over," *Wall Street Journal,* May 6, 1997, p. A24.

[115]"The Desperate Efforts to Block the Road to Doomsday," pp. 23–24. See also "Anything You Can Do . . . ," *The Economist,* May 10–16, 1997, pp. 36, 41.

[116]Barbara Crossette, "Security Council Closes Its Ranks Against Baghdad," *New York Times,* August 7, 1998, p. A6. Iraqis admitted to inspectors of the U.N. Special Commission (Unscom) that they had filled over 100,000 warheads with chemical weapons in the 1980s during their war with Iran and repeatedly have refused to provide full information to inspectors about their chemical and biological weapons programs. The Sudanese facility, the Al Shifa factory, was believed to be making components for VX nerve gas. Judith Miller, "U.S. Suspected Deadly Production Line," *New York Times,* August 21, 1998, p. A10.

[117]Cited in Amy Dockser Marcus, "U.S. Drive to Curb Doomsday Weapons in Mideast Is Faltering," *Wall Street Journal,* September 6, 1996, p. A1.

[118]Philip Shenon, "U.S. to Transfer Most of Its Force in Saudi Arabia," *New York Times,* July 18, 1996, pp. A1, A4.

[119]Michael R. Gordon, "U.S. Says Russians Hide Bid to Develop Deadly Poison Gas," *New York Times,* June 23, 1994, pp. A1, A4; Clifford Krauss, "U.S. Tells Russia to Stop Making Nerve Gas," *New York Times,* February 6, 1997, p. A8.

[120]Barbara Crossette, "Iraq Supplies U.N. with New Details on Germ Weapons," *New York Times,* August 23, 1995, pp. A1, A6.

[121]Erhard Geissler, "Biological Weapon and Arms Control Developments," in *SIPRI Yearbook 1994,* pp. 715–716. According to U.S. intelligence, Libya, which has not signed the

CWC, is building the world's largest chemical weapons plant, and U.S. officials have alluded to possible military action to prevent its completion. Tim Weiner, "Libya Completing Huge Plant for Chemical Arms, U.S. Says," *New York Times,* February 25, 1996, sec. 1, p. 6.

[122]"Bosnia Produced Chemical Arms, Report Says," *New York Times,* December 4, 1996, p. A11; Philip Shenon, "Yugoslav Army Is Suspected of Having Chemical Arms," *New York Times,* March 28, 1997, p. A5.

[123]Cited in Geissler, "Biological Weapon and Arms Control Developments," p. 713. In January 1998 President Clinton promised to confront the danger of biological weapons in the hands of "outlaw states, terrorists and organized criminals," and in May he announced a plan to stockpile vaccines around the United States "to protect our civilian population." However, little has been accomplished to date. William J. Broad and Judith Miller, "Germ Defense Plan in Peril As Its Flaws Are Revealed," *New York Times,* August 7, 1998, pp. A1, A12.

[124]Compellance is similar to what Alexander L. George calls "coercive diplomacy." See Alexander L. George, *Forceful Persuasion: Coercive Diplomacy as an Alternative to War* (Washington, DC: United States Institute of Peace Press, 1992).

[125]Schelling, *Arms and Influence,* pp. 71–72. Emphasis in original.

[126]Had the missiles become operational, U.S. leaders would have had the additional task of deterring their use against the United States. The United States had the problem of deterring Soviet action against targets such as West Berlin, which, it was feared, might be challenged in response to U.S. action against Cuba.

[127]Tet is Vietnam's New Year. The offensive, though a military defeat for the communists, was a political triumph because it showed that not even a half-million U.S. soldiers could pacify the country.

[128]Cited in Barton Gellman, "Is This 'Immaculate Coercion'?" *Washington Post National Weekly Edition,* April 6, 1999, pp. 6–7; Craig R. Whitney, "Peacekeepers in Kosovo Have Tough Job Ahead, Allied Commander Says," *New York Times,* June 12, 1999, p. A7. Recent and less successful efforts to apply compellance include China's use of missile tests and military maneuvers to coerce Taiwan to forget about seeking independence, and Israel's bombardment of southern Lebanon to force Syria to rein in Hizbollah. Steven Erlanger, "'Ambiguity' On Taiwan," *New York Times,* March 12, 1996, pp. A1, A7; Amy Dockser Marcus, "Israel Uses Bombardment of Lebanon to Press Syria to Control Militant Group," *Wall Street Journal,* April 15, 1996, p. A11.

Chapter 12

International Political Economy: Where Economics and Politics Meet

Until recently, theorists of global politics largely ignored economics. The realist Hans J. Morgenthau argued that "the concept of interest defined in terms of power . . . sets politics as an autonomous sphere of action and understanding apart from other spheres, *such as economics (understood in terms of interest defined as wealth)*. . . ."[1] Nevertheless, economic factors greatly affect the political arena, and politics conditions the economic sphere. Although Adam Smith (1723–1790), the author of *Wealth of Nations* and acknowledged father of modern capitalism, held a chair in *political economy* at Glasgow University and Karl Marx (1818–1883) and his followers referred to themselves as political economists, the discipline was mostly ignored in the United States until recent decades.

This lapse betrays ignorance of history. For example, the practice of slavery and the American Civil War were linked to economic relations between North and South, and Europe's colonial expansion had economic motives. Developments in recent decades, especially the growth of a global capital market, have reduced the capacity of governments to regulate their countries' economies. Capital flows freely from country to country in pursuit of profit and foreign exchange, and bond markets can overwhelm governments' monetary and fiscal policies.[2] In recent years, economic markets have been globalized as the value of gross foreign direct investment as a percentage of global gross domestic product doubled between 1986 and 1996.[3] In addition, regional economic integration has taken place in virtually every area of the world, and in Europe, as we shall see in the next chapter, a single currency, the euro, is replacing national currencies like the French franc and the German Deutschmark.

One can hardly avoid reflecting on the interdependence of politics and economics, whether one is describing American efforts to pressure oil companies to build a pipeline for Caspian Sea oil that would cross Turkey[4] or the efforts of Israeli business leaders to persuade their government to show moderation on security issues.[5] Such cases illustrate that "economic power is the new determinant of international stature."[6] One observer of U.S.-Japanese negotiations over opening Japan's market to U.S. auto parts commented wryly that "car parts never quickened Henry Kissinger's pulse. But one doesn't have to be in Geneva long to discover that divisions between America and Japan are the arms-control negotiations of the '90s with terms like 'massive retaliation,' 'containment,' and 'verification' applied to trade relations."[7]

In this chapter we examine the relationship between economic. First, we describe the actors and issues in the liberal economic order War II, and then we turn to economic issues that help determine politica. among actors today.

Politics of the Liberal Economic Order

The current economic order has its roots in decisions made as World War II ended. Western leaders sought to foster reconstruction and a global market system based on the principles of liberal capitalism. They tried to create institutions that would increase efficiency and growth[8] and prevent adoption of the competitive and destructive *beggar-thy-neighbor policies* that had intensified the Great Depression in the 1930s and contributed to fascism's rise. They assumed that actors try to maximize efficiency and growth and that the purpose of economic institutions is to allocate resources for these ends. Such allocation, in their view, is best achieved by an open system without impediments to trade or capital flows. In such a system, actors focus on producing what they can most efficiently and enjoy *comparative advantage*— specializing in producing only those goods that they can produce most efficiently. That system, they hoped, if allowed to operate without interference, would lead to prosperity for all. Today, as in the past, the United States remains a vigorous advocate of economic liberalism and tries to export its free-market values through international economic institutions.[9]

The Bretton Woods System

The first steps in building a *liberal economic order* were taken at a 1944 conference at *Bretton Woods,* New Hampshire. The conferees agreed to found three organizations to manage the global economy—the *International Monetary Fund (IMF)*, the *General Agreement on Tariffs and Trade (GATT),* and the International Bank for Reconstruction and Development (the IBRD or *World Bank*).

The IMF.   The IMF was built to promote economic health by regulating monetary policy. Global trade and investment require payment in money, which is possible only when rules determine the value of different national currencies. The main task was to stabilize *exchange rates* by assisting states with *balance-of-payments* difficulties—when more funds are leaving a country than entering it. Such stability, it was believed, was critical to inspire confidence in the system. To meet its task, the IMF provided short-term loans and set up a system or *fixed monetary exchange rates* and *currency convertibility* that would enable countries to use their own currency to purchase "international" or hard currencies, like the U.S. dollar and British pound, that were acceptable everywhere.[10]

The United States provided much of the initial IMF funding, and other currencies were pegged to the dollar's value. As a result, the health and stability of the U.S. economy were crucial to the health of the global economy. Adding another element of stability to the system, the United States fixed and guaranteed the value

America's ideology of free enterprise is a source of soft power. Its attraction is symbolized in this photo of a McDonald's restaurant in Beijing, China. *(Jeffrey Aaronson/Network Aspen)*

of the dollar against gold: U.S. dollars could be converted to gold at $35 an ounce. The Bretton Woods accord worked well until the early 1970s.

In recent years, the IMF role has changed. Today, its principal task is to lend funds to countries whose currency is under speculative attack and which are struggling with heavy debt.[11] The idea is that such funds can be used by countries to purchase their own currencies, thereby maintaining their value and restoring global confidence in them. In this capacity, the IMF played a mayor role in rescuing Mexico in 1994 and in trying to help first those Asian countries suffering financial turmoil in 1997— Thailand, Indonesia, and South Korea—and then Russia and Brazil, as the crisis spread from one to another developing economy.

When it lends funds under these conditions, however, the IMF requires that borrowers agree to stringent reforms. They must reduce government spending and subsidies to reduce deficits, eliminate protection of weak industries and banks, privatize state enterprises, give local financial institutions greater transparency (accessibility to outside scrutiny), create greater labor flexibility, institute high interest rates to attract foreign investment, eliminate bad loans and restructure local banks to make sure that political influence will no longer determine who receives loans, and open local markets to foreign goods and investment. This *conditionality* entails severe austerity in debtor countries and causes slower economic growth, higher prices and interest rates, and higher unemployment. IMF conditions reflect the free-market orthodoxy of its largest contributors, who dominate its twenty-four member executive board.[12] However, the failure of these policies to provide rapid improvement in Asia and elsewhere has triggered debate about the wisdom of setting these conditions.

The growing instability in global currency markets that accompanied Asia's economic crisis provoked a lively debate about reforming the IMF and the monetary system more generally. Some, including U.S. and IMF officials, saw little reason for major changes in IMF policy.[13] Others, including a majority in the U.S. Congress, demanded that the IMF be more accountable for its actions. Thus, before providing the IMF with $18 billion in funds requested by the Clinton administration to replenish reserve accounts depleted by loans to states in financial trouble,[14] Congress, arguing that IMF assistance gave profligate states an opportunity to avoid putting their economic houses in order, demanded an end to the IMF practice of lending at below-market interest rates and required that loans be repaid in a much shorter time than had been the case.[15] And at a meeting of finance ministers from the world's major economies held in Washington, D.C., in October 1998, a variety of ideas were put forward: the Clinton administration proposed that the IMF provide assistance to states threatened by capital flight *before* an economic crisis struck; Japanese and other Asian leaders spoke of reimposing "capital controls" to limit the unfettered movement of short-term investments; and the French sought to increase IMF accountability. In the end, there was little consensus.[16]

The GATT.   A second element of Bretton Woods was movement toward a liberal trading order. Most economists agree that free trade increases the overall volume of trade and, therefore, the total number of jobs in an economy. However, there are losers as well as winners. Those who support trade barriers do so to protect jobs that would be lost to low-wage foreign competitors, but one result is higher costs to consumers and lower overall economic growth. Thus trade barriers in twenty-one U.S. industries saved 191,000 jobs at a cost to consumers of $170,000 per job.[17]

Although the original conferees envisioned an ambitious International Trading Organization (ITO), they compromised on the General Agreement on Tariffs and Trade (GATT) after the U.S. Congress balked.[18] The GATT sought to reduce trade barriers on manufacturing and to establish the principle of *most-favored-nation (MFN) status.* That principle requires that actors treat each other equally by according the same (lowest) tariff rates on imports from all countries. The GATT sponsored a series of "negotiating rounds" to remove obstacles to free trade. In GATT's fifty years, world trade quintupled and average industrial tariffs were reduced to one-tenth of their 1948 level, and since 1950 global trade has exploded sixteen-fold, far surpassing the growth in gross domestic product (GDP).[19] After 1980, the task of liberalizing trade became more complex, as the GATT turned from reducing industrial tariffs to knottier issues of reducing *nontariff barriers* (such as quotas or orderly marketing agreements) and liberalizing trade in services and agriculture.

The World Bank.   The third leg of the Bretton Woods system was the World Bank. The Bank's initial aim was to aid postwar reconstruction, but it soon turned to economic development. It is funded by member states' contributions and by

ACTORS SPEAK

Following the failure of the IMF and its policies to overcome the economic crisis that first struck Asia in 1997 and then spread elsewhere, a debate began about whether the organization needs to be reformed. Some officials argued that IMF policy was fundamentally correct and that what was needed was patience. Others argued that the IMF "cure" worsened the "illness" it was intended to overcome.

Every place you turn you read the same story, that we came in, that we made things worse. We frequently get the blame, some of it well deserved. But it is politically convenient for governments around the world to cry, "The I.M.F. made us do it," and pin their mistakes on us. That's fine. We'd rather be loved, but more than that we'd like to be effective. (Stanley Fischer, Deputy Managing Director of the IMF, as cited in David E. Sanger, "As Economies Fail, the I.M.F Is Rife with Recriminations," *New York Times,* October 2, 1998, p. A10)

Last year the standard that all of us were given came down to this: "We have the I.M.F and the World Bank and they know best." Then they said that everything that went wrong was our fault. But now, now I think people know that much of the problem came from the outside, and we need something better. (Ali Alatas, Indonesian Foreign Minister, as cited in David E. Sanger, "As Economies Fail, the I.M.F Is Rife with Recriminations," *New York Times,* October 2, 1998, p. A10)

borrowing on global capital markets, and its lending decisions are based on market principles—loan rates and prospects for repayment. About a decade after the World Bank was founded, the International Finance Corporation was added to provide loans to private enterprises whose activities would contribute to poor countries' development. In 1960, the International Development Association was established to provide interest-free loans on a long-term basis (usually fifty years) to poor countries. All three banking institutions are overseen by a Board of Governors consisting of member states and twenty-two executive directors, five of whom are appointed by the largest contributors. In practice, these requirements mean that a few wealthy states, led by the United States, enjoy great influence in these institutions.

With these institutions—and the shared rules and norms they promoted—Bretton Woods created a liberal monetary and trading regime to manage the global economy. It was able to do so for three reasons.[20] First, the system enabled wealthy countries in North America and Western Europe to amass economic power, and excluded the command economies of the Soviet bloc. Second, these states shared a commitment to market principles and economic freedom, albeit mixed with limited government intervention, which they promoted by cooperating with one another. Third, and most important, the United States was willing to underwrite the system. The IMF and World Bank had their headquarters in Washington, and the United States assumed a leading role in both. As the strongest economic power, it was in an ideal position to assume this role. Both the U.S. dollar and domestic market were major elements in reviving the world economy, and U.S. leaders were prepared to bear economic burdens for political stability.

Criticized for doing little to alleviate global poverty, the World Bank has in recent years turned its attention increasingly to that task. It has also been grudgingly drawn into assisting the IMF in providing funds to countries whose currencies are under speculative attack.[21]

| The Collapse of Bretton Woods | The Bretton Woods system fell apart in the early 1970s, beginning with a dramatic announcement by the Nixon administration—the *"Nixon shock."*[22] Although the institutions remained, the rules and practices governing them changed dramatically. To combat inflation and a spiraling balance-of-payments deficit, the administration decided that the United States could no longer afford to subsidize global trade by maintaining a strong dollar that encouraged imports to the United States but discouraged the purchase of U.S. exports. On August 15, 1971, the United States announced it would no longer maintain a system of fixed exchange rates, that the convertibility of U.S. dollars into gold would cease, and that a surcharge would be levied on all imports. After an agreement among the major trading partners in December 1971 an effort to maintain fixed exchange rates and dollar convertibility collapsed, and all convertible currencies were permitted to "float" in relation to one another. With the exception of countries like Hong Kong and Argentina, which peg the value of their currencies to the U.S. dollar, floating exchange rates remain the norm today, but the movement of huge amounts of money around the world can rapidly undermine the integrity of a country's currency, thereby casting doubt on the wisdom of floating rates. |

Why did the Bretton Woods system fall apart so quickly? Most explanations show how tightly politics and economics are enmeshed. First, as monetary interdependence deepened, it became difficult to coordinate so many actors' policies. Transnational banks and corporations had learned how to take advantage of even slight fluctuations in interest and currency rates. Their actions—for example, purchasing "cheap" gold and selling dollars in the belief that the dollar was overvalued— were beyond effective control by the Bretton Woods regime and placed pressure on the system.

Second, with vigorous economies, the Europeans and Japanese had recovered much of the self-confidence they had lost during World War II and wanted to reduce their dependence on the United States and seek a more independent political role for themselves. Moreover, American spending to wage war in Vietnam and simultaneously combat poverty at home stimulated harmful global inflation. American inflation meant that U.S. dollars were worth less, but, since adjustment was impossible with fixed exchange rates, America's inflation was transmitted to its allies' economies.

The Nixon administration tried to stem the decline in America's trading position. A strong dollar reduced U.S. competitiveness worldwide by making American goods expensive, but, under Bretton Woods, the United States could not devalue the dollar to reduce the cost of U.S. exports to others. Previously, Washington had absorbed this cost to open U.S. markets to allies' goods, helping their recovery and stimulating the global economy by affording *liquidity,* that is, dollars available to help allies pay for imports. By 1973, however, devaluation of the dollar was seen as necessary to reduce America's growing payment deficits and end Japanese and European discrimination against U.S. exports. The only way to confront these issues, the administration believed, was to move decisively away from fixed exchange rates.

Issues in the Global Economy: The First World[23]

Since the collapse of Bretton Woods, several economic issues have plagued relations among the wealthy states. These include protectionism, fluctuating exchange rates, global energy prices, and national budget deficits and unemployment. In recent decades, several strategies have been proposed to deal with these issues, but none has been entirely satisfactory. We briefly review these issues and the strategies used to cope with them.

Floating Exchange Rates

Since *floating exchange rates* were adopted in the early 1970s, the developed countries have tried to muddle through, responding to monetary crises in an ad hoc way. The issue is contentious because it directly affects domestic economic health in most countries. Under a system of floating exchange rates, the value of a currency depends on perceptions of a country's economic condition as reflected by its trade balance, rate of economic growth, and level of inflation. The perceptions of speculators who buy and sell currency (thereby determining its value) are also influenced by other factors that predict an economy's future health, such as political stability and strength of political institutions. If the currency they purchase loses value, they will lose money; if it increases in value, they will profit. It was growing concern about the economies of Southeast Asia—especially their enormous debt burden and high number of "nonperforming" loans (loans with little prospect of being repaid) held by local banks—that triggered the sale of local currencies by investors in the summer of 1997 and so began what became a global economic crisis.

Although the U.S. dollar is no longer the global benchmark currency it was when pegged to gold, stabilizing the dollar has remained a key objective of developed countries because of its importance in world trade. A fluctuating dollar harms world trade because it creates instability by making it difficult for trading partners to predict the prices of goods they wish to buy and sell.

In the 1970s, the dollar weakened—its value fell—because of high inflation in the United States and mushrooming U.S. trading deficits abroad and budget deficits at home. Other countries' goods became more expensive in the United States, fueling domestic inflation, and the dollars they received for their goods could buy less. As energy prices, calculated in dollars, soared in the 1970s, other countries suffered a double whammy: rising energy costs and less-valuable dollars with which to purchase expensive oil. The weak dollar was a thorn to the United States for other reasons as well. As the dollar's value declined, other countries sold dollars and bought stronger currencies like Japanese yen, which further weakened the dollar (because demand for dollars was declining but the supply of dollars was growing). For Americans, this weakness meant that everything from overseas cost more, thereby lowering their standard of living.

In the 1980s, conditions changed, and an opposite problem appeared—a strong U.S. dollar—which made it difficult for Americans to sell products overseas and opened a yawning trade deficit between the United States and its trading partners. The strong dollar owed much to a lower rate of inflation (especially a lower price for oil), high interest rates, and restored confidence in the management of America's economy. As America's trade deficit grew and interest rates remained high, foreign investors bought dollars and invested them in the United States for high returns. These investments, especially by the Japanese, paid for U.S. budget deficits in the Reagan-Bush years. Although European and Japanese export industries thrived, the flight of capital to the United States drained resources that were vital to business expansion and employment in Europe and elsewhere.

Soaring budget deficits, yawning trade deficits, and low interest rates, combined with the Clinton administration's effort to increase U.S. exports by reducing the dollar's value relative to Japanese and German currencies, sent the dollar's value plummeting in 1994 and 1995. In 1994, it declined 11 percent against the mark and the yen, down about two-thirds from its 1960s value against these currencies. However, any concern that the dollar had ceased serving as a genuine international *reserve currency* were put to rest when fears about Asian economies in 1997 and 1998 caused a flight of funds to the safety of the dollar. This event dramatically raised the dollar-denominated debts of those countries, and, along with a weak yen that reduced Japanese demand for imports from others in Asia, reduced the value of peoples' savings and standard of living first in Asia and then elsewhere as the economic crisis spread.

Thus monetary issues, though apparently "technical," generate strong passions. In 1994, France suddenly devalued the African (CFA) franc—the currency in fourteen West African countries that were formerly French colonies—from 50 per French franc (its value since 1948) to 100.[24] After years of subsidizing imports to its former colonies, France wanted to force them to produce rather than import more.[25] However, the move doubled the price for most goods in these countries and triggered a wave of violence, strikes, and turmoil throughout West Africa.[26]

Political Efforts to Manage Monetary Problems

One strategy was reflected in a number of multilateral and unilateral efforts initiated by the United States. To prop up the weak dollar in the late 1970s, the Carter administration first sought to coordinate macroeconomic policy with its allies. Specifically, it urged other rich states, especially Germany and Japan, to pursue expansionist economic policies to encourage demand for U.S. goods and services in those countries and so strengthen the dollar. When this effort failed, partly because of U.S. unwillingness to make sensitive domestic budget cuts and impose energy-conservation measures, the U.S. Federal Reserve intervened actively in foreign-exchange markets, buying dollars to prop up their value and reducing the money supply at home to slow inflation.

The Reagan administration also pursued a policy of unilateralism, promoting U.S. economic interests even to the detriment of some of its allies. In the end, the efforts of Presidents Carter and Reagan increased the value of the U.S. dollar.[27] Although a strong dollar dampened U.S. inflation and helped allied economic growth, it also had negative effects, including skyrocketing U.S. trade and budget deficits. Elsewhere, dollars were purchased, and capital investment fled to American shores, shrinking economic growth. By the mid-1980s, a monetary-management crisis produced an effort to achieve a multilateral solution.

In September 1985, the finance ministers of the United States, Japan, Germany, France, and Great Britain—the so-called G-5 nations—gathered in New York City to address the problems posed by a strong U.S. dollar. They agreed in what was called the Plaza Accord that "further orderly appreciation of the main non-dollar currencies against the dollar is desirable,"[28] shortly after the United States had dumped dollars in exchange for yen and marks, forcing down the dollar's value. Thereafter, additional multilateral steps were taken to confront monetary instability. In rapid succession, four other informal and formal commitments were made to stabilize exchange rates. In October 1986, the United States and Japan agreed to stabilize the yen-dollar exchange rate and increase Japan's domestic demand for imports to stimulate trade between the two countries. In February 1987, the Louvre Accord (after the palace in Paris at which the meeting took place) was reached among the G-6 (the original five plus Canada). It called for maintaining exchange rates among the dollar, yen, and mark within a narrow range.[29] Two additional agreements later in 1987 refined the commitment by the G-7 nations (now including Italy) to multilateral exchange-rate stability.[30]

Between 1990 and 1992, the Bush administration tried to stimulate the American economy by letting the value of the dollar fall, and the Clinton administration continued the policy. Unfortunately, this fall was accompanied by lower U.S. interest rates at a time of high German interest rates, creating a rush to sell dollars, buy German marks, and invest at higher rates in German securities. High German rates were intended to attract capital for reconstructing the eastern region of the country, but the difference in U.S. and German policies placed intense pressure on the dollar.

Eroding state capacity to stabilize global exchange rates became evident in the 1990s. Between 1987 and 1992, rate fluctuations remained more modest than in the late 1970s and early 1980s, but then the dollar began its precipitous slide, showing the growing clout of private speculators. This was apparent as the central banks of the G-7 were unable to slow the dollar's fall. After the Naples summit of July 1994, two observers wrote, "Less than a decade ago, under U.S. leadership, the world's big economies successfully pushed the dollar in the direction they wanted it to go—at that time, down—with a mixture of strong words and market intervention. Today, governments acknowledge they are increasingly powerless in the face of currency markets."[31]

Monetary stability will be continually tested by new events, and individual governments will be tempted to go it alone. At best, monetary management remains fragile.

Trade Issues and the First World

A second set of issues involves trade relations and the effort to move toward a freer market in services and agriculture. Table 12.1 shows the growing importance of trade to the developed states in recent years. "Asian tigers" like Hong Kong and Singapore are more deeply enmeshed in globalized trade than other countries, but increases in trade for other wealthy states since 1986 are significant. These countries, sometimes called *newly industrializing countries (NICs),* achieved prosperity by creating "export

Country*	Trade as a Percent of GDP	
	1986	1996
Canada	45.6	58.5
France	33.7	45.4
Hong Kong	111.8	247.6
Italy	28.0	39.6
Japan	21.5	26.1
Netherlands	86.7	106.4
New Zealand	29.7	45.0
Norway	67.8	80.3
Singapore	191.0	316.0
South Korea	33.6	46.7
Spain	18.4	36.8
Sweden	61.5	87.2
Switzerland	67.4	89.8
United Kingdom	33.3	46.3
United States	14.0	19.4

*Data for Germany unavailable.

Trade has played a a major role in the economies of most developed states, especially since the 1970s. Although U.S. dependence on international trade has grown, it still remains less than that of most other major countries. SOURCE: *World Development Indicators 1998*, pp. 310–312.

machines."[32] For the world as a whole, the value of trade measured as a share of gross domestic product (GDP) rose from 20.7 to 29.1 percent. In the case of the United States, the increase was from 14.0 to 19.4 percent.[33] Others are far more dependent on trade than the United States. For example, the value of trade for Hong Kong and Singapore as a percentage of GDP was 247.6 and 316.0 percent, respectively.

International trade, though historically a smaller element in the U.S. economy than in other economically advanced countries, has grown in recent years, and overseas markets are growing more important to U.S. producers. The leading trading partners of the United States are Canada, Japan, and Mexico, and the United States is Japan's and Europe's leading trading partner.

Events that disrupt or alter these trade patterns or change relative amounts of trade among partners can provoke economic and political turmoil. The inevitable political dimension of trade issues frustrates economists.

On the one hand, we have our theory, descended from Adam Smith and David Ricardo, which stresses all the benefits of open markets and unrestricted exchange between nations based on underlying differences of comparative advantage. On the other hand, we have the real world, where forces of . . . protection always seem rampant. . . . Rarely in the economics profession do we encounter greater dissonance between what we are taught in principle and what we observe in practice.

And try as we might to find logical reasons for all this in the tenets of our own discipline, ultimately we are tempted simply to throw up our hands and proclaim "It's all politics!"[34]

In recent years, turmoil in trade relations has been the rule. As the threat of communism receded, the United States, Germany, Japan, and others were less willing to compromise economic differences to maintain political solidarity. As a result, changes in the global political environment have directly influenced the global economic environment.

Managing Trade Relations Politically

Three strategies have been used to manage trade differences within the First World.[35] The first is global, involving the General Agreement on Tariffs and Trade (GATT). This strategy involves coordinated efforts to reduce tariffs by multilateral negotiations (or "rounds") among members. A second strategy is using multilateral economic summits among the Western allies and Japan to coordinate economic policies. These summits have been held yearly since 1975. A third strategy, to which we turn in the next chapter, is the use of bilateral negotiation to overcome frictions.

Negotiations centering on the GATT have passed through eight rounds.[36] The Dillon and Kennedy rounds in the 1960s reduced tariff and nontariff barriers for several industrial sectors and agricultural commodities.[37] The Tokyo Round (1973–1979) made deep tariff cuts and launched a search for agreement on subjects such as favorable treatment for poor countries and eliminating subsidies and countervailing duties. The *Uruguay Round*[38] (1986–1993) took GATT a step further by addressing such nettlesome issues as agricultural subsidies, trade in services (such as insurance), rules for governing *intellectual property rights,* and *nontariff barriers.* Few issues link the domestic and global arenas as much as these, complicating attempts to reach agreement.[39] Efforts to reduce agricultural subsidies were violently opposed by Japanese and European, especially French, farmers and raised grave doubts in the electorally important U.S. Midwest, and the issue, exacerbated by global recession, was a major barrier to completion of the Uruguay Round. In 1992 the United States and Europe narrowly avoided a trade war because of U.S. retaliation (increasing tariffs on selected European exports, including white wines) for French reluctance to limit acreage growing subsidized oilseeds.[40]

Although the original goal was to complete the Uruguay Round by 1990, the issues it raised were so contentious that, even though it was expected to add $200 billion a year to the world economy by the year 2000, completion was delayed until mid-December 1993. President Clinton argued that "for middle-class Americans who work hard and play by the rules, more trade and fair trade means more and higher wage jobs."[41] Nevertheless, the agreement was fought in the United States by a coalition of labor unions, environmentalists, farmers, consumer advocates, liberal Democrats, and conservative Republicans.[42] The 124-nation agreement was finally approved by Congress in December 1994.

In the end, agricultural subsidies were cut (though not as much as originally hoped);[43] protection for intellectual property was expanded;[44] rules for investment and trade in services were set; and tariffs were slashed by an average of one-third.[45] Since 1993, additional agreements have been reached to lower trade barriers in telecommunications, financial services, and information technology. And barriers still exist to free trade in agriculture (where global tariffs average 40 percent), textiles, and services.[46] Other areas that must be discussed in future trade negotiations include foreign direct investment and competition (antitrust) policy.[47]

The treaty's most important step was replacing the GATT with a powerful new *World Trade Organization (WTO)* with authority to constitute arbitration panels that would decide if countries are violating the agreement, to make them correct such violations and pay for damages, and even to authorize retaliation against violators.[48] In the first nine months of 1995, eighteen complaints were brought to the WTO, six of which involved the United States as complainant and three as defendant, and by the end of 1996 it had received over sixty cases.[49] One of most acerbic of the cases involving the U.S. was brought by the European Union (EU) against an American law that would penalize foreign companies that conduct business in Cuba using assets seized from American companies. Initially, the United States threatened to invoke a "national security exemption" to prevent the WTO from hearing the case, but in the end a settlement was reached between the U.S. and EU that avoided a WTO hearing. In another dispute, the WTO ruled that the EU had not carried its earlier judgment that Europe could not favor banana imports from former Caribbean colonies over imports from Central America, and authorized the United States to impose sanctions on selected European goods.[50]

Critics argue that the WTO could erode U.S. interests and sovereignty and gut its consumer-protection and environmental and labor regulations. Since in a globalized market firms may produce goods anywhere in the world, they may seek to cut expenses by moving to countries with cheap labor and few environmental standards. And, as frontiers grow more porous, the poor will immigrate, both legally and illegally, in order to obtain even low-paying or unpleasant jobs.[51] Although WTO rules permit countries to legislate trade restrictions for environmental or health reasons, it is not always clear whether such legislation is the result of genuine concerns or whether it has a protectionist intent. Thus, in the first decision to be made by the WTO Appellate Body, the United States was told that regulations issued under the Clean Air Act discriminated against foreign oil refiners.[52] Other environment-related cases before the WTO have included a European ban on American hormone-treated beef (lost by the European Union) and a U.S. law banning imported shrimp from countries that do not use special nets to protect sea turtles (lost by the United States).

Regarding labor, a 1996 WTO summit adopted voluntary guidelines for "core standards." Public pressure in the United States forced major apparel companies such as Nike, Reebok, and L.L. Bean to abide by a code of conduct on wages and working conditions in their factories in *less-developed countries* (hereafter LDCs) in order to eliminate "sweatshop" conditions, and efforts are growing to combat child labor.[53] Not surprisingly, many poor countries believe that both the environmental and labor regulations proposed by rich countries are intended to reduce their advantage in lower wage costs.

Unlike the strategy of global participation in the GATT and the WTO, the second strategy—regular *economic summits* among the leading industrial democracies—is a limited multilateral mechanism for sustaining the international trade regime. The idea was proposed by French President Valery Giscard d'Estaing in 1975 in response to challenges to economic stability, especially the collapse of the Bretton Woods system and the 1973 Arab oil embargo.[54] The first summit was held near Paris and was attended by the heads of government of the United States, Britain, West Germany, Italy, Japan, and France. The Canadian prime minister and the president of the EC Commission were invited to the summits beginning in 1976 and 1977, respectively, and, starting in 1994, Russia's president has been allowed to join summit political discussions. Summits have been held yearly, rotating among the participants—at Puerto Rico, London, Tokyo, Bonn, Ottawa, Versailles, Williamsburg, Munich, Naples, Halifax, Denver, and Birmingham (UK), among others.

The meetings have four advantages. First, they are small, encouraging flexibility with personal rapport and avoiding bureaucratic obstacles to agreement that usually arise at lower levels. Second, the summits treat global economic problems as important political issues. Third, the leaders are in a unique position to implement the agreements they reach. Finally, the summits also focus on other issues—Soviet intervention in Afghanistan, INF deployment in Western Europe, global terrorism, war in Bosnia, violence in Kosovo, and India's nuclear tests—to coordinate policy.

The economic summits have had a mixed record. Two observers judge that, of the first twelve, only six earned a grade of B or better for cooperation, and six achieved little, including three that accomplished "nothing significant."[55] With one exception, the summits that accomplished least were in the 1980s, and those that achieved most were in the 1970s. Summits in the early 1990s were also disappointing even though they began to address economic reform in Eastern Europe and Russia.

To get a sense of the summits, let us review some of them. The 1978 Bonn summit was a success because it completed a comprehensive plan for dealing with pressing global problems: Japan and West Germany agreed to expand their economies; France agreed to cut its deficit; and the United States committed itself to find a more effective energy policy. The 1979 summit, held after a dramatic rise in oil prices, set a target for participants' oil imports for the following years. The 1991 and 1992 summits achieved some coordinating of relief efforts to Russia, Ukraine, and other Soviet successor states. The 1993 Tokyo summit reached preliminary agreement to eliminate tariffs in eight industrial sectors, breathing new life into the flagging Uruguay round of the GATT. At the 1994 Naples meeting, leaders declared the "unacceptable waste" of unemployment their biggest problem, pressed Russia to remove its troops from the Baltic republics, endorsed Bosnian peace efforts, pledged to approve the GATT agreement, and agreed to increase aid to Ukraine to assist in privatizing industries and replace the Chernobyl nuclear plant.[56] Much of the time at the 1995 Halifax summit was spent trying to solve bilateral disputes, especially the U.S.-Japanese quarrel over auto imports. The most important decisions involved reforming the IMF. With memories of Mexico's currency collapse still fresh, the leaders agreed to make IMF members provide timely data about emerging economic problems, create an emergency IMF loan fund, and study a plan for an international bankruptcy court to help states recover from insolvency.[57] At the 1996 summit, the leaders pledged to fight terrorism, and at the 1997 meeting, a quarrel broke out when President Clinton refused to commit the United States to a specific target in reducing carbon dioxide emissions.[58] In Birmingham, England, in 1998, the leaders discussed a variety of issues ranging from the need for Japanese economic recovery to the IMF approach to the Asian financial crisis.

Finally, LDCs have acted bilaterally and unilaterally in managing trade issues. In Chapter 13, we shall address these efforts in more detail, but suffice it to say that, despite some agreements, the developed countries still differ about trade relations.

Issues in the Global Economy: North-South Relations

The economic gulf between the First World and the LDCs—countries with a per capita GNP below $9,385 as of 1995—continues to grow, and that gap is one of the greatest challenges in world affairs. Consider sub-Saharan Africa, site of many of the world's poor. There, per capita GNP declined between 1980 and 1995,[59] and it will take forty years to regain the per capita income level of the mid-1970s; debt burden in 1996 for many African countries exceeded 100 percent of GNP (411 percent in Mozambique and 310 percent in Angola),[60] and Africa's share of world trade became so small that "it is almost as if the continent has curled up and disappeared from the map of international shipping lanes and airline routes that rope together Europe, North America and the booming Far East."[61] Violence is widespread.[62] And much of Africa is afflicted by both new diseases like AIDS and ebola[63] and old diseases like malaria, hepatitis, cholera, and tuberculosis.[64] Ten million people, or 90 percent of the world's AIDS deaths, have been in Africa,[65] and the resulting decline in life expectancy will significantly reduce populations in stricken countries.[66] The rate of AIDS infection exceeds 50 cases per 100,000 people in Botswana, Namibia, Zimbabwe, and Djibouti.[67]

In Africa and elsewhere, the poor have little reason to be satisfied by the liberal international economic order, which, in their eyes, perpetuates their poverty, and unmet economic and social problems may lead them to "desperate politics" against the rich.[68] Alternative approaches to global economics thus have found greater favor in the LDCs than in the First World. By the early 1970s, more and more states in Africa, Asia, and Latin America found the global economic system inimical to their interests and called for a "new international economic order."

Radical and Nationalist Alternatives

Liberal market theory contrasts with radical explanations[69] of how the global economy works. For radicals, equality and autonomy matter more than productivity and efficiency. Free trade, they believe, works to the advantage of rich states and perpetuates poor states' dependence on the rich. Foreign investment and open markets do less to benefit poor states than to open their human and natural resources to plundering. As a result, the system actually prevents development in the LDCs, and widening economic disparities reinforce political inequality.

The most fully developed radical analysis is *Modern World System theory*.[70] World-system theorists believe that political life revolves around class struggle that is reflected in relations between rich and poor states. Global capitalism, represented by a wealthy "core" (societies that are the source of capital), perpetuates economic underdevelopment at the expense of an impoverished "periphery" (societies with little economic clout) whose wealth is exploited. This relationship, in which a global division of labor prevents the economic development of dependent economies, it is argued, has its roots in the birth of Western capitalism in the sixteenth and seventeenth centuries and has remained essentially unchanged. The forces of modern capitalism are seen as running the global economy in their own interest, and "uneven" development results as profits and resources are siphoned from periphery to core.

In contrast, *economic nationalism* or *neomercantlism* holds that economic activities should be directed to building state power and subordinated to national security. Neomercantilists reverse the radicals' belief in the primacy of economic over political forces, arguing that wealth is the basis of political and military power. They aim to reduce the influence of market forces, to accumulate economic resources for the state, and to make the state as self-sufficient as possible. More than do liberals, neomercantilists believe that domestic political demands are crucial in the global economy.

Economic nationalism can take several forms, from efforts to shelter and isolate infant industries from global competition to policies that directly challenge the global economic order. High tariff barriers, nontariff impediments to trade, import-substitution arrangements, and industrial subsidies[71] are among the weapons of economic nationalists. More aggressive forms—"malevolent nationalism"[72]—include imperial expansion and economic warfare. *Embargoes*—refusal to sell goods to another state—or boycotts—refusal to buy goods—are forms of economic warfare.

All three economic perspectives have been criticized. Liberals retain an idealistic belief in the separation of politics and economics. Radicals fail to recognize the substantial domestic political constraints against capitalist societies' sustained economic expansion, and nationalists underestimate how important the market is in producing efficient economies. Nevertheless, the nonliberal variants shed light on some of the issues that radical and nationalist critiques of economic liberalism raise and help explain the tensions between the North (rich) and South (poor).

The Poverty Gap

The economic disparity between rich and poor both within and among countries has grown in recent decades.[73] Currently, about a billion people live in poverty, and 13 to 18 million die annually of poverty-related causes.[74] In some countries, over half the population live on less than $1 a day, and in a few that figure exceeds 80 percent (e.g., Guinea-Bissau and Zambia).[75] Figure 12.1 reveals that, between 1979 and 1993, *the gap between the developed and developing worlds actually widened.* Per capita GDP in rich countries in 1995 averaged $16,241, compared with an average of $1,362 in poor countries.[76] Consumption patterns reflect this gap. The world's richest fifth consumes 86 percent of global goods and services, over half the world's energy, and nearly half its meat and fish. Americans spend $8 billion a year on cosmetics, and Europeans $11 billion on ice cream, yet the world cannot find the $6 billion needed to provide basic education or the $9 billion that the U.N. believes is needed to give all people schooling and access to clean drinking water and sanitation. Indeed, in Africa an average household consumes 20 percent less today than it did twenty-five years ago.[77]

Examination of Figure 12.2 shows that Africa and South Asia are the poorest regions in the world and that most high-income countries are European or of European ancestry. It is discouraging that poor countries (excluding China and India) experienced lower annual average growth (0.1 percent) in per capita GNP between 1980 and 1992 than the richest (2.2 percent).[78] By 1996, seventy countries

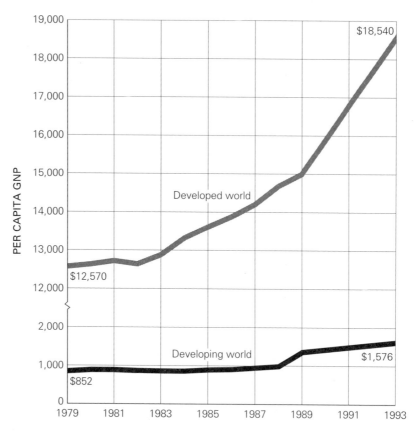

FIGURE 12.1
Per Capita GNP for Developing and Developed Worlds

Between 1979 and 1993, the standard of living of citizens in the developed
world, as measured by per capita GNP, increased substantially, far faster
than the standard of living of citizens of the less-developed countries. SOURCE:
World Military Expenditures and Arms Transfers 1993–1994, Table 1, p. 43.

had lower average incomes than in 1980. Of these, forty-three were actually poorer
than they had been in 1970.[79] Of the sixty-seven high-income economies (countries and possessions defined by the World Bank), all but nine are European or of
European descent. By contrast, of the sixty-one low-income economies, thirty-
eight are in sub-Saharan Africa and eleven are in Asia.[80]

Although per capita income is an important measure, others can more vividly
portray the gap between the two worlds. Poor countries have made gains but still
lag far behind. In 1995, for example, average life expectancy in rich countries was
almost seventy-four years, whereas in poor countries it was only fifty-one.[81] This
discrepancy reflects factors such as the availability of medical care, the level of violence, and the presence of diseases. Infant mortality rate, adult literacy, daily calo-
rie supply, and access to safe water are also useful measures of standard of living.

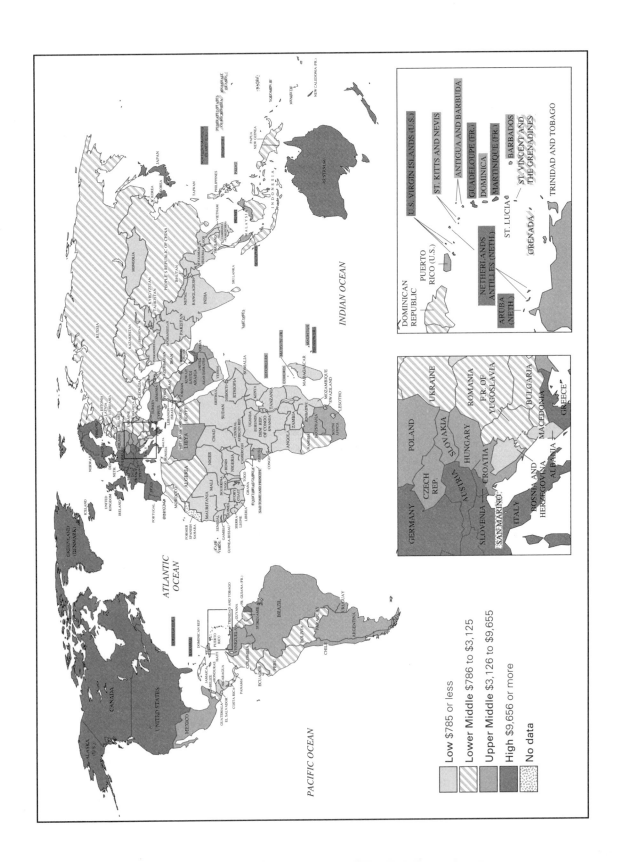

Several efforts have been made to combine indicators like those described above to arrive at a composite score for *quality of life*.[82] All are posited on the belief that wealth alone cannot measure how well people live. Each consists of a somewhat different basket of indicators. One, Economic and Social Rank, lists states according to eleven variables—five involving health, five for education, and one for per capita GNP. A second, the Physical Quality of Life (PQLI) Index, is based on infant mortality, life expectancy, and literacy. A third, the Index of Social Progress, consists of forty-four indicators touching on health, education, welfare, economics, political stability, and so forth. A final scale, the *Human Development Index (HDI),* developed by the U.N. Development Program, has three components—the percentage of people expected to die before age forty, the rate of illiteracy, and per capita income.[83] Table 12.2 shows the Human Development Index for a selection of states with composite scores ranging from 0 (lowest HDI) to 1,000 (highest HDI). In a summary way, it reveals how much the human condition differs and shows again that Europeans or those of European descent enjoy a much higher quality of life than the poor in Africa, Asia, or the Middle East.

In view of such gaps, it is hardly surprising that there are differences between North and South on economic issues. The North-South distinction is geographic in the sense that most rich countries are in the Northern Hemisphere. The rich have *knowledge economies* because their future economic growth lies in the production, storage, and distribution of knowledge, whether as a good (e.g., computers) or a service (e.g., education). By contrast, most of the world's poor live in the Southern Hemisphere. The distinction is imperfect, however, for the Southern Hemisphere has such relatively rich countries as Argentina, Australia, and New Zealand. In time, the South translated economic dissatisfaction into political demands for an overhaul of the international economic order. In the early 1970s, at about the time the Bretton Woods system collapsed, the poor countries proposed a *New International Economic Order (NIEO).*

Call for a New International Economic Order

FIGURE 12.2
The World by Income

Most of the poor countries are in the Southern Hemisphere, and most of the rich are in the Northern Hemisphere. SOURCE: *World Development Report, 1998/99,* p. 189. Copyright © 1998 by the International Bank for Reconstruction and Development/The World Bank. Used by permission of Oxford University Press Inc.

Demands that the global economic system be reformed date from the formation of the *nonaligned movement* in Belgrade, Yugoslavia, in 1961 and the establishment of the U.N. Conference on Trade and Development (UNCTAD) and the "Group of 77" in 1964.[84] UNCTAD was created to deal with global economic issues from the poor countries' perspective and challenge the GATT system, which favored rich states. Gradually, the nonaligned movement's platform expanded beyond political issues to economic reform, thereby creating links with the Group of 77. Late in the 1960s, the Group of 77 adopted the Charter of Algiers, which demanded global economic reform.[85] Similar proposals were discussed at other meetings in the early 1970s—in Zambia in 1970, Peru in 1971, and Guyana and Algeria in 1973. This last meeting was crucial because it instructed Algeria's President Hovari Boumedienne, then chairman of the nonaligned group, to deliver the Economic Declaration and the Action Programme For Economic Cooperation to the Sixth Special Session of the United Nations.

The passage of U.N. Resolutions 3201 and 3202 on May 1, 1974, at this special session, marked the formal call for the New International Economic Order (NIEO). The resolutions set out principles to improve economic relations between rich and poor. These resolutions were also outlined as controversial demands in the

TABLE 12.2
HDI Ranking, 1998

High Human Development				Low Human Development		
HDI rank	**Country**	**HDI value**		**HDI rank**	**Country**	**HDI value**
1	Canada	0.960		131	Myanmar (Burma)	0.481
2	France	0.946		132	Cameroon	0.481
3	Norway	0.943		133	Ghana	0.473
4	USA	0.943		134	Lesotho	0.469
5	Iceland	0.942		135	Equatorial Guinea	0.465
6	Finland	0.942		136	Laos	0.465
7	Netherlands	0.941		137	Kenya	0.463
8	Japan	0.940		138	Pakistan	0.453
9	New Zealand	0.939		139	India	0.451
10	Sweden	0.936		140	Cambodia	0.422
11	Spain	0.935		141	Comoros	0.411
12	Belgium	0.933		142	Nigeria	0.391
13	Austria	0.933		143	Dem. Rep. of Congo	0.383
14	United Kingdom	0.932		144	Togo	0.380
15	Australia	0.932		145	Benin	0.378
16	Switzerland	0.930		146	Zambia	0.378
17	Ireland	0.930		147	Bangladesh	0.371
18	Denmark	0.928		148	Ivory Coast	0.368
19	Germany	0.925		149	Mauritania	0.361
20	Greece	0.924		150	Tanzania	0.358
21	Italy	0.922		151	Yemen	0.356
22	Israel	0.913		152	Nepal	0.351
23	Cyprus	0.913		153	Madagascar	0.348
24	Barbados	0.909		154	Central African Rep.	0.347
25	Hong Kong, China	0.909		155	Bhutan	0.347
26	Luxembourg	0.900		156	Angola	0.344
27	Malta	0.899		157	Sudan	0.343
28	Singapore	0.896		158	Senegal	0.342
29	Antigua and Barbuda	0.895		159	Haiti	0.340
30	South Korea	0.894		160	Uganda	0.340
				161	Malawi	0.334
				162	Djibouti	0.324
				163	Chad	0.318
				164	Guinea-Bissau	0.295
				165	Gambia	0.291
				166	Mozambique	0.281
				167	Guinea	0.277
				168	Eritrea	0.275
				169	Ethiopia	0.252
				170	Burundi	0.241
				171	Mali	0.236
				172	Burkina Faso	0.219
				173	Niger	0.207
				174	Sierra Leone	0.185

SOURCE: *World Development Report 1998*, pp. 128–130. Copyright © 1998 by the International Bank for Reconstruction and Development/The World Bank. Used by permission.

Charter of Economic Rights and Duties of States, passed by the General Assembly in December 1974. They outlined six areas of economic reform that were necessary to forestall conflict between the First World and the LDCs:

1. Regulating transnational corporations
2. Transferring technology from rich to poor
3. Reforming the trading order to assist poor states' development
4. Canceling or renegotiating poor countries' debt
5. Increasing economic aid from rich to poor countries
6. Revising voting procedures in international economic institutions to provide poor countries with greater influence

The response from the First World was initially negative. American policy-makers expressed anger at the idea of "demands." They viewed the NIEO as a "screwball effort" and a "rip-off" and as a way to "beat the West and the North over the head." Some of the proposals were described as "unrealistic," "economically meaningless," and "framed in a naive way."[86] In time, this harsh rhetoric gave way to efforts by wealthy states to address the issues raised by the NIEO. Denunciations have been replaced by dialogue between North and South.

Regulating Transnational Corporations

Many critics of the existing global economic system call for regulating the activities of *transnational corporations (TNCs),* which raises questions about the role of such corporations in poor states and their effect on them. Many corporations, though not all, originate in the First World and, like the governments of those countries, advocate a free market. Their sheer number, size, and clout frighten poor countries. As noted in Chapter 7, many TNCs have economic interests in every corner of the world, and they enjoy access to resources and policy flexibility that most states can only envy. For good reason, poor countries see them as agents of the rich.

Critics argue that TNCs often simply expropriate a local resource and export it for the company's benefit, and poor countries lose control over their own assets. Such TNCs, the argument continues, return a disproportionate share of profits to their home countries, plowing little back into their hosts. As a result, TNCs are less beneficial to poor countries than if they were locally controlled. Critics also contend that TNCs create little employment in host countries and hire few locals for senior positions. A variant of this argument is that TNCs seek low taxes, cheap labor, and a warm business climate and move operations to get them. And even when they do create jobs, the result is greater local economic inequality and privileged urban elites with little stake in fostering local development. In addition, TNCs increase demand for unhealthy or even dangerous products in poor countries, like cigarettes, that are regulated in the First World.[87] Finally, it is argued that TNC economic power is translated into political influence. Allegations have been made about TNC interference in local politics, ranging from outright bribery of government officials to illicit campaign contributions for local candidates.

A number of reforms have been suggested to curb these abuses. Poor countries tried to establish a code of conduct with norms limiting TNC activity in LDCs.[88] However, the response has been minimal. Global standards for corporate behavior remain almost nonexistent. Although the United Nations proposed a code of conduct early in the 1970s and a few national groups such as the U.S. Chamber of Commerce have done the same, only three steps have been taken toward regulating TNCs. The first was the establishment of a voluntary code of conduct among the Organization for Economic Cooperation and Development (OECD) countries in 1976. The code was very general and vague, and no mechanisms were provided to enforce it. A second step was establishing two centers in the mid-1970s to render TNC activity more "transparent." The Center on Transnational Corporations collects and disseminates information about TNCs to familiarize the global community with their range of activities,[89] and the Commission on Transnational Corporations checks on complaints against TNCs and manages the Center. Finally, more recently, the OECD banned bribery by corporations seeking contracts. This reform was a long time coming. In 1977, following the discovery that Lockheed Corporation had bribed Japanese officials, the United States banned such practices in the Foreign Corrupt Practices Act.[90] Not until 1996 were the other members of the OECD persuaded that bribes paid to local officials should no longer be tax deductible.[91]

Not surprisingly, the most vigorous efforts to regulate TNCs have been undertaken by host countries themselves. Some have joined in regional groups to establish their own codes of conduct. Among the first to impose restrictions on TNCs was the Andean Group, founded in 1969 by Bolivia, Colombia, Ecuador, Peru, and Venezuela. The Andean Group placed limits on repatriation of profits from TNCs investing in their countries, set standards for transferring corporate technology to host countries, and required that, eventually, foreign ownership of local affiliates be surrendered.[92] In other cases, hosts have required at least majority local control before permitting TNC investments. Some countries simply prohibited TNC investment in specified industries, believing that it would infringe upon their sovereignty and increase their economic dependency. Finally, a few countries have nationalized TNC property. Late in the 1960s and early in the 1970s, Peru, Libya, and Venezuela, among others, nationalized foreign petroleum industries in their countries, and Bolivia and Chile nationalized the tin and copper industries inside their borders.[93] Nationalization is a dangerous path, however, because it spurs conflict with rich states and brings an end to investment and foreign aid.

The threat of nationalization has lessened as poor countries' bargaining leverage has improved. As the number of TNCs increased, hosts became more selective about which TNCs they permit to operate. Some countries can now exploit competition among TNCs to get better contracts and investments. Larger numbers of TNCs also reduce the prospect that corporations will pull up stakes, because others can replace them. The most important development in recent years, however, has been the growing pursuit of free-market policies in the LDCs accompanied by rising TNC investment in countries like China, Brazil, Indonesia, Malaysia, and India. As the climate for investment improved, TNC investment in the LDCs climbed, reaching $97 billion in 1995.[94]

Technology Transfer and the LDCs

A second issue is the *transfer of technology* from rich to poor. Poor countries complain that high technology is too costly to get from advanced countries or TNCs, that the price is artificially high, and that no mechanism exists to facilitate technology transfer. Since advanced technology is necessary to be competitive in the global economy, the result, according to critics, is to perpetuate the dependency of the poor countries.[95]

A somewhat different criticism is that the advanced technology used by TNCs and the products they produce are unsuited to local needs. For example, TNCs sell automobiles that only a few very rich people can afford and for which a poor country has to import expensive oil. Instead, local economies need *appropriate technology,* such as bicycles or mopeds that can be used by poor peasants.

Criticisms about technology transfer focus on four issues. First, technology is expensive because patents are held by rich countries. By one estimate, only 30,000 of more than 3.6 million patents were held by citizens of poor countries. Second, the technology TNCs use in poor countries is capital-, not labor-intensive, doing little to reduce chronic unemployment and underemployment. Third, either the cost of technology is too high for poor countries to purchase or the manner in which it is sold reduces its value for the poor. Finally, research-and-development facilities are mainly located in the First World, resulting in a *brain drain* from the LDCs as scientists, engineers, and technicians seek jobs in rich countries.

Poor states sought three reforms. First, they asked that rich countries facilitate technology transfer and create technology appropriate for them. Second, they asked the First World to help them strengthen scientific and technological institutions. Finally, they sought agreement on guidelines for technology transfer.[96]

If anything, the First World has been less responsive in facilitating technology transfer than in regulating TNCs. Although conferences on technology transfer have been sponsored by the United Nations, the rich countries and TNCs continue to protect their technological monopoly, for at least three reasons.[97] First, because costly technology is often developed by the private sector, it is not considered part of the "global commons." Protection of copyrights and patents is seen as a vital aspect of commercial success. Second, corporations believe that, when technology transfer does occur, it should be at a "fair market price" to enable them to recoup their investment and to profit from their innovations. Third, technology transfer may weaken the competitive edge of those who formerly enjoyed its exclusive use. Nevertheless, there is informal technology transfer from rich to poor countries because of the export of high-technology jobs by TNCs to countries like India, where salaries are lower.

Trade Reform

Trade reform, especially changes in trading rules, is crucial to economic development. This means altering the pricing of commodities and raw materials, establishing a system of preferential trade treatment for LDC products, and changing the overall direction of global trade. Poor countries argue that the composition of world trade is disadvantageous to them. An overwhelming proportion (70 percent) is among the rich, and too little is between the First World and the LDCs.[98]

Another issue is the nature of trade between rich and poor. In general, rich countries export capital goods (for example, machine tools) and finished products (for example, computers) to poor countries, and the latter export raw materials (for example, tin) and agricultural commodities (for example, coffee). Although this division of labor may seem reasonable, the *terms of trade*—the relationship between the prices of imports and those of exports—favor rich countries. The price of capital goods and finished products tends to rise more quickly than that of raw materials, and commodity prices fluctuate dramatically depending on conditions outside producers' control. This is one reason for the widening gap between North and South.

Another source of friction is tariffs. Industrial countries have historically raised tariff barriers against products from poor countries. They bar not only manufactured goods like textiles (where one might expect rich countries to protect their industries from the products of cheap labor) but also agricultural products. Such barriers impede poor countries' efforts to modernize.

Several reforms have been suggested to improve the LDCs' trade position. First, all states were asked to cooperate in dismantling obstacles to and improving the framework for conducting trade. Second, First World countries were asked to stabilize prices for primary products. Third, poor countries called for preferential treatment for their exports to gain access to the markets of rich countries without granting the same privilege to those rich countries, thereby abandoning the principle of reciprocity in trade. Fourth, poor countries called for addressing the terms-of-trade issue, arguing for price adjustments in their exports in relation to prices of their imports. Finally, the LDCs sought to establish commodity cartels and multilateral commodity agreements to maintain higher prices for primary products.[99]

The First World has been reasonably responsive to trade demands. The European Community (EC) in the mid-1970s began to provide preferential arrangements. In 1975, the EC concluded the first of the Lomé agreements (named after the capital of Togo, where it was negotiated) granting special access to Europe for products from seventy selected poor countries. Under these agreements, several African, Caribbean, and Pacific (ACP) countries—mainly former European colonies—were granted privileged access to the EC. The EC and the ACP countries also worked out an arrangement to stabilize prices for commodities purchased from these LDCs. However, the Lomé Convention is due to end in 2000 and, in any event, failed to have the positive impact its sponsors had wished. In addition, economic globalization has made the arrangement obsolete.[100]

The United States has also granted preferential trading status to products from some poor states, albeit not as liberally as the Europeans. By the 1974 Trade Act, the United States established a general system of preference by granting access to 2,000 items from poor countries. Although critics argue that the items granted this status were minor, the principle of preferential access is important. In 1982, the Reagan administration proposed the Caribbean Basin Initiative (CBI), a preferential trading arrangement for countries bordering on the Caribbean (except Cuba). Under this plan, exports from these countries could enter the United States without duties, and tax incentives would be granted to U.S. firms investing in the Caribbean Basin. In 1991, the Bush administration started the Enterprise for the Americas Initiative, which was also intended to promote trade between the United States and Latin America,[101] and in recent years the United States has sought to establish a U.S.-Africa Economic Forum to generate greater trade and investment with Africa and to encourage direct private investment in Africa.[102]

Efforts to stabilize commodity prices, improve terms of trade, and institute general reform in the trading order have not progressed very far. A North-South conference (the Conference on International Economic Cooperation) convened in

Paris for three years (1975–1977) to address these and other development issues. Although the First World committed itself in principle to establish a Common Fund to support the prices of commodities, the idea never got off the ground because of inadequate funding. The Tokyo Round of the GATT (1973–1979) took up trading preferences for poor states, but results were minimal, leading to a LDC boycott of the concluding ceremony. And, because of lower agricultural subsidies and the diminished importance of the Lomé Convention as a result of the overall reduction in trade barriers, the big losers in the 1993 GATT agreement were African states.[103]

Global Debt   A fourth demand was aid for poor countries with debt burdens. Although the debt problem was already serious in the early 1970s, it became a crisis early in the 1980s that deepened until early in the 1990s. Although progress has been made toward reducing the debt burden of the poor, the issue remains a source of friction between rich creditor and poor debtor states, and it has been complicated by the debt problems of countries like South Korea and Russia that were caught up in the financial crisis that erupted in Asia in 1997.

The global debt crisis originated in several trends in the 1970s and 1980s. First, steeply rising oil prices hurt both rich and poor countries. Poor countries needed loans to finance oil purchases and pay off earlier loans. The demand for loans triggered higher global interest rates, exacerbating the problem. A second price rise in oil late in the 1970s pushed interest rates and inflation to double digits, burying poor countries under mountainous debt and forcing them to devote much of their annual budgets to interest payments. A global recession in 1974–1975 and an accompanying decline in commodity prices made it even harder for these states to pay their bills. Finally, some LDCs, like Mexico and Nigeria, counting on higher earnings from oil sales, borrowed heavily for domestic projects. When oil prices plummeted in the 1980s and 1990s, they were left with huge debt burdens. From 1970 until late in the 1980s, the poor countries' debt rose from $67 billion to more than $1 trillion.

A global debt crisis became evident with one event: Mexico's inability to meet its debt-service obligations in 1982. Mexico was not earning enough from exports to meet payments, mostly to big money-center banks like Bank of America and Citicorp. By the mid-1980s, other LDCs—Bolivia, Brazil, Argentina, Nigeria, the Philippines—were also close to bankruptcy. *Debt-service ratios*—the ratios of the principal and interest due on debts to export earnings—were estimated at between 20 and 50 percent for non-oil-producing LDCs worldwide in 1985.[104] Latin American countries had a debt-service ratio of 47 percent; African countries, 27 percent; and Middle Eastern countries, 26 percent. Between one-quarter and one-half of poor countries' export earnings were assigned to meet loan-repayment schedules.

The debt issue affected the welfare of both the First World and the LDCs. Poor countries, with less of their export earnings available for new projects, faced declining standards of living and growing domestic instability. Rich countries were able to sell less to the LDCs and thus lost jobs at home and had increasing trade deficits. By one estimate, 400,000 U.S. jobs were lost early in the 1980s as the Latin America export market dried up,[105] and the need to reschedule debt payments or make additional loans to finance repayments threatened major banks in North America and Europe.

Even before global debt exploded early in the 1980s, poor countries were trying to restructure debt burdens, reduce interest rates, and cancel debt. Poor states sought case-by-case renegotiation to cancel or reschedule debts. They argued that dramatic action was needed if they were to have any chance to develop, and a one-time cancellation would be equivalent to a grant by the rich to the poor.

The First World's early response to demands for debt relief was negative, but this attitude changed in the 1980s and 1990s. Debt cancellation was at first vigorously opposed, especially by Germany and the United States, for two reasons. First, it was argued that if debts were canceled, poor states would spend irresponsibly, expecting additional debt cancellation. Second, debt cancellation would disrupt rich countries' economies, reducing profits and endangering the solvency of the banks that had made the loans. Instead, rich countries preferred restructuring debt conditioned on stringent domestic reforms.

As the debt issue festered in the 1980s, rich countries took a number of initiatives. The Reagan and Bush administrations proposed two plans to cope with global debt. The first, the *Baker Plan* (named after Treasury Secretary James Baker) involved *restructuring debt.* Under the proposal, commercial banks worldwide would aid the most deeply indebted countries, and the international lending institutions would provide additional new resources. The United States would provide additional funding for the international financial institutions and commit itself to opening up further its domestic markets to products from poor states.[106] Nevertheless, the crisis intensified, and, by late in the 1980s, the Western leaders decided to confront the issue more decisively. Treasury Secretary Nicholas Brady acknowledged for the first time that canceling debt might be necessary. The *Brady Plan* included a number of specific schemes, three of which were especially innovative.

One proposal was to encourage the international lending institutions to provide more assistance to poor countries to pay off a portion of their debt to commercial banks at a discount. The banks would get most of their money back, although they would have to write off some debt. A second strategy was for *debt-equity swaps*—trading the debt owed to a bank or commercial institution for stock in a debtor country's industries. A more sophisticated version of this idea was for banks to sell a portion of their loans to TNCs at a discount. The TNCs would convert the loans into local currency that would be reinvested in host countries. By this plan the poor countries would reduce their debt without having to sell off assets, and the banks would get much of the money owed them. A third idea was for *debt-commodity swaps* under which commercial banks would form companies to export debtors' commodities, retaining some of the profits for repaying debt. This plan was designed to boost LDC exports while allowing creditors to be repaid in hard currency.[107]

By 1994, the Brady Plan seemed to be working. Between 1985 and 1994 banks had written down LDC debt by about $90 billion. Between 1980 and 1993 Brazil, the largest LDC debtor, had reduced the ratio of its debt service to the value of its exports from 63 to 24 percent.[108] Brazil reached agreement with its 750 creditor banks in 1994. The agreement represented the sort of debt cancellation suggested in the Brady Plan, reducing Brazil's debt and providing new longer-term loans at lower interest. Declared a prominent American banker: "The architects of the

Brady Plan have never been given enough credit. As a result of the plan, banks were able to liquefy and recover much of what we had lent out."[109]

Although the debt picture had improved, the predicament of some countries was worse than ever. According to a 1996 study, the cost of reducing the debts of the world's poorest countries to raise their economic growth rate ranged from $5.6 to $7.7 billion over six years.[110] Despite rescheduling Russia's debt in 1993 and 1994 to allow repayment over a longer period of time, the country effectively defaulted on its loans in 1998. By 1995, poor countries still had to pay about $43 per capita in debt servicing, compared to $35 per capita on health and education.[111] Also, little progress has been made toward relieving the debt burdens of African countries. Of the thirty-six most severely indebted countries in 1996, twenty-nine were African.[112] Thus abatement of the debt crisis varied by region, with an eye toward reducing the threat to Western banks and stabilizing politically important societies.

In a highly innovative decision, the World Bank and the IMF in 1996 agreed to forgive loans to about twenty poor countries that had made major efforts to reform their economies.[113] Uganda, whose annual debt payments were almost equal to its expenditure on education and health, was the first to benefit from this program.[114]

Foreign Assistance A fifth demand was for increased bilateral and multilateral aid from rich countries. First, most rich states had failed to live up to the goals the United Nations set out in its three Development Decades. For the first decade, the United Nations had called for an annual transfer of 1 percent of GNP from each developed state in the form of development assistance to poor states. In the second and third decades, the United Nations lowered that target to 0.7 percent of GNP, hoping that the other 0.3 percent could be made up by private contributions.

In fact, the percentage of official aid from the developed world (members of the Organization for Economic Cooperation and Development) has declined. In 1965, the average official development assistance as a portion of GNP transferred from rich to poor was 0.48. By 1996, it had declined to 0.25, or about $68 per capita.[115] Some countries have done better than others. Scandinavian countries have approached and occasionally exceeded the 1 percent target, whereas the United States has been at or near the bottom, declining from 0.58 percent of GNP in 1970 to 0.12 in 1996.[116] Even as aid effort, measured by percent of GNP, has declined, the overall amount of official development assistance has increased. In 1965, rich countries provided about $6.5 billion to poor countries. This rose to $14 billion in 1975, $29 billion in 1985, and $55.5 billion in 1996.[117] By 1996, Japan's foreign aid exceeded that of the United States.

Beyond general criticism of inadequate total assistance, poor countries complained about the kind of aid and the way it was provided. First, most is bilateral rather than multilateral and often has political strings attached by donors. For instance, U.S. aid to Egypt and Israel was provided as a condition for concluding peace with each other in 1979. Also, much of the aid is in the form of loans, not grants, and much of it is tied to the recipients' purchase of goods from donor countries.[118] Using loans as a vehicle for aid ensures that poor states will amass debt. Although *tied aid* may make sense for the donor who wants to sell the idea of foreign aid to a dubious public, the requirement prevents poor countries from getting the best products and prices. Third, some donors, such as the former U.S.S.R., were criticized for emphasizing large-scale, showy projects that were less helpful to poor countries than modest projects that focused on basic needs, especially in the agricultural sector. LDC leaders, especially those who after independence sought to build their reputations on such projects (for instance, Kwame Nkrumah of Ghana and Ahmed Sukarno of Indonesia), must assume some of the blame.

To address these criticisms, NIEO advocates called for several changes in the amount and composition of aid from rich to poor. They asked that states promote more resources to LDCs from all sources. They also advanced what was called the 20-20 proposal, by which donors would earmark 20 percent of foreign aid for basic social needs such as schools and hospitals and recipients would allocate 20 percent of their expenditures for the same needs.[119] NIEO proponents wanted to rely less on private contributions and investments and more on government-to-government assistance. In addition, they wanted grants, rather than loans, to make up most of the aid and wanted it to be untied. Finally, NIEO advocates asked major food-producing countries to extend special grants and assistance to poor countries in need.

The First World has generally responded poorly to demands for more foreign aid. An economic slowdown in the West during the 1990s and the election of Republican majorities in the U.S. Congress in 1994 dampened any ardor to provide greater aid to the LDCs. In addition, there is serious doubt that foreign aid is effective, especially where there is an inadequate pool of trained people or where corruption is widespread.[120] Some claim that aid creates dependency and waste and discourages entrepreneurial activity in the LDCs. Others argue that economic aid does not produce development. "In terms of human development," declared a British scholar, "I looked at things like primary school enrollment, infant mortality and life expectancy in 97 countries between 1970 and 1990, and there was no correlation between these sorts of indicators and development assistance."[121]

Although amounts of aid have not increased significantly, some improvements have been made in the way in which aid is provided and in the kind of aid. In 1973 the U.S. Congress adopted a new aid strategy. One aim of the new legislation was to "give the highest priority to undertakings submitted by host governments which directly improved the lives of the poorest of the poor."[122] Aid projects would be directed toward meeting the basic needs of the world's poorest people—food, health, and education. Another objective was to empower the poor by encouraging them to participate directly in planning projects. Two years later, the U.S. food aid program was altered to target aid to the "poorest of the poor," and Congress directed that 75 percent of food aid sales go to the world's neediest as defined by the World Bank.[123]

Partly in response to the U.S. initiative, other rich countries also agreed to target more of their assistance to the world's poorest populations. In 1977, the Development Assistance Committee of the OECD approved a policy statement recommending that aid programs be directed toward meeting the basic survival needs of the poor. During the 1980s, the United States paid little attention to demands for foreign aid. The Reagan administration moved away from emphasizing basic needs and again focused on countries that were crucial to U.S. policy in the Cold War, and U.S. aid was tied to recipients' establishing a free market. The administration took the position that private-sector investment should be the principal mechanism for producing economic development. The end of the Cold War removed a primary domestic justification in the United States for providing assistance, and domestic budget deficits made foreign aid—with no domestic constituency—even less popular politically than in the past. In response to this pressure, the Clinton administration was forced to halve its pledge of annual food aid in 1995,[124] and overall food aid in 1996 was the lowest since the 1970s.[125] Under pressure to reduce foreign aid, the Clinton administration, like its predecessors, targeted countries important for U.S. interests, for example, Kazakhstan, which received aid to advance political reform, dismantle nuclear weapons, and back U.S. oil companies that are investing heavily in that country.[126]

Other rich states did little better than the United States. In Germany, a three-year study concluded that great obstacles confronted that country's effort to alter its aid strategy.[127] Although Japan has become a major donor, complaints are regularly heard that Tokyo lavishes most of its aid on a few countries in Southeast Asia and that it is directed toward big industrial projects that benefit Japanese companies.[128]

International Organizations and LDCs

A final demand was for restructuring international organizations to provide poor states with more influence. Critics argue that, because voting procedures in organizations like the World Bank and the IMF are based on the proportional financial contribution of members, these "clubs for the rich" are controlled by a few rich states and reflect their conservative economic views. Decisions made by these organizations directly affect poor states' welfare by determining, for example, whether they receive loans and under what conditions, and LDC leaders seek greater influence in those decisions. They also want to move discussions about reforming the global economic system out of international organizations dominated by rich countries to those like UNCTAD where they have more influence.

No change has been made in voting procedures to provide a larger voice for the world's poor. A flurry of conferences and meetings put the spotlight on this issue and raised global consciousness about poverty, but accomplished little of substance. Nowhere was the First World's unwillingness to compromise more evident than at a meeting of leaders from fourteen poor countries and eight rich countries in Cancún, Mexico, in October 1981. President Reagan succinctly articulated his country's attitude when he called for the LDCs to rely more on their own initiative and on the free market. He envisioned a development strategy enabling "men and women to realize freely their full potential, to go as far as their God-given talents will take them. Free people build free markets that ignite dynamic development for everyone."[129]

By the 1990s, the traditional international economic organizations—the World Bank, WTO, and IMF—were still the principal forums for North-South dialogue, and the tone of North-South rhetoric had moderated. It was clear as early as the 1983 meeting of nonaligned states in New Delhi, India, that the LDCs had decided to adopt a more conciliatory strategy. Rich countries remain unconvinced that restructuring the global economic order to enhance development in the LDCs will benefit them. And, from time to time, LDC frustration with failure by the rich to respond again erupts, as it did at the U.N. Conference on the Environment and Development held in Rio de Janeiro in June 1992, where one LDC delegate after another denounced the rich states for seeking environmental reforms that would hobble their efforts to achieve growth while failing to provide adequate assistance.

However, there are some promising developments. In 1997, the United States agreed to recommend that three permanent seats on the U.N. Security Council be given to LDCs.[130] In addition, the World Bank has begun to reorient its mission toward aiding the poorest of the poor.[131] Increasingly, too, the provision of small loans, or *microcredit,* to help poor people start small businesses is growing and has become an effective means of promoting economic development. Such loans, declared one observer, "are more efficient than public-sector spending because once the poor have incomes they can look after themselves."[132] Finally, the end of the Cold War made it easier for Western leaders to consider factors other than "strategic importance" in disbursing scarce aid and to take account of humanitarian factors.

However, the LDCs have little cause for optimism. First, the end of the Cold War reduced the visibility of many poor countries still further because they are no longer able to play one side against the other. Second, economic woes at home further reduced public sympathy in the First World for foreign aid, and repeated disasters such as genocide in Rwanda and famine in Somalia produced *donor fatigue.* The election of President Clinton in 1992 on a pledge to pay more attention to domestic economic issues and of Republican congressional majorities two years later were harbingers of declining U.S. interest in the LDCs. Third, growing quarrels among rich states began to absorb much of the time and attention of First World diplomats. Finally, Russia, Eastern Europe, and the other states of the former U.S.S.R. are competing for scarce foreign aid. The anger of the LDCs at this competition caused them to veto a special IMF lending program to aid them and Russia in 1994.[133]

The Globalized World Economy

Although we have discussed the LDCs and First World separately, in fact they are enmeshed in a globalized economic system in which individuals, states, and other actors around the world are dependent on the global market and, therefore, one another's decisions for prosperity and security. Although *globalization* is a feature of postinternational politics more generally, it encompasses "the integration of markets, trade, finance, information, and corporate ownership around the globe."[134] In a very real sense, production and distribution processes have become global in scope, and the world has become "a single machine."[135]

It is in the sphere of economics where the erosion of state sovereignty is most advanced. Governments are increasingly forced to obey the imperatives of the global market, and globalization is difficult to resist because, as the historian Ronald Steel puts it, "You try to shut the door and it comes in through the window. You try to shut the window and it comes in on the cable. You cut the cable, it comes in on the Internet. And it's not only in the room with you. You eat it. It gets inside you."[136]

Decisions made by individual consumers and investors in the United States or by their government may determine the prosperity of countless Africans, Asians, and Latin Americans, just as decisions by the latter will have an impact on Americans. In addition, the ability of giant investment institutions known as "hedge funds" to move massive amounts of money almost instantaneously into extremely risky ventures contributes to global economic uncertainty.[137] Government efforts to use the Keynesian tools of macroeconomic policy developed in the 1930s to combat recession and inflation—interest rates and government spending—are often frustrated by the global market. Thus, if a government reduces interest rates to stimulate the economy and reduce unemployment, this action will trigger an outflow of foreign and domestic funds in search of higher interest rates, thereby draining the country of the very investment needed to help jump-start an economy in recession.

In a globalized world, physical distance means little, and no one is "remote" from anyone else. Proximity no longer defined who are "neighbors" in global politics. One observer speaks of a novel *"neighborhood effect"*:

> In the aftermath of the latest Mexican crisis, financial markets moved to attack currencies in Thailand, Spain, Hong Kong, Sweden, Italy, and Russia, substantially weakening them. . . . [I]ncreasingly financial markets tend to cluster those countries perceived to be in the same "neighborhood" and to treat them roughly along the same lines. This time, however, the neighborhood is no longer defined solely in terms of geography. The main defining criterion is the potential volatility of the countries; the contagion spreads inside risk-clusters, or volatility neighborhoods.[138]

In other words, "neighbors" are defined not by their location but by the similarities in their economic situation.

The Asian Contagion

Nowhere was the neighborhood effect or the consequences of globalization more visible than in the economic and financial crisis that struck Asia in the summer of 1997 and then spread to other emerging markets. The first inkling of trouble ahead came in Thailand at the beginning of July 1997 when the value of the local currency (the baht) plunged.

From Thailand, the financial meltdown spread to Indonesia, Malaysia, and the Philippines, and then northward to South Korea and Hong Kong.[139] Although each case was unique, there were a number of common features. Throughout Asia, cozy relations among bankers, businessmen, and politicians—called *"crony capitalism"*—often exacerbated by official corruption,[140] led to the proliferation of loans to projects that were economically unsound. This was exacerbated by lax supervision of banks and corporations and the lack of transparency about debt.[141] In addition, during the early 1990s, Western and Japanese mutual funds had invested heavily in Asia, and Asian governments and private enterprises had borrowed huge amounts of dollars short-term to finance showy projects and business expansion, even though profit margins were small.

With foreign banks demanding repayment of loans in dollars, foreign investors pulling out of local stock and bond markets, and hedge funds selling local currencies

Following economic turmoil in Asia, the IMF provided assistance, but only under conditions including greater austerity. Pictured here is a participant in a demonstration in South Korea by those who lost their jobs as a result of the austerity measures. *(Agence France Presse)*

for dollars, Asian stock markets and currencies took a nose dive. Investors in Southeast and East Asia were in a panic, desperately trying to get their money out. Fifteen months after the Asian crisis had begun, lenders were stuck with $1 trillion in bad loans, $2 trillion in capital investment had fled the region, and countries had lost $3 trillion in GDP growth.[142] As the value of Asian currencies fell, Asian consumers were able to buy fewer and fewer imported products, and their exports, especially to Europe and the United States, climbed.

First, Thailand and Indonesia and then South Korea sought dollar infusions from the IMF and from Europe and the United States in order to buy back local currencies and to stabilize their value, as well as to provide the liquidity necessary to keep local economies functioning. However, before the IMF provided additional funds, it set tough conditions, including austerity policies that increased unemployment, raised the prices of staple goods, and caused bank failures and corporate bankruptcies. Such policies produced anger on the part of large numbers of people[143] and, in the case of Indonesia, were instrumental in setting off savage violence against Chinese shopkeepers and forcing the resignation of President Suharto, who had governed his country since 1965.[144]

World leaders initially believed that Asia's economic crisis was, as President Clinton put it, "a few small glitches on the road."[145] After a year during which the economic crisis spread and deepened, concern had grown dramatically that Asia's problems might push the world into a recession or worse. "This is off the radar screens in terms of severity," declared one economist. "It is the single most negative economic event since the Great Depression in the United States."[146] The changed attitude of the Clinton administration was reflected in the words of one of the president's top advisors. "Just look at how our view of this has changed in the past year. First it was all about Thailand. Then it was about containing this all to Southeast Asia And look at where all this is headed in the next year: Russia, Japan, maybe China—the superpowers."[147]

Like the ripples in a pond, the impact of the Asian crisis spread further and further from where it had begun. As Asian demand for commodities like oil, metals, and timber declined—by almost 10 percent between February and July 1998 alone—producer countries were hurt. Falling prices for oil slowed economies as geographically disparate as Russia, Mexico, Venezuela, and Saudi Arabia Declining demand for copper hurt Zambia and Chile, and Canada witnessed declining demand for its coal and timber. Japan, already in the grip of a recession, was further hurt by reduced demand for its exports elsewhere in Asia and by the devaluation of other Asian currencies, which made Japanese exports relatively less competitive. Above all, it appeared that Japan's banking system was on the verge of drowning under a sea of bad debt.[148] In 1997 alone, the Asian crisis cost Japan's GDP 1.4 percent, leading an American economist to declare: "We're seeing how the contagion process can flow both ways and be self-reinforcing. The Asian crisis is contributing to Japan's decline, while Japan's own internal problems are affecting the rest of Asia."[149]

In the summer of 1998, the contagion leapfrogged from Asia to Russia. Despite the infusion of funds from the IMF, Russia reneged on its foreign debt and the ruble collapsed. Repeatedly, Russia seemed unable or unwilling to fulfill the conditions for its loans, and the Russian economy teetered on the brink of collapse.[150] When the IMF withheld funds to force Russian leaders to adopt economic reforms, the Russians threatened large-scale default.[151] Events in Russia affected the Greek, German, Polish, and, most importantly, the Brazilian economies. It appeared that Latin America and perhaps even China[152] were next. In Brazil's case, large government deficits produced fear that the country's currency would have to be devalued, and in only a month its foreign reserves plummeted from $70 to $42 billion.[153] In order to qualify for IMF aid, the Brazilian government promised an $80 billion package of additional taxes and spending cuts.[154] American leaders were sufficiently concerned that they were prepared to lend Brazil billions of dollars to prevent an economic meltdown in that country, much as they did for Mexico some years earlier.[155] "We're witnessing an unprecedented crisis," declared India's finance minister, "with whole regions engulfed, not just countries. It's a global challenge."[156]

Despite reduced Asian demand for their exports, the United States and Europe actually benefited in some ways at first. The lower price of oil alone was a bonanza for big energy consumers like Europeans and Americans, and fears about Asian stability triggered a flight of foreign funds into the United States, thereby reducing long-term U.S. interest rates and relieving inflationary pressures.[157] Nevertheless, it soon became apparent that declining U.S. exports to Asia would bring the Asian crisis closer to home.[158]

Conclusion

A number of points merit repeating. First, global politics has a critical economic dimension. The economist C. Fred Bergsten captures the relationship between the political and economic spheres when he declares:

> The central task in shaping a new American foreign policy is to set priorities and select central themes. These choices must derive from America's national interests, which have shifted sharply in the direction of economics. . . . With the elimination of the principal threat to world peace, the priorities most countries attach to economic issues will rise substantially.[159]

The Clinton administration shared this view of global politics and devoted much attention to opening Japanese, European, and Chinese markets and to getting approval for NAFTA and the Uruguay Round agreement.

Second, the domestic and global arenas for most issues of international political economy are linked in complex ways. Economic events and decisions within a country directly affect the global economy and vice versa. Third, the gap between rich and poor remains a defining characteristic of today's world. A positive response by the rich to the poor will ultimately enhance the economies of the former by creating greater purchasing power in the LDCs. It will also reduce instability in the LDCs and the likelihood of conflict between rich and poor.

Fourth, and most important, economic markets have become globalized, linking peoples around the world in complex ways that they only dimly understand. Governments can no longer protect themselves against the gales of economic change that blow from one to another corner of the world in defiance of geography.

In the next chapter, we continue our examination of the global political economy by focusing on relations among the four economic giants: the United States, Europe, Japan, and China. The question is whether the major participants in the global economy can contain quarrels in the face of sharply divergent economic interests.

Key Terms

appropriate technology
Baker Plan
balance of payments
beggar-thy-neighbor policies
Brady Plan
brain drain
Bretton Woods system
comparative advantage
conditionality

crony capitalism
currency convertibility
debt-commodity swaps
debt-equity swaps
debt restructuring
debt-service ratios
donor fatigue
economic nationalism
economic summits

embargoes
exchange rates
First World
fixed monetary
   exchange rates
floating exchange rates
General Agreement on Tariffs and
   Trade (GATT)
globalization

Human Development Index (HDI)   neighborhood effect   reserve currency
intellectual property rights   neomercantilism   technology transfer
International Monetary Fund   New International Economic   terms of trade
  (IMF)   Order (NIEO)   Third World
knowledge economies   newly industrializing countries   tied aid
less-developed countries (LDCs)   (NICs)   transnational corporations
liberal economic order   Nixon shock   (TNCs)
liquidity   nonaligned movement   Uruguay Round
microcredit   nontariff barriers   World Bank
Modern World System theory   political economy   World Trade Organization (WTO)
most-favored-nation (MFN) status   quality of life

End Notes

[1]Hans J. Morgenthau, *Politics Among Nations,* 6th ed., rev. by Kenneth W. Thompson (New York: Alfred A. Knopf, 1985), p. 5. Emphasis added.

[2]"The World Economy," special section, *The Economist,* October 7-13, 1995.

[3]*World Development Indicators 1998* (Washington, DC: World Bank, 1998), p. 312. The distinction between direct and indirect or portfolio investment should be kept in mind. *Direct investment* refers to the purchase or construction of fixed assets such as factories and real estate. *Indirect* or *portfolio investment* refers to the purchase of stock, bonds, or other securities.

[4]Stephen Kinzer, "U.S., Pushing Its Route for Pipeline, Aids Turkey," *New York Times,* October 22, 1998, p. A1.

[5]Joseph Berger, "Israeli Executives Urge Moderation on Netanyahu," *New York Times,* June 8, 1996, p. 3.

[6]Congressman Lee H. Hamilton, "A Democrat Looks at Foreign Policy," *Foreign Affairs* 71:3 (Summer 1992), p. 34.

[7]David E. Sanger, "In Geneva, Diplomats Talk of Mufflers, Not Warheads," *New York Times,* June 26, 1995, p. A2.

[8]Robert Gilpin, *The Political Economy of International Relations* (Princeton: Princeton University Press, 1987), p. 28. For an analysis of the impact of the IMF and GATT on economic interdependence, see Miles Kahler, *International Institutions and the Political Economy of Integration* (Washington, DC: Brookings, 1995), pp. 22-79.

[9]David E. Sanger, "Playing the Trade Card," *New York Times,* February 17, 1997, pp. 1, 27.

[10]Robert O. Keohane and Joseph S. Nye, *Power and Interdependence,* 2nd ed. (Glenview, IL: Scott, Foresman, 1989), pp. 78-82.

[11]Jacob M. Schlesinger, "IMF Drafts Plan to Avert Another Mexico," *Wall Street Journal,* December 31, 1996, p. 4.

[12]See Graham Bird, "The International Monetary Fund and Developing Countries: A Review of the Evidence and Policy Options," *International Organization* 50:3 (Summer 1996), pp. 477-511.

[13]Mark Landler, "Rubin Defends I.M.F. Policies and Continues His Asian Tour," *New York Times,* June 30, 1998, p. A12; Stanley Fischer, "Lessons from a Crisis," *The Economist,* October 3-9, 1998, pp. 23-24, 27.

[14]Richard W. Stevenson, "I.M.F. Says It Will Borrow from Members," *New York Times,* July 14, 1998, p. A9.

[15]Philip Shenon, "Budget Deal in Congress to Give Clinton the Full $18 Billion Sought for the I.M.F.," *New York Times,* October 15, 1998, p. A10.

[16]Michael M. Phillips, "IMF and Critics Debate Accounting Principles," *Wall Street Journal,* September 28, 1998, p. A1; David E. Sanger, "As Economies Fail, the I.M.F. Is Rife with Recriminations," *New York Times,* October 2, 1998, pp. A1, A10; David E. Sanger, "Economic Leaders Differ in Strategy on Halting Crisis," *New York Times,* October 4, 1998, sec. 1, pp. 1, 6.

[17]*New York Times,* November 12, 1993, p. C1.

[18]The ITO was established by the 1947 Havana Charter. Congress feared that the ITO would mean a loss of national sovereignty.

[19]"Where Next?" special section, *The Economist,* October 3-9, 1998, p. 3. Gross domestic product (GDP) is a country's gross national product (GNP) minus foreign earnings.

[20]Joan E. Spero and Jeffrey A. Hart, *The Politics of International Economic Relations,* 5th ed. (New York: St. Martin's Press, 1997), pp. 21-24.

[21]Paul Lewis, "World Bank Worried by Pressure for Quick-Fix Fiscal Action," *New York Times,* October 5, 1998, p. A6.

[22]The following discussion draws on Spero and Hart, *Politics of International Economic Relations,* pp. 16-24, and Gilpin, *Political Economy of International Relations,* pp. 134-140.

[23]Wealthy states constitute the *First World,* and those states that are economically less developed are collectively called the *Third World.* The very poorest are sometimes called the *Fourth World.* With the end of the Soviet bloc—the *Second World*—some have suggested that the term Third World is obsolete. The best term is probably *LDCs (less-developed countries).*

[24]Howard W. French, "The French Keep Africa Under Economic Wing," *New York Times,* September 11, 1994, p. 9.

[25]The devaluation achieved its aim and brought economic growth back to West Africa after years of declining production, investment, and exports. Thomas Kamm, "After a Devaluation, Two African Nations Fare Very Differently," *Wall Street Journal,* May 10, 1995, pp. A1, A15.

[26]Kenneth B. Noble, "French Currency Move Provokes Unrest in Africa," *New York Times,* February 23, 1994, pp. A1, A6.

[27]I.M. Destler and C. Randall Henning, *Dollar Politics: Exchange Rate Policymaking in the United States* (Washington, DC: Institute for International Economics, 1989), p. 22.

[28]Robert D. Hormats, "The World Economy Under Stress," in William G. Hyland, ed., *America and the World 1985* (New York: Pergamon Press, 1986), p. 469.

[29]See Yoichi Funabashi, *Managing the Dollar: From the Plaza to the Louvre,* 2nd ed. (Washington, DC: Institute for International Economics, 1989), pp. 183-187.

[30]Destler and Henning, *Dollar Politics,* pp. 61-67.

[31]Peter Gumbel and Bob Davis, "G-7 Countries Show Limits of Their Power," *Wall Street Journal,* July 11, 1994, p. A3.

[32]Other countries beside Singapore and Hong Kong thought of as NICs include Taiwan, South Korea, Malaysia, and Thailand. Ireland is sometimes called a European NIC because of its impressive economic record in recent years.

[33]*World Development Indicators 1998,* p. 312. These data include power parity conversion factors. About one-third of U.S. trade takes place *within* TNCs in the course of producing components in one country and shipping them to others for assembly. "Where next?" p. 13.

[34]Benjamin J. Cohen, "The Political Economy of International Trade," *International Organization* 44:2 (Spring 1990), pp. 261-262.

[35]Beth V. Yarbrough and Robert M. Yarbrough, "Cooperation in the Liberalization of International Trade: After Hegemony, What?" *International Organization* 41:1 (Winter 1987), pp. 1-26.

[36]For a discussion of negotiating strategies at GATT, see Bernard M. Hoekman, "Determining the Need for Issue Linkages in Multilateral Trade Negotiations," *International Organization* 43:4 (Autumn 1989), pp. 693-714.

[37]Named, respectively, after former U.S. Secretary of the Treasury Douglas Dillon and President John F. Kennedy.

[38]The talks were begun in the Uruguayan resort of Punta del Este.

[39]See Charles E. Hanrahan, "The Uruguay Round: Impact on Agriculture," in *Trade and Investment: The Changing International Framework* (Washington, DC: Congressional Research Service, February–March, 1992), p. 8.

[40]Roger Cohen, "Impasse over World Trade Pact Poisons Ties to U.S., France Says," *New York Times,* November 6, 1993, p. A5.

[41]Cited in Helene Cooper and John Harwood, "Major Shifts in Trade Are Ensured as GATT Wins U.S. Approval," *Wall Street Journal,* December 2, 1994, p. A1.

[42]Keith Bradsher, "Foes Set for Battle on GATT," *New York Times,* October 3, 1994, pp. C1, C8.

[43]The volume of subsidized exports must be reduced by 21 percent over six years. U.S. quotas on sugar, peanuts, and dairy products must end, as well as Japanese and South Korean bans on rice imports.

[44]The agreement provided 7 years protection for trademarks, 20 for patents, and up to 50 for copyrights.

[45]The industrialized countries eliminated all tariffs among themselves in ten industries: beer, construction equipment, distilled spirits, farm machinery, furniture, medical equipment, paper, pharmaceuticals, steel, and toys. U.S. industries that benefited most were electronics, pharmaceuticals, and chemicals; the big losers were textiles and apparel makers and filmmakers. "The Trade Pact's Key Provisions," *Wall Street Journal,* December 2, 1994, p. A6.

[46]"Fifty Years On," *The Economist,* p. 22; "Where Next?" pp. 7-8; Seth Schiesel, "Global Agreement Reached to Widen Law on Copyright," *New York Times,* December 21, 1996, pp. 1, 22; Edmund L. Andrews, "67 Nations Agree to Freer Markets in Communications," *New York Times,* February 16, 1997, sec. 1, pp. 1, 6.

[47]"Co-operate on Competition," *The Economist,* July 4-10, 1998, p. 16.

[48]Unlike in the GATT, members cannot veto WTO decisions. Floyd Norris, "A Quick Ramble in a Thicket of Rules," *New York Times,* November 27, 1994, sec. 4, p. 3.

[49]It is unlikely that the U.S. record will be as favorable in the WTO as in the GATT, where it won 47 percent of its complaints. Eduardo Lachica, "U.S. May Be Losing Its Trade-Bully Status," *Wall Street Journal,* October 13, 1995, p. A11. See also Helene Cooper, "U.S. Faces a Loss on Underwear Quota," *Wall Street Journal,* October 22, 1996, p. A2; "All Free Traders Now?" *The Economist,* December 7-13, 1996, pp. 21-23; Larry Rohter, "Trade Storm Imperils Caribbean Banana Crops," *New York Times,* May 9, 1997, p. A6.

[50]David E. Sanger, "Europe Takes U.S. to Court in Trade Flap," *New York Times,* October 2, 1996, p. A4; David E. Sanger, "Europe Postpones Challenge to U.S. on Havana Trade," *New*

York Times, February 13, 1997; David E. Sanger, "U.S. Rejects Role for World Court in Trade Dispute," *New York Times,* February 21, 1997, pp. A1, A9; David Sanger, "Ruling Allows Tariffs by U.S. over Bananas," *New York Times,* April 17, 1999, pp. C1, C21. The U.S., though not a source of bananas, was seeking to aid U.S. corporations like Chiquita Brands that exported Central American bananas.

[51]See, for example, Laurie P. Cohen, "With Help from INS U.S. Meatpacker Taps Mexican Work Force," *Wall Street Journal,* October 16, 1998, pp. A1, A8.

[52]David F. Sawyer, "U.S. Defeated in Trade Case at World Body," *New York Times,* April 30, 1996, pp. A1, C6.

[53]Steven Lee Myers, "Clothing Makers Taking Steps to Limit Child Labor Abroad," *New York Times,* October 21, 1996, p. A4; Steven Greenhouse, "Group Vows Fight over Child Labor," *New York Times,* February 14, 1997, pp. A1, A9; Steven Greenhouse, "Apparel Industry Group Moves to End Sweatshops," *New York Times,* April 9, 1997, p. A11.

[54]The following discussion draws on Robert D. Putnam and Nicholas Bayne, *Hanging Together: Cooperation and Conflict in the Seven-Power Summits,* rev. ed. (Cambridge: Harvard University Press, 1987).

[55]Ibid., Table 11.1, p. 270.

[56]R. W. Apple, Jr., "Unclimbed Summit," *New York Times,* July 11, 1994, p. A4.

[57]Bob Davis, Peter Gumbel, and Rick Wartzman, "Disputes Between G-7 Nations Crowd Out Big Issues at Summit," *Wall Street Journal,* June 19, 1995, pp. A2, A5.

[58]Thomas Kamm and Michael K. Frisby, "Group of Seven Industrial Nations Vows Stronger Campaign Against Terrorism," *Wall Street Journal,* June 28, 1996, p. A8; Steven Erlanger, "8 Leaders Issue Long Wish List to End Meeting," *New York Times,* June 23, 1997, pp. A1, A7.

[59]*World Development Indicators 1998,* p. 185.

[60]Ibid., pp. 242-243.

[61]John Darnton, "In Decolonized, Destitute Africa Bankers Are the New Overlords," *New York Times,* June 20, 1994, p. A6. There are a few bright spots, such as growing South African investment in neighboring states. GDP in sub-Saharan Africa increased 3.8 percent in 1995. "Inching Ahead," *The Economist,* May 11-17 1996, pp. 42-44.

[62]"A Continent Goes to War," *The Economist,* October 3-9, 1998, pp. 47-48.

[63]Howard W. French, "Sure, Ebola Is Bad. Africa Has Worse," *New York Times,* June 11, 1995, sec. 4, p. 3.

[64]Nicholas D. Kristof, "Malaria Makes a Comeback, and Is More Deadly Than Ever," *New York Times,* January 8, 1997, pp. A1, A7.

[65]Michael Specter, "Doctors Powerless as AIDS Rakes Africa," *New York Times,* August 6, 1998, p. A7. To reduce the rate at which infants are infected by the HIV virus that causes AIDS, some U.N. officials are reversing decades of nutritional advice in recommending against breast-feeding. Lawrence K. Altman, "To Fight AIDS, the U.N. Warns on Breast-Feeding," *New York Times,* July 26, 1998, sec. 1, pp. 1, 8.

[66]Youssef M. Ibrahim, "AIDS Is Slashing Africa's Population, U.N. Survey Finds," *New York Times,* October 28, 1998, p. A3.

[67]*Human Development Report 1998* (New York: Oxford University Press, 1998), pp. 158-159. In one Zimbabwe community, 60 percent of pregnant women were HIV-positive, and in another in Botswana, 48 percent of such women were HIV-positive. Ibid., p. 35.

[68]Richard Falk, "What's Wrong with Henry Kissinger's Foreign Policy," *Alternatives* 1 (1975), p. 99.

[69]Robert S. Walters and David H. Blake, *The Politics of Global Economic Relations,* 4th ed. (Englewood Cliffs, NJ: Prentice-Hall, 1992), pp. 5-12. The radical perspective evolved from Marxist assumptions.

[70]See André Gunder Frank, *Latin America: Underdevelopment or Revolution?* (New York: Monthly Review Press, 1970); Immanuel Wallerstein, *The Modern World System* (New York: Academic Press, 1974), and Wallerstein, *The Modern World-System II* (New York: Academic Press, 1980).

[71]An example is U.S. subsidies to private industry to develop advanced computer display screens. Keith Bradsher, "U.S. to Aid Industry in Computer Battle with the Japanese," *New York Times,* April 27, 1994, pp. A1, C5.

[72]Gilpin, *Political Economy of International Relations,* p. 32.

[73]Barbara Crossette, "U.N. Survey Finds World Rich-Poor Gap Widening," *New York Times,* July 15, 1996, p. A3.

[74]Barbara Crossette, "U.N. Planning Ambitious, and Risky, Conference on Poverty," *New York Times,* January 23, 1995, p. A5.

[75]*World Development Indicators 1998,* pp. 64-66. The World Bank has developed two versions of a human poverty index. *Human Development Report 1998,* p. 15.

[76]*Human Development Report 1998,* pp. 128, 130.

[77]Barbara Crossette, "Most Consuming More, and the Rich Much More," *New York Times,* September 13, 1998, sec. 1, p. 3. Impure water is the cause of some 3,100,000 cases of diarrhea, 200,000 cases of schistosomiasis, and 130,000 cases of trypanosomiasis in the developing world per year. Nicholas D. Kristof, "For Third World, Water Is Still a Deadly Drink," *New York Times,* January 9, 1997, p. A6.

[78]*World Development Report 1995* (New York: Oxford University Press, 1995), Table 1, pp. 162-163.

[79]"A Global Poverty Trap?" *The Economist,* August 20-26, 1996, p. 34.

[80]*World Development Report 1998/99* (New York: Oxford University Press, 1999), pp. 250-251.

[81]*Human Development Report 1998,* pp. 128, 130. "Averages" hide a significant range within groups. For example, even though the average life expectancy for poor countries in 1995

was fifty-six years, in Sierra Leone, average life expectancy was under thirty-five years, whereas in Pakistan it was almost sixty-three.

[82]Michael J. Sullivan III, *Measuring Global Values* (New York: Greenwood Press, 1991), pp. 218-219.

[83]*Human Development Report 1998,* p. 15.

[84]Nonaligned states remained outside Cold War alliances, seeking to avoid political entanglements while seeking economic aid from both sides. By 1995, the Group of 77 consisted of 130 developing nations.

[85]This chronology draws on James M. McCormick, "The NIEO and the Distribution of American Assistance," *Western Political Quarterly* 37 (March 1984), pp. 100-119.

[86]The quotations are from interviews with members and staff of the House Foreign Affairs Committee and officials at the U.S. Agency for International Development during the early 1980s, as reported in James M. McCormick, "Congressional-Executive Attitudes Toward the NIEO," *International Studies Notes* 10 (Spring 1983), pp. 12-17.

[87]Glenn Frankel, "The Tobacco Pushers," *Washington Post National Weekly Edition,* November 25-December 1, 1996, pp. 6-9.

[88]Charter of Economic Rights and Duties of States," as reprinted in Guy F. Erb and Valeriana Kallab, *Beyond Dependency: The Developing World Speaks Out* (Washington, DC: Overseas Development Council, 1975), p. 206.

[89]See United Nations Centre on Transnational Corporations, *Transnational Corporations in World Development* (New York: United Nations, 1988).

[90]Although some U.S. corporations, including Goodyear and Napco International, have been caught violating this law, most have developed legal practices that help them to compete, such as using middlemen or making small "facilitation" payments. Dana Milbank and Marcus W. Brauchli, "How U.S. Concerns Compete in Countries Where Bribes Flourish," *Wall Street Journal,* September 29, 1995, pp. A1, A14.

[91]Marlise Simons, "U.S. Enlists Other Rich Countries in a Move to End Business Bribes to Foreign Officials," *New York Times,* April 12, 1996, p. A7. Corporate behavior has improved in recent years. "Companies and Their Consciences." *The Economist,* July 20-26, 1996, pp. 15, 16.

[92]Walters and Blake, *Politics of Global Economic Relations,* p. 148.

[93]Richard J. Barnet and Ronald E. Muller, *Global Reach* (New York: Simon & Schuster, 1974), p. 188. Some of these industries were later returned to their corporate owners.

[94]Fred R. Bleakley, "Multinational Firms Spent $325 Billion in 1995 on Foreign Direct Investment," *Wall Street Journal,* June 5, 1996, p. A2.

[95]Walters and Blake, *Politics of Global Economic Relations,* pp. 120, 169. The authors define technology transfer as "the flow of purposeful knowledge across national boundaries" (p. 167). See also pp. 169-173.

[96]Erb and Kallab, *Beyond Dependency,* p. 208.

[97]Walters and Blake, *Politics of Global Economic Relations,* pp. 174-188.

[98]Developed countries produce more goods demanded by consumers in other developed countries than do poor countries.

[99]Erb and Kallab, *Beyond Dependency,* pp. 206, 208, 209, 211.

[100]"Wanted: Some African Tigers," *The Economist,* November 30-December 6, 1996, p. 41.

[101]Patricia Lee Dorff, "Chronology 1991," *Foreign Affairs* 71:1 (1992), p. 219.

[102]Michael E. Phillips, "U.S. Is Seeking to Build Its Trade with Africa," *Wall Street Journal,* June 2, 1997, p. A1.

[103]Helene Cooper, "Sub-Saharan Africa Is Seen as Big Loser in GATT's New World Trade Accord," *Wall Street Journal,* August 15, 1994, p. A8.

[104]Table B-3 in John W. Sewell, Richard E. Feinberg, and Valeriana Kallab, eds., *U.S. Foreign Policy and the Third World: Agenda 1985-86* (Washington, DC: Overseas Development Council, 1985), p. 174.

[105]"Opening Statement by Senator Bill Bradley," Subcommittee on International Debt, Senate Finance Committee, March 9, 1987.

[106]S. Karene Witcher, "Baker's Plan to Relieve Debt Crisis May Spur Future Ills, Critics Say," *Wall Street Journal,* November 15, 1985, p. 1.

[107]On these schemes, see Peter Dombrowski, *Policy Responses to the Globalization of American Banking* (Pittsburgh: University of Pittsburgh Press, 1996), pp. 99-146.

[108]*World Development Report 1995,* p. 207.

[109]Cited in Kenneth N. Gilpin, "Brazil Reaches an Agreement with Big Banks on Its Debt," *New York Times,* April 17, 1994, sec. 1, p. 8.

[110]Paul Lewis, "Debt-Relief Cost of the Poorest Nations," *New York Times,* June 10, 1996, p. C2.

[111]Barbara Crossette, "U.N. Parley Ponders Ways to Stretch Scarce Aid Funds," *New York Times,* March 7, 1995, p. A6.

[112]*World Development Report 1996* (New York: Oxford University Press, 1996), pp. 240-241. "Severely indebted" means that the value of a country's debt service to GNP is 80 percent or higher or that the value of debt service to exports is 220 percent or greater.

[113]For an illustration, see Donald G. McNeil, Jr., "Mozambique's Way with Austerity Puts It on Brink of an Economic Boom," *New York Times,* September 13, 1998, sec. 1, p. 10.

[114]Lewis, "Debt-Relief Cost of the Poorest Nations"; Richard W. Stevenson, "Global Banks Offer a First: Forgiveness on Some Debt," *New York Times,* March 12, 1997, p. A10. Of the wealthy countries, Japan has urged debt cancellation most vigorously.

[115]*World Development Report, 1990* (New York: Oxford University Press, 1990), p. 214; *World Development Indicators, 1998,* p. 340.

[116]*World Development Report,1995,* p. 196; *World Development Indicators, 1998,* p. 340.

[117]Ibid. The increase is much lower if controlled for inflation.

[118]"Beyond Band-Aids," *The Economist,* March 23-29, 1996, pp. 15-16.

[119]Crossette, "U.N. Parley Ponders Ways to Stretch Scarce Aid Funds," p. A6.

[120]See, for example, "It's the Government, Stupid," *The Economist,* June 28-July 4, 1997, pp. 71-72; "Poorer and Angrier," *The Economist,* August 15-21, 1998.

[121]Cited in Howard W. French, "Donors of Foreign Aid Have Second Thoughts," *New York Times,* April 7, 1996, sec. 4, p. 5.

[122]*AID's Challenge in an Interdependent World* (Washington, DC: Agency for International Development, 1977), p. 11.

[123]McCormick, "Congressional-Executive Attitudes Toward the NIEO," p. 14.

[124]Steven Greenhouse, "U.S. to Cut Overseas Food Aid by Nearly Half," *New York Times,* April 2, 1995, sec. 1, p. 8.

[125]Donatella Lorch, "Even with Peace and Rain, Ethiopia Fears Famine," *New York Times,* January 3, 1996, p. A3.

[126]Gwen Ifill, "U.S. Will Triple Its Foreign Aid to Kazakhstan," *New York Times,* February 15, 1994, p. A3.

[127]Brian H. Smith, *More Than Altruism: The Politics of Private Foreign Aid* (Princeton: Princeton University Press, 1990), p. 104.

[128]See Robert M. Orr, *The Emergence of Japan's Foreign Aid Power* (New York: Columbia University Press, 1990), pp. 109-131.

[129]Excerpts from Reagan Speech on U.S. Policy Toward Developing Nations," *New York Times,* October 16, 1981, p. A12.

[130]Barbara Crossette, "U.S. Offers Third World a Wider Role at the U.N.," *New York Times,* July 17, 1997, p. A7.

[131]"Time to Roll out a New Model," *The Economist,* March 1-7, 1997, pp. 71-72.

[132]Cited in Paul Lewis, "Small Loans May Be Key to Helping Third World," *New York Times,* January 26, 1997, sec. 1, p. 5. For a less optimistic view, see Ken Wells, "Microcredit Arrives in Africa, but Can It Match Asian Success?" *Wall Street Journal,* September 29, 1998, pp. A1, A15.

[133]The proposal involved creating additional Special Drawing Rights, international credit units that entitle countries to draw foreign currencies from the IMF. David Wessel, "Developing Nations Exert Power, Blocking IMF Aid Plan for Russia," *Wall Street Journal,* October 4, 1994, p. A14.

[134]Thomas L. Friedman, "Big Mac II," *New York Times,* December 11, 1996, p. A21.

[135]"Meet the Global Factory," special section, *The Economist,* June 20-26, 1998, p. 3.

[136]Cited in ibid.

[137]For a less critical view, see "The Risk Business," *The Economist,* October 17-23, 1998, pp. 21-23.

[138]Moisés Naím, "Mexico's Larger Story," *Foreign Policy* 99 (Summer 1995), p. 125.

[139]"Unpegged," *The Economist,* July 19-25, 1997, pp. 35-36; Mark Landler, "Hong Kong Surprise," *New York Times,* July 1, 1998, pp. A1, A11.

[140]See, for example, Glenn R. Simpson and Michael M. Phillips, "World Bank Sounds Alarm at Jakarta Corruption," *Wall Street Journal,* October 23, 1998, p. A12.

[141]The world's largest accounting firms failed to use accounting rules that would have provided warning of a looming financial crisis. Melody Peterson, "U.N. Report Faults Big Accountants in Asia Crisis," *New York Times,* October 24, 1998, pp. B1, B4.

[142]"Still Sick and Gloomy, Now Rebellious," *The Economist,* July 11-17, 1997, pp. 41-42; Darren McDermott, "Asia Waits in Vain for Money to Return," *Wall Street Journal,* October 14, 1998, p. A7.

[143]"Trouble upon Trouble for Kim," *The Economist,* August 29-September 4, 1998, pp. 40-41.

[144]"Indonesia Awakes, South-East Asia Starts to Wonder," *The Economist,* June 6-12, 1998, pp. 37-38; Jay Solomon and Wayne Arnold, "Racial Unrest Mars Indonesia's Recovery," *Wall Street Journal,* July 17, 1998, p. A12.

[145]Cited in David E. Sanger, "After a Year, No Letup in Asia's Economic Crisis," *New York Times,* July 6, 1998, p. A1. For analysis of how U.S. leaders failed to understand the extent of the crisis, see David Wessel and Bob Davis, "How Global Crisis Grew Despite Efforts of a Crack U.S. Team," *Wall Street Journal,* September 24, 1998, pp. A1, A10.

[146]Cited in Sanger, "After a Year, No Let up in Asia's Economic Crisis," p. A6.

[147]Cited in ibid., p. A1.

[148]David E. Sanger, "Japanese Tell U.S. That Their Banks Are in Big Trouble," *New York Times,* October 5, 1998, pp. A1, A6.

[149]Cited in Eduardo Lachica, "Japan to Lose 1.4% of Its 1997 GDP Due to Asia's Turmoil, Study Says," *Wall Street Journal,* July 8, 1998, p. C12.

[150]Jacob M. Schlesinger, "Russia's Challenge to Capitalism, Part II," *Wall Street Journal,* August 17, 1998, p. A1.

[151]Celestine Bohlen, "Russia Warns It Might Default If Western Aid Is Withheld," *New York Times,* September 25, 1998, p. A10; David E. Sanger, "I.M.F. Resists 'Blackmail' by Russia and U.S.," *New York Times,* September 25, 1998, p. A10. Foreign loans intended to stabilize the Russian ruble were lost in currency transactions.

[152]"Red Alert," *The Economist,* October 24-30, 1998, pp. 23-26.

[153]Diana Jean Schemo, "Possible I.M.F. Bailout Stirs Brazilians' Bitter Memories of 80's," *New York Times,* October 1, 1998, p. A17.

[154]Diana Jean Schemo, "Brazil Introduces $80 Billion Plan for Economic Ills," *New York Times,* October 29, 1998, pp. A1, C4.

[155]David E. Sanger, "U.S. Plans to Shield Brazil's Economy," *New York Times,* October 25, 1998, sec. 1, pp. 1, 12.

[156]Cited in Lewis, "World Bank Worried by Pressure for Quick-Fix Fiscal Action," p. A6. For a more optimistic view, see "The Darkest Hour Comes Just Before Dawn," *The Economist,* October 17–23, 1998, pp. 85–87.

[157]Lachica, "Japan to Lose 1.4% of Its 1997 GDP Due to Asia's Turmoil, Study Says," pp. C1, C12; Michael M. Phillips, "How Long Can the U.S. Stay Immune to What Ails the World Economy?" *Wall Street Journal,* February 5, 1999, pp. A1, A10.

[158]Sam Howe Verhovek, "Northwest Farms and Industry Feel Pinch of Asia Fiscal Crisis," *New York Times,* October 1, 1998, pp. A1, A18; David E. Sanger, "U.S.Trade Deficit Shows the Effect of Global Turmoil," *New York Times,* October 26, 1998, pp. A1, C4.

[159]C. Fred Bergsten, "The Primacy of Economics," *Foreign Policy* 87 (Summer 1992), pp. 4, 5.

Chapter 13

Economic Competitors or Partners: The United States, Japan, China, and Europe

Although the world seems unipolar militarily, from an economic perspective, it already has three poles—the United States, the Pacific Rim, and Western Europe. It is in these regions that state institutions remain strongest. Economically, the United States no longer enjoys its postwar domination.[1] This decline has been accompanied by sharp economic quarrels among the United States, Japan, China, and the European Union. So important are these quarrels that beginning in 1993 the Clinton administration asked the intelligence community to improve collection and analysis of information on trade negotiations, tactics foreigners use to win business, and financial crises. To this end, the National Security Agency (NSA) secretly eavesdropped on conversations among Japanese bureaucrats and auto executives about U.S.-Japanese trade negotiations. "It was a remarkable performance," declared a senior U.S. official, "because the intelligence agencies finally realized this was the World Series—the arms control talks of the new age."[2] Unfortunately, the intelligence agencies had little experience with economic issues, and, following the onset of Asia's economic woes, one senior intelligence official admitted that the CIA "hasn't a clue how to deal with this kind of crisis, where the enemy is the markets or a finance ministry that lies about a country's currency reserves."[3]

Will conflict between East and West be replaced by conflict among competitive trading blocs: North America (with the United States as its leader), Western Europe (with Germany at the helm), and East Asia (revolving around Japan or China)? What if America's competitors play by different rules? Lester Thurow tells of a secret meeting held in Singapore in 1990 between the two largest business conglomerates in the world—Japan's Mitsubishi group and Germany's Daimler Benz-Deutsche Bank group—to consider a global alliance. He writes:

> In the United States banks cannot own industrial firms and businesses cannot sit down behind closed doors to plan joint strategies. Those doing so get thrown into jail for extended periods of time. Yet in today's world Americans cannot force the rest of the world to play the economic game as Americans think it should be played.[4]

And will Japan, China, and Europe exercise their economic clout in parochial ways?[5] Or will the end of the Cold War and the interdependence of the United States, Europe, and Asia produce a dynamic and open global economic system in which growing prosperity makes resort to arms irrational and obsolete? Finally, how will changes in the distribution of economic resources affect political relations among leading actors?

In this chapter we examine relations among the economic top dogs and discuss prospects for their future cooperation or conflict in the context of a globalized economic system. Until recently, the United States, Japan, China, and Western Europe did not compete with one another directly. Instead, each occupied an economic niche in which the products one made did not threaten producers and workers in the others. This condition has so changed that, economist Lester Thurow writes, the twenty-first century will be seen "as a century of head-to-head competition."

> Starting from approximately the same level of economic development, each country or region wants exactly the same industries. . . . *Niche competition* is win-win. Everyone has a place where they can excel; no one is going to be driven out of business. *Head-to-head competition* is win-lose. . . . Some will win; some will lose.[6]

Some fear that the United States is losing the competition. "Everyone's been saying for a long time that foreign policy is becoming economic," declared former U.S. Treasury Secretary Lloyd Bentsen, "but like everything it's taken a while for the message to sink in around here."[7]

Declining American Hegemony?

During the 1980s and the early 1990s, there was considerable speculation about declining American economic power. In less than a decade, the United States shifted from being the world's leading creditor to the world's leading debtor. Until 1996, foreign indebtedness—the difference between the value of Americans' overseas investments and foreigners' investments in the United States—stood at over $831 billion.[8] From virtual self-sufficiency, the United States grew increasingly dependent on world trade yet continued to suffer from a trade deficit. Throughout the 1980s, America's productivity performance—output per hour of work—was poor.[9] Once self-sufficient in energy, the United States depended ever more on foreign oil. Most telling perhaps from the *declinist perspective* was America's need to go hat in hand to its allies to finance the Persian Gulf War.

At that time, observers began to wonder whether it were possible to remain a political and military leader or hegemon without also enjoying dominant economic influence. Some claim that *imperial overextension* brings economic decline, which spells the end of political influence. Historian Paul Kennedy argues that "the difficulties experienced by contemporary societies which are militarily top-heavy merely repeat those which, in their time, affected Phillip II's Spain, Nicholas II's Russia, and Hitler's Germany."[10] British hegemony in the nineteenth century ended when that country, the world's trading and financial hub, was overtaken by new economic giants—the United States and Germany. Does the same fate await the Cold-War superpowers? The Soviet collapse in 1991 under extensive military burdens lends weight to the argument.

The question of whether the United States is in decline is not a simple one. Is a country weaker because it is a debtor rather than a creditor? Is foreign investment a source of vigor or weakness? Is the loss of manufacturing industries a sign of economic weakness, or are service industries the wave of the future?[11] What high-tech areas are most critical for the future? As World War II ended, the United States stood alone, an economic colossus dominating every economic sector. That supremacy has vanished. The dollar is no longer undisputed king of global currencies, and U.S. dominance of world financial markets, manufacturing, and trade has diminished. During the 1970s and 1980s, global economic clout shifted to the Pacific Rim, especially Japan and the newly industrializing countries (NICs)—Singapore, Hong Kong, South Korea, Malaysia, and Taiwan—and to Europe.

Is America's seeming economic decline an illusion based on the echo Joseph Nye calls the *"vanishing World War II effect"* in which "the American share of global power resources exaggerated by World War II went through a natural and steady decline during the next quarter century and then stabilized"?[12] The year 1945 was hardly typical. Europe was in shambles; Japanese cities were reduced to rubble; and, of all the world's industrial regions, only America remained unscarred by war. If Nye's view is correct, then what appears to be a sustained decline is really a return to normalcy after a rare moment of supremacy. Thus the pessimists who warn of America's fall from grace may be drawing conclusions from faulty time periods. Looking at trends from the immediate postwar period may overstate America's "normal" dominance.[13]

As other regions rebuilt their shattered infrastructures after 1945, America's preeminence necessarily declined. Indeed, a primary goal of U.S. postwar foreign policy was to aid allies, and their prosperity today reflects successful policies like the Marshall Plan (1948–1952) and preferential access to U.S. markets for Japanese and European products. Using data on gross national product (GNP), military expenditures, and manufacturing production from 1945, one observer concludes that "the United States retains on all these indicators a degree of dominance . . . that compares well with the U.S. position in 1938." Thus "the basis of American hegemony may have declined, but it has hardly vanished."[14]

In sum, despite a decline from the lofty economic heights it once occupied, the United States still enjoys a gross national product (GNP)[15] of some $7.43 trillion (in 1996 dollars), about the same as the GNP of Japan and Germany combined ($7.51 trillion).[16] Although America's per capita GNP ($28,020) as of 1996 was lower than Japan's ($40,940),[17] the figures are distorted by fluctuating currency exchange rates and differences in purchasing power. When purchasing power is taken into account, real GNP per capita in the United States was the highest in the world.[18] Other indicators, such as home ownership, leisure time, and accessibility of higher education, also suggest that Americans still enjoy a higher standard of living than their Japanese or German counterparts.

When we examine America's economic position from a longer perspective, the picture changes. Looking at U.S. percentage of world product from 1900 through

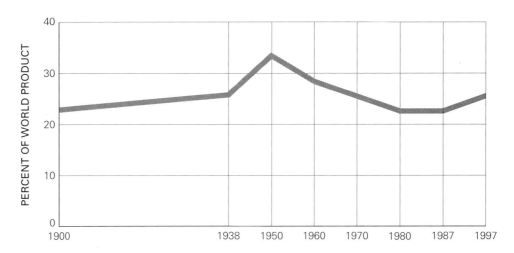

FIGURE 13.1
The Shape of American Decline

The U.S. share of global production peaked after World War II and has since declined to where it stood earlier in the century. SOURCE: From *Bound to Lead: The Changing Nature of American Power* by Joseph S. Nye, Jr. Copyright © 1990 by Basic Books, Inc. Reprinted by permission of Basic Books, Inc; 1997 data from OECD, www.oecd.org/std/nahome.htm.

1987 (Figure 13.1), it is clear that although the U.S. share dropped from a peak in the late 1940s and early 1950s, it has really only settled back to a position comparable to the early part of the century. By 1997, the United States still accounted for more than 25 percent of world GNP.[19] As shown in Figure 13.2, between the end of World War II and 1980, the U.S. share of world manufacturing production declined from a high of almost 45 percent (1953), but only to what it had been in 1938. Finally, as Table 13.1 shows, the decline of America's share of the export of technology-intensive products between 1970 and 1986—an area emphasized by policy-makers—was modest, and this decline was strongly reversed during the following decade. Then, too, as shown in Table 13.2, the bases of influence have gradually shifted so that the history of former hegemons may be a poor guide to the future.

It is tempting to confuse others' prosperity with U.S. decline. Japan's great strides in various technologies have not been at the expense of the United States, nor is America's economic revival in the late 1990s at Japan's expense. In 1993, four U.S. and six Japanese corporations were among the top ten receiving patents in the United States.[20] Japan's growing share of high-tech exports between 1980 and 1989 was accompanied by U.S. losses in computers, precision equipment, aerospace, telecommunications equipment, and machine tools, but, at the same time, the United States gained larger shares of exports of microelectronics, medicine and biological products, and organic chemicals.

Pessimists cited such trends as declining educational performance, a shrinking pool of skilled laborers, and low U.S. savings rates[21] as causes for alarm. For seven of the ten years in the 1970s and for every year in the 1980s, the United States had deficits in its merchandise trade account, and in the second quarter of 1995, the

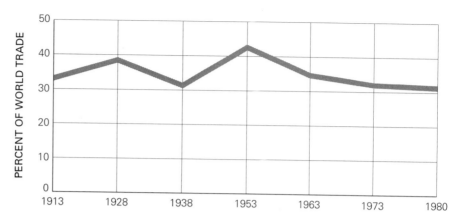

FIGURE 13.2
American Share of World Manufacturing Production

Despite fears about the erosion of America's industrial base, data suggest that the U.S. share of world manufacturing has stabilized. SOURCE: From *Bound to Lead: The Changing Nature of American Power* by Joseph S. Nye, Jr. Copyright © 1990 by Basic Books, Inc. Reprinted by permission of Basic Books, Inc.

U.S. trade deficit reached a record $43.62 billion.[22] Economists argued that if savings exceed investment, as in Japan, a trade surplus must follow, whereas if savings are less than investment, as in the United States, there will be a trade deficit.[23] A weak U.S. dollar encouraged foreigners to purchase U.S. assets and created fear of "dependency" on "outsiders."[24] Such anxiety was reflected in Michael Crichton's novel and film *Rising Sun*. "What if foreigners acquire a monopoly in industries that make strategic products for the Pentagon," asks Paul Kennedy, "or if an important military-related item is made only abroad? What if the country becomes ever more reliant upon foreign capital—will it one day pay a political price as well as a financial one for that dependency?"[25]

Even if America had suffered a relative economic decline, U.S. *soft power*—"cultural attraction, ideology, and international institutions"[26]—was increasing, meaning that the United States was enjoying new sources of influence. If the Soviet system collapsed partly because its ideology was bankrupt, America's strength may lie less in its laboratories and factories than in its ideals of liberal democracy and free enterprise.[27] In the words of a German youth, "Just about everything we have that's fun comes from the United States. If it weren't for Americans, we wouldn't have baseball caps. We wouldn't have malls or fast food shops or skateboards."[28] One historian explains that Oxford University is creating an Institute for American Studies, because "American culture is so dominant in the world."[29] In a word, cultural and economic globalization seem to be marching hand in hand with Americanization.

Perhaps America's future depends on whether the country "will have the political leadership and strategic vision to convert these power resources into real influence in a transitional period of world politics."[30] Today, in contrast to their strident criticisms of U.S. interference during the Cold War, many developing countries complain more about the absence of U.S. leadership.[31]

TABLE 13.1
*World Export Shares
of Technology-
Intensive Products,
1970–1997*

Country	1970	1980	1986	1997
United States	27.0%	22.9%	20.9%	26.1%
Japan	10.9	14.3	19.8	21.4
France	7.1	8.5	7.9	8.5
West Germany	16.8	16.3	16.0	10.6*
Great Britain	9.8	10.8	9.0	9.3

*United Germany

SOURCE: From *Bound to Lead: The Changing Nature of American Power* by Joseph S. Nye Jr.
Copyright © 1990 by Basic Books, Inc. Reprinted by permission; 1997 data from
www.oecd.org/std/nahome.htm

Nowhere was the key role of U.S. leadership more vividly apparent than in the rapid sequence of events beginning in late 1995 with NATO airstrikes against Bosnian Serb positions, followed by a cease-fire in Bosnia and culminating in a peace agreement among Croatians, Serbs, and Bosnian Muslims in Dayton, Ohio, at the end of November. During four years of war, to the frustration of America's NATO allies, the United States refused to get materially involved in the Bosnian morass. However, following revelations of Bosnian Serb atrocities after the fall of the Bosnian Muslim enclave of Srbrenica, this policy changed. In the end, the application of U.S. military and diplomatic pressure, as well as the commitment of 20,000 U.S. troops (of an international peace force of 60,000), was decisive. In a speech on November 27, 1995, President Clinton repeatedly alluded to the key role of soft power in American leadership. "It is the power of our ideas," he declared, "even more than our size, our wealth and our military might, that makes America a uniquely trusted nation."

My duty as President is to match the demands for American leadership to our
strategic interests and to our ability to make a difference. . . . Now the war is over.
American leadership created the chance to build peace and stop the suffering. . . .
And as NATO's leader . . . , the United States must be an essential part of the mission. If we're not there, NATO will not be there.[32]

American leadership was again evident in NATO's bombing of Serbia, which began in March 1999 in an effort to force Serbia to acquiesce in an agreement that would give the Albanian ethnic majority in Kosovo greater autonomy. The dramatic upturn in U.S. economic fortunes in the 1990s, even as Japan's economy slumped, largely ended talk of American decline. As American corporations downsized and became more efficient and as the American economy was deregulated, America's competitive position improved.[33] Between 1987 and 1992, U.S. enterprises accounted for 37 percent of sales and 48 percent of profits in global markets (compared with 15.5 and 31.5 percent and 36.8 and 31.1 percent for Japan and Europe, respectively). American industries accounted for over 50 percent of global sales in such sectors as energy equipment (92.7 percent), aerospace (75.8 percent), data processing and reproduction (73.2 percent), electronic components and instruments (61.8 percent), beverages and tobacco (63.4 percent), and forest products and paper (51 percent). Between 1990 and 1995, U.S. industry regained much of its competitive edge.[34]

TABLE 13.2
*Leading States and
Major Power
Resources*

Historical period	Leading state	Major resources
16th century	Spain	Gold bullion, colonial trade, mercenary armies, dynastic ties.
17th century	Netherlands	Trade, capital markets, navy.
18th century	France	Population, rural industry, public administration, army.
19th century	Britain	Industry, political cohension, finance and credit, navy, liberal norms, island location (defensibility).
20th century		Economic scale, scientific and technical leadership, universalistic culture, military forces and alliances, liberal international regimes, hub of transnational communications.

SOURCE: From *Bound to Lead: The Changing Nature of American Power* by Joseph S. Nye, Jr. Copyright © 1990 by Basic Books, Inc. Reprinted by permission.

Declared investment banker Felix Rohatyn: "We never realized how much we did in the 1980's to restructure American business and capitalize on new technology."[35] American corporations are the most thoroughly globalized in the world, producing about twice as much overseas as Japanese or European TNCs.[36] Although America's trade deficit continued to grow, much of it was due to the rising value of the dollar, America's buoyant consumers, and the flight of Asian investment to the safety of American securities.[37]

After 1986, the United States increased its share of exports of manufactured goods, regaining its position as the world's largest exporter by 1989. Inflation remained low, and unemployment was below that of other developed countries. Layoffs and cost-cutting made U.S. workers the most productive in the world, dropping U.S. unit labor costs below Japan's or Germany's,[38] and Americans began to lecture Europeans and Asians about the need to deregulate their economies, reduce state intervention, and open their markets. Declared the real estate developer and publisher Mortimer B. Zuckerman: "Let us celebrate an American triumph. The mantra is privatize, deregulate and do not interfere with the market."[39] American *triumphalism*—belief in the superiority of America's free-wheeling version of capitalism—had replaced the earlier declinism.

Who is likely to challenge America's economic primacy in the twenty-first century? Despite current economic woes in Asia, most observers still regard that continent—especially Japan, China, and the "tigers" such as Hong Kong, Singapore, Taiwan, South Korea, Thailand, and Malaysia—as the site of much of the world's economic growth in coming decades. Before Asia experienced the economic crisis that began in the summer of 1997, the World Bank had forecast an annual average economic growth of 7.6 percent in East Asia between 1994 and 2003 compared to 2.7 percent for rich industrial countries.[40]

It was the belief in Asia's rosy economic future that led the United States to follow up a suggestion made by Australian Prime Minister Bob Hawke for an enormous free-trade area to span the Pacific Ocean.[41] In 1993, the leaders of fifteen countries that abut the Pacific—Australia, Brunei, Canada, China, Hong Kong,[42]

ACTORS SPEAK

Has there been a genuine renaissance of the American economy in the 1990s, or is American's apparent prosperity simply a willingness on the part of Americans to limit their economic horizons and expectations? The first quotation reflects the former belief and the second reflects the latter.

People had written off the innovative character of American entrepreneurs and their workers, and they were wrong. They had emphasized our troubles, the slower economic growth, the downsizing, the uneven distribution of income. These are real issues, but they had gotten out of proportion to the industrial renaissance that has been taking place. (President of the National Association of Manufacturers, Jerry J. Jasinowski, as cited in Louis Uchitelle, "The Rehabilitation of Morning in America," *New York Times,* February 23, 1997 sec. 4, p. 1)

It is a little like people are saying, "I am not earning enough to get by, but it is not as bad as it could be," while in the 60's they thought, "How good can it get?" When you make that downward change in your standard of judgment, that makes a great deal of difference in the national outlook. (Director of the University of Michigan's Survey Research Center, Richard T. Curtin, as cited in Louis Uchitelle, "The Rehabilitation of Morning in America," *New York Times,* February 23, 1997 sec. 4, pp. 1, 4)

Indonesia, Japan, Malaysia, New Zealand, the Philippines, Singapore, South Korea, Taiwan, Thailand, and the United States (Mexico, Chile, and Papua New Guinea were added later)—with a combined GNP of $14 trillion, gathered in Seattle for the first *Asia-Pacific Economic Cooperation (APEC)* forum. As of 1997, these countries accounted for over half the world's economic output in goods and services,[43] and the value of U.S. exports to the original fourteen rose from $92 billion in 1988 to $129 billion in 1992.[44] That year the value of U.S.-Pacific Rim exports and imports was $343 billion, compared with $206 billion with European Union (EU) members.[45] The United States exports more to Taiwan than to France, and has greater trade with China than with Britain or France.[46]

American leaders have high hopes for APEC, and it symbolizes growing U.S. attention to the Pacific Rim and its booming markets. The American objectives that it serves include establishing a regular forum to negotiate with China, providing a means to bring diplomatic pressure on the European Union, and reducing Asian suspicions about the United States.[47] President Clinton declared that APEC "is about the jobs and futures and incomes of the American people," and then U.S. Secretary of State Warren Christopher called the 1993 meeting a "vision statement," comparing it to "a NATO meeting in 1950."[48] Carrying the comparison further, one observer wrote: "If Harry S Truman was the midwife who attended the birth of new Atlantic institutions such as NATO in the years following victory in World War II, President Clinton pictures himself as the godfather of new linkages in the Pacific in the aftermath of the Cold War."[49]

The optimistic tone of a meeting of APEC finance ministers in Honolulu in March 1994 contrasted with the gloom at a jobs conference among the leaders of the seven major industrialized states (G-7) held in Detroit shortly before. Referring to European concerns about unemployment, the Malaysian foreign minister remarked:"We couldn't have been invited to Detroit. Our problem is a labor shortage."[50] At a second meeting in Jakarta in 1994, APEC members reached a nonbinding "declaration of common resolve" called the *Bogor Declaration* to establish "free and open trade and investment" among themselves by the year 2020 (2010 for industrial members),[51] but, at the third meeting in 1995, with a dubious Republican majority in Congress and President Clinton unable to attend because of a budget stalemate in Washington, little progress was made toward realizing the APEC idea.[52] Although the APEC summit held in the Philippines in late 1996 endorsed a nonbinding plan to reduce tariffs on information technologies, American efforts to speed up reduction of trade barriers among APEC members met resistance from the Asians.[53] The following year Peru, Vietnam, and Russia were invited to join APEC.

For the most part, however, the 1997 APEC summit in Vancouver was preoccupied with Asia's financial woes, and Asia's optimism about its economic future turned to gloom in the midst of collapsing currencies and stock markets. As economic turmoil engulfs Asia, the continent's economic and political future continues to center on two traditional adversaries—Japan and China. America's relations with both have had ups and downs, and Asia's economic future and, indeed, the world's economic future depend heavily on events in those two countries.

Japan—Rising or Falling?

Japan's economy is eight times larger than China's and twice as big as the rest of Asia's.[54] Until recently, Japan was viewed as the principal challenger to U.S. economic dominance. Its transformation from a devastated and occupied nation in 1945 to a prosperous power in the 1990s is one of the most remarkable stories of the late twentieth century. The question remains whether Japan's recent economic woes are long-term or short-term and whether the country has the will and capacity to become a hegemonic leader in the future and, if so, what sort of leader it will be.

Pre–World War II Japan   Japan left feudal isolation[55] after a U.S. fleet arrived in Tokyo Bay in 1853. Emulating the West, Japan then became Asia's first industrialized nation. As a result of its victory in the Sino-Japanese War of 1894–1895, Japan gained Taiwan (called Formosa) and, like its imperial rivals in Europe, made territorial inroads in China. In 1902, Japan became the first Asian state to conclude an alliance with a European power (Great Britain), and this treaty (which aimed to balance Russian power in Asia) gave Japan a claim on German colonies in Asia after World War I. With its defeat of a European power in the Russo-Japanese War of 1904–1905, Japan's influence in Asia grew. By 1910, Japan had annexed Korea and extended its involvement in Manchuria at the expense of China and Russia.

In the following years, Japan expanded its influence in Asia. A desperate search for markets during the Great Depression set off its seizure of Manchuria and growing involvement in the rest of China. Rivalry with Russia (in Mongolia), fear of Soviet communism, and friction with the United States and Britain caused Japan to cast its lot with the Axis in the Anti-Comintern Pact (1936).

With militarists controlling the cabinet, Japan invaded China in 1937 despite U.S. opposition. In 1940, Japanese leaders began to plan to extend Tokyo's influence in Asia and eliminate the Western presence in the region. Alarmed by U.S. economic sanctions, Japan called for a "Greater East Asia Co-prosperity Sphere" that would include Japan, Manchuria, China, and Southeast Asia. On December 7, 1941, Japan attacked the U.S. Pacific fleet and sent its armies into Southeast Asia. At its peak, the Japanese Empire included all of Southeast Asia, Indonesia, and the island chains in the South Pacific and stretched to the frontiers of Alaska, Australia, and British India. And, in the course of their conquests, as one observer recalls, "Japanese atrocities were infamous."

> In 1937 the Japanese army slaughtered at least 100,000 Chinese, mostly civilians, when it captured Nanjing. Japan forced at least 100,000 women into sexual servitude as "comfort women." Medical units indulged in thousands of experiments, including vivisection on Chinese civilians and allied prisoners of war. The sacking of Manila, the dreadful treatment of prisoners of war, about a third of whom died in captivity, the enforced Bataan march in the Philippines (which killed 33,000 out of 78,000 allied prisoners on it), are all an indictment of Japan's brutal militarism.[56]

Postwar Reconstruction   The attack on Pearl Harbor was the beginning of the end of Japan's stab at global preeminence. Japan's defeat was complete. The United States demanded Japan's unconditional surrender,[57] called for Tokyo to renounce war, and restricted Japan's sovereignty. The Allies also placed stringent conditions on Japan's reconstruction, calling for new political institutions and weakening the country's powerful *zaibatsu,* its giant industrial and financial institutions. The country remained under U.S. occupation until 1952 and was governed by General Douglas MacArthur, who directed Japan's reconstruction and its adoption of a new constitution.

As a consequence of defeat and occupation, Japanese society was restructured. First, military influence on political life was eliminated, and Article 9 of the new constitution proclaimed that "the Japanese people forever renounce war as a sovereign right of the nation and the threat or use of force as means of settling international disputes" and "land, sea, and air forces, as well as other war potential, will never be maintained."[58] Second, a new generation was thrust into leadership, and the old prewar conservative elements lost power. Third, efforts were made to increase workers' power with a revitalized trade-union movement. In this way, Japanese society was restructured in a manner more compatible with Western values.

The reconstruction of Japan after 1945 was rapid. The new democratic constitution was promulgated by early 1947. Economic recovery was a key objective.

Entrepreneurial activity was encouraged, emphasizing new technologies. By 1950, helped by the Korean War, Japan had embarked on a period of accelerated economic growth. Growth rates averaged about 10 percent a year in the 1960s and 1970s and continued to outpace those of most other industrial societies in the 1980s.

With economic and political reform under way, Japan was ready to regain its independence. In 1952, fifty-one former enemies signed a Treaty of Peace with Japan,[59] and Washington and Tokyo signed a mutual-security pact. The United States committed itself to protect Japan from external attack, thereby allowing Tokyo to emphasize economic growth without the burden of military spending. The mutual-security treaty ushered in an extended period of close bilateral ties between the two countries.

For much of the Cold War, the United States was willing to provide security for Japan, even at significant cost. The arrangement not only served the policy of containment but harnessed a mighty economic engine to the forces opposed to Soviet communism. As the Cold War waned and the Japanese economic challenge grew, the United States became less willing to underwrite the security relationship.

Japanese Economic Power

As Japan recovered after World War II, it mobilized its economy to promote exports by capturing and holding foreign markets in key sectors, especially those at the high end of the technological chain. In the initial postwar decades, Japan dominated low-cost and low-technology sectors and, with each success, moved into more sophisticated sectors. The economy became a veritable export machine in which the Ministries of Finance and of International Trade and Industry worked hand in hand with big business to promote industries that would enhance the country's global competitiveness.

Japan's industrial policy contrasted with America's free-market approach. Its economic ministries attracted the country's most talented university graduates (unlike in the United States), and bureaucrats single-mindedly pursued the goal of increasing exports no matter what the preferences of elected politicians.[60] "The real equivalent of the Japanese Ministry of International Trade and Industry (MITI) in the United States," declared one observer, "is not the Department of Commerce but the Department of Defense, which by its very nature and functions shares MITI's strategic, goal-oriented outlook."[61]

Japan's emphasis on exports led to its dominance of some key industries. On a worldwide scale, Japanese automobiles—Toyota, Honda, Mitsubishi, Mazda, Nissan, Isuzu—began to dominate the market in many countries and were highly regarded for quality and dependability.[62] In the electronics and communications industries, Japanese corporations like Sony and Matsushita became world leaders. "Under the leadership of its elite bureaucracy," wrote one Japanese critic, "Japan's homogeneous, group-oriented society has striven to improve its standard of living and to avoid dependence on or intrusion by outsiders. It has done so by ... focusing all of its enormous energy on building an industrial structure with comparative advantage and bargaining power."[63]

In trade, Japan became a superpower. As the U.S. trade deficit worldwide increased, Japan enjoyed record trade surpluses, and the United States relied on Japanese investment to help pay its budget deficits. Throughout the 1970s and 1980s, except for the oil crises in 1973–1974 and 1979–1980, Japan had a positive trade balance. Following both crises, Japan's export economy rebounded, and its current account surplus (the difference between exports and imports) ballooned. In recent years, recession at home combined with a relatively cheap yen are increasing Japanese trade surpluses again (over $66 billion in 1996),[64] after a period during which they had begun to shrink.

As Japanese industry began to outperform American industry in highly visible sectors, some observers predicted growing U.S. dependence on Japan for high-technology products. "As a result of the hollowing of its industry," wrote one Japan-basher, "the United States no longer makes hundreds of products, ranging from ceramic semiconductor packages to bicycle tires to VCRs. . . . The composition of the trade has made the United States look ever more like a developing country. It imports high technology goods and capital from Japan and . . . exports to it mostly commodities, such as logs and soybeans. . . ."[65]

Not surprisingly, the growth of Japanese economic power created unease in the United States. Between 1970 and 1992, Japanese GDP increased almost twenty times, more than doubling West Germany's and making it almost ten times the size of Russia's, prompting two observers to write:

> At the end of the 1980s, the biggest problem the world economy posed to Japan was . . . how to recycle the staggering wealth of its external assets. These assets have been estimated to reach $470 billion in 1990, more than twice the combined external assets of the members of the Organization of Petroleum Exporting Countries (OPEC) at the height of the second oil crisis. . . .[66]

The volume of trade between the two countries is high. Japan is America's second-largest trading partner, and the United States is Japan's largest source of imports. However, as the U.S.-Japanese trade imbalance grew, their relations frayed. In 1982, the United States had a trade deficit of $19 billion with Japan. Five years later the deficit hit $60 billion[67] and surged past that in 1993 and 1994 because of recession in Japan, U.S. economic recovery, and a strong yen that inflated the dollar value of Japan's surplus.[68] American purchases of Japanese cars and auto parts ($40.1 billion in 1994 compared with $3.1 billion in Japanese purchases of U.S. cars and auto parts)[69] accounted for the largest portion of the deficit.[70] The United States and Europe accounted for about two-thirds of Japan's total 1992 trade surplus of $132.3 billion (up from $63.5 billion in 1990).[71] During the 1990s, however, healthy expansion of the U.S. economy and the growing competitiveness of U.S. industry, combined with Japan's prolonged recession, reduced U.S. unease.

Changing patterns of foreign investment were a second indicator of Japan's growing economic role. Between 1985 and 1990 Japan invested more than $650 billion abroad, nearly half of which went to the United States,[72] and Japanese purchases of U.S. government securities helped pay the interest costs on America's budget deficit.[73] However, in 1991, after five years in which Japan's direct overseas investment outstripped U.S. direct foreign investment, the United States regained the lead and has held it since. A combination of recession and an inflated yen reduced the rate of direct Japanese foreign investment from $48 billion in 1990 to $18 billion in 1994. In 1993, U.S. direct foreign investment jumped to $69 billion, or three times the next biggest investor, and in the first nine months of 1995 the annual rate was up to $74 billion, more than double the 1992 figure.[74] Americans again accounted for the lion's share of total foreign investment, much of which went to China.[75]

By the late 1990s, the Japanese banking system was on the verge of collapse, burdened by nonperforming loans and declining assets. How had this happened? A fall in the yen's value in the mid-1980s made Japanese exports less competitive and forced Japanese firms to increase their borrowing dramatically. Loans were guaranteed by real estate and corporate stock. In the early 1990s, however, Japan's stock market plummeted and property values collapsed. Rather than reducing loans, Japanese banks loaned more and more money to bail out borrowers.[76] By mid-1998, bad loans were the equivalent of 12 percent of Japan's GDP,[77] and pressure was building to make Japan clean up its banking mess.[78]

During the heyday of Japan's economic growth, its currency—the yen—challenged the U.S. dollar in investor's eyes. Wide fluctuations in the dollar's value, U.S. budget deficits, and the continuing boom-bust cycle in the U.S. economy made the yen a desirable haven for investors. In June 1994, the dollar slid below 100 yen for the first time (having sold as late as 1985 at 250 to a dollar),[79] and, in April 1995, the yen hit an all-time high, selling below 80 to the dollar.[80] Even the concerted efforts of the U.S. Federal Reserve and fifteen other central banks did not end the slide until late summer 1995.[81] The dollar's plunge was partly intentional U.S. policy, because a weak dollar reduces American imports and lowers the cost of American exports, thereby reducing the trade deficit. Other factors in the dollar's decline were high U.S. budget deficits, talk of tax cuts in Washington, fallout from the collapse of the Mexican peso, and relatively low U.S. interest rates.

One result of the strong yen was to make goods produced in Japan for export more expensive and to reduce the value of Japanese investments in the United States.[82] Another was the movement of Japanese industry offshore to other countries, especially in Asia, and to some extent the United States as well. By the mid-1990s, Canon, the giant Japanese camera company, was making 70 percent of its cameras in Taiwan, Malaysia, and China, and Japan's auto manufacturers were increasingly assembling cars for the U.S. market at plants in North America. This trend meant higher unemployment in Japan and led one angry Japanese minister to say that America was using "very diligent Japanese" as "slaves."[83] It also meant a decline in Japan's trade surplus as Japanese-owned plants in other countries exported back to Japan.[84] The weak dollar had other effects, including raising the costs of U.S. operations overseas. In 1995, the drop in the dollar's value meant that Pentagon costs overseas jumped by $700 million and State Department costs rose by $20 million.[85]

A number of other events in the 1990s clouded Japan's future. In 1993 the Liberal Democratic Party (LDP) that had ruled Japan since World War II[86] splintered, ushering in a period of political instability,[87] and by 1998 it appeared that a two-party system might be emerging.[88] In addition, Japan was the victim of various disasters, such as the Kobe earthquake and a poison gas attack on the Tokyo subway that reduced the country's aura of invincibility.

Most importantly, while the U.S. economy surged, Japan remained mired in recession, one result of which has been to cast doubt on the continued value of the Japanese economic model. By mid-1998, after two quarters of economic contraction, Japan was officially in recession, and the yen had fallen from its peak by some 45 percent against the dollar.[89] With foreign-exchange reserves of more than $200 billion, however, Japan was not hobbled to the extent of its Asian neighbors.[90] However, instead of fearing Japanese economic might, observers were concerned that Japan could not lead Asia out of its economic crisis and that an economic collapse in Japan itself was not out of the question.[91]

In consequence, foreign pressure mounted on Japanese leaders to adopt economic reforms like deregulation, new banking regulations, and reduction of corporate debt and to jump-start its economy by permanently reducing taxes at home in order to stimulate domestic demand. Unfortunately, the absence of strong political leadership in Japan, its deeply entrenched interest groups, and the continued influence of its permanent bureaucrats make it difficult for the country to undertake the vigorous reforms[92] needed to restore economic health.[93]

United States–Japanese Economic Frictions

On June 28, 1995, mere hours before U.S. imposition of $5.9 billion in tariffs on Japanese luxury cars, negotiators stepped back from the brink of a U.S.-Japanese trade war over Japanese purchases of U.S. cars and auto parts.[94] For months, the two countries had been on a collision course, with U.S. demands that Japan modify its auto-inspection system to make it easier for U.S. companies to sell parts, increase the number of dealers who sell U.S. cars in Japan, and set numerical targets for purchases of U.S.-made auto parts as part of a "results-oriented approach" to judging trade progress.

Many Americans resent restrictions on access to the Japanese market and the "dumping" of Japanese goods at unfairly low prices on the U.S. market. One observer described Japan's trade relations as "a monstrous burden on the world's trade system,"[95] and U.S. industries that fare poorly against Japanese competitors complain that the "playing field" is not even, because of regulations that act as non-tariff barriers. For example, Tokyo required that imported tulips be inspected individually for germs and that imported pharmaceutical products like Tylenol be tested on Japanese clinical subjects.[96] Complicated rules and procedures—excessive red tape—and chummy alliances (called *keiretsu* relationships) among Japanese manufacturers, suppliers, and distributors prevented foreign companies from entering the Japanese market. Thus Eastman-Kodak claims that Fuji Photo Film Company keeps Kodak out of the Japanese market by pressuring Japan's four big film distributors. Fuji has stock in two of them, owns banks that lend to them, and provides them with year-end rebates. Fuji also controls hundreds of photofinishing labs.[97]

Bilateral trade negotiations going back to 1978, when the United States demanded that Japan increase import quotas on beef and citrus,[98] have resembled elaborate chicken games, with U.S. demands and threats against Japan followed by Japanese promises at the last minute. Repeatedly, talks between what a Japanese newspaper called "American lawyers who do not know economics" and "Japan's stone-headed bureaucrats" produced vague agreements that the two sides interpreted differently.[99] In 1993, the United States threatened sanctions against Japanese construction companies unless Japan opened its public-works market to foreign bidders,[100] and pressed Tokyo to ease complex regulations that frustrated foreign companies.[101] At a 1993 Tokyo summit, President Clinton and Japanese

Are the Big Three simply ignoring Japan's open car market?

Who's the biggest winner if Japanese cars are restricted in the U.S.? Ford, GM and Chrysler, of course. And now that the Big Three have successfully used their muscle to persuade the Administration to ban certain Japanese cars from the market, consumers want to know why.

The Big Three have been ignoring Japan's auto market for years. Yet now they claim that the Japanese are shutting them out. But that's not the case when you take a look at the facts:

JAPANESE AUTO MARKET FACTS	THE BIG THREE
60% of the Japanese market is small cars	Do not offer one U.S.-built small car
20% of the Japanese market is midget cars	Do not make a single midget car
Imported autos account for 28% of large car sales in Japan	Wrongly claim the Japanese market is closed

The facts don't lie. The Big Three want to ban Japanese auto imports while they ignore the Japanese market.

And the Administration is going along for the ride.

JAMA
Japan Automobile Manufacturers Association, Inc.
1050 17th Street, NW • Washington, DC 20036

American auto companies repeatedly argue for limits on Japanese exports of cars to the United States, claiming that Japan's market is closed to their exports. This advertisement presents the Japanese side of the issue, arguing that America's "Big Three" (GM, Ford, and Chrysler) have simply failed to produce cars with the features that Japanese consumers want. (*Japan Automobile Manufacturers Association*)

Prime Minister Kiichi Miyazawa tried to paper over differences with a vague "framework" calling for lower U.S. budget deficits and easier access to Japanese markets.[102] In 1994, the United States successfully pressured Japan to open up a range of previously closed financial markets and then demanded that Tokyo change its policies regarding cellular telephones, civil aviation, medical equipment, government procurement practices, patent policies, glass, and insurance.[103] Within days of the auto settlement, the United States was again threatening Japan, this time over international air routes.[104]

Many Japanese resent U.S. pressure tactics. In a 1993 poll, almost two-thirds of Japanese respondents described U.S.-Japanese relations as "unfriendly," and only 6 percent had "favorable" feelings about President Clinton. Eighty-five percent thought "the United States is blaming Japan for its own economic problems."[105]

Some bilateral talks tried to deal with underlying sources of U.S.-Japanese trade quarrels. In 1989 the United States and Japan agreed to the *Structural Impediments Initiative (SII)* to study impediments to U.S. economic efficiency and competitiveness such as low savings and investment patterns and Japanese barriers to free trade such as land use and retail and distribution practices.

Unfortunately, the SII mainly inflamed public opinion and demonstrated how intractable are social and cultural barriers. By 1991, most Japanese (70 percent) believed that Americans "look down on the Japanese," and resent Japan's economic success.[106] The real problem, they believed, was that Americans were unwilling "to respect the differences among people who live outside the United States."[107] American society is "deteriorating," declared one Japanese diplomat: "Everyone is either fighting or hiring lawyers, and America's ability to integrate different elements into a melting pot is weakening. So Americans are looking for scapegoats and blaming Japan."[108]

To tame protectionist sentiment at home, U.S. leaders tried to get Japan to agree to subtle forms of joint protectionism, most importantly, *orderly marketing agreements* that place quotas on imports or guarantee exporters a specified share of a market. Such agreements, which limit free trade and avoid uncertainty, constitute *managed trade.* In 1991, under U.S. pressure, Japan set a numerical target under which imported computer chips would have 20 percent of Japan's market by the end of 1992. When imports fell below this target in 1993, the United States placed added pressure on Japan.[109] Since then, U.S. negotiators have pressed Japan to specify numerical targets for other U.S. products because voluntary plans to buy more U.S. goods had not worked. Recalling the computer-chip agreement, the Japanese argue that such targets are used by Americans to interfere with the decisions of private corporations.

In 1993 the Clinton administration demanded specific targets for reducing Japan's trade surplus but settled for a pledge of a "significant" reduction, and the 1995 autos agreement only included vague goals by Japan's auto companies to increase production at plants in the United States and purchase more U.S. auto parts. At the same time as Americans fear that compromise with Japan will make others like South Korea[110] and China unwilling to open markets to U.S. exports, Japan has become more willing to say no to U.S. demands, and some Japanese fear the prospect of U.S. hegemony.[111] Cooler heads in both countries realize that, if the pattern of U.S. bullying and Japanese intransigence persists, it may harm bilateral political and military ties, which are important to both. Says one observer: "The president [Clinton] may have fancied that he would have the glory of 'opening Japan,' as a sort of modern-day Commodore Perry. That historical parallel will not work. The tragedy is that, by persisting in the current policy, he may put two great nations on a course that may repeat history in less agreeable ways."[112]

American anger over Japanese trade barriers was exacerbated by exaggerated fears in the early 1990s of Japanese investments in the United States.[113] American sensitivity to Japanese investment was intensified by perceived Japanese unwillingness to accept U.S. investment in Japan. Before the 1980s, Japan limited foreign investment in various ways, entirely excluding it in some sectors. And even with legal barriers eliminated, foreign investment is still restricted by exclusive national industrial associations, unavailability of stock in Japanese firms that is held by other Japanese firms, and nationalist sentiments that promote purchase of Japanese products even when they are more expensive than imports.

Some of the strain Japanese investment produced in the United States eased after lower U.S. interest rates in the 1990s induced Japanese investors to look elsewhere for higher yields, and large Japanese corporations began to enter into consortiums and joint ventures with former U.S. adversaries like Intel rather than trying to buy them up. Such alliances, involving research and marketing, were an innovative response to the high costs of getting new high-technology products to the market.[114]

Frictions in U.S.-Japanese trade relations also began to ease as the U.S.-Japan trade imbalance moderated in the 1990s.[115] Slowly, the *keiretsu* system has begun to loosen,[116] and foreign firms have begun to penetrate the Japanese market.[117] Japanese-owned factories in the United States provided jobs for Americans, reduced the need to import certain products, and increased exports from the United States to Asia. In addition, the aging of Japan's population may reduce the country's rate of saving and increase its consumption rate.[118] Most importantly, greater productivity means that American firms can now compete with anyone.

Whether U.S.-Japanese trade friction will explode again in the coming years is unclear. Japan's prolonged recession has reduced the Japanese appetite for foreign goods, and a weak yen gives Japanese exporters an opportunity to increase exports to the United States.[119] Economic turmoil in Asia and the depreciation of most Asian currencies have dramatically reduced the demand for Japanese goods, thereby increasing the importance of the American market for Japanese exporters. If Japan tries to work its way out of its economic malaise by exporting rather than by deregulating and opening its economy, U.S.-Japanese trade relations will again worsen.[120]

Economic conflicts exacerbate general cultural and social differences between the two societies. Americans emphasize individual achievement, whereas Japanese stress collective success. Thus Americans seek a higher personal standard of living, whereas many Japanese derive satisfaction through their corporation and nation. Americans are, as a rule, less willing than Japanese to postpone gratification and so spend more of their income on consumption and save less. However, the Japanese pay a steep price for saving as much as they do. Spending little on personal consumption, many live in cramped housing and enjoy less leisure than their American counterparts. Barriers to foreign imports raise prices and reduce the quality and variety of goods available to Japan's consumers, who "have enjoyed less than their full share of Japan's economic growth."[121]

Economic frictions also strain the two countries' political relations. In recent years, Washington has pressed Tokyo to shoulder more of its security burden[122] by increasing defense spending, assuming greater responsibility for keeping Asian sea lanes open, and paying a bigger share of the costs of basing more than 60,000 U.S. military personnel in Japan.[123] Washington's demand that Japan pay much of the cost of the Gulf War also strained the U.S.-Japanese relationship.

By 1995, relations were so frayed that a dispute broke out within the U.S. government, with an assistant secretary of defense declaring that Japan might alter its long-term strategy of alliance with the United States to free itself from U.S. pressure and an undersecretary of commerce answering, "We have no intention of undermining the security relationship with Japan or using our military presence there as a tool of trade."[124] Japanese anger at U.S. soldiers was heightened by a series of highly publicized incidents including the rape of a young girl on Okinawa.[125] From Japan's perspective, there remain serious potential security problems, most importantly rivalry with China,[126] and in 1997 the United States and Japan agreed to cooperate militarily beyond Japan's boundaries.[127]

Will Japan transform its economic assets into political and military leverage? It has the technology to become a nuclear military power, and its aid programs and investments in cash-starved economies can provide political clout. Russia and China compete for Japanese investment and technology; Southeast Asia depends on Tokyo for prosperity; and even the United Nations is trying to harness Japanese economic might to peacekeeping efforts. To date, Japan has been reluctant to assert itself politically, anxious that it might arouse memories of World War II. But, if history provides any lessons, one is that an economic power—for example, the United States after 1919—cannot long evade the political and military responsibilities that follow.

China: Coming Pacific Superpower?

Modern China dates from the efforts of the Kuomintang (National Party) led by Jiang Jieshi (Chiang Kai-shek) and aided by Soviet advisers in 1926–1927 to overcome China's warlords and reunify the country. Between 1923 and 1927, the Kuomintang cooperated with China's Communist Party, but in April 1927 Jiang turned upon his former allies in what one observer declares "a bloody betrayal."[128] For more than two decades thereafter, even during China's war of resistance against Japan (1937–1945), the country remained in the grip of civil war between Jiang's followers and the communists led by Mao Zedong (Mao Tse-tung). To escape their nationalist foes, the communists in late 1934 embarked on their epic "Long March" of over 6,000 miles from Jiangxi to the remote vastness of Shaanxi. There, they established the base they would use to fight both China's Japanese invaders and their Kuomintang enemies.

Despite mediation efforts by American emissaries, notably Generals Patrick J. Hurley and George C. Marshall, communist-nationalist hostilities intensified as World War II drew to an end. Jiang's strategy of maintaining control of China's cities, combined with Kuomintang corruption and mismanagement, squandered public support and whatever military advantages the nationalists enjoyed. In contrast, Mao's strategy of guerrilla warfare was highly effective. In 1949 Jiang's regime collapsed, and the nationalists fled to Taiwan. Mao proclaimed the People's Republic of China on October 1, 1949.

From Mao's Communist Revolution to Deng's Reforms

Chinese communist hostility to the United States intensified when, after the beginning of the Korean War in 1950, the United States embraced Jiang's regime on Taiwan and refused to recognize the communist government in Beijing. When the Chinese communists intervened in the Korean War in October 1950, the hostility deepened. However, the zero-sum perceptions that dominated U.S.-Chinese relations in the 1950s began to erode when the Chinese communists had a falling out with the Soviet Union in the mid-1960s, culminating in violent clashes along their common frontier in 1968 and 1969.

In 1958, Mao launched what he called the *"Great Leap Forward."* John King Fairbank describes this as "a mighty paroxysm of round-the-clock labor. The face of the country was changed with new roads, factories, cities, dikes, dams, lakes, afforestation, and cultivation, for which the 650 million Chinese had been mobilized in nationwide efforts of unparalleled intensity and magnitude."[129] The Great Leap lasted until 1960, during which time, declares Fairbank, "some 20 to 30 million people lost their lives through malnutrition and famine because of the policies imposed upon them by the Chinese Communist Party."[130] The Great Leap proved an economic disaster; ideological zealotry was no substitute for economic and managerial competence.

Only six years later the same zealotry was unleashed by Mao in China's *"Cultural Revolution,"* which lasted until 1976 ("ten years of turmoil"). Fearing that the Communist Party and government bureaucrats, aided by China's intellectuals, were undermining his revolution and abandoning its radical roots, Mao mobilized his followers, especially teenage students called the Red Guards, to attack party and state institutions and their leaders. Thousands of Chinese officials, including then party secretary-general Deng Xiaoping, were denounced, purged, publicly humiliated, and, in many cases, imprisoned or even murdered. It was as though, in Fairbank's words, "the president in Washington urged high school students all over the United States to put on armbands, accost, upbraid, and harass citizens on the streets and in their homes and finally take over city hall, local business firms, government services, and institutions."[131]

Mao died on September 9, 1976, but already China was in the hands of Mao's wife Jiang Qing and three of her supporters (later called the Gang of Four). They were, however, outmaneuvered by Deng Xiaoping, who by 1978 had become China's "paramount leader." The Gang of Four were put on trial and convicted in 1977 for their misdeeds during the Cultural Revolution, and Deng began to lead his country down a very different road than it had traveled before. Deng's reforms were both in foreign and domestic policy.

In foreign policy, Deng completed the normalization of relations with the United States that had begun in 1972 with President Richard Nixon's visit to China, and full diplomatic relations were established in 1979.[132] At home, Deng began to decentralize and privatize agriculture, which led to enormous gains in productivity, and in industry he opened his country to foreign trade, technology, and investment. Under Deng, China embarked upon the "four modernizations": agriculture, industry, science, and defense. By the time of his death in 1997, China had privatized much of the country's industry, was providing incentives for entrepreneurial initiatives, had become the target of enormous direct foreign investment, and had established a modernized sector of its economy, especially in Guangdong Province, coastal regions adjacent to Hong Kong and further south around Shanghai.

Indeed, one can speak of two Chinas, one the modernized urban areas witnessing a capitalist revolution, and increasingly integrated in a globalized economic system, and the other, much of rural China and the northern cities, especially Beijing, in which is located much of China's remaining state-owned industry (much of which is actually owned and operated by the People's Liberation Army). The new China "might be called the 'blue' China: coastal, outward-looking, cosmopolitan, tolerant and increasingly sophisticated." By contrast, the old or "brown" China "embodied in much of the Communist Party" is "inward-looking, suspicious of markets, authoritarian or corrupt, and generally dirt poor."[133] Already as many as 100 million Chinese have been made unemployed by economic reforms, and the next and perhaps most worrisome challenge will be privatizing the country's remaining state enterprises and the inevitable unemployment and political discontent that will accompany that reform.

Embracing capitalism created a conundrum for Chinese leaders. Aware of the fact that economic liberalization in the Soviet Union had been accompanied by political turmoil and the collapse of communism, Chinese leaders are seeking a middle way that will provide the benefits of a (semi)open market while maintaining the authoritarian rule of the Chinese Communist Party.

Whether this is possible remains unclear. On the one hand, China's prosperous pockets of free enterprise enjoy unprecedented independence from Beijing, and its citizens are coming to enjoy many of the material benefits associated with the postinternational world in the West. On the other hand, economic modernization and integration into the globalized world economy have been accompanied by growing demands, especially among the young, for political democracy and is viewed by Chinese leaders as highly threatening. It is this perception that explains the brutal crackdown on June 3, 1989, on students who were demonstrating in Beijing's Tiananmen Square for greater democracy. That crackdown and China's subsequent violations of human rights remained one of the leading obstacles to better U.S.-Chinese relations, at least until President Clinton's landmark journey to Beijing nine years later.

The Emerging Economic and Political Colossus

China today is, in an economic context, much like Japan in the 1960s, growing rapidly, a huge exporter and target of foreign investment, but with high barriers to foreign imports. Thus American officials seek to avoid the mistakes made in earlier decades with Japan, moving Mickey Kantor to say: "We're determined not to get into the same position we got into with Japan."[134] Another observer declared that "the Chinese have read the Japanese playbook."[135]

Between 1992 and 1997, China's economy grew an average of 12 percent a year, with rising exports fueling a major part of this growth.[136] In 1996 alone, China attracted $40 billion in foreign investment, second only to the United States, and more private investment than all of Eastern Europe. Among the major transnational corporations that made commitments to invest heavily in China in 1995 and 1996 were Intel, Motorola, Sony, and Matsushita Electric, and they were following the lead of Proctor & Gamble, Coca-Cola, and Nestle.[137] Indeed, foreign companies are responsible for about three-quarters of China's exports. In 1985, foreign-owned factories produced only 1 percent of China's exports, but by 1996 that had increased to 44 percent.[138]

According to the World Bank, China will pass America as the world's biggest economy by about the year 2020.[139] As China's economy has grown and as America's economic ties with China have deepened, trade frictions have also intensified. China's explosive economic growth involves ever greater exports to the United States, especially of low-tech products. China sells roughly four times as much to the United States as it buys.[140] It accounts for about 27 percent of U.S. imports of consumer goods, including 69 percent of all toys sold in the United States (as any child who has collected toys at McDonald's knows).[141] And Chinese imports of U.S. capital goods doubled between 1991 and 1996.[142] Between 1980 and 1995, total trade between China and the United States grew from $4.8 billion to $57.3 billion, making China America's sixth-largest trading partner and providing an estimated 170,000 jobs for Americans.[143] Currently, China's exports are largely low-tech, like those of Japan to the United States in the 1950s and 1960s, but many observers anticipate that China will increasingly move into the production and export of high-tech products, as did Japan. In 1996, China passed Japan as the largest source of the U.S. trade deficit,[144] a deficit that by 1998 was over $50 billion.[145]

A variety of disagreements continue to bedevil U.S.-Chinese relations. One major source of contention, as we will see in Chapter 15, is Chinese human-rights abuses, especially against its pro-democracy activists and ethnic minorities, especially Tibetans.[146] The reason this is such a problem for bilateral relations is that the issue is deeply enmeshed in domestic politics in both China and the United States. Chinese authorities interpret efforts to impose human-rights reforms as interference in the country's domestic affairs aimed at loosening the Communist Party's authoritarian control. In the United States, the cause of Chinese dissidents has been taken up by an improbable coalition of liberals in the Democratic Party and social conservatives, especially Christian fundamentalists, in the Republican Party.

China's trade surplus produces howls of pain from American labor unions, which argue that U.S. jobs are being lost, and U.S. business, which claims that the Chinese have erected barriers to U.S. imports.[147] In addition, China's failure to prevent piracy of U.S. software, movies, and music led Washington to impose trade sanctions before a deal was struck and the Chinese began to carry out their promises to crack down on such piracy.[148] Chinese failure to open markets more fully to foreign goods is the reason given by the United States for its refusal to endorse China's entry into the World Trade Organization (WTO).[149] As Mickey Kantor declared: "We have continued concerns over market access in China within the industrial and agricultural sectors. We've been heartened to some degree by China's willingness to implement the second intellectual property agreement, but we've not made appreciable progress with regard to their accession to the W.T.O."[150] The Chinese have made an effort to meet American objections, but, until Beijing agreed to a variety of concessions in April 1999 during Premier Zhu Ronji's visit to the United States, it was difficult to get the United States to agree to China's admission to the WTO.[151] And the human-rights and trade-surplus issues are cited in annual efforts in the U.S. Congress[152] to block renewal of most-favored-nation (MFN) status for China.[153]

Another source of U.S.-Chinese conflict has been Chinese sales of sensitive military equipment that can facilitate nuclear proliferation.[154] For example, China apparently provided Pakistan with specialized magnets that were needed to enrich uranium for nuclear weapons.[155] The Chinese have also exported missile technology to Iran and probably others as well. Alleged Chinese theft of U.S. missile warhead technology aggravated relations in 1999. In addition, China's efforts to modernize its own military forces have disconcerted American leaders.

Perhaps the thorniest issue in U.S.-Chinese relations involves the status of Taiwan, which is regarded by Beijing as an integral part of China. American support of and aid to Jiang Jieshi's regime on Taiwan following the onset of the Korean War was regarded by the communists as intervention in China's civil war.

Until the early 1970s, the United States prevented Beijing from replacing Taiwan as China's representative in the United Nations, and the U.S. Seventh Fleet regularly patrolled the Taiwan Strait to deter any attack on Taiwan from the mainland. Since the early 1950s, Taiwan has enjoyed considerable influence within the Republican Party, and an American president has to tread warily lest he invite domestic controversy.[156] The Taiwan question heated up in 1995, when the United States permitted Taiwain's President Lee Teng-hui to visit the U.S. And, in March 1996, shortly before Taiwan's first presidential elections, China sought to intimidate the Taiwanese by conducting war games and missile tests in the Taiwan Strait. In response, the United States sent two aircraft carriers to the region. Beijing was concerned lest Taiwan seek sovereign independence.

After several years of severely strained relations, American and Chinese leaders have gingerly sought a rapprochement. China's President Jiang Zemin visited the United States in October 1997, and President Bill Clinton reciprocated by visiting China in June 1998. While in China, Clinton was permitted to go on television and speak directly to Chinese viewers.[157] This rapprochment was set back by the U.S. destruction of China's embassy in Belgrade in 1999.

During President Jiang's visit to Washington, the Chinese leader pledged to stop aiding Pakistan's nuclear program and to stop sending missiles to Iran. Agreement was reached to establish a hotline between Washington and Beijing (which was first used in May 1998 after India tested a nuclear device). During his trip to China, President Clinton publicly reaffirmed the so-called three "noes": (1) that there was only one China and that the United States favored the eventual (peaceful) reunification of Taiwan with the mainland, (2) that Taiwan should not be regarded as a government of China, and (3) that Taiwan should not be independent.

The two sides also agreed to stop targeting missiles at each other. In addition, the Chinese announced new trade and investment deals with American firms worth about $1.6 billion, in marked contrast to earlier purchases of European aircraft when relations with Washington were poor.[158] The Chinese are also making efforts to open up their domestic market and reduce impediments to foreign imports.[159] In human rights, China has agreed to sign the two major U.N. human-rights covenants though its willingness to abide by them is questionable. China has also agreed to reduce exports of high-tech weapons technology and is working closely with the United States to bring a halt to the nuclear arms race that is under way on the Indian subcontinent and to reduce tensions between the two Koreas. It is hardly surprising that talk of building a new "strategic partnership" between the United States and China was disconcerting to America's allies, especially Japan.[160]

Challenge from the West: The European Union and Germany

Another economic challenger is an enlarged European Union (EU). The reconstruction of Europe (and Germany in particular) has parallels to Japan's rebirth after 1945. Like Japan, Europe had suffered devastation, and many of its famous cities lay in ruins. Germany was divided and occupied, and even the victors' economies were badly weakened. Europe's reconstruction required massive infusions of U.S. economic aid.

European Integration   The first step in helping Europe was creating an environment in which reconstruction could take place. Following a European initiative—the Brussels Treaty (1948)—the United States and its European friends formed a military alliance—NATO (1949). Washington also began economic assistance with the Marshall Plan, contingent on Europeans coordinating their economies.[161] The two U.S. commitments—one providing a security environment to facilitate reconstruction and the other affording the tools for that reconstruction—enabled Europeans to start rebuilding. A primary U.S. objective was to encourage movement toward a united Europe as a counterweight to the threat from the East, as a tonic for the anemic postwar global economy, and as a way of preventing future European conflicts.

The idea of a united Europe—some spoke of a "United States of Europe"—led to a proposal in 1951 for establishing the *European Coal and Steel Community (ECSC)*. That scheme called for Belgium, West Germany, France, Italy, Luxembourg, and the Netherlands to pool coal and steel production under a supranational institution. The ECSC's aims were economic and political: to rehabilitate the German economy within a larger European context that would prevent a resurgence of German nationalism. Some of the ECSC founders had a more ambitious goal: to launch European regional integration. Once established in 1952, the ECSC had just that effect. Although a proposal for an integrated European army (the European Defense Community) died in 1954,[162] foreign ministers of "the Six" met in Messina, Sicily, in 1955 to examine other ways to advance European integration. The result was two treaties establishing the *European Atomic Energy Community (EURATOM)* and the *European Economic Community (EEC)* that were signed in Rome in March 1957. These reflected the neofunctionalist claim that integration has a "snowballing effect."

In contrast with EURATOM, which coordinated policy in a single sector, the EEC sought to expand economic cooperation into several areas of European life. It provided for common agricultural, industrial, and trade policies, eliminated tariff barriers, and established a common external tariff. Taken together, the pacts aimed "to preserve and strengthen peace, to achieve economic integration for the benefit of all the peoples of Europe through the creation of a large economic area, and to work towards political union."[163]

Novel political institutions were created in the EEC framework: a dual executive (Council of Ministers and European Commission), a legislature with limited powers (European Parliament), and a judiciary (European Court of Justice). Further institutional elaboration followed. The ECSC, EEC, and EURATOM integrated their executive structures in 1965, and a single Council of Ministers and Commission was established to govern all three communities, collectively renamed *European Community (EC)* and renamed *European Union (EU)* in 1993.

Institutional growth was accompanied by membership growth. In 1973, the members of a rival trading bloc, the European Free Trade Association (EFTA), were invited to join,[164] and three—Britain, Ireland, and Denmark—did so.[165] Greece followed in 1981, Spain and Portugal in 1986, and Sweden, Finland, and Austria in 1995.[166] In 1997, Poland, the Czech Republic, Estonia, Hungary, and Slovenia were invited to join the EU, having met the political (guarantees of democracy, human rights, and protection of minorities) and economic criteria (market economy, capacity to cope with a single market, and acceptance of the single European currency). Of the other countries that had expressed interest in joining, Slovakia did not meet the political criteria and Bulgaria, Romania, Lithuania, Latvia, and Malta did not meet the economic requirements.[167] Cyprus may join in 2002, an arrangement that infuriates the Turks, who were not even invited to begin negotiating with the EU.[168]

The European Community's greatest achievement was the prosperity that followed its creation. Several other goals were pursued, some meeting with greater success than others. First, the EC sought to eliminate customs duties on member states' products and establish a common external tariff. This was accomplished by 1968. Second, the EC sought to promote free movement by workers and capital and give citizens of member states the right to provide services anywhere in the community. These goals are approaching realization. Finally, the EC sought to foster common policies in various areas: agriculture, corporate mergers, transport, energy, and research. In agriculture, however, little policy coordination was achieved until the 1990s.

A major step toward integration was establishment of the *European Monetary System (EMS)* in 1978 to stimulate trade within Europe and to emulate centralized American monetary policy. The EMS created a new mechanism to calculate currency exchange rates, the European Currency Unit (ECU), whose value reflected a "basket" of European currencies. Currencies would be allowed to fluctuate in a narrow range before a state could intervene in foreign-exchange markets. However, Portugal and Spain (until 1989) remained outside the system, and Britain and Greece refused to accept the EMS exchange-rate mechanism. British reluctance was troubling because the pound sterling is a *reserve currency*—a currency that countries hold because of its strength and stability.

Although tariffs no longer obstructed trade, national standards and regulations impeded common policy. Recognizing these impediments, the EC proposed the *Single Market Act* of 1985 to create an area in "which persons, goals, and capital shall move freely under conditions identical to those obtaining within a Member State."[169] The EC was to become a free internal market for all goods and services by December 31, 1992, unobstructed by tariff or nontariff barriers. Completing "Europe '92" provided a formidable task. This ambitious project required numerous specific community-wide changes to standardize laws ranging from those governing corporate mergers to those setting tax rates.[170] The European Commission developed 282 directives to eliminate technical, fiscal, and physical barriers to trade.

"Europe '92" got a push when members completed a 250-page draft treaty for economic and political union at a meeting in Maastricht, the Netherlands, in December 1991. Members agreed to establish common foreign and defense policies and to create a single currency by the end of the century. They also agreed to an *exchange-rate mechanism (ERM)*, under which currencies could fluctuate only in a narrow range, thereby giving muscle to the 1979 European Monetary System (EMS). The treaty represented genuine "spillover" because the EU was granted greater authority over more issues than in the past.

The *Maastricht Treaty* (also called the Treaty on European Union) required members' unanimous ratification, and difficulty in achieving this, especially in Denmark, France, and Great Britain,[171] showed how hard it is to move from economic to political and monetary union.[172] The obstacles to monetary integration were evident when Europe's exchange-rate mechanism virtually collapsed in speculative storms in the autumn of 1992 and the summer of 1993. The two crises[173]—the consequence of different macroeconomic policies of Germany, its partners, especially France, and the United States—provided further evidence that governments no longer had adequate resources to control global monetary flows. They also reinforced the doubts of euroskeptics, as well as the conviction of euro-enthusiasts that currency stability could only be achieved with a single currency.

Despite all the obstacles, the EU is achieving economic and monetary union (EMU), with a common currency (called the euro) and a European Central Bank in Frankfurt to regulate monetary policy,[174] but the road was a bumpy one[175] before final agreement was reached in May 1998. For a time, it appeared that virtually no EU member could meet the strict economic criteria set at Maastrict for joining the EMU—an annual budget deficit of no more than 3 percent of GNP, total public debt of no more than 60 percent of GNP, short-term interest rates below 6.8 percent, and inflation below 3 percent.[176] The difficulty lay partly in Europe's poor economic performance during much of the 1990s, but an upturn in economic fortunes beginning in the late 1990s, combined with austerity policies, made it possible for all that wished to join to do so except Greece.[177]

In the end, the conversion rates of Europe's currencies were "irrevocably fixed," and eleven EU member states agreed "to surrender a central pillar of national sovereignty, control over their currencies," and begin euro-based electronic transactions on January 1, 1999.[178] Enthusiasts argue that the European-wide euro will rival the U.S. dollar for primacy in the global economic system, while pessimists fear that the states of Europe will no longer be able to use monetary and fiscal policy to overcome recession or inflation.[179]

Monetary union will not, however, overcome other obstacles to European integration. Europe's failure to forge a cohesive foreign policy toward Albania, Bosnia, Rwanda, Iraq, or the Middle East[180] and quarrels, such as that which accompanied the EU's ban of British beef during the "mad cow" scare, are evidence that national self-interest remains strong even in Europe.[181] It also proved difficult to remove border controls within the EU.[182] The EU even found it difficult to achieve consensus on agricultural policy for completing the Uruguay Round of the GATT. Agricultural subsidies of almost $47 billion a year consume most of the EU's budget and cause quarrels with other agricultural exporters, especially the United States. Josef Joffe described the issue's Janus faces:

> The French government . . . was facing national elections in March 1993, so it did not matter that France had been outvoted in the EC council. What did matter were French peasants who stood ready for yet another storm on the Bastille. . . . The French message . . . was: our peasants are more important than Europe.[183]

Finally, the institutions of the EU are still far from fully independent of national influence. The European Parliament remains largely advisory, and the European

Commission, with twenty commissioners and over sixteen thousand officials, is "squeezed" between the Council of Ministers and the parliament.[184] Accusations of corruption forced the resignation of all the commissioners in Spring 1999.

The final movement toward Europe's integration is difficult to predict. Progress continues, but few people think of themselves as "European first."[185] However, if the movement achieves its goal, the EU will be a formidable political and economic player.

Reconstructing Germany

The "German problem" haunted Europe for more than a century (see Figure 13.3). Following unification in 1871, Germany sought dominance in Central Europe. Under the "Iron Chancellor" Otto von Bismarck, it defeated France in the Franco-Prussian War of 1870–1871 in a contest for continental hegemony and then used balance-of-power policies to stabilize Europe with such alliances as the Three Emperor's League (1872) and the Dual Alliance of Germany and Austria-Hungary (1879). These alliances divided Europe into hostile military camps.

After Wilhelm II became emperor in 1890 and dismissed Bismarck, Germany abandoned caution for an ambitious *Weltpolitik* (world politics) in which Berlin challenged British supremacy at sea and sought a "place in the sun." In only a few decades, the country was transformed from an agrarian society into Europe's largest industrial power, boasting a growing navy and the world's best army. Germany's growing power unnerved its neighbors and made them seek security against German truculence. In 1902, Britain entered an alliance with Japan. Two years later, Britain and France overcame colonial conflicts and entered into a "friendly understanding" *(entente cordiale),* and a few years later Russia joined them in the Triple Entente.[186]

Germany continued to rattle sabers, thwarting French and Russian colonial ambitions and meddling in the tottering Ottoman Empire. When the Balkans were set alight by wars and crises, Russia and Austria-Hungary squared off to claim the spoils from the Ottoman retreat. The Balkans were the fuse that lit the European powder keg, and alliance politics brought Germany into the crisis.

Germany was defeated in World War I and subjected to the harsh Treaty of Versailles. "This is not a treaty," was the prescient comment of French Marshal Ferdinand Foch. "It is an armistice for twenty years."[187] Germany was forced to admit its war "guilt," disarm, give up its colonies, and cede territories that accounted for much of its wealth. Berlin was also forced to pay large reparations, even while being deprived of the means to pay.[188] In 1933, Adolf Hitler was swept to power on promises to overthrow Versailles and reverse the 1918 verdict.

Following defeat in 1945, Germany was divided into zones of occupation and became a Cold War battleground. The zones became separate states in 1949: the western Federal Republic of Germany (FRG) and the eastern German Democratic Republic (GDR). This division lasted forty years, during which time the two states took opposite social and political paths. In the end, West Germany's capitalist course became the model for a reunited Germany.

During its separate existence, the FRG established democratic institutions and achieved an "economic miracle." It accomplished these goals because of farsighted leadership by chancellors beginning with Konrad Adenauer (1949–1963), who appreciated the importance of strong ties to the United States and Germany's

1945

NORWAY
Oslo
Stockholm
SWEDEN
FINLAND
Helsinki
Leningrad

North Sea
Baltic Sea

DENMARK
Copenhagen

Incorporated into
U.S.S.R., 1945

From Finland,
1940–1956

ESTONIA
to U.S.S.R.
1940

LATVIA
to U.S.S.R.
1940

SOVIET
UNION
1917

LITHUANIA
to U.S.S.R.
1940

U.S. Zone

NETHERLANDS
Amsterdam

Bremen
British Zone
Soviet Zone
Berlin
EAST
GERMANY

Gdansk
(Danzig)

WHITE RUSSIA

Brussels
BEL.
Bonn
WEST
GERMANY

Incorporated into
Poland, 1945

Warsaw

Brest
From Poland
1940–1947

LUX.

POLAND
1947

UKRAINE

FRANCE
French
Zone
U.S. Zone
Munich
Prague

CZECHOSLOVAKIA
1948

From Czechoslovakia,
1945–1947

From Romania,
1940–1947

Berne
SWITZERLAND
French
Zone
U.S.
Zone
Vienna
AUSTRIA
British Zone
Soviet
Zone
Budapest

BESSARABIA

Milan
From Italy,
1945
HUNGARY
1949
ROMANIA
1947

Crimea
Yalta

ITALY

Corsica
(Fr.)

Adriatic Sea

Belgrade
Bucharest

From Romania,
1940–1947

Black Sea

YUGOSLAVIA
1945

Rome
Sardinia
(Italy)

BULGARIA
1946
Sofia

Tirane
ALBANIA
1944

Istanbul

GREECE

TURKEY

Sicily
Mediterranean Sea

Athens

Crete

CYPRUS

EAST
GERMANY
Soviet
Sector
East
Berlin
EAST
GERMANY
British Sector
West
Berlin
Soviet
Sector
U.S. Sector
Potsdam
— Berlin Wall (1961–1989)

— Postwar national boundaries, to 1989
▓ Allied occupation of Germany and Austria 1945–1955
▨ Territory lost by Germany
▨ Territory gained by Soviet Union
1945 Year communist control of government gained
— "Iron Curtain" to 1989

0   400   800 Km.
0   400   800 Mi.

Post-1990

DENMARK
THE NETHERLANDS
Berlin
POLAND
BELGIUM
GERMANY
LUXEMBURG
CZECH REP.
FRANCE
LIECHTENSTEIN
AUSTRIA
SWITZERLAND

FIGURE 13.3
The Changing Faces of Germany

The German issue has been a key factor in global politics since the nineteenth century. Between 1863 and 1870 Gemany was united by a series of wars. Since then, World Wars I and II and the Cold War have caused it to expand, shrink, and finally, in 1990, be reunified.

European neighbors, especially France. Under Adenauer, the FRG pursued policies that tied Germany tightly to the West. The FRG's entry into NATO in 1955 returned it to full sovereignty and ensured a secure context for reconstruction.[189] Adenauer was an early proponent of European integration, believing that membership in the EC would anchor Germany in the West. By 1957 the FRG's economy had recovered, and prosperity was in sight. While West Germany was establishing a mutually beneficial partnership with its allies, the GDR was being exploited by the U.S.S.R. and governed by a pro-Soviet puppet regime.

Reunifying Germany   West Germany was "an economic giant but a political dwarf,"[190] and sought an independent political course to match its economic power. In 1969, Chancellor Willy Brandt introduced the policy of *Ostpolitik* (east policy) based on negotiation and accommodation with the GDR. This was possible because of superpower détente and West Germany's economic might. Among its results were the Basic Treaty of 1972, by which the FRG and GDR agreed to exist side by side in "one German nation," and a new four-power agreement governing access to Berlin. As U.S.-Soviet relations soured in the early 1980s, West Germans tried to keep détente alive, worrying that the U.S.-West German alliance too might unravel.

American efforts to apply sanctions against the U.S.S.R. after the invasion of Afghanistan (1979) and the declaration of martial law in Poland (1981) caused a deep U.S.-West European political rift. American efforts to prevent subsidiaries of U.S. corporations in Europe from participating in a Soviet-European gas deal infuriated Europeans, who saw this claim to extraterritorial jurisdiction as arrogant interference in their domestic affairs. European and American interests differed. "To the Europeans, Soviet natural gas was a means of necessary diversification of their imports of energy. . . . For the Reagan administration, the pipeline was doubly condemned not only for the . . . dependency that it imposed on Western Europe . . . but also for the contribution that it made to Soviet economic well-being and ultimately to Soviet military gains."[191]

Chancellor Helmut Kohl's decision to limit FRG overtures to the East, along with a thaw in U.S.-Soviet relations during the last of the Reagan years, mended U.S.-Germany ties. Kohl also sought a larger role for Germany in Europe's affairs, necessitating a special relationship with France. Franco-German ties increasingly became the fulcrum for actions in Europe, and combining German economic clout and French nuclear weapons provided a basis for potential political influence.[192] In this way German influence could be exercised through "Europe," and Germany could be an economic engine for its EU partners.

Events in Central Europe unfolded rapidly late in the 1980s. Between November 9, 1989, and December 1, 1990, Germany was reunited and all-German democratic elections were held. This rapid change began with a mass exodus of East Germans to the West in the autumn of 1989. In November, the Berlin Wall fell. In February 1990, the four World War II victors and the two Germanys agreed on the outlines for reunification. That summer the FRG and GDR economies were reunited, and political reunification was declared on October 3, 1990.

Reunification turned German attention to the East, siphoned resources into reconstructing the eastern territories and underwriting withdrawal of Soviet troops, and eroded coordination of economic policy with EU partners. In

Germany itself, declining economic competitiveness,[193] recession (exacerbated in the East by the wrenching shift from a socialist to a capitalist system), budget pressures caused by reunification (some $500 billion in cash transfers, including a net transfer of $108 billion in 1995 alone from West to East),[194] tensions between West ("Wessis") and East Germans ("Ossis"),[195] refugee pressures from the East, rising right-wing popularity,[196] and antiforeigner violence sapped self-confidence.[197] As reunification problems and recession began to wane, however, signs of German self-confidence began to reappear, and Germans began to articulate interests apart from their allies'.[198] When German troops were assigned to assist NATO forces in the Balkans, it was the first time since World War II that German forces operated beyond NATO's borders.[199] Perhaps the clearest sign of a "new" Germany was the election of Gerhard Schröder as Germany's chancellor in 1998. Schroder is the first postwar chancellor born after 1945.

The Challenge of European Economic Power

The birth of the *European Economic Area (EEA)* on January 1, 1994, consisting of the EU's twelve members and EFTA's five, created a free-trade area of 372 million people whose number will grow with the addition of new members from the East. The eleven members of the European Monetary Union have an annual output of about $6.28 trillion (compared with America's $8.1 trillion) and are the center of a $2 trillion bond market.[200] As of 1995, thirty-four of the world's one hundred largest corporations were European (12 German, 11 French, 3 Italian, 2 Swiss, 2 Dutch, 2 British-Dutch, 1 British, 1 Austrian).[201] In 1996, EU members alone accounted for more than 39 percent of global exports.[202] Transatlantic trade is worth about $225 billion a year, roughly a fifth of total U.S. and European exports and imports,[203] and the eleven initial members of the EMU have a larger share of global trade and larger foreign-exchange reserves than the United States.[204]

The EU has become a foreign-investment Mecca. Between 1984 and 1988, Japanese investment in the EU grew from $7 billion to about $30 billion, and U.S. investment increased by $55 billion. Investments by EU countries in the United States have also been substantial. In 1987 alone, EU investments in the United States—in petroleum, manufacturing, finance, real estate, and publishing—totaled $325 billion, and in 1995 British investments in the United States exceeded those of Japanese.

Germany alone has a GDP of more than $1.5 trillion and a population of more than 80 million, making it Europe's largest economy[205] and creating apprehension on the part of EU partners.[206] Like the U.S. dollar and the Japanese yen, the mark is a highly prized currency, and the euro may rival the dollar as a world reserve currency. Germany is the largest contributor to the EU budget (28 percent in 1993),[207] and its strong economy gives it regional political influence, which it has used to promote greater European integration. Germany and German TNCs have also taken the lead in linking Central European and Russian economies to the EU and in investing in Eastern Europe.[208]

United States-European relations are plagued by some of the same issues that divide the United States and Asia. Relations are complicated by the possibility that a single European state can undermine a U.S.-EU agreement. Several possible approaches might manage transatlantic friction. One is using transatlantic institutions like NATO, which celebrated its fiftieth anniversary in April 1999, to cope with post–Cold War issues or to create links between newer institutions like the

EU and NAFTA. Efforts to manage trade and investment between the European and North American blocs are likely because the two share many common political and economic interests with respect to third parties.

However, this is not always the case. Europeans take strong issue with American efforts to isolate Cuba and Iran,[209] adopt a less combative stance toward Saddam Hussein, and are ready to accept economic opportunities that are offered by American efforts to use economic sanctions against countries such as China and Iran. Europeans and Canadians are especially irked by the efforts of the U.S. Congress to exert extraterritorial control over the foreign policies of America's allies and their corporations.

Thus, with an eye to the 1996 elections, the Republican-dominated Congress first passed the *Helms-Burton Act* requiring the U.S. government to punish foreign companies that "traffic" in property confiscated after the 1959 Cuban revolution, and a month later passed the *D'Amato law,* which would impose sanctions on foreign companies such as Italy's Agip, France's Total SA, Russia's Gazprom, Malaysia's Petronas, and others that invest in the oil and gas industries of Libya or Iran. Referring to the latter, the European Commission's vice-president declared: "It establishes the unwelcome principle that one country can dictate the foreign policy of others."[210]

Agriculture remains a special thorn in U.S.-European relations. On both sides of the Atlantic, farmers are small but politically important domestic interests. The EU's *Common Agricultural Policy (CAP)* limits the free market by supporting artificially high domestic prices for European produce. Prices are kept high by purchasing surpluses and excluding commodities from outside the EU. Mountains of surplus food have resulted, and the EU has chosen to subsidize their export, entering markets traditionally enjoyed by U.S. farmers. However, U.S. hands are hardly clean, because, since the 1930s, the U.S. government has maintained agricultural prices by buying domestic commodities, controlling production, and giving export subsidies. On the whole, however, government intervention in agriculture is less in the United States (and is diminishing still further), and U.S. farmers are more efficient than European farmers.

In one sense, a united Europe should be welcomed by those committed to an open-market environment. Eliminating internal trade barriers has produced greater efficiency and growth among members. Uniform national standards and simpler government procurement of products from other countries benefit Europe's trading partners. American investors also benefit because U.S. companies in Europe enjoy easier access to all EU states. Companies that have already set up shop in Europe can comply with requirements necessary to avoid the EU's uniform external tariffs.

Some Americans and Japanese fear that Europe's unity will boost policies to protect the EU market and that members will pay less attention to the needs of "third countries" as they bargain among themselves. As Europeans change their definition of a European product ("rules of origin") and place *local-content requirements* on them (that is redefining the meaning of "manufactured in Europe"), other countries may be left out. EU aid for high-tech industries—computers, semiconductors, and telecommunications equipment—illustrates what non-Europeans fear. These industries compete directly with U.S. exporters, and the

Clinton administration responded with aid to selected U.S. industries,[211] as well as by sending officials abroad to lobby for purchases of U.S. products.[212] European efforts to limit U.S. and Japanese economic penetration reflect fear of technological backwardness, job losses, and a decline in European competitiveness. Such fears fuel economic espionage by rival intelligence agencies. As a result, the open-trading order suffers.

A third general area of U.S.-European friction results from incompatible macroeconomic policies. In recent years, Americans have urged Europe and Japan to pursue expansionist economic policies to energize the world economy and increase imports of U.S. goods. If Germany and Japan were willing to increase government spending at home and accept more inflation, Americans argue, the number of jobs at home and abroad would be increased by greater international trade. European complaints about the United States mirror those of the Japanese, focusing, until recently, on America's budget deficits, which reduced funds available for European investment at home. Despite U.S. rhetoric about protectionism, they point out that the United States also protects such inefficient industries as steel.

Like the United States and Japan, the EU and the United States have engaged in multilateral, regional, and bilateral negotiations to iron out differences. Talks have dealt with controversial issues such as European import restrictions on U.S. agricultural products, European barriers to importing U.S. beef that has been fed growth hormones, European subsidies to domestic industries engaged in export, government aid to commercial aircraft industries,[213] and industrial and regulatory standards for products like appliances and pharmaceuticals.[214]

Although one can imagine extensive conflicts between the United States and the EU in coming years, leaders are likely to contain them. To this end, the United States and the EU signed a broad trade and security accord called the New Transatlantic Agenda in December 1995, which committed them to cooperate in 150 specific policy areas, such as cutting international crime, slowing nuclear proliferation, and forming a Transatlantic Marketplace to cut trade barriers.[215] The Janus faces of politics are visible on both sides of the Atlantic in the contradictory imperatives from domestic constituencies fearing lost jobs and declining export markets and the global system in which free markets and greater trade benefit all. More important is recognition that, if what former U.S. trade representative Mickey Kantor calls "commercial engagement"[216] is not contained, it may infect the political bonds that helped Americans and Europeans win the Cold War.

Free Trade and North American Economic Power

The United States met the challenging economic power of Japan and the EU by establishing a regional free-trade area with its North American trading partners Canada and Mexico. These countries are, respectively, America's largest and (after Japan) third largest trading partners. By establishing a new trade bloc, the United States created a larger market for its goods and limited inroads by Japan and the EU in North America. The project began with the *U.S.-Canada Free Trade*

Agreement (FTA) of 1989. In August 1992, the more ambitious *North American Free Trade Agreement (NAFTA)* was initialed by U.S., Mexican, and Canadian representatives and went into effect on January 1, 1994, creating a larger free-trade area than the EU.

The FTA was meant to eliminate trade barriers between Canada and the United States over a ten-year period. Under the treaty, U.S. firms in Canada and Canadian firms in the United States enjoyed the same treatment as indigenous enterprises. Some industries, which are important to their country's cultural sovereignty—broadcasting, publishing, and films—were left out of the agreement.[217] Each country had competing and complementary motives for pursuing the arrangement and was influenced by trends in the global economic system and its domestic economies.[218] The pact with Canada was an opportunity to increase the competitiveness of industries in both countries and was a model for liberal trade worldwide in the way it addressed issues of nontariff barriers and trade subsidiaries.[219]

The NAFTA, signed in August 1992, enlarged the free-trade area to take in America's southern neighbor. The pact called for removing tariffs and other trade impediments in advertising, agriculture, automobile, banking, energy, insurance, textiles, trucking, and other sectors, while preventing other countries from eluding U.S. tariffs by going through Mexico. It was immediately hailed by business leaders like Eastman Kodak's CEO as an agreement that "could unleash a surge of trading activity with Mexico, already [the U.S.'s] third largest trading partner and fastest-growing export market."[220] Supporters argued that the enlarged free-trade area would enhance prosperity in all three countries by creating a regional bloc of 370 million people in which more jobs and lower production costs, especially in agriculture, would bring benefits to consumers and producers in the three countries.[221] As Mexico privatized industry,[222] and wages and working conditions become more like those of their northern neighbors, Mexican workers, it was hoped, would have less incentive to emigrate across the Rio Grande.

Opposition to the pact was strong in the United States. Opponents feared a loss of jobs to low-cost Mexican competition and a watering-down of U.S. environmental laws.[223] President Clinton lobbied vigorously, placating special interests such as wheat and peanut growers before he could muster a congressional majority for NAFTA in November 1993.[224]

In fact, despite Mexico's 1995 devaluation of the peso and the flight of capital from the country,[225] NAFTA's effect on the United States has been modest. Rather than accelerating the loss of U.S. jobs, there has been a shift from exporting U.S. jobs to Asia to exporting them to Mexico.[226] Mexico has benefited as it has become a manufacturing center for all of North America. In addition, American and Mexican firms have set up joint ventures.[227] Politically, NAFTA reflects the growing interdependence of the United States and Mexico and has encouraged Mexicans to pursue greater democratization.

American leaders saw NAFTA as only a beginning, and, at a trade summit in Washington, D.C., in December 1994, agreement was reached to expand free trade to the entire Western Hemisphere ("Free Trade Area of the Americas") beginning in the year 2005. "When our work is done," declared President Clinton, "the free trade area of the Americas will stretch from Alaska to Argentina."[228] However, NAFTA's adversaries continue to portray NAFTA as a disaster for the United States, and a coalition of labor unions and liberal Democrats prevented a renewal of *fast-*

track authority necessary for President Clinton to negotiate additional trade agreements which Congress could either vote up or down but could not amend. As a result, progress toward realizing a hemisphere-wide free trade area has ground to a halt.[229]

Conclusion

Rapid change in global politics makes it difficult to discern the future shape of relations among the world's economic leaders, all of which except China were Cold-War allies. Fears of America's economic decline proved premature, as the United States enjoyed one of the longest peacetime economic booms in its history in the 1990s. By contrast, Japan and Germany found themselves mired in a prolonged slump. No longer do observers believe that Americans cannot compete with Asia and Europe.

What do the economic rivalries between the three centers of economic power portend for the twenty-first century? What effect will growing Asian economic dependence on troubled Japan and China's explosive economic growth have, and what effect will its sometimes belligerent policies have? Will Europe's voyage toward unity produce cooperation or rivalry with the rest of the world? And what does NAFTA presage? Will we see "islands of prosperity" sharply divided from and competing with one another—Pacific Rim versus NAFTA or NAFTA versus the European Union? Or are we on the verge of greater global cooperation and prosperity as actors recognize their global interdependence? Is a new world economy forming in which government and business will be closer partners and change things so that "the choice is no longer between free trade and protectionism?"[230] Perhaps the most important unanswered question is whether the United States, long an advocate of free trade, will remain so. America's willingness to bypass multilateral procedures, its reluctance to provide additional funding for the IMF, and congressional refusal to grant President Clinton "fast track" trade authority indicate a retreat from the commitment to an open trading system.[231]

If the past was prologue, then rivalry rather than cooperation would seem the order for tomorrow, but the future is not simply the past warmed over. Some trends promise greater cooperation. Japan's economic recession in the 1990s with steep declines in stock-market prices and domestic real-estate values makes it recognize its stake in universal prosperity. Japan is slowly realizing that it has to face the economic and social challenges already faced in the West, such as reforming its banking system, integrating women into the work force, and meeting growing demands for leisure. For its part, China's stake in the world economy has grown dramatically, and Chinese leaders recognize that political conflict with the country's leading trading partners is bad business. On the other side of the world, Europe is moving ahead to institute a common currency that will integrate further the economic life of member states in the EU. Resolving the complex issues in unifying Europe will consume more time than originally anticipated and stretch those decisions into the new century even as the Pacific Rim confronts economic crisis.

Such trends may either accelerate divisions among economic powers or encourage the cooperation that the West enjoyed after 1945.

How will economic rivalries affect political ties among these actors? Will economic friction reinforce political rivalries? Will Japan and Germany seek political and military power commensurate with their economic power? Will China emerge as a new superpower, and will warmer U.S.-Chinese relations diminish Japan's standing?[232] Will APEC dwarf the EU and NAFTA and become the foundation of a new global economic hierarchy, or will political differences preclude this? American efforts to play off Asia against Europe have already led to a European initiative to hold an annual "Europe-Asia" summit.[233]

The inevitable question is whether political frictions will stay manageable. They have thus far, and prospects are good that they will continue to do so. Although Japan and Germany are growing more independent, they can continue to value their political and military ties to the United States. Both are constrained militarily by constitutional restrictions,[234] and both are committed to democracy. Finally, both countries, as well as China to an increasing degree, are deeply enmeshed in a global web of complex interdependence. Their commitments could be altered, but not easily or inexpensively. Japan and Germany will become more active in their own regions and in the United Nations, but neither is likely to become an adversary of the United States. Instead, Germany, Japan, and the United States are likely to remain friendly adversaries, less constrained than in the past (by a common foe) about bringing disagreements into the open, but fearful of collision that would harm all of them.

Key Terms

Asia-Pacific Economic Cooperation (APEC)

Bogor Declaration

Common Agricultural Policy (CAP)

Cultural Revolution

D'Amato law

declinist perspective

European Atomic Energy Community (EURATOM)

European Coal and Steel Community (ECSC)

European Community (EC)

European Economic Area (EEA)

European Economic Community (EEC)

European Monetary System (EMS)

European Union (EU)

exchange-rate mechanism (ERM)

fast-track authority

Great Leap Forward

head-to-head competition

Helms-Burton Act

imperial overextension

keiretsu

local-content requirements

Maastricht Treaty

managed trade

niche competition

North American Free Trade Agreement (NAFTA)

orderly marketing agreements

Ostpolitik

reserve currency

Single Market Act

soft power

Structural Impediments Initiative (SII)

triumphalism

U.S.-Canada Free Trade Agreement (FTA)

vanishing World War II effect

Weltpolitik

zaibatsu

End Notes

[1]Helen Milner and Jack Snyder, "Lost Hegemony?" *International Organization* 42:4 (Autumn 1988), p. 749.

[2]Cited in David E. Sanger and Tim Weiner, "Emerging Role for the C.I.A.: Economic Spy," *New York Times,* October 15, 1995, sec. 1, p. 1. The CIA has admitted spying on France to find out the French position on world trade talks. Tim Weiner, "C.I.A. Confirms Blunders During Economic Spying on France," *New York Times,* March 13, 1996, p. A8.

[3]Cited in David E. Sanger, "After a Year, No Letup in Asia's Economic Crisis," *New York Times,* July 6, 1998, p. A6.

[4]Lester Thurow, *Head to Head: The Coming Economic Battle Among Japan, Europe, and America.* (New York: William Morrow, 1992), p. 35.

[5]See, for example, Hanns W. Maull, "Germany and Japan: The New Civilian Powers," *Foreign Affairs* 69:5 (Winter 1990/91), p. 91.

[6]Thurow, *Head to Head,* pp. 29, 30. Emphasis added.

[7]Cited in David E. Sanger, "Foreign Relations: Money Talks, Policy Walks," *New York Times,* January 15, 1995, sec. 4, p. 1.

[8]"Home Debts from Abroad," *The Economist,* July 12–18, 1997, p. 24.

[9]Thurow, *Head to Head,* p. 165. Between 1980 and 1990, U.S. productivity grew at 1.2 percent per year compared with 3.1 percent per year for Japan.

[10]Paul Kennedy, *The Rise and Fall of the Great Powers* (New York: Random House, 1987), p. 444.

[11]"Meet the Global Factory," *The Economist,* special report, June 20–26, 1998.

[12]Joseph S. Nye, Jr., *Bound to Lead* (New York: Basic Books, 1990), p. 72.

[13]U.S. hegemony is compared to earlier British supremacy. Robert O. Keohane points out, however, that the comparison is flawed because "Britain had never been as superior in productivity to the rest of the world as the United States was after 1945." *After Hegemony* (Princeton: Princeton University Press, 1984), p. 37. See Bruce M. Russett, "The Mysterious Case of Vanishing Hegemony; Or, Is Mark Twain Really Dead?" *International Organization* 39:2 (Spring 1985), p. 211.

[14]Russett, "Mysterious Case of Vanishing Hegemony," p. 211.

[15]GDP is the value of the total output of goods and services. GNP is GDP plus net income from abroad.

[16]*World Development Indicators 1998* (Washington, DC: World Bank, 1998), Table 1.1, pp. 12–14.

[17]Ibid.

[18]Ibid. Japan ranked fifth.

[19]*World Development Report 1998/99* (New York: Oxford University Press, 1999), Table 1, pp. 190–191.

[20]These four were IBM, Eastman Kodak, General Electric, and Motorola. The Japanese companies were Toshiba, Canon, Mitsubishi, Hitachi, Matsushita, and Fuji. Sabra Chartrand, "U.S. Gains on Japan in Patents," *New York Times,* March 14, 1994, pp. C1, C2.

[21]Paul Kennedy, *Preparing for the Twenty-First Century* (New York: Random House, 1993), p. 199. In 1991, Japan's gross domestic savings was more than twice America's.

[22]Helene Cooper, "Trade Gap Grew to $43.62 Billion in Second Quarter," *Wall Street Journal,* September 13, 1995, p. A2.

[23]Nicholas D. Kristof, "Japan's Secret Weapon Is the Piggy Bank," *New York Times,* May 21, 1995, sec. 4, p. 1.

[24]See Thomas Omestad, "Selling Off America," *Foreign Policy* 76 (Fall 1989), pp. 119–140. Typical of earlier European fears of U.S. dominance is J. J. Servan-Schreiber, *The American Challenge* (New York: Atheneum, 1968).

[25]Kennedy, *Preparing for the Twenty-First Century,* pp. 299, 301.

[26]Nye, *Bound to Lead,* p. 188.

[27]See, for example, Matt Moffett, "Key Finance Ministers in Latin America Are Old Harvard-MIT Pals," *Wall Street Journal,* August 1, 1994, pp. A1, A8; Charles Trueheart, "The All-American Age," *Washington Post National Weekly Edition,* August 21–27, 1995, pp. 16–17.

[28]Cited in Stephen Kinzer, "The G.I.s' Legacy: Basketball and Sweet Memories," *New York Times,* September 27, 1994, p. A8. For a discussion of how the WTO represents a powerful instrument of U.S. soft power, see David E. Sanger, "Playing the Trade Card," *New York Times,* February 17, 1997, pp. 1, 27.

[29]Cited in John Darnton, "New Oxford Fashion: United States Studies," *New York Times,* September 6, 1995, p. A6.

[30]Nye, *Bound to Lead,* p. 260.

[31]Barbara Crossette, "Look Who Wants U.S. As a Leader," *New York Times,* February 12, 1995, sec. 4, p. 5.

[32]"Clinton's Words on Mission to Bosnia: 'The Right Thing to Do'," *New York Times,* November 28, 1995, p. A6.

[33]T.R. Reid, "In Japan, the Sun Shines on 'Rising Sam'," *Washington Post National Weekly Edition,* February 28–March 6, 1994, p. 21.

[34]"Back on Top?" special report, *The Economist,* September 16–22, 1995.

[35]Cited in Louis Uchitelle, "The Rehabilitation of Morning in America," *New York Times,* February 23, 1997, sec. 4, p. 1.

[36]G. Pascal Zachary, "Behind Stocks' Surge Is An Economy in Which Big U.S. Firms Thrive," *Wall Street Journal,* November 22, 1995, p. A5.

[37]Michael M. Phillips, "Foreign Executives See U.S. as Prime Market," *Wall Street Journal,* February 3, 1997, p. A1; Bernard Wysocki, Jr., "Foreign Money Keeps Flooding Into the U.S.," *Wall Street Journal,* May 19, 1997, p. A1; Gregory Zuckerman, "U.S. Bond Market Is Likely to Stay Strong," *Wall Street Journal,* June 6, 1998, p. A1.

[38]Sylvia Nasar, "The American Economy, Back on Top," *New York Times,* February 27, 1994, sec. 3, pp. 1, 6.

[39]Cited in Louis Uchitelle, "Puffed Up by Prosperity, U.S. Struts Its Stuff," *New York Times,* April 27, 1997, sec. 4, p. 1.

[40]"The Global Economy," special report, *The Economist,* October 1-7, 1994, pp. 3-6.

[41]A.F. Cooper, Richard A. Higgott, and Kim Richard Nossel, *Relocating Middle Powers: Australia and the Changing World Order* (Vancouver: University of British Columbia Press, 1993), pp. 92-94.

[42]Hong Kong was returned to China in the summer of 1997.

[43]Todd S. Purdum, "Free Trade Gains Backing by Asians," *New York Times,* November 26, 1996, pp. A1, A6.

[44]Steven Greenhouse, "Clinton Pushing Business with Asia," *New York Times,* November 11, 1993, p. A7.

[45]Roger Cohen, "Like U.S., West Europe Steps Up Its Asia Trade," *New York Times,* November 24, 1993, p. A6.

[46]Michael M. Weinstein, "Limits of Economic Diplomacy," *New York Times,* April 8, 1999, p. C1. China is finally beginning to open its markets to foreign trade. Ian Johnson and Leslie Chang, "China Offers an Array of Reforms," *Wall Street Journal,* March 25, 1999, p. A18.

[47]David E. Sanger, "Clinton's Asian Card," *New York Times,* November 26, 1996, p. A6.

[48]Cited in David E. Sanger, "Clinton in Seattle for Pacific Talks to Seek Markets," *New York Times,* November 19, 1993, pp. A1, A7.

[49]R.W. Apple, Jr., "Godfather to Pacific Era?" *New York Times,* November 21, 1993, p. 1. Not surprisingly, Europeans are concerned about America's growing focus on Asia. R.W. Apple, Jr., "On Eve of NATO Talks, President Seeks to Ease Fear that His Focus Is on Asia," *New York Times,* January 10, 1994, pp. A1, A4.

[50]Cited in Thomas L. Friedman, "Asia Pacific Economic Alignment Is Off to an Upbeat Start," *New York Times,* March 21, 1994, p. A5.

[51]Elaine Sciolino, "Leaders Agree On Free Trade for the Pacific," *New York Times,* November 16, 1994, p. A6.

[52]Andrew Pollack, "A Pacific Vision Now in Search of Reality," *New York Times,* November 14, 1995, p. C2.

[53]In early 1997, the U.S., Japan, China, Singapore, Australia, and Hong Kong established the "Six Markets Group," an Asian equivalent of the G-6. David Wessel, "U.S., Five Asian Nations Plan to Meet, Aiming at Counterpart to Group of Seven," *Wall Street Journal,* February 24, 1997, p. A2; Robert Steiner, "G-6 to Dive into Technical Details, Avoiding Politics at Initial Summit," *Wall Street Journal,* March 3, 1997, p. A15.

[54]Nicholas D. Kristof, "Japanese Politicians Jockeying to Succeed Resigning Premier," *New York Times,* July 19, 1998, p. A1.

[55]Japan had been closed to all foreigners except the Dutch since the seventeenth century.

[56]"No End of Lessons," *The Economist,* May 6-12, 1995, p. 23. Japan refuses to acknowledge the extent of the atrocities committed or apologize for them. "The Japan that Cannot Say Sorry," *The Economist,* August 12-18, 1995, pp. 31-33; "Japan's Many Memories of War," *The Economist,* August 19-25, 1995, pp. 29-30.

[57]In the end, Japan's surrender was not unconditional. The emperor was allowed to remain, though he would no longer be regarded as divine.

[58]Reprinted in Robert A. Scalapino, "The Foreign Policy of Japan," in Roy C. Macridis, ed., *Foreign Policy in World Politics* (Englewood Cliffs, NJ: Prentice-Hall, 1992), p. 194. Japan gave Article 9 as its reason for not sending troops to join the U.S.-led coalition against Iraq. In September 1992, a controversy erupted in Japan when the government claimed that Article 9 permitted sending combat troops as part of a U.N. contingent helping Cambodia.

[59]John Foster Dulles, later U.S. secretary of state, was the architect of the treaty. Of the major powers, only the U.S.S.R. remained in a state of war with Japan. Efforts to end the state of war fell victim to disagreement over four small islands in the Kurile chain north of Japan that the Soviet Union seized in 1945.

[60]See Suzuta Atsuyuki, "The Way of the Bureaucrat," in Daniel I. Okimoto and Thomas P. Rohlen, eds., *Inside the Japanese System* (Stanford, CA: Stanford University Press, 1988), pp. 196-203; James Sterngold, "Japan Trade Talks: Good Will Meets Bureaucracy," *New York Times,* January 16, 1994, sec. 1, p. 3.

[61]Chalmers Johnson, "Market Rationality vs. Plan Rationality," in ibid., p. 217. Japan's export orientation allows it to use surplus industrial capacity and maintain domestic employment. See Kozo Yamamura, "Japanese Industrial Policy: International Repercussions," in ibid., pp. 221-222.

[62]American auto makers are catching up. See, for example, Andrew Pollack, "Detroit's Japan-Friendly Cars Go to Tokyo," *New York Times,* October 25, 1995, pp. A1, C6.

[63]Clyde V. Prestowitz, Jr., *Trading Places* (New York: Basic Books, 1988), p. 489.

[64]*World Development Indicators 1998,* Table 4.16, p. 235. By contrast, the U.S. trade deficit in 1996 was almost $149 billion.

[65]Prestowitz, *Trading Places,* p. 491.

[66]Henrik Schmiegelow and Michele Schmiegelow, "How Japan Affects the International System," *International Organization* 44:4 (Autumn 1990), pp. 560-561.

[67]Steven R. Weisman, "Japan and U.S. Struggle with Resentment," *New York Times,* December 3, 1991, pp. A1, A6.

[68]"Trading in Confusion," *The Economist,* May 28–June 3, 1994, p. 24.

[69]James Bennet, "Hearty Cheers In Detroit as Japan Renews Earlier Goals," *New York Times,* June 29, 1995, p. C4.

[70]Barnaby J. Feder, "Business Chiefs Praise Clinton for Stand on Japan," *New York Times,* February 21, 1994, p. C1.

[71]James Sterngold, "Japan Offers to Back Loans to Help Trim Trade Surplus," *New York Times,* September 8, 1993, p. C1.

[72]James Sterngold, "Hollywood 1, Japanese 0," *New York Times,* April 16, 1995, sec. 4, p. 5.

[73]Ronald E. Dolan and Robert L. Worden, eds., *Japan: A Country Study,* 5th ed. (Washington, DC: U.S. Government Printing Office, 1992), Table 31, pp. 500–501. As Japanese investment tapered off in 1994, it was partly replaced by investment from the developing world. Keith Bradsher, "U.S. Is Attracting New Money Pool," *New York Times,* July 31, 1994, sec. 1, pp. 1, 6.

[74]G. Pascal Zachery, "U.S. Companies Again Hold Wide Lead Over Rivals in Direct Investing Abroad," *Wall Street Journal,* December 6, 1995, p. A2; Allen R. Myerson, "American Money Makes the Whole World Sing," *New York Times,* December 17, 1995, sec. 4, pp. 1, 14.

[75]Fred R. Bleakley, "Foreign Investment in U.S. Surged in 1994," *Wall Street Journal,* March 15, 1995, p. A2.

[76]Jathon Sapsford, "It's Japan's Paradox: Troubled Banks Buoy Their Ailing Borrowers," *Wall Street Journal,* July 7, 1998, pp. A1, A10.

[77]"Fallen Idol," *The Economist,* June 20–26, 1998, p. 22.

[78]In July 1998, Japan announced a plan to end its banking crisis. Jathon Sapsford and Norihiko Shirouzu, "Focus Shifts to Japan's Follow-Through on Key Pledges," *Wall Street Journal,* July 6, 1998, p. A11.

[79]Michael R. Sesit and Laura Jereski, "Dollar Slides Below 100 Yen, Hits Postwar Low," *Wall Street Journal,* June 22, 1994, pp. C1, C6.

[80]Anthony Ramirez, "Dollar Sets Lows vs. Yen and Mark," *New York Times,* April 19, 1995, pp. A1, C8.

[81]Thomas L. Friedman, "16 Central Banks Are Thwarted in Huge Effort to Prop Up Dollar," *New York Times,* June 25, 1994, pp. 1, 24. In July 1995, Japan's trade surplus fell 23 percent, and, as the yen began to fall in August, Japanese exporters breathed a sigh of relief, anticipating that exports would again rise. David P. Hamilton, "Japan's Trade Surplus Fell 23% in July, As the Growth in Imports Accelerated," *Wall Street Journal,* August 16, 1995, p. A6; Michael Williams, "Japan Counts Blessings of a Falling Yen," *Wall Street Journal,* August 17, 1995, p. A7; David E. Sanger, "Dollar Recovers to Above 100 Yen," *New York Times,* September 13, 1995, pp. A1, C8.

[82]"Dial C for Chaos," *The Economist,* March 11–17, 1995; Peter Passell, "Weak Dollar and Its Costs," *New York Times,* April 21, 1995, pp. A1, C3.

[83]Sheryl WuDunn, "U.S. Accused of Enslaving the Japanese," *New York Times,* April 30, 1995, sec. 1, p. 8.

[84]Andrew Pollack, "Japan's Companies Moving Production to Sites Overseas," *New York Times,* August 29, 1993, pp. 1, 11. Toyota began to export cars assembled in its plant in Kentucky to South Korea. Valerie Reitman, "Toyota to Export U.S.-Made Cars to South Korea," *Wall Street Journal,* February 9, 1996, p. A8.

[85]Steven Greenhouse, "Sinking Dollar Raises Costs of U.S. Operations Abroad," *New York Times,* April 24, 1995, p. A4.

[86]The LDP received significant CIA support. Tim Weiner, "C.I.A. Spent Millions to Support Japanese Right in 50's and 60's," *New York Times,* October 9, 1994, sec. 1, pp. 1, 11.

[87]"Japan's Long March," *The Economist,* August 1–7, 1994, pp. 42, 44, 46.

[88]Kristof, "Japanese Politicians Jockeying to Succeed Resigning Premier," pp. A1, A8.

[89]Sandra Sugawara, "Sayonara, Japan Inc.," *Washington Post National Weekly Edition,* March 17, 1997, pp. 18–19; Sheryl WuDunn, "Japan's Economy Appears Bleaker," *New York Times,* June 13, 1998, pp. A1, B2; "As Japan Goes?" *The Economist,* June 20–26, 1998, pp. 15–16; David P. Hamilton, "So, How Far Has Japan Fallen? Take a Look at These Numbers," *Wall Street Journal,* July 2, 1998, p. A19.

[90]"What Goes Round. . . ," *The Economist,* February 8–14, 1997, p. 79.

[91]"If Japan Should Crash," *The Economist,* April 11–17, 1998, p. 9; "Worse to Come," *The Economist,* April 11–17, 1998, pp. 13–15.

[92]Some reforms aimed at opening Japanese markets have taken place. See Nicholas D. Kristof, "Real Capitalism Breaks Japan's Old Rules," *New York Times,* July 15, 1997, pp. A1, A6.

[93]"The Japan Puzzle," *The Economist,* March 21–27, 1998, p. 15; "Hurtling Toward Paralysis," *The Economist,* March 21–28, 1998, pp. 21–23. Just when it appeared Japan might be serious about reforms, parliamentary elections gave the ruling LDP such a beating that Prime Minister Ryutaro Hashimoto had to resign. Nicholas D. Kristof, "Japanese Rebuke Governing Party in National Vote," *New York Times,* July 13, 1998, pp. A1, A8.

[94]David E. Sanger, "U.S. Settles Trade Dispute, Averting Billions in Tariffs on Japanese Luxury Autos," *New York Times,* June 29, 1995, pp. A1, C4. The agreement was signed two months later. Helene Cooper, "U.S., Japan Sign Agreement on Autos, but Comments Hint at Long Struggle," *Wall Street Journal,* August 24, 1995, p. A2. Washington thought the talks so important that the CIA spied on Japan's negotiators. David E. Sanger, "U.S. Won't Admit or Explain Its Trade Espionage to Japan," *New York Times,* October 28, 1995, p. 4.

[95]James C. Abegglen, "Japan's Ultimate Vulnerability," in Okimoto and Rohlen, eds., *Inside the Japanese System,* p. 258.

[96]Sheryl WuDunn, "But Is Japan Indeed Protectionist?" *New York Times,* June 30, 1995, p. C5. Average Japanese and American tariff rates are about the same. American rice was

entirely banned until Japan's rice shortage of 1993 forced a temporary opening of that market. David E. Sanger, "Ending Sacred Trust, Japan Will Open Rice Market," *New York Times,* December 8, 1993, pp. C1, C2.

[97]Fuji makes similar accusations against Kodak. Wendy Bounds, "Fuji Accused by Kodak of Hogging Markets, Spits Back: 'You Too'," *Wall Street Journal,* July 31, 1995, pp. A1, A4; Sheryl WuDunn, "It's Trouble Selling Kodak in Japan Land of Fuji," *New York Times,* June 11, 1996, pp. C1, C5.

[98]James Sterngold, "Intractable Trade Issues With Japan," *New York Times,* December 4, 1991, p. C4.

[99]Cited in Andrew Pollack, "Japanese Express Skepticism Over Trade Deal With U.S.," *New York Times,* October 3, 1994, p. A1.

[100]Bob Davis and Jathon Sapsford, "Japan Escapes U.S. Sanctions, Offering Plan to Open Up Public-Works Market," *Wall Street Journal,* October 27, 1993, p. A2.

[101]James Sterngold, "Tokyo Panel Calls for Loosening of Regulatory Bonds on Business," *New York Times,* November 9, 1993, p. A4.

[102]Paul Blustein, "Giving a Little, Taking a Little," *Washington Post National Weekly Edition,* July 19-25, 1993, p. 20.

[103]David E. Sanger, "Japan Will Widen Wall St.'s Access," *New York Times,* January 11, 1994, pp. A1, C5; David P. Hamilton and Jathon Sapsford, "U.S. Puts Pressure on Japan Over Trade in Aviation and Medical Equipment," *Wall Street Journal,* March 17, 1994, p. A12; Helene Cooper, "U.S. Declares Japanese Government Purchasing Practices Hurt U.S. Firms," *Wall Street Journal,* August 1, 1994, pp. A2, A20; Teresa Riordan, "U.S., Japan in Accord On Patents," *New York Times,* August 17, 1994, pp. C1, C2; "Big Deal," *The Economist,* October 8-14, 1994, p. 76; Bob Davis and David P. Hamilton, "U.S.-Japan Pact on Trade Marks a Balancing Act," *Wall Street Journal,* October 3, 1994, pp. A2, A8; Sheryl WuDunn, "Accord Is Set on U.S. Access to Japanese Insurance Market," *New York Times,* December 16, 1996, p. A7.

[104]"Chocks Away," *The Economist,* February 8-14, 1997, pp. 65-67. More recently, shipping became a divisive issue. See Sandra Sugawara, "The One-Man Trade Barrier," *Washington Post National Weekly Edition,* April 7, 1997, p. 19.

[105]David E. Sanger, "64% of Japanese Say U.S. Relations Are 'Unfriendly'," *New York Times,* July 6, 1993, pp. A1, A6. Some are concerned about U.S. indifference toward and ignorance of Japan. See Kevin Sullivan, "Blissfully Ignorant About Japan," *Washington Post National Weekly Edition,* p. 21.

[106]Steven R. Weisman, "A Deep Split in Attitudes is Developing," *New York Times,* December 3, 1991, p. A6.

[107]Kazuo Ogura, director of cultural affairs in Japan's foreign ministry, as cited in Asra Q. Nomani, "U.S., Japan 'Far Apart' in Trade Talks," *Wall Street Journal,* January 3, 1994, pp. 3, 38.

[108]Cited in Weisman, "Japan and U.S. Struggle With Resentment," p. A6.

[109]Keith Bradsher, "Share of Foreign Chips in Japan's Market Slips," *New York Times,* September 23, 1993, p. C2. Another

case of numerical targets was Japan's agreement to import U.S. cellular telephones. Andrew Pollack, "America as Trade Micro-Manager," *New York Times,* March 14, 1994, pp. C1, C2. U.S. and Japanese firms control 80 percent of the chip market, but a worldwide glut in chips intensified competition among manufacturers. "When the Chips are Down," *The Economist,* March 23-29, 1996, pp. 19-21.

[110]Robert S. Greenberger and Nancy Keates, "U.S. and Seoul Agree on Steps to Open Market," *Wall Street Journal,* September 29, 1995, pp. A2, A4.

[111]Jathon Sapsford, "Japan's Mr. No Has Fresh U.S. Charges," *Wall Street Journal,* June 9, 1998, p. A15.

[112]Jagdish Bhagwati, "Samurais No More," *Foreign Affairs* 73:3 (May/June 1994), p. 12. The author is alluding to the events leading up to World War II. Also Bob Davis and Jacob M. Schlesinger, "Trade War? Unlikely, but Shifting Relations Do Increase the Risk," *Wall Street Journal,* February 18, 1994, pp. A1, A7.

[113]Between 1986 and 1994 Japanese investors sold many of their holdings at huge losses and overall lost more than $320 billion on their U.S. investments. James Sterngold, "Sony, Struggling, Takes a Huge Loss on Movie Studios," *New York Times,* November 18, 1994, pp. A1, C2. "In a great many instances the Japanese investors paid way too much, often got fleeced, and rarely understood what they were in for." James Sterngold, "Hollywood 1, Japanese 0," *New York Times,* April 16, 1995, sec. 4, p. 5.

[114]Kyle Pope, Asra Q. Nomani, and David P. Hamilton, "Japan Suggests It May Want to Join U.S. Consortium of Chip Companies," *Wall Street Journal,* January 31, 1994, p. B6.

[115]Michael Williams, Jennifer Cody, and David P. Hamilton, "Japan's Imports Rise, And U.S. Companies Are Gaining New Sales," *Wall Street Journal,* April 15, 1994, pp. A1, A6; Andrew Pollack, "Japan's Trade Surplus Shrinks for the First Time in Five Years," *New York Times,* January 24, 1996, pp. A1, C7; "The Shrinking Surplus," *The Economist,* February 3-9, 1996, p. 31.

[116]Low economic growth, antitrust enforcement, and foreign competition have helped weaken these arrangements. David P. Hamilton and Norihiko Shirouzu, "Japan's Business Cartels Are Starting to Erode, but Change Is Slow," *Wall Street Journal,* December 4, 1995, pp. A1, A6.

[117]David E. Sanger, "Sales of U.S. Autos Up 50% in Japan Since Trade Accord," *New York Times,* April 12, 1996, pp. A1, C2; Sandra Sugawara, "A Crack in the Foundation," *Washington Post National Weekly Edition,* March 18-24, 1996, p. 24.

[118]Andrew Pollack "Waiting Out Japan's Trade Surplus," *New York Times,* October 7, 1994, pp. C1, C5.

[119]David P. Hamilton, "Japan's Love Affair with Imports Wanes," *Wall Street Journal,* October 30, 1996, p. A15; Keith Bradsher, "Imports Again Hurt U.S. Cars as Dollar Rises," *New York Times,* December 6, 1996, pp. A1, C3; Helene Cooper, "Dollar's Rise Hurts Japanese Units in U.S.," *Wall Street Journal,* December 30, 1996, p. A2; David P. Hamilton, "Japan's Exporters Grow Bolder, Stronger," *Wall Street Journal,* February 13, 1997, p. A2;

"Rising Surplus, Rising Wrath," *The Economist,* March 22-28, 1997, pp. 43-44.

[120]David E. Sanger, "Clinton Warns Japan Leader On Trade Gap," *New York Times,* April 26, 1997, pp. 21, 23.

[121]Richard J. Samuels, "Consuming for Production: Japanese National Security, Nuclear Fuel Procurement, and the Domestic Economy," *International Organization* 43:4 (Autumn 1989), p. 625.

[122]Nicholas D. Kristof, "Finally, Japan May Have a Future in the Military," *New York Times,* April 21, 1996, sec. 4, p. 5.

[123]Japan contributed $6 billion in 1994 for U.S. bases in Japan. James Sterngold, "Some Leaders in Japan Begin to Question U.S. Bases," *New York Times,* August 28, 1994, sec. 1, p. 7. However, even while asking the United States to maintain troop strength in Japan, Tokyo made large military cuts in late 1995. Nicholas D. Kristof, "Japan to Cut Own Military, Keeping G.I.'s," *New York Times,* November 29, 1995, p. A5.

[124]Cited in David E. Sanger, "The Corrosion at the Core of Pax Pacifica," *New York Times,* May 14, 1995, sec. 4, p. 1. See also "Is Japan Normal?" *The Economist,* June 24-30, 1995, pp. 25-26; and Joseph S. Nye, Jr., "The Case for Deep Engagement," *Foreign Affairs* 74:4 (July/August 1995), pp. 90-102.

[125]Nicholas D. Kristof, "Welcome Mat Is Wearing Thin for G.I.'s in Asia," *New York Times,* December 3, 1995, sec. 1, p. 6. Environmental issues also pose a problem. See Nicholas D. Kristof, "Suit in Japan Seeks to Ban Night Flights at U.S. Base," *New York Times,* April 11, 1996, p. A6.

[126]"Japan's Unspoken Fears," *The Economist,* October 7-13, 1995, pp. 35-36.

[127]Although not explicit, the arrangement was meant to allow for Japanese logistical aid in the case of a flare-up in Korea. Most Japanese still oppose expanding the country's military responsibilities overseas. "Friends in Need," *The Economist,* April 13-19, 1998.

[128]John King Fairbank, *China: A New History* (Cambridge, MA: The Belknap Press of Harvard University Press, 1992), p. 284.

[129]Ibid., p. 371.

[130]Ibid., p. 368.

[131]Ibid., p. 383.

[132]U.S. diplomatic relations with Taiwan were broken at the same time, but were in fact continued by means of the American Institute on Taiwan and the Coordination Council for North American Affairs in the United States.

[133]"The New, and Improved China Awaiting Clinton," *The Economist,* June 27-July 3, 1998, p. 39.

[134]Cited in David E. Sanger, "In a Trade Pact with China, a Ghost of Japan," *New York Times,* February 20, 1995, p. C5. The analogy also applies to South Korea. Robert Keatley, "U.S. Tests Way to Solve Disputes With Seoul, Progressing Little by Little," *Wall Street Journal,* July 15, 1994, p. A5.

[135]Cited in "America's Dose of Sinophobia," *The Economist,* March 29-April 4, 1997, p. 36.

[136]Seth Faison, "9.5% Growth in China Stuns Experts Again," *New York Times,* July 23, 1997, p. C6.

[137]Marcus W. Brauchli, "China Stays a Magnet for Overseas Money," *Wall Street Journal,* January 14, 1997, p. A14. China is developing its own highly efficient firms that can compete effectively with foreign firms, especially in high-tech areas. "Silicon Valley, PRC," *The Economist,* pp. 64-65.

[138]Joseph Kahn "Foreigners Help Build China's Trade Surplus," *Wall Street Journal,* April 7, 1997, p. A1.

[139]"The Global Economy," special report, *The Economist,* October 1-7, 1994.

[140]Robert D. Hershey, Jr., "Trade Deficit Grew Sharply Last Year," *New York Times,* February 20, 1997, p. 4.

[141]Marcus W. Brauchli, "In a Trade War, China Takes the Bigger Hit," *Wall Street Journal,* May 17, 1996, p. A10.

[142]"The Eastern Question," *The Economist,* May 24-30, 1997, p. 28.

[143]Eric Schmitt, "House Defeats Bill to End Trade Privileges for China," *New York Times,* June 28, 1996, p. A4.

[144]Robert D. Hershey, Jr., "China Has Become Chief Contributor To U.S. Trade Gap," *New York Times,* August 21, 1996, p. A1.

[145]"U.S. Says China Trade Gap May Grow," *Wall Street Journal,* July 2, 1998, p. A17.

[146]Seth Faison, "Dalai Lama Move Imperils Disney's Future in China," *New York Times,* November 26, 1996, pp. A1, A6. Tibet was occupied and incorporated into China in 1950.

[147]Chinese and American officials cannot agree on the size of the imbalance, the problem being how to measure Chinese goods that go through Hong Kong. Many of these goods are improperly labeled "Made in Hong Kong." Raymond Bonner, "Altering Labels, Not Clothes, China Sidesteps Trade Limits," *New York Times,* April 17, 1997, pp. A1, A4. See also Seth Faison, "China Announces Trade Penalty as Reply to Similar U.S. Move," *New York Times,* November 11, 1996, p. A6.

[148]David E. Sanger, "President Imposes Trade Sanctions on Chinese Goods," *New York Times,* February 5, 1995, sec. 1, pp. 1, 6; Seth Faison, "China Warns U.S. of Retaliation in Trade Dispute," *New York Times,* May 10, 1996, p. A7; David E. Sanger, "This One Just Might Be a Real Trade War," *New York Times,* May 19, 1996; sec. 4, p. 6; Seth Faison, "U.S. and China Agree on Pact to Fight Piracy," *New York Times,* June 18, 1996, pp. A1, A8; Seth Faison, "China Appears to Crack Down on CD Pirating," *New York Times,* April 7, 1997, pp. A1, A6; and Seth Faison, "Chinese Crack Down—for Now—on Pirated Video Disks," *New York Times,* on the web, June 24, 1998.

[149]Ian Johnson, "Traders Skeptical of China's WTO Efforts," *Wall Street Journal,* February 24, 1997, p. A2.

[150]Cited in Richard W. Stevenson, "U.S. Trade Deficit Worsens, and Gap with China Grows," *New York Times,* November 21, 1996, p. C6.

[151]David E. Sanger, "China Reported Ready to End Some Barriers," *New York Times,* February 12, 1997, pp. C1, C5; David E. Sanger, "China Faces Test of Resolve to Join Global

Economy," *New York Times,* March 2, 1997, sec. 1, pp. 1, 8; Johnson and Chang, "China Offers an Array of Reforms." Chinese leaders, especially Premier Zhu Ronji, have indicated that they will reduce subsidies, forcing state-owned industries to make it on their own or go bankrupt. If this leads to additional large-scale unemployment, social discontent may ensue.

[152]Alison Mitchell, "Clinton Launches Effort to Renew China Trade Ties," *New York Times,* May 20, 1997, pp. A1, A5.

[153]If China were a member of the WTO, it would not be necessary for the United States to renew China's MFN status annually.

[154]Robert S. Greenberger and Kathy Chen, "Washington Makes an Overture to China," *Wall Street Journal,* November 21, 1996, p. A16.

[155]Paul Blustein and R. Jeffrey Smith, "Where China's Concerned, Money Talks," *Washington Post National Weekly Edition,* February 9-25, 1996, p. 20.

[156]For its part, Beijing apparently sought to increase its influence in American political circles by contributing funds to President Clinton's 1996 reelection campaign. See David E. Sanger, "'Asian Money,' American Fears," *New York Times,* January 5, 1997, sec. 4, pp. 1, 4.

[157]John M. Broder, "Jiang Held Cards Till Final Moment," *New York Times,* June 30, 1998, pp. A1, A9.

[158]Laurence Zuckerman, "$1.6 Billion in Deals Can't Mask U.S. Disappointment," *New York Times,* June 30, 1998, p. A10; "China Plays the Europe Card," *The Economist,* May 11-17, 1996, pp. 33-34.

[159]See, for example, Seth Faison, "U.S.-China Textile Trade Pact," *New York Times,* February 3, 1997, p. A6.

[160]"Welcome to China, Mr. Clinton," *The Economist,* June 27-July 3, 1998, p. 17; Nicholas D. Kristof, "Albright Hugs Wary Tokyo Smarting from Beijing Trip," *New York Times,* July 5, 1998, sec. 1, p. 4.

[161]The Organization of European Economic Cooperation (OEEC) was Europe's response. The OEEC became the Organization for Economic Cooperation and Development (OECD) in 1960, with additional members including the United States, Canada, and Japan.

[162]The objective of rearming West Germany in a European context to help meet the Soviet threat was achieved by creating the Western European Union with West Germany as a member and then admitting the FRG to NATO.

[163]Klaus-Dieter Borchardt, *European Unification* (Luxembourg: Office for Official Publications of the European Communities, 1987), p. 19.

[164]Established in 1959, EFTA fostered free trade but rejected further integration.

[165]British entry followed a long fight. Through the 1950s, Britain resisted supranational proposals; and, when the British changed their minds, their membership application was vetoed by French President Charles de Gaulle in January 1963. De Gaulle argued that Britain depended too much on the United States and was insufficiently committed to Europe.

[166]In a 1994 referendum, Norway became the first country to turn down an invitation to join the EU. John Darnton, "Vote in Norway Blocks Joining Europe's Union," *New York Times,* November 29, 1994, pp. A1, A3. Swiss voters decided not to apply for membership.

[167]"European Union Names Possible Additions," *New York Times,* July 11, 1997, p. A6; "Eastward Ho, They Said Warily," *The Economist,* July 19-25, 1997, pp. 43-44. All the countries in Eastern Europe pose special problems because they are relatively poor and will drain resources from the EU's wealthier members.

[168]Stephen Kinzer, "Europeans Shut the Door on Turkey's Membership in Union," *New York Times,* March 27, 1997, p. A9.

[169]Cited in Derek W. Urwin, *The Community of Europe* (London: Longman, 1991), p. 231.

[170]"A Survey of The European Community: An Expanding Universe," *The Economist,* July 7-13, 1990.

[171]Alan Riding, "Union in Europe Strongly Backed by Danish Voters," *New York Times,* May 19, 1993, pp. A1, A4; Alan Riding, "French Approve Unity Treaty, But Slim Margin Leaves Doubts," *New York Times,* September 21, 1992, pp. A1, A6; John Darnton, "British Legislators Approve Pact Forging Greater European Unity," *New York Times,* May 21, 1993, pp. A1, A7.

[172]Josef Joffe, "The New Europe: Yesterday's Ghosts," *Foreign Affairs* 72:1 (1992/93), p. 36.

[173]"In Their Hands," *The Economist,* August 7-13, 1993, pp. 21-22; "Shooting the Messengers," *The Economist,* August 7-13, 1993, pp. 23-24.

[174]Although the position of bank president is supposed to be nonpolitical, a nasty spat erupted between Germany, which supported a Dutch candidate, and France, which sought the post for its own candidate. Only a last-minute compromise to divide the president's first term between the two candidates kept matters on track.

[175]See "A Funny New Emu," *The Economist,* March 4-10, 1995, pp. 49-50; "Is the Single Market Working?" *The Economist,* February 17-23, 1996, p. 50.

[176]Edmund L. Andrews, "The Euro Creates European Turmoil," *New York Times,* May 29, 1997, p. C3; Thomas Kamm and Matt Marshall, "Europeans Grapple With EMU Criteria," *Wall Street Journal,* June 13, 1997; Edmund L. Andrews, "The Dollar Soars As Europe Doubts Its Currency Plan," *New York Times,* July 15, 1997, pp. A1, C6. Germans took a hard line on these criteria to assuage domestic fears that the new currency would be weaker than the mighty Deutschemark. "Bridging a Continental Gap," *The Economist,* December 21, 1996–January 3, 1997, pp. 61-62. Yet even Germany was hard pressed to make the grade. Matt Marshall, "Germany Won't Meet EU Debt Target, Imperiling Schedule for Single Currency," *Wall Street*

Journal, June 13, 1996, p. A9; Matt Marshall, "Germany Considers Oil Sale to Ease Budget Crisis and Gain EMU Entry," *Wall Street Journal,* June 13, 1997, p. A14; Thomas Kamm and Greg Steinmetz, "Europeans See March to One Currency Hit New Stumbling Blocks," *Wall Street Journal,* June 2, 1997, pp. A1, A12.

[177]"The Ghosts at the EMU Feast," *The Economist,* November 30-December 6, 1996, pp. 43-45; "Figure It In," *The Economist,* April 26-May 2, 1997, p. 47.

[178]Edmund L. Andrews, "11 Nations Take Key Step Toward Unified Currency," *New York Times,* on the web, April 26, 1998. Actual bills and coins will not be circulated until 2002.

[179]With only a single currency and with policy made by a single central bank, all members will have to follow the same macroeconomic policies whether or not they are at the same point in their economic cycle.

[180]"The 15 at Sixes and Sevens," *The Economist,* May 18-24, 1996, pp. 50-52; Celestine Bohlen, "Europeans Celebrate Unity and Chafe at New Frictions," *New York Times,* March 26, 1997, p. A5.

[181]Alan Cowell, "Mad Cow Disease Tests European Cooperation," *New York Times,* March 28, 1996, p. A6; Sarah Lyall, "This Calls for Beefeaters: Britain Cudgels the European Union," *New York Times,* May 24, 1996, p. A4.

[182]In 1995, only seven EU members (called the Schengen group) removed such controls. Alan Cowell, "7 Members of the European Union Launch a Passport-Free Zone," *New York Times,* March 27, 1995, p. A4. Europe strictly regulates the movement of outsiders seeking to enter the EU. "Open to Us, Closed to Them," *The Economist,* July 13-19, 1994, pp. 43-45. There is fear that refugees and terrorists might gain admission to a country with porous borders, such as Italy or Greece, and then enjoy free movement throughout Europe.

[183]Joffe, "The New Europe," p. 40. French farmers are a militant group, willing to use violent tactics to maintain subsidies.

[184]"The Big Squeeze," *The Economist,* February 8-14, 1997, pp. 55-56.

[185]Support is weakest in Greece, Portugal, Ireland, Spain, and Denmark. "More-or-Less European Union," *The Economist,* August 26-September 1995, p. 46.

[186]A secret Franco-Russian military alliance was signed in 1894.

[187]Cited in Winston S. Churchill, *The Gathering Storm* (Boston: Houghton Mifflin, 1948), p. 7.

[188]A young member of the British delegation at Versailles, John Maynard Keynes, denounced the treaty as a catastrophe. Keynes, *Economic Consequences of the Peace* (New York: Harcourt Brace Jovanovich, 1920).

[189]Bonn had to renounce atomic, biological, and chemical weapons.

[190]Jonathan Carr, *Helmut Schmidt: Helmsman of Germany* (London: Weidenfeld and Nicolson, 1985), p. 86.

[191]Miles Kahler, "The United States and Western Europe: The Diplomatic Consequences of Mr. Reagan," in Kenneth A. Oye, Robert J. Lieber, and Donald Rothchild, eds., *Eagle Resurgent? The Reagan Era in American Foreign Policy* (Boston: Little, Brown, 1987), p. 313.

[192]In recent years, France and Germany have discussed adding a European nuclear deterrent apart from NATO. Craig R. Whitney, "France and Germany to Discuss Nuclear Deterrent," *New York Times,* January 25, 1997, pp. 1, 3.

[193]Rick Atkinson, "Germany Prepares to Face the Music, and It's No Waltz," *Washington Post National Weekly Edition,* February 28-March 6, 1994, p. 17.

[194]"The Eagle's Embrace," *The Economist,* September 30-October 6, 1995, p. 21-22, 24; Alan Cowell, "Only Economic Jitters Unite Germans Now," *New York Times,* October 3, 1995, p. A5. West Germans had to pay a 7.5 percent "solidarity surcharge" on income tax.

[195]Craig R. Whitney, "Germans, 5 Years Later: Bitter and Still Divided," *New York Times,* January 24, 1995, p. A3.

[196]Craig R. Whitney, "Right Wing Gains in Elections in State in Western Germany," *New York Times,* March 8, 1993, p. A4.

[197]Stephen Kinzer, "Where Is Optimism in Germany? Among the Bedraggled Easterners," *New York Times,* December 27, 1993, pp. A1, A6.

[198]"Germany Resolves to Pursue its Interests," *The Economist,* July 13-19, 1996, pp. 45-46.

[199]Alan Cowell, "German Air Force Planes Fly Reconnaissance Over Bosnia," *New York Times,* September 2, 1995, p. 2; "Normal Army = Normal Country?" *The Economist,* September 7-13, 1996, p. 46; "No Longer Shy About Being German," *The Economist,* November 9-15, 1996, p. 58; Alan Cowell, "Germans Plan Combat Troops Outside NATO, A Postwar First," *New York Times,* December 14, 1996, p. 3.

[200]Andrews, "11 Nations Take Key Step Toward Unifiied Currency."

[201]*Fortune,* August 7, 1995, pp. F-1, F-2.

[202]*World Development Indicators 1998,* Table 6.6, p. 328.

[203]"Who Ya Gonna Call?" *The Economist,* August 5-11, 1995, p. 49.

[204]"An Awfully Big Adventure," special report, *The Economist,* April 11-17, 1998, p. 17.

[205]Central Intelligence Agency, *World Factbook 1994-95* (Washington, DC: Brassey's, 1994), p. 146.

[206]"Germany's Europe," *The Economist,* June 11-17, 1994, pp. 45-46.

[207]"Ghosts of Handbags Past," *The Economist,* January 29-February 4, 1994, p. 55.

[208]William Drozdiak, "Germany's Economic Push to the East," *Washington Post National Weekly Edition,* April 21, 1997, p. 15.

[209]Europe and Japan look toward improving economic ties with these countries as a way of modifying their behavior. See Robert S. Greenberger, "Iran's Economic Problems Could Spark Friction Between U.S. and Its Allies," *Wall Street Journal,* January 3, 1994, p. 8; David E. Sanger, "Japan Tells U.S. It Will not Join Embargo on Iran," *New York Times,* June 10, 1995, p. 1.

[210]Cited in "Total War," *The Economist,* August 10-16, 1996, p. 37. Conflict over Helms-Burton and D'Amato was muted and the EU did not file a complaint with the WTO because the Clinton Administration waived indefinitely any attempt to impose sanctions on foreign companies. See Adrian Croft, "EU, U.S. Tackle Obstacles to Helms-Burton Pact," *Yahoo! News,* May 12, 1998, http://dailynews.yahoo.../stories/europe_1.html. Had the EU's complaint gone forward, the U.S. would have invoked a "national security exemption," thereby preventing WTO consideration. David E. Sanger, "Europe Postpones Challenge to U.S. On Havana Trade," *New York Times,* February 13, 1997, pp. A1, A6.

[211]John Markoff, "A Declaration of Chip Independence," *New York Times,* October 6, 1994, pp. C1, C13.

[212]See, for example, Edmund L. Andrews, "AT&T Wins $4 Billion Saudi Project," *New York Times,* May 10, 1994, pp. D1, D7.

[213]Eduardo Lachica, "U.S., EC Agree on Terms to Curb Subsidies for Airbus and Its Rivals," *Wall Street Journal,* April 2, 1992, p. A10.

[214]Brian Coleman, "U.S., EU Draft Pact on Trade-Product Standards," *Wall Street Journal,* May 29, 1997, p. A2.

[215]Nathaniel C. Nash, "Showing Europe that U.S. Still Cares," *New York Times,* December 3, 1995, p. 12; Mark M. Nelson and Brian Coleman, "U.S. and EU Sign Trade, Security Pact, Boosting Trans-Atlantic Cooperation," *Wall Street Journal,* December 4, 1995, p. A11.

[216]Sanger, "Foreign Relations: Money Talks, Policy Walks," p. 4.

[217]*U.S.-Canada Free Trade Agreement* (Washington, DC: U.S. Department of State, June 1988). France is also sensitive about maintaining cultural sovereignty. See Marlise Simons, "Bar English? French Bicker on Barricades," *New York Times,* March 15, 1994, pp. A1, A6.

[218]Peter Morici, *Making Free Trade Work* (New York: Council on Foreign Relations Press, 1990), p. 3.

[219]Ibid., p. 15.

[220]Cited in Keith Bradsher, "Economic Accord Reached by U.S., Mexico and Canada Lowering Trade Barriers," *New York Times,* August 13, 1992, p. A1.

[221]See, for example, Peter Behr, "In the NAFTAmath, Some Texas-Sized Gains," *Washington Post National Weekly Edition,* August 29-September 4, 1994, p. 19.

[222]Anthony DePalma, "Mexico Unloads State Companies, Pocketing Billions, but Hits Snags," *New York Times,* October 27, 1993, pp. A1, A6.

[223]Keith Bradsher, "Nafta: Something to Offend Everyone," *New York Times,* November 14, 1993, sec. 1, p. 10; Anthony DePalma, "Nafta Environmental Lags May Delay Free Trade Expansion," *New York Times,* May 21, 1997, p. A4. Some regions have benefited more than others. See Carl Quintanilla, "Midwest Boom Fueled by Mexico Trade," *Wall Street Journal,* April 21, 1997, p. A2; Sam Howe Verhovek, "Benefits of Free-Trade Pact Bypass Texas Border Towns," *New York Times,* June 23, 1996, pp. A1, A16.

[224]Gwen Ifill, "56 Long Days of Coordinated Persuasian," *New York Times,* November 19, 1993.

[225]Tod Robberson, "NAFTA's One-Way Street," *Washington Post National Weekly Edition,* August 28-September 3, 1995, p. 17.

[226]James Sterngold, "In Nafta's Complex Trade-Off, Some Jobs Lost, Others Gained," *New York Times,* October 9, 1995, pp. A1, A7.

[227]"When Neighbors Embrace," *The Economist,* July 5-11, 1997, pp. 21-23; Robert S. Greenberger, "Nafta Is Good for U.S., Clinton Study Says," *Wall Street Journal,* July 11, 1997, p. A2.

[228]Cited in James Brooke, "U.S. and 33 Hemisphere Nations Agree to Create Free-Trade Zone," *New York Times,* December 11, 1994, sec. 1, p. 1.

[229]Jonathan Friedland and Robert S. Greenberger, "Talks on Free Trade Area of Americas Are Postponed, in a Rebuff to the U.S.," *Wall Street Journal,* May 19, 1997, p. A15.

[230]Peter F. Cowhey and Jonathan D. Aronson, "A New Trade Order," *Foreign Affairs* 72:1 (1992/93), p. 183.

[231]Paul Lewis, "U.S. Trade Pullback," *New York Times,* July 4, 1995, p. 29; "Buy My Cars or Else," *The Economist,* May 13-19, 1995, pp. 16-17; Robert S. Greenberger and Jonathan Friedland, "Latin Nations, Unsure of U.S. Motives, Make Their Own Trade Pacts," *Wall Street Journal,* January 9, 1996, pp. A1, A4.

[232]Marcus W. Brauchli, "Clinton's Trip Sets Off Ripples Beyond China," *Wall Street Journal,* July 6, 1998, pp. A11-A12.

[233]"As Europe Meets Asia," *The Economist,* March 2-8, 1996, pp. 16-17.

[234]Germany's Constitutional Court and parliament cleared the way for German forces to take part in overseas military operations. Craig R. Whitney, "Court Permits German Troops a Foreign Role," *New York Times,* July 13, 1994, pp. A1, A5.

Part Four

The Search for Solutions

Part Four focuses on two issues that transcend the state and that will challenge all of us as we enter the twenty-first century: the global environment and human rights. Chapter 14 looks at a series of interrelated environmental issues, such as the population explosion, that threaten everyone's survival. Chapter 15 examines the relationship between the state and individual citizens in the context of human-rights abuses. Chapter 16 ends the book by summarizing the relative impact of globalizing and localizing trends in global politics.

Chapter 14

The State and the Species: Environmental Dilemmas

Growing threats to the global environment constitute what many think is the greatest challenge to human well-being as the millennium begins. These threats redefine the essential meaning of "national security," posing problems to humanity as a whole that do not respect political boundaries, that are interrelated, and that are beyond the capacity of individual states to solve.[1] Thus the problem created by China's declining capacity to feed itself because of depleted sources of fresh water and the need to import grain "is now *so clearly linked to global security* that the U.S. National Intelligence Agency... has begun to monitor the situation with the kind of attention it once focused on Soviet military maneuvers."[2] Threats such as these foster a perception of a common destiny among people around the world, but they also provoke angry disputes among states about who is to blame and who should pay to overcome these problems.

Environmental threats epitomize the paradox of "collective goods" that we discussed in Chapter 1. In other words, it is in our collective interest to deal with these threats, but it is also in the interest of each individual and state to pay as little as possible to do so. Indeed, all of us can cite a variety of reasons why others should pay instead of us. Thus the rich argue that burgeoning populations in less-developed countries will put dramatically greater burdens on the global environment, and the poor declare that the rich use a disproportionate share of global resources. If others pay, we can be "free riders," enjoying benefits without having to pay for them.[3]

As we shall see, states sometimes have the political will to undertake common efforts to deal with collective environmental threats, especially by creating international regimes. More often than not, however, because of the tension between "national interest" and "collective interest," they fail to do so or do so only imperfectly. As a consequence, like other collective challenges that characterize the postinternational world—such as drugs, disease, terrorism, and capital flows—they "involve a diffusion of power away from states to private actors and require organizing states for cooperative responses."[4] Transnational groups have emerged to press states to deal with environmental threats and sometimes take direct action to force states to do so.

The best known of these is Greenpeace, founded in 1971 by Canadians opposed to U.S. nuclear testing in Alaska. Organized like a transnational corporation, Greenpeace's global income grew from $40 million to $179 million between 1985 and 1991. Today, the organization has 3.1 million contributors and a budget of $145 million. It supports forty-three offices in thirty countries, a staff of 1,200, and thousands of volunteers.[5] Sometimes Greenpeace's efforts bear fruit. Thus, in 1994, after a ten-year effort, Greenpeace's toxic-trade team achieved a great victory with the Basle Convention, which restricts exports of hazardous wastes from rich to poor countries.[6]

Greenpeace specializes in visible confrontations to gain sympathetic publicity for environmental causes. In 1985, as its ship the *Rainbow Warrior* prepared to sail to Mururoa Atoll, France's nuclear test site in the South Pacific, French agents blew it up in the harbor of Auckland, New Zealand. Ten years later *Rainbow Warrior II* once more sought to disrupt French nuclear testing but was seized by French commandos before it could put protesters ashore,[7] and, in another incident, Greenpeace divers managed to hide in a testing platform.[8] In 1995, Greenpeace "commandos" rallied opposition among Europe's environmentalists to Shell Oil Company when they were lowered from a helicopter onto an oil-storage platform in the North Atlantic that Shell was about to sink.[9] Groups like Greenpeace teach that everyone has a stake in the survival issues described in this chapter.

Burgeoning Populations

Now that the Cold War has ended and the threat of large-scale nuclear war has receded, burgeoning populations and their environmental impact may be the greatest overall peril to human well-being. Population growth, especially if not accompanied by economic development, will, at best, reduce standards of living and amenities for everyone. The case of China, where as many as 100 million peasants have emigrated to cities in what the Chinese call the "blind flow,"[10] illustrates the population-environment link. According to one report, "China presents ecological problems so severe that they constitute a collective crisis, with global implications."[11] The World Bank is providing $500 million a year for environmental programs in China, where "acid rain nibbles at the Great Wall; the Grand Canal... resembles an open sewer; part of Shanghai is slowly sinking as its water table is depleted; and Benxi, in Manchuria, is so thick with air pollution the city doesn't appear in satellite pictures."[12] China's heavy reliance on coal to industrialize will make it the world's leading producer of climate-warming carbon dioxide in two or three decades, and *global warming* will inundate China's coastal plain, displacing some 67 million people in and around Shanghai and Guangzhou.[13]

High birth rates in the poorest societies among people who live in crowded conditions with inadequate sanitary and medical facilities provide fertile soil for spreading diseases such as AIDS (acquired immune deficiency syndrome), malaria, and cholera and resurgent death rates among children.[14] Leading off the U.N. Conference on Population and Development in Cairo late in 1994, Secretary General Boutros Boutros-Ghali declared that "the future of human society" depended on dealing successfully with the population explosion and that "indifference and inaction are the real crimes against conscience."[15]

The population issue is part of a larger problem, the gap between rich and poor. Population control is critical if poor countries are to develop their economies, and, as development takes place, population growth rates will decline and then stabilize. However, some from the developing countries look with suspicion on efforts to limit their populations, pointing out that the pressures on global resources come from the developed, not the developing world.[16]

Two centuries ago, Thomas Malthus (1766–1834), an English economist and clergyman, predicted a growing imbalance between populations and food supply. He argued that world population would be kept in balance with resources only by catastrophes such as famine, disease, and war. Malthus left open the possibility that changes would occur to forestall his dire predictions, and global productivity has continued to grow because of emigration, agricultural technology, industrialization, and what Thomas F. Homer-Dixon calls "ingenuity"—ideas applied to technical and social problems.[17] Whether or not a "neo-Malthusian"[18] future lies ahead remains to be seen.

Culture, Tradition, and Population

Discussions of population generate passion, for they touch individuals' cultural, economic, and ethical beliefs. Preference for large numbers of children has deep roots. In some developing societies, large numbers of male offspring are wanted to help parents in the fields, compensate for a high infant mortality rate, and provide social insurance for parents in old age. In some cases, economic incentives are reinforced by patriarchal traditions that treat children as symbols of prestige. Thus, in Rwanda, where large families give men prestige, women bear an average of 8.5 children, the highest rate in the world.[19] From the individual's point of view, many children may make sense, even though it is harmful to society as a whole; the individual's private good and society's collective good are in conflict.

The conventional view of population control is that changes in customs and values are needed and that birth control alone is not the answer. Social and economic upheavals that increase wealth, education, and urbanization alter individual incentives and bring down birthrates. Some countries, such as Singapore, have enjoyed great success in lowering rates by combining economic incentives with cultural norms and coercion. Wealth and education arouse new interests outside the home and bring knowledge about opportunities for personal growth that are only possible with a small family. As women in developing societies join the work force, their interests (as well as those of spouses) change in ways that reduce birthrates. Finally, urbanization and government social-security policies reduce economic incentives to have large families and create practical constraints such as insufficient housing.

Can population growth be arrested without first going through economic development? In Zimbabwe, where before independence there was widespread suspicion that birth control was a white plot to limit the numbers of blacks, 800 women ride bicycles to deliver contraceptive advice to peasant women, and population growth has been reduced to 2.3 percent, well below most of Africa.[20] Along with Zimbabwe, the experience of Bangladesh, the most densely populated territory on earth (behind Hong Kong) and still among the world's poorest countries, where fertility rates declined 21 percent between 1970 and 1991, leads some experts to conclude: "If fertility rates are to fall, don't wait around for the forces of modernization to slowly work their way. Make family planning available, and you

ACTORS SPEAK

Growing population pressures and environmental deterioration pit the interests of individual states against the collective good of humanity. Economic interest groups persuade states to balk at accepting trade-offs between environmental well-being and economic growth. For these reasons, transnational groups have formed to lobby governments, sometimes dramatically, and to press them to act in the interest of the world as a whole. Poor states argue that the wealthy ones, which industrialized earlier, want them to bear disproportionate costs for cleaning up the environment, including foregoing economic development.

We try to keep it simple. One, we raise environmental awareness. Two, we want to push the world toward solutions, using the most egregious examples. The whole point is to confront; we try to get in the way. Confrontation is critical to get coverage in the press or to reach the public some other way. (Steve D'Esposito, executive director of Greenpeace International, as cited in Marlise Simons, "For Greenpeace Guerrillas, Environmentalism Is Again a Growth Industry," *New York Times*, July 8, 1995, p. 3)

There's an interest that there be no development here. There are 219 international groups concerned with saving the Amazon. Of those, I would say that 218 don't even know where the Amazon is. (Gilberto Mestrinho, governor of Amazonas, Brazil, as cited in Don Podesta, "A Burning Issue in Brazil," *Washington Post National Weekly Edition*, October 18-24, 1993, p. 18)

might be surprised by the number of couples that use them." In other words, "contraceptives are the best contraceptives."[21] However, contraceptive prevalence varies dramatically in the developing world, ranging from 86 percent in Hong Kong to 2 percent in Guinea.[22]

Developing countries that reduce death rates, emphasize the education of women as agents of change, and offer family planning in community settings have done best in reducing birth and fertility rates, even in the face of opposition from religious institutions. Muslim Indonesia, for instance, reduced its birthrate from 5.6 per woman to 3.0 between 1971 and 1991. (Birthrate refers to the annual number of births per thousand, and fertility rate is the average number of children born alive to women in a population.) Another example is Colombia, a Catholic country where, according to the executive director of the leading family-planning organization, "couples see no contradiction between their religious beliefs, which they take care of on Sundays, and their family planning the rest of the week."[23]

Colombia offers families a wide range of birth-control options and has reduced its fertility rate from 7.1 children per woman to 2.9 in three decades.

Combining economic development and coercion can make a significant difference, as shown by China's recent experience. In 1988, China, with 22 percent of the world's population but only 7 percent of its arable land, imposed a harsh family-planning policy, setting population quotas for local officials. Between 1987 and 1992, China's birthrate dropped from 23.3 to 18.2 per thousand population, and the country's fertility rate dropped to its lowest point in recorded history.[24] Chinese officials use abortion, sterilization, marriage bans, and even public tracking of women's menstrual cycles on village chalkboards[25] to limit births and to "avoid new births of inferior quality and heighten the standards of the whole population."[26] However, as many as 20 percent of Chinese births may go unrecorded as families, especially in rural areas, exceed the official limit.[27]

In some societies, traditional religion is a powerful deterrent to birth control. In Pakistan, mass distribution of birth-control devices has little effect because women in traditional Islamic families cannot make men use them.[28] In Catholic countries, the church rails against artificial birth control and abortion, attacking what a Vatican journalist called "'contraceptive colonialism' by rich countries of poor countries."[29] The church's influence over behavior has waned in such Catholic countries as Brazil, where the average number of children born per family dropped from 5.75 in 1970 to 2.35 today. Italy, where 97 percent of the population is Catholic, has the world's lowest fertility rate. "Not many of our friends worry about the church," declared an Italian schoolteacher. "They get married in church and have their children baptized in church, but it's out of tradition, not belief."[30]

The Vatican formally objected to those parts of the final declaration of the Cairo Conference that endorsed providing women with a range of family-planning and health-care options, including abortion in countries where it is legal.[31] Declaring that life is sacred from the moment of conception and fearing that the conference would be a victory for what he called "the culture of death," Pope John Paul II warned against "the temptation of a dangerous shortcut—focusing all efforts on the reduction, by whatever means possible, of the birth rate."[32] Malta and several Latin American countries endorsed the Vatican position, prompting a Colombian participant to declare, "These Latin American nations are trying to make the Vatican happy. But in 2,000 years the Vatican has never been happy."[33] Vatican opposition frustrated a number of conference participants. Egypt's population minister asked, "Does the Vatican rule the world? We respect the Vatican. We respect the Pope. But if they are not going to negotiate, why did they come?"[34] The conference secretary general spoke of the frustration of African delegates that "are complaining to me bitterly that we have spent days on one paragraph when they wanted to discuss broad population policy and issues like how aid will be channeled to them."[35]

Muslim opponents of the conference's draft declaration were equally outspoken. A Saudi Arabian journalist decried it as "an attempt to tear the values and beliefs of Islam from their roots. It is a ferocious attack on Islam and Muslims and their most holy beliefs,"[36] and the highest Saudi religious official, Mufti Abdel-Aziz bin Baz, urged Muslims to boycott the conference. Egypt's Al Azhar University denounced the conference's draft plan as sanctioning abortion, homosexuality, and extramarital sex "in such a manner as to demolish the values upheld by all the

One of the greatest threats to human well-being and even survival in the post–Cold War world is the population explosion which, if unabated, may cause environmental collapse and may trigger "green wars" for dwindling natural resources like fresh water. *(Toles,* The Buffalo News. *Copyright © 1984. Dist. by Universal Press Syndicate. Reprinted with permission. All rights reserved.)*

revealed religions" and argued that the U.N. recommendation that countries "promote responsible and healthy reproductive behavior" meant they should "encourage secret illicit sex."[37]

At best, getting control over spiraling birthrates is painful. As industrialization proceeds and land-hungry peasants flock from countryside to cities seeking jobs, urban services feel the pressure. Sewage, water, power, transportation, and police services break down under burdens larger than they were intended to bear. In India, for example, the increase in population of some 550 million people since independence has brought the country's infrastructure to the verge of collapse, reflected in train wrecks, floods, and fires.[38] *Shantytowns* with few amenities sprout up to house burgeoning numbers of urban poor and present daunting environmental threats to inhabitants—impure water, toxic air, inadequate sanitation—that constitute a *"brown agenda"* for environmentalists. Nevertheless, newly available cheap labor attracts foreign industry, which, in turn, draws more people from the countryside.[39]

All this change has hastened global urbanization, drastically changing the location of big cities. By the year 2025, two-thirds of the world's population will live in urban areas, compared with 37 percent in 1970.[40] London, the world's second largest city in 1960, will drop out of the top twenty by the year 2000. By that time, there will be 391 cities with more than a million inhabitants (compared with 288 in 1990) and 30 "megacities" with more than 10 million (21 in the developing world),[41] including Seoul (South Korea), Teheran (Iran), Manila (Philippines), Lagos (Nigeria), New Delhi (India), and Karachi (Pakistan).

A Crowded World

Fast-growing population is relatively recent (see Figure 14.1). It took from the beginning of history until 1830 for world population to reach one billion, and population doubled again by 1927.[42] Since the middle of the eighteenth century (about one-quarter of 1 percent of human history), world population has increased sixfold, and the rate of increase is accelerating. Each year population grows by about 88 million, or somewhat more than Mexico's population. Declared U.S. Vice President Al Gore: "It took roughly 10,000 generations for the world to reach a population of 2 billion. And yet in my 46 years, we have gone from a little over 2 billion to almost 6 billion."[43] This explosion is the result of several interacting factors: improved health and health care (especially for infants), growing agricultural production, and greater wealth and economic productivity.

At current U.N. projections, world population will soar from 5.7 billion in 1992 to 9.4 billion by the middle of the next century, with 95 percent of the increase in the developing world. The twenty-year U.N. Population Fund "program of action" accepted by the Cairo conference involves raising annual funding from $5 billion to $17 billion for population control by the year 2000 and making family planning available to the estimated 350 million people who do not have access to such programs today. If carried out, it would stabilize world population at about 7.8 billion by the year 2050.[44]

As world population shifts to the poorest societies, population pressures are becoming ever less evenly distributed. More people live in Asia than in the rest of the world combined. *Population density* in Asia and Europe is ten times that of North America and thirty times that of Oceania.[45] At one extreme is Bangladesh, with 920 people per square kilometer, and at the other is Australia, with 2 people per square kilometer.[46] The United States, with a land area sixty-five times that of Bangladesh, has a population density of 29 per square kilometer. Consider that North America has about two acres of arable land[47] per inhabitant, whereas Asians have about a third of an acre of arable land each.

At current rates, regional differences in population density will grow. Population has stabilized in North America and Europe, but, without profound change, the less-developed countries will have enormous population increases in coming decades. Almost all the projected population increases will take place there. Population will double in the less-developed countries by 2037, two hundred years earlier than in the rich countries (see Table 14.1).

Table 14.2 shows the disparity in population density and annual growth for a range of countries. Although First World countries such as the Netherlands and Japan have high population density, their growth (except by immigration) has mostly ceased. At the other extreme, India's population will have grown by almost 250 million by 2015.

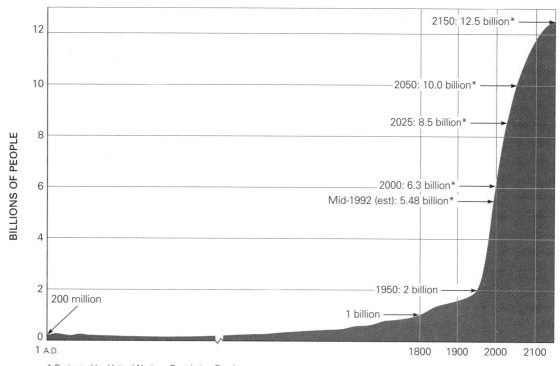

* Projected by United Nations Population Fund

FIGURE 14.1
World Population Growth

Most of the world's burgeoning population growth has occurred in recent centuries. For much of human history, world population was stable.

Population Trends and Global Consequences

Population growth has major political implications. Historically, a large population was regarded as an element of power that made it possible to recruit armies and support labor-intensive industries at low wages. For some, a large population provided emigrants for overseas colonization that added to the power of the mother country. Overpopulation in the city-states of classical Greece allowed for settlements in Asia Minor, North Africa, and elsewhere that spread Greek culture to the corners of the known world. The poor from Great Britain settled North America and Australia, and excess population from many societies, by emigration, contributed their talents to building the United States.[48] For such reasons, countries competed to encourage growth in population. In the 1930s Benito Mussolini offered rewards to Italian mothers with many children. Today, Iran's Arab neighbors express fear of that country's burgeoning population; Palestinians denounce Russian Jews' immigration to Israel as a ruse to displace them, and Israelis are uneasy about the high birthrate in the country's Arab population.

Rapidly increasing populations today are a source of political weakness and instability in countries as different as Rwanda and Pakistan. As population outstrips

TABLE 14.1
Population Trends 1970–2015

	Estimated population (millions)			Annual population growth rate (%)		Population doubling date (at current growth rate)	Total fertility rate	Contraceptive prevalence rate, any method (%)
	1970	1995	2015	1970–1995	1995–2015	1995	1995	1990–95
All developing countries	2,616.1	4,394.0	5,892.2	2.1	1.5	2037	3.2	56
Least developed countries	285.7	542.5	873.7	2.6	2.4	2022	5.3	22
Industrial countries	1,043.5	1,233.1	1,294.7	0.7	0.2	2223	1.7	70
World	3,659.6	5,627.1	7,186.9	1.7	1.2	2046	2.9	58

SOURCE: Adapted from *Human Development Report 1998*, p. 177. Copyright © 1998 by the International Bank for Reconstruction and Development/The World Bank. Used by permission of Oxford University Press, Inc.

increases in production, employment, wealth, and government services, discontent spreads, often becoming violent. Thus much of what we earlier called postmodern war takes place in societies that have been unable to slow population growth.

An Increase in Young and Old.   Rapid population growth increases the numbers of young people in a society, and declining or stabilizing growth rates produce an aging or graying society. Each trend entails different problems with consequences for global politics. Young people place special burdens on a society's economic and social infrastructure. The very young need medical care and day care so that parents can work. To contribute to society, they need education. Above all, they need land or jobs, and, in much of the developing world, these are scarce. If the educated have no opportunity to realize their aspirations, they become disillusioned, often rejecting the political system that has failed them. Some may be ripe for radical movements and become terrorists, criminals, or revolutionaries. The young were the backbone in Europe's fascist and communist movements in the 1930s, just as they are found in fundamentalist Islamic groups today.

Aging populations also create problems for societies, such as labor shortages, high medical and social-security costs, and a small tax and investment base.[49] Labor shortages in countries such as Italy, the first country with more people over the age of 65 than under the age of 15,[50] help developing societies because they provide opportunities for them to "export" workers who then send money home. Low birthrates all across Europe mean that foreign workers will be needed to pay the pensions of retired workers in the coming century.

Increasing Conflict?   Rapid population growth is associated with war. One hypothesis is that a growing population translates into demands for resources, which, if unmet, generate *lateral pressures* as countries try to satisfy their need for space and resources at the expense of one another.[51] Another aspect of this argument

TABLE 14.2
Estimated Population Growth of Selected Countries

Country	Population (1996)	Density* (1997)	Annual Increase (%)	Projected population, 2010
Third World				
India	945,000,000	313	1.3	1,129,700,000
China	1,215,000,000	129	0.7	1,349,100,000
Rwanda	7,000,000	244	3.5	11,000,000
First World				
United States	265,000,000	29	0.7	294,000,000
Netherlands	16,000,000	456	0.3	16,000,000
Japan	126,000,000	333	0.1	127,000,000

*Number of people per square kilometer

SOURCES: UNESCO, *1998 Statistical Yearbook,* Table 1.1; *World Development Report 1998/99,* pp. 190–191; *Human Development Report 1998,* pp. 176–177; *World Development Indicators 1998,* pp. 42–44.

is that population density and economic inequality combine to produce *land hunger* in agrarian societies. Small elites own disproportionate amounts of arable land, leaving large numbers of poor peasants to share the rest, which is not enough to support them. Land hunger and economic inequality are an explosive combination that revolutionaries can exploit.[52]

Land hunger was a key factor behind the civil war that raged in El Salvador in the 1980s. More than half of El Salvador's people and three-quarters of those in rural areas lived in absolute poverty between 1980 and 1990, and its population is expected to double between 1995 and 2026.[53] The U.S.-supported Salvadoran government resisted decisive land reform, and Marxist guerrillas seized large estates and distributed them to landless peasants. Although a 1992 agreement ended the war in El Salvador, continuing population pressures may rekindle social tension in the future, and similar conditions exist elsewhere in Central America.

Some analysts believe that crowding, which is a consequence of population density, triggers violence. One describes urban conditions as a "human zoo":

> Only in the cramped quarters of zoo cages do we find anything approaching the human state.... But even the least experienced zoo director would never contemplate crowding and cramping a group of animals to the extent that man has crowded and cramped himself in his modern cities and towns. *That* level of abnormal grouping, the director would predict with confidence, would cause a complete fragmentation and collapse of the normal social pattern of the animal species concerned.[54]

In this perspective, urban crime and war have common roots. We would expect violence to be greater in densely populated areas such as Calcutta, where there are more than 88,000 people per kilometer,[55] than in sparsely populated ones, and the high murder and crime rates of rapidly growing cities such as Bogota and Rio de

Janeiro reflect the explosive combination of crowding and poverty.[56] In Karachi, a city of 10 million that by current trends will be 19 million by the year 2019, "middle-class suburbs are virtually under siege from urban guerrillas, armed with automatic rifles, bombs and rocket-launchers.[57]

AIDS and Population.   An offshoot of population growth has been the spread of AIDS, which infected almost nine million people between 1980 and 1994, of whom 90 percent died. By 1997, more than thirty million people were living with AIDS, or the *human immunodeficiency virus (HIV)* that produces AIDS,[58] and the death toll is revising population estimates downward. The less-developed countries have already been especially hard-hit by AIDS. They account for 92 percent of HIV infections since 1980, and the disease is spreading rapidly in densely populated areas of Asia. Southeast Asia had 1.7 million new cases of HIV in 1994, and Asia will probably soon pass Africa in terms of new AIDS cases.[59] Sub-Saharan Africa has been hardest hit, accounting for over two-thirds of those infected by AIDS/HIV.[60] Among urban high-risk groups in Uganda, Rwanda, and Zimbabwe, over 86 percent are infected with HIV,[61] and, because of AIDS, life expectancy in Zimbabwe has plummeted from 64 to 42 years.[62] All this leads one observer to predict a Malthusian fate for Africa: "If there is no cure found for AIDS in the next few years, then Africa's high fertility rates could be checked by worsening mortality rates."[63]

No region is immune to the epidemic. In the United States, AIDS is the leading cause of death of men between the ages of 25 and 44.[64] In Europe, a German company distributed AIDS-infected blood to German hospitals and foreign clients, and similar scandals rocked France and Switzerland.[65] In Eastern Europe, open borders and growing mobility have increased the prospects of an AIDS epidemic.[66] And, where there are AIDS-weakened populations, diseases like tuberculosis also take root.[67] The World Health Organization declared a global tuberculosis emergency in April 1993.[68]

The AIDS disease has been attacked globally by research, treatment, and education, but little of this has taken place in the regions most severely affected by the disease. Too few countries recognize how massive the problem is, and national efforts have been poorly coordinated.

Deteriorating Global Ecology

Population growth diminishes our physical space and strains to bursting the earth's physical, social, and political environments. Already, wealthy countries are running out of space in which to dump solid waste, some of it violently toxic, and, in some cases, have exported it to poor countries.[69] Environmental crises are not new. A popular explanation for the Roman Empire's fall was declining birthrates caused by the use of lead in water pipes. Industrialization in the West was also accompanied by environmental disasters. The madness of the Mad Hatter in *Alice in Wonderland* was caused by mercury used in making hatbands. In the nineteenth century, entire species of animals such as the American bison were threatened by overhunting, and others were wiped out.

Nevertheless, the current global crisis is unprecedented. According to the Worldwatch Institute, some current environmental trends are the following:

- The ozone shield in heavily populated latitudes of the northern hemisphere is thinning twice as fact as scientists thought a few years ago.

- At least 140 plant and animal species become extinct each day.

- Levels of heat-trapping carbon dioxide are now 26 percent higher than the preindustrial concentration, and continue to climb.

- The earth's surface is warmer today than at any time since record keeping began in the mid-nineteenth century.

- Forests are vanishing at an annual rate of 17 million hectares.

- Annual world population growth is roughly equal to adding another Mexico each year.[70]

All this leads the author to conclude: "The roots of environmental damage run deep. Unless they are unearthed soon, we risk exceeding the planet's carrying capacity to such a degree that a future of economic and social decline will be impossible to avoid."[71]

Too Little Food   The mass famine that Malthus feared has been postponed by technology, including genetic engineering, new strains of plants, improved fertilizers, and mechanized agriculture.[72] Nevertheless, in some regions per capita food consumption is outstripping food production.[73] African food production in the early 1990s was 20 percent lower than two decades earlier.[74] In China, with population growing by 14 million a year, loss of 20 percent of cropland since the late 1950s to industrialization, along with soil erosion, salting of irrigation systems, and global warming, Lester Brown foresees a decline of 20 percent in grain production between 1990 and 2030, leaving a shortfall of 216 million tons—*a level that exceeds the world's entire 1993 grain exports of 200 million tons.*"[75]

Sufficient food is still available globally, but distributing it to those in need is difficult. Both local and global political problems have shaped efforts to address that imperative demand. Somalia is a frightening illustration. After the global community's response to starvation in Somalia had been an "abject failure,"[76] a U.S.-led intervention late in 1992 tried to arrest famine in that country until continued violence led to the withdrawal of U.S. forces in March 1994. As in prior famines in Ethiopia and the Sudan, the world community reacted late, only after starvation was widespread. Part of the reason is that, in dealing with such hunger, knotty local political issues have to be addressed. Ethiopia, the Sudan, and Somalia all suffered intractable political problems—petty warlords, weak central government, and ethnic rivalry—which make external assistance ineffective. Even if the global community wants to help, food assistance often fails to reach those who need it most and may create local dependency slowing the agricultural reform needed to make a country self-sufficient.

Sadly, food is used as a weapon in global politics. As more countries depend on a few food exporters, the latter may provide or withhold food exports to coerce political concessions, as did the Carter administration when it halted grain shipments to the U.S.S.R. after the 1979 invasion of Afghanistan. The United States provides inexpensive credits to countries it wishes to reward so that they can purchase surplus U.S. grain. Foreign leaders, including Presidents Anwar Sadat and Hosni Mubarak of Egypt, Iraq's Saddam Hussein, and Russia's Boris Yeltsin, have received such credits. Food has also become a political football in civil wars. In the Sudan, the Islamic government and its enemies withhold food from areas controlled by their rival. Food has also been used as a weapon in Afghanistan, Bosnia, Somalia, and Iraq.

Inadequate food spurs efforts to increase food production, but such efforts risk leaving a damaged environment for future generations.

Vanishing Forests

Environmental factors enter into the equation describing world food needs. Intensive farming may contribute to *soil erosion, salinization, deforestation,* and *desertification*. Among the most visible effects of deforestation is southward expansion of the Sahara in Africa and sandbars created in the Bay of Bengal by silt runoff from the Himalayas. Many Bengalis who try to live on these islands perish during annual cyclones. Another effect of deforestation is the carbon dioxide, methane, and nitrous oxide pouring ever faster into the atmosphere by burning trees and diminishing the ability of remaining forests to absorb carbon dioxide by photosynthesis. These gases contribute to the *greenhouse effect* (warming of the earth's atmosphere), and nitrous oxide also helps destroy the *ozone layer*, which protects us from the sun's ultraviolet rays.[77]

At the 1992 U.N. Conference on Environment and Development, or *Earth Summit*, in Rio de Janeiro, a plan was adopted to halt desertification. This Convention on Desertification establishes a "Global Mechanism" to seek money for and coordinate projects to slow the spread of deserts and migration from arid areas. However, little new money has been pledged for this task. An effort to limit logging was blocked by the United States, and international efforts to achieve "the missing Rio conventions" have been unsuccessful.[78]

A special problem is posed by disappearing jungles. Already, vast Third World jungle tracts have been denuded to slake the world's thirst for Southeast Asian, South Pacific, and Latin American[79] hardwood and local demand for living space and fuel. Every year an area the size of Belgium is cleared of jungles under pressure of population. Losing that much jungle reduces the earth's ability to produce oxygen, alters patterns of rainfall, and creates new deserts and enlarges old ones. In Brazil's Amazon basin, home to half the world's plant and animal species and source of as much as 20 percent of all fresh water flowing into oceans, economic needs are colliding head-on with the imperatives of global survival. That region, drained by the Amazon River, covers 800 million acres, an area almost as large as Australia. Although rain forests absorb huge amounts of carbon dioxide, more than 11 percent of the jungle has been burned away since 1975—an area the size of Morocco—in fires that contribute more to global air pollution and global warming than did burning Kuwait's oil fields by retreating Iraqi troops in 1991.[80] In September 1993, the space shuttle *Discovery* reported clouds of smoke over the Amazon, and in 1997 much of Southeast Asia was blanketed with smoke from Indonesia's burning forests.[81] Despite the Earth Summit, conditions in the Amazon continued to deteriorate as burnings reached their worst level after 1995.[82] As jungle is destroyed, animal and plant life are lost, and deforestation sends to extinction perhaps one hundred species *every day*. Among the plants pushed to extinction are those with high medical potential. Plants that may help cure or prevent cancer or AIDS tomorrow are being destroyed today.

Several factors combined to induce land hunger among Brazilian peasants. Steep population growth was accompanied after World War II by agricultural unemployment caused by drought, mechanization,[83] and crop shifts (from rubber and coffee to soybeans). By 1989, about 81 percent of Brazil's farmland was owned by fewer than 5 percent of the population.[84] Brazil's cities attracted many rural poor, some 31 million between 1960 and 1980. The cities could not absorb such numbers, and Brazil's political and social fabric was headed toward collapse. To hard-pressed Brazilians, the enormous Amazon region seemed an answer, and Brazil's military supported the idea of opening the Amazon as part of a campaign to suppress guerrilla and drug-related violence. Brazilian entrepreneurs too were excited about potential riches from lumber, oil, bauxite, gold, and hydroelectric power.[85] In 1970, the government launched a vast program to colonize the basin. Any farmer could have one hundred acres free. But the land is poor; the rain-forest trees gather their own nutrients but store little in the soil, which, once cleared of jungle, can produce crops for only one or two seasons. Thereafter nothing grows; the remaining soil blows away and the farmer must move elsewhere.

The fight to reduce slashing and burning of the Amazon has been led by foreign and local ecologists and by those who use the jungle to tap rubber (a harvest that does not destroy trees).[86] Resulting violence included the 1988 murder of Chico Mendes, a leader in protecting the rain forest and helping the rubber workers, and the murder of indigenous Yanomami Indians by gold prospectors in August 1993. Mendes's martyrdom turned Brazilian public opinion against the business interests that were exploiting the Amazon. In June 1991, Brazilian President Fernando Collor de Mello took steps to save the Amazon: abolishing tax subsidies for farmers and ranchers, firing the head of Brazil's Indian Protection Agency, establishing the Chico Mendes Extraction Reserve, and, most important, embarking on a new policy of debts-for-nature swaps. These actions plus an economic recession slowed but did not halt deforestation of the Amazon rain forest.

The *debts-for-nature swap* is an approach suggested by Thomas Lovejoy in 1984 to reducing friction with indebted developing states that are asked to bear a large share of the costs of global environmental reform. Lovejoy's idea was that a government or environmental group pay off part of a debtor's obligation at reduced interest. In return, the debtor would use the funds it would have paid in interest for environmental ends. The proposal attracted attention when it became apparent that some loans would never be repaid and banks became willing to accept partial repayment rather than confront a loan default.[87] The debts-for-nature tactic was used for the first time in 1987 in Ecuador. Another innovation involves the purchase by rich countries from poor ones of "carbon bonds" that allow the purchaser to continue emitting current levels of carbon while providing funds to poor countries to save forests and jungles.[88]

Water: Dying Seas and Drying Wells

Environmental stress is evident in the world's oceans and seas, which are used as open sewers, as if the oceans were so large that they could bear any abuse. In March 1989, the supertanker *Exxon Valdez* lost enough oil to poison Prince William Sound in Alaska;[89] in January 1993, the tanker *Braer* spilled 630,000 barrels of oil on the Shetland Islands coastline;[90] a 1994 oil-pipeline spill three times larger than the size of the *Exxon Valdez* spewed oil across Russia's tundra;[91] in April 1995, a Russian natural gas pipeline exploded, turning clouds bright red;[92] in recent years, Colombian guerrillas have blown up pipelines, spilling more millions of barrels of crude oil; and, for thirty years, the Soviet Navy dumped its radioactive waste in the Barents and Kara Seas in the Arctic.[93] Coral reefs, which support rich concentrations of life, have begun to die.[94] Plastic debris and oil slicks have killed countless sea birds, and whales, seals, turtles, and fish are victims of deadly toxins and viruses caused by chemical discharges. And this problem will worsen as we acquire the technology to exploit the wealth stored in ocean seabeds and rock chimneys—new microbes and minerals such as zinc, copper, silver, and gold as well as potential oil reserves.[95]

Eleven of the world's fifteen major fishing areas and almost 70 percent of the world's fishing stocks are presently overharvested.[96] Common food fish like tuna and swordfish are more and more heavily polluted, and species of food fish that were once common— cod, haddock, flounder, perch, pollock, halibut—have been overfished to the point where they are threatened by extinction.[97] So overfished were the waters off Newfoundland that they were closed in 1992, and two years later Georges Bank, once one of the world's richest fishing grounds, was also closed to allow stocks to replenish.[98] In thirteen of the world's fifteen largest fishing regions, the catch has shrunk until "the oceans are nearly fished to the limits."[99]

Scarcity intensifies competition for what remains and deepens tension between the collective good of conservation and the individual incentive to catch as many fish as possible while they remain. American and Canadian fishermen heatedly argue over the distribution of declining stocks of Pacific salmon,[100] and, in 1994, Canada passed a law authorizing the seizure of foreign fishing boats in the Grand Banks beyond the two-hundred-mile limit.[101] The following year Canadians and Spaniards virtually came to blows over dividing Greenland halibut around Canada, as depleted stocks in European waters increased the Spanish presence in the North Atlantic. Another contentious issue is commercial whaling. Most countries have agreed to end the practice that has endangered some species, such as the blue whale, the ocean's largest creature, but Japan and Norway refuse to do so.[102]

Supplies of fresh water are diminishing. Only 3 percent of the earth's water is fresh, and current demand is roughly thirty-five times as great as it was three hundred years ago. Agriculture accounts for about 66 percent of the fresh water that is used, industry 25 percent, and human consumption only about 9 percent. Figure 14.2 shows the global distribution of fresh water resources. In China, according to the country's water resource's minister, "in rural areas, over 82 million people find it difficult to procure water."[103] Global per capita fresh water is a third lower now than in 1970, and eighty countries with 40 percent of the world's population, located mainly in Africa and the Middle East, are water-scarce.[104] And much of the fresh water in the less-developed countries is polluted, contributing to the death of between 3.8 and 5 million children each year from diarrhea.[105]

More mouths and less water engender conflicts. During the severe drought that struck California early in the 1990s, Los Angeles had to compete with the state's influential agricultural interests for diminishing supplies. Only after a considerable struggle were limitations placed on agriculture's extravagant consumption of water. Without long planning and care, California may find itself in the tragic position confronting Central Asia in Kazakhstan and Russia as a result of the pollution of the Aral, Caspian,

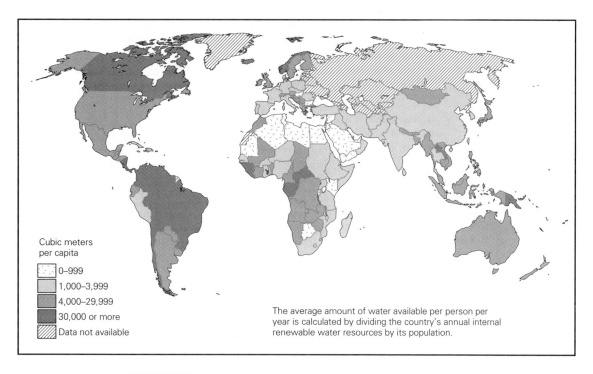

FIGURE 14.2

Annual Renewable Water Sources

Water has become a scarce human resource. As this map illustrates, large areas of the world lack adequate sources of renewable fresh water. As populations grow, conflicts over water resources will intensify. SOURCE: *World Development Report 1992* (New York: Oxford University Press, 1992), p. 217. Copyright © 1992 by the International Bank for Reconstruction and Development/The World Bank. Used by permission of the Oxford University Press, Inc.

and Black Seas. Since 1960, so much water has been diverted from rivers that feed the Aral Sea (Ama Darya and Syr Darya) to irrigate the region's cotton crop that the Aral is drying up. By 1994, the sea's surface area had been halved and its salinity tripled. Toxic chemicals used to fertilize cotton have leeched into the region's groundwater, increasing infant mortality and producing typhoid, dysentery, and birth defects.[106] The U.S.S.R., Turkey, and others used the Black Sea to dump vast quantities of toxic chemicals, and only five of twenty-six species of fish caught there in the 1960s remain.[107]

Global Energy Needs and the Environment

Energy issues illustrate how environmental and economic imperatives collide and how global actors have divergent views of trade-offs between the two. Actors in less-developed countries are willing to sacrifice environmental benefits to achieve rapid economic development at the same time as developed societies demand more stringent global environmental standards.[108] Let us examine these trade-offs by identifying various sources of energy, evaluating their environmental consequences, and describing attempts to balance safeguards for the environment with energy needs.

Fossil Fuels and Economic Development

Harnessing new energy sources tells much about how human society has modernized. The nineteenth-century industrial revolution was possible only because machinery was invented to replace human and animal labor, and that revolution was built on mountains of cheap, plentiful fossil fuels such as coal and coke. Transportation and distribution networks were built on the internal-combustion engine—trains, planes, and automobiles. In recent decades, the revolution in high technology has been brought about by computers that, using relatively little energy, can store and combine previously unimaginable quantities of information. If the engine of progress in earlier centuries depended on substitutes for physical labor, the present revolution is fueled by substitutes for brainpower.

Economic progress is never without cost, however. It changes lifestyles and cultural traditions and destabilizes communities. Before labor unions, many people, including women and children, were forced to work long hours for little pay and live in squalor. Working-class conditions in nineteenth-century Europe and America influenced Karl Marx and Friedrich Engels (who wrote *The Condition of the Working Class in England*). Charles Dickens and Émile Zola vividly depicted in their novels how workers lived. Unfettered industrialism left terrible environmental scars. Smog, toxic compounds, and other side effects of the workplace inflicted disease and premature death. Air and water were poisoned; coal miners contracted tuberculosis and black lung; and coal burned for heat made London notorious for its pea-soup fogs.

The global community today is more sensitive to the relationship between energy and environment and better understands how both are needed for prosperity and health. The economic and political sides of the equation received great attention during the *oil shocks* in 1973 and 1979. When gasoline was hard to find and its price inflated following the Arab-Israeli war of 1973, interest picked up in alternative sources of energy such as solar, geothermal, wind, nuclear, and even thermonuclear power. The oil shocks showed the world it was depending ever more on oil from the Middle East. All over the world, geologists feverishly sought new sources of oil, especially offshore in the North Sea, the South China Sea, the Pacific Ocean off California, and the Gulf of Mexico. High oil prices in the 1970s also spurred conservation, especially in smaller cars with improved mileage, and global use of oil dropped from 65 million barrels a day in 1979 to 59 million in 1985.[109] Conservation and cleaner energy promised to reduce air pollution.

If the world was sensitized to environmental issues in the 1970s, new burdens were piled on the global environment in the 1980s. Efforts to cope with some challenges (for example, air pollution caused by sulfur) complicated programs to cope with others (for example, global warming and holes in the ozone layer). The upsurge in oil exploration and production set off by earlier shortages and price hikes, combined with reliance on market forces in the West and a weakened OPEC, brought prices down and produced an oil glut. One consequence was a reduction in conservation efforts. People again began to buy "gas-guzzling" cars and to pay less attention to conservation measures, and dependence on Middle Eastern oil began to climb again. The energy crunch will grow again in coming decades because of surging demand in the developing world.[110] Nevertheless, there is some cause for optimism because the price of renewable energy sources (other than nuclear and hydro power) is beginning to decline. Renewable sources, like solar and wind energy, are especially suitable for the roughly two billion people, most of whom live in the tropics, who still do not have electricity.[111]

Nuclear Energy

As rising oil prices awakened interest in alternative energy sources, nuclear energy became more popular.[112] By 1996, 476 nuclear plants were operating or being built worldwide.[113] As the number of power plants grew, events made it appear that the cure might be worse than the illness.

On March 28, 1979, a malfunctioning valve set in train events at *Three-Mile Island* nuclear power plant near Harrisburg, Pennsylvania that uncovered the nuclear reactor core. Although little nuclear material escaped, the fear of nuclear meltdown gripped many in the United States. Then, on April 26, 1986, Reactor No. 4 of the *Chernobyl* nuclear power plant, near Kiev in the Soviet Union, blew up, sending toxic nuclear debris across much of Western and Central Europe and forcing the evacuation of 134,000 people living near the plant. Although relatively few people were killed in the initial blast, estimates of future cancer deaths from radiation range as high as 45,000. Thyroid cancers are 285 times pre-Chernobyl levels in Belarus,[114] and if the experience of Hiroshima and Nagasaki is a guide, rates of chromosome aberration, immune deficiency disease, and genetic diseases in Ukraine and Belarus will also be abnormal. High-risk reactors similar to Chernobyl No. 4 (RMBK-1000) operate in Chernobyl, as well as near Ignalia in Lithuania, Bohunice in Slovakia, Kozloduy in Bulgaria, and Kola in Russia.[115] American companies are involved in completing Soviet-designed reactors in the Czech Republic, but they are reluctant to work on Russian and Ukrainian reactors without an international nuclear liability treaty by which the U.S. government would help pay for damage caused by overseas nuclear accidents.[116]

Memories of Chernobyl and other incidents, such as the 1957 explosion of a liquid-waste holding tank in the Urals, the 1993 release of toxic debris from a Russian facility near the East Siberian city of Tomsk, and an accident at Japan's prototype fast-breeder reactor in 1995,[117] have fired public fear about nuclear power in many countries. In Germany, mass protests greeted efforts to ship nuclear waste,[118] and the socialist-green coalition that took office in Germany in late 1998 promised to phase out nuclear power. Public fear intensifies when publics learn about earlier nuclear tragedies such as the sinking of the Soviet nuclear submarine *Komsomolets* off the Norwegian coast in 1989.[119] The United States is pressing for a global ban on dumping of low-level radioactive waste at sea (to reinforce an existing ban on dumping high-level radioactive wastes),[120] but no solution is in sight for the large amount of radioactive debris leaking from Russian nuclear reactors in space that threaten other satellites.[121] Between 1947 and 1967, radioactive waste from uranium mining in Soviet Kirgizstan was dumped in twenty-three open sites,[122] and to avoid surface leaks of nuclear waste, the U.S.S.R. secretly injected liquid nuclear material directly into the earth, a process described by a U.S. Nobel laureate in physics as "the largest and most careless nuclear practice that the human race has ever suffered."[123]

Even discounting dramatic events like Chernobyl, nuclear power carries environmental hazards. Among the worst is low-level and high-level radioactive waste—"everything from piping-hot irradiated [used] fuel to mildly radioactive clothes worn by operators."[124] One issue is how to dispose of this "hot" trash safely. Some radioactive waste remains dangerous practically forever. Plutonium-239 is poisonous for a quarter of a million years, and spent fuel rods from nuclear power plants must be stored for more than one hundred years. Regional compacts among U.S. states to deal with low-level waste have proved difficult to forge.

The problem of nuclear waste is complicated by rusting tanks of toxic by-products from manufacturing nuclear weapons during the Cold War.[125] That problem has been made more serious because arms-control agreements require the United States and Russia to dismantle many of these weapons. Nuclear production plants in the United States are located at Piketown, Ashtabula, and Fernald, Ohio; Oak Ridge, Tennessee; Richland, Washington; Aiken, South Carolina; Denver, Colorado; and Amarillo, Texas, and nuclear weapons are being dismantled at the Pantex plant in Amarillo and at Oak Ridge.[126] These facilities are responsible for widespread contamination of soil and water. At least one defense contractor (Rockwell International), which operated the Rocky Flats Plant near Denver between 1975 and 1989 that built atomic triggers for hydrogen bombs, was convicted of criminal felonies because of illegally incinerating nuclear waste and dumping radioactive water at the plant in the middle of the night.[127] In 1989, the U.S. Department of Energy closed several of these facilities and launched a multi-billion-dollar cleanup, which has made little progress;[128] the effort at Hanford Nuclear Reservation alone costs almost $3,000 a minute with little to show for the $7.5 billion already spent there.[129]

So far, despite imaginative proposals, no solution has been found for disposing of different nuclear wastes. One approach was to construct Defense Waste Processing Facilities in South Carolina, New York, and Washington in Order to encase highly radioactive liquid wastes in huge blocks of glass suitable for storage. The first of these facilities, to have been completed in 1989, began to operate in Aiken, South Carolina, in March 1996.[130] Since 1981, the government has been studying the construction of a Waste Isolation Pilot Plant (WIPP) for permanently disposing of nuclear-weapons waste in salt caverns at Yucca Mountain, near Las Vegas, and near Carlsbad, New Mexico.[131] The Carlsbad facility accepted its first shipment of nuclear waste in spring 1999.[132] Few people want such facilities in their back yard. Consequently, at more than four hundred sites around the world, nuclear waste is being stored where it was produced, and the problem will become overwhelming as these temporary storage sites reach capacity.

Future Energy Needs and the Environment

Without viable alternatives, the world, for the foreseeable future, will continue to rely on fossil fuels. One consequence of this is killer smogs that envelop cities like Mexico City, New Delhi, and Athens (where it is slowly destroying the Parthenon and other treasures of classical antiquity). The pollution is so great in Mexico City that it is the equivalent of smoking two packs of cigarettes a day.[133] Rural smog in less-developed countries from wood and dung fires in poorly ventilated huts accounts for most of the four million children who die from respiratory distress.[134] Another consequence of air pollution is *acid rain,* which has denuded forests of eastern Canada, New England, Germany, and Central Europe and eliminated fish from countless lakes, leaving them little "dead seas." Americans in the Midwest, where many of the pollutants that cause acid rain are produced, quarrel with its victims in New York, New England, and Canada, and airborne garbage from North America crosses the Atlantic to Western Europe.[135] In the future, air pollution may also menace food production.[136]

Still worse are environmental problems that menace the earth as a whole. *Chlorofluorocarbons (CFCs)*[137] released at ground level threaten to destroy the earth's ozone layer. As a result, the rate of skin cancer is likely to jump in coming decades. A 1992 international agreement (amending the 1987 Montreal Protocol) called for completely phasing out chlorofluorocarbon production in developed countries by 1996 and in developing countries by 2010. A second agreement was reached in 1995 to phase out the production of methyl bromide, the only remaining ozone-destructive industrial chemical.[138] Although the ban on CFCs has spawned a lively illegal trade in them,[139] it has already had positive results.[140]

The carbon dioxide, CFCs, nitrous oxides, and methane that we release are mostly responsible for the growing threat from heating the earth's atmosphere, the greenhouse effect. These gases, produced by burning oil, coal, and other fossil fuels, trap heat just as a glass greenhouse does. Though sunlight can pass through these gases, they also reflect it back to earth's surface as infrared radiation, and it can no longer escape into space.[141] The earth's average temperature in 1998 was the highest since people began to measure it, and seven of the ten warmest years on record have occurred since 1990.[142] Even small temperature changes may have big effects on the world as we know it. The earth 130,000 years ago was between 2 and 3 degrees (centigrade) warmer than it is today, and tropical swamps thrived where London now sits. Sea levels were higher, and areas in Europe and the United States that are now coastal dry land were under water.

As the earth's temperature increases, the polar ice caps may melt and flood populated coasts and islands. Island countries in the Caribbean, Indian, and Pacific Oceans such as the Marshall Islands, Tonga, Trinidad and Tobago, and the Maldives would disappear beneath the waves, and low areas like parts of Egypt and Bangladesh would be inundated.[143] Weather changes may make previously fertile areas in tropical zones desertlike, and crops that thrive in temperate zones may become difficult to grow in those regions. Higher temperatures may also cause droughts in grain-growing areas of America's Midwest and deplete the underground aquifer on which the region depends. Massive coastal erosion would follow, and salt water would poison freshwater systems. Secondary effects may include death for freshwater life forms and immense property damage.[144]

At the 1992 Rio Earth Conference, agreement was reached for industrialized countries to reduce carbon emissions to 1990 levels by the year 2000 (see Figure 14.3). However, the Commission on Sustainable Development that was set up to monitor the Rio commitment declared that the target was not being met,[145] and at a 1995 Berlin conference to review the Rio commitment, a coalition of oil-producing states and a few industrial states continued to oppose strong emissions curbs.[146]

In a speech to a special session of the U.N. General Assembly called in 1997 again to assess the environmental progress made since the 1992 Earth Summit, President Clinton spoke of these consequences and then described the collective

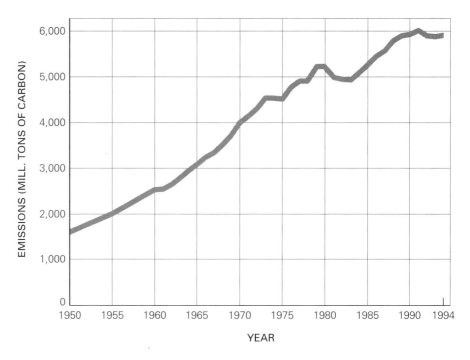

FIGURE 14.3
World Carbon Emissions from Fossil Fuel Burning, 1950–1994

World carbon emissions increased dramatically from 1950 to 1991. SOURCE: Lester R. Brown, Nicholas Lenssen, and Hal Kane, Eds., *Vital Signs 1995,* (New York: Norton, 1995), p. 67. Copyright © 1995 by the Worldwatch Institute. Reprinted by permission of W.W. Norton and Company, Inc.

nature of the issue: "No nation can escape this danger. None can evade its responsibility to confront it, and we must all do our part, industrial nations that emit the largest quantities of greenhouse gases today, and developing nations whose greenhouse gas emissions are growing rapidly."[147]

Indeed, as shown in Table 14.3, the United States is responsible for over one-fifth of world carbon dioxide emissions, yet it has lagged behind other rich countries in meeting the responsibility described by President Clinton. Significant political resistance at home from Republican foes in Congress and industrial interests who feared the impact of an agreement on economic growth, partly because of Americans' dependence on automobiles,[148] limited the administration's ability to negotiate an acceptable environmental agreement. Thus Republican Representative Dana Rohrabacher of California declared global warming "at best, to be unproven and, at worst, to be liberal claptrap, trendy but soon to go out of style in our Newt Congress."[149] As a result, the president refused to make any clear commitment of targets for American emissions reductions at the 1997 U.N. conference, and the United States was strongly criticized by some of its closest allies.[150] The 1997 U.N. conference did set the stage for a second conference that was held in Kyoto, Japan, later that year.

TABLE 14.3
National Sources of Carbon Dioxide

Country	Total million metric tons		Per capita metric tons	
	1980	1995	1980	1995
First World				
United States	4,515.3	5,468.6	19.9	20.8
Norway	90.4	72.5	22.1	16.6
Australia	202.8	289.8	13.8	16.0
Canada	420.9	435.7	17.1	14.7
France	482.7	340.1	9.0	5.8
Less-developed countries				
China	1,476.8	3,192.5	1.5	2.7
India	347.3	908.7	0.5	1.0
Indonesia	94.6	296.1	0.6	1.5
Iran	116.1	263.8	3.0	4.3
World	13,585.7	22,700.2	3.4	4.1
Richest	8,772.1	11,112.7	12.0	12.5
Poorest	2,037.8	4,503.7	0.9	1.4

SOURCE: *World Development Indicators 1998,* pp. 146–148.

In order to make a global agreement on reducing greenhouse gas emissions palatable to political foes at home, the Clinton administration sought to get a commitment for emissions reductions from the less-developed countries, especially China and India.[151] In addition, the United States demanded that any agreement include issuing rights or permits—*emissions credits*—that could be bought or sold, thereby allowing one country to pay another to reduce emissions to meet global targets. Thus the United States could pay other countries to reduce their emissions without having to reduce its own. The Kyoto conference accepted the American demands in principle, thereby reaching agreement—with the *Kyoto Protocol*—for major reductions in greenhouse gas emissions within ten to fifteen years. At Kyoto, agreement was also reached on providing funds and technology for energy efficiency projects in the less-developed countries. For its part, the Clinton administration committed itself to cutting U.S. emissions within that time to a level 7 percent below 1990s emissions. However, by the time follow-up negotiations were held in Buenos Aires, Argentina, in November 1998, little progress had been made.[152]

Global warming reveals the tension between global needs and states' perceived interests. Island countries threatened by rising oceans lobby for strong action. "Each tick of the clock," declared the Maldives' representative, "could be time lost for saving some 30 small island nations from drowning in a sea of rising tides."[153] By contrast, OPEC countries and coal-producing countries like Australia oppose vigorous action to limit global warming because it entails reducing demand for their fossil fuels.

Poor countries believe the burden of reducing carbon emissions should be borne by the rich, and, according to some critics, global warming is less of a problem for the poor than other hazards being ignored by rich countries.[154] Nevertheless, they will bear the brunt of a policy based on conservation and limiting heavy industry and the internal combustion engine. Western prosperity was built on intensive use of energy, and cities such as Pittsburgh and Glasgow were highly polluted during the industrial revolution. Demand for energy will grow dramatically in the less-developed countries in coming decades. Nevertheless, energy use is currently lower in poor than in rich societies, and the latter still consume far more resources and produce more waste per capita than the former. Economically advanced countries are responsible for three-quarters of the carbon released into the atmosphere, mainly from fossil fuels burned in automobiles.

Do not people in developing countries have the same "right" to develop their economies as Europeans and Americans did in earlier centuries? Why, they ask, should we not be able to exploit our jungles to feed, clothe, and heat our growing population? What right do others have to tell us how to use our own resources, especially when they already enjoy a high standard of living? Why should the rich, whose societies have 20 percent of the world's population but account for 80 percent of worldwide carbon dioxide emissions as well as for 86 percent of the world's private consumption,[155] not cut their standard of living for the common good rather than demand that we accept limits to growth?

Such questions have no simple answers. Even prosperous societies meet resistance at home to trade-offs between the environment and prosperity. Passionate conflicts arise between Americans who exploit forests and wetlands for jobs and profit and those who wish to preserve them; between those who wish to drill for offshore oil in the Arctic and off California and those who fear environmental damage; and between those who wish to develop "clean" nuclear power rapidly and those who fear new Chernobyls. Everyone bears some responsibility. On the one hand, consumers in developed societies use more resources, including energy, and produce more waste than the poor. On the other hand, the poor use energy less efficiently, invest little in controlling pollution, and have larger populations. Solutions require imaginative strategies enabling each actor to perceive that it can benefit by adopting measures to improve its economy and, at the same time, preserve the environment. Such proposals would entail capital transfers from the rich to the poor in exchange for greater environmental commitment and would create trade pacts to encourage development, even as environmental standards are raised.

Conclusion

Will individual states continue to pursue their own selfish interests even though these imperil the species by thwarting global cooperation to achieve collective goods? The World Bank's establishment of a Global Environment Facility to support environmental programs in the developing world is a hopeful sign. The June 1992 Earth Summit was evidence that people around the world were taking seriously the ecological threats to their survival and were slowly recognizing that, in the words of one observer, "Homo Sapiens rivals grand forces like the movement of continents, volcanic eruptions, asteroid impacts and ice ages as an agent of global change."[156] Another hopeful sign was the reversal of U.S. opposition to signing the *Convention on Biological Diversity*—to preserve diverse plant and animal life—which came into force in 1994.[157] Finally, the World Bank is beginning to make loans available for environmental purposes, providing Russia with funds to start cleaning up the contaminated rivers, polluted industrial sites, and toxic waste caused by decades of communist indifference to the environment.[158] There are now more than 170 environmental treaties and many other accords, most of them since the 1972 *U.N. Conference on the Human Environment* in Stockholm "first put the environment on the international agenda."[159]

The challenges discussed in this chapter are so linked that any effort to solve one problem will affect others. Feeding more mouths by clearing more land, growing new strains of crops, and using fertilizers to increase productivity mean fewer trees to absorb carbon dioxide and produce oxygen, greater competition for scarce water supplies, seepage of toxic chemicals into aquifers, and even more extensive soil erosion. Everything is tied to everything else. Cooperation on many issues and by the whole global community is indispensable to ensure survival. Some limited success has been achieved for the environment, but it has been so hard to get broad agreements that we will probably continue to see piecemeal agreements on environmental issues.

A debate has raged for decades about earth's capacity to sustain continued growth. Although some disagree about defining that capacity and when it will be reached, consensus is growing about *limits to growth,* beyond which environmental collapse is inevitable. Whichever answer is correct, it is clear that, as one observer says, the "scale and pressure of human demands on the environment is little appreciated, and it is growing: in 1975 every single man, woman and child in the United States used on average 40,000 pounds of *mineral* matter alone. . . . And all this was used in commonplace ways—just in making buildings, roads, furniture, packaging, hamburgers . . . things we take for granted. [T]he majority represent destruction of the environment *somewhere*."[160]

No one should assume that solutions will be found to our collective problems. Such solutions necessarily entail limitations on national sovereignty and will involve restricting state autonomy. We have no guarantee that such solutions are possible or that actors have either the imagination or will to cooperate for the collective good. Most species that existed on this earth have already disappeared. Only the future can tell whether *Homo sapiens* will be another casualty of failure to adapt to changing conditions.

Key Terms

acid rain
brown agenda
Chernobyl
chlorofluorocarbons (CFCs)
Convention on Biological
   Diversity
debts-for-nature swap
deforestation

desertification
Earth Summit
emissions credits
global warming
greenhouse effect
human immunodeficiency virus
   (HIV)

Kyoto Protocol
land hunger
lateral pressure
limits to growth
oil shocks
ozone layer
population density

salinization

shantytowns

soil erosion

Three-Mile Island

U.N. Conference on the Human

Environment

End Notes

[1]See, for example, A.J. McMichael, *Planetary Overload: Global Environmental Changes and the Health of the Human Species* (Cambridge, UK: Cambridge University Press, 1993).

[2]Lester R. Brown and Brian Halweil, "China's Water Shortage Could Shake World Food Security," *World Watch* 11:4 (July/August 1998), p. 10. Emphasis added. For a skeptical view, that China poses a threat to world food supplies, see "Chinese Grist to the Malthusian Mills," *The Economist*, May 4-10, 1996, pp. 33-34.

[3]See, for example, John Gerard Ruggie, "Collective Goods and Future International Cooperation," *American Political Science Review* 66:3 (September 1972), pp. 874-893; Todd Sandler and Jon Cauley, "The Design of Supranational Structures: An Economic Perspective," *International Studies Quarterly* 21:2 (June 1977), pp. 251-276.

[4]Joseph S. Nye, Jr., *Bound to Lead* (New York: Basic Books, 1990), pp. 20-21.

[5]Marlise Simons, "For Greenpeace Guerrillas, Environmentalism Is Again a Growth Industry," *New York Times*, July 8, 1995, p. 3. For critical commentary on Greenpeace, see "A Surprise in the Woods," *The Economist*, July 19-25, 1997, p. 31; "The Limits to Growth?" *The Economist*, August 1-7, 1998, pp. 67-68.

[6]"Greenpeace Means Business," *The Economist*, August 19-25, 1995, pp. 59, 62.

[7]Craig R. Whitney, "Paris Defends Seizing Ship in Pacific," *New York Times*, July 11, 1995, p. A4.

[8]Philip Shenon, "France Seizes 2 Ships Owned by Greenpeace," *New York Times*, September 2, 1995, pp. 1, 3.

[9]Cacilie Rohwedder and Peter Gumbel, "Shell Bows to German Green's Muscle," *Wall Street Journal*, June 21, 1995, p. A10.

[10]Lena H. Sun, "The Dragon Within," *Washington Post National Weekly Edition*, October 17-24, 1994.

[11]Patrick E. Tyler, "A Tide of Pollution Threatens China's Prosperity," *New York Times*, September 25, 1994, sec. 1, p. 3. For a discussion of urban air pollution, water shortage, and deforestation and resulting flooding in China, see Elisabeth Rosenthal, "Beijing Officially Uncaps Filter on Its Staggering Pollution Data," *New York Times*, June 14, 1998, sec. 1, pp. 1, 6; Patrick Tyler, "China's Fickle Rivers: Dry Farms, Needy Industry, a Growing Crisis," *New York Times*, May 23, 1996, pp. A1, A6; Erik Eckholm, "Stunned by Floods, China Hastens Logging Curbs," *New York Times*, September 27, 1998, sec. 1, p. 3.

[12]Marcus W. Brauchli, "China's Environment Is Severely Stressed as Its Industry Surges," *Wall Street Journal*, July 25, 1994, p. A1.

[13]Patrick E. Tyler, "China's Inevitable: Coal Equals Growth," *New York Times*, November 29, 1995, pp. A1, A10.

[14]Barbara Crossette, "Study Says Deaths Rise for World's Poor Children," *New York Times*, May 9, 1992, p. 3.

[15]Cited in Barbara Crossette, "Population Meeting Opens with Challenge to the Right," *New York Times*, September 6, 1994, p. A6. The Cairo meeting was the third world population conference, following a 1974 meeting in Bucharest and a 1984 meeting in Mexico City.

[16]See Mahbub ul Haq, *The Poverty Curtain: Choices for the Third World* (New York: Columbia University Press, 1976), pp. 122-136.

[17]Cited in William K. Stevens, "Feeding a Booming Population Without Destroying the Planet," *New York Times*, April 5, 1994, p. B5.

[18]"Apocalypse Soon," *The Economist*, July 23-29, 1994, p. 26.

[19]Jane Perlez, "In Rwanda, Births Increase and the Problems Do, Too," *New York Times*, May 31, 1992, pp. 1, 10. Rwandan refugees in Zaire had a birth rate of 50 to 60 births per 1,000, and more than 2,800 infants were born in the camps each month. James C. McKinley, Jr., "Anguish of Rwanda Echoed in a Baby's Cry," *New York Times*, February 21, 1996, pp. A1, A4.

[20]Bill Keller, "Zimbabwe Takes a Lead in Use of Contraceptives," *New York Times*, September 4, 1994, sec. 1, p. 7; "Shrinking Families," *The Economist*, July 30-August 5, 1994, p. 37.

[21]Cited in William K. Stevens, "3rd-World Gains in Birth Control: Development Isn't Only Answer," *New York Times*, January 2, 1994, sec. 1, pp. 1, 4. Also see John F. Burns, "Bangladesh, Still Poor, Cuts Birth Rate Sharply," *New York Times*, September 13, 1994, p. A5.

[22]*Human Development Report 1998* (New York: Oxford University Press, 1998), pp. 176-177.

[23]Cited in Barbara Crossette, "A Third-World Effort on Family Planning," *New York Times*, September 7, 1994, p. A6.

[24]Nicholas D. Kristof, "China's Crackdown on Births: A Stunning, and Harsh, Success," *New York Times*, April 25, 1993, sec. 1, pp. 1, 6. American policy between 1981 and 1993 was to withhold aid for birth-control programs involving abortion. This policy was reversed by President Clinton, but when Republicans took control of Congress in 1995, they sought to go back to the old policy.

[25]Patrick E. Tyler, "Population Control in China Falls to Coercion and Evasion," *New York Times*, June 25, 1995, sec. 1,

pp. 1, 6. Houses may be blown up and property confiscated if birth-control laws are violated. Chinese leaders are rethinking their harsh policies. Elisabeth Rosenthal, "For One-Child Policy, China Rethinks Iron Hand," *New York Times,* November 1, 1998, sec. 1, pp. 1, 16.

[26]Cited in Steven Mufson, "In China, Survival of the Certified Fittest," *Washington Post National Weekly Edition,* December 27-January 2, 1994, p. 17.

[27]"The Lost Girls," *The Economist,* September 18-24, 1993, p. 38; "China's Illegal Families," *The Economist,* February 10-16, 1996, p. 36.

[28]Barbara Crossette, "Population Debate: The Premises Are Changed," *New York Times,* September 14, 1994, p. A3.

[29]Cited in Alan Cowell, "Is This Abortion? Vatican vs. U.S.?" *New York Times,* August 11, 1994, p. 4.

[30]Cited in Alan Cowell, "Legendary Big Italian Family Becoming a Thing of the Past," *New York Times,* August 28, 1993, p. 5.

[31]Alan Cowell, "U.N. Population Meeting Adopts Program of Action," *New York Times,* September 14, 1994, p. A2. The Vatican was embarrassed when its Pontifical Academy of Sciences declared that there was an "unavoidable need to contain births globally" and urged limits on family size. Alan Cowell, "Scientists Associated with Vatican Call for Population Curbs," *New York Times,* June 16, 1994, p. A4.

[32]Cited in Alan Cowell, "U.S. Negotiators Push for a Truce over Population," *New York Times,* September 5, 1994, p. 2.

[33]Cited in Barbara Crossette, "Vatican Holds Up Abortion Debate at Talks in Cairo," *New York Times,* September 8, 1994, p. A6.

[34]Cited in ibid., p. A1.

[35]Cited in Alan Cowell, "Despite Abortion Issue, Population Pact Nears," *New York Times,* September 9, 1994, p. A6.

[36]Cited in Michael Georgy, "Saudis Scrap Plans to Go to Cairo Conference," *New York Times,* August 30, 1994, p. A3.

[37]Cited in "Al Azhar Joins the Vatican," *The Economist,* August 27-September 2, 1994, p. 34.

[38]John F. Burns, "Blaze in India Kills Over 300, Mostly Youths," *New York Times,* December 24, 1995, sec. 1, pp. 1, 4.

[39]The implications of urbanization were discussed at the 1996 U.N. Conference on Human Settlements, held in Istanbul. Barbara Crossette, "Hope and Pragmatism, for U.N. Cities Conference," *New York Times,* June 3, 1996, p. A3.

[40]Hal Kane, "Leaving Home," in Lester R. Brown, Nicholas Lenssen, and Hal Kane, eds., *State of the World 1995* (New York: Norton, 1995), table 8.2, p. 144.

[41]William Claiborne, "The Greens and the Browns Find Common Ground," *Washington Post National Weekly Edition,* October 3-9, 1994, p. 38.

[42]David Hargreaves, Monica Eden-Green, and Joan Devaney, *World Index of Resources and Population* (Aldershot, UK: Dartmouth, 1994), p. 10.

[43]Cited in David S. Broder, "A Return to Leadership," *Washington Post National Weekly Edition,* September 12-18, 1994, p. 4.

[44]Paul Lewis, "U.N. Conference to Discuss Population Plan," *New York Times,* April 3, 1994, sec. 1, p. 4; Barbara Crossette, "World Is Less Crowded Than Expected, the U.N. Reports," *New York Times,* November 17, 1996, sec. 1, p. 3.

[45]Australia, New Zealand, Melanesia, Micronesia, and Polynesia.

[46]*World Development Report 1998/99* (New York: Oxford University Press, 1998), table 1, pp. 190-191.

[47]Land under temporary crops, meadows for pasture, or gardens, and land lying fallow.

[48]Indonesia is trying to deal with population pressures on Java by resettling people on less crowded islands such as Sumatra. Seth Mydans, "Indonesia Resettles People to Relieve Crowding on Java," *New York Times,* August 25, 1996, sec. 1, p. 4.

[49]"Japan's Debt-Ridden Future," *The Economist,* August 3-9, 1996; Nicholas D. Kristof, "Baby May Make 3, but in Japan That's Not Enough," *New York Times,* October 6, 1996, sec. 1, p. 3; Michael Specter, "Population Implosion Worries a Graying Europe," *New York Times,* July 10, 1998, pp. A1, A6.

[50]Alan Cowell, "In an Affluent Europe, the Problem is Graying," *New York Times,* September 8, 1994, p. A4.

[51]Robert C. North and Nazli Choucri, *Nations in Conflict* (San Francisco: Freeman, 1975); and North and Choucri, "Economic and Political Factors in International Conflict and Integration," *International Studies Quarterly* 27:4 (December 1983), pp. 443-461.

[52]Land reform may reduce social tension, but where peasant populations are large, resulting farms may be too small to be efficient.

[53]*Human Development Report 1998,* pp. 164, 177.

[54]Desmond Morris, *The Human Zoo* (New York: Dell, 1969), pp. 77-78. Emphasis in original. See Robert D. Kaplan, "Cities of Despair," *New York Times,* June 6, 1996, p. A27.

[55]*Human Development Report 1994,* p. 173.

[56]"Fast Growth, Pollution and Crime Are Stifling Bogota," *New York Times,* September 9, 1993, p. A8; James Brooke, "Crime Now Reigns in Brazilian City Renowned as the Source of Romance," *New York Times,* October 25, 1994, p. A4.

[57]"Asia's Answer to Beirut," *The Economist,* July 1-7, 1995, p. 30. The guerrillas are members of the Mohajir Qaumi Movement (MQM) composed of Muslims who fled to Pakistan from India in 1947.

[58]*World Development Indicators 1998* (Washington, DC: World Bank, 1998), p. 40.

[59]Philip Shenon, "AIDS Epidemic, Late to Arrive, Now Explodes in Populous Asia," *New York Times,* January 21, 1996, sec. 1, pp. 1, 8.

[60]*World Development Indicators 1998,* p. 40.

[61]Ibid., p. 102. See also Howard W. French, "Migrant Workers Take AIDS Risk Home to Niger," *New York Times,* February 8, 1996, p.A3; James C. McKinley, Jr., "A Ray of Light in Africa's Struggle with AIDS," *New York Times,* April 7, 1996, sec. 1, pp. 1, 6.

[62]*World Development Indicators 1998,* p. 40.

[63]Paul Kennedy, *Preparing for the Twenty-First Century* (New York: Random House, 1993), p. 28.

[64]"AIDS Becomes Top Killer of Men 25 to 44 Years Old, U.S. Reports," *New York Times,* October 31, 1993, p. 13.

[65]Marlise Simons, "Swiss Red Cross Faces AIDS Probe," *New York Times,* May 22, 1994, sec. 1, pp. 1, 9.

[66]Jane Perlez, "With New Freedom, Risk of AIDS," *New York Times,* September 14, 1993, p. A4.

[67]"Surge of Tuberculosis in Africa Is Reported," *New York Times,* October 15, 1993, p. A3.

[68]"Agency Cites Urgent Need To Fight Increase in TB," *New York Times,* November 16, 1993, p. 15.

[69]Steve Coll, "Dumping on the Third World," *Washington Post National Weekly Edition,* April 18-24, 1994, pp. 9-10. The export of nuclear waste is the most controversial of these cases. "Dump and Be Damned," *The Economist,* January 18-27, 1997, p. 38; "The Wasteland," *The Economist,* May 31-June 6, 1997, p. 39.

[70]Sandra Postel, "Denial in the Decisive Decade," in Lester R. Brown et al., *State of the World 1992* (New York: Norton, 1992), p. 3.

[71]Sandra Postel, "Carrying Capacity: Earth's Bottom Line," in Lester R. Brown et al., *State of the World 1994* (New York: Norton, 1994), p. 5.

[72]See, for example, Boyce Rensberger, "Building a Better Ear of Corn," *Washington Post National Weekly Edition,* July 4-10, 1994, p. 38; Keith Schneider, "New Rice Variety Could Raise Yields by 20%," *New York Times,* October 24, 1994, p. A5.

[73]Lester R. Brown, "Facing the Prospect of Food Scarcity," in Brown et al., *State of the World 1997,* pp. 22-41. By U.N. estimates, 800 million people in poor countries were chronically undernourished in 1990. "The Food Crisis That Isn't, and the One That Is," *The Economist,* November 25-December 1, 1995, p. 41. For a more optimistic perspective, see "Will the World Starve?" *The Economist,* June 10-16, 1995, pp. 39-40.

[74]Marguerite Michaels, "Retreat from Africa," *Foreign Affairs* 72:1 (1992/93), pp. 95-96.

[75]Lester R. Brown, "The Makings of a Feeding Frenzy," *Washington Post National Weekly Edition,* September 5-11, 1994, p. 23. Emphasis in original. See also Lester R. Brown, "Struggling to Raise Cropland Productivity," in Brown et al., *State of the World 1998,* pp. 79-95. Megan Ryan and Christopher Flavin, "Facing China's Limits," in ibid., pp. 113-131; "Malthus Goes East," *The Economist,* August 12-18, 1995, p. 29.

[76]Jeffrey Clark, "Debacle in Somalia," *Foreign Affairs* 72:1 (1992/93), p. 109.

[77]For a summary of the causes and effects of tropical deforestation, see Nicholas Guppy, "Tropical Deforestation: A Global View," *Foreign Affairs* 62:4 (Spring 1984), pp. 928-965.

[78]Marlise Simons, "Nations Sign an Agreement to Halt Spread of Deserts," *New York Times,* October 16, 1994, sec. 1, p. 11; Paul Lewis, "World Forestry Talks End in Split on Curbing Logging," *New York Times,* February 22, 1997, p. 4; Janet N. Abramovitz, "Sustaining the World's Forests," in *State of the World 1998,* pp. 21-40.

[79]Julia Preston, "It's Indians vs. Loggers in Nicaragua," *New York Times,* June 25, 1996, p. A5; Seth Mydans, "To Conquer Cambodia, Rivals for Power Denude It," *New York Times,* December 22, 1996, sec. 1, p. 3. Timber interests prevented the addition of mahogany to a treaty to control global trade in endangered species.

[80]Frederic Golden, "A Catbird's Seat on Amazon Destruction (Monitoring of Illegal Agricultural Burning by Remote Sensing Satellites)," *Science* 246, October 13, 1989, p. 201; Reginald Newell, Henry Reichle, Jr., and Wolfgang Seiler, "Carbon Monoxide and the Burning Earth," *Scientific American,* October 1989, pp. 82-88.

[81]Don Podesta, "A Burning Issue in Brazil," *Washington Post National Weekly Edition,* October 18-24, 1993, p. 18. Brazil's president argued that conditions had improved; "only" 64,999 fires were detected in the first half of September 1992, compared with 219,941 detected in September 1991. Air pollution from slash-and-burn fires in Indonesia produced so much air pollution that two ships collided off Singapore in 1994 because of poor visibility. "Some Vision," *The Economist,* October 8-14, 1994, p. 36.

[82]Between 1991 and 1998, matters dramatically deteriorated. Diana Jean Schemo, "Burning of Amazon Picks Up Pace, With Vast Areas Lost," *New York Times,* September 12, 1996, p. A4. Diana Jean Schemo, "Fires Posing Greater Risk As Amazon Grows Drier," *New York Times,* September 13, 1998, sec.1, p. 4.

[83]A tractor replaces about nineteen farm workers.

[84]Nicholas Hildyard, "Adiós Amazonia? A Report from the Altimira Gathering," *The Ecologist* 19:2 (1989), pp. 53-62.

[85]In the United States, political collisions have pitted environmentalists against business interests over felling trees in national forests and drilling for oil in the Alaskan tundra and off the California coast.

[86]The harvesting of rubber from wild trees in the Amazon can no longer compete with rubber plantations in southern Brazil. James Brooke, "Rubber Trees Grow Again in Brazil," *New York Times,* July 9, 1995, sec. 1, p. 7.

[87]Peter Passell, "Washington Offers Mountain of Debt to Save Forests," *New York Times,* January 22, 1991, p. C1.

[88]"Your Pollution, Our Forests," *The Economist,* June 27-July 3, 1998, pp. 36, 38.

[89]Keith Schneider, "In Aftermath of Oil Spill, Alaskan Sound Is Altered," *New York Times,* July 7, 1994, pp. A1, A9.

[90]William E. Schmidt, "As Oil Calamities Go, Shetland Spill Was a Wimp," *New York Times,* September 3, 1993, p. A3.

[91]Steve Liesman, "Spring Thaw Unleashes Winter Oil Spill in Tundra," *Wall Street Journal*, April 28, 1995, p. A8.

[92]Allanna Sullivan and Anne Reifenberg, "Decrepit Oil Arteries Threaten Health of Russia," *Wall Street Journal*, April 28, 1995, p. A8.

[93]Patrick E. Tyler, "Soviets' Secret Nuclear Dumping Raises Fears for Arctic Waters," *New York Times*, May 4, 1992, pp. A1, A4.

[94]See, for example, William J. Broad, "Coral Reefs Endangered in Jamaica," *New York Times*, September 9, 1994, p. A11.

[95]William J. Broad, "Strange Oases in Sea Depths Offer Map to Riches," *New York Times*, November 16, 1993, pp. B5, B6. China, Japan, and South Korea are quarreling over a few uninhabited islets (the Senkakus) in the East China Sea because of the resource potential of the area. Nicholas D. Kristof, "Asian Tensions Rise Over Sea's Wealth," *New York Times*, May 19, 1996, sec. 1, p. 4.

[96]Anne Platt McGinn, "Promoting Sustainable Fisheries," in *State of the World 1998*, p. 60.

[97]Michael Specter, "The World's Oceans Are Sending an S.O.S.," *New York Times*, May 3, 1992, p. E5; David E. Pitt, "Fishing Countries Split On Harvest," *New York Times*, August 1, 1993, sec. 1, p. 6. In an innovative response, a consortium of public and private groups—the Atlantic Salmon Federation, the National Fish and Wildlife Foundation, and the U.S. State Department—pooled resources to pay the Greenland fishing industry not to catch salmon for two years to replenish stocks. Peter Bodo, "U.S. Buys 2-Year Timeout for the Atlantic Salmon," *New York Times*, August 2, 1993, p. A7.

[98]"Leaving the Feeding Grounds," *The Economist*, August 7-13, 1993, p. 40; Clyde H. Farnsworth, "Cod Gone, Will a Culture Follow?" *New York Times*, May 14, 1994, p. 4; John H. Cushman, Jr., "Panel Recommends Virtual End to Fishing Fleet in Georges Bank," *New York Times*, October 27, 1994, pp. A1, A4. Fishermen from the Georges Bank then descended on other fishing areas, creating conflict there. "New England Fleets Are Battling for New Coastal Fishing Ground," *New York Times*, March 5, 1995, sec. 1, p. 9.

[99]Peter Weber, "Protecting Oceanic Fisheries and Jobs," in Brown et al., *State of the World 1995*, p. 21.

[100]"Salmon War on Two Fronts," *The Economist*, June 28-July 4, 1997, p. 36; "Net Losses" *The Economist*, June 20-26, 1998, p. 38.

[101]Clyde W. Farnsworth, "Canada to Seize Boats Fishing Outside Its Zone," *New York Times*, May 22, 1994, sec. 1, p. 4.

[102]The Japanese eat whale meat and have an exemption from the whaling ban allowing them to kill minke whales for "scientific purposes." "Whaling Around Antarctica Is Banned by World Body," *New York Times*, May 27, 1994, p. A2. America's once secret integrated undersea-surveillance system (IUSS), a network of sensors on the ocean floor used to track Soviet submarines, is now used to track whales as part of a global effort to save them. "Swords into Sensors," *The Economist*, January 29-February 4, 1994, pp. 85-86.

[103]Cited in Patrick E. Tyler, "China Lacks Water to Meet Its Mighty Thirst," *New York Times*, November 7, 1993, p. 1. Also Patrick E. Tyler, "China Proposes Huge Aqueduct to Beijing Area," *New York Times*, July 19, 1994, pp. A1, A7.

[104]Paul Lewis, "U.N. Report Warns of Global Water Shortage," *New York Times*, January 20, 1997, p. A6. See also Paul Lewis, "5 Years After Earth Summit, U.N. Seeks to Fill in Gaps," *New York Times*, April 7, 1997, p. A3.

[105]Gregg Easterbrook, "Forget PCB's. Radon. Alar.," *New York Times Magazine*, September 11, 1994, p. 61.

[106]"No More Caviar," *The Economist*, October 15-21, 1994, p. 38.

[107]John Pomfret, "The Black Sea Is Becoming the Dead Sea," *Washington Post National Weekly Edition*, June 27-July 3, 1994, p. 16.

[108]See Bob Davis, "U.S. Is Hoping to Blend Environmental, World Trade Issues at Morocco Meeting," *Wall Street Journal*, June 10, 1994, p. A10. For a discussion of the economics of reducing pollution, see "How Clean Can You Get?" *The Economist*, February 17-23, 1996, p. 37.

[109]Consumption has risen again since 1985, especially in the United States, where oil imports account for 50 percent of consumption (up from 35 percent in 1973). Allen R. Myerson, "U.S. Splurging on Energy After Falling off Its Diet," *New York Times*, October 23, 1998, pp. A1, C6.

[110]"Power to the People," special report, *The Economist*, June 18-24, 1994.

[111]"The Battle for World Power," *The Economist*, October 7-13, 1995, pp. 23-24, 26.

[112]Long before its environmental hazards were fully understood, radioactivity had done great damage to human health. See Matthew L. Wald, "Study Finds Destruction in the Making of A-Bombs," *New York Times*, July 26, 1995, p. A8.

[113]"U.N. Says Atom Pact Is in Effect Worldwide," *New York Times*, October 25, 1996, p. A4.

[114]Barbara Crossette, "Chernobyl Fund Depleted as Problems Rise," *New York Times*, November 29, 1995, p. A11; "Inherited Damage Is Found In Chernobyl Area Children," *New York Times*, April 25, 1996, p. A7.

[115]William J. Broad, "U.S. Lists 10 Soviet-Built Nuclear Reactors as High Risks," *New York Times*, July 20, 1995, sec. 1, p. 4. Chernobyl remains dangerous because the tomb encasing it is deteriorating. James Rupert, "The Cloud over Chernobyl," *Washington Post National Weekly Edition*, June 26-July 2, 1995, pp. 6-7. Ukraine has promised to replace the Chernobyl nuclear plant with a thermal energy plant by the year 2000. "Ukraine Reaches Agreement to Replace Chernobyl Plant," *New York Times*, May 28, 1995, sec. 1, p. 8.

[116]Douglas Frantz, "Global Plan on Nuclear Liability," *New York Times*, May 31, 1994, pp. C1, C3; Douglas Frantz, "U.S. Backing Work on Czech Reactors by Westinghouse," *New York Times*, May 22, 1994, sec. 1, pp. 1, 8.

[117]"Leakproof?" *The Economist,* January 20–26, 1996, p. 36; Andrew Pollack, "Reactor Accident in Japan Imperils Energy Program," *New York Times,* February 24, 1996, pp. 1, 5; "Political Meltdown," *The Economist,* April 19–25, 1997, p. 41.

[118]Alan Cowell, "Nuclear Waste Convoy Rouses Protests and Potential Saboteurs in Germany," *New York Times,* March 4, 1997, p. A6.

[119]Craig R. Whitney, "Russia Halts the Dumping of Nuclear Wastes in Sea," *New York Times,* October 22, 1993, p. A4; William J. Broad, "Russia Admits to Accidents in Atom Plants in Cold War," *New York Times,* November 27, 1994, sec. 1, p. 10. Two U.S. nuclear submarines sank in the 1960s. William J. Broad, "Navy Says 2 Sunken Submarines Show No Sign of Nuclear Contamination," *New York Times,* November 7, 1993, p. 13. The United States and Norway agreed to aid Russia's efforts to dispose of nuclear submarine reactors and other radioactive waste dumped into the Barents and Kara Seas. "Effort to Clean Russian Nuclear Waste," *New York Times,* October 8, 1996, p. A16.

[120]David E. Pitt, "U.S. to Press Ban on Atomic Dumping," *New York Times,* November 2, 1993, p. A5. The Pentagon resisted the ban. David E. Pitt, "Pentagon Fights Wider Ocean-Dumping Ban," *New York Times,* September 26, 1993, p. A4.

[121]William J. Broad, "Soviets' Radioactive Debris Threatening Satellites," *New York Times,* February 26, 1995, sec. 1 pp. 1, 8.

[122]"Deadly Secret," *The Economist,* December 3–9, 1994, pp. 45–46.

[123]Cited in William J. Broad, "Nuclear Roulette for Russia: Burying Uncontained Waste," *New York Times,* November 21, 1994, p. A8.

[124]Nicholas Lenssen, "Confronting Nuclear Waste," in Brown et al., *State of the World 1992,* p. 50. Radiation caused by medical and dental x-rays and radiopharmaceuticals may produce higher doses for the population than do nuclear plants. John R. Lamarsh, *Introduction to Nuclear Engineering,* 2nd ed. (Reading, MA: Addison-Wesley, 1983), p. 428.

[125]Matthew L. Wald, "Stored Plutonium May Be a Danger, Government Says," *New York Times,* December 7, 1994, pp. A1, A11.

[126]Ray Perkins, Jr., *The ABCs of the Soviet-American Nuclear Arms Race* (Pacific Grove, CA: Brooks/Cole, 1991), p. 35. Matthew L. Wald, "Nation Considers Means to Dispose of Its Plutonium," *New York Times,* November 15, 1993, pp. A1, A9; Matthew L. Wald, "Disassembly of A-Bombs Stopped After Inspectors Find Violations," *New York Times,* October 4, 1994, pp. A1, A11; "Blowing in the Wind," *The Economist,* November 26–December 2, 1994, p. 31.

[127]Matthew L. Wald, "Rockwell's Guilty Plea Accepted on Nuclear Arms-Plant Charges," *New York Times,* June 2, 1992, pp. A1, A8; James Brooke, "Plutonium Stockpile Fosters Fear of 'a Disaster Waiting to Happen'," *New York Times,* December 11, 1996, p. A16.

[128]"Nuclear Grunge," *The Economist,* August 21, 1993, p. 23; Matthew L. Wald, "U.S. Reaches Pact on Plant Cleanup," *New York Times,* October 3, 1993, p. A5; "Not Here, Please," *The Economist,* November 26–December 2, 1994, p. 31.

[129]Timothy Aeppel, "Mess at A-bomb Plant Shows What Happens If Pork Gets into Play," *Wall Street Journal,* March 28, 1995, pp. A1, A10. John J. Fialka, "Regulators Abound for Trouble-Shooter at Hanford Waste Cleanup," *Wall Street Journal,* July 13, 1998, p. A16.

[130]Matthew L. Wald, "Encase Excess Plutonium in Glass, U.S. Urged," *New York Times,* November 17, 1994, p. A10; Matthew L. Wald, "Factor Is Set to Process Dangerous Nuclear Waste," *New York Times,* March 13, 1996, p. A13. Some scientists claim that stored nuclear wastes might explode, poisoning air and water. William J. Broad, "Theory on Blast Threat at Nuclear Dump Gains Support," *New York Times,* March 23, 1995, p. A9.

[131]Matthew L. Wald, "The Long Radioactive Goodbye," *New York Times Magazine,* July 26, 1998, p. 28; Gary Putka, "Court Rules U.S. Energy Department Broke Vow to Rid Plants of Nuclear Fuel," *Wall Street Journal,* November 2, 1998, p. A14. Currently, about one quarter of all Americans live within fifty miles of a military nuclear-waste storage site. James Brooke, "Deep Desert Grave Awaits First Load of Nuclear Waste," *New York Times,* March 26, 1999, p. A17.

[132]Brooke, "Deep Desert Grave Awaits First Load of Nuclear Waste," pp. A1, A17.

[133]Julia Preston, "A Fatal Case of Fatalism," *New York Times,* February 14, 1999, sec. 4, p. 3. In 1995, pollution levels in Mexico City exceeded Mexico's "own lenient standard of acceptability" on 324 days. Julia Preston, "The City That Can't Fix the Air," *New York Times,* February 4, 1996, sec. 4, p. 4. Mexican air pollution is also a problem for Texas. Sam Howe Verhovek, "A Diplomatic Haze Pervades Park's Air Pollution Dispute," *New York Times,* June 7, 1996, pp. A1, A12.

[134]Easterbrook, "Forget PCB's, Radon, Alar," p. 61.

[135]The Acid Rain Control Program created in 1990 by amendments to the 1970 U.S. Clean Air Act brought a decline in sulfur dioxide emissions that cause acid rain. Tim Hilchey, "Government Survey Finds Decline in a Building Block of Acid Rain," *New York Times,* September 7, 1993, p. B8.

[136]"Air Pollution May Damage Food Supply in 3 Decades," *New York Times,* April 3, 1994, sec. 1 p. 9.

[137]These chemicals are released by air conditioners and other forms of refrigeration.

[138]William K. Stevens, "100 Nations Move to Save Ozone Shield," *New York Times,* December 10, 1995, sec. 1, p. 6.

[139]Carey Goldberg, "A Chilling Change in the Contraband Being Confiscated at Border Crossings," *New York Times,* November 10, 1996, sec. 1, p. 1; John H. Cushman, Jr., "U.S. Prosecutors in 6 Cities File Charges of Smuggling Refrigeration Gas," *New York Times,* January 10, 1997, p. A10.

[140]"Data Point to Ultimate Closing of Ozone Hole," *New York Times,* May 31, 1996, p. A11.

[141]Richard Houghton and George Woodwell, "Global Climatic Change," *Scientific American* 260:4 (April 1989), pp. 36–44.

142William K. Stevens, "Earth Temperature in 1998 Is Reported at Record High," *New York Times,* December 18, 1998, p. A26. Although there has been a debate about whether or not the high temperatures of recent years represent more than a long-term cycle, most scientists are now persuaded that human activity is causing global warming. William K. Stevens, "Experts Confirm Human Role in Global Warming," *New York Times,* September 10, 1995, sec. 1, pp. 1, 6; Christopher Flavin, "Last Tango In Buenos Aires," *World Watch* 11:6 (November/December 1998), pp. 10-18.

143William K. Stevens, "Scientists Say Earth's Warming Could Set Off Wide Disruptions," *New York Times,* September 18, 1995, pp. A1, A5.

144Edward Barbier, "The Global Greenhouse Effect," *Natural Resources Forum,* February 1989, pp. 20-29.

145Paul Lewis, "U.N. Panel Finds Action on Environment Lagging," *New York Times,* May 29, 1994, sec. 1, p. 6.

146Stephen Kinzer, "New Limits on Carbon Dioxide Emission Unlikely," *New York Times,* April 2, 1995, sec. 1, p. 8.

147"Clinton on the Global Environment: Some Progress but Much More Still to Be Done," *New York Times,* June 27, 1997, p. A7. See also James Bennet, "Clinton Urges Action on Global Warming," *New York Times,* May 10, 1997, p. 6.

148John H. Cushman, Jr., "Push Begins for New Global Warming Pact," *New York Times,* July 16, 1997, p. A10. As long as governments subsidize petroleum products, coal mining, and other environmentally destructive practices, there will be economic incentives to oppose restricting these practices. Barbara Crossette, "Subsidies Hurt Environment, Critics Say Before Talks," *New York Times,* June 23, 1997, p. A5. The Senate Appropriations Committee slashed funds sought by the Clinton administration to fulfill its Kyoto commitment.

149Cited in William K. Stevens, "With Energy Tug of War, U.S. Is Missing Its Goals," *New York Times,* November 28, 1995, p. A12.

150John H. Cushman, Jr., "Europe Leaders Fault U.S. At U.N. Environment Talks," *New York Times,* June 24, 1997, p. A6; Barbara Crossette, "Half-Hearted Global Warming Conference Closes Gloomily," *New York Times,* June 28, 1997, p. 3.

151Other industrial countries were prepared to go forward without a commitment from the less-developed countries in order to get an agreement.

152The United States signed the Kyoto Protocol in November 1998, but it has not been ratified by the Senate. John H. Cushman, Jr., "U.S. Signs a Pact to Reduce Gases Tied to Warming," *New York Times,* November 13, 1998, pp. A1, A12.

153Cited in Stephen Kinzer, "New Limits on Carbon Dioxide Emission Unlikely," *New York Times,* April 2, 1995, sec. 1, p. 8.

154Easterbrook, "Forget PCB's. Radon. Alar." pp. 60-63.

155Barbara Crossette, "Most Consuming More, and the Rich Much More," *New York Times,* September 13, 1998, sec. 1, p. 3.

156William K. Stevens, "Humanity Confronts Its Handiwork: An Altered Planet," *New York Times,* May 5, 1992, p. B5.

157David E. Pitt, "Biological Treaty, with the Goal of Saving Species, Becomes Law," *New York Times,* January 2, 1994, sec. 1, p. 4.

158David E. Sanger, "Russia Gets First Installment on Aid to Clean Environment," *New York Times,* November 9, 1994, p. A4.

159Hilary F. French, "Forging a New Global Partnership," in Brown et al., *State of the World 1995,* p. 172.

160Guppy, "Tropical Deforestation," pp. 930-931. Emphasis in original.

Chapter 15

The State Versus the Individual: Human Rights in the Global Arena

A s a rule we think of governments as their citizens' servants and guardians. In democratic societies such as our own, that is the relationship, but in others, the government may be the citizens' enemy and a danger to individual health and safety. For many reasons, from ideology to fear, goverments may treat citizens as enemies from whom they must extract obedience or as potential opponents whom they must repress. Some in power try to impose ideological, linguistic, religious, and political views on citizens, and some regimes are led by individuals whose thirst for power and glory or whose pathological personality makes them behave as despots. Around the world, governments illegally imprison, torture, and kill their citizens. Even the United States has been accused of "a persistent and widespread pattern of human rights violations" in its criminal justice system.[1]

Rogue regimes have carried out genocidal campaigns, deliberately and systematically exterminating national or ethnic groups. During World War II, the Nazis murdered more than six million Jews and sought to exterminate other groups, such as gypsies and homosexuals. Between 1975 and 1979, Pol Pot's Khmer Rouge government in Cambodia murdered between one and one-and-one-half million of its eight-million citizens and perhaps more.[2] And in 1994 the Hutu-dominated government of Rwanda set out to exterminate the minority Tutsis.[3] According to a twelve-year-old boy, Hutu soldiers arrived at his village by helicopter "and gathered all of us in a church. They were screaming. They asked us our ethnic group. Then they began to kill us. Busloads of people came with machetes. They killed my family with machetes. They thought I was dead and they left me."[4]

Genocide refers to the effort to exterminate an entire race or ethnic group and is, therefore, the most extreme example of human-rights violation. The Nigerian army shot unarmed Ogoni villagers, burned their homes, and gang-raped their women to silence their demand for a share of revenues generated by oil from their lands.[5] Russian soldiers opened fire on unarmed people and burned villages in Chechnya.[6] Slavery is still practiced in Mauritania and the Sudan, and street children are murdered by police *death squads* in Rio de Janeiro.[7] Colombian vigilantes have undertaken "social-cleansing" killings of street children, vagrants, and other undesirables called "disposables."[8] Indeed, children are often victims of human-rights abuses. In some countries, they are virtually enslaved and are bought and sold.[9] The Haitian military targeted orphans as "enemies of the state."[10] The "disappearance" of real and imagined government foes at the hands of rightist death squads (often consisting of police and soldiers) was common practice in Argentina, where political prisoners were drugged and then thrown from airplanes,[11] and in Uruguay in the 1970s and in Guatemala, Honduras, and El Salvador in the 1970s and 1980s. Victims were called *los desaparecidos* ("the ones who disappeared").

After war erupted in 1992, systematic violation of *human rights* was practiced by Bosnian Serbs to force Croatians and Muslims from their homes by murder, starvation, and intimidation.[12] This policy, euphemistically called *"ethnic cleansing,"* has been compared to Nazi policies in Yugoslavia during World War II. With acquiescence by Serbian authorities, Bosnian Serbs used terrorist tactics, including systematic rape, to force Bosnian Muslims to flee their homes and villages. The Serbs meant to alter the map of Bosnia and get control of most of the country, and efforts to halt the carnage and provide humanitarian relief for besieged Muslims in Sarajevo and elsewhere were conspicuously unsuccessful until 1995. After the fall of the town of Srebrenica—a U.N. "safe area"—to Bosnian Serbs in July 1995, Bosnian Muslims were brutally expelled; thousands of men were loaded into trucks, delivered to killing sites, and shot in the worst war crime in Europe since World War II.[13] After photos from U.S. space satellites provided evidence of the genocide, Madeleine K. Albright, then U.S. delegate at the U.N., declared: "The perpetrators of these atrocities have—literally—not covered their tracks. The physical evidence of what they have done—the bodies discarded in their fields—will bear silent witness."[14] More recently, Serbian authorities have used similar tactics against civilians in the province of Kosovo, which is home to a largely Muslim Albanian population.[15]

After an inauspicious start, the International Criminal Tribunal for Yugoslavia in the Hague, which was set up to try those accused of genocide, other war crimes, and crimes against humanity in the former Yugoslavia, proved to be a valuable and impartial instrument of justice. Although high- ranking accused war criminals like Radovan Karadzic remain at liberty,[16] a growing number of those accused—Bosnian Serbs, Croatians, and Muslims alike—have been arrested and are being or have been tried.[17] The tribunal has also begun to collect evidence of crimes against humanity committed by Serbians, including top leaders, during the expulsion of ethnic Albanians from Kosovo, and Serbian leader Slobodan Milosevic has been indicted.

The human-rights issue exemplifies a more general problem: *citizens versus states in global politics.* We begin by assessing the relationship between states and their citizens and how human rights fit into this relationship. Next, we consider various definitions of human rights and survey the current state of human rights along these dimensions. Third, we identify factors that account for human-rights abuses and discuss ways of monitoring, protecting, and improving human rights worldwide.

The State and the Individual

How is the state related to the individual, and what rights do individuals have? These questions have vexed political philosophers from Plato to Marx. Do states determine the rights of individuals? Do individuals possess intrinsic rights, whether or not states recognize them? And if individuals have rights, what are they, and what are their limits? Do outside efforts to end states' violations of human rights violate state sovereignty?[18] Such questions have no definitive answers.

The modern conception of human rights is derived from natural rights and natural law.[19] The idea of *natural law,* that God and nature confer dignity on all human beings, dates back to Greek Stoicism and Roman law. This tradition places obligations on both individuals and the societies of which they are a part. The demands of natural law were seen as duties of states.

During the late Middle Ages and the Renaissance, popular movements sought to limit rulers' arbitrary behavior. Natural-law doctrine as a basis for natural rights began to change form. Instead of a code with which societies should comply, natural law was seen as a basis for asserting the individual's natural rights. Two reasons help explain this transformation. First, states seemed to be flouting natural law more often. Second, the Renaissance, and later the Protestant Reformation and Enlightenment, affirmed that the individual and individual liberty were ends in themselves, not merely means to state power.

A new emphasis on individual rights suggested itself as early as the Magna Carta (1215).[20] With the English Bill of Rights (1689), the American Declaration of Independence (1776), and the French Declaration of the Rights of Man (1789), the push for individual rights accelerated. Such events were "testimony to the increasingly popular view that human beings are endowed with certain eternal and inalienable rights, never renounced when humankind 'contracted' to enter the social from the primitive state and never diminished by the claim of 'the divine right of kings.'"[21] The doctrine of natural rights was transformed into a doctrine of human rights neither quickly nor smoothly. Political philosophers such as David Hume and Jeremy Bentham argued against basing individual rights on natural law because such law lacked an empirical foundation. Others, including John Stuart Mill and Friedrich Karl von Savigny, contended that human rights could be grounded in their utility for society only as a whole. Rights were necessarily bounded by *cultural relativism:* That which one society deemed a fundamental right might be denied by others, so that human rights were limited to those that society granted by law.

Nazi and Japanese atrocities renewed the call for enforcing human rights. The trial and conviction of Germans accused of crimes against humanity and war crimes by an international tribunal at Nuremberg were widely regarded as a path-breaking precedent in human rights. In 1948, the United Nations adopted the *Universal Declaration of Human Rights.* Although the declaration was not binding on states, it set a tone for renewed attention to human rights that was reinforced by two further U.N. covenants: the *International Covenant on Civil and Political Rights* and the *International Covenant on Economic, Social and Cultural Rights.* Both imposed obligations on U.N. members and codified human rights.

During the Cold War, the superpowers often marginalized human rights when they got in the way of political objectives. Neither let the issue stand in the way of good relations with regimes that repressed individual rights. The United States maintained close relations with dictators like Francisco Franco in Spain, Augusto Pinochet in Chile, Syngman Rhee in South Korea, Ferdinand Marcos of the Philippines, Anastasio Somoza in Nicaragua, and Sese Seko Mobuto of Zaire, despite their repressive policies. The Soviet Union, too, routinely violated human rights, as did communist regimes in Cuba, China, and Eastern Europe.

With a U.S. president committed to human rights, the issue gained new prominence in the mid-1970s. During the first year of President Jimmy Carter's administration, human rights dominated Washington's agenda.[22] Although the Carter administration argued publicly for human rights, its behavior reflected the need to compromise with a difficult reality. Repeatedly, Washington seemed more willing to enforce its human-rights policy on small countries than on large ones, and on enemies rather than friends. Thus, even though Indonesia committed serious human-rights abuses against the people of East Timor, the Carter administration refused to act because Indonesia was a U.S. ally. Subsequent U.S. administrations again played down human rights. The Reagan administration had to deal with complaints that its policy in Central America did not take human-rights violations into account, ignoring death squads in El Salvador.[23] The Bush administration confronted similar challenges to continued political and economic ties with China after the June 1989 Tiananmen Square massacre of students demonstrating for democracy, and both the Bush and Clinton administrations were accused of indifference to atrocities committed in the former Yugoslavia.

The Content of Human Rights

There is still no consensus about defining human rights. Do economic, social, and political rights qualify as human rights? Are some more important than others? Is there a "third generation" of human rights consisting of rights to peace, a healthy environment, and economic development?[24] Can we identify a core of human rights? A good beginning is political scientist Jack Donnelly's definition: "Human rights are the rights one has simply by virtue of being a human being."[25] Donnelly acknowledges that including humanness in the definition omits a divine influence in their origin, and argues that a right involves an entitlement that an individual can use to make a moral claim on others who are bound to respect that right. In this sense, violations of rights are fundamental wrongs.[26]

Human rights then are not merely goals that proper conduct directs us to follow, nor are they obligations that momentary expedience may compel people to obey. Rather, they are individuals' fundamental moral obligations toward each other. Rights are fundamental in another sense; they "logically and morally . . . take precedence over the rights of the state and society."[27]

Cultural Differences and Human Rights

Although human rights *as rights* derive mostly from Western traditions, demands that governments respect human dignity also have a basis in non-Western traditions. The source of this respect is mostly in reciprocal "duties" for rulers and ruled rather than a conception of inherent "rights," and examples from Islam, traditional African societies, Confucian China, and Hindu India be adduced to support this judgment.[28] Islamic scholars contend that "the basic concepts and principles of human rights had from the very beginning been embodied in Islamic law" and that "Muslims are enjoined constantly to seek ways and means to assure to each other what in modern parlance we call 'human rights.'" On closer inspection, these rights resemble the proper conduct that individuals should follow rather than fundamental entitlements.

Similar claims are made for other cultures. The Chinese language did not have a word for "rights" until late in the nineteenth century. If rights were defended, they were placed among the rulers' duties toward the people as part of rulers' heavenly and earthly responsibilities. The twenty-five-hundred-year-old Confucian tradition in China includes reciprocal duties between rulers and ruled in which relations are dominated by human dignity and virtue without need for coercion. One historian writes: "Of crucial importance was the initiative of the ruler, who . . . could initiate benevolent government and win over the people. The people's confidence was essential to the state, more important than arms or even food."[29]

Is a universal claim for human rights thus undermined? The idea of individual human rights, even if Western in origin, has steadily gained global acceptance, leading one observer to conclude that "the connection to universal jurisdiction [of several global treaties] plus state public pronouncements and the bulk of applied policy clearly and universally indicate opposition to certain practices on grounds of a fundamental denial of human rights. . . . No exceptions are acknowledged because of culture or any other reason. . . ."[30]

This claim is not universally accepted. Some Asian and less-developed regimes argue that human rights should be interpreted differently in non-Western settings.[31] They contend that economic development for their countries may require limiting individual liberties or that women in Islamic societies must be treated differently than men. Declared Iran's foreign minister: "Human rights in Iran are based on Islamic values, and we will not accept the values of foreign countries imposed on us under the cover of human rights."[32] The General Assembly resolution creating a U.N. Human Rights Commissioner implicitly accepted part of this view in calling for the appointment of a person who has "knowledge and understanding of diverse cultures."[33] Dismissing such arguments, U.S. Secretary of State Warren Christopher declared in a speech to the U.N. World Conference on Human Rights in Vienna in June 1993: "We cannot let cultural relativism become the last refuge of repression."[34]

One way to think about individual entitlements is to conceive of human rights as negative or positive by their relationship to state actions. *Negative rights* are those that prevent a government from interfering with individual liberty and autonomy. In the United States, these are readily familiar to us as the first ten amendments (the Bill of Rights) to the Constitution. Negative rights usually involve political and civil rights and liberties such as freedom of speech.[35] The idea of *positive rights* implies the government's obligation to provide for citizens' social and economic welfare—housing, employment, health care, education, and so on. Soviet leaders emphasized positive rights as prerequisites for negative rights, and, in general, Marxists argue that individual liberty is meaningless without economic and social equality. By contrast, American society gives relatively little weight to positive rights. Nearly all governments today give some attention to these rights, but they disagree about how far they must go in securing and promoting positive rights.[36]

Ethnic cleansing,
1943

Ethnic cleansing,
1995

They are coming by the thousands. Some with only the clothes on their backs. They are camping in mosquito-infested fields. Their numbers are growing by the hour.

They are Bosnian refugees being ethnically cleansed from what were yesterday's "U.N. safe areas"– Srebrenica, Zepa, and soon Gorazde. Will Sarajevo be next?

"The only sounds heard were the plaintive wails of babies and small children," reports *The New York Times*, July 14, 1995. Women speak of rapes, throats slit and "bodies left hanging from trees and littering streets."

For the past 3 years, the International Rescue Committee has saved thousands of lives in Bosnia. We have provided tons of supplies such as wood-burning stoves, seeds to grow vegetables and fruits, soap, anti-biotic drugs, winter coats and shoes.

We rebuilt the water system in Sarajevo and laid miles of natural gas pipeline to bring heat to thousands of apartment dwellers. Mental health support groups have been established to ease the pain of women who have been raped. Our Children's Medical Project has treated over 400 war-injured or chronically ill children who could not get the care they needed because of the war.

Now we are helping these latest victims of the Bosnian tragedy. We urgently need your help to provide food, clothing, medicines and shelter.

The U.N. Forces may withdraw but the IRC will stay as long as possible to be with and to help the refugees. It has been our mission for over 62 years, and it will not change.

Founded in 1933 by Albert Einstein to assist refugees fleeing Hitler's Germany, the International Rescue Committee is today working in 24 countries helping refugees who flee political, religious and racial persecution.

You can't stop the ethnic cleansing in Bosnia, but you can save a life. Perhaps a thousand lives.

Please give generously.

International Rescue Committee
Attn: Mr. Robert P. DeVecchi, President
122 East 42nd Street, 12th Floor
New York, NY 10168-1289

Enclosed is my tax-deductible contribution to help Bosnian refugees.

☐$40 ☐$75 ☐$100 ☐$500 ☐$—

Name _____

Address_____

City_____

State _____ ZIP_____

This ad paid for by private contributions. You can obtain the latest financial audit from IRC or the Office of Charities Registration, NY Department of State, Albany, NY 12231.

One of the most serious violations of human rights in Bosnia was the forcible removal of people of one ethnic group from their homes and villages by members of other ethnic groups. This practice, called "ethnic cleansing," is compared in this advertisement to the genocide of Europe's Jews by the Nazis in World War II. *(International Rescue Committee. Reprinted by permission.)*

International Bill of
Human Rights

Recently, attempts have been made to identify and codify human rights. Three documents—the Universal Declaration of Human Rights, the International Covenant on Civil and Political Rights, and the International Covenant on Economic, Social and Cultural Rights—are recognized as covering the core of universal human rights and are collectively labeled the *International Bill of Human Rights*. Some observers consider other agreements, such as the Covenants on Genocide and Torture, as part of the International Bill of Human Rights.[37]

The Universal Declaration of Human Rights declares its aim as setting "a common standard of achievement for all peoples and nations" in observing human rights. Its thirty articles identify a range of political, civil, economic, social, and cultural rights, including "the right to life, liberty and security of person," freedom from "inhuman or degrading treatment or punishment" and "arbitrary arrest, detention or exile," freedom of "movement and residence," "the right to freedom of thought, conscience and religion," "the right to property," and "the right to take part in" government. The Declaration endorses democracy: "The will of the people shall be the basis of the authority of government . . . expressed in periodic and genuine elections which shall be by universal and equal suffrage. . . ." It also identifies positive rights—"the right to work," "the right to equal pay for equal work," "the right to rest and leisure," "the right to education," and "the right to a standard of living" adequate for health and well-being.[38] To codify, expand, and make binding the rights set out in the Universal Declaration, the U.N. General Assembly adopted the International Covenant on Civil and Political Rights and the International Covenant on Economic, Social, and Cultural Rights in 1966.

By 1994, 127 states had acceded to the International Covenant on Economic, Social, and Cultural Rights, and 125 had acceded to the International Covenant on Civil and Political Rights. Only 72 countries had acceded to the Optional Protocol to the International Covenant on Civil and Political Rights, which recognized individuals as subjects of international law, and only 19 to the second Optional Protocol aimed at the abolition of the death penalty.[39] The United States has signed the two Covenants but not the Optional Protocols. Because many countries have not acceded to these agreements, it is too early to conclude that these standards are universally accepted.

The end of the Cold War again turned attention to human-rights issues. Neither the United States nor Russia felt the same pressure as before to support regimes that violate human rights to secure allies against each other. As a result, countries like Turkey or Indonesia that abuse human rights can no longer assume that they will get unquestioning support from the United States or Western Europe. Human rights has also partly replaced anticommunism as a rationale for Western intervention in Haiti and Kosovo.

The Global Human-Rights Record

Several efforts have been made to determine how well human rights are respected globally, but the results are ambiguous. In some countries, regimes change quickly and so too do human-rights policies. In others, regimes are too weak to prevent police or military officials from committing human-rights abuses. In addition, there are legitimate differences over what constitutes cruelty or suppression of political dissent. Westerners believe that punishments such as amputating a limb that are called for by the Koran are unnecessarily harsh, but many Muslims disagree. Some countries believe the death penalty is cruel and unusual punishment, while others, including the United States, do not. Some regimes like that of China contend that allegations made by political dissidents are lies and that so-called political prisoners are really common criminals. Some leaders admit human-rights violations but claim they are justified by political or military necessity. Whatever the ambiguities, the overall human-rights picture is bleak.

Protecting the "Integrity of the Person"

One examination of 122 countries found that more than half held political prisoners "often" or "very often."[40] Another third "sometimes" held political prisoners, and only eight did not commit human-rights violations of this kind. Torture was less frequent but still widespread. Forty-six countries "often" or "very often" resorted to torture, and another forty-seven used torture "sometimes" or "rarely." Only twenty-nine countries in the sample never used torture. When a similar analysis was conducted for 135 countries a few years later (1987), the results were equally discouraging.[41] Just under 60 percent of the countries in the sample often or very often held political prisoners, and only 10 percent never arbitrarily imprisoned individuals. About 37 percent frequently resorted to torture, and only 25 percent never did so. Overall, countries such as the United States, Switzerland, Ireland, Japan, and Finland did well by these measures, whereas others such as Sri Lanka did poorly.

Protecting Political and Civil Rights

Several assessments of compliance with political and civil liberties demonstrate that most nations do *not* allow free exercise of political and civil rights. The best known was conducted by Freedom House, a U.S.-based nonprofit organization. Since 1978, this organization has published a yearly country-by-country evaluation of political and civil rights called the "comparative survey of freedom." Of the 169 nations in a recent survey, only 61 were declared "free," while 62 were described as "unfree," results that have changed little.[42] A number of countries that have been embarrassed by Freedom House tried to have it barred from U.N. conferences.[43]

The U.S. government also evaluates the status of human rights country by country. Since the mid-1970s, Congress has required the Department of State to report on human rights in countries that receive U.S. economic or military assistance, later enlarging this requirement to all U.N. members. Like the Freedom House reports, these focus on three components of human rights: "the right to be free from governmental violations of the integrity of the person," "the right to enjoy civil rights," and "political rights, or the right of citizens to change their government."[44] In general, the portrait that these reports paint is that, despite lip service, human rights are not widely observed.

Promoting Economic and Social Rights

Most studies measure observance of economic and social rights indirectly, and, as with other human rights, the results are disappointing. One way to measure global economic rights is to compare per capita GNP for individual countries. Between 1980 and 1992 the average annual increase in GNP per capita in low- and middle-income countries rose more slowly (0.9 percent) than in high-income countries

(2.3 percent). In the Middle East and North Africa, sub-Saharan Africa, and Latin America, average per capita GNP actually declined in this period. By 1997, individuals in high-income countries enjoyed average incomes ($25,700) more than twenty-one times larger than those in low- and middle-income countries ($1,250).[45]

Other indicators of economic and social well-being address more directly the enormous gap between rich and poor. For example, as of 1993, there was only one medical doctor for every 7,143 persons in the least-developed countries, while developed countries had one doctor for every 348 persons.[46] The "health gap" between rich and poor is enormous. Other indicators of access to health care and education reflect the same disparity between rich and poor. Since 1990, as we have seen, the U.N. Development Program has published the Human Development Index (HDI), described as "a measure of human happiness," which maps progress in dealing with economic and social challenges. Income alone does not produce happiness; some countries, such as the Netherlands and Spain, produce human development more effectively with limited resources than others, like the United Arab Emirates and Qatar.[47]

Gender and Human Rights

Women have systematically been deprived of positive and negative human rights for centuries, but only in recent decades has this issue earned a prominent place on the global agenda. Thus the percentage of World Bank funding for "gender concerns" rose from 10 percent to more than a third in the last decade.[48] Women were the first to be fired when Asia's economies began to shrink in 1997, and physical abuse of women is widespread.[49] In 1993, for the first time, the U.S. State Department focused on women in its annual human-rights report, describing forced sterilizations and abortions in China, Burmese and Thai girls forced into prostitution, maids beaten in Saudi Arabia, and Sudanese and Somali girls ritually mutilated. The report on 193 countries also highlighted the day-to-day discrimination faced by women—less schooling of women than men in the Congo, adultery as illegal for women but not men in the Republic of the Congo, excusing the murder of a wife committing adultery in Morocco but not a husband, and so forth.[50] American authorities now recognize that women fleeing rape in Bosnia or Haiti, forced abortion in China, or imprisonment in Iran, as well as others who fear for their freedom and safety, are human-rights victims who merit *political asylum* in the United States.[51]

Feminist International-Relations Theory

Male dominance has historically been reinforced by legal and economic institutions and by religious and cultural norms.[52] The power-politics tradition, feminist theorists argue, focuses on "issues that grow out of men's experiences"[53] and, presumably, would be greatly modified if account were taken of women's experiences. Argues Christine Sylvester:

> IR theory does not spin any official stories about such people or evoke "womanly" characteristics. . . . Feminists, however, find evocations of "women" in IR as the Chiquita Bananas of international political economy, the Pocohantas's of diplomatic

ACTORS SPEAK

The global status of women has become a hotly debated human-rights issue. If human rights are culturally based, then women's reproductive rights are limited to societies in which they find approval. If human rights are universal, then women should enjoy reproductive freedom even in societies where dominant religious or cultural norms run counter to such freedom. This question occupied center stage at the 1994 Conference on Population and Development in Cairo and at the 1995 Fourth World Conference on Women in Beijing.

It is time for us to say here in Beijing, and the world to hear, that it is no longer acceptable to discuss women's rights as separate from human rights. It is a violation of human rights when babies are denied food, or drowned, or suffocated, or their spines broken, simply because they are born girls. . . . It is a violation of human rights when women are doused with gasoline, set on fire and burned to death because their marriage dowries are deemed too small. (Hillary Clinton, as cited in Patrick E. Tyler, "Hillary Clinton in China, Details Abuse of Women," *New York Times,* September 6, 1995, p.A1)

In this document, the Holy See sees pressure of an ideological nature, which seems to want to impose on women of the entire world a particular social philosophy, belonging to certain sectors within Western countries. (Vatican spokesman Joaquín Navarro-Valls, as cited in Celestine Bohlen, "Vatican Will Champion the Role of Mothers at a U.N. Conference," *New York Times,* June 21, 1995, p.A4)

practice, the women companions for men on military bases, and the Beautiful Souls wailing the tears of unheralded social conscience at the walls of war. Moreover, "men" are in IR too, dressed as states, statesmen, soldiers, decision makers, terrorists, despots and other characters with more powerful social positions than "women."[54]

How does the world look from a feminist perspective? Feminist theory, it is argued, views the world from the perspective of the disadvantaged and takes greater account of economic inequality, ecological threats, and human rights in defining security than conventional (male) international-relations theory, which focuses on military issues.[55] Some argue that a feminist perspective must abandon strict empiricism (or "science") because of "the contamination of its knowledge by the social biases against women."[56] Knowledge is not value-free, and feminist theory is skeptical about claims of "objective" knowledge and the meanings attached to such knowledge. Although there are several feminist approaches to global politics, they share the premise that male views dominate international relations.[57]

**The Global Status
of Women**

Increasingly we recognize the inferior position to which women have been consigned in global politics. In 1983, UNESCO asked the Commission on the Status of Women to set up a procedure to review complaints of sex discrimination.[58] The Commission set up a working group to review complaints and bring to the Commission's attention evidence of "a consistent pattern of reliably attested injustice and discriminatory patterns against women."[59] A decade later, the World Conference on Human Rights brought the status of women into the mainstream of human-rights concerns, and the Vienna Declaration and Programme of Action endorsed the appointment of a new Special Rapporteur on violence against women.[60]

The Gender Gap.   The disadvantaged status of women is reflected by the fact that nowhere do women enjoy the same opportunities as men. Table 15.1 shows that, when account is taken of gender disparities in the three components of the Human Development Index, no society treats its women as well as its men. Of 1.3 billion people living in absolute poverty, 70 percent are women, and women and children make up about 80 percent of all refugees.

The *gender gap* is narrowest in Scandinavia. By contrast, Ireland, Spain, and Arab states such as Saudi Arabia and Libya treat women poorly, dropping significantly in HDI rank when we account for gender. Between 1970 and 1992, Nepal, Tunisia, Botswana, Saudi Arabia, and Ethiopia showed the most dramatic improvement in women's status.[61] Declared the administrator of the U.N. Development Program: "Gender gaps in human capabilities . . . have been halved in the last two decades. There have been huge increases in the capacity of women. . . . But when you go beyond the preparatory phase of life, women overwhelmingly still lack access to economic and political opportunities."[62]

Turning to individual indicators, the education gap is especially large in African and Middle Eastern countries such as Chad, Benin, Togo, and Yemen, and, of those between the ages of fifteen and nineteen who are illiterate in China, 70 percent are women.[63] Women actually do better than men on school enrollment in some countries, including the United States, Portugal, and Uruguay. The gap is most striking in share of earned income. In no country do women account for more than 50 percent of earned income, and in a number of Islamic societies (Oman, Saudi Arabia, and Qatar) they account for only about 10 percent. A highly innovative effort to aid women in less-developed countries economically was developed by a Bangladesh economist, Muhammad Yunus, who founded the Grameen Bank in 1976 to extend small loans or "micro-credit" to women for "micro-enterprises" like raising sheep or knitting shirts. In this way, the bank has aided two million families in 35,000 Bangladesh villages, and the idea is spreading.[64]

The United Nations uses an index called the *Gender Empowerment Measure (GEM)* to determine the economic (share of earned income), political (share of parliamentary seats), and professional (share of professional, technical, and managerial jobs) participation of women in 116 countries (see Table 15.2). By this measure, Scandinavia and Canada do best, and African and Islamic societies do worst. Indeed, in Afghanistan, self-appointed conservative Islamic councils used the threat of violence to stop women from working for U.N. agencies in that country.[65]

The United States ranks fourth on the GEM, pulled down by the relatively few seats (11.2 percent) held by women in Congress. In no country, except Sweden,

TABLE 15.1
Gender-Related Development Index: Selected Countries

HDI rank	Gender-related development index (GDI) rank	Life expectancy at birth (years) 1995		Adult literacy rate (%) 1995		School enrollment ratio (%) 1995		Share of earned income (%) 1995		GDI value 1995
		Female	Male	Female	Male	Female	Male	Female	Male	
High human development	–	76.8	70.3	95.3	96.2	79.2	75.9	34.4	65.6	0.861
1 Canada	1	81.8	76.3	99.0	99.0	100.0	100.0	38.0	62.0	0.940
2 France	7	82.6	74.4	99.0	99.0	91.0	87.0	39.1	60.9	0.925
3 Norway	2	80.5	74.7	99.0	99.0	93.0	92.0	42.4	57.6	0.935
4 USA	6	79.7	73.0	99.0	99.0	98.0	93.0	40.3	59.7	0.927
7 Netherlands	12	80.4	74.5	99.0	99.0	88.0	93.0	34.1	65.9	0.905
8 Japan	13	82.8	76.7	99.0	99.0	77.0	79.0	34.1	65.9	0.902
9 New Zealand	8	79.4	73.9	99.0	99.0	96.0	91.0	38.8	61.2	0.920
10 Sweden	3	80.8	75.9	99.0	99.0	84.0	81.0	44.7	55.3	0.932
11 Spain	19	81.3	74.1	96.1	98.2	94.0	87.0	29.7	70.3	0.877
12 Belgium	14	80.3	73.5	99.0	99.0	86.0	86.0	33.6	66.4	0.893
13 Austria	15	79.8	73.3	99.0	99.0	85.0	88.0	33.6	66.4	0.891
14 United Kingdom	11	79.4	74.2	99.0	99.0	86.0	85.0	37.6	62.5	0.907
15 Australia	9	81.1	75.3	99.0	99.0	80.0	77.0	40.0	60.0	0.918
16 Switzerland	18	81.6	74.8	99.0	99.0	73.0	78.0	32.5	67.5	0.887
17 Ireland	27	79.1	73.7	99.0	99.0	89.0	87.0	26.8	73.2	0.859
18 Denmark	10	78.0	72.7	99.0	99.0	90.0	87.0	41.8	58.2	0.917
19 Germany	17	79.5	73.0	99.0	99.0	79.0	83.0	34.8	65.2	0.888
20 Greece	20	80.5	75.3	95.3	98.3	80.0	83.0	31.8	68.2	0.876
21 Italy	23	81.0	74.7	97.6	98.6	74.0	72.0	31.2	68.8	0.868
22 Israel	22	79.2	75.5	93.0	97.0	76.0	74.0	33.1	66.9	0.873
23 Cyprus	30	79.4	75.0	91.0	98.0	80.0	73.3	27.9	72.1	0.847
24 Barbados	16	78.3	73.3	96.8	98.0	79.1	73.7	39.6	60.4	0.889
25 Hong Kong, China	33	81.8	76.1	88.2	96.0	69.9	61.9	25.6	74.4	0.836
26 Luxembourg	32	79.3	72.7	99.0	99.0	59.0	57.0	28.7	71.3	0.836
27 Malta	44	78.8	74.3	92.0	91.0	75.0	79.0	21.1	78.9	0.788
28 Singapore	29	79.3	75.0	86.3	95.9	66.6	57.6	31.9	68.1	0.848
30 Korea, Rep. of	37	75.4	68.1	96.7	99.3	78.4	65.9	29.2	70.8	0.826

TABLE 15.1
Gender-Related Development Index: Selected Countries (continued)

HDI rank	Gender-related development index (GDI) rank	Life expectancy at birth (years) 1995		Adult literacy rate (%) 1995		School enrollment ratio (%) 1995		Share of earned income (%) 1995		GDI value 1995
		Female	Male	Female	Male	Female	Male	Female	Male	
High human development	–	76.8	70.3	95.3	96.2	79.2	75.9	34.4	65.6	**0.861**
31 Chile	46	78.0	72.2	95.0	95.4	72.1	64.7	22.0	78.0	0.783
36 Argentina	48	76.2	69.1	96.2	96.2	80.6	68.7	22.1	77.9	0.777
39 Czech Rep.	25	75.4	69.3	99.0	99.0	70.0	69.0	39.0	61.0	0.864
42 Slovakia	26	75.6	66.5	99.0	99.0	73.0	71.0	40.7	59.3	0.861
43 Bahrain	60	74.7	70.4	79.4	89.1	85.9	78.1	15.0	85.0	0.746
46 Venezuela	43	75.3	69.5	90.3	91.8	68.4	58.0	27.1	72.9	0.790
47 Hungary	34	73.8	64.3	99.0	99.0	68.0	66.0	38.5	61.5	0.834
48 United Arab Emirates	66	75.9	73.5	79.8	78.9	72.1	66.1	10.2	89.8	0.718
49 Mexico	49	75.1	69.2	87.4	91.8	66.1	64.0	25.7	74.3	0.774
52 Poland	35	75.7	66.6	99.0	99.0	80.0	79.0	39.0	61.0	0.834
53 Colombia	41	73.1	67.7	91.4	91.2	70.7	62.7	33.5	66.5	0.810
54 Kuwait	50	77.7	73.7	74.9	82.2	57.9	52.6	25.3	74.7	0.773
57 Qatar	67	74.8	69.4	79.9	79.2	72.8	65.2	10.0	90.0	0.714
59 Thailand	40	72.3	66.9	91.6	96.0	55.5	49.4	36.7	63.3	0.812
60 Malaysia	45	73.7	69.3	78.1	89.1	62.0	60.0	30.4	69.6	0.785
62 Brazil	56	70.7	62.8	83.2	83.3	71.8	69.1	29.3	70.7	0.751
64 Libyan Arab Jamahiriya	79	66.3	62.8	63.0	87.9	89.0	85.5	16.3	83.7	0.664
Medium human development	–	69.7	65.4	76.9	89.5	63.7	64.9	36.4	63.6	**0.656**
69 Turkey	55	70.9	66.1	72.4	91.7	53.7	59.9	35.5	64.5	0.753
70 Saudi Arabia	102	72.5	69.3	50.3	71.5	54.4	55.1	10.0	90.0	0.589
71 Oman	104	72.7	68.4	46.0	71.0	58.1	60.1	10.6	89.4	0.580
72 Russian Federation	53	72.1	59.2	99.0	99.0	82.0	75.0	41.3	58.7	0.757
78 Iran, Islamic Rep. of	92	69.1	67.9	59.3	77.7	62.6	67.0	18.9	81.1	0.643
81 Syrian Arab Rep.	94	70.3	66.0	55.8	85.7	57.8	61.2	19.8	80.2	0.638
82 Algeria	96	69.4	66.8	49.1	73.9	62.0	66.7	19.1	80.9	0.627
84 Jamaica	65	76.3	71.9	89.1	80.8	68.9	63.4	39.2	60.8	0.724

TABLE 15.1
Gender-Related Development Index: Selected Countries (continued)

HDI rank		Gender-related development index (GDI) rank	Life expectancy at birth (years) 1995		Adult literacy rate (%) 1995		School enrollment ratio (%) 1995		Share of earned income (%) 1995		GDI value 1995
			Female	Male	Female	Male	Female	Male	Female	Male	
High human development		–	69.7	65.4	76.9	89.5	63.7	64.9	36.4	63.6	0.656
85	Cuba	69	77.6	73.9	95.3	96.2	67.3	62.1	31.5	68.5	0.705
86	Peru	80	70.2	65.3	83.0	94.5	76.1	72.0	23.8	76.2	0.664
87	Jordan	90	70.8	67.0	79.4	93.4	66.0	66.0	19.1	80.9	0.647
89	South Africa	74	67.2	61.2	81.7	81.9	82.9	75.4	30.9	69.1	0.680
90	Sri Lanka	70	74.8	70.3	87.2	93.4	67.9	64.7	35.5	64.5	0.700
91	Paraguay	89	71.4	66.8	90.6	93.5	63.0	61.1	23.2	76.8	0.651
96	Indonesia	88	65.8	62.2	78.0	89.6	59.1	61.3	33.0	67.0	0.651
98	Philippines	82	69.3	65.6	94.3	95.0	81.8	70.9	35.0	65.0	0.661
102	Ukraine	83	73.8	63.1	98.0	98.0	78.0	75.0	42.4	57.6	0.660
106	China	93	71.3	67.3	72.7	89.9	61.5	64.1	38.1	61.9	0.641
112	Egypt	111	66.1	63.6	38.8	63.6	63.4	68.9	25.0	75.0	0.555
127	Iraq	127	59.7	57.3	45.0	70.7	45.4	55.1	13.9	86.1	0.443
Low human development		–	57.5	55.9	38.3	63.0	39.5	52.2	28.6	71.4	0.388
133	Ghana	121	58.9	55.2	53.6	75.9	38.1	48.6	43.3	56.7	0.466
134	Lesotho	123	59.5	57.0	62.3	81.1	61.0	51.3	30.5	69.5	0.457
137	Kenya	122	55.1	52.5	70.0	86.3	50.9	51.8	41.8	58.2	0.459
138	Pakistan	131	63.9	61.8	24.4	50.0	27.0	53.1	20.6	79.4	0.399
139	India	128	61.8	61.4	37.7	65.5	46.5	60.1	25.4	74.6	0.424
142	Nigeria	133	53.0	49.8	47.3	67.3	43.7	53.9	30.0	70.0	0.375
147	Bangladesh	140	57.0	56.9	26.1	49.4	30.9	39.6	23.1	76.9	0.342
156	Angola	145	49.1	45.9	29.0	56.0	27.5	31.8	39.2	60.8	0.331
157	Sudan	151	53.6	50.8	34.6	57.7	28.8	33.1	22.4	77.6	0.318
158	Senegal	149	51.3	49.3	23.2	43.1	27.9	36.5	35.1	64.9	0.326
159	Haiti	144	56.3	52.9	42.2	48.1	28.0	29.6	36.0	64.0	0.335
160	Uganda	146	41.4	39.6	50.2	73.7	34.2	41.9	40.6	59.4	0.331
161	Malawi	150	41.4	40.5	41.8	72.0	71.4	79.7	42.0	58.0	0.325

TABLE 15.1
Gender-Related Development Index: Selected Countries (continued)

HDI rank	Gender-related development index (GDI) rank	Life expectancy at birth (years) 1995		Adult literacy rate (%) 1995		School enrollment ratio (%) 1995		Share of earned income (%) 1995		GDI value 1995
		Female	Male	Female	Male	Female	Male	Female	Male	
Low human development	–	57.5	55.9	38.3	63.0	39.5	52.2	28.6	71.4	0.388
163 Chad	152	48.9	45.7	34.7	62.1	16.7	37.2	37.2	62.8	0.301
164 Guinea-Bissau	153	44.9	41.9	42.5	68.0	29.0	29.0	33.0	67.0	0.284
165 Gambia	154	47.6	44.4	24.9	52.8	34.0	42.6	37.5	62.5	0.277
166 Mozambique	156	47.8	44.8	23.3	57.7	20.5	29.0	41.9	58.1	0.264
167 Guinea	157	46.0	45.0	21.9	49.9	16.2	32.4	40.2	59.8	0.258
168 Eritrea	155	51.8	48.7	25.0	25.0	25.1	31.8	34.3	65.7	0.269
169 Ethopia	158	50.3	47.2	25.3	45.5	15.1	24.1	33.3	66.7	0.241
170 Burundi	159	46.1	42.9	22.5	49.3	20.1	25.1	42.3	57.7	0.230
171 Mali	160	48.7	45.4	23.1	39.4	13.9	22.3	39.1	60.9	0.229
172 Burkina Faso	161	47.4	45.3	9.2	29.5	14.9	23.5	39.6	60.4	0.205
173 Niger	162	49.2	45.9	6.7	20.9	10.7	18.6	37.1	62.9	0.196
174 Sierra Leone	163	36.3	33.3	18.2	45.4	23.7	35.7	29.2	70.8	0.165
All developing countries	–	63.6	60.7	61.7	78.8	53.0	58.9	32.4	67.6	0.564
Least developed countries	–	52.3	50.0	39.3	59.2	30.9	40.3	34.3	65.7	0.332
Industrial countries	–	77.9	70.4	98.5	98.8	84.0	81.6	38.0	62.0	0.888
World	–	65.3	61.9	71.4	83.7	58.0	62.5	33.7	66.3	0.736

SOURCE: *Human Development Report 1998*, pp. 128–133. From *World Development Report, 1998/99* by the World Bank. Copyright © 1998 by the International Bank for Reconstruction and Development/The World Bank. Used by permission of Oxford University Press, Inc.

TABLE 15.2
Gender Empowerment Measure: Selected Countries

HDI rank	Gender empowerment measure (GEM) rank	Seats in parliament held by women (%)	Female administrators and managers (%)	Female professional and technical workers (%)	Women's share of earned income (%)	GEM value
High human development	–	14.1	–	–	35	–
1 Canada	7	21.2	42.2	56.1	38	0.720
2 France	31	9.0	9.4	41.4	39	0.489
3 Norway	2	36.4	31.5	61.9	42	0.790
4 USA	11	11.2	42.7	52.6	40	0.675
5 Iceland	6	25.4	27.7	53.5	42	0.723
6 Finland	5	33.5	25.3	62.5	42	0.725
7 Netherlands	9	28.4	20.3	44.0	34	0.689
8 Japan	38	7.7	8.9	43.3	34	0.472
9 New Zealand	4	29.2	34.0	49.1	39	0.725
10 Sweden	1	40.4	38.9	64.2	45	0.790
11 Spain	16	19.9	31.9	43.0	30	0.617
12 Belgium	19	15.8	18.8	50.5	34	0.600
13 Austria	10	24.7	23.9	46.1	34	0.686
14 United Kingdom	20	11.6	32.9	44.2	38	0.593
15 Australia	12	20.5	43.3	25.5	40	0.664
16 Switzerland	13	20.3	28.3	24.9	32	0.654
17 Ireland	21	13.7	22.6	45.0	27	0.554
18 Denmark	3	33.0	19.2	46.8	42	0.739
19 Germany	8	25.5	25.8	49.0	35	0.694
20 Greece	51	6.3	22.0	44.2	32	0.438
Medium human development	–	–	–	–	36	–
65 Suriname	53	15.7	12.1	61.8	26	0.434
69 Turkey	85	2.4	10.1	32.6	36	0.281
78 Iran, Islamic Rep. of	87	4.9	3.5	32.6	19	0.261
81 Syrian Arab Rep.	79	9.6	2.9	37.0	20	0.319
82 Algeria	93	3.2	5.9	27.6	19	0.241
83 Tunisia	74	6.7	12.7	35.6	25	0.345
85 Cuba	25	22.8	18.5	47.8	31	0.523
87 Jordan	97	1.7	4.6	28.7	19	0.211
89 South Africa	23	23.7	17.4	46.7	31	0.531

TABLE 15.2
Gender Empowerment Measure: Selected Countries (continued)

HDI rank	Gender empowerment measure (GEM) rank	Seats in parliament held by women (%)	Female administrators and managers (%)	Female professional and technical workers (%)	Women's share of earned income (%)	GEM value
Medium human development	–	–	–	–	36	–
106 China	33	21.0	11.6	45.1	38	0.483
112 Egypt	88	2.0	11.5	29.5	25	0.258
Low human development	–	7.9	–	–	25	–
132 Cameroon	86	5.6	10.1	24.4	30	0.268
134 Lesotho	50	11.2	33.4	56.6	30	0.451
135 Equatorial Guinea	90	8.8	1.6	26.8	29	0.256
138 Pakistan	100	2.6	3.9	19.5	21	0.179
139 India	95	7.3	2.3	20.5	25	0.228
146 Zambia	81	9.7	6.1	31.9	39	0.304
147 Bangladesh	80	9.1	4.9	34.7	23	0.305
149 Mauritania	101	0.7	7.7	20.7	37	0.177
154 Central African Rep.	98	3.5	9.0	18.9	39	0.205
157 Sudan	96	5.3	2.4	28.8	22	0.225
159 Haiti	71	3.6	32.6	39.3	36	0.356
161 Malawi	89	5.6	4.8	34.7	42	0.256
165 Gambia	94	2.0	15.5	23.7	38	0.239
166 Mozambique	55	25.2	11.3	20.4	42	0.430
171 Mali	72	12.2	19.7	19.0	39	0.351
172 Burkina Faso	77	10.8	13.5	25.8	40	0.339
173 Niger	102	1.2	8.5	8.1	37	0.121
All developing countries	–	8.6	–	–	32	–
Industrial countries	–	15.3	–	–	37	–
World	–	11.8	–	–	33	–

SOURCE: *Human Development Report 1998*, pp. 134–136. From *World Development Report, 1998/99* by the World Bank. Copyright © 1998 by the International Bank for Reconstruction and Development/The World Bank. Used by permission of Oxford University Press, Inc.

do women account for more than 40 percent of parliamentary seats, and in Kuwait, they account for none. Only in Italy do women account for more than half of administrators and managers, but they do better in professional and technical categories, accounting for half or more in thirty-one countries.

Women and Traditional Societies. In traditional societies, males control "public" life and women are relegated to "private" life—that is, the home and family. Women hold only about 10 percent of the seats in national parliaments and 3.5 percent of cabinet posts, although as of 1995 they were the elected leaders in nine countries (Bangladesh, Dominica, Iceland, Ireland, Nicaragua, Norway, Pakistan, Sri Lanka, and Turkey).[66] Women who remain pregnant during their fertile years may find themselves politically and economically dependent on men who were being educated, earning money, and building careers. In modern societies, women have acquired greater independence and have assumed new roles as birth control has become available, but, even in a modern society like Japan, women are still denied equal status—they are refused education, kept in the kitchen, or relegated to menial jobs.[67]

Traditional societies value male children more than females because males are thought to be more valuable for economic and military purposes and enhance the father's "macho" image. Females are considered burdensome dependents who must be fed and clothed until they can be married off.[68] Such traditions reflect male dominance and led to customs such as polygamy, "exposing" females (leaving them outside to die)—which until recently was common in China—suttee, a former Hindu practice in India in which a widow immolated herself on her husband's funeral pyre, and abducting and selling women into slavery.[69] Declared Pakistan's Prime Minister Benazir Bhutto: "How tragic it is that the pre-Islamic practice of female infanticide still haunts a world we regard as modern. . . . [T]he cries of the girl child reach out to us."[70] Perhaps the most repugnant tradition is genital mutilation (sometimes wrongly called "female circumcision"), which is still common in Africa and the Middle East, where men demand that those they marry be virgins who cannot succumb to sexual temptation afterward.[71]

Modern technology has not overcome these prejudices: Families in India and China use prenatal amniocentesis and ultrasound scanning to discover the gender of fetuses, thereafter aborting females.[72] According to one report, of 8,000 abortions in Bombay in which gender had been determined, all but one of the fetuses was female.[73] Said an Indian physician, "Of course, the women want only a boy. If we tell them it is a girl, they will feel very sorry, there will be a sadness in their face, and they will be looking as though they will have a nervous breakdown. And the husband will be saying right away, 'O.K., you are going for an abortion.'"[74] Because of mobile ultrasound machines, gender selection has become so common in India that the ratio of females to males in the population dropped from 972 per 1,000 in 1901 to 927 per thousand in 1991.[75] And in China the ratio of boy babies to girl babies rose from 107.2 in 1982 to 111.3 in 1989. Where a mother already had one girl, the ratio jumped to 149.4, and where she had two, it rose to 224.9.[76] China's population ratio of three men to two women promises serious social problems in the future.[77]

In some countries, resurgent religious fundamentalism has denied women freedoms that they had previously enjoyed. In Algeria, the Armed Islamic Group has killed at least twenty women who refused to marry militant Muslims and has threatened to kill women for failing to wear a veil and for seeking education.[78] In Afghanistan, the Taliban has imposed tight restrictions on women.[79] After Iran's Shah was overthrown and the Ayatollah Khomeini took power, women were denied access to birth control, and the country's birthrate shot up, reaching 3.9 percent in 1985.[80] In some Islamic countries, women are subject to purdah (seclusion in the home from the sight of men or strangers). And in Bangladesh, angry Muslim zealots demanded the death of a woman writer, Taslima Nasrin, accusing her of blaspheming the Koran by saying it should be "revised thoroughly" and forcing her to flee to Sweden.[81] Militant Muslims offered a $5,000 reward for her death, and Ms. Nasrin denounced Muslim fundamentalism for "spreading darkness in many parts of the world."[82]

Rape. One of the most brutal manifestations of male hostility toward women is rape in wartime. From the Roman conquest of the Sabines in 290 B.C. to the Japanese enslavement of Korean, Chinese, Filipino, and Dutch "comfort women" in military brothels,[83] rape has been used to affirm male domination of women. In recent years, Bosnian and Croatian Serbs and Serbs in Kosovo have used systematic rape to terrorize women as part of the policy of "ethnic cleansing."[84] During the massacre of Tutsis between April 1994 and April 1995 in Rwanda, almost 16,000 women and girls were raped by Hutu militiamen, who, according to a report financed by a French humanitarian agency, used rape "as a weapon of ethnic cleansing to destroy community ties." "From our sources, it appears that every adult woman and every adolescent girl spared from a massacre by militias was then raped."[85] The use of rape to terrorize populations is increasingly characteristic of what we call postmodern wars, whether in Africa, the Balkans, or Indonesia.[86]

The Beijing Conference. Many of these themes came together at the U.N.-sponsored *Fourth World Conference on Women,* which convened in Beijing in September 1995. Some 50,000 people from over 180 countries, including first lady Hillary Rodham Clinton, attended the official U.N. gathering or the enormous Nongovernmental Organization forum composed of thousands of women's groups trying to influence the U.N. conference.[87] The preamble of the final conference declaration decisively rejected claims that national custom or religious tradition could justify unequal treatment of women: "It is the duty of states, regardless of their political, economic and cultural systems, to promote and protect all human rights and fundamental freedoms."[88]

The final declaration declared the "full realization of all human rights and fundamental freedoms of all women" to be "essential for the empowerment of women." It focused on six key gender issues: (1) women's right to decide freely matters related to their own "sexuality," (2) prohibition of violence against women, including rape in wartime, domestic abuse, genital mutilation, and sexual harassment in the workplace, (3) discrimination against female infants and girls, (4) women's need for access to credit and other instruments of economic power, (5) the equal right of women to inherit, and (6) the need to strengthen, protect, and support the family as the basic unit of society.[89]

Human Rights and Reproductive Issues

No global problem so clearly reflects the gender issue as does the population explosion. Population control is greatly complicated by patriarchal cultural and traditional religious values—Christian, Islamic, and Jewish.[90] Declared Peru's president: "The Catholic Church has quite a strong power, and with a very large and influential network, and this is one of our obstacles in succeeding in family planning."[91] In some countries, birth-control devices are unobtainable; and population pressures, along with grinding poverty and the specter of famine, encourage widespread resort to abortion for birth control. Thus Romania has what Western doctors call "an abortion culture," and in Russia repeated abortions left many women unable to have children.[92]

In the United States, too, abortion is highly controversial, with opponents seeking to prevent the sale of abortion drugs[93] and U.S. aid to institutions that they believe promote abortions. Since many of those institutions are involved in promoting birth control that is necessary for economic development, the Clinton administration has opposed limiting such funding. "One of the most important ways we contribute to sustainable development," declared U.S. Secretary of State Madeleine K. Albright, "is through our support for international family planning."[94] According to one estimate, a 35 percent reduction in U.S. family planning assistance would lead to about four million more unintended pregnancies and, paradoxically, to a dramatic increase in abortions worldwide.[95] Many women believe that questions of reproductive rights and birth control, including abortion, are equivalent to the issue of women's control over their own bodies.

Abortion is more an issue of health than population control in poor countries, where women become pregnant at an early age and thereafter bear children at short intervals. The World Health Organization estimates that in the less-developed countries maternal causes are among the leading causes of death among women aged between 15 and 44.[96] In at least seventeen countries, mainly in sub-Saharan Africa, maternal mortality exceeds 1,000 per 100,000 live births each year.[97] In Brazil, where abortion is mainly illegal, about 1.4 million women each year abort unwanted pregnancies, often in a midwife's shack, and 400,000 women are hospitalized yearly (compared to about 10,000 in the United States) for abortion-related complications.[98] In Kenya, where most abortions are also illegal, one-third of maternal deaths are due to unsafe abortions, and as many as 10,000 girls a year drop out of school because of unwanted pregnancies.[99] And in India as many as six million illegal abortions a year take place partly because of the bureaucratic barriers that impede legal abortions.[100]

The 1994 *U.N. Conference on Population and Development* in Cairo was a major step toward recognizing women's reproductive rights as a serious issue.[101] Birth-control and reproductive issues featured prominently at the conference. One analyst with a New York-based health group argued that women needed "a holistic form of quality care, a one-shop stop for women," and that safe abortion was only one of a range of health services women needed.[102] Norwegian Prime Minister Gro Harlem Bruntland was blunter: "Morality becomes hypocrisy if it means accepting mothers' suffering or dying in connection with unwanted pregnancies and illegal abortions and unwanted children."[103] The conference's final

"Program of Action" proclaimed the right of women to make their own decisions about their families and children and recommended controlling population by improving the status of women worldwide, especially by providing access to education and birth control.[104] This approach was applauded by the director of the International Women's Health Coalition as "ending 2,000 years of ecclesiastical authority or jurisdiction over marriage and women's lives. Medicine and science, not religion and belief, will govern family planning."[105]

This approach was vigorously challenged by Catholic and Islamic religious leaders. Shortly before the conference opened, 114 of the world's 139 Catholic cardinals decried "cultural imperialism" in which "abortion on demand, sexual promiscuity and distorted notions of the family are proclaimed as human rights."[106] A spokesperson for the NGO Population Action International responded: "Women should not die or suffer irreparable physical harm as a result of unsafe abortions because of a group of 114 celibate men."[107] Controversy swirled around the passages in the conference draft report that read:

> Reproductive health . . . implies that people are able to have a satisfying and safe
> sex life and that they have . . . the freedom to decide if, when and how often to do
> so. Implicit in this last condition are the right of men and women to be informed
> and to have access to safe, effective, affordable and acceptable methods of fertility
> regulation of their choice. . . . Reproductive health care in the context of primary
> health care should, inter alia, include: family planning counseling, information,
> education, communication and services. . . . All governments . . . are urged to deal
> openly and forthrightly with unsafe abortion as a major public health concern.[108]

Although U.S. Vice President Al Gore tried to reassure critics that these passages were warrants to improve women's health conditions, not to establish abortion or sex outside of marriage as global human rights, his explanation did not satisfy Vatican spokesmen, who opposed all forms of artificial contraception and argued that life is sacred from the moment of conception.[109] "After the epic duel with Moscow and the Polish Communist Party to save Solidarity," declared an Italian journalist, "this is the biggest battle for Pope John Paul II. The stake is the family and the aim is to subdue the United Nations, defeat Clinton and force the Cairo conference to rewrite its manifesto so as to eliminate any reference to abortion laws."[110] So heated was the conference debate that, in one five-hour closed session in which the Vatican stood alone in blocking a Pakistani proposal, Vatican diplomats were booed by other participants.[111]

Muslim spokesmen also opposed the draft document, even though many Muslims have long approved of birth-spacing and contraceptive use. Saudi Arabia refused to attend the conference, and some Egyptian clerics denounced the Cairo conference as "corrupt," "immoral," and a "Zionist and imperial assault against Islam."[112] Egypt's Islamic Group murdered several U.N. aid officials shortly after having threatened to attack foreign delegates to the Cairo conference.[113]

The Beijing Conference was even more outspoken on the right of women to make uncoerced sexual decisions. Said a spokeswoman for Population Action International: "This is a major step forward in defining human rights. It is recognition that a woman is not just a reproductive machine, but a sexual being with rights." Added an American delegate: "What we're trying to do is ensure that a woman has the right to say 'no.'That is good for everyone."[114] Although the Vatican objected to phrases like "reproductive rights," it took a far more conciliatory line in Beijing than in Cairo.[115]

Explaining Human-Rights Violations

What accounts for violations of human rights around the world? There is no simple answer, and it is likely that several factors explain why states are repressive and do not respect human rights. Economic, social, and political factors have been cited to explain human-rights abuses.

Economic Explanations

One explanation focuses on economic conditions and their effect on countries' use of political repression. Deteriorating economic conditions are associated with spreading debt slavery (forced labor to pay off a debt) in some societies.[116] Said former U.S. Secretary of Defense and World Bank President Robert McNamara: "There can . . . be no question but that there is an irrefutable relationship between violence and economic backwardness."[117] By this logic, the poorer a country, the more likely it is that human-rights abuses will occur. According to one analysis, the greater the social and economic deprivation and inequality in a society, the more likely its government is to engage in repression.[118]

The opposite claim is made by political scientist Samuel Huntington, who argues that the poorest countries are likely to be ultrastable because citizens are busy making ends meet and cannot imagine how they might alter their condition. "People who are really poor," Huntington contends, "are too poor for politics and too poor for protest."[119] But societies that are beginning to modernize and improve social and economic conditions, such as Iran under the Shah, are susceptible to demands for change. As citizens make greater demands and as governments are less able to satisfy them, greater repression will follow.

Neo-Marxists provide an economic explanation for human-rights abuses that goes beyond the conditions in one country to include that country's external ties. They argue that countries that are deeply enmeshed in the global capitalist system try to control the growth and influence of trade unions, repress revolutionary activities that threaten the regime in power, and control protest activities.[120]

Political Explanations

The first factor that many in the West think of to explain respect for human rights is a state's type of political regime. Democratic or "liberal" states are believed to have greater respect for human rights than authoritarian states.[121] The arguments are straightforward. Liberal regimes have the "requisite conception of human dignity" to make possible observance of human rights and are founded on a belief in individual liberty. Democracy is identified not only with the people's right to govern their own affairs but with the belief that individual rights should be observed.[122] In some authoritarian societies, on the other hand, the state's interests are given higher priority than those of citizens.

Back in 1979, Jeanne Kirkpatrick, then U.S. Ambassador to the United Nations, distinguished among nondemocratic states, arguing that some are worse than others in observing human rights. *Totalitarian states* (which she tended to equate with states under communist control), she argued, leave the individual defenseless. *Authoritarian regimes* (such as Latin American military governments), she believed, though also repressive, do not penetrate so deeply into the fabric of society, exercise less control of individual conduct, and are more "susceptible of liberalization" than their totalitarian counterparts.[123] Events in the former Soviet Union and Eastern Europe cast doubt on her claim because those societies have reformed further and faster than many authoritarian regimes.

Research does indicate that democratic states respect human rights better than nondemocratic states, though the relationship is not perfect.[124] The distinction between totalitarian and authoritarian regimes is less useful.[125] In short, the type of political regime matters, but other factors also contribute to respect for human rights, including cultural and ethnic features.

Cultural Explanations

A society's cultural divisions also help explain human-rights violations. If a society is fractured along ethnic, racial, economic, religious, or ideological lines, and if these cleavages reinforce one another, political repression is more likely. According to political scientist Ted Robert Gurr:

> In ethnically and religiously diverse societies, social cohesion tends to be low; hence, challenges to the regime are more common and elites are more likely to respond violently. This is not only because of the frequency and intensity of challenges, but because compliance with regime policies is not likely to be given freely.[126]

Many states today are a patchwork of ethnic, religious, and racial groups, and only a few are homogeneous. According to one analysis, 93 of 127 countries have at least one "politicized minority," and those minorities account for some 915 million people.[127] Although systematic studies of the relationship between social cleavages and political repression are few, evidence suggests that heterogeneity is linked to human-rights abuses.

From its creation after World War I, Yugoslavia, for example, was a hodgepodge of ethnic adversaries. During World War II, Croatian and Serbian nationalists waged a cruel war against each other, and the country's unity was maintained after the war only by the authoritarian policies of Marshal Tito and the communist party. After the country broke up, religious and ethnic hatred contributed to widespread violations of human rights in Croatia and later in Bosnia and Kosovo. Conflicts between Tamils and Sinhalese in Sri Lanka, Hindus and Muslims in Kashmir, and Catholics and Protestants in Northern Ireland reinforce the impression that religious and ethnic divisions may have bloody consequences. New York Senator Daniel Patrick Moynihan expresses the issue:

> What is to be the basis of a legitimate political order? The will of the people? Well, yes. But which people? The cold war kept that question at bay. No longer. . . . The barbarians had gone; barbarism had returned. Europe . . . had become the setting of sealed trains, "ethnic cleansing," murderous hate. . . . In what had been Yugoslavia, a Serb militiaman . . . told of his village burnt, his brother-in-law dead, "Serbs, naked and tortured." He responded in kind. "I have cut the throats of three Turks[128] so far, and I don't ever have nightmares."[129]

Improving Human Rights

Efforts to protect individual human rights have been pursued through various channels. The issue mobilizes individuals, nongovernmental organizations, governmental agencies, and international organizations. Indeed, NGOs have played a larger role in fostering human rights than in any other policy area, with the possible exception of the environment. A brief survey of the groups and individuals and the kind of work that they undertake depicts global activity on behalf of human rights.

The Individual's Role   In many countries, improving human rights owes much to a few dedicated, courageous individuals, often risking imprisonment or worse at the hands of outraged officials. President Jimmy Carter's personal campaign to place human rights on the global agenda in the 1970s exemplifies what a major public figure can do, as well as the limits on such work. Nelson Mandela's exertions on behalf of South African blacks under a repressive regime showed great personal courage. Mandela, imprisoned himself almost thirty years for his political activities, continued to wage his campaign for majority rule even while behind bars. Others include Wei Jingsheng, who was jailed in China for all but seven months between 1979 and 1995; Harry Wu, who spent nineteen years in Chinese labor camps until freed in 1979, returned to China several times, often under assumed names, to document human-rights abuses until being arrested once again (and released) in 1995; Wole Soyinka, Nobel Prize–winning Nigerian playwright, who urged the world to impose an economic boycott on his country to protest its military regime;[130] and Jennifer Harbury, whose persistence finally forced the CIA to provide information about the death of her husband at the hands of a CIA-connected Guatemalan army officer.[131]

The quiet work of many individuals has begun to receive recognition. Several recent winners of the Nobel Prize for Peace have been human-rights advocates. The 1992 recipient, Rigoberta Menchu of Guatemala, campaigned tirelessly for the rights of indigenous people and sought to end the violence committed by the Guatemalan army against the rural poor. In 1991, the Burmese opposition leader, Day Aung San Suu Kyi (daughter of the country's founder), was awarded the prize for opposing military rule in her country. Other human-rights activists who have received this award include two women from Belfast, Northern Ireland, Mairead Corrigan and Betty Williams (1976), who sought to start a dialogue between Catholics and Protestants; Mother Teresa of Calcutta (1979) for her work among the poor of India; Adolfo Pérez Esquivel (1980) for advocating human rights in Argentina when that country was ruled by a military dictatorship; the former leader of the Polish trade union Solidarity (and later president of Poland), Lech Walesa (1983); the South African antiapartheid leader, Bishop Desmond Tutu (1984); the anti-Nazi activist Elie Wiesel (1986); and the exiled Tibetan leader, the Dalai Lama (1989).

Despite such recognition, much of the work by individuals goes unnoticed. These range from an Argentine mothers' campaign to locate and identify their sons and relatives who "disappeared" during the military regime's "dirty war" late in the 1970s and early in the 1980s to the many thousands of ordinary citizens who demonstrated for political freedom in Leipzig, East Germany, or Vilnius, Lithuania, early in the 1990s or who gathered in Moscow to thwart an attempt to overthrow President Mikhail Gorbachev in a coup d'état. Clearly individuals can make a difference.

Nongovernmental Organizations

More and more often, nongovernmental organizations monitor and publicize human-rights compliance worldwide. The most prominent and successful of these, *Amnesty International (AI)*, was originally named the "Appeal for Amnesty, 1961" and began as a campaign by lawyers and writers in London. The campaign gained attention when one of them (a lawyer named Peter Berenson) wrote an essay in a London paper expressing his outrage at global human-rights violations and calling for world-wide action to stop them:

> Open your newspaper any day of the week and you will find a report from some-where in the world about someone being imprisoned, tortured, or executed because his opinions or religion are unacceptable to his government. . . . The newspaper reader feels a sickening sense of impotence. Yet if these feelings of disgust all over the world could be united into common action, something effective could be done.[132]

The AI Charter succinctly summarizes its principal goal, "to contribute to the observance throughout the world of human rights as set out in the Universal Declaration of Human Rights" and promote "the indivisibility and interdependence of all human rights and freedoms."[133]

After more than three decades, AI has grown into a worldwide movement with more than 1,100,000 members, subscribers, and donors in more than 150 countries.[134] Local AI groups petition for changes in their country's constitution or their government's adherence to international conventions. Amnesty International also provides support for individuals held as "prisoners of conscience," works to improve the conditions under which such prisoners are held, and publicizes the plight of political detainees. At the end of 1993, AI was working on more than 3,507 human-rights cases (or "Action Files") involving 8,960 individuals, and had initiated 551 new cases involving torture (179), political killing (100), "disappearance" (76), judicial execution (95), threats to safety (110), and legal concerns such as detention without trial (108).[135]

The publicity that AI gives human-rights abuses through annual reports on human-rights conditions in specific countries and through massive letter-writing campaigns makes a difference in the way governments deal with political dissent, because fear of publicity induces caution and restraint. AI's work is so influential that the organization was awarded the Nobel Prize for Peace in 1977.

Other nongovernmental humanitarian groups operate as human-rights monitors, seeking to improve global conditions. Humanitarian groups such as *Médecins Sans Frontières* (Doctors Without Borders) publicize human-rights violations, and the Women's Environment and Development Organization pressures governments to improve the status of women worldwide. Human Rights Watch does an annual survey of human-rights abuses,[136] as do three regional human-rights organizations called Americas Watch, Asia Watch, and Africa Watch. Americas Watch, founded in 1981, carries out fact-finding missions in the Western Hemisphere. Asia Watch has complained about the treatment of Vietnamese refugees and has campaigned to improve human rights in China. Africa Watch did much to focus world attention on famine in Somalia in 1992, genocide in Rwanda two years later, and most recently, violence in Burundi. Physicians for Human Rights has conducted forensic examinations at mass graves in Rwanda and Bosnia. Such groups lobby individual goverments, as well as the U.N. Human Rights Commission.[137]

Other nongovernmental organizations focus on international law and legal advocacy to protect human rights worldwide. The Human Rights Advocates International is a New York-based group with attorneys in forty countries who represent individuals or groups in courts. Another, the International Human Rights Law Group, promotes worldwide human rights by applying international law. Still a third, the Lawyers Committee for Human Rights, relies on the legal norms in the Universal Declaration of Human Rights to guide its work.[138]

Church groups are also deeply involved in monitoring human rights, especially in Central America. In El Salvador, a church group repeatedly challenged the Reagan administration's claim in the mid-1980s that the U.S.-supported government was improving its human-rights record. Finally, NGOs working for human rights have emerged in academic circles, and the study of human rights and human-rights abuses has become a growth industry. Thus collaboration between a German university and the German Red Cross led to the creation of the Berlin Treatment Center for Torture Victims in 1992.[139]

In sum, NGOs' ability to publicize abuses sometimes helps mobilize world public opinion, and some governments restrain their behavior to avoid such publicity and the resulting condemnation. The influence of such NGOs arises from the legitimacy they enjoy, their reputation for good works, and the information they can provide. Where governments are prepared to bear the costs of negative publicity, however, as in the case of China, NGOs can do little, and some observers wonder whether human-rights reports matter at all. Thus a conservative U.S. political observer declared: "The public at large pays absolutely no attention to them [reports], unless they get reported extensively in the media. Even then it's not the reports so much that drives public opinion, it's television."[140]

International Organizations

The United Nations is the main international organization with responsibility to monitor human rights. One of its principal organs, the Economic and Social Council, has this specific responsibility. In 1946, shortly after the United Nations was founded, UNESCO established the *Commission on Human Rights,* which has the responsibility to evaluate human rights worldwide and investigate complaints.

The Commission and its Sub-Commission on Prevention of Discrimination and Protection of Minorities discuss violations of human rights and set up fact-finding groups. One report described amputations, maiming, and branding of dissidents in Iraq, which was called one of "the worst offenders of human rights since the Second World War."[141] Individuals may bring complaints of human-rights violations to the United Nations, and, under the "1503" procedure (named after the resolution by which it was established in 1970), their allegations are summarized in confidential documents for the Commission and Sub-Commission.[142] In recent years, the Commission and the Sub-Commission have sponsored public meetings in which alleged human-rights violations are discussed.

The Commission on Human Rights and the United Nations as a whole have initiated several other actions to promote human rights worldwide. An international Human Rights Day is observed every December 10, and the International Day for the Elimination of Racial Discrimination is observed annually on March 21. The year 1968 was declared the International Year for Human Rights, and a human-rights conference was held on the twentieth anniversary of the adoption of the Universal Declaration of Human Rights. Finally, the United Nations provides governments with experts, training programs, and fellowships to promote observance of human rights.[143]

The 1993 U.N. World Conference on Human Rights in Vienna, though beset by disagreements among participating states, began a process that led to establishing a U.N. *High Commissioner for Human Rights.* Representatives of more than 1,000 NGOs attended the Vienna conference. The High Commissioner's mandate is to promote and protect human rights worldwide, work with governments to improve human rights, coordinate U.N. human-rights activities, and publicize human-rights programs.[144] The position acquired a higher profile when President Mary Robinson of Ireland was selected by Secretary General Kofi Annan for the office in 1997.[145]

Some regional organizations also have committees or commissions to monitor and address human-rights violations.[146] Europe and, to a lesser extent, Latin America have the most highly developed institutions for dealing with human-rights abuses. Both regions have human-rights courts in addition to human-rights commissions. In Europe, a Commission on Human Rights is responsible for implementing the European Convention on Human Rights and for investigating human-rights abuses brought to its attention by governments, individuals, or groups.[147] Where it seems necessary, the Commission can refer a matter to the European Court of Human Rights in Strasbourg, France, for further adjudication. The European Court has issued legal judgments, with which states usually comply.[148]

Governments

Governments can improve their human-rights records in two ways. First, they can initiate domestic reforms that demonstrate adherence to human-rights norms. Second, a government or group of governments may take punitive action toward a state that violates human rights and demand that abuses cease. Both strategies are difficult to implement successfully, despite several partial successes.

Human-rights improvements in Central Europe and Russia during the 1990s following communism's demise show that governments can make dramatic changes in the way they treat citizens. At no time in recent history have so many people's civil rights improved so quickly. Reforms in Russia, so often portrayed as a violator of human rights, demonstrate convincingly that a government (or, perhaps more accurately, a determined population) can put an end to repressive policies.

There are other recent cases in which governments have improved the climate for human rights in their societies. However, it is difficult to confront the past, and, even after abuses have ended, it may prove impossible to bring to justice those who perpetrated them.[149] The perpetrators may retain powerful positions in the army or police, and bringing them to justice risks touching off a military coup. With democracy restored, Argentina undertook a concerted campaign to publicize the abuses committed by the military regime during the "dirty-war" period and was almost the first country to be tried in an American court for human-rights abuses committed against a Jewish businessman.[150] A similar undertaking began in Chile when Patricio Aylwyn Azocar was elected president in December 1989, following sixteen years of repressive military rule under General Augusto Pinochet Ugarte.[151] Elsewhere in South America, including Brazil and Paraguay, efforts have been made to confront an authoritarian past.[152] After a decade-long war in Central America, El Salvador has publicized and confronted its past human-rights violations.[153] In the Philippines, Nigeria, and Guatemala governments have also come to power that are less oppressive than their predecessors. And when the president of Guatemala in spring 1993 tried to overthrow the democratic order in his country, he was thwarted by an alliance between human-rights activists and the military. Both Rwanda and Ethiopia have sought to bring to trial officials who were responsible for human-rights violations.[154] Finally, South Africa has made a successful transition from a repressive white-minority regime to a vibrant democracy and has sought to come to terms with its past by establishing a Truth and Reconciliation Commission chaired by Archbishop Desmond Tutu, a Nobel Peace Prize laureate. Those who had abused human rights during the apartheid era—both blacks and whites—could admit their deeds before the Commission and be forgiven for them.[155]

Nevertheless, major exceptions remain to the improving picture of human rights. Repressive regimes persist in many parts of the world, such as in China, Cuba, Iraq, and parts of Africa, and relying upon internal reform alone is a weak reed for improving human rights in those countries. Authoritarian leaders have few incentives to cede power voluntarily, and outsiders have few levers that will bring about their overthrow.

The other option for governments is to use diplomatic, economic, and, as in the cases of Panama and Haiti, military instruments against states that abuse human rights. Such efforts have had mixed success. For almost two decades the United States has had a legislatively mandated policy that denies foreign aid to states engaged "in a consistent pattern of gross violations of internationally recognized human rights." And most evidence is that human rights worldwide have not been improved by this policy, for several reasons. Strategic considerations still interfere with consistently applying the policy, and target states resist interference in matters that they claim to be their domestic affairs.[156]

Governments have also tried to employ *economic sanctions* against offending states. Again, the overall record is mixed. Sanctions against the white minority government in Rhodesia (now Zimbabwe) were influential in bringing about majority rule, and sanctions against South Africa encouraged reform there. In some cases, however, sanctions harm innocent people,[157] and in others they have little effect. United States sanctions against the People's Republic of China after the massacre of prodemocracy demonstrators in Tiananmen Square were blunted by the target's intransigence and fear of serious political and economic consequences.

Trade Versus Human Rights: The China Case

With the Cold War ended, balancing economic interests with the effort to improve human rights is difficult. Winston Lord, U.S. Assistant Secretary of State for East Asian and Pacific Affairs, captures the dilemma:

> There are still security considerations, but increasingly the thrust of the debate is economics versus human rights. When I was working for Henry Kissinger in the

1970's, I tended to meet with think-tankers and academics, purely on political-security issues. Today, I find myself going from a meeting with Amnesty International or Asia Watch in the morning to one with the Chamber of Commerce in the afternoon.... I think we can promote the interests of both. But clearly in the short run there are sometimes tough trade-offs.[158]

The issue of human rights in China illustrates the dilemma.[159] Efforts to make China improve its dismal human-rights record, which includes repressing dissent in Tibet, exporting goods made in Chinese prisons,[160] and transplanting organs from executed prisoners,[161] run up against the lure of the country's vast and growing market. During the 1992 presidential campaign, candidate Bill Clinton charged President Bush with "coddling" the Chinese government and, after the election, continued the policy of making annual renewal of China's most-favored nation (MFN) trade status contingent on improvement of its human-rights performance.[162]

Like his predecessor, however, Clinton found himself pressured by those who believed that it was not worth risking a deterioration of U.S.-Chinese, political and economic relations to try to improve human rights in China.[163] The fear of jeopardizing America's $9 billion in exports to China and the more than 200,000 American jobs it represents,[164] not to mention surrendering economic opportunities to other countries, was a powerful incentive for Washington to accept vague Chinese promises in return for MFN renewal.[165]

In May 1994, President Clinton severed the link between China's human-rights record and renewal of its MFN status, admitting what was already evident, that U.S. political and economic interests outweighed human-rights interests. The president declared: "China has an atomic arsenal and a vote and a veto in the U.N. Security Council. It is a major factor in Asian and global security.... China is also the world's fastest growing economy."[166] The new policy was hailed by U.S. companies, which had been lobbied by Chinese officials,[167] and roundly criticized by human-rights activists. Declared Representative Nancy Pelosi of California: "We know money talks in Washington, but in the case of China ... it rules."[168] Said the director of Asia Watch, "If 'commercial diplomacy' means anything, responsible members of the corporate community should be doing everything they can to convince the Chinese that respect for human rights is fundamental to doing business in China."[169] Indeed, one result of President Clinton's trip to China in 1998 was Chinese business deals with companies like Boeing, IBM, and General Electric.

If the United States hoped that its concession in delinking trade and human rights would be reciprocated by a quiet improvement in China's human-rights performance, it was soon disappointed.[170] Chinese prodemocracy dissidents were again jailed and given stiff prison sentences, and, in June 1995, human-rights activist Harry Wu, a U.S. citizen, was arrested, an act described by a human-rights observer as a "declaration of war against the United States on the human-rights issue."[171] In part, China's poor human-rights record reflects leaders' fears of political instability during its transition to an increasingly open economic system.[172] Although China has finally signed both the International Covenants on Economic, Social and Cultural Rights and on Civil and Political Rights, this has not ended human-rights abuses in that country.[173]

Refugees: Human-Rights Crisis of the 1990s[174]

In 1951, the United Nations created the office of the High Commissioner for Refugees, responsible for implementing the Convention Relating to the Status of Refugees and upholding the principle that asylum should be granted to those fleeing because of "a well-founded fear of persecution."[175] In practice, this meant dealing with those escaping from the communist bloc. However, in recent years this limited responsibility has expanded dramatically to include humanitarian relief for millions.[176]

Refugees With slow economic growth in the 1990s, countries were less willing than in the past to accept desperate refugees fleeing violence, persecution, and hardship. The sagas of Vietnamese boat people who were victimized by pirates and then refused entry into other Asian countries, of fleeing Cubans drowning off Florida, or of Albanians and Haitians fleeing hardship and tyranny being turned away by Italy and the United States, respectively, are well known. Having lost special refugee status in 1994, many of the 800,000 refugees who fled Vietnam after 1975 languished in crowded detention camps in Indonesia, the Philippines, Thailand, Hong Kong, Malaysia, and elsewhere, some for decades. Because of demands from these countries, the U.N. High Commissioner for Refugees endorsed an agreement (the Comprehensive Plan of Action) to repatriate these refugees to Vietnam, forcibly if necessary, and close most of the camps by 1996. Thereafter, violence erupted in some of the camps, and some refugees inflicted wounds on themselves to prevent forcible repatriation.[177]

As the collapse of communism and the loosening of border controls in the former Soviet bloc made those countries conduits for illegal immigration to the West, Western Europe began erecting immigration barriers.[178] In 1992, over 438,000 people requested political asylum in Germany, which at the time allowed such refugees to remain, sometimes for many years, until asylum claims were investigated. In 1993, the country changed its liberal asylum law to permit authorities to send back unqualified applicants at the point of entry.[179] And a new flood of refugees from the Serbian province of Kosovo threatened to intensify Europe's refugee problem as some 800,000 ethnic Albanians were sent fleeing into Albania, Macedonia, and Montenegro by Serbian forces in March–April 1999.[180]

The issue also surfaced in the United States, where illegal aliens from Mexico, China, and Central America have created resentment among those who believe they compete for scarce jobs and strain scarce public resources.[181] President Clinton used the Coast Guard to return Haitian boat people trying to flee to U.S. shores, to intern Cuban refugees in Panama and Guantanamo, and to intercept boatloads of Chinese workers.[182] This policy, which was upheld by the U.S. Supreme Court in 1993, violated the principle of "nonrefoulement" (after *refouler,* French for "to force back") that people not be returned to a country where they may suffer persecution.[183]

Growing resistance to refugees is partly a result of the rapid increase in those fleeing civil disorder, famine, war, and repression. Overall, there has been an explosion in

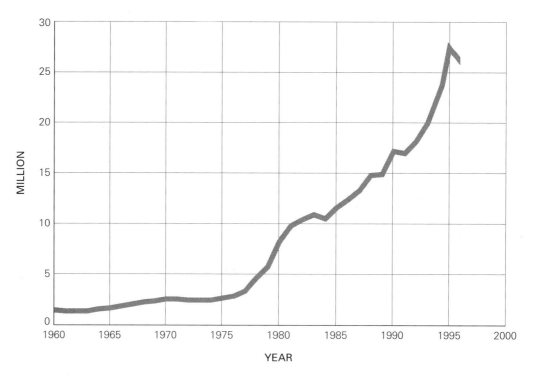

FIGURE 15.1
A Growing Tide of Refugees

Beginning in the mid-1970s, the number of refugees receiving U.N. assistance worldwide began to explode, reaching 27.4 million by 1995. SOURCE: Lester R. Brown, Michael Renner, Christopher Flavin, *Vital Signs 1997: The Environmental Trends That Are Shaping Our Future,* p. 183. Copyright © 1997 by the Worldwatch Institute. Reprinted by permission of W.W. Norton & Sons.

the world's refugee population—from about 4.6 million in the early 1970s to some 18.9 million in 1993[184] and 23 million in 1995.[185] Figure 15.1 summarizes this trend. An equally large problem is posed by refugees who flee one part of a country for another to escape war and famine. Today, almost thirteen million people are displaced in their own country.[186] More than 6 million Afghans were displaced by war in that country after 1979. Between 3.5 and 5 million out of a population of 23 million (including 1.3 million of 4.4 million in Bosnia) were displaced after 1989 in the former Yugoslavia,[187] and innumerable refugees were created by turmoil in Iraq, Somalia, Ethiopia, Mozambique, Liberia, and the Central Asian republics of the former U.S.S.R.

The number of refugees skyrocketed in 1994 as a result of the flight of as many as 4 million Hutus from Rwanda, sometimes at a rate of 30,000 an hour, to the Congo (Zaire), Tanzania, and Burundi following the Hutu massacre of Tutsis and the victory of the Tutsi-dominated Rwanda Patriotic Front.[188] A year later 2.2 million remained in the camps that sprang up, many terrorized by former Hutu officials.[189] After efforts to entice these people back to Rwanda failed, a Tutsi army in the Congo led by Laurent Kabila and supported surreptitiously by the Rwandan and Ugandan governments drove the Hutu refugees away from the Rwandan border and far back into the jungles of the Congo, where many were massacred or allowed to die.[190]

The costs of caring for refugees doubled between 1990 and 1992, and the main contributors to the U.N. High Commission for Refugees were less willing than in the past to give. Refugees place heavy burdens on host countries such as the Congo, Pakistan, Austria, Jordan, and Iran and on humanitarian organizations like the International Red Cross. Africa alone has nearly 7.5 million refugees; Europe 6 million; Asia 5.7 million; and the former Soviet republics 2.3 million.[191] It is hardly surprising that the explosion in illegal immigration has spawned a variety of people-smuggling criminal gangs.[192]

Guest Workers

Guest workers are migrants from poor countries like Algeria, Turkey, and Vietnam[193] to wealthy countries with labor shortages. Many guest workers settled in Western Europe in prosperous times, and by local law their children enjoy citizenship.[194] With deepening recession in the 1990s, local resentment against guest workers intensified. Europeans, who had been willing to let guest workers do work that they had spurned, came to see them as competitors. With economic hard times, racist xenophobia intensified among Europeans against immigrant guest workers. Africans and Asians were accused of refusing to assimilate and of having large families that burdened Europe's generous social-welfare systems. Antiforeign sentiment boosted the electoral fortunes of right-wing political parties in France and Germany. In response, Germany tried to stem the flood of refugees from the East and rising neo-Nazi violence aimed at them, and France set a zero-immigration goal.[195]

Guest workers are not only a European phenomenon. Israel's security is complicated by the many Palestinians from Gaza and the West Bank who work in vital sectors of Israel's economy. Oil-wealthy Middle East countries with small populations, such as Kuwait, "import" foreign workers, including Palestinians, Egyptians, Filipinos, and Pakistanis, while labor-rich countries such as South Korea make deals with labor-short countries to send teams of construction workers. And following the downturn in Asia's economies in 1997–98, many guest workers were expelled from South Korea and the countries of Southeast Asia.

Before the Iraqi invasion, Kuwaitis had been a minority in their own country, and their prosperity depended heavily on the muscle and brains of foreign laborers and entrepreneurs, especially Palestinians. During the war, however, some Palestinians in Kuwait collaborated with the Iraqi occupiers. In revenge, after its liberation in February 1991 Kuwait expelled 400,000 Palestinians and treated with suspicion those who remained.[196] This reaction has historical parallels. In 1492, in the midst of the Inquisition, Spain's Christian rulers expelled the Jews and Moors (Muslim Spaniards), thereby losing some of their most talented citizens.

The largest migration of workers from a developing to a developed country is that of Mexicans to the United States, especially to California and Texas, where they provide cheap labor for U.S. agribusiness. Despite reforms to ease their plight, many Mexican migrants work for low wages and enjoy no health, unemployment, social-security or welfare benefits. Many Americans, especially union members, seek more effective law enforcement to slow illegal migration, but U.S. businesses that employ low-cost migrant labor have little interest in enforcing the law. Even the Mexican government does not want the law enforced too vigorously because of the social and economic benefits the country gets from exporting surplus labor.

Conclusion

We have described how global human rights have evolved and assessed the state of these rights in today's world politics. Human rights in much of the world remain precarious. Civil and political (negative) rights and social and economic (positive) rights are not widely respected. The reasons are rooted in political, economic, and cultural differences within and across different countries. Impediments to improving human-rights conditions remain formidable. Although sensitivity has been greater toward individuals' rights in the international community in recent decades and in some states, overall improvement is disappointing. For the most part, state sovereignty remains an obstacle to eliminating human-rights abuses, but the efforts of humanitarian groups and international organizations on behalf of human rights are challenging the sovereign "right" of states to abuse their citizens.

With the end of the Cold War and the birth of a new era in global politics, have prospects for human rights become any brighter? On the surface, the answer appears to be a cautious yes. With more democratic states presumably committed to human rights and with more government and nongovernment agencies attending to human rights, future prospects should be good.

On the other hand, we should remain guarded in our conclusions for several reasons. First, governments remain primarily responsible for addressing the human-rights issue, and many, like China, continue to resist pressure that would limit their domestic freedom of action. Second, despite expansion in global human-rights NGOs, their influence is still mostly limited to moral suasion, and they have little enforcement capability. Third, even with new democracies in Europe, Latin America, and Asia, sustaining protection for human rights remains a tough problem for regimes confronting immense economic and political difficulties. Finally, the end of the Cold War released powerful national and ethnic feelings that lead to human-rights violations.

Key Terms

Amnesty International (AI)
authoritarian regime
cultural relativism
death squads
economic sanctions
ethnic cleansing
Fourth World Conference on
    Women
Gender Empowerment Measure
    (GEM)

gender gap
genocide
guest workers
High Commissioner for Human
    Rights
human rights
International Bill of Human
    Rights
International Covenant on Civil
    and Political Rights

International Covenant on
    Economic, Social, and Cultural
    Rights
natural law
negative rights
political asylum
positive rights
totalitarian regime
U.N. Commission on Human
    Rights

U.N. Conference on Population
and Development

Universal Declaration of Human
Rights

End Notes

[1]Barbara Crossette, "Amnesty Finds 'Widespread Pattern' of U.S. Rights Violations," October 5, 1998, p. A11.

[2]Barbara Crossette, "Waiting for Justice in Cambodia," *New York Times,* February 25, 1996, sec. 4, p. 5. This atrocity is recorded in the book and film *The Killing Fields.*

[3]Richard D. Lyons, "U.N. Investigators Accuse Hutu of Genocide in Rwanda Killings," *New York Times,* December 3, 1994, p. 4; Barbara Crossette, "Former Rwandan Officers Focus of Atrocity Inquiries," *New York Times,* March 28, 1996, p. A4.

[4]Cited in Donatella Lorch, "Children's Drawings Tell Horror of Rwanda in Colors of Crayons," *New York Times,* September 16, 1994, p. A1.

[5]Howard W. French, "Rights Group Accuses Nigeria of a Civil War," *New York Times,* March 28, 1995, p. A5. In November 1995, Nigeria's military government hanged nine critics who had denounced the treatment of the Ogoni, including Ken Saro-Wiwa, a prominent author and environmentalist. Howard W. French, "Nigeria Executes Critics of Regime: Nations Protest," *New York Times,* November 11, 1995, pp. 1, 5; "Nigeria's Foaming," *The Economist,* November 18-24, 1995, pp. 15-16. The West was slow to take action against Nigeria's military government because of its thirst for Nigerian oil. Paul Lewis, "U.S. Seeking Tougher Sanctions to Press Nigeria for Democracy," *New York Times,* March 12, 1996, pp. A1, A6; John Darnton, "Shell Makes a Big Oil Discovery Off Nigeria," *New York Times,* March 12, 1996, p. A6.

[6]Michael Specter, "Killing of 100 in Chechnya Stirs Outrage," *New York Times,* May 8, 1995, pp. A1, A4.

[7]Charles Jacobs and Mohamed Athie, "Bought and Sold," *New York Times,* July 13, 1994, p. All; "When Death Squads Meet Street Children," *The Economist,* July 31-August 5, 1993, p. 39; Diana Jean Schemo, "Rio Ex-Officer Is Convicted In Massacre of Children," *New York Times,* May 1, 1996, p. A5.

[8]"Vigilantes in Colombia Kill Hundreds of 'Disposables,'" *New York Times,* October 31, 1994, p. A7.

[9]Orville Schell, "China's 'Places of No Return'," *Wahington Post National Weekly Edition,* January 15-21, 1996, p. 24; Nicholas D. Kristof, "Asian Childhoods Sacrificed to Prosperity's Lusts," *New York Times,* April 14, 1996, sec. 1, pp. 1, 6; G. Pascal Zackary, "Estimate of Child-Labor Levels Triples," *Wall Street Journal,* November 12, 1996 p. A2.

[10]Rick Bragg, "Orphans of Haiti Disappear, Targets of Murderous Thugs," *New York Times,* September 9, 1994, pp. A1, A4.

[11]Calvin Sims, "Argentine Tells of Dumping 'Dirty War' Captives into Sea," *New York Times,* March 13, 1995, pp. Al, A5; Calvin Sims, "National Nightmare Returns to Argentine Consciousness," *New York Times,* April 5, 1995, pp. A1, A8.

[12]"Blood and Earth," *The Economist,* September 23-29, 1995, pp. 16-18.

[13]Stephen Engelberg and Tim Weiner, "Srebrenica: The Days of Slaughter," *New York Times,* October 29, 1995, sec. 1, pp. 1, 6, 8.

[14]Cited in ibid, p. 7. See also "Harvesting Evidence in Bosnia's Killing Fields," *New York Times,* April 7, 1996, sec. 4, pp. 1, 3.

[15]Jane Perlez, "In Kosovo Death Chronicles, Serb Tactic Revealed," *New York Times,* September 27, 1998, sec. l, p.10; Jane Perlez, "Another Kosovo Village, Burned Down by Serbs," *New York Times,* September 28,1998, p. A3; Jane Perlez, "New Massacre by Serb Forces in Kosovo Villages," *New York Times,* September 30, 1998, pp. A1, A6.

[16]Chris Hedges, "Wanted Serb Not Only Lives Free, but Prospers," *New York Times,* April 6, 1997, sec. 1, p. 4. A civil suit was brought against Karadzic in New York by two Bosnian refugees. "Thugs Brought to Book," *The Economist,* March 22-28, 1997, pp. 31-32.

[17]Marlise Simons, "War Crimes Panel in First Verdict," *New York Times,* November 30, 1996, pp. 1,4; Marlise Simons, "A War-Crimes Trial, but of Muslims, Not Serbs," *New York Times,* April 3, 1997, p. A3; Chris Hedges, "Zagreb Extradites Croat to War Crimes Trial," *New York Times,* April 29, 1997, p. A7; "U.N. Panel Convicts Bosnian Serb of War Crimes," *New York Times,* May 8, 1997, pp. A1, A13; Steven Lee Myers, "Hague Tribunal Makes First Arrest, Holding a Serb for the Massacre of 261 Croats," *New York Times,* June 28, 1997, p. 5; Steven Erlanger, "Bosnian Serb General Is Arrested by Allied Force in Genocide Case," *New York Times,* December 3, 1998, pp. A1, A18.

[18]Kelly Kate Pease and David P. Forsythe, "Human Rights, Humanitarian Intervention, and World Politics," *Human Rights Quarterly* 15 (May 1993), pp. 290-314.

[19]See Burns Weston, "Human Rights," *Human Rights Quarterly* 6 (August 1984), pp. 257-283. For a review of evolving human rights, emphasizing cultural relativism, see David P. Forsythe, *The Internationalization of Human Rights* (Lexington, MA: DC Heath, 1991), pp. 1-26.

[20]Technically, this was less a new emphasis than a reaffirmation of the individualism of classical Athens. The Athenian conception was less than complete: Women and slaves were denied the rights given free male citizens.

[21]Weston, "Human Rights," p. 259.

[22]For an argument that the Carter and Reagan administrations differed little on human rights, see David Carleton and Michael Stohl, "The Foreign Policy of Human Rights: Rhetoric and Reality from Jimmy Carter to Ronald Reagan," *Human Rights Quarterly* 7 (May 1985), pp. 205-229.

[23]"See, for example, Clifford Krauss, "U.S., Aware of Killings, Worked with Salvador's Rightists, Papers Suggest," *New York Times,* November 9, 1993, p. A4.

[24]David P. Forsythe, "Human Rights After the Cold War," *Netherlands Quarterly of Human Rights* 11: 4 (1993), p. 398.

[25]Jack Donnelly, "Human Rights and Foreign Policy," *World Politics* 34:4 (July 1982), p. 575. See also Jack Donnelly, *International Human Rights* (Boulder, CO: Westview Press, 1993).

[26]Jack Donnelly, "Human Rights and Human Dignity: An Analytic Critique of Non-Western Conceptions of Human Rights," *American Political Science Review* 76:2 (June 1982), p. 304.

[27]Ibid., p. 305.

[28]The examples and passages are from ibid., pp. 306-309.

[29]Conrad Schirokauer, *A Brief History of Chinese Civilization* (New York: Harcourt Brace Jovanovich, 1991), p. 31.

[30]Forsythe, *Internationalization of Human Rights,* p. 9. Also Donnelly, *International Human Rights,* pp. 34-38.

[31]Daniel Williams and Clay Chandler, "Things Aren't So Pacific in Our Far East Relations," *Washington Post National Weekly Edition,* May 9-15, 1994, p. 19.

[32]Cited in "Walk in Fear," *The Economist,* July 23-29, 1994, p. 39.

[33]Cited in Paul Lewis, "U.N. Assembly Agrees on Creating a Human Rights Commissioner," *New York Times,* December 14, 1993, p. A7.

[34]Cited in Elaine Sciolino, "At Vienna Talks, U.S. Insists Rights Must Be Universal," *New York Times,* June 15, 1993, p. A1.

[35]Writers and journalists are among the first targets of authoritarian rule.

[36]For a discussion of economic rights as they relate to development, see Rhoda Howard, "Human Rights, Development and Foreign Policy," in David P. Forsythe, ed., *Human Rights and Development* (New York: St. Martin's Press, 1989). China criticized the United States for failing to provide positive rights. Seth Faison, "China Turns the Tables, Faulting U.S. on Rights," *New York Times,* March 5, 1997, p. A7.

[37]See Lawrence J. LeBlanc, *The United States and the Genocide Convention* (Durham, NC: Duke University Press, 1991).

[38]*Everyone's United Nations,* 10th ed. (New York: U.N. Department of Public Information, 1986), pp. 462-466.

[39]*Amnesty International Report 1994* (New York: Amnesty International, 1994), app. 6, pp. 341-349.

[40]Neil J. Mitchell and James M. McCormick, "Economic and Political Explanations of Human Rights Violations," *World Politics* 40:4 (July 1988), table 1, p. 487.

[41]Neil J. Mitchell and James M. McCormick, "Global Human Rights and the Reagan Administration," paper presented at the International Studies Association, Vancouver, Canada, March 1991. For some examples, see Nicholas D. Kristof, "Torture in North Korea Labor Camps," *New York Times,* July 14, 1996, sec. 1, p. 4; "U.N. Panel Rules Israel Uses Torture," *New York Times,* May 10, 1997, p. 6.

[42]Steve Chan, *International Relations in Perspective* (New York: Macmillan, 1984), p. 372.

[43]Barbara Crossette, "Human Rights Group Is Denied Accreditation for U.N. Event," *New York Times,* June 29, 1995, p. A4.

[44]*Country Reports on Human Rights Practices for 1984,* Report Submitted to the Committee on Foreign Relations and Committee on Foreign Affairs, U.S. House of Representatives, by the Department of State (Washington, DC: Government Printing Office, 1985), p. 2. See Steven Erlanger, "U.S. Rights Report Faults China, Nigeria and Cuba," *New York Times,* January 30, 1997, p. A6.

[45]*World Development Report 1995* (New York: Oxford University Press, 1994), p. 163; *World Development Report 1998* (New York: Oxford University Press, 1998), p. 191.

[46]*Human Development Report 1998* (New York: Oxford University Press, 1998), p. 159.

[47]Ibid., pp. 128-129.

[48]Barbara Crossette, "The Second Sex in the Third World," *New York Times,* September 10, 1995, sec. 4, p. 3.

[49]Nicholas D. Kristof, "Do Korean Men Still Beat Their Wives? Definitely," *New York Times,* December 5, 1996, p. A4; Nicholas D. Kristof, "As Asian Economies Shrink, Women Are Squeezed Out," *New York Times,* June 11, 1998, pp. A1, A12.

[50]Steven Greenhouse, "State Dept. Finds Widespread Abuse of World's Women," *New York Times,* February 3, 1994, pp. A1, A6.

[51]Deborah Sontag, "Women Asking U.S. Asylum Expand Definition of Abuse," *New York Times,* September 27, 1993, pp. A1, C8; Ashley Dunn, "U.S. Eases Rules on Women Seeking Political Asylum," *New York Times,* May 27, 1995, pp. 1, 7.

[52]J. Ann Tickner, *Gender in International Relations* (New York: Columbia University Press, 1992), p. 15.

[53]Ibid., p. 4. See V. Spike Peterson and Anne Sisson Runyan, *Global Gender Issues* (Boulder, CO: Westview Press, 1993).

[54]Christine Sylvester, *Feminist Theory and International Relations in a Postmodern Era* (New York: Cambridge University Press, 1994), pp. 4-5.

[55]Tickner, *Gender in International Relations,* pp. 19, 22-23.

[56]Sylvester, *Feminist Theory and International Relations,* p. 31.

[57]For a taste of the growing literature in feminist approaches to international relations, see Jean Bethke Elshtain, *Women*

and War (New York: Basic Books, 1987); Cynthia Enloe, *Bananas, Beaches, and Bases: Making Feminist Sense of International Relations* (London: Pandora, 1989); Sylvester, *Feminist Theory and International Relations.*

[58]The U.N. Children's Fund is responsible for monitoring the 1989 Convention on the Rights of the Child. See Barbara Crossette, "Unicef to Avoid Buying Goods Made by Children," *New York Times,* May 25, 1994, p. A7.

[59]*Everyone's United Nations,* p. 307.

[60]*Amnesty International Report 1994,* p. 32.

[61]*Human Development Report 1995,* pp. 78-79, 80.

[62]Cited in Barbara Crossette, "U.N. Documents Inequities for Women as World Forum Nears," *New York Times,* August 18, 1995, p. A3.

[63]Patrick E. Tyler, "China's Country Schools Are Failing," *New York Times,* December 31, 1995, sec. 1, p. 5.

[64]Joseph Kahn and Miriam Jordan, "Women's Banks Stage Global Expansion," *Wall Street Journal,* August 30, 1995, p. A8; Paul Lewis, "Small Loans May Be Key to Helping Third World," *New York Times,* January 26, 1997, p. 5; "The Other Government in Bangladesh," *The Economist,* July 25-31, 1998, p. 42.

[65]Barbara Crossette, "Afghanistan Islamic Pressure on U.N. over Hiring Women," *New York Times,* November 8, 1995, p. A4.

[66]Anjali Acharya, "Women Slowly Accepted as Politicians," in Lester R. Brown et al., *Vital Signs 1995* (New York: Norton, 1995), p. 134.

[67]Sheryl WuDunn, "Japanese Women Fight Servility," *New York Times,* July 9, 1995, sec. 1, p. 6. According to the Population Council, the worldwide erosion of traditional families is related to the improved status of women. Tamar Lewin, "The Decay of Families Is Global, Study Says," *New York Times,* May 30, 1995.

[68]See, for example, "India's Rich Little Poor Girls," *The Economist,* March 11-17, 1995, p. 40. Sheryl WuDunn, "Korean Women Still Feel Demands to Bear a Son," *New York Times,* January 14, 1997, p. A3.

[69]Barbara Crossette, "In Cairo, Pleas to Stop Maiming Girls," *New York Times,* September 11, 1994, sec. 1, p. 6; Seth Faison, "Women as Chattel: In China, Slavery Rises," *New York Times,* September 6, 1995, pp. A1, A4.

[70]Cited in Patrick E. Tyler, "Hillary Clinton in Beijing as Women's Conference Opens," *New York Times,* September 5, 1995, p. A3.

[71]Neil MacFarquhar, "Mutilation of Egyptian Girls: Despite Ban, It Goes On," *New York Times,* August 8, 1996, p. A3; Celia W. Dugger, "African Ritual Pain: Genital Cutting," *New York Times,* October 5, 1996, pp. 1, 4. The practice even goes on among immigrants in the United States, where it is illegal, and African women have been granted political asylum in the United States because they oppose the practice. Celia W. Dugger, "Women's Plea for Asylum Puts Tribal Ritual on Trial," *New York Times,* April 15, 1996, pp. A1, A12; Celia W. Dugger, "U.S.

Grants Asylum to Women Fleeing Mutilation Rite," *New York Times,* June 14, 1996, pp. A1, A13; Celia W. Dugger, "New Law Bans Genital Cutting in United States," *New York Times,* October 12, 1996, pp. 1, 6.

[72]In amniocentesis, a sample of amniotic fluid is taken from a pregnant woman's uterus to discover possible genetic defects. Information about the fetus's gender is a by-product of the test. See Nicholas D. Kristof, "Peasants of China Discover New Way to Weed Out Girls," *New York Times,* July 21, 1993, p. A1.

[73]"Ultrasound effects," *The Economist,* August 5-11, 1995, p. 34.

[74]Cited in John F. Burns, "India Fights Abortion of Female Fetuses," *New York Times,* August 27, 1994, p. 5.

[75]India and China have banned the use of ultrasound for gender selection. Burns, "India Fights Abortion of Female Fetuses"; "China to Ban Sex-Screening of Fetuses," *New York Times,* November 15, 1994, p. A7.

[76]"The Lost Girls," *The Economist,* September 18-24, 1993, p. 38. Also, "More Than Ever, Chinese Abandon Baby Girls," *New York Times,* April 22, 1999, p. A10.

[77]Philip Shenon, "China's Mania for Baby Boys Creates Surplus of Bachelors," *New York Times,* August 16, 1994, pp. A1, A4.

[78]Youssef M. Ibrahim, "Algeria Militant Vow to Kill Women Linked to Government," *New York Times,* May 4, 1995, p. A3; Youssef M. Ibrahim, "Algerians Hope for Better Life and War's End," *New York Times,* June 6, 1995, pp. A1, A6.

[79]Barbara Crossette, "Afghans Draw U.N. Warning Over Sex Bias," *New York Times,* October 8, 1996, pp. A1, A7; John F. Burns, "Afghan Says Restrictions Will Not Be Eased," *New York Times,* October 9, 1996, p. A8; Barabara Crossette, "U.N.'s Impatience Grows over Afghan Restrictions on Aid Workers," *New York Times,* July 15, 1998, p. A4.

[80]Later the government realized that this rate would produce intolerable burdens on society. By changing course and advocating birth control, Iran managed to reduce the rate to 2.7 percent; even at this rate, Iran's population will have grown from 37 million in 1979 when the Shah was overthrown to over 100 million early in the next century. Caryle Murphy, "Iran's Second Revolution: Population Control," *Washington Post National Weekly Edition,* May 18-24, 1992, p. 15; Neil MacFarquhar, "With Iran Population Boom, Vasectomy Receives Blessing," *New York Times,* September 8, 1996, sec. 1, pp. 1, 6.

[81]John F. Burns, "A Writer Hides. Her Country Winces," *New York Times,* July 31, 1994, sec. 4, p. 3; John F. Burns, "A Feminist Writer's Defiance Fuels Militants in Bangladesh," *New York Times,* July 13, 1994, p. A3.

[82]Cited in William E. Schmidt, "Bangladesh Writer Vows to Fight from Exile," *New York Times,* August 19, 1994, p. A7. Claiming she was misunderstood, Ms. Nasrin returned to Bangladesh, where she was tried and found innocent. Fundamentalism is causing a backlash against women in Bangladesh. See "Backlash," *The Economist,* October 22-28, 1994.

[83]Andrew Pollack, "Japan to Offer Reparations for Wartime Brothel Abuse," *New York Times,* August 31, 1994, pp. A1, A5; Nicholas D. Kristof, "Japanese Try to Rescue Fund For War's 'Comfort Women'," *New York Times,* May 13, 1996, p. A11.

[84]Paul Lewis, "Rape Was Weapon of Serbs, U.N. Says," *New York Times,* October 22, 1993, pp. A1, A4; Marlise Simons, "Bosnian Rapes Go Untried by the U.N.," *New York Times,* December 7, 1994, p. A8; Carlotta Gall, "Refugees Crossing Kosovo Border Tell of Rapes and Killings," *New York Times,* April 20, 1999, p. A7. The precedent of considering rape a war crime was set at the Hague trial of alleged war criminals in Bosnia. Marlise Simons, "Far from Former Yugoslavia, First War Crimes Trial Opens," *New York Times,* May 8, 1996, p. A6.

[85]Cited in Donatella Lorch, "Wave of Rape Adds New Horror to Rwanda's Trail of Brutality," *New York Times,* May 15, 1995, p. A4.

[86]Barbara Crossette, "An Old Scourge of War Becomes Its Latest Crime," *New York Times,* June 14, 1998, sec. 4, pp. 1, 6.

[87]Rochelle Sharpe, "A Nervous China Awaits Women of the World: Huge Gathering Stars Feminists, Heads of State," *Wall Street Journal,* August 28, 1995, pp. B1, B6. Fearing that members of these NGOs would try to make their voices heard on sensitive topics, the Chinese government relegated the forum to a town far from the U.N. site in Beijing.

[88]Cited in Patrick E. Tyler, "Forum on Women Agrees on Goals," *New York Times,* September 15, 1995, p. A3.

[89]"Key Points from Women's Conference," *New York Times,* September 15, 1995, p. A3.

[90]In 1993, for example, under pressure from the Catholic Church, Poland reversed its decades-old policy of easy access to abortion. See Jane Perlez, "A Painful Case Tests Poland's Abortion Ban," *New York Times,* April 2, 1995, sec. 1, p. 3.

[91]Cited in Patrick E. Tyler, "At Women's Forum, Peru's Leader Defies Church," *New York Times,* September 13, 1995, p. A3. Speaking of Peru's family-planning program, the country's Roman Catholic Primate said: "My feeling is one of deep sadness because at this moment, when Peru needs God's protection to emerge from many problems, the country accepts a law that goes against the law of God." Cited in ibid.

[92]Jane Perlez, "Romania's Communist Legacy: 'Abortion Culture'," *New York Times,* November 21, 1996, p. A3; Michael Specter, "Climb in Russia's Death Rate Sets Off Population Implosion," *New York Times,* March 6, 1994, p. A1. This has begun to change because of the growing availability of contraceptives in Russia, and abortions fell from 4.6 million in 1988 to 2.5 million in 1997. Celestine Bohlen, "Russian Women Turning to Abortion Less Often," *New York Times,* March 29, 1999, p. A3.

[93]Douglas Lavin, "Hoechst Will Stop Making Abortion Pill," *Wall Street Journal,* April 9, 1997, pp. A3, A4.

[94]Cited in Katherine Q. Seelye, "Family Planning and Foreign Policy Are Linked, Albright Tells House Panel," *New York Times,* February 12, 1997, p. A12.

[95]Steven A. Holmes, "U.S. Assistance to International Birth-Control Programs Faces Further Cuts," *New York Times,* September 12, 1996, p. A6. See also Katherine Q. Seelye, "Clinton Pushes for More Birth Control Money," *New York Times,* February 1, 1997, p. 7.

[96]Alan Thomas, et al., *Third World Atlas,* 2nd ed. (Washington, DC: Taylor & Francis, 1994), p. 60.

[97]*Human Development Report 1998,* pp. 156-157.

[98]James Brooke, "With Church Preaching in Vain, Brazilians Embrace Birth Control," *New York Times,* September 2, 1994, pp. A1, A3.

[99]Donatella Lorch, "Unsafe Abortions Become a Big Problem in Kenya," *New York Times,* June 4, 1995, sec. 1, p. 3.

[100]"Losing Babies, and Statistics," *The Economist,* July 1-7, 1995, p. 28.

[101]Barbara Crossette, "Women's Advocates Flocking to Cairo, Eager for Gains," *New York Times,* September 2, 1994, p. A3.

[102]Cited in Alan Cowell, "Conference on Population Has Hidden Issue: Money," *New York Times,* September 12, 1994, p. A8.

[103]Cited in Barbara Crossette, "Population Meeting Opens with Challenge to the Right," *New York Times,* September 6, 1994, pp. A1, A6.

[104]Chris Hedges, "Key Panel at Cairo Talks Agrees on Population Plan," *New York Times,* September 13, 1994, p. A5.

[105]Cited in Barbara Crossette, "Population Debate: The Premises Are Changed," *New York Times,* September 14, 1994, p. A3.

[106]Cited in Alan Cowell, "Vatican Attacks Population Stand Supported by U.S.," *New York Times,* August 9, 1994, p. A4.

[107]Cited in Alan Cowell, "Vatican Fights Plan to Bolster Role of Women," *New York Times,* June 15, 1994, p. A6.

[108]"Sections of Draft U.N. Document," *New York Times,* September 1, 1994, p. A9. In the end, the language on abortion was diluted. Alan Cowell, "Despite Abortion Issue, Population Pact Nears," *New York Times,* September 9, 1994, p. A6.

[109]John H. Cushman, Jr., "Gore Wants U.N. to Leave Abortion Up to Each Nation," *New York Times,* August 26, 1994, p. A2; Alan Cowell, "Vatican Says Gore Is Misrepresenting Population Talks," *New York Times,* September 1, 1994, pp. A1, A9; "Rome and Latins," *The Economist,* August 14-20, 1993, p. 39.

[110]Cited in Alan Cowell, "Is This Abortion? Vatican vs. U.S.?" *New York Times,* August 11, 1994, p. A4.

[111]Alan Cowell, "Vatican Rejects Compromise on Abortion at U.N. Meeting," *New York Times,* September 7, 1994, p. A1.

[112]"Muslim Militant Preachers in Egypt Condemn U.N. Population Conference," *New York Times,* August 23, 1994, p. A4.

[113]Michael Georgy, "Egypt's Islamic Group Issues a Warning," *New York Times,* August 28, 1994, sec. 1, p. 4; Chris Hedges, "5 on U.N. Aid Mission Killed; Egyptian Militants Suspected," *New York Times,* September 18, 1994, sec. 1, p. 8.

[114]Cited in Seth Faison, "Women's Meeting Agrees on Right to Say No to Sex," *New York Times,* September 11, 1995, pp. A1, A8.

[115]John Tagliabue, "Vatican Attacks U.S.-Backed Draft for U.N. Women's Conference in China," *New York Times,* August 26, 1995, p. 5.

[116]James Brooke, "Slavery on Rise in Brazil, as Debt Chains Workers," *New York Times,* May 23, 1993, sec. 1, p. 3.

[117]Cited in Samuel Huntington, *Political Order in Changing Societies* (New Haven: Yale University Press, 1968), p. 41.

[118]Conway W. Henderson, "Conditions Affecting the Use of Political Repression," *Journal of Conflict Resolution* 35: 1 (March 1991), pp. 124, 125.

[119]Huntington, *Political Order in Changing Societies,* p. 52. Huntington's argument is directed more at the general question of political instability than at human rights, but its implications are applicable.

[120]See Mitchell and McCormick, "Economic and Political Explanations of Human Rights Violations"; Henderson, "Conditions Affecting the Use of Political Repression"; and Kathleen Pritchard, "Human Rights and Development: Theory and Data," in Forsythe, ed., *Human Rights and Development,* pp. 329-345. Pritchard examines political, civil, and socioeconomic rights and finds that economic factors are positively associated with greater respect for all three.

[121]Rhoda Howard and Jack Donnelly, "Human Dignity, Human Rights, and Political Regimes," *American Political Science Review* 80:3 (September 1986), pp. 801-818.

[122]One problem in analyzing democracy to explain respect for human rights is that it may be a tautological or circular argument. The same factor that is used to explain human-rights violations (the absence of democracy) is used to define democracy (respect for human rights).

[123]Jeanne Kirkpatrick, "Dictatorships and Double Standards," *Commentary* 88 (November 1979), pp. 34-45.

[124]Henderson, "Conditions Affecting the Use of Political Repression."

[125]Mitchell and McCormick, "Economic and Political Explanations of Human Rights Violations," pp. 494-495.

[126]Ted Robert Gurr, "The Political Origins of State Violence and Terror: A Theoretical Analysis," in Michael Stohl and George A. Lopez, eds., *Government Violence and Repression* (Westport, CT: Greenwood Press, 1986), p. 58.

[127]Ted Robert Gurr, *Minorities at Risk* (Washington, DC: United States Institute of Peace Press, 1993), p. 10. Gurr identifies 233 minorites.

[128]Bosnian Muslims.

[129]Daniel Patrick Moynihan, *Pandaemonium: Ethnicity in International Politics* (New York: Oxford University Press, 1993), pp. 143-145.

[130]Steven Greenhouse, "Nigerian Author Urges Boycott Against Rulers," *New York Times,* December 7, 1994, p. A9; Howard W. French, "Nigerian Nobel Winner Faces Treason Charges," *New York Times,* March 13, 1997, p. A7.

[131]Anthony DePalma, "U.S. Wife's Resolute Quest Shakes Guatemala," *New York Times,* November 6, 1994, sec. 1, p. 3; Tim Weiner, "In Guatemala's Dark Heart, C.I.A. Tied to Death and Aid," *New York Times,* April 2, 1995, sec. 1, pp. 1, 3.

[132]Peter Benenson, "The Forgotten Prisoners," *The Observer Weekend Review* (London), May 28, 1961, p. 21.

[133]*Amnesty International Report 1994,* app. 2, p. 332.

[134]Amnesty International is suffering growing pains as it debates whether to take on new issues. Raymond Bonner, "Trying to Document Rights Abuses," *New York Times,* July 26, 1995, p. A4.

[135]*Amnesty International Report 1994,* app. 8, p. 352. The categories are not mutually exclusive.

[136]See, for example, Steven Lee Myers, "Report Says Business Interests Overshadow Right," *New York Times,* December 5, 1996, p. A8.

[137]Paul Lewis, "Rights Groups Pressing U.N. and U.S.," *New York Times,* February 1, 1997, sec. 1, p. 4.

[138]Thomas P. Fenton and Mary J. Heffron, *Human Rights: A Directory of Resources* (Maryknoll, NY: Orbis Books, 1989), pp. 6, 9, and 10.

[139]Stephen Kinzer, "German Aid for Victims of Torture," *New York Times,* December 14, 1995, p. A4.

[140]Cited in Steven A. Holmes, "Tidings of Abuse Fall on Deaf Ears," *New York Times,* February 5, 1995, sec. 4, p. 4.

[141]Barbara Crossette, "U.N. Report Tells of 'Heinous' Abuses in Iraq," *New York Times,* February 28, 1995, p. A6; Barbara Crossette, "Rising Variety of Groups Vie for Attention at U.N. Rights Forum," *New York Times,* March 31, 1996, sec. 1, p. 7.

[142]*Everyone's United Nations,* pp. 304-307.

[143]Ibid., pp. 305-306.

[144]*Amnesty International Report 1994,* pp. 33-34. One human-rights triumph at the United Nations was the decline in abuses in Guatemala. See Julia Preston, "In a U.N. Success Story, Guatemalan Abuses Fall," *New York Times,* March 27, 1996, p. A5.

[145]Barbara Crossette, "Irish President Picked for U.N. Human Rights Post," *New York Times,* June 13, 1997, p. A6.

[146]Jack Donnelly, "Human Rights in the New World Order," *World Policy Journal* 9 (Spring 1992), p. 252.

[147]A. Glenn Mower, *Regional Human Rights: A Comparative Study of the West European and Inter-American Systems* (Westport, CT: Greenwood Press, 1991), pp. 89-108, 131-145.

[148]Donnelly, "Human Rights in the New World Order," p. 252; Sarah Lyall, "Rights Panel for Europe Stirs Anger in Britain," *New York Times,* May 6, 1996, p. A4.

[149]See, for example, Calvin Sims, "Growls from Military Echo in Peru and Chile," *New York Times,* June 20, 1995, p. A5; "The Past Raises Its Ugly Head," *The Economist,* July 1-7, 1995, p. 31.

[150]Tim Golden, "Argentina Settles Lawsuit by a Victim of Torture," *New York Times,* September 14, 1996, p. 6. See also Marlise Simons, "Unforgiving Spain Pursues Argentine Killers," October 24, 1996, p. A3.

[151]When General Pinochet visited London for medical reasons in 1998, he was placed under house arrest while British courts tried to determine whether he could be extradited to Spain for crimes committed while he was Chile's head of state. "Bringing the General to Justice," *The Economist,* November 28-December 4, 1998, pp. 23-25.

[152]"Human Rights, Political Wrongs," *The Economist,* May 18-24, 1996, p. 43; "The Challenge of the Past," *The Economist,* October 24-30, 1998.

[153]Larry Rohter, "Where Countless Died in '81, Horror Lives On in Salvador," *New York Times,* February 12, 1996, pp. A1, A4.

[154]James C. McKinley, Jr., "Ex-Mayor on Trial, a Rwanda Town Remembers," *New York Times,* September 27, 1996, p. A3; James C. McKinley, Jr., "Ethiopia Tries Former Rulers In 70's Deaths," *New York Times,* April 23, 1996, pp. A1, A6.

[155]"South Africa Looks for Truth and Hopes for Reconciliation," *The Economist,* April 20-26, 1996, pp. 33-34. The Commission completed its work by late 1998.

[156]See James M. McCormick and Neil J. Mitchell, "Human Rights and Foreign Assistance: An Update," *Social Science Quarterly* 70 (December 1989), pp. 969-979. Sometimes U.S. aid decisions are effective. The Carter administration's cutting off aid to the Somoza regime in Nicaragua reduced that regime's ability to survive.

[157]Howard W. French, "Study Says Haiti Sanctions Kill Up to 1,000 Children a Month," *New York Times,* November 9, 1993, pp. A1, A6. Saddam Hussein claims U.N. sanctions on Iraq have led to the death of many Iraqi children.

[158]Cited in Thomas L. Friedman, "Trade vs. Human Rights," *New York Times,* February 6, 1994, p. A1.

[159]The dilemma exists elsewhere as well, for example, in Burma. David E. Sanger, "Unocol Signs Burmese Gas Deal; U.S. May Ban Such Accords," *New York Times,* February 1, 1997, p. 4; Steven L. Myers, "Trade vs. Rights: A U.S. Debate with a Burmese Focus," *New York Times,* March 5, 1997, p. A7.

[160]"China's Secret Economy," *The Economist,* October 2-8, 1993, p. 33; Robert S. Greenberger, "Lawmakers Support Report Charging China Still Exports Prison-Made Goods," *Wall Street Journal,* May 19, 1994, p. A16.

[161]"Of Car and Body Parts," *The Economist,* September 3-9, 1994, p. 40. See also "China's Arbitrary State," *The Economist,* March 23-29, 1996, pp. 31-32.

[162]Elaine Sciolino, "State Dept. Says China Has Failed to Improve Human Rights Record," *New York Times,* January 12, 1994, pp. A1, A4.

[163]Robert S. Greenberger, "U.S. Loath to Penalize China on Trade Despite Insufficient Human-Rights Steps," *Wall Street Journal,* January 13, 1994, pp. A2, A4.

[164]Patrick E. Tyler, "Awe-Struck U.S. Executives Survey the China Market," *New York Times,* September 2, 1994, pp. C1, C2.

[165]Patrick E. Tyler, "U.S. and Chinese Seen Near a Deal on Human Rights," *New York Times,* February 24, 1997, pp. A1, A6. It was clear that neither European nor less-developed states would support sanctions against China. Barbara Crossette, "China Outflanks U.S. to Avoid Scrutiny of Rights Record," *New York Times,* April 24, 1996, p. A7; "China Defeats a U.N. Resolution Criticizing Its Rights Record," *New York Times,* April 16, 1997, p. A6.

[166]"Clinton's Call: Avoid Isolating China on Trade and Rights," *New York Times,* May 27, 1994, p. A4; China has made clear that it can retaliate if the United States links trade to human rights by concluding a number of deals with European firms instead of Boeing. Craig R. Whitney, "China Signs Deal with Airbus Jets for $1.5 Billion," *New York Times,* April 11, 1996, pp. A1, A6.

[167]Louis Uchitelle, "Back to Business on China Trade," *New York Times,* May 27, 1994, p. C1. The Business Council, a group of CEOs from 100 of the largest U.S. companies, has urged the United States not to impose sanctions on China that would endanger their ability to compete in that country. Richard W. Stevenson, "Tread Lightly with China, Business Leaders Urge U.S.," *New York Times,* May 11, 1996, p. 4.

[168]Cited in Paul Blustein and R. Jeffrey Smith, "Where China's Concerned, Money Talks," *Washington Post National Weekly Edition,* February 19-25, 1996, p. 20.

[169]Cited in Tim Weiner, "U.S. Envoy Allowed to Visit Crusader Jailed in China," *New York Times,* July 11, 1995, p. A4. The phrase "commercial diplomacy" was introduced by U.S. officials to explain Clinton's new China policy. Patrick E. Tyler, "U.S. Delegation Pursues Business in China," *New York Times,* August 30, 1994, p. A6.

[170]Elaine Sciolino, "State Dept. Study Says China Lags on Human Rights," *New York Times,* February 1, 1995, pp. A1, A6; Robert S. Greenberger, "U.S. Report Cites Continued Abuses of Rights in China," *Wall Street Journal,* March 6, 1996, p. A9.

[171]Cited in Patrick E. Tyler, "Beijing Arrests Rights Defender," *New York Times,* July 9, 1995, sec. 1, p. 1.

[172]During a state visit to China, President Clinton appeared on Chinese television and before student groups, describing China's social and economic transformation as "remarkable" and urging China to permit greater personal freedom. Kathy Chen and Jackie Calmer, "New China-U.S. Pacts Total $1.1 Billion," *Wall Street Journal,* June 30, 1998, pp. A12, A15.

[173]"Chinese Agree to Sign a Key Rights Treaty," *New York Times,* April 19, 1997, p. A4; Erik Eckholm, "After Signing Rights Accord, Beijing Begins a Crackdown," *New York Times,* October 28, 1998, pp. A1, A3.

[174]For an excellent treatment of this issue, see Myron Weiner, *The Global Migration Crisis* (New York: HarperCollins, 1995).

[175]"Economic refugees" are not entitled to political asylum.

[176]John Darnton, "U.N. Faces Refugee Crisis That Never Ends,"

New York Times, August 8, 1994, pp. A1, A5.

[177]Philip Shenon, "Thousands of Boat People Face Return to Vietnam," *New York Times,* April 3, 1995, p. A4; Philip Shenon, "Riots by Vietnamese Imperil Plan to Send Them Home," *New York Times,* June 9, 1995, p. A3; Steven Erlanger, "U.S. Negotiates to Send Vietnamese Home From Asian Camps," *New York Times,* March 4, l996, p. A4; Edward A. Gargan, "200 Vietnamese Refugees Flee Detention Camp in Hong Kong," *New York Times,* May 11, 1996, p. 4.

[178]Raymond Bonner, "New Road to the West for Illegal Migrants," *New York Times,* June 14, 1995, p. A8; "Keep Them Out," *The Economist,* April 27–May 3, 1996, p. 53. See also "Go West and North—If You Can," *The Economist,* January 13-19, 1996, p. 52.

[179]For German resistance to the growing tide of refugees, see Alan Cowell, "For Migrants to Germany, Welcome Turns Sour," *New York Times,* March 24, 1996, sec. 1, p. 3; Alan Cowell, "Bavaria, Acting Alone, Begins Ousting Bosnian Refugees," *New York Times,* October 10, 1996, p. A8; Alan Cowell, "2 Bosnian Refugees Expelled by City of Berlin," *New York Times,* March 14, 1997, p. A5.

[180]"Exporting Misery," *The Economist,* April 17-23, 1999, pp. 23-24, 27.

[181]"So Does America Want Them or Not?" *The Economist,* July 19-25, 1997, pp. 25-27.

[182]During 1993, one boatload of Chinese ran aground off New York City, costing a number of lives, and several other boatloads were interned in Mexico. Anthony DePalma, "Refugees Are Sent Back to China Hours After They Dock in Mexico," *New York Times,* July 18, 1993, sec. 1, p. 1. See also Roberto Suro, "China's Growing Trade in Smuggled Humans," *Washington Post National Weekly Edition,* June 13-19, 1994, p. 33; Sam Dillon, "Thwarting a Trend, U.S. Breaks Up Ring That Smuggled Asian Aliens Through Mexico," *New York Times,* May 30, 1996, p. A6.

[183]Deborah Sontag, "Reneging on Refuge: The Haitian Precedent," *New York Times,* June 27, 1993, sec. 4, p. 1. About 2,000 Hutu refugees were killed when Rwandan authorities tried to make them go home. Donatella Lorch, "As Many as 2,000 Are Reported Dead in Rwanda," *New York Times,* April 24, 1995, pp. A1, A4.

[184]*Wall Street Journal,* April 23, 1993, p. A1.

[185]Barbara Crossette, "This Is No Place Like Home," *New York Times,* March 5, 1995, sec. 4, p. 3.

[186]"Exporting Misery," p. 27.

[187]"Nations on the Move," *The Economist,* August 19-25, 1995, p. 42.

[188]"The Flight of a Nation," *The Economist,* July 23-29, 1994, p. 37.

[189]James C. McKinley, Jr., "Rwandan Exiles Find They Can't Go Home," *New York Times,* February 7, 1996, p. A6. The U.N. High Commissioner for Refugees refused to oppose the forceful return of refugees to Rwanda. Raymond Bonner, "U.N. Shift on Rwandans A Bow to 'New Realities'," *New York Times,* December 21, 1996, p. 4.

[190]James C. McKinley, Jr., "Rebels Forced 80,000 Hutu to Flee to Jungle, U.N. Says," *New York Times,* April 26, 1997, p. 5; James C. McKinley, Jr., "Machetes, Axes and Rebel Guns: Refugees Tell of Attacks in Zaire," *New York Times,* March 30, 1997, pp. A1, A8; Donald G. McNeil, Jr., "Reports Point to Mass Killings of Refugees in Congo," *New York Times,* May 27, 1997, pp. A1, A6.

[191]Crossette, "This Is No Place Like Home."

[192]"The New Trade in Humans," *The Economist,* August 5-11, 1995, pp. 45-46.

[193]Alan Cowell, "Vietnamese Wait for End of German Dream," *New York Times,* October 13, 1995, pp. A1, A5.

[194]Germany, an exception to this, took steps to extend citizenship to immigrants following the 1998 election, which brought the Social Democrats to power, "2 German Parties Reach Deal to Relax Law on Citizenship," *New York Times,* October 15, 1998, p. A11.

[195]"Shut the Door," *The Economist,* August 3-9, 1996, pp. 45, 53. Subsequently, police opposition forced the government to back down.

[196]Youssef M. Ibrahim, "A Peace That Still Can't Recover from the War," *New York Times,* May 6, 1992, p. A4.

Chapter 16

From International to Postinternational Politics

The central theme of this book has been that limiting our vision of the world around us to the interactions of sovereign states and thinking solely in terms of their national interest and relative power is inadequate. "The absolutes of the Westphalian system—territorially fixed states where everything of value lies within some state's borders; a single secular authority governing each territory and representing it outside its borders; and no authority above states—are all dissolving."[1] With the end of the Cold War, old identities and issues resurfaced and new ones emerged; some are linked, and some isolated; some are subnational, others transnational, and still others global; some generate conflict and others cooperation.

Fragmegration

What is perhaps most puzzling about global politics today is the appearance of larger networks of interdependence such as global financial markets and regional trading blocs that are visible alongside the dissolution of political life into tiny islands of self-identification based on ethnicity, tribalism, and nationality. These processes—on the one hand, *globalization* and, on the other, *localization*—pull the state apart in two directions and erode its autonomy and capacity. According to political scientist James N. Rosenau, globalization includes whatever "has the potential of an unlimited spread that can readily transgress national jurisdictions"[2] and facilitates the movement of people, goods, information, and ideas across national frontiers. Localization, by contrast, impedes such movement and leads to new boundaries that separate ever smaller and smaller groups from one another. *Fragmegration* is a term coined by Rosenau for the fragmentation and integration of authority produced by the two processes.[3]

Complexity is heightened because the two trends affect each other. Fragmentation makes it difficult for people to meet economic needs or see to their security, whereas the emergence of "mega-collectivities" like the World Trade Organization increases the psychological and physical distance between decision-makers and those on whom decisions have an impact. This, in turn, produces yearnings for smaller collectivities that are closer to citizens. Thus religious fundamentalism, whether Islamic or other, involves a rejection of the globalized, modern, and secular culture ("Coca-Cola, jeans, and rap and rock") that is undermining traditional society and culture. Speaking of economic issues, one observer declares, "the big corporations and institutions shaping the world economy seem so remote that many people turn to local ethnic groups and obscure languages for their identity, furthering the world's political fragmentation." He speculates that there is emerging a new kind of state "something akin to a corporate holding company—with the central government little more than a shell and power residing in the regions."[4]

As we noted in the first chapter, the basis of the state system is control of territory, but the time has come to escape this "territorial trap."[5] Whether describing a speculative attack on Asian currencies, a terrorist attack on U.S. embassies and U.S. retaliation using cruise missiles aboard ships and planes, the start of cyberwar against a country's computer systems, or advertising on CNN, we are dealing with phenomena that are not greatly affected by physical distance or that depend on territory.

Then too, the past, present, and future are more tightly bound than ever before. From day to day, our ancestors could expect that the society into which they were born—its technology, ethics, and modes of behavior—would remain more or less intact in their lifetimes. As they grew older, they would notice gradual changes (about which they might complain because "things were better in the old days"), but the contours of the life they had known in their youth would still be recognizable. We cannot do as they did. Accelerated change has telescoped the future; each of us will experience not one but several generation gaps as the years pass, and there will be growing cleavages between old and young.[6]

The Globalized Side of Things

In a globalized world, persons, things, and ideas speed across frontiers; populations are more and more specialized, literate, and urban; and "security" and "insecurity" have drastically altered their meaning. The wall between domestic and global politics is falling, and security means more than safety from military attack. Defenses have to be built against financial meltdown, overpopulation, resource depletion, ethnic upheavals, and terrorist outrages.

Globalization reduces state autonomy in a variety of ways. In such a world the fates of individuals everywhere are linked, and "*the conditions* of happiness for the mass of the people . . . involve a high degree of collective action. . . ."[7] Just as most individuals cannot by their own striving meet their needs for food, shelter, health, and old age, as their agrarian ancestors did in "simpler" times, individual states cannot shield their citizens from all threats, nor can they cope with emerging issues. But if states seek parochial gains at each other's expense, they only impede those equipped to confront grand challenges. As individuals diversify and specialize their occupation and role in society, the world mimics them, and we have increasingly specialized international and nongovernmental actors and institutions. Such actors and institutions may work with states in dealing with global challenges or in coping with the forces that threaten to destroy states, even while quietly usurping their sovereign prerogatives.

At the same time, citizens' expectations expand, and the demands they place on states and on the global system more generally multiply.[8] No longer do people meekly accept the status and destiny that come with birth. Expanding claims tax national and international institutions, pressuring them to alter the ways in which they operate. Overall, we are probably less secure in our collective existence than in earlier epochs, when our survival depended on our own exertion and imagination.

In a globalized world, people depend for prosperity and health on decisions arrived at far beyond their state frontiers. They are also enmeshed in global networks either as employees or as purchasers of goods and services. The trade in narcotics illustrates the impact of transnational networks on our lives and how futile it is for states to go it alone. Latin American peasants grow coca (for cocaine) because of global demand for their product, and they will not cease doing so until they find a profitable substitute. If the supply of cocaine reaching the United States from one or another of these countries is reduced, street prices soar in U.S. cities; crime increases as users seek more money, and more people find it profitable to get into the narcotics industry. Thus America's war on drugs is doomed to fail until global solutions are found and enforced.[9]

The tidy world of states pursuing narrow national interests was never an accurate depiction of reality, and it is a dangerous fiction if people act as if it were real. More than national interest and power politics will be needed to fix global problems like AIDS. And the new issues are themselves linked. The transnational drug issue is connected, for example, when the heroin plague sweeping China brings with it an AIDS epidemic.[10] Like ecological catastrophe, disease does not respect national frontiers. By late 1998, some 30 million people worldwide had been infected by the HIV virus that causes AIDS, and the disease had reached pandemic proportions in 34 African countries. "In looking at global epidemics," declared Lester Brown, president of World Watch Institute, "one has to go back to the 16th century and the introduction of smallpox in the Aztec population of what is now Mexico to find anything on that scale, and before that, to the bubonic plague in Europe in the 14th century, to see that kind of heavy toll."[11]

Those who focus on globalization are especially impressed by the economic dimension of global politics. Regional economic organizations are expanding, and new ones are forming. Leading this trend is the European Union, developing and expanding despite setbacks. Virtually all of Europe's trade barriers have disappeared, and efforts continue to move toward economic and political union, with a common currency, a central bank, and common foreign and defense policies. Elsewhere, similar efforts are under way. The North American Free Trade Agreement and Mercosur reflect growing economic integration in the Western Hemisphere. In Asia, the Association of Southeast Asian Nations and the Asia-Pacific Economic Cooperation promise greater economic integration along the Pacific Rim. Finally, a new GATT agreement was signed and set up by the World Trade Organization, with authority to arbitrate trade disputes among member states.

Some predict that the expanding web of economic interdependence and cooperation, driven by the *"four forces"* of communication, corporations, capital, and consumers, combined with growing demands for democracy in countries as diverse as

Mexico, Indonesia, and Nigeria, means that nationalism and resort to force are obsolete. As people look to the global economic system for prosperity, the importance of states declines and the incentive for separatism grows. Are globalists on to something, or are they a new generation of idealists?

Sadly, globalization does not mean an end to violence or poverty in world politics. In the economic sphere, it allows corporations to exploit workers, including women and children in poor countries. Democracy promotes instability in some countries,[12] while others stubbornly maintain authoritarian institutions. Moreover, doubts about the benefits of a globalized economic system are growing, especially since the Asian economic crisis, and countries like Malaysia are reimposing impediments to the free movement of capital.[13]

The species as a whole is threatened by environmental catastrophes, and environmental pressures will incite *"green wars."* Bitter disputes between Canada and Spain, the United States and Canada, Japan and South Korea, and Japan and Australia over declining fishing stocks auger intensifying conflict caused by growing resource scarcities that can only be averted by collective action. "Wars of the next century," declares the World Bank "will be over water,"[14] and growing friction over water between countries such as India and Bangladesh, Turkey and Syria, and Jordan and Israel buttress this prediction.[15] At the very moment when critical issues demand global attention, coordination, and planning, actors continue to satisfy parochial constituencies and assess their well-being *relative to others*. If everyone fares poorly, what does it matter that some fare less poorly than others?

As these examples illustrate, globalization promises both opportunities and perils, but so does localization.

The Localized Side of Things

The impact of localization is most visible in the collapse or splitting of states confronted by ethnic, religious, and national conflicts and in the violence that has engulfed many of these states. Even as the threat of nuclear war between the superpowers recedes, violent ethnic and national conflicts are erupting that President Clinton described as the "disease" of "militant nationalism" which eats "away at states" and leaves "their people addicted to the political pain-killers of violence and demagoguery."[16] Because of intense nationalism and larger segments of societies taking part in politics, political elites throughout the world find themselves forced to make painful foreign-policy choices as they respond to local pressures. And, if such nationalism continues to rage unchecked, in the words of former U.S. Secretary of State Warren Christopher, "We'll have 5,000 countries rather than the hundred plus we now have."[17]

And many of these countries would be incapable of protecting or caring for their citizens. Already, according to two observers, "From Haiti in the Western Hemisphere to the remnants of Yugoslavia in Europe, from Somalia, Sudan, and Liberia in Africa, to Cambodia in Southeast Asia, a disturbing new phenomenon is emerging: the *failed nation-state*, utterly incapable of sustaining itself as a member of the international community."[18] An apocalyptic picture of failed states is painted by Robert D. Kaplan:

Disease, overpopulation, unprovoked crime, scarcity of resources, refugee migrations, the increasing erosion of nation-states and international borders, and the empowerment of private armies, security firms, and international drug cartels are now most tellingly demonstrated through a West African prism.[19]

As a result, many of the less-developed countries are experiencing "the withering away of central governments, the rise of tribal and regional domains, the unchecked spread of disease, and the growing pervasiveness of war." Political maps are lies because "the classificatory grid of nation-states is going to be replaced by a jagged-glass pattern of city-states, shanty-states, nebulous and anarchic regionalisms."[20]

Political scientist Samuel Huntington has interpreted the upsurge in ethnic and national conflict as auguring an end to the (European) epoch of interstate war and the onset of "the clash of civilizations" pitting "nations and groups of different civilizations" against one another.[21] His most compelling evidence has been ethnic violence in the former Yugoslavia and Soviet Union, much of which seems to reflect a clash between Islam, on the one hand, and Western and Slavic-Orthodox civilizations, on the other. "In Eurasia," Huntington declares, "the great historic fault lines between civilizations are once more aflame. This is particularly true along the boundaries of the crescent-shaped Islamic bloc of nations from the bulge of Africa to central Asia. . . . Islam has bloody borders."[22]

Yugoslavia fragmented into a number of warring countries. The former Yugoslav army, mostly Serbs, sought to stop Slovenes, Croatians, and Bosnian Muslims from declaring independence[23] and thereafter set out to create a "Greater Serbia." Fierce fighting broke out in Croatia between Croats and the Serb minority in the Krajina region of that republic, and the war continued until ethnic Serbian areas had been wrested from Croatian control. Savage ethnic violence also erupted among the Croats, Muslim Slavs, and Serbs in Bosnia. Neither the European Union nor the United Nations could end the communal violence, and Bosnian Serbs resorted to a policy of ethnic cleansing (murdering or forcibly removing non-Serbians from their homes and land), and violence continued until the Dayton peace accord of 1995 was imposed on the belligerents by NATO. The conflict was "the first surrogate war of the post–Cold War era, with Russia quietly helping the Serbs, the Arab world increasingly helping the Muslims and the United States supporting the Muslim-Croat federation however it can."[24] Thereafter, Serbia itself was threatened by fragmentation, as Albanian Muslims in Kosovo sought independence.

Bloody clashes also broke out among ethnic and tribal groups in the former Soviet republics and the newly noncommunist Eastern European countries following the dissolution of the Soviet Union. In the Caucasus, Chechnya sought to secede from Russia, and the Russian effort to crush Chechen separatism was seen by Muslims as another attack on their brethren by non-Muslims. Armenia and Azerbaijan went to war over the tiny area of Nagorno-Karabakh, which is inhabited mainly by Armenians but is within Azerbaijan. Azerbaijan itself was the scene of coups and counter-coups, and a secessionist movement in the isolated region of Nakhichevan. Next door, Georgia struggled to put down a secessionist movement in Abkhazia with the help of Russian troops. In Tajikistan, civil war pitted former communists, aided by Russia, against Muslim fundamentalists who crossed back and forth from Afghanistan. The Crimea, mostly inhabited by ethnic Russians, sought independence from Ukraine. Slavic separatists challenged the government of Moldova, a new country largely inhabited by ethnic Romanians. Civil War gripped Georgia, and tension was high between ethnic Russians and majority populations in the Baltic states of Latvia, Lithuania, and Estonia.

Ethnic conflict also threatens to balkanize the Middle East, India, and Africa. Afghanistan is divided into three ethnic regions—one in the north with Uzbeks and Tajiks, a second in the south around Kabul with Pathans, and a third in the west controlled by Afghans with close ties to Iran.[25] Palestinian and Jewish extremists seek to undermine the fragile Israeli-PLO accord; Indian Hindus and Muslims are at each other's throats; Arabs and Turks fight Kurds, and Kurds fight each other; and Shi'ite and Sunni Muslims continue to battle in the Middle East and South Asia. Tribal and clan conflicts are endemic in Africa, where Hutu massacres of Tutsi and the subsequent flight of Hutus from Rwanda to neighboring countries are omens of a grim future not only for Rwanda but for the rest of central Africa.

The "New World Order"—Or Will We Miss the Cold War?

On May 6, 1992, in a speech at Westminster College in Missouri, where Winston Churchill had delivered his iron curtain address four decades earlier, Mikhail Gorbachev declared: "We live today in a watershed era. One epoch has ended and a second is commencing. No one yet knows how concrete it will be—no one."[26] His uncertainty reflects a more general doubt about the future. As in 1945, old expectations, rules, and norms have disappeared, and we do not yet know what the new ones will look like. The end of the Cold War has produced a world of diffuse threats. Enemies and friends are no longer clear. As President Bill Clinton aptly observed, in the absence of a single overriding issue like the Cold War, "there seems to be no mainframe explanation for the PC world in which we're living."[27] Will global politics be more or less peaceful than the years of Cold War?

Optimists see the Cold War's passing as an opportunity to break out of power politics and confront mushrooming global problems. "For the first time since 1815," declares a former diplomat, "no great powers are threatening each other."[28] Communism and the Soviet Union have failed; and unprecedented East-West arms-control agreements have been concluded, shrinking the specter of nuclear war and giving all a chance to reduce tensions worldwide.

Optimists point out that with no more Cold War to worry about, many regional disputes have slackened around the world. In Europe, there have been steps toward ending the durable conflict in Northern Ireland. In the Middle East following Saddam Hussein's defeat, unprecedented peace talks among Arabs, Israelis, and Palestinians led to agreements between Israel and the PLO, a peace treaty between Jordan and Israel, and even an Israeli-Syrian dialogue. In Africa, conflicts in Ethiopia and Mozambique ended; Namibia achieved independence; and the racial-discrimination system in South Africa crumbled. In Asia, the Soviets ended their occupation of Afghanistan in 1988. In 1989 Vietnamese troops left Cambodia, and shortly thereafter a U.N.-brokered agreement ended that country's civil war.

ACTORS SPEAK

Although many observe that state autonomy is eroding, there is disagreement about whether the anarchic system of states is giving way to a more integrated and globalized world or to a world divided into still smaller and more localized political entities. Those like the author of the first passage can point to revolutions in knowledge, communication, and economic exchange that are binding together peoples in distant places, especially in the First World. Those like the second author can point to the explosion of violent nationalism and ethnicity, especially in the less-developed countries, and the collapse of states that are wracked by civil strife, environmental catastrophe, and economic deterioration.

Consider the global system of transnationalized microeconomic links. Perhaps the best way to describe it . . . is that these links have created a nonterritorial "region" in the world economy—a decentered yet integrated space-of-flows, operating in real time, which exists alongside the space-of-places that we call national economies. . . . In the nonterritorial global region, however, the conventional distinctions between internal and external . . . are exceedingly problematic, and any given state is but one constraint in corporate global strategic calculations. This is the world in which IBM is Japan's largest computer exporter, and Sony is the largest exporter of television sets from the United States. . . . (John Gerard Ruggie, "Territoriality and Beyond: Problematizing Modernity in International Relations," *International organization* 47:1 [Winter 1993]," p. 172)

Imagine cartography in three dimensions, as if in a hologram. In this hologram would be the overlapping sediments of various group identities such as those of language and economic class, atop the two-dimensional color distinctions among city-states and the remaining nations, themselves confused in places by shadows overhead, indicating the power of drug cartels, mafias, and private security agencies that guard the wealthy in failing states and hunt down terrorists. . . . To this protean cartographic hologram one must add other factors, such as growing populations, refugee migrations, soil and water scarcities and . . . vectors of disease. This future map will be an ever-mutating representation of cartographic chaos. . . . (Robert D. Kaplan, *The Ends of the Earth: A Journey to the Frontiers of Anarchy* [New York: Random House, 1996], pp. 336–337)

And in Central America, which captured so much American attention in the 1980s, negotiated settlements ended conflicts in El Salvador and Nicaragua.

Pessimists, by contrast, argue that the end of the Cold War portends the rebirth of traditional power politics and conflicting nationalisms. One Cassandra[29] calls the Cold War something that "we will soon miss."[30] The U.S.-Soviet nuclear stalemate and the bipolar distribution of power had made a "long peace" and provided order and stability for forty years. With that conflict over, pessimists believe, world politics will return to a multipolar, conflict-prone world, reminiscent of the twentieth century before 1945. It will then be a more dangerous place because weapons of mass destruction will be available to more and more actors.

During the Cold War, argue the pessimists, the superpowers provided guarantees to allies that were sufficient to prevent their seeking their own weapons of mass destruction and in some cases twisted arms to prevent countries from acquiring such weapons. That era is over, and the world is becoming more dangerous because of the availability of weapons of mass destruction to terrorists and "rogue states" such as North Korea and Iraq. Nowhere is the salience of this problem clearer than in the recurrent crises in 1997 and 1998 involving Iraq's refusal to allow U.N. inspectors to do their job to verify that Saddam Hussein has actually destroyed his weapons of mass destruction and the means to produce them.

Pessimists also foresee economic conflict, not cooperation. Efforts toward economic integration and toward creating larger economic groupings, they believe, will inflame rather than extinguish economic rivalry. First, regional blocs may become regional adversaries. Second, though members may initially cooperate, eventually they will become rivals because some will be seen as gaining more than others from free trade. Economic transactions may breed conflict rather than harmony. Only time will tell whether John Mearsheimer's provocative observation is correct: "Interdependence.... is as likely to lead to conflict as cooperation, because states will struggle to escape the vulnerability that interdependence creates."[31]

Conclusion: Change and Its Consequences

Under conditions of dramatic and rapid change, we can no longer use the same tools as Machiavelli or Thucydides for interpreting events. But change itself is not "good" or "bad." We have no grounds for assuming that global politics will yield better outcomes in the future than in the past. Naive optimism is as out of place as paralytic pessimism. Changes in global politics brought on by factors like technological innovation do not necessarily improve our lot. If every problem has a solution, every solution creates new problems. Thus, as medical science overcomes old diseases, it accelerates population growth, intensifying pressure on the environment and creating greater financial burdens for an ever-smaller number of young people. Nuclear power reduces energy costs even as it produces serious environmental risks. Policies that are intended to improve our lives always have *unintended consequences*—results that were neither predicted nor desired—and trends that seem to promise a brighter future may throw up unanticipated dilemmas. Hence, growing economic productivity improves standards of living but generates unemployment and more waste, exhausting finite natural resources.

The great mathematician-philosopher Alfred North Whitehead wrote, "It is the business of the future to be dangerous."[32] As change accelerates, the world becomes in many ways a more dangerous place. The faster the pace of change, the more difficult it is for leaders to grasp its implications and grapple with it effectively. In the best of times, policy-makers have short time horizons. Busy coping with the crises of the instant, they are thinking about what they can accomplish in the few years they will be in office. They guess, follow their political instincts, and use shallow analogies to past events when they lack information or when (more often) they are overwhelmed by it. Short-run and long-run imperatives have always collided, but that collision's cost is growing ominously. It is sobering to recall the *"law of gambler's ruin,"* as defined by political scientist Karl Deutsch:

> If one looks over the major decisions about initiating war … the probability of a major decision being realistic may well have been less than one-half, on the average. That is to say, if in the last half-century statesmen made major decisions on matters of war and peace, the chances were better than even that the particular decision was wrong.[33]

Still, to this point we have muddled through. New institutions and actors, whether international organizations or transnational humanitarian and environmental groups, provide unprecedented institutional resources to confront burgeoning global challenges. Innovative technology, while creating new problems, also provides us with capabilities—including accumulation of and access to knowledge undreamed of in earlier epochs. We cannot assume that technology will allow us to cope successfully with postinternational issues, but it does provide us with a reason to believe we can do so.

Key Terms

failed states	globalization	localization
four forces	green wars	unintended consequences
fragmegration	law of gambler's ruin	

End Notes

[1] Jessica Matthews, "Power Shift," *Foreign Affairs* 76:1 (January/February 1997), p. 50.

[2] James N. Rosenau, *Along the Domestic-Foreign Frontier: Exploring Governance in a Turbulent World* (Cambridge, UK: Cambridge University Press, 1997), p. 81.

[3] Ibid., p. 38.

[4] Bob Davis, "Growth of Trade Binds Nations, but It Also Can Spur Separatism," *Wall Street Journal,* June 20, 1994, p. A1.

[5] John Agnew and Stuart Corbridge, *Mastering Space* (New York: Routledge, 1995), p. 80.

[6] The French historian Fernand Braudel distinguishes three types of change. The fastest encompasses daily events in individual lives; the second, which is slower, entails economic and political change that is the result of aggregating daily events; and the slowest, which was almost imperceptible in past centuries, includes fundamental changes in the way people live. *On History,* trans. by Sarah Matthews (Chicago: University of Chicago Press, 1980), pp. 3 ff. These three types have begun to merge in the modern world.

[7] Daniel Bell, "The Study of the Future," *The Public Interest* 1 (Fall 1965), p. 120. Emphasis in original.

[8] Modern citizens enjoy many advantages that were unavailable to their ancestors, but their expectations have risen even faster. As a result, their *relative* satisfaction may decline even as their absolute well-being grows.

[9]Since criminals operate transnationally, U.S. law-enforcement agencies are increasingly forced to do the same. David Johnston, "Strength Is Seen in a U.S. Export: Law Enforcement," *New York Times,* April 17, 1995, pp. A1, A8.

[10]Patrick E. Tyler, "Heroin Influx Ignites a Growing AIDS Epidemic in China," *New York Times,* November 28, 1995, p. A3.

[11]Cited in Youssef M. Ibrahim, "AIDS Is Slashing Africa's Population, UN. Survey Finds," *New York Times,* October 28, 1998, p. A3.

[12]See, for example, Marcus W. Brauchli, "More Nations Embrace Democracy—and Find It Often Can Be Messy," *Wall Street Journal,* June 25, 1996, pp. A1, A6.

[13]David E. Sanger, "The Invisible Hand's New Strong Arm," *New York Times,* September 13, 1998, sec. 4, pp. 1, 3.

[14]Cited in "Flowing Uphill," *The Economist,* August 12-18, 1995, p. 36.

[15]Sweeter Waters," *The Economist,* November 16-22, 1996, p. 37; Stephen Kinzer, "Restoring the Fertile Crescent to Its Former Glory," *New York Times,* May 29, 1997, p. A4; "Jordan Asks for More," *The Economist,* May 17-23, 1997, p. 52.

[16]Cited in Maureen Dowd, "Clinton Warns of Violent Nationalism," *New York Times,* June 8, 1994, p. A4.

[17]Cited in David Binder with Barbara Crossette, "As Ethnic Wars Multiply, U.S. Strives for a Policy," *New York Times,* February 7, 1993, p. 1.

[18]Gerald B. Helman and Steven R. Ratner, "Saving Failed States," *Foreign Policy* 89 (Winter 1992-93), p. 3. See Paul Johnson, "Colonialism's Back—and Not a Moment Too Soon," *New York Times Magazine,* April 18, 1993, pp. 22, 43, 44, for a provocative analysis of why many states are unable to govern themselves.

[19]Robert D. Kaplan, "The Coming Anarchy," *The Atlantic Monthly,* February 1994, p. 46.

[20]Ibid., pp. 48 and 72.

[21]Samuel P. Huntington, "The Clash of Civilizations?" *Foreign Affairs* 72:3 (Summer 1993), p. 22. Huntington defines a civilization as "a cultural entity" (p. 23), eight of which he identifies— "Western, Confucian, Japanese, Islamic, Hindu, Slavic-Orthodox, Latin American and possibly African civilization" (p. 25).

[22]Ibid., pp. 34-35.

[23]Yugoslavia shrunk from six (Serbia, Montenegro, Slovenia, Croatia, Bosnia-Herzegovina, and Macedonia) to two republics (Serbia and Montenegro).

[24]Roger Cohen, "Out of the Mud, into the Morass," *New York Times,* April 16, 1995, sec. 4, p. 1.

[25]Edward A. Gargan, "Afghanistan, Always Riven, Is Breaking into Ethnic Parts," *New York Times,* January 17, 1993, pp. 1, 6.

[26]"Gorbachev's Talk: Building on the Past," *New York Times,* May 7, 1992, p. A6.

[27]Cited in Todd S. Purdum, "Clinton Cautions Against a Retreat into Isolationism," *New York Times,* October 7, 1995, p. 1.

[28]Charles William Maynes cited in Barbara Crossette, "Discord Over Renewing Pact on Spread of Nuclear Arms," *New York Times,* April 17, 1995, p. A4.

[29]A prophetess, whose prophecies, though true, were never believed.

[30]John J. Mearsheimer, "Why We Will Soon Miss the Cold War," *The Atlantic Monthly* 266 (August 1990), p. 35 ff. See his "Disorder Restored," in Graham Allison and Gregory F. Treverton, eds., *Rethinking America's Security* (New York: W.W. Norton and Company, 1992), pp. 213-237.

[31]Mearsheimer, "Why We Will Soon Miss the Cold War," p. 45.

[32]Alfred North Whitehead, *Science and the Modern World* (New York: Macmillan, 1929), p. 298.

[33]Karl W. Deutsch, "The Future of World Politics," *Political Quarterly* 13 (January-March 1966), p. 13.

Glossary

ABM Treaty: A 1972 U.S.-Soviet agreement to forego deploying antiballistic missiles except at two sites in each country. *(p. 347)*

Accuracy of nuclear weapons: The ability of nuclear weapons to hit targets. Greater accuracy reduces strategic stability. *(p. 339)*

Acid rain: Precipitation made acidic by sulfur dioxide and nitrogen oxides that are produced by industry, automobiles, and power plants. Acid rain and snow devastate forests and acidify lakes and streams, leaving them uninhabitable for fish. *(p. 468)*

Action-reaction model: A simplified view of foreign policy focused on states' actions toward each other and the reactions that are elicited. Sometimes called the *stimulus-response model.* *(p. 168)*

Actors in global politics: Individuals or groups who seek to enhance their value satisfaction by participating directly in global politics. *(p. 13)*

Affective approach: Analyzing leaders' perceptual distortions as caused by emotions such as insecurity and hostility. *(p. 170)*

Aggression: The initiation of actions that violate the rights and interests of other actors. *(p. 297)*

Alliances: Groupings of actors that pool their resources and coordinate their policies to increase joint security. *(p. 145)*

Amnesty International (AI): A nongovernmental organization that monitors and publicizes human-rights compliance worldwide. *(p. 504)*

Analogies from the past: The propensity of leaders reacting to crisis, but having no information, to draw comparisons between historical and present events. *(p. 272)*

Anarchy: In global politics, the absence of a central government. Widely considered a source and cause of conflict. *(pp. 61, 140)*

Anthropomorphizing: Ascribing human form or attributes to a thing not human. *(p. 13)*

Appropriate technology: Technology suitable for the society in which it is introduced. Often used to describe technology suitable for use in the less-developed countries. *(p. 389)*

Arms control: Any approach designed to regulate levels and types of arms in a manner that reduces adversaries' incentives to initiate war. *(p. 343)*

Arms race: Rivalry among actors trying to outdo each other in quantity or quality of their armaments. *(p. 302)*

Asia-Pacific Economic Cooperation (APEC): A group of fifteen countries that abut the Pacific Ocean that plan to form a free-trade area early in the coming century. See **Bogor Declaration.** *(p. 414)*

Authoritarian regime: A political system in which individual freedom is subordinate to the power of the state, concentrated in one person or small group that is not accountable to the people. *(p. 502)*

Autonomy: An actor's ability to formulate and pursue its own goals. *(p. 72)*

Baker Plan: An initiative by Secretary of State James Baker to overcome the LDC debt crisis by domestic economic reform and loans from private banks. *(p. 392)*

Balance of payments: A summary of a country's financial dealings with other countries, usually over a year, indicating whether more funds are leaving the country ("deficit") or entering ("surplus"). *(p. 369)*

531

Balance-of-power theory: The belief that peace or stability or both are most secure under conditions in which power is more or less equally distributed among five or more actors. Under such conditions, it is believed that no one actor or group of actors can dominate the others, because defensive alliances are formed and reformed. *(pp. 45, 49)*

Barbarian: A label that the ancient Greeks and Chinese applied to those who did not speak their language and whom they, therefore, considered uncivilized. *(p. 29)*

Bargaining reputation: The reputation actors have for standing behind or reneging on their commitments. *(p. 267)*

Beggar-thy-neighbor policies: Policies meant to alter a country's trade balance by devaluing its currency and raising barriers to imports from other countries. *(p. 369)*

Beliefs: Actors' convictions about the world around them and about what is right or wrong in that world. *(p. 154)*

Berlin blockade: The first of a series of Cold-War crises over Berlin that began in June 1948 and lasted until May 1949. The crisis involved a Soviet effort to strangle Berlin by blocking land traffic to the city. The Soviet effort was countered by a Western airlift of supplies to the city. *(p. 109)*

Berlin Wall: A wall built by East Germany in 1961 to divide East and West Berlin, thereby ending the flight of East Germans to the West. The wall was dismantled in 1989. *(p. 111)*

Billiard-ball model: A metaphor depicting global politics as a game in which billiard balls (unitary states) collide with each other in a continuous sequence of action and reaction. The model disregards factors within the actors. *(p. 166)*

Biological and Toxins Weapons Convention: A 1972 treaty requiring the destruction of all biological weapons and prohibiting their production. *(p. 356)*

Bipolarity: A political system divided into two centers of power. *(pp. 10, 63)*

Black-boxing a state: Analyzing a state's foreign policy as though its internal setting had no influence on behavior. *(p. 166)*

Blitzkrieg (lightning war): An offensive strategy devised by Nazi Germany employing close cooperation between armored units and bombers. *(p. 308)*

Bluffing: A tactic that seeks to mislead by bold action. *(p. 266)*

Bogor Declaration: A nonbinding "declaration of common resolve" by the members of Asia-Pacific Economic Cooperation to establish "free and open trade and investment" among themselves by the year 2020 (2010 for industrial members). *(p. 415)*

Bolt from the blue: A surprise attack. *(p. 333)*

Boundaries of a system: The demarcation between what is inside and what is outside the system. *(p. 137)*

Bounded rationality: A definition of rationality recognizing that human limitations constrain a decision-maker's ability to select the best of all alternatives. See **Comprehensive rationality.** *(p. 176)*

Brady Plan: A plan that U.S. Secretary of the Treasury Nicholas Brady put forward to resolve the debt crisis of the less-developed countries by renegotiating or reducing their overall debt burden. *(p. 392)*

Brain drain: The emigration of highly educated and skilled citizens from the less-developed countries to the First World. *(p. 389)*

Bretton Woods system: The postwar agreement reached at Bretton Woods, New Hampshire, which shaped international monetary arrangements until 1973. The agreement led to establishment of the International Monetary Fund (IMF) and the World Bank (IBRD). *(p. 369)*

Brinksmanship: A sequence of threats and counterthreats involving bluff that runs a serious risk of war. *(p. 336)*

Brown agenda: A set of environmental problems—impure water, toxic air, inadequate sanitation, and so on—associated with the less-developed countries. *(p. 455)*

Bureaucratic-politics model: An approach to the study of foreign policy that focuses on bargaining and compromises among governmental organizations and agencies pursuing their own interests. *(p. 173)*

Capabilities: Resources available to actors that can be used to influence other actors. *(pp. 68, 147)*

Capacity: An actor's ability to tap and use its citizens' resources. *(p. 72)*

Capitalism: An economic system based on the private ownership of property and the means of production and a free market that allows competition. *(p. 106)*

Cartel: A group of producers that sets out to limit competition among its members, often by restricting production to keep prices high. *(p. 253)*

Chameleon effect: The illusion that one actor is influencing another when the former is merely correctly predicting the behavior of the latter. *(p. 67)*

Chemical Weapons Convention: A 1993 treaty requiring the destruction of chemical weapons and prohibiting their production. *(p. 356)*

Chernobyl: The Ukrainian nuclear plant that was the site of a nuclear meltdown in 1986. *(p. 467)*

Chicken game: A game-theory relationship in which actors find themselves in a dangerous conflict spiral. *(p. 266)*

Chlorofluorocarbons (CFCs): A group of chemicals whose release causes ozone depletion. *(p. 469)*

City-state: An independent political entity consisting of a city and its outskirts that dominated international politics in ancient Greece and Renaissance Italy. Singapore is among the few contemporary examples. *(p. 34)*

Coercion: Negative incentives such as threats or punishment for generating influence. *(p. 69)*

Cognitive approach: Analyzing how leaders' perceptions are distorted by ambiguous information. *(p. 170)*

Cognitive consistency: The balance between feelings about and attitudes toward a phenomenon and the information that is received about it. If feelings and information seem to contradict each other, the result is *cognitive dissonance*. *(pp. 171, 298)*

Cold War: A period of intense conflict and competition short of open war between the United States and its allies and the Soviet Union and its allies that lasted from the mid-1940s until 1991. *(p. 97)*

Cold War consensus: The general fear and loathing of communism and acceptance of the national-security burden in the United States that accompanied the Cold War. *(p. 112)*

Collective good: A benefit such as clear air and water or military security from which individuals cannot be selectively excluded. Beneficiaries may wish the good but have no incentive to pay for it. *(p. 20)*

Collective security: A security system designed after World War I under which any actor's aggression would be met by all other actors' combined might. *(p. 225)*

Commitment: A pledge or guarantee by an actor to fight under certain conditions. *(p. 333)*

Commodity cartel: An organization consisting of major producers of some commodity or raw material that seeks higher prices for its product. *(p. 253)*

Common Agricultural Policy (CAP): A European Union policy to maintain common, artificially high prices for local agricultural products by purchasing surpluses and placing tariffs on agricultural imports. The policy stimulates overproduction and the exporting of food surpluses with help from export subsidies. *(p. 436)*

Communism: A political and economic system prescribing government ownership and management of the means of production and distribution and relying on central planning rather than markets to achieve economic goals. *(p. 6)*

Comparative advantage: The theory that every country can benefit from international trade if it concentrates on goods that it can produce most efficiently. *(p. 369)*

Compatibility of goals: The degree to which the aims of actors in a system do not conflict. *(p. 145)*

Compellance: Thomas C. Schelling's name for the threat or use of force to make an adversary cease doing something or undo something it has already done. See **Coercive diplomacy.** *(p. 358)*

Comprehensive rationality: Selection of the best policy from among all possible alternatives. See **Bounded rationality.** *(p. 176)*

Concern about the future: Capacity to weigh the future consequences of one's behavior, especially the costs of conflict. *(p. 270)*

Concert of Europe: A security system developed after the Napoleonic Wars with regular conferences among Europe's great powers. *(p. 52)*

Conditionality: Providing loans or aid subject to the recipient's adhering to certain conditions such as reducing government spending or raising interest rates. *(p. 370)*

Conference on Security and Cooperation in Europe (CSCE): A series of meetings initiated by the 1976 Helsinki Accords among NATO, former Soviet bloc, and neutral European countries to build confidence among participants about their national security. *(p. 348)*

Confidence-building measures: Actions and agreements aimed at improving communication and trust between potential adversaries and reducing the possibility of misunderstandings and misperceptions that could lead to war. *(p. 348)*

Containment: A strategy suggested by George Kennan to prevent Soviet expansionism by exerting counterpressure along Soviet borders. *(p. 108)*

Contract state: A state expending much money and manpower on defense. See **Garrison state.** *(p. 320)*

Convention on Biological Diversity: A treaty signed at the 1992 U.N. Conference on the Environment and Development to assemble a world inventory of plants and animals and make plans to protect endangered species. *(p. 472)*

Cooperation: Acting together for a common purpose. *(p. 262)*

Costs of power: The tangible (such as budget and manpower) and intangible (such as time) costs associated with exercising power. *(p. 70)*

Counterforce strategy: A deterrence plan targeting an enemy's military forces and weapons systems. *(p. 337)*

Counterproliferation: A policy aimed at preventing additional states from acquiring nuclear weapons. *(p. 354)*

Countervalue strategy: A deterrence scheme targeting an enemy's cities and industrial centers. *(p. 343)*

Credibility of deterrence: The degree to which others believe that an actor will carry out its commitments. *(p. 334)*

Crimes against humanity: One class of charges—ill treatment of civilians—brought against defendants at the Nuremberg trials. *(p. 279)*

Crimes against peace: A novel class of charges—planning aggressive war—brought against defendants at the Nuremburg trials. *(p. 279)*

Crisis: A situation threatening prized goals, imposing time constraints, and surprising decision-makers. A moment of danger, often at the second stage in an issue cycle, during which adversaries seek to determine the rules of the game. *(pp. 97, 170)*

Crisis of overproduction: A central aspect of Vladimir Lenin's theory of imperialism, stating that capitalist economies produce more than citizens can afford to consume and so have to seek overseas markets. *(p. 300)*

Crony capitalism: A modified form of state capitalism characterized by nepotism, political favoritism, and even bribery in determining the distribution of jobs, loans, and investments. *(p. 397)*

Cuban missile crisis: The most dangerous U.S.-Soviet confrontation (1962) of the Cold War that began when the U.S.S.R. secretly deployed nuclear-armed missiles in Cuba. A major step in making both sides realize the perils of nuclear war. *(pp. 109, 110)*

Cult of the offensive: European belief before World War I that war could be won only by rapidly mobilizing armies and at once launching offensive operations. *(p. 307)*

Cultural relativism: The claim that ethical beliefs

are different in different cultures so that there are few or no universal ethical principles. *(p. 482)*

Cultural Revolution: A campaign launched by Mao Zedong in China between 1966 and 1976 to remove his political opponents within the communist party and revitalize China's revolutionary spirit. *(p. 425)*

Currency convertibility: Interchangeability of one national currency into another or into gold. A country must have convertible currency to participate in international trade. *(p. 369)*

Cybernetic model: An approach to foreign policy that focuses on bureaucrats' attempt to control uncertainty by relying on simplified procedures, using limited information. *(p. 177)*

D'Amato law: A 1996 law sponsored by New York's Senator Alphonse D'Amato to impose sanctions on foreign companies that invest in the oil and gas industries of Libya or Iran. *(p. 436)*

Death instinct: Psychologist Sigmund Freud's claim that human beings have an innate impulse toward destruction. *(p. 297)*

Death squad: A group that assassinates its political opponents. *(p. 480)*

Debt-commodity swaps: A strategy for dealing with the international debt crisis under which commercial banks form companies to export the debtor's commodities, putting aside some of the profit for repaying debt. *(p. 392)*

Debt-equity swaps: A strategy for dealing with the international debt crisis under which debt owed to banks is traded for stock in the debtor's industries or loans are sold at a discount to transnational corporations. *(p. 392)*

Debt restructuring: Renegotiation between borrowers and lenders of a loan, usually to lengthen the repayment time or reduce interest rates. *(p. 392)*

Debt-service ratio: The ratio between the amount of interest and principal due on loans and export earnings. *(p. 391)*

Debts-for-nature swap: An imaginative strategy for reconciling environmental and economic objectives under which a government or environmental group pays off part of a debtor's obligation at reduced interest. In return, the debtor uses the funds it would have paid in interest for environmental ends. *(p. 463)*

Decision-makers: Government officials whose views are critical in formulating foreign policy. *(p. 169)*

Decision-making approach: An approach to foreign policy focusing on domestic factors, especially decision-makers and the setting and situations in which they find themselves. It is contrasted with the unitary-actor model, which exclusively considers the external setting of states to explain foreign policy. *(p. 169)*

Declinist debate: A debate pitting those who believe the United States is a declining world power against those who believe such a decline is not occurring. *(p. 408)*

Defense conversion: The process of transforming defense industries into industries that can be used for nonmilitary purposes. *(p. 322)*

Definition of the situation: A decision-maker's interpretation of a problem or an issue. *(p. 169)*

Deforestation: Massive loss of forests with environmental consequences such as reduced production of oxygen and extensive erosion of soil. *(p. 462)*

Demonstration effect: The propensity of geographically separated individuals and groups to copy each other's behavior. *(pp. 82, 205)*

Desertification: The spread of deserts as a result of soil erosion, overfarming, and desforestation. *(p. 462)*

Destructiveness: The extent of damage caused by nuclear weapons. *(p. 339)*

Détente: Relaxation of tensions between adversaries. *(p. 111)*

Deterrence: A strategy aimed at preventing an adversary from pursuing its aims by threatening to use military force in retaliation. *(p. 334)*

Disarmament: Agreements to reduce or eliminate weapons or categories of weapons. Such agreements arise from the assumption that possession of weapons is a cause of war. *(p. 343)*

Distribution of attitudes: The manner in which identities, expectations, beliefs, and goals are distributed among actors in a political system.

This distribution predicts what is likely to take place within the system. *(p. 154)*

Distribution of influence: The distribution among actors in a system of a capacity to change the behavior of others. *(p. 145)*

Distribution of resources: Distribution within a political system of factors that contribute to actors' capability. This distribution predicts what is possible within the system. *(p. 145)*

Domain of power: The persons or things over which an actor enjoys influence. *(p. 67)*

Donor fatigue: The growing unwillingness of actors to provide humanitarian relief because of the repeated demands for such aid. *(p. 396)*

Dual-track decision: The decision by NATO in 1979 to deploy intermediate-range nuclear missiles in Europe while trying to negotiate an INF arms-control agreement with the U.S.S.R. *(p. 274)*

Earth Summit: See **U.N. Conference on the Environment and Development (UNCED).** *(p. 462)*

Economic and Social Council: The organ that coordinates the economic and social affairs of the United Nations, including the U.N. specialized agencies. *(p. 234)*

Economic nationalism: Theories about international political economy stressing the need to reduce imports and increase exports using protectionist measures if necessary. Sometimes called *neomercantilism*. See **Mercantilism.** *(p. 382)*

Economic sanctions: Efforts to exert influence on other actors by limiting or serving economic relations. *(p. 507)*

Economic socialism: See **Socialism.** *(p. 6)*

Economic summits: Annual meetings of the leaders of the world's leading industrial states. *(p. 379)*

Embargo: Prohibiting trade with another country. *(p. 382)*

Emergent property: Characteristic of a group of actors that is the unforeseen consequence of interaction among them. *(p. 135)*

Emissions credits: Rights or permits issued to countries that allow them to pay one another to reduce carbon emissions, thereby avoiding the need to reduce their own emissions. *(p. 471)*

Empirical theory: Knowledge that is derived from experiment and experience. *(p. 32)*

End of history: A phrase popularized by Francis Fukuyama to express his belief that the end of the Cold War marked the triumph of democratic liberalism around the world. *(p. 97)*

End-of-the-world game: An interaction that takes place only once and does not permit reciprocity. *(p. 270)*

Escalation: An upward spiral in level of conflict or violence. *(p. 135)*

Ethnic actor or group: A group of people of the same race or nationality who share a distinctive culture. *(pp. 77, 208)*

Ethnic cleansing: A euphemism for the forced and brutal removal of members of one ethnic group from a city or region by members of another ethnic group. Applied to Serbians' and Croatians' campaign to remove each other and by both to clear areas of Bosnian Muslims during civil strife in the former Yugoslavia starting in 1992. *(p. 481)*

Eurocentric theory: Theory based only on Europe's experience. *(p. 30)*

European Atomic Energy Community (EURATOM): One of the original institutions of the European Community, EURATOM was to promote European cooperation in the development of peaceful nuclear energy. *(p. 429)*

European Coal and Steel Community (ECSC): An intergovernmental organization established in 1952 to ensure adequate supplies of coal and steel at a reasonable price. *(p. 429)*

European Community (EC): A regional intergovernmental organization established in 1967 consisting of the European Economic Community (EEC), the European Atomic Energy Community (EUROATOM), and the European Coal and Steel Community (ECSC). *(p. 429)*

European Economic Area (EEA): The single regional common market formed by merging the European Community and the European Free Trade Association in 1993. *(p. 435)*

European Economic Community (EEC): A

regional free market established in Western Europe in 1958. *(p. 429)*

European Monetary System (EMS): Endeavor by European Community members to stabilize the value of their currencies in relation to each other and the dollar. *(p. 430)*

European Union (EU): The new name given the European Community in 1993 following the Maastricht Treaty. *(pp. 249, 429)*

Exchange rate: The price of one currency compared with those of other currencies or gold. *(p. 369)*

Exchange-rate mechanism (ERM): An agreement among European Community members to link closely the value of their currencies. *(p. 430)*

Expectations: The outcomes that actors in global politics anticipate. *(p. 154)*

Expected-utility theory: An approach to war predicated on the belief that leaders are rational and seek to maximize gains. *(p. 299)*

Expertise: Skills or knowledge that provide influence. *(p. 70)*

Extended deterrence: The effort to deter an adversary from attacking one's allies. *(p. 336)*

External setting: Outside factors that influence foreign policy. *(p. 170)*

Failed state: States whose institutions of statehood, including central government, have melted away and whose inhabitants depend on outsiders for the essentials of survival. *(pp. 73, 528)*

Fast-track authority: A congressional grant of authority to the President of the United States allowing him to negotiate trade agreements with foreign governments that Congress may approve or disapprove only *in their entirety;* congressional amendments of specific passages in such agreements are not permitted. *(p. 438)*

Feedback: Information that an actor receives regarding the consequence(s) of its act(s). *(p. 135)*

Feudalism: A social and economic system based on holding of lands in fief or fee and on the resulting relations between superior (lord) and inferior (vassal). *(p. 43)*

First-strike capability: A nuclear power's ability to launch an attack and succesfully destroy an adversary's capability to retaliate. *(p. 335)*

First World: The wealthy industrialized countries, most of which are members of the OECD. *(p. 402)*

Fission: The splitting of the nucleus of an atom into nuclei of lighter atoms, accompanied by the release of nuclear energy. *(p. 332)*

Fixed monetary exchange rates: Currency exchange rates that prevail when actors agree to maintain their relative value at established levels. *(p. 374)*

Flexible response: A NATO military doctrine instituted in the 1960s under which response to a military provocation would be adjusted to the level of the provocation and would change as necessary in response to an enemy's willingness to cease or escalate. Under the doctrine NATO would not use nuclear weapons in responding to the first stages of an enemy's conventional-weapons attack. *(p. 334)*

Floating exchange rates: Currency exchange rates that prevail when actors allow the market to determine their relative value. *(p. 374)*

Foreign policy: The sum of an actor's goals and purposive actions in global politics. In studying foreign policy we seek to explain and predict those goals and actions. *(p. 164)*

Formal role: Patterns of behavior, preferences, and actions associated with all officials occupying similar official positions in a political system. *(p. 70)*

Four forces of economic interdependence: Communications, corporations, capital, and consumers. *(p. 522)*

Fourteen Points: The conditions outlined for the postwar world by President Woodrow Wilson in a 1918 speech. They included national self-determination, collective security, free trade, open diplomacy, and freedom of the seas. *(p. 225)*

Fourth World Conference on Women: A 1995 U.N.-sponsored conference in Beijing, China, to discuss and make plans to overcome the inferior status of women around the world. *(p. 498)*

Free-market capitalism: See **Capitalism** and **Free market.** *(p. 6)*

Frustration-aggression models: Theories that explain conflicts as caused by impediments in the path of human desires and inducing frustration that in turn causes aggression to eliminate those impediments. *(p. 297)*

Functionalism: A theory that conflict eventually can be eliminated if actors cooperate in dealing with relatively noncontroversial technical issues like health, communications, travel, or environmental protection. Functionalists believe that cooperative habits acquired in one area will spread to others and that functional international organizations will increasingly assume the responsibilities currently carried out by nation-states. See **Spillover** and **neo-functionalism.** *(p. 225)*

Fusion: Release of nuclear energy—radiation and high-speed neutrons—by fusing light atoms, especially hydrogen. Used in the hydrogen or thermonuclear bomb. *(p. 332)*

Games: Interactions among actors characterized by rules and strategies in which each actor's outcome depends partly on what other actors do. *(p. 263)*

Gangster capitalism: The free-wheeling capitalist system that characterizes Russia in which criminals and criminal activities play a major role. *(p. 121)*

Garrison state: A state in which the military exercises undue influence and seeks to maintain international tension to preserve its status and privileges. See **Contract state.** *(p. 320)*

Gender Empowerment Measure (GEM): An index based on per capita income, share of parliamentary seats, and share of professional, technical, and managerial jobs to measure the participation status of women. *(p. 490)*

Gender gap: The difference between the status of men and women in global politics. *(p. 490)*

General Agreement on Tariffs and Trade (GATT): A U.N.-affiliated organization established in 1947–1948 as a forum for promoting international trade. The GATT was replaced in December 1993 by the World Trade Organization. *(p. 369)*

General Assembly: The main U.N. deliberative body in which all U.N. member states are represented and each has an equal vote. *(p. 231)*

Genesis: The first stage of the issue cycle during which an issue is placed on the global agenda. *(p. 97)*

Genocide: Deliberate or systematic extermination of a national or racial group. *(p. 480)*

Geopolitics: Study of the relationship between politics and geography. *(p. 148)*

Glasnost: Policy of openness initiated by Soviet President Mikhail Gorbachev. *(p. 115)*

Global agenda: Issues that attract the attention of major actors and to which those actors are prepared to devote resources. *(p. 98)*

Global civic society: An arena formed by nonstate actors in which people engage in spontaneous, customary, and nonlegalistic forms of association. *(p. 196)*

Global norms: Behavior in global politics that significant actors consider appropriate. *(pp. 270, 275)*

Global warming: Warming of earth's climate caused by release of "greenhouse" gases trapping heat from the earth that would otherwise escape into outer space. Also known as the *greenhouse effect. (p. 451)*

Globalization: Those processes that knit people together around the world and link their fates. *(pp. 4, 396, 520)*

Goal: An outcome that actors in global politics seek. *(pp. 154, 158)*

Governance: Authoritative demands, goals, directives, and policies of any actor, whether a government or not. *(pp. 4, 196)*

Great Leap Forward: A campaign undertaken by China between 1958 and 1960 to mobilize China's economy and increase economic production through ideological guidance and indoctrination. *(p. 424)*

Great power: In the eighteenth century, the name for a European state that could not be conquered by the combined might of other European states. More recently applied to countries regarded as among the most powerful in the global system. *(p. 49)*

Green war: A war fought over scarce resources such as fresh water. *(p. 523)*

Guest workers: Laborers who migrate from poor countries where unemployment is high, such as Egypt and Turkey, to wealthier countries where unemployment is lower and wages are higher, such as Germany and Switzerland. *(p. 511)*

Hard shell of impermeability: In the eighteenth century, the protection afforded inhabitants by the impenetrable frontiers of states. *(p. 49)*

Head-to-head competition: An international economic system in which different countries and regions seek the same industries, thereby threatening the economic status and security of each other's workers and producers. *(p. 408)*

Hegemon: A dominant state that uses its military and economic power to impose and maintain customs and rules aimed at preserving the existing world order and its position in that order. *(p. 284)*

Hegemonic war: A war initiated by a hegemon to preserve its status or by a challenger seeking to overthrow the hegemon. *(p. 64)*

Helms-Burton Act: A 1996 law proposed by North Carolina's Senator Jesse Helms and Indiana Congressman Dan Burton to impose sanctions on foreign companies that purchase property in Cuba that had been confiscated by American citizens after 1959. *(p. 436)*

Heterogeneous state: A state in which society is deeply cleaved by ethnicity, religion, language, or other differences. *(p. 13)*

High Commissioner for Human Rights: Chief U.N. official responsible for promoting and protecting human rights. *(p. 506)*

Historical experience: Past relations among actors that affect their current behavior toward each other. *(p. 271)*

History of rewarding cooperation: A situation in which actors have benefited from prior experiences of having acted together for a common purpose. *(p. 270)*

Holy Roman Empire: A Germanic empire beginning in the ninth century and lasting until 1806. *(p. 43)*

Homogeneous state: A state with relatively few ethnic, religious, linguistic, or other cleavages among citizens. *(p. 13)*

Horizontal nuclear proliferation: An increase in the number of states or other actors that possess nuclear weapons. *(p. 332)*

Hot money: A multitrillion-dollar pool of capital in private hands that races around the world's stock, bond, and currency markets in search of the highest returns each day. *(p. 13)*

Human Development Index (HDI): A summary index developed by the United Nations comparing countries by life expectancy, literacy, and income. *(p. 385)*

Human immunodeficiency virus (HIV): The viral infection that causes AIDS. *(p. 460)*

Humanitarian intervention: International intervention in the internal affairs of a country to save lives and provide citizens with relief from famine, disease, or violence. *(p. 242)*

Human-nature theories: Theories about war and other behavior that start from a belief that such behavior is inherent in human beings and cannot be altered. *(p. 297)*

Human rights: The rights that individuals in all countries enjoy by virtue of their humanness. *(p. 481)*

Identities: The shared self-identifications or self-descriptions of peoples indicating how psychologically close they are. *(p. 154)*

Ideology: A closed system of closely linked concepts and theories purporting to offer a coherent and comprehensive explanation for reality. *(p. 31)*

Image: An individual's perception of reality that is influenced by experience and beliefs. *(p. 169)*

Imperialism: The policy of extending a country's rule over other countries. *Neoimperialism* connotes subtle forms of foreign influence such as control over exports or raw materials. *(p. 300)*

Imperial overextension or overstretch: A condition in which a country's overseas commitments exceed its ability to honor them. *(p. 408)*

Incremental bias: A preference for making decisions that involve small steps rather than fundamental changes. *(p. 177)*

Individual rationality: The ability of an individual to select the best of all alternatives on the basis of costs and benefits. *(p. 299)*

Intangible resources: Nonmaterial resources difficult to observe or measure that contribute to an actor's power. *(p. 146)*

Intellectual property rights: Ownership of ideas as reflected in patents. A contentious issue in the Uruguay Round of the GATT and between the United States and China. *(p. 378)*

Intelligence failure: The inability of the intelligence community to predict key events such as the overthrow of the Shah of Iran or the Japanese attack on Pearl Harbor. *(p. 265)*

Intentions: An actor's attitudes toward the effect of its actions and policies. *(p. 147)*

Interagency group (IG): Experts from various U.S. foreign-policy bureaucracies who review and develop policy options that are passed on to a Senior Interagency Group (SIG). *(p. 177)*

Interdependence: A relationship in which two or more actors are sensitive and vulnerable to each other's behavior and in which actions taken by one affect the other. *(p. 89)*

Intergovernmental organization (IGO): An international organization consisting of representatives of sovereign states. *(p. 223)*

Intermediate-Range Nuclear Force (INF) Treaty: A 1987 agreement between the United States and Soviet Union to remove intermediate-range nuclear missiles. The path-breaking agreement was the first that entailed eliminating many nuclear weapons. *(p. 349)*

Internal setting: Factors within a state that influence foreign policy. *(p. 169)*

International Bill of Human Rights: Collective codification of global human rights in the Universal Declaration of Human Rights, the International Covenant on Civil and Political Rights, and the International Covenant on Economic, Social, and Cultural Rights. *(p. 486)*

International Court of Justice (ICJ): A U.N. organ established to adjudicate disputes referred by member states and to provide advisory opinions on legal questions to other U.N. organs. The ICJ, often called the World Court, is the successor to the League of Nations Permanent Court of International Justice. *(p. 234)*

International Covenant on Civil and Political Rights: A U.N. covenant dealing with "negative rights" and defining the sphere of freedoms of individuals from government interference. *(p. 482)*

International Covenant on Economic, Social, and Cultural Rights: A U.N. covenant dealing with "positive rights" and stipulating what services governments should provide for individuals. *(p. 482)*

International Criminal Court: A proposed permanent U.N.-sponsored court to hear and try individuals accused of crimes against humanity and war crimes. *(p. 281)*

International law: A body of principles and rules derived from custom and treaties commonly observed by states in their dealings with each other. *(pp. 47, 277)*

International Monetary Fund (IMF): A U.N. agency established at Bretton Woods to provide a multilateral system of payments and help stabilize currency rates necessary for expanding international trade. *(p. 369)*

International politics: Interactions among sovereign territorial states. *(p. 2)*

International regime: A set of rules, norms, and decision-making procedures that govern actors' behavior in an international area of activity. *(p. 282)*

Iron curtain: A metaphor Winston Churchill coined in a 1946 speech to describe the line separating the Soviet sphere of interest from the "free" countries in Western Europe. *(p. 105)*

Islamic fundamentalism: The belief by some Muslims that the tenets of Islam are the sole source of political authority. *(p. 213)*

Issue cycle: A cycle of four stages through which an issue passes between the time it is placed on the global agenda and the time it leaves that agenda. See **Genesis, Crisis, Ritualization, Resolution.** *(p. 97)*

Issues in global politics: Contentions among actors over proposals for distributing among them valued objects and ends. *(p. 13)*

Janus faces of foreign policy: The idea that foreign policy is produced by forces both within and outside of states. Janus was a two-faced Roman god. *(p. 164)*

Janus faces of politics: See **Janus faces of foreign policy.** *(p. 16)*

Juridical statehood: The legal rather than empirical attributes of statehood. *(p. 79)*

Keiretsu: Chummy alliances among Japanese manufacturers, suppliers, and distributors that prevent foreign companies from entering the Japanese market. *(p. 420)*

Knowledge economies: Countries whose future economic growth lies in production, storage, and distribution of knowledge. *(p. 385)*

Korean War: A war beginning with North Korea's invasion of South Korea in June 1950 that ended indecisively with an armistice in 1953. The war was a major step in militarizing the Cold War, and American troops remain in Korea to this day. *(p. 109)*

Kyoto Protocol: A 1997 agreement for major reductions in green house gas emissions as part of the efforts to limit global warming. *(p. 471)*

Land hunger: A country's condition when its land is inadequate to support its population. *(p. 459)*

Lateral pressure: Stress or pressure that is directed sideways. *(p. 458)*

Launch vehicle: The means for delivering nuclear weapons—planes or missiles. *(p. 347)*

Law of gambler's ruin: A gambler who keeps betting double-or-nothing on the same outcome will ultimately lose all. *(p. 528)*

Leaders in mufti: National political leaders who are in their nation's military forces. *(p. 319)*

League of Nations: An intergovernmental organization established by the Versailles Treaty after World War I mainly to promote international peace and security. *(p. 227)*

League Covenant: The rules of the League of

Nations, including the obligations of member states. *(p. 227)*

Learning: A process of trial and error in which actors come to understand the rules of the game in global politics. *(pp. 270, 272)*

Legitimate power: Power derived from an actor's ability to alter a target's attitude by using legitimate authority, expertise, or charisma. *(p. 69)*

Less-developed countries (LDCs): The world's poorer countries. *(pp. 379, 402)*

Levée en masse: The general conscription introduced in France after the French Revolution. *(p. 304)*

Liberal economic order: The belief that global prosperity can be achieved by establishing a free market and eliminating political impediments to the free movement of capital, goods, and labor. *(pp. 369, 401)*

Limits-to-growth theory: A theoretical perspective on the global environment claiming that earth's ability to support life has inherent limits and that if any critical resources such as supplies of fresh water are depleted large numbers of deaths will ensue. *(p. 473)*

Liquidity: Hard currency available to purchase imports. *(p. 374)*

Local-content requirement: The requirement that an imported product incorporate parts that are manufactured locally. *(p. 436)*

Localization: Those processes that erode centralized authority in global politics. *(p. 520)*

Long Telegram: A 1946 report by George F. Kennan, then a counselor in the U.S. Embassy in Moscow, that viewed relations between the United States and the Soviet Union as basically incompatible. *(p. 104)*

Maastricht Treaty: An agreement signed by European Community (EC) leaders in December 1991 that outlined steps toward increased European political and economic unity, including renaming the group the European Union and establishing a single currency for member states. *(p. 431)*

Managed trade: A policy to limit free trade by agreements among countries involving export-import limits, trade goals, and import-export quotas. *(p. 422)*

Marshall Plan: A U.S. program of grants and loans conceived in 1947 to assist postwar West European recovery. *(p. 109)*

Marxism-Leninism: Marxist theory as interpreted by Soviet leader V. I. Lenin and his successors. *(p. 8)*

Massive retaliation: The U.S. strategic posture during the Eisenhower administration under which the United States threatened to use nuclear weapons against the U.S.S.R. in response to conventional challenges by the U.S.S.R. or its allies. *(p. 333)*

Maximin strategy: A strategy, derived from game theory, that allows players to minimize their potential losses. Also called *minimax. (p. 141)*

Melian Dialogue: A passage in Thucydides' *History of the Peloponnesian War* in which Athens threatens to destroy Melos unless the latter becomes an ally. The passage illustrates power politics in action. *(p. 60)*

Mercantilism: The doctrine that exports should be encouraged and imports discouraged to accumulate national wealth and power. *(p. 49)*

Microcredit: Small loans available to the poor to start up small businesses. *(p. 396)*

Military-industrial complex: The idea articulated by President Dwight Eisenhower that private defense interests, Congress, and the Pentagon cooperate to keep U.S. defense spending high. *(p. 320)*

Mirror image: The propensity of groups and individuals to have similar perceptions of each other—that is, we see in others what they see in us. *(p. 105)*

Missile Technology Control Regime (MTCR): An effort, begun by the West in 1986 and later joined by the U.S.S.R. and China, to restrict the transfer of missiles to other countries. *(p. 354)*

Modern World System Theory: A theory of international political economy associated with Immanuel Wallerstein which sees the world divided between a wealthy "core" and a poor "periphery." *(p. 381)*

Modernity: Substituting brain power for muscle power in development and acquiring secular and rational attitudes toward the outside. *(p. 150)*

Mogadishu line: A term from the U.S. intervention in Somalia to designate the moment when soldiers shift from peacekeeping to peace enforcement. *(p. 243)*

Most-favored-nation (MFN) status: The principle that tariff preferences that are granted to one actor for its exports must be granted to all trading partners. *(p. 371)*

Multicentric world: A world of state and non-state actors. *(p. 196)*

Multilocalism: A combination of being transnational and having sensitivity to local tastes and customs. *(p. 199)*

Multiple independently targetable reentry vehicles (MIRV): Missiles with several nuclear warheads that can be programmed to hit different targets. *(p. 339)*

Multipolarity: A political system having three or more dominant power centers. *(p. 64)*

Multipurpose global IGOs: International organizations that perform a variety of functions and include as members states from all over the world. *(p. 248)*

Multipurpose regional IGOs: International organizations that perform a variety of functions and include as members states from a particular geographic region such as Europe or Africa. *(p. 248)*

Mutual assured destruction (MAD): A nuclear-deterrence strategy based on each nuclear state's ability to launch devastating nuclear retaliation even if an enemy attacks it first. *(p. 334)*

Nation: A collection of people loyal to each other because of perceived ethnic, linguistic, or cultural affinity. *(p. 52)*

National interest: The idea that a state has a corporate interest, the result of its relative power, geograhic location, or other factors, that determines its political behavior. *(pp. 9, 61, 80)*

Nationalism: Exclusive attachment to a national or ethnic group. *(pp. 51, 157)*

National security: A state's capacity to ensure its fundamental economic and political independence and survival, and its citizens' safety and well-being. Sometimes used by politicians to justify policies and activities not related to national survival. *(p. 81)*

Natural law: Principles of law considered as derived from nature, right reason, or God. *(p. 482)*

Near abroad: Regions along Russia's periphery that were formerly Soviet republics and that Moscow regards as critical to its national security. *(p. 123)*

Negative or corrective feedback: Information that brings about a change in policy and produces different behavior. *(p. 136)*

Negative rights: Individuals' rights not to suffer from undue government interference in personal independence and autonomy. Sometimes called *political and civil rights. (p. 484)*

Neighborhood effect: Treating countries with similar economic profiles in the same way. *(p. 397)*

Neofunctionalism: A revised version of functional theory positing that organizations established by agreements among states may create political interests and pressures for broadening or strengthening their own authority or even for establishing additional organizations. *(p. 225)*

Neomercantilism: See **Economic Nationalism.** *(p. 382)*

Neorealism: A variant of realism emphasizing the causal importance of the global system's anarchic structure and the role of power as an *intervening,* rather than an *independent,* variable. *(p. 63)*

New International Economic Order (NIEO): A composite of demands by the less-developed countries for reforming the international economic system and redistributing global resources. *(p. 385)*

Newly industrializing countries (NICs): A group of rapidly industrializing export-oriented countries, including Singapore, Hong Kong, South Korea, Taiwan, and Malaysia. *(p. 376)*

New thinking: Changes introduced in Soviet policies after 1986 by Mikhail Gorbachev, including more openness and democracy at home and conciliation and cooperation with other countries. *(p. 115)*

Nixon shock: The 1973 announcement by President Richard Nixon that the United States was suspending convertibility of dollars into gold. That move brought an end to the Bretton Woods system. *(p. 373)*

Nonaligned movement: A group, originally established in 1961, currently consisting of more than one hundred countries that do not wish to be associated with great-power alliances and try to further the interests of the less-developed countries. *(p. 385)*

Nongovernmental organization (NGO): See **International Nongovernmental Organization (INGO).** *(p. 196)*

Nonstate actors: Actors consisting of individuals and groups other than governments or their surrogates. *(p. 196)*

Nontariff barrier: A restriction on free trade other than tariffs, such as quotas or complex requirements and inspection procedures. *(pp. 371, 378)*

Normative theory: Beliefs about what is moral and immoral. *(p. 32)*

North American Free Trade Agreement (NAFTA): An agreement among the United States, Mexico, and Canada to form a free-trade zone. Strongly opposed by organized labor and some environmental groups in the United States that feared that jobs would move to Mexico and that corporations would use the treaty to get around tough U.S. environmental laws. *(p. 437)*

Novikov Telegram: A secret 1946 report from the Soviet ambassador in the United States claiming that the United States was an aggressive threat to Soviet security. *(p. 105)*

NSC–68: A 1950 National Security Council report summarizing the official U.S. perspective on the danger from the Soviet Union and international communism. *(p. 107)*

Nuclear Nonproliferation Treaty (NPT): An international agreement signed in 1968 and renewed in 1995 to prevent horizontal proliferation of nuclear weapons. *(p. 352)*

Nuclear winter: A period of life-threatening

darkness and cold on earth that could follow nuclear war. *(p. 342)*

Nuremberg trials: International trials of accused Nazi war criminals after World War II. *(p. 275)*

Oil shocks: Rapid increases in the price of oil following the 1973 Arab-Israeli war, the 1979 revolution in Iran, and the 1990 Iraqi invasion of Kuwait. *(p. 466)*

One-shot game: A gamelike interaction in which players interact only once. *(p. 270)*

Open Skies Treaty: A 1992 confidence-building measure permitting observation flights over countries that are parties to the agreement. *(p. 348)*

Orderly marketing agreement: An agreement violating free-trade principles to set quotas on imports and exports of selected products from participating states. *(p. 422)*

Organizational-process model: An approach to studying foreign policy focused on the routine output of large bureaucracies. *(p. 173)*

Organization of Petroleum Exporting Countries (OPEC): A worldwide organization of petroleum-producing countries established in 1960 to coordinate and unify members' petroleum policies and stabilize international oil prices. *(p. 253)*

***Ostpolitik* (East policy):** The policy initiated by West Germany toward East Germany in 1969 for systematic accommodation, negotiation, and economic aid with the aim of gaining influence over events there. *(p. 434)*

Ottoman Empire: A Muslim-Turkish Empire founded in 1300 and surviving until 1919 that held sway over much of the Middle East and the Balkans. For much of the nineteenth and twentieth centuries, it was referred to as the *sick man of Europe. (p. 40)*

Ozone layer: A region in the upper atmosphere where most atmospheric ozone is concentrated. The ozone layer protects us from dangerous solar radiation. *(p. 462)*

Paradox of power: Actors with greatest capabilities may find it difficult to achieve objectives because their power sows fear, envy, and hatred among other actors. *(p. 68)*

Participation explosion: The growing interest of mass publics in and knowledge about foreign policy and their willingness to become directly involved in world politics. *(p. 83)*

Payoff: The value of losses or gains of alternatives in game theory. *(p. 264)*

Peace dividend: Funds and other resources made available by cuts in defense spending following the end of the Cold War. The dividend is less than many optimists had hoped. *(p. 315)*

Peace enforcement: Vigorous international action, including military force, to end aggression. *(p. 235)*

Peaceful coexistence: The doctrine made popular by Soviet leader Nikita Khrushchev in 1956 claiming that war between capitalist and socialist states was not inevitable and that the two blocs could compete peacefully. *(p. 113)*

Peacekeeping: Using military forces to prevent fighting, separate combatants, or ensure by observation that peace agreements are kept. The forces are provided by neutral third parties under an international organization such as the United Nations or the Organization of American States, and must be invited by the belligerents. *(p. 235)*

Perception: The version of reality held by an observer or decision-maker. If that version differs from reality, it is called *misperception. (p. 169)*

Perestroika: Economic-restructuring policy initiated by Soviet President Mikhail Gorbachev. *(p. 115)*

Players: Actors in situations characterized by rules and strategies. *(p. 264)*

Polarity: Distribution of power centers in a political system. *(p. 301)*

Political asylum: A haven provided for refugees fleeing political persecution. *(p. 488)*

Political democracy: See **Democracy.** *(p. 6)*

Political economy: The study of the relationship of politics and economics. *(p. 368)*

Political organization: The manner in which individuals and groups join one another and cooperate for political ends. *(p. 31)*

Population density: Ratio of population to arable land. *(p. 456)*

Positive or amplifying feedback: Information that reinforces policy and produces more of the same behavior. *(p. 135)*

Positive rights: Individuals' rights to have their essential needs such as food and health seen to by the government. Sometimes called *economic and social rights. (p. 484)*

Postinternational politics: Political scientist James N. Rosenau's name for the presence in global politics of new structures, processes, and relations other than sovereign states and the relations among them. *(p. 3)*

Postmodern war: War in which armies and peoples become indistinguishable, where states are replaced by informal groupings, and in which civilians are the main victims. *(p. 309)*

Potential power: Capabilities that can be directed toward constructing a power relationship. *(p. 68)*

Potsdam Conference: The last of the wartime summits between the United States, Britain, and the Soviet Union, held in the Berlin suburb of Potsdam in July 1945. At the conference, it was decided to divide Germany into occupation zones, turn over German territory to Poland and the U.S.S.R., and require that Germany pay reparations. *(p. 103)*

Power: A psychological relationship in which one actor influences another to behave differently than it would have if left to its own devices. *(p. 66)*

Power-cycle theory: An approach to understanding war focused on the factors and conditions that enable some states in a system to rise above others and aspire to hegemony. *(p. 302)*

Power elite: Individuals in a political system who enjoy disproportionate political influence either by occupying political and economic positions or by having access to those who do. *(p. 320)*

Power politics: An intellectual tradition affirming that outcomes in global politics are determined by distribution of power and changes in that distribution. See **Realism.** *(p. 59)*

Power-preponderance theory: The belief that peace is ensured when one actor or group of actors in a political system enjoys hegemony. *(p. 301)*

Power vacuum: According to power theorists, an area not under the control of a strong state that strong states may wish to control to prevent others from doing so. *(p. 106)*

Preventive diplomacy: Inserting U.N. peacekeepers in a conflict, especially in the less-developed countries, to prevent intervention and possible confrontation between the superpowers. *(p. 235)*

Prisoner's dilemma game: A relationship among actors described in game theory to illustrate the problem of trust under conditions of anarchy. *(p. 141)*

Private good: A benefit that is enjoyed only by some and need not be shared with others. *(p. 20)*

Quality of life: The level of well-being, happiness, and satisfaction enjoyed by citizens. *(p. 385)*

Rational analysis: Selection of the best of *all* alternatives based on a calculation of costs and benefits. *(p. 10)*

Realism: A theoretical approach, dominant in the United States after World War II, that sees sovereign states as leading actors in global politics, power and its distribution as the determinants of state behavior, and war as the main issue in global politics. *(p. 62)*

Realpolitik: Policy based on power and expediency rather than principles. *(p. 59)*

Reason of state: Idea that a state has a corporate interest that determines its policies. See **National interest.** *(p. 60)*

Reciprocity: Strategy by which one actor behaves toward others as they have behaved toward it. *(p. 270)*

Recognition of states: Act by which states declare that a new state is legitimate and by which the new state acquires legal sovereignty. *(p. 71)*

Relative military-spending burden: The comparative burden of states as measured by the ratio of defense spending to GNP. *(p. 70)*

Reserve currency: See **Hard currency.** *(pp. 375, 430)*

Resolution: The final stage in an issue cycle during which agreement is reached or the issue loses actors' attention. *(p. 99)*

Rewards: Positive incentives used to generate influence. *(p. 69)*

Riga Axioms: Unlike the Yalta Axioms, the belief that Soviet policy was driven by ideology rather than power. *(p. 104)*

Ritualization: The third stage in an issue cycle during which routine patterns of behavior and rules for managing an issue evolve among actors. *(p. 99)*

Role: The manner in which an individual's official position affects the individual's attitudes and behavior. *(p. 180)*

Rules of the game: Widely understood and accepted global norms that actors follow out of habit and self-interest. *(pp. 264, 275)*

Salami tactics: An aggresive strategy in which an actor makes small demands that collectively constitute something more significant. *(p. 272)*

Salinization: Causing infertile soil by adding excess salt. *(p. 462)*

SALT I: The Strategic Arms Limitation Treaty signed in 1972, which limited the deployment of antiballistic missiles. *(p. 347)*

SALT II: The Strategic Arms Limitation Treaty signed in 1979 but not approved by the United States because the U.S.S.R. invaded Afghanistan. Its provisions were honored by the signatories anyway. *(p. 347)*

Samurai: Member of the hereditary warrior class in feudal Japan. *(p. 318)*

Satellite effect: A situation in which two actors behave in tandem, and observers mistake which one is influencing the other. *(p. 67)*

Satisficing: Propensity of decision-makers to select alternatives that meet minimally acceptable standards. *(p. 177)*

Schlieffen Plan: German military plan before World War I for a two-front war against France and Russia, in which victory would be achieved by rapidly invading France through Belgium. *(p. 307)*

Scope of power: Aspects of a target's behavior that are subject to an influence relationship. *(p. 67)*

Second-order feedback: Information that brings about a change in actors' goals as well as in their behavior. *(p. 136)*

Second-strike capability: A nuclear power's ability to absorb an enemy first strike and then launch a devastating retaliatory strike. Second-strike capability is achieved by making nuclear-weapons systems invulnerable to a first strike by hardening them or making them mobile. *(p. 335)*

Secretariat: The U.N. executive organ; it manages the organization's bureaucracy and finances and oversees the operation of all organs and personnel. *(p. 233)*

Security: See **National security.** *(p. 14)*

Security Council: The most powerful U.N. organ which deals largely with questions of peace and security; its five permanent members can veto decisions thereby preventing them from being carried out. *(p. 231)*

Security dilemma: Actors' inability under anarchic conditions to trust each other because of the absence of reliable enforcement. *(p. 140)*

Self-help: The principle that, under anarchic conditions, actors must rely on themselves for security in global politics. *(p. 265)*

Senior interagency group (SIG): A group of senior U.S. bureaucrats from various foreign-policy agencies that reviews policy options made by an Interagency Group (IG). The SIG's recommendations are forwarded to the National Security Council and ultimately the president. *(p. 177)*

Sensitivity interdependence: The speed with which events in one part of the world affect other parts of the world and the magnitude of those effects. *(p. 89)*

Seven sisters: The seven petroleum corporations that controlled production, refining, and distribution of Middle East oil between the 1920s and the 1960s. *(p. 200)*

Shantytown: An extremely poor section in a city. *(p. 455)*

Shi'ite Muslims: The smaller of the two major branches of Islam, consisting of those who regard 'Ali, son-in-law of Muhammad, as the Prophet's legitimate successor. Many Shi'ites believe that the Koran is the only source of political authority. See **Islamic fundamentalism.** *(p. 213)*

Side payment: A special or private benefit provided to an actor or individual in return for supporting a policy involving collective goods. See **Collective good.** *(p. 20)*

Single Market Act: A 1985 agreement among members of the European Community to create a free internal market for all goods and services by December 31, 1992, unobstructed by tariff or nontariff barriers. *(p. 430)*

Situational power: Power derived from an actor's ability to manipulate the situation of a target by using rewards and coercion. *(p. 69)*

Size: The absolute level of resources controlled by an actor or to which it has access. Such resources predict the actor's potential influence in global politics. *(p. 161)*

Social and economic development: The per capita level of resources controlled by an actor. Social and economic development predicts how effectively an actor can use its total resources. *(p. 149)*

Social structure: The way in which individuals and groups in a society relate to one another, e.g., as equals, as leaders and followers, and so forth. *(p. 169)*

Socialism: An ideology critical of capitalism that advocates collective control of production and marketing facilities in order to achieve the well-being and equality of citizens. *(p. 107)*

Society of states: A group of states conscious of common interests and bound by a common set of rules and norms. *(p. 270)*

Soft power: Influence based on cultural attraction, ideology, and role in international institutions. *(p. 411)*

Soil erosion: Loss of fertile soil owing to the effects of wind and flooding. Often caused by deforestation. *(p. 462)*

Sovereign equality: The principle that states are legal equals and under which threatening or using force against any state is prohibited. *(p. 71)*

Sovereignty: The status of states as legal equals under international law, according to which

they are supreme internally and subject to no higher external authority. *(p. 46)*

Specialized agencies: A group of U.N.-affiliated organizations seeking to promote the common welfare by carrying out functional tasks. *(p. 234)*

Specialized IGOs: Organizations of states such as military alliances that have limited purposes. *(p. 248)*

Special relationship: Name for U.S.-British relations since the nineteenth century. For most of that time, the two countries have been close allies, sensitive to each other's problems and needs. *(p. 271)*

Sphere of influence: An area under the influence of a major state. *(p. 102)*

Stability of a system: The ability of a system's structural features to maintain themselves over time and change slowly and predictably. *(p. 145)*

Stag-hare parable: A parable told by political philosopher Jean-Jacques Rousseau to illustrate how anarchy produces conflict. *(p. 140)*

Standard operating procedures (SOPs): Established routines that bureaucracies follow to carry out recurring tasks and duties. *(p. 176)*

State: A political entity that is sovereign and is said to enjoy exclusive control over a defined territory and population. *(p. 12)*

State-centric approach: A perspective on global politics that sees states as the sources of all important activities. *(pp. 9, 166)*

State-centric world: The system of sovereign states. *(p. 196)*

Status: An actor's ranking or prestige in the global hierarchy as defined by other actors. *(p. 152)*

Status inconsistency: An imbalance between an actor's ranking in the global hierarchy and its resources. Such inconsistency may be dangerous as actors seek to bring the two factors into balance. *(p. 153)*

Stimulus-response model: See **Action-reaction model.** *(p. 168)*

Strategic Arms Reduction Treaty I (START I): A 1991 U.S.-Soviet agreement to make major cuts in nuclear warheads. *(p. 349)*

Strategic Arms Reduction Treaty II (START II): A 1992 agreement between the United States and Russia to reduce nuclear arsenals on both sides by 50 percent. *(p. 350)*

Strategic Arms Reduction Treaty III (START III): A 1997 agreement between the United States and Russia requiring a cut of 80 percent of warheads. As of 1999, the treaty had not been ratified by Russia. *(p. 350)*

Strategic Defense Initiative (SDI or Star Wars): A plan President Ronald Reagan initiated to deploy an antiballistic missile system using space-based lasers. *(p. 340)*

Strategic stability: Condition in which leaders have few incentives to try to launch a military first strike. *(p. 337)*

Strategy: A plan or method for obtaining a specific goal. *(p. 264)*

Strong state: A state that has extensive autonomy and capacity. *(p. 72)*

Structural Impediments Initiative (SII): A 1989 agreement between the United States and Japan to study conditions in the two countries that affect free trade between them. *(p. 421)*

Subnational group: A political party located in one state. *(p. 196)*

Subsystem: Specialized group of actors whose relations show more interaction and interdependence than those in the larger global system. *(p. 137)*

Sunni Muslims: The dominant branch of Islam consisting of those who regard the first four caliphs as legitimate successors of Muhammad. *(p. 213)*

Supranational organization: A body with the authority to make decisions binding on states without requiring their approval. *(p. 223)*

System: An abstraction referring to a set of units complexly interrelated by interaction. *(p. 135)*

System boundaries: The border dividing a system from its environment. *(p. 137)*

System stability: See **Stability of a system.** *(p. 145)*

System structure: Distribution of resources and attitudes among actors in a political system. *(p. 139)*

Tangible resources: Material resources that contribute to an actor's power. *(p. 146)*

Technology transfer: The movement of advanced technology from wealthy, developed countries to poor less-developed countries. *(p. 388)*

Tectonic-plates model: A metaphor associated with neorealists comparing foreign policy to the folds in the earth's crust whose movement causes earthquakes. *(p. 167)*

Terms of trade: The ratio between prices of exports and those of imports that determines a state's ability to prosper from international trade. *(p. 389)*

Terrorism: Calculated use of violence against innocent civilians for political ends, especially to gain public attention. Terrorism can be undertaken by state authorities or nonstate groups and individuals. *(p. 203)*

Theocracy: A form of government based on religion and in which religious leaders have a major role. *(p. 39)*

Third World: All the less-developed countries, most of which are in Africa, Asia, Latin America, and the Middle East. *(p. 402)*

Thirty Years' War: The war fought from 1618 to 1648 in central Europe between Catholic and Protestant supporters, creating the conditions for the modern sovereign state. *(p. 46)*

Three-Mile Island: A nuclear power plant near Harrisburg, Pennsylvania, at which a malfunctioning valve on March 28, 1979, led to uncovering the nuclear reactor core. *(p. 467)*

Throw weight: The load of nuclear bombs and warheads that can be delivered by a country's bombers and missiles. *(p. 347)*

Tied aid: Foreign aid that is tied to the recipients' purchase of goods from the donor country. *(p. 393)*

Tokyo Round of GATT: Multilateral trade negotiations held between 1973 and 1979.

Totalitarian state: A form of authoritarianism exercising control over even the minute details of individual lives, often by means of technology and an omnipresent political party. *(p. 502)*

Traditional society: An agrarian society in

which inhabitants follow preindustrial customs and in which religion and superstition continue to be highly influential in individual and group decisions. *(p. 29)*

Transnational corporation (TNC): A firm headquartered in one country and having operations in one or more other countries. *(pp. 197, 387)*

Transnational model: An approach to analyzing global politics that goes beyond the assumptions that territorial states are the only important actors, that conflict is the dominant characteristic in global relations, that actors must rely on self-help, and that anarchy is the dominant feature of the global system. *(p. 181)*

Transnational relations: Direct interactions or transactions across national frontiers involving nongovernmental actors or social groups. *(p. 34)*

Transnational war: War waged by nonstate groups across state frontiers. *(p. 295)*

Tribe: A political group united by descent (real or fictitious) from a common ancestor. *(p. 30)*

Tripwire: A wire tightly stretched so that touching it sets off a trap or alarm. The name applied to the presence of troops whose task is not to defend a position so much as to trigger threatened retaliation if attacked. *(p. 336)*

Triumphalism: Belief in the superiority of America's brand of capitalism. *(p. 413)*

Truman Doctrine: The policy announced by President Harry S Truman in 1947 stating that the United States would support all countries threatened by external or internal communism. Many feel the policy marked the beginning of the Cold War. *(p. 108)*

Trusteeship Council: The U.N. organ established to administer trust territories placed under the U.N. trusteeship system and to help prepare them for eventual independence. *(p. 234)*

U.N. Charter: Document describing the objectives, organization, and function of the United Nations. *(p. 229)*

U.N. Commission on Human Rights: A UNESCO commission with the responsibility to evaluate human rights worldwide and investigate complaints. *(p. 505)*

U.N. Conference on Population and Development: A U.N.-sponsored conference held in Cairo late in 1994 to discuss proposals for dealing with the world population explosion. *(p. 499)*

U.N. Conference on the Environment and Development (UNCED): A U.N.-sponsored conference held in Rio de Janiero, Brazil, in June 1992 to discuss and plan improvement of global ecology.

U.N. Conference of the Human Environment: A 1972 U.N.-sponsored conference in Stockholm, Sweden, that first put the environment on the global agenda. *(p. 473)*

Unintended consequences: Outcomes from foreign-policy initiatives that were not foreseen. *(p. 527)*

Unitary-actor approach: An approach to understanding global politics assuming that actors' internal attributes or differences among such attributes do not affect behavior. *(p. 9)*

United Nations (U.N.): A global intergovernmental organization established in 1945 to maintain peace and security and to improve its members' economic and social conditions. The United Nations consists of six principal organs: the General Assembly, the Security Council, the Economic and Social Council, the Trusteeship Council, the Secretariat, and the World Court. *(p. 227)*

Uniting for Peace Resolution: A procedure adopted by the U.N. General Assembly at the time of the Korean War to get around the veto provision in the Security Council. *(p. 233)*

Universal Declaration of Human Rights: A 1948 U.N. declaration consisting of thirty articles that identify a range of political, civil, economic, social, and cultural rights. The declaration is at the heart of the International Bill of Human Rights. *(p. 482)*

Uruguay Round of GATT: Multilateral trade negotiations from 1986 to 1993 to consider such issues as nontariff barriers, agricultural trade, and intellectual property rights. Agreement established the World Trade Organization to replace the GATT. *(p. 378)*

U.S.-Canada Free Trade Agreement (FTA): A 1989 agreement establishing a free-trade area between the two countries. *(p. 437)*

Vanishing World War II effect: The illusion of American economic decline because the U.S. share of global power resources was exaggerated by World War II. *(p. 409)*

Variable-sum game: A relationship in which the gains and losses of actors do not add up to zero but instead vary. In some cases, all actors gain, and in others all lose. *(p. 264)*

Versailles Conference: A peace conference held after World War I that produced the global structure of the interwar period (1919–1939). *(p. 100)*

Vertical nuclear proliferation: An increase in the nuclear capabilities of actors that already possess nuclear weapons. *(p. 332)*

Vietnam War: The war (1956–1975) between non-communist South Vietnam, communist North Vietnam, and communist insurgents in South Vietnam which ended in the victory of the North and reunification of Vietnam (1976). Growing American participation in the war to aid South Vietnam starting in 1961 provoked domestic opposition, especially after 1968. *(p. 112)*

Vulnerability of nuclear weapons: The degree to which an actor's nuclear retaliatory force can be destroyed by an enemy first strike. Greater vulnerability reduces strategic stability. *(p. 337)*

War: Organized violence within (civil war) or between (interstate war) states. *(p. 293)*

War crimes: Abuse of enemy soldiers or prisoners of war during wartime. *(p. 279)*

Weak state: A state whose ministries and beaurocracies are deeply penetrated by societal forces in the form of interest groups and which, as a result, are unable to behave autonomously. *(p. 92)*

***Weltpolitik* (world policy):** The policy of Germany under Kaiser Wilhelm II, challenging British supremacy at sea and seeking additional colonies. *(p. 432)*

World Bank: See IBRD. *(p. 369)*

World Trade Organization (WTO): An agency established in December 1993 to replace the GATT. The WTO has authority to constitute three-member arbitration panels to decide if countries are violating trade rules, make them correct such violations, and pay for damages. *(p. 379)*

Worst-case analysis: Foreign policy-planning based on the assumption that an adversary will seek to do as much harm as possible. *(p. 265)*

Yalta Axioms: The belief of American leaders before the Cold War that it was possible to bargain with the Soviet Union and that the latter was much like other states that designed foreign policies based on power. *(p. 106)*

Yalta Conference: A 1945 summit meeting with Franklin D. Roosevelt, Josef Stalin, and Winston Churchill at which major postwar issues were discussed, such as the status of Poland and voting arrangements in the United Nations. *(p. 102)*

Zaibatsu: The great industrial or financial enterprises of Japan. *(p. 416)*

Zero option: A 1981 proposal by the Reagan administration for the worldwide elimination of INF missiles. *(p. 274)*

Zero-sum game: A relationship in which a gain for one actor is equal to a loss for another actor. *(pp. 10, 264)*

Name Index

Subject Index